D0072806

AMERICAN FAMILIES

AMERICAN FAMILIES

A Research Guide
and
Historical Handbook

Edited by
JOSEPH M. HAWES
and
ELIZABETH I. NYBAKKEN

Greenwood Press
New York • Westport, Connecticut • London

Library of Congress Cataloging-in-Publication Data

American families : a research guide and historical handbook / edited
  by Joseph M. Hawes and Elizabeth I. Nybakken.
      p. cm.
    Includes bibliographical references and index.
    ISBN 0–313–26233–0 (alk. paper)
    1. Family—United States—History.   I. Hawes, Joseph M.
  II. Nybakken, Elizabeth I.
  HQ535.A585   1991
  306.85′0973—dc20   90–25221

British Library Cataloguing in Publication Data is available.

Library of Congress Catalog Card Number: 90–25221
ISBN: 0–313–26233–0

First published in 1991

Greenwood Press, 88 Post Road West, Westport, CT 06881
An imprint of Greenwood Publishing Group, Inc.

Printed in the United States of America

∞™

The paper used in this book complies with the
Permanent Paper Standard issued by the National
Information Standards Organization (Z39.48–1984).

10 9 8 7 6 5 4 3 2 1

Contents

Preface

Recently there has been a noticeable increase in the amount of literature pertaining to the history of the American family. Our purpose in publishing this collection is to provide a preliminary guide to the emerging literature. We say preliminary because we believe family history to be a robust field that will continue to yield solid scholarship for many years to come. At the same time, however, the amount of material currently available seems to require an aid to accessibility and a solid point of departure.

The chapters that follow are both chronological and topical—because the field of family history is organized in both ways. Such an organization will result in some overlap of coverage, but it will also make our readers aware of the different ways of looking at the history of the American family.

At this stage in the life cycle of family history, a great deal of literature is to be found primarily in scholarly articles. We hope that this guide will make that material more accessible and that, as one result of the efforts of all the contributors, more studies, both monographic and synthetic, will result.

A second purpose of our collection is to give some organization and shape to the burgeoning field of family history. For the most part we have left this task to our contributors, each of whom is a recognized authority in his or her specialty. We have sought to describe the resulting general pattern or trend in the literature in our introduction. In the chapters themselves, the authors have reviewed the literature and assessed the relative merits of some of the recent work, while identifying classics as well. In addition, they have commented on some of the emerging patterns in their areas of specialization.

We hasten to add one caution: this book is conceived as an introductory guide. As such it does not seek to be definitive. Our goal is to emphasize important recent work and to serve those whose knowledge of the history of the American family is relatively limited.

Joseph M. Hawes
Elizabeth I. Nybakken

Acknowledgments

Our first duty is to acknowledge that primary credit for this work belongs to the contributors whose chapters follow. Our task has been one of assembling, compiling, and assisting the scholars whose work we present. This project also owes a great deal to Cynthia Harris, History Editor at Greenwood Press, to Joanne V. (Jan) Hawks of the Sarah Isom Center for Women's Studies at the University of Mississippi for providing us with a place to meet and work, and to Peggy Bonner and Lonna Reinecke for a wide variety of assistance. We also wish to thank the departments of history at Mississippi State University and Memphis State University for their assistance, as well as both universities for their support.

I

Introduction to the Study of the American Family

1

The Study of the American Family

Joseph M. Hawes and Elizabeth I. Nybakken

Many contemporary authorities and experts think that the American family is in trouble and out of synchronization with society. "In many ways the family represents a historically older form of life," assert the authors of *Habits of the Heart: Individualism and Commitment in American Life*. They find it amazing that the family, with its strong emphasis on interdependence, has survived in a nation that emphasizes independence and self-reliance. The historian Christopher Lasch agrees that "the family has been slowly coming apart for more than a hundred years."[1] Perhaps the family is coming apart, but the study of its history is flourishing.

The vigor of family history is demonstrated by the existence of the *Journal of Family History*, which has not only enjoyed years of success, but has also published a special issue on the field as a whole.[2] Family history now routinely is included in a variety of journals. Several major new syntheses have recently appeared, among them Carl Degler's splendid *At Odds: Women and the Family in America from the Revolution to the Present* (1980), Robert V. Wells's *Revolutions in Americans' Lives* (1982), and more recently, *Domestic Revolutions: A Social History of American Family Life* (1988) by Steven Mintz and Susan Kellogg and *The Social Origins of Private Life* (1988) by Stephanie Coontz. There is an anthology of scholarly work on the family, currently in its third edition, *The American Family in Social-Historical Perspective* edited by Michael Gordon, and an impressive collection of primary sources edited by Ronald M. Scott and Bernard Wishy, *America's Families, A Documentary History* (1982).

Until the 1960s, the American family had received little attention from historians. It is odd that it took so long for an interest in the family to arise, since historians traditionally have used institutional frameworks that support a society as a means to analyze it, compare it with others, and chart its changes. The family is, perhaps, the most central institution in any society.

Possibly this early neglect stemmed from the fact that the study of the family is so difficult. Most institutions fulfill a single function; families are involved in the whole range of human activity on many levels. It is not easy to incorporate the changing demographic form and structure of the family, with its equally fluid internal dynamics, and mesh all of this with an external environment in flux. Sources also present a problem. Since a single type of source will illuminate only one aspect of the multifaceted activity of families, a variety of sources is necessary to flesh out the picture.

The predilections of historians might also have been at fault for this neglect of family history. History developed its standards at the end of the nineteenth century when families were considered to be the private business of their members and of no concern to "outsiders," least of all scholarly investigators. Finally, it became imperative to generate a precise definition of what was being studied, since history has offered a wide variety of domestic arrangements through time and across cultures. Early studies of the family were therefore scattered and impressionistic. Arthur W. Calhoun's *A Social History of the American Family* (1917–1919), Alice Morse Earle's *Child Life in Colonial Days* (1899), and Edmund Morgan's *Puritan Family: Religious and Domestic Relations in Seventeenth-Century New England* (1944; 1966) paralleled the work of sociologists in Chicago, who briefly evinced an interest in the interaction between urban life and immigrant families in the 1930s.

Now that family history has moved to the forefront, historians and social scientists have managed to develop distinct definitions for the terms *family, household,* and *kinship,* which are often intermingled in popular usage. Such jargon offers some precision for comparisons across cultures and ages and allows changes and distinctions to be charted with more rigor. Household refers only to a residential unit of kin and nonkin who live together. Family, as a general term, refers to a kinship and legal unit based on marriage or on parent-child linkage. There are many types of families under this umbrella, however. The nuclear or conjugal family of husband, wife, and dependent children has been the most prevalent arrangement in America and serves as the operational definition in the chapters that follow. "Consanguineal" families with a single parent and children were not the norm in the past, but their numbers are increasing. "Complex" families, based either on generational ties (such as a three-generation household) or on lateral ties (such as two married siblings with their spouses and children) were usually a temporary arrangement as families shifted in response to their changing needs. Kinship connotes genealogical relationships among groups of families, sometimes called extended families or kindred. Kinship usually is figured by descent:

patrilineal, if based on ties through the father; matrilineal, if based on ties through the mother; or cognitive, if based on ties through either or both parents. These careful definitions, however, do not bring complete precision to the study of American families. Nonrelated godparents, for instance, played a central role in some families, as Selma Berrol has noted, and one individual might have been a member of several types of families during a lifetime. Nevertheless, the use of common terms facilitated the conduct and sharing of research.

Interest in family history reawakened in the post–World War II era with the dawning of the "new" social history, concerned more with the inarticulate masses than with the literary elite who left records. Historians of this period were conversant with models developed by social scientists, such as Talcott Parsons. They focused on life on the small scale and then related it to larger social structures and processes. Charles Tilley spearheaded the movement to relate the concrete experience of living in families at various points in space and time to the larger society.

Eschewing the impressionistic studies of the past, historians began looking at records that could be subjected to statistical analysis. Church and government records allowed them to study demography and reconstitute families on a macro level. The earliest use of this technique was by a group of French demographers associated with the so-called *Annales* school in the 1950s. They used parish records to estimate rates of marriage, births, and deaths for past European societies. The Cambridge University Group for the History of Population and Social Structure, headed by Peter Laslett in England, used available records to reconstruct the organizational structure of families, size of households, kinship networks, inheritance systems, and migration patterns. Perhaps the most striking revision that has emerged from this work is that the preindustrial family in much of Europe was found to be nuclear, not extended, and that the industrial revolution did not spark the rise of the nuclear family. The Group's conclusions were presented lucidly by Lawrence Stone as he charted the rise of the "affective family" in *The Family, Sex and Marriage in England, 1500–1800* (1977).

Similar work was done in the United States on families in New England, where tidy records allowed John Demos, Philip J. Greven, Jr., Kenneth Lockridge, and others to make analogous statements about colonial families, with Greven adding an emphasis on generational changes. Demography continues to augment our knowledge of families in the Chesapeake, middle colonies, and even the southern back country, providing a quantitative dimension to the study of the family. By viewing the family as a household unit at one or several points in time, however, this approach has difficulty charting and explaining changes or reconstructing the internal texture and dynamics of families.

A second generation of historians in the 1970s drew on these demographic techniques and on models developed by sociologists in their quest to account for transitions in the family. Possibly it was the rapid social change of the era, which seemed to be altering families, that both prompted their inquiries and provided an audience for their work.[3] The family-cycle approach, as developed by sociologist Reuben Hill, measured role changes in the family unit as it moved from stage to stage over the life of its members. The family was still viewed as a unit, but as a unit that changed over time. In focusing on this developmental aspect, the family-cycle approach has illuminated the actions and decisions of the family as a collective unit, which changed in relation to the roles and social characteristics of its members and in response to external conditions. Historians have found, for instance, that the structure of late nineteenth-century households varied in accordance with patterns of migration, the availability of housing, and changing economic needs. Likewise, families changed their collective economic strategy at certain stages to survive in times of economic insecurity.

At this point, the dialogue between historians and other social scientists increased as the latter began to acknowledge the importance of historical development in their models. Historians have tended to refine the models developed by sociologists whose a priori stages were based on modern families and, thus, were of limited use with the varieties of families found in earlier times and milieus. Life-cycle work showed that families were in constant flux. The one stable factor was the individual who may have changed but who retained an identity that could be studied, either as that of an individual or a member of a group or cohort.

This emphasis on individuals within the family coincided with the increasing concern in Western society with the independence of the individual and with the growing contributions of other subfields of social history that focused on particular family members—women, men, children, adolescents, and the aged—and their involvement in society. The life-course approach that emerged has employed the life-cycle representation of stages in parenthood but has expanded its vision to include all family individuals, their interactions within the family unit over time and under changing historical conditions, and their interactions as individuals and as family members with the external society. Longitudinal studies are an important component of this research. Historians of recent families can draw on data banks created by sociologists; those surveying an earlier period must make imaginative use of sources, especially in attempting to recreate the *mentalité* of the family and its members.

All historians of the family are interested in three major areas that overlap. The structure of the family—its size, mortality and fertility rates, length of child dependency, and life stages—must be ascertained before the question of how, when, and why changes occurred can be posed. Historians with a more cultural lens focus on the values, expectations, roles, and functions of the family and the emotional interactions that both reflected and fostered changes. A third emphasis is on the world external to the family and how changes there both affected and were affected by changes in the structural and internal dynamics of the family. The role of the family in the modernization process has attracted much attention by intellectual historians such as Robert V. Wells. These interests cut across methodology, conceptual framework, and historiographical "schools" by which one might categorize family historians. One of the most sophisticated works that relates family to its larger society, *Family Time and Industrial Time* (1982), is by Tamara K. Hareven, an early proponent of the life-cycle approach who now advocates the life-course perspective. Glen Elder, Jr., suggests that these two approaches are compatible if the focus is on the household arrangement of individuals over time instead of the household unit per se.[4] Maris A. Vinovskis and Laura McCall advocate only the life-course approach in their chapter but have widened their vision to include external influences on the individual's involvement in that course, thus bringing them to a more cultural or intellectual emphasis. Together, historians have used these methodologies and conceptual schemes to develop a broad-ranging body of scholarship on the history of the American family.

In the course of this volume, a number of theoretical schemes appear, focusing on relations within the family, and between the family and the larger society and state. All attest to the process of individuation as one of the central dynamics of the history of the family in the United States. Perhaps the simplest way to conceptualize these relationships through time is to borrow characteristics that Darrett Rutman has developed for facilitating the study of early American communities.[5] A family, after all, can be viewed as a kind of community that has both horizontal (space, way of life, collective action) and vertical dimensions, both as a unit and as a group of individuals.

1. Space: A family is a social unit that occupies a limited space. That space, however, has changed. The trend toward smaller families and larger dwellings suggests that individual family members have increased their privacy and that the family as a unit spends much less time in common interior spaces.

2. Way of life: Families have their own distinctive ways of ordering their institutions, articulating their values, and generally distinguishing themselves from other families, in the same time period as well as in different geographical regions. A focus on economic strategies, for instance, highlights the preference of one family for educating its children and of another for sending them into the work force. We observe that over the course of time, as family prosperity has increased so has the family's desire to educate female children and thereby broaden their individual opportunities.

3. Collective action: Families operate as a unit but the degree of collective action

varies over time and among families. It is one of our observations that, over time, all families have been given less to collective action as individual members have pursued their independent goals.

4. External associations or vertical ties: Family members always have had relationships with larger social and political units, both as individuals and as members of a family unit. It seems that in more recent families, these external relationships are maintained more by individuals than by the unit.

These categories correspond with some of the ways historians of the family have conceived of their task and set about the process of developing a body of information about how American families have changed both in horizontal and in vertical directions.

INDIVIDUATION AND THE AMERICAN FAMILY

The history of the American family is a story of the conflict between the "family ideal" in American society and the core value of individualism. An analysis of this struggle provides a framework for understanding the history of the American family.[6] In clinical usage individuation is a psychological process whereby an infant discovers that he or she is in fact separate from his or her parents. If this concept is extended to the entire life course of an individual, then the process of psychological and economic separation from one's family of origin can also be labeled "individuation."[7] How this ideology of individualism and efforts to put it into practice have interacted with the family as an institution is the central question explored in this introduction.

The history of the American family falls into three distinct periods: before 1815, from 1815 to 1930, and since 1930. The turning points between these periods in family history are marked by major shifts in the behavior of family members as they become more individuated. In the early colonial period, for example, young people were so undifferentiated that their parents chose their marriage partners for them. By the nineteenth century, however, young people had claimed the right to choose their own mates. In that same period young men, responding to the ideal of self-improvement, strove to surpass their fathers in economic success. By the twentieth century young women had begun to claim the same rights as their brothers for self-improvement—including the right to be both economically and psychologically independent.

As family members became more differentiated from the group, the primary purpose of the family also shifted. To put it another way, changes in the relationship between the family and the society accompanied changes within the family. In the earliest period the primary purpose of the family had been economic survival. As society became more affluent, it became possible for the family to stress the psychological and economic development of its individual members. Formerly, the family had sought to advance as a unit, requiring its members to sacrifice their own interests for the benefit of the whole; now the family stressed individual growth and demonstrated its affluence by means of conspicuous consumption. This emphasis on upward social mobility continued more or less unabated until the Great Depression of the 1930s, which forced most families to cut back on their investment in self-fulfillment as times became hard.

Economic advancement and personal self-fulfillment were the goals of the process of individuation for young men as they left home to seek fame and fortune. Young women, while they enjoyed more personal freedom than their mothers and grandmothers had, did not, as a general rule, leave home to seek their fortunes and self-fulfillment until the twentieth century had entered its third decade. Thus the process of individuation had different meanings for sons and daughters.

Consumption provides one measure of the process of individuation. Over time, as the members of the family became more differentiated, items for the use of particular members accumulated. For example, excavations of archaeological sites dating from seventeenth- and eighteenth-century Massachusetts reveal that the number of dinner plates and chamber pots for single households increased dramatically. According to James Deetz this indicated a shift from an "older, corporate emphasis wherein sharing technomic objects was the norm" to "a one-to-one match, with each person having his own plate and chamber pot."[8]

If chamber pots could be individualized, so too could a host of other things. The nineteenth century saw a great extension in the range of goods available for sale as the industrial revolution transformed the household economy. As the nineteenth century gave way to the twentieth, planned obsolescence vastly magnified the market potential of the nation and made the process of conspicuous consumption never-ending. As a result, all members of the family became consumers in their own right. Today, among affluent families, even preteens possess large stereo sets, televisions, video cassette recorders, and microcomputers of their very own.[9]

We also see the process of individuation in other aspects of family life: the decline of dependence, the extension of the family's socialization function to new social institutions, and the separation of birth and death from the family. As individuation becomes more prominent, the family loses many of its former functions so that members relate to each other more on psychological and emotional bases and less because of economic dependence.[10]

The preindustrial family witnessed both birth and death at home. Children were born at home in the nineteenth century, but increasingly mothers chose male obstetricians to attend the birth. As the nineteenth century gave way to the twentieth, childbirth moved to the hospital. At about the same time death also moved to the hospital. This elimination of basic life-course events from the home is related to the process of individuation and reflects a major change in the family since the colonial period.[11]

The care of dependents consumed a major portion of the time of a preindustrial family. Rarely over the course of the life cycle of that family would it be free from the need to care for children, younger servants, or the elderly. But by the nineteenth century families spent less time caring for dependents because they had fewer children, and also because poorhouses and orphan asylums had appeared. The twentieth century saw the emergence of "retirement," which produced a new class of the idle elderly who provided for their own care or turned their care over to institutions when they had become incapacitated. Nursing homes for the elderly and day-care facilities for children were established to provide care for these dependents.

By creating new institutions, which took control of children for longer and longer time spans, reformers began removing parts or all of the socialization process from the home, thus accelerating the process of individuation. The story of the rise of various social institutions, including schools, public welfare agencies, juvenile justice institutions, and guidance clinics, indicates that society sought to supplement (and in some cases replace) the socialization function of the family.

Recently the historian and social critic Christopher Lasch has argued that the rise of public institutions and the appearance of experts on the family aid and abet the process of individuation and that the process itself leads to cultural and social disaster.[12] By contrast Daniel Yankelovich in *New Rules* is much more positive about contemporary society and the effects of individuation on family life. He believes that a new ethic of commitment is emerging in American society, a movement toward closer and deeper personal relationships, which reflects a switch from instrumental to "sacred expressive" values.[13]

Thus the family has evolved through these distinct phases. The preindustrial family, which many clinicians would label "enmeshed," gave way to the nineteenth-century middle-class family that sought to produce individualism and self-reliance in young men. For the most part in this nineteenth-century family the process of individuation was confined to sons who sought to outdistance their fathers and frequently chose careers in new fields. Daughters, in contrast, tended to sustain their "corporate" identity. Then, by the third decade of the twentieth century young women sought their own separation from the family by leaving home for gainful employment or by seeking advanced education.

In tracing this process of individuation in broad outline, we have focused on the culturally dominant family type, thereby homogenizing the distinctive variations that reflect ethnicity, race, class, and gender. Discussions of these variables within the context of family history typically occur at two levels— the level of ideas or larger cultural patterns and the level of human behavior. Family history necessarily includes both, and at times the distinctions become blurred. One of the aims of this new discipline is to discover the larger patterns in order to improve the ability to generalize about how the family has changed. This introduction focuses on larger cultural patterns, but the essays themselves point to a rich diversity of family arrangements and relationships.

Class is the variable that presents the most difficulty for family historians. While most of them recognize its importance and attempt to address it as an issue, few studies have focused on it alone. Nevertheless, anyone familiar with the history of the family recognizes the extent to which income affects family life. Nineteenth-century cities contained thousands of homeless people, including many children who lived on the city streets because their families had disintegrated. Other families, slightly more fortunate, remained together only because they relied on the labor of all the family members. Ironically, the poorest families witnessed a kind of involuntary individuation that resulted from the vagaries of life. More fortunate families fostered the individuation of their members themselves.[14]

Clearly race, class, ethnicity, and gender have had an effect on the American family. Selma Berrol and Karen Anderson point out that ethnicity and race interacted with economic class structure within a dominant culture that contained chauvinism and racism to create a variety of family arrangements within both the black and ethnic communities. Recent trends among these families reflect the general tendency in American life toward greater homogeneity, especially among middle-class Americans, regardless of their ethnicity. Still, race and ethnicity continue to retain their power as identifying symbols that differentiate one family from another.

The variable of gender is important mainly as the most obvious way to study the process of individuation that characterizes the evolution of the American family. Females remained an undifferentiated part of the collective family long after males were viewed as individuals. Women have followed the paths trod by their fathers, brothers, and sons, albeit forty paces behind. Only recently has American society come to realize that the process of individuation is no longer gender-bound.

As American families continue to respond to changes in the economic, technological and social environment, they will reflect the manner in which this most basic unit of society provides for its members—both collectively and individually. These chapters detailing the current state of the field of American family history should not only supply information on earlier families but also provide a perspective for understanding contemporary domestic arrangements. It is both expected and desirable that, as the study of American families continues along the lines suggested in these chapters, an even more complete understanding of American families will emerge.

NOTES

1. Robert N. Bellah et al., *Habits of the Heart: Individualism and Commitment in American Life* (Berkeley: University of California Press, 1985), 87; Christopher Lasch, *Haven in a Heartless World: The Family Besieged* (New York: Basic Books, 1977), xx.

2. Vol. 12, nos. 1–3 (1987).

3. Among them might be included Glen H. Elder, Jr., Tamara K. Hareven, John Modell, Maris A. Vinovskis, Howard P. Chudacoff, Carl F. Kaestle, and Michael B. Katz.

4. Glen H. Elder, Jr., "Families and Lives: Some Developments in Life-Course Studies," *Journal of Family History* 12 (1987): 187.

5. Darrett B. Rutman, "The Social Web: A Prospectus for the Study of Early American Community," in *Insights and Parallels: The Problems and Issues of American Social History*, ed. William O'Neill (Minneapolis, Minn.: Burgess Publishing Co., 1973), 57–89.

6. For a definition of the family ideal see Elizabeth Pleck, *Domestic Tyranny: The Making of American Social Policy against Family Violence from Colonial Times to the Present* (New York: Oxford University Press, 1987), 7–11. For a discussion of individualism as a core value in American society, see Bellah et al., 90, 111–12, 143.

7. For a discussion of the idea of individuation, see Margaret S. Mahler, Fred Pine, and Anni Bergman, *The Psychological Birth of the Human Infant: Symbiosis and Individuation* (New York: Basic Books, 1975), 3–15. See also Murray Bowen, *Family Therapy in Clinical Practice* (New York: Jason Aronson, 1978), chs. 21–22.

8. James Deetz, *In Small Things Forgotten: The Archaeology of Early American Life* (Garden City, N.Y.: Doubleday and Co., 1977), 58–59.

9. Christopher Lasch, *The Minimal Self: Psychic Survival in Troubled Times* (New York: W. W. Norton & Company, 1984), 185–86, 192.

10. Perhaps the best and most succinct account of this process is to be found in the conclusion to John Demos, *A Little Commonwealth: Family Life in Plymouth Colony* (New York: Oxford University Press, 1970).

11. Judith Walzer Leavitt, *Brought to Bed: Childbearing in America, 1750–1950* (New York: Oxford University Press, 1986); Philippe Aries, *Western Attitudes toward Death from the Middle Ages to the Present*, trans. Patricia M. Ranum (Baltimore, Md.: Johns Hopkins University Press, 1974), ch. 4.

12. Lasch, *Minimal Self*, passim.

13. Daniel Yankelovich, *New Rules: Searching for Self-Fulfillment in a World Turned Upside Down* (New York: Random House, 1981), 254–55.

14. For a cogent discussion of the impact of industrialization and urbanization

on family life, see Pleck, *Domestic Tyranny*, and Christine Stansell, *City of Women: Sex and Class in New York, 1789–1860* (Urbana: University of Illinois Press, 1987).

REFERENCES

Aries, Philippe. *Western Attitudes toward Death from the Middle Ages to the Present.* Patricia M. Ranum, trans. Baltimore, Md.: Johns Hopkins University Press, 1974.

Bellah, Robert N., et al. *Habits of the Heart: Individualism and Commitment in American Life.* Berkeley, Calif.: University of California Press, 1985.

Bowen, Murray. *Family Therapy in Clinical Practice.* New York: Jason Aronson, 1978.

Deetz, James. *In Small Things Forgotten: The Archeology of Early American Life.* Garden City, N.Y.: Doubleday and Co., 1977.

Demos, John. *A Little Commonwealth: Family Life in Plymouth Colony.* New York: Oxford University Press, 1970.

Elder, Glen H., Jr. "Families and Lives: Some Developments in Life-Course Studies." *Journal of Family History* 12 (1987): 179–99.

Lasch, Christopher. *Haven in a Heartless World: The Family Besieged.* New York: Basic Books, 1977.

Lasch, Christopher. *The Minimal Self: Psychic Survival in Troubled Times.* New York: W. W. Norton & Company, 1984.

Leavitt, Judith Walzer. *Brought to Bed: Childbearing in America, 1750–1950.* New York: Oxford University Press, 1986.

Mahler, Margaret S., Fred Pine, and Anni Bergman. *The Psychological Birth of the Human Infant: Symbiosis and Individuation.* New York: Basic Books, 1975.

Pleck, Elizabeth. *Domestic Tyranny: The Making of American Social Policy against Family Violence from Colonial Times to the Present.* New York: Oxford University Press, 1987.

Rutman, Darrett B. "The Social Web: A Prospectus for the Study of Early American Community." In *Insights and Parallels: The Problems and Issues of American Social History.* Ed. William O'Neill, 57–89. Minneapolis, Minn.: Burgess Publishing Co., 1973.

Stansell, Christine. *City of Women: Sex and Class in New York, 1789–1860.* Urbana: University of Illinois Press, 1987.

Yankelovich, Daniel. *New Rules: Searching for Self-Fulfillment in a World Turned Upside Down.* New York: Random House, 1981.

2

Changing Approaches to the Study of Family Life

Maris A. Vinovskis and Laura McCall

One of the newest and most exciting fields in history today concerns the family. Except for a few works, such as Arthur Calhoun's three-volume social history of the American family and Alice Morse Earle's study of child life in colonial America, the subject of family history has been virtually uncharted until recent times.[1] Beginning with Edmund Morgan's pioneering study of the Puritan family in 1944 and aided by the growing post–World War II interest in European families, historians during the past three decades began to study American family life in earnest.[2]

Despite the recent outpouring of research, there is considerable methodological confusion and disagreement over how the American family should be studied. Most historians are unaware of these differences and simply use the concept of the family rather casually in their research and writings. Those who pay more attention to these issues differ amongst themselves on how to organize the study of family life. Some prefer to compare and contrast generations, while many have employed simple indices of family life, such as mean household size. Others, borrowing from their sociology colleagues, use more sophisticated analytic approaches, such as family-cycle models or life-course analysis.

This chapter will review and critique some of the alternate approaches to the study of American family life in the past. Particular attention will be paid to the relative strengths and weaknesses of the family-cycle model and its main competitor today—life-course analysis. Finally, the chapter will suggest the need for reintegrating the study of individuals and families in the past with the broader social and cultural phenomena that shaped their lives and experiences.[3]

EARLY EFFORTS IN THE STUDY OF FAMILY LIFE

The first studies of families were mainly descriptive and usually focused exclusively upon the literate elites who left written records of their lives. While the dearth of materials available about the more average family still plagues historians, the use of quantification has enabled scholars to study common families through the use of vital and census records.

Most of the early efforts to study American family life using quantitative information were based upon family reconstitution. Estimating birth, marriage, and death rates by reconstructing the lives of individuals from their church and community vital records, these scholars portrayed the residents of colonial New England as having a high fertility rate and a surprisingly low adult mortality rate in the countryside.[4] Subsequent demographic work on the Chesapeake in the seventeenth and eighteenth centuries found lower fertility and much higher childhood and adult mortality rates than in New England.[5]

Demographic indices of early Americans were reported in a variety of ways, which has made comparisons difficult. Some analysts give the vital rates by the birth or marriage cohort of individuals. Others summarize the data by the broad chronological periods in which they occurred. Some provide demographic indices for the different generations.[6]

Since much of the early work on colonial families focused on the transmission of property from fathers to sons, the use of the concept of generations was frequently employed. Philip Greven, for example, analyzed the first settlers of Andover, Massachusetts, and grouped their descendants by generations.[7] While the concept of generations sometimes is useful in comparing the experiences of immigrants and their offspring, by the third or fourth generation it loses most of its analytical rigor as there is a considerable overlap among later generations. In other words, given the wide dispersion of births over the entire life course in colonial America, many members of the third and fourth generations were of the same age, lived at the same time in Andover, and probably did not distinguish themselves from each other in generational terms.[8] Indeed, David Kertzer warns social scientists against any use of generational analysis as it has limited analytic value in most circumstances.[9]

Another early approach, adopted primarily by European historians, was the analysis of mean household size. Their concerns were primarily whether European households were extended or nuclear and the implications this had for population growth, family structure, and the pace of industrialization. Rejecting the conventional wisdom that the shift from home to factory production shattered the premodern extended family, Peter Laslett demonstrated empirically that Western European families had always been relatively small and nuclear.[10] However, mean household size is not always a clear indicator of whether a family is extended or nuclear—scholars must know the exact composition of its residents. A large household may not necessarily indicate a complex extended family; in colonial New England, for example, households were large not because of the presence of various relatives but because of high fertility.[11] Further, as Lutz Berkner suggested in his study of eighteenth-century Austrian families, household composition changed among nuclear, extended, and stem-family arrangements depending upon time and circumstance.[12] As a result, the use of mean household size has been almost entirely abandoned by historians as providing too static and too simplistic a portrait of family life in the past.

FAMILY-CYCLE MODELS

Use of these pioneering approaches to family history—simple demographic indices, generational studies, or measurement of mean household size—rarely capture the attention of present-day scholars. Currently, two different approaches to the study of families in the past are more commonly used and reflect a more developmental emphasis. The first uses household or family cycles as a way to portray family dynamics in history.

European scholars tend to study family cycles in order to ascertain economic well-being of family life, particularly the availability of labor within the household. Berkner, for example, discovered that while mean family size changed hardly at all in eighteenth-century Austrian households, the labor available within these households could change dramatically according to the presence and age of the children. When children were either very young or had reached maturity and left home, the family had to hire workers or take in boarders to satisfy the labor requirements of that household.[13]

Like most other European historians who have adopted the family-cycle approach, Berkner uses the age of the male head of household to document these changes in family composition. His stages are also quite simple: while the parents are alive, the family is extended; when the parents die, the heir reigns over a nuclear family; and when the heir retires, his own son marries and the extended family reemerges.[14]

There are several problems with most analyses that utilize this particular type of family-cycle model. Almost all select the age of the male head of household to conceptualize their stages, but there is little agreement among the Europeanists as to the number of age groupings or at what age to begin a new category. Further, many of these scholars focus too heavily on the male head of household as the linchpin of their analyses, often ignoring other changes in family structure such as children leaving home or entering school.

Table 2.1
Evelyn Duvall's Eight-Stage Model of the Family Cycle

Stage I	Beginning families (married couple without children)
Stage II	Childbearing families (oldest child, birth to 30 months)
Stage III	Families with preschool children (oldest child 2 1/2 to 6 years)
Stage IV	Families with schoolchildren (oldest child 6 to 13 years)
Stage V	Families with teenagers (oldest child 13 to 20 years)
Stage VI	Families as launching centers (first child gone to last child's leaving home)
Stage VII	Families in middle years (empty nest to retirement)
Stage VIII	Aging families (retirement to death of one or both spouses)

American scholars, on the other hand, have been more assiduous in their attempts to capture the complexity of family cycles. Many have been influenced by the models of sociologists. For instance, Evelyn Duvall's eight-stage model of the family cycle reflects her belief that the social functioning of the family is largely determined by the age of the eldest child (see Table 2.1). As he or she enters school or leaves home permanently, the character of the family can change profoundly.[15]

The Duvall family-cycle model is limited because it only takes into consideration the presence and activities of the first child. The role of additional children, particularly important historically when couples had much larger families than today, is ignored altogether. When Roy Rodgers attempted to modify Duvall's scheme by taking into consideration both the youngest and the eldest child, the result was an unwieldy twenty-four-stage family-cycle model that has been virtually ignored by other analysts.[16]

Duvall's model is also limited historically because the relationship between parents and institutions such as schools varied over time. In colonial America parents were expected to provide primary education for their children at home rather than sending them to a private or public school. Yet by the mid-nineteenth century, public education had become widespread throughout most of the United States.[17] Since Duvall's family-cycle model is driven in large measure by school attendance, it is less relevant in periods and regions where children received their education at home.

Another classic sociological family-cycle model is the one developed by Reuben Hill. He proposed a nine-stage family-cycle model that is somewhat broader than Duvall's because it recognizes the potential importance of other children as well as the impact of the retirement of the father from the labor force (see Table 2.2).[18]

Table 2.2
Reuben Hill's Nine-Stage Model of the Family Cycle

Stage I	Establishment (newly married, childless)
Stage II	New parents (infant–3 years)
Stage III	Preschool family (child 3–6, and possible younger siblings)
Stage IV	School-age family (oldest child 6–12, possible younger siblings)
Stage V	Family with adolescent (oldest 13–19, possible younger siblings)
Stage VI	Family with young adult (oldest 20 until first child leaves home)
Stage VII	Family as launching center (from departure of first to last child)
Stage VIII	Postparental family, the middle years (after children have left home until father retires)
Stage IX	Aging family (after retirement of father)

While Hill's family-cycle model is an improvement upon Duvall's more narrow construction, it too suffers from the lack of sufficient information about the number and activities of the children within the family. Since adolescents often worked in the past, otherwise comparable families with a larger proportion of older children in the labor force than in school experienced fewer economic difficulties. In addition, although Hill's model acknowledges the importance of the father working, it does not provide an opportunity for incorporating the effects of any work or career changes on the well-being of the family. Furthermore, the concept of retirement itself is really a twentieth-century phenomenon as most colonial and nineteenth-century Americans continued to work until they were incapacitated or died.[19]

Dissatisfaction with the existing sociological family-cycle models has led scholars to call for more appropriate ones that are more relevant historically. In 1974 Tamara Hareven urged that a more culturally and historically appropriate family-cycle model be developed:

Family research in the next few years will have to determine what type of family cycles existed and what the significant stages of transition were. Historians of the life cycle (childhood, adolescence, youth) have already demonstrated the fact that stages of psychobiological development are socially defined, and that it would be impossible, therefore, to rely on universal stages. Similarly, stages in the family cycle are not governed simply by biological age grades. In their analysis of contemporary groups, family sociologists are grappling with the classification of stages of the family cycle. Historians will not only need to define such stages for past societies, but to interpret their relationship in the historical accounts.[20]

Table 2.3
Katz, Doucet, and Stern's Twelve-Stage Model of the Family Cycle

Stage I	Young (wife under 25), no children
Stage II	Young (wife under 25), all children aged 1–6
Stage III	Early midcycle (wife 25–34), no children
Stage IV	Early midcycle (wife 25–34), all children aged 1–14
Stage V	Late midcycle (wife 35–44), no children
Stage VI	Late midcycle (wife 35–44), all children aged 1–14
Stage VII	Late midcycle (wife 35–44), at least one male child 15 or over
Stage VIII	Late midcycle (wife 35–44), all children 15 or over, female
Stage IX	Late cycle (wife 45 or over), at least one male child 15 or over
Stage X	Late cycle (wife 45 or over), all children 15 or over, female
Stage XI	Late cycle (wife 45 or over), no children
Stage XII	Late cycle (wife 45 or over), other

Hareven's challenge for the development of a new family-cycle model more appropriate for historical analyses remains unanswered. Several historians have incorporated the concept of family cycle in their works, but they have not carefully defined or specified the particular model they are employing.[21]

There has been one recent effort to provide a more detailed family-cycle model appropriate for historical analysis. This model was proposed by Michael Katz, Michael Doucet, and Mark Stern in their study of family life in Hamilton, Canada, during the second half of the nineteenth century (see Table 2.3). Instead of accepting the traditional approach to family-cycle models, which focuses upon the age of the male head of household, Katz and his colleagues chose instead the age of the wife. Their chief concern is how the presence of children placed economic strains on the family.[22]

This model is creative, and its implications for the study of women are intriguing. However, the focus of the Hamilton study was economic, and the selection of a wife's age, particularly in the nineteenth century, could mask important shifts in the family's financial status. Since so few married women worked outside of the home, the mother's age is not necessarily a good barometer of family income. In addition, they failed to distinguish between children who were at school (a potential burden on the family) and children who worked and may have alleviated financial strains. Further, their stages are based upon intact, two-parent families exclusively, and thus they do not address the experiences of families living in one-parent households. Finally, since some of their stages are mutually exclusive, this is not really a family-cycle model that depicts stages through which all or most families must pass.

LIFE-COURSE ANALYSIS

All of these models of the family cycle possess limitations for the historian: many fail to take into account historical contexts, most ignore the experiences of individuals within families, and few are sensitive to the varied social environments of the past. None of these family-cycle models takes into consideration the effects of differences among individuals or families in the timing or sequencing of events. Given these inadequacies, many historians have concluded that the family-cycle approach usually is unworkable and have begun to turn to life-course analysis, which focuses on the individual rather than the family as the unit of analysis:

Life-course analysis in some ways signifies a radical departure from earlier efforts to study the family. Rather than trying to categorize and analyze developments in the family as a whole, the life course focuses only on the more limited experiences of the members of that family. Life-course analysis, however, is derived from the earlier efforts to study life histories and pays particular attention to three components of an individual's life—approximate stage of biological development, age-related social roles, and historical position.[23]

Whereas the family-cycle models are easy to describe and follow since they consist of only a few stages, life-course analysis is more difficult to use because it is more of a perspective than a specific prescription for analysis. Perhaps the best summary of it comes from one of its most articulate proponents, Glen Elder:

The life course refers to pathways through the age-differentiated life-span, to social patterns in timing, duration, spacing, and order of events; the timing of an event may be as consequential for life experience as whether the event occurs and the degree or type of change. Age differentiation is manifested in expectations and options that impinge on decision processes and the course of events that give shape to life stages, transitions, and turning points. Such differentiation is based in part on the social meanings of age and the biological facts of birth, sexual maturity, and death. These meanings have varied through social history and across cultures at points in time, as documented by evidence on socially recognized age categories, grades, and classes. . . . Over the life course, age differentiation also occurs through the interplay of demographic and economic processes, as in the relation between economic swings and timing of family events. Sociocultural, demographic, and maternal factors are essential in a theory of life-course variation.[24]

Unlike the family-cycle approach, the life course focuses more squarely upon individuals in order to discover how not only their families, but also peer groups, institutions, and historical events impact their lives. It is particularly concerned with the transitions in an individual's life within the broader cultural and historical contexts in which they occur.

Since the early 1970s considerable work has been done on the family using a life-course perspective. Peter Uhlenberg's pioneering studies of female birth cohorts born from 1830 to 1920 and from 1890 to 1931 found more white women conforming to the traditional life patterns of marriage and motherhood over time.[25] Albert Chevan and Gordon F. Sutton, who examined life-course differentials by race and sex, discovered important differences in family experiences resulting from social norms that dictated appropriate behavior for blacks and whites or men and women.[26] Elder has explored skillfully the effects of the Great Depression and World War II on the cohorts of children born in Oakland between 1920 and 1921 and in Berkeley between 1928 and 1929.[27] Hareven has studied the lives of textile mill workers in Manchester, New Hampshire in the early twentieth century.[28] And a group of historians have used life-course analysis to investigate the lives of the residents of Essex County, Massachusetts in 1860 and 1880 using cross-sectional federal census data.[29]

Much has already been written about the conceptual and methodological problems involved in using a life-course perspective to study family life in the past.[30] Therefore, it is not necessary to repeat those earlier discussions. Instead, we want to focus in more detail on the need to develop a broader historical and normative context in which to use life-course analysis. As Elder recently observed:

The life course has become a prominent framework for demographic analysis, especially in relation to family transitions generally and the adult transition in particular. By comparison, cultural influences on the life course remain noteworthy for their acknowledged importance *and* lack of development. We still lack research on the normative patterning of the life course.[31]

Scholars have been calling for greater linkages between historical processes such as cultural change and the impact of outside events upon the family for a long time. Nevertheless, those utilizing the life course as a methodological tool too often consider only the experiences within families. However, under what conditions should we look at the family as a self-contained unit? Individuals within a family also interact with other institutions and peer groups that may influence their attitudes and behavior. For example, Norman Ryder places great emphasis on schooling as a "cohort creator," but what do children actually learn in schools that might influence their future life courses?[32] Studies of textbook content would provide one direction for exploration. An intriguing approach would be to examine cohorts as peer groups: in other words, what do people in the same birth cohort teach each other?

Trying to ascertain the social norms of a group is extremely difficult. One new method might examine prescriptive literature of the past or the electronic media of the present and determine the frequency of messages proclaiming a certain style of life. This might enable the scholar to examine not only external events like wars or depressions, but also cultural messages learned or reinforced through sermons, novels, textbooks, editorials, television, and movies. The problem is determining the function of prescriptive materials. Do they clarify, reinforce, modify, or reflect attitudes and behavior? Who are the readers and viewers? The earliest studies engaging these questions made distinctions between "highbrow" and "lowbrow" art and engaged in lively debates about the position of art in a culture. Many assumed that literature does indeed mirror the times in which it was written and that, in addition, "it confirms and strengthens cultural norms."[33] Others suggested that literature is more symptomatic than causal.

Thus the prime effect of the media is to reinforce already-existing behavior and attitudes, rather than to create new ones. . . . Moreover, a society's art, information and entertainment do not develop in a vacuum; they must meet the standards of form and substance which grow out of the values of the society and the needs and characteristics of its members.[34]

Other investigations, however, argue that popular literature is biased toward the elite and economically powerful; they have reported that statistical characteristics of a society are not reproduced in its fiction.[35] This last study, however, failed to look at normative messages that may have been universal to the culture. Furthermore, the depiction of wealthy and powerful characters provides glimpses of a life-style toward which the middle and lower classes may have aspired or which they sought to emulate.

Recent studies more carefully examine the readers and writers of popular art forms and are discovering that exposure to them affects people in considerable ways. Jane Tompkins, in her study of best-selling novels published during the early national period, persuasively argues that fiction "offers powerful examples of the way a culture thinks about itself, articulating and proposing solutions for the problems that shape a particular historical moment." Tompkins asserts that not only did nineteenth-century writers actively engage in the discussion and evaluation of actual events, but they also regarded themselves as shapers of public morality.[36] Laura McCall discovered the same phenomenon in her study of novels published between 1820 and 1860. Most were highly didactic and contained lengthy asides in which the authors virtually preached to their readers.[37]   Janice Radway found that consumers of romantic fiction, particularly those stories that featured weak or foolish heroines, served as gentle reminders concerning their own behavior.

In reading some of those "namby-pamby books about the women who let the man dominate them," Dot explained, the readers "are thinking 'they're nerds.' And they begin to reevaluate. 'Am I acting like that?' " They begin to say to themselves, she added, "Hey, wait a minute—my old man kinda tends to do this." And then, "because women are capable of learning from what they read," they begin "to express what they want and sometimes refuse to be ordered around any longer."

Later, Radway suggests that, although romantic novels exert a conservative influence upon women because they emphasize women's roles as wives and mothers, they also depict heroines who "find their identity through the care of a nurturant protector and sexual partner." In so doing, the readers "might well be teaching themselves to believe in the worth of such a route to fulfillment and encouraging the hope that such a route might yet open up for them as it once did for the heroine."[38]

The "teaching" function of popular art forms may be even more pervasive with the introduction of electronic media, particularly the television. George Gerbner and Larry Gross assert that television "is the central cultural arm of American society, serving to socialize most people (especially children) into standardized roles and behaviors."[39] Other studies even suggest that heavy television watchers have a different sense of reality. Queries of both daytime and prime-time viewers have found that they believe there are more murders, abortions, jailings, and divorces than actually exist in society.[40]

Central to scholars of the life course must be an examination of the frequency of certain messages during the lifetimes of a particular birth cohort, especially during its youth.[41] A powerful methodological tool in the study of prescriptive sources is content analysis, which enables researchers to code and categorize information in a systematic fashion. The use of a carefully designed and tested coding sheet permits the examination of limitless variables, including an evaluation of the hypotheses of other scholars. For students of the life course, content analysis could be used to measure changes in attitudes and behavior over time and to discover whether there are any connections between the values expressed in popular art forms and the actions of a contemporaneous birth cohort.

Next comes the problem of integrating popular materials with a life-course analysis. John Modell, who has not relied heavily upon prescriptive materials, and in fact has challenged the validity of using legal or literary sources to understand families, does suggest a method.[42] In his recent study of twentieth-century American youth, he introduces his chapter on the baby boom with a 1959 short story published in *True Love* magazine. Entitled "Coke for Breakfast," it describes two sixteen-year-olds who impetuously marry after a high-school dance. Their indulgent parents accept the marriage itself but insist that the young couple abandon certain childish practices like drinking Coca-Cola for breakfast. Modell suggests that these rather benign parental injunctions, which the young people refuse to obey, coupled with the acceptance of the marriage demonstrate "a further assumption by adolescents of prerogatives formerly their parents'." Furthermore, their early marriages and the possibility that young Jill is pregnant (later disconfirmed) reflect the "downward revision of the timetable for family-building" that occurred in the 1950s. The young people assert their values despite parental objections; Modell suggests this was possible because of permissive parents who "liked their goofy children quite well" and because the prosperity of the age would ensure their economic survival.[43] The integration of his statistical findings with popular fiction not only reveals a new pathway for life-course studies, but also it deepens his analysis.

CONCLUSION

The study of family history has undergone a clear evolution from anecdotal recitals of family life to examinations of generations, mean household size, family-cycle models and life-course analyses. Although the life-course approach currently holds the greatest promise for those seeking to understand family dynamics, it still needs greater grounding within specific historical periods and a better appreciation of the impact of social organizations and norms on the lives of individuals. This chapter suggests that a systematic examination of didactic and literary materials may provide one method by which scholars can integrate and elaborate upon changes and continuities in social norms which may have affected or influenced the behaviors of family members living during a particular historical moment.

NOTES

1. Arthur W. Calhoun, *A Social History of the American Family*, 3 vols. (New York: Barnes and Noble, 1917–1919). Alice Morse Earle, *Child Life in Colonial Days* (New York: Macmillan Co., 1899).

2. Edmund S. Morgan, *The Puritan Family: Religion and Domestic Relations in Seventeenth-Century New England*. 1944. Revised edition. (New York: Harper and Row, 1966).

3. For some overviews of American family life in the past, see Stephanie

Coontz, *The Social Origins of Private Life: A History of American Families, 1600–1900* (London: Verso, 1988); Carl N. Degler, *At Odds: Women and the Family in America from the Revolution to the Present* (New York: Oxford University Press, 1980); Steven Mintz and Susan Kellogg, *Domestic Revolutions: A Social History of American Family Life* (New York: The Free Press, 1988).

4. John Demos, *A Little Commonwealth: Family Life in Plymouth Colony* (New York: Oxford University Press, 1970); Philip J. Greven, Jr., *Four Generations: Population, Land, and Family in Colonial Andover, Massachusetts* (Ithaca, N.Y.: Cornell University Press, 1970); Kenneth A. Lockridge, *A New England Town: The First Hundred Years, Dedham, Massachusetts, 1636–1736* (New York: W. W. Norton & Company, 1970).

5. Darrett B. Rutman and Anita H. Rutman, *A Place in Time: Middlesex County, Virginia, 1650–1750* (New York: W. W. Norton & Company, 1984); Allan Kulikoff, *Tobacco and Slaves: The Development of Southern Cultures in the Chesapeake, 1680–1800* (Chapel Hill: University of North Carolina Press, 1986).

6. Maris A. Vinovskis, "Recent Trends in American Historical Demography: Some Methodological and Conceptual Considerations," *Annual Review of Sociology* 4 (1978): 603–27.

7. Greven, *Four Generations*.

8. Maris A. Vinovskis, "From Household Size to the Life Course: Some Observations on Recent Trends in Family History," *American Behavioral Scientist* 21 (November/December 1977): 263–87.

9. David I. Kertzer, "Generation and Age in Cross-Cultural Perspective," in *Aging from Birth to Death: Sociotemporal Perspectives*, ed. Matilda White Riley, Ronald P. Abeles, and Michael S. Teitelbaum (Boulder, Colo.: Westview Press, 1982): 27–50.

10. Peter Laslett, *The World We Have Lost: England before the Industrial Age* (New York: Charles Scribner's Sons, 1965); Peter Laslett, ed., *Household and Family in Past Time* (Cambridge: Cambridge University Press, 1972).

11. John Demos, "Families in Colonial Bristol, Rhode Island: An Exercise in Historical Demography," *William and Mary Quarterly* 3rd ser., 25 (October 1968): 40–57.

12. Lutz Berkner, "The Stem Family and the Development Cycle of the Peasant Household: An Eighteenth-Century Austrian Example," *American Historical Review* 77 (April 1972): 398–418.

13. Berkner, "Stem Family and the Development Cycle."

14. For examples of other studies in European history using the family-cycle approach, see Peter Czap, " 'A Large Family: The Peasant's Greatest Wealth': Serf Households in Mishino, Russia, 1814–1858," in *Family Forms in Historic Europe*, ed. Richard Wall, Jean Robin, and Peter Laslett (Cambridge: Cambridge University Press, 1983): 105–51; Richard Wall, "Does Owning Real Property Influence the Form of the Household? An Example from Rural West Flanders" in ibid., 379–407.

15. Evelyn M. Duvall, *Family Development* (Philadelphia, Pa.: J. B. Lippincott, 1967).

16. Roy H. Rodgers, *Improvement in the Construction and Analysis of Family Life Cycle Categories* (Kalamazoo: Western Michigan University Press, 1962).

17. Maris A. Vinovskis, "Family and Schooling in Colonial and Nineteenth-

Century America," *Journal of Family History* 12 (1987): 19–37.

18. Reuben Hill, "Methodological Issues in Family Development Research," *Family Process* 3 (March 1964): 186–206.

19. William Graebner, *A History of Retirement: The Meaning and Function of an American Institution, 1885–1978* (New Haven, Conn.: Yale University Press, 1980); Carole Haber, *Beyond Sixty-Five: The Dilemma of Old Age in America's Past* (New York and Cambridge: Cambridge University Press, 1983).

20. Tamara K. Hareven, "The Family Process: The Historical Study of the Family Cycle," *Journal of Social History* 7 (Spring 1974): 322–29.

21. For examples see Michael R. Haines, "Poverty, Economic Stress, and the Family in a Late-Nineteenth-Century American City: Whites in Philadelphia, 1880," in *Philadelphia: Work, Space, Family, and Group Experiences in the Nineteenth Century: Essays toward an Interdisciplinary History*, ed. Theodore Hershberg (New York: Oxford University Press, 1981), 245–76; Mary P. Ryan, *Cradle of the Middle Class: The Family in Oneida County, New York, 1790–1865* (Cambridge: Cambridge University Press, 1981); Robert V. Wells, *Uncle Sam's Family: Issues in and Perspectives on American Demographic History* (Albany: State University of New York Press, 1985). For a critique of these approaches, see Maris A. Vinovskis, "The Historian and the Life Course: Reflections on Recent Approaches to the Study of American Family Life in the Past" in *Life-Span Development and Behavior*, ed. Paul B. Baltes, David L. Featherman, and Richard M. Lerner, Vol. 8 (Hillsdale, N.J.: Lawrence Erlbaum Associates, 1988): 33–59.

22. Michael B. Katz, Michael J. Doucet, and Mark J. Stern, *The Social Organization of Early Industrial Capitalism* (Cambridge, Mass.: Harvard University Press, 1982).

23. Maris A. Vinovskis, "American Families in the Past," in *Ordinary People and Everyday Life: Perspectives on the New Social History*, ed. James B. Gardner and George Rollie Adams (Nashville, Tenn.: American Association for State and Local History, 1983), 119.

24. Glen Elder, Jr., "Family History and the Life Course" (pp. 21–22), in Tamara K. Hareven, ed., *Transitions: The Family and the Life Course in Historical Perspective* (New York: Academic Press, 1978): 17–64. See also Charles Tilly, "Foreword," in ibid., xi–xv.

25. Peter Uhlenberg, "A Study of Cohort Life Cycles: Cohorts of Native Born Massachusetts Women, 1830–1920," *Population Studies* 23 (1969): 407–20: Peter Uhlenberg, "Cohort Variations in Life Cycle Experiences of U. S. Females," *Journal of Marriage and the Family* 36 (May 1974): 284–92.

26. Albert Chevan and Gordon F. Sutton, "Race and Sex Differentials in the Life Course," in *Life Course Dynamics: Trajectories and Transitions, 1968–1980*, ed. Glen H. Elder, Jr. (Ithaca, N.Y.: Cornell University Press, 1985), 282–301.

27. Glen H. Elder, Jr., *Children of the Great Depression: Social Change in Life Experience* (Chicago: University of Chicago Press, 1974); Glen H. Elder, Jr., "Military Times and Turning Points in Men's Lives," *Developmental Psychology* 22 (March 1986): 233–45.

28. Tamara K. Hareven, *Family Time and Industrial Time: The Relationship between the Family and Work in a New England Industrial Community* (Cambridge: Cambridge University Press, 1982).

29. Hareven, *Transitions*.

30. Elder, "Family History and the Life Course"; Vinovskis, "The Historian and the Life Course." See also David L. Featherman, "Biography, Society, and History: Individual Development as a Population Process," in *Human Development and the Life Course: Multidisciplinary Perspectives*, ed. Aage B. Sorensen, Franz E. Weinert, and Lonnie R. Sherrod (Hillsdale, N.J.: Lawrence Erlbaum Associates, 1986): 99–149; and Martin Kohli, "The World We Forgot: A Historical Review of the Life Course," in *Later Life: The Social Psychology of Aging*, ed. Victor W. Marshall (Beverly Hills, Calif.: Sage Publications, 1986): 271–303.

31. Glen H. Elder, Jr., "Families and Lives: Some Developments in Life-Course Studies," in *Family History at the Crossroads: A Journal of Family History Reader*, ed. Tamara Hareven and Andrejs Plakans (Princeton, N.J.: Princeton University Press, 1987): 179–80.

32. Norman B. Ryder, "The Cohort as a Concept in the Study of Social Change," *American Sociological Review* 30 (December 1965): 854.

33. M. C. Albrecht, "The Relationship of Literature and Society," *American Journal of Sociology* 59 (March 1954): 428.

34. Herbert J. Gans, *Popular Culture and High Culture* (New York: Basic Books, 1974), 32, 67.

35. B. Berelson and Patricia J. Salter, "Majority and Minority Americans: An Analysis of Magazine Fiction," *Public Opinion Quarterly* 10 (Summer 1946): 188.

36. Jane Tompkins, *Sensational Designs: The Cultural Work of American Fiction, 1790–1860* (New York: Oxford University Press, 1985), xi, 44–45.

37. Laura McCall, "Symmetrical Minds: Literary Men and Women in Antebellum America" (Ph.D. diss., University of Michigan, 1988), esp. 144–46, 246, 282, 301.

38. Janice A. Radway, *Reading the Romance: Women, Patriarchy, and Popular Literature* (Chapel Hill: University of North Carolina Press, 1984), 102, 187.

39. George Gerbner and Larry Gross, "The Scary World of TV," *Psychology Today* 9 (1976): 41–45, cited in Muriel G. Cantor and Suzanne Pingree, *The Soap Opera* (Beverly Hills, Calif.: Sage Publications, 1983), 138.

40. See N. Buerkel-Rothfuss and S. Mayes, "Soap Opera Viewing: The Cultivation Effect," *Journal of Communication* 31 (Summer 1981): 108–15; and R. Carveth and A. Alison, "Learning from Television Whether You Intend to or Not: Reality Exploration and the Cultivation Effect" (paper presented at the annual meetings of the Eastern Communication Association, Hartford, Conn., 1982). Both of these studies are summarized in Cantor and Pingree, *The Soap Opera*, 139–40.

41. Both Norman Ryder and Bernice Neugarten and her collaborators emphasize the importance of youth in pushing the boundaries of accepted social norms. See Ryder, "The Cohort as a Concept in the Study of Social Change," 849, 852; and Bernice L. Neugarten, John W. Moore, and John C. Lowe, "Age Norms, Age Constraints, and Adult Socialization," *American Journal of Sociology* 70 (May 1965): 710–17.

42. John Modell, "Changing Risks, Changing Adaptations: American Families in the Nineteenth and Twentieth Centuries," in *Kin and Communities: Families in America*, ed. Allan J. Lichtman and Joan R. Challinor (Washington, D.C.: Smithsonian Institution Press, 1979): 119–44.

43. John Modell, *Into One's Own: From Youth to Adulthood in the United States, 1920–1975* (Berkeley: University of California Press, 1989), 213–16.

REFERENCES

Albrecht, M. C. "The Relationship of Literature and Society." *American Journal of Sociology* 59 (March 1954): 425–36.

Berelson, B., and Patricia J. Salter. "Majority and Minority Americans: An Analysis of Magazine Fiction." *Public Opinion Quarterly* 10 (Summer 1946): 168–90.

Berkner, Lutz. "The Stem Family and the Developmental Cycle of the Peasant Household: An Eighteenth-Century Austrian Example." *American Historical Review* 77 (April 1972): 398–418.

Buerkel-Rothfuss, N., and S. Mayes. "Soap Opera Viewing: The Cultivation Effect." *Journal of Communication* 31 (Summer 1981): 108–15.

Calhoun, Arthur W. *A Social History of the American Family*, 3 vols. New York: Barnes and Noble, 1917–1919.

Canter, Muriel G., and Suzanne Pingree. *The Soap Opera*. Beverly Hills, Calif.: Sage Publications, 1983.

Chevan, Albert, and Gordon F. Sutton. "Race and Sex Differentials in the Life Course." In *Life Course Dynamics: Trajectories and Transitions, 1968–1980*, ed. Glen H. Elder, Jr., 282–301. Ithaca, N.Y.: Cornell University Press, 1985.

Coontz, Stephanie. *The Social Origins of Private Life: A History of American Families, 1600–1900*. London: Verso, 1988.

Czap, Peter. " 'A Large Family: The Peasant's Greatest Wealth': Serf Households in Mishino, Russia, 1814–1858." In *Family Forms in Historic Europe*, ed. Richard Wall, Jean Robin, and Peter Laslett, 105–51. Cambridge: Cambridge University Press, 1983.

Degler, Carl N. *At Odds: Women and the Family in America from the Revolution to the Present*. New York: Oxford University Press, 1980.

Demos, John. "Families in Colonial Bristol, Rhode Island: An Exercise in Historical Demography." *William and Mary Quarterly* 3d Ser., 25 (October 1968): 40–57.

———. *A Little Commonwealth: Family Life in Plymouth Colony*. New York: Oxford University Press, 1970.

Duvall, Evelyn M. *Family Development*. Philadelphia, Pa.: J. B. Lippincott, 1967.

Earle, Alice Morse. *Child Life in Colonial Days*. New York: Macmillan Co., 1899.

Elder, Glen H., Jr., *Children of the Great Depression: Social Change in Life Experience*. Chicago: University of Chicago Press, 1974.

———. "Families and Lives: Some Developments in Life-Course Studies." In *Family History at the Crossroads: A Journal of Family History Reader*, ed. Tamara Hareven and Andrejs Plakans, 179–99. Princeton, N. J.: Princeton University Press, 1987.

———. "Family History and the Life Course." In *Transitions: The Family and the Life Course in Historical Perspective*, ed. by Tamara K. Hareven, 17–64. New York: Academic Press, 1978.

———. "Military Times and Turning Points in Men's Lives." *Developmental Psy-*

chology 22 (March 1986): 233–45.

———. "Perspectives on the Life Course." In *Life Course Dynamics: Trajectories and Transitions, 1968–1980*, ed. Glen H. Elder, Jr., 23–49. Ithaca, N.Y.: Cornell University Press, 1985.

Featherman, David L. "Biography, Society, and History: Individual Development as a Population Process." In *Human Development and the Life Course: Multidisciplinary Perspectives*, ed. Aage B. Sorensen, Franz E. Weinert, and Lonnie R. Sherrod, 99–149. Hillsdale, N.J.: Lawrence Erlbaum Associates, 1986.

Gans, Herbert J. *Popular Culture and High Culture*. New York: Basic Books, 1974.

Graebner, William. *A History of Retirement: The Meaning and Function of an American Institution, 1885–1978*. New Haven, Conn.: Yale University Press, 1980.

Greven, Philip J., Jr. *Four Generations: Population, Land, and Family in Colonial Andover, Massachusetts*. Ithaca, N.Y.: Cornell University Press, 1970.

Haber, Carole. *Beyond Sixty-Five: The Dilemma of Old Age in America's Past*. Cambridge: Cambridge University Press, 1983.

Haines, Michael R. "Poverty, Economic Stress, and the Family in a Late-Nineteenth-Century American City: Whites in Philadelphia, 1880." In *Philadelphia: Work, Space, Family, and Group Experiences in the Nineteenth Century: Essays Toward an Interdisciplinary History*, ed. Theodore Hershberg, 245–76. New York: Oxford University Press, 1981.

Hareven, Tamara K. "The Family Process: The Historical Study of the Family Cycle." *Journal of Social History* 7 (Spring 1974): 322–29.

———. *Family Time and Industrial Time: The Relationship between the Family and Work in a New England Industrial Community*. Cambridge: Cambridge University Press, 1982.

———, ed. *Transitions: The Family and the Life Course in Historical Perspective*. New York: Academic Press, 1978.

Hill, Reuben. "Methodological Issues in Family Development Research." *Family Process* 3 (March 1964): 186–206.

Katz, Michael B., Michael J. Doucet, and Mark J. Stern. *The Social Organization of Early Industrial Capitalism*. Cambridge, Mass.: Harvard University Press, 1982.

Kertzer, David I. "Generation and Age in Cross-Cultural Perspective." In *Aging from Birth to Death: Sociotemporal Perspectives*, ed. Matilda White Riley, Ronald P. Abeles, and Michael S. Teitelbaum, 27–50. Boulder, Colo.: Westview Press, 1982.

Kohli, Martin. "The World We Forgot: A Historical Review of the Life Course." In *Later Life: The Social Psychology of Aging*, ed. Victor W. Marshall, 271–303. London: Sage Publications, 1986.

Kulikoff, Allan. *Tobacco and Slaves: The Development of Southern Cultures in the Chesapeake, 1680–1800*. Chapel Hill: University of North Carolina Press, 1986.

Laslett, Peter, ed. *Household and Family in Past Time*. Cambridge: Cambridge University Press, 1972.

———. *The World We Have Lost: England Before the Industrial Age*. New York: Charles Scribner's Sons, 1965.

Lockridge, Kenneth A. *A New England Town: The First Hundred Years, Dedham,*

Massachusetts, 1636–1736. New York: W. W. Norton & Company, 1970.

McCall, Laura. "Symmetrical Minds: Literary Men and Women in Antebellum America." Ph.D. diss., University of Michigan, 1988.

Mintz, Steven, and Susan Kellogg. *Domestic Revolutions: A Social History of American Family Life.* New York: The Free Press, 1988.

Modell, John. "Changing Risks, Changing Adaptations: American Families in the Nineteenth and Twentieth Centuries." In *Kin and Communities: Families in America,* ed. Allan J. Lichtman and Joan R. Challinor, 119–44. Washington, D.C.: Smithsonian Institution Press, 1979.

———. *Into One's Own: From Youth to Adulthood in the United States, 1920–1975.* Berkeley: University of California Press, 1989.

Morgan, Edmund S. *The Puritan Family: Religion and Domestic Relations in Seventeenth-Century New England.* 1944. Revised edition. New York: Harper and Row, 1966.

Neugarten, Bernice L., John W. Moore, and John C. Lowe. "Age Norms, Age Constraints, and Adult Socialization." *American Journal of Sociology* 70 (May 1965): 710–17.

Radway, Janice A. *Reading the Romance: Women, Patriarchy, and Popular Literature.* Chapel Hill: University of North Carolina Press, 1984.

Rodgers, Roy H. *Improvement in the Construction and Analysis of Family Life Cycle Categories.* Kalamazoo: Western Michigan University Press, 1962.

Rutman, Darrett B., and Anita H. Rutman. *A Place in Time: Middlesex County, Virginia, 1650–1750.* New York: W.W. Norton & Company, 1984.

Ryan, Mary P. *Cradle of the Middle Class: The Family in Oneida County, New York, 1790–1865.* Cambridge: Cambridge University Press, 1981.

Ryder, Norman B. "The Cohort as a Concept in the Study of Social Change." *American Sociological Review* 30 (December 1965): 843–61.

Tilly, Charles. "Foreword." In *Transitions: The Family and the Life Course in Historical Perspective,* ed. Tamara K. Hareven, xi–xv. New York: Academic Press, 1978.

Tompkins, Jane. *Sensational Designs: The Cultural Work of American Fiction, 1790–1866.* New York: Oxford University Press, 1985.

Uhlenberg, Peter. "Cohort Variations in Life Cycle Experiences of U.S. Females." *Journal of Marriage and the Family* 36 (May 1974): 284–92.

———. "A Study of Cohort Life Cycles: Cohorts of Native Born Massachusetts Women, 1830–1920." *Population Studies* 23 (1969): 407–20.

Vinovskis, Maris A. "American Families in the Past." In *Ordinary People and Everyday Life: Perspectives on the New Social History,* ed. James B. Gardner and George Rollie Adams, 115–137. Nashville, Tenn.: American Association for State and Local History, 1983.

———. "Family and Schooling in Colonial and Nineteenth-Century America." *Journal of Family History* 12 (1987): 19–37.

———. "From Household Size to the Life Course: Some Observations on Recent Trends in Family History." *American Behavioral Scientist* 21 (November/December 1977): 263–87.

———. "The Historian and the Life Course: Reflections on Recent Approaches to the Study of American Family Life in the Past." In *Life-Span Development and Behavior,* ed. Paul B. Baltes, David L. Featherman, and Richard M.

Lerner. Vol. 8: 33–59. Hillsdale, N.J.: Lawrence Erlbaum Associates, 1988.

————. "Recent Trends in American Historical Demography: Some Methodological and Conceptual Considerations." *Annual Review of Sociology* 4 (1978): 603–27.

Wall, Richard. "Does Owning Real Property Influence the Form of the Household? An Example from Rural West Flanders." In *Family Forms in Historic Europe*, ed. Richard Wall, Jean Robin, and Peter Laslett, 379–407. Cambridge: Cambridge University Press, 1983.

Wells, Robert V. *Uncle Sam's Family: Issues in and Perspectives on American Demographic History*. Albany: State University of New York Press, 1985.

II

Periods in the Study of the Family

3

The Preindustrial Family (1600–1815)

Ross W. Beales, Jr.

Few fields in American history have grown as quickly, or produced such substantial scholarship, as the history of the family. Although the field hardly existed in the 1960s,[1] the development of social history in general, new methodologies, the example of British and French scholarship, and a growing interest in everyday life led American scholars, especially younger members of the profession, to begin the systematic exploration of family history. Not surprisingly, the first efforts focused on New England, where generations of town clerks, antiquarians, and genealogists had compiled exceptionally rich records. The work of three scholars, John Demos, Philip J. Greven, Jr., and Kenneth A. Lockridge, seemed to burst onto the historiographical landscape in 1970 with the publication of their book-length studies of Plymouth Colony, Andover, and Dedham, Massachusetts.[2] Today scholars devoted to the study of family history are legion, their methodologies sophisticated, and their debates numerous, and only recently have historians begun to attempt to synthesize the work of a generation of scholarship.[3]

This chapter describes major developments in the history of the American family from the seventeenth century to the early nineteenth century, starting with the background and characteristics of immigration to the colonies, the demographic development of the major mainland regions, and broad changes in family patterns, including topics in the history of the family cycle from the formation to the dissolution of family units.

Fundamental to understanding the history of the family in colonial America are the characteristics of the immigrants who formed the sometimes unstable nucleus of settlement and growth. Considerable scholarly energy has focused on the social origins, motivations, and demographic profile of seventeenth-century immigrants to America. Thanks to the work of English demographers and historians, there is a rich body of works about late sixteenth- and early seventeenth-century English society. The work of Peter Laslett and the Cambridge Group for the History of Population and Social Structure has been especially important. Laslett's *The World We Have Lost* presents an English society in which geographic mobility (or instability, if one prefers) was an important characteristic.[4] The land from which immigrants came to America was one of extraordinary movement, and as Bernard Bailyn, Jack P. Greene, and others have suggested, the movement to America was an extension of patterns of movement both within England and to other parts of the world. As Greene notes, "probably no fewer than 240,000 and perhaps as many as 295,000 people left Britain before 1660" to such varied destinations as Ireland, the Chesapeake, Bermuda, New England, and the West Indies.[5]

Immigrants to the Chesapeake were overwhelmingly young, male, and single, and typically came as indentured servants.[6] As a result, there was a marked imbalance between men and women, and some men, although reliable estimates do not exist, would never marry or, at best, marry relatively late in their lives. The immigrants, whether men or women, had to complete their servitude before striking out on their own, thereby delaying the establishment of family units (although not necessarily limiting sexual activity). For immigrant women, several years of potential childbearing were sacrificed as a precondition for immigration, but once a woman had completed her indenture, she was likely to marry very quickly.

The second major influence on family life in the Chesapeake colonies was the hostile disease environment, for disease and death rates among immigrants and their children were exceptionally high. This, too, had a dramatic impact on the character of family life. Many servants did not live to the end of their indentures, and those who did survive entered into family relationships that were frequently broken by death, whether of husband, wife, or children. Traditional family units, as we might define them in terms of a nuclear family, were short-lived, and the recombination of family fragments—widows, widowers, and orphans—into new family units resulted in families, kin relationships, and households that were complex and highly mutable.[7]

These two principal circumstances—the age structure, marital status, gender imbalance, and legal restraints affecting servants on the one hand, and the hostile disease environment on the other—shaped seventeenth-century Chesapeake society in profound ways. With nuclear families fragile, individuals came to rely on wider kin networks for some of the emotional, legal, and educational services and functions that could not be provided by truncated nuclear families. In addition, the high death rates placed a premium on early independence for children and resulted in an especially important role for the orphans' courts in protecting the interests of minors.[8] With early death far more than an abstract possibility, emotional ties may have been attenuated in the face of almost certain and frequent bereavement.[9] The large numbers of single males posed a political threat, most clearly manifested during Bacon's Rebellion, which affected not only politics in Virginia but possibly also decisions about the racial composition of the labor force.[10]

Only toward the end of the seventeenth century were there the beginnings of significant change. With shifts in immigration patterns—from English indentured servants to African slaves—the composition of the white population began to change. American-born children, or "creoles" as Chesapeake scholars have come to denote them, survived in relatively equal numbers, male and female, and thus the native-born population in the second and subsequent generations was more evenly balanced by gender. There appear also to have been changes in life expectancy, with lower death rates. In addition, native-born children could, and did, marry earlier than their parents. Conceiving children at younger ages, and sometimes out of wedlock, creole women bore greater numbers of children.

Conditions of life and death were far different in seventeenth-century New England than in the Chesapeake region. A brief, if infamous, "starving time" at Plymouth and some initial difficulties in Massachusetts Bay were followed by generally prosperous demographic conditions. Immigrants to New England, acting under different motives, arrived in family groups far more frequently than immigrants to the Chesapeake. While winters were harsh and the soil unyielding, New England posed few of the dangers that settlers faced in the Chesapeake. Indeed, from a demographic perspective, New England provided one of the most salutary environments available to Europeans in the seventeenth century. Children married relatively young compared with old England—although among women ages at marriage were significantly higher than their creole sisters of Virginia and Maryland. Maternal mortality rates were lower, as was infant and childhood mortality. The character of immigration to New England and a more favorable environment resulted in larger, more stable families and significantly longer life expectancies. Women bore more children because they lived longer; completed families (those in which the mother survived to age forty-five, that is, until menopause) were more common; more children survived the perils of infancy and childhood; life expectancies were high; and a majority of men and women married only once.

The results of the dramatically contrasting conditions between the seventeenth-century Chesapeake and New England colonies can be seen in the growth of population in the two regions. Between 1635 and 1699 more than 80,000 persons arrived in Virginia, and in the years 1634 to 1681 between 23,500 and 38,000 Europeans came to Maryland, but by

1700 Virginia's population was only about 60,000 and Maryland's 19,000. By contrast, immigration to New England was concentrated in the 1630s, when it numbered slightly more than 20,000.[11] Primarily through natural increase this initial population grew to nearly 100,000 by 1700. Thus, in the Chesapeake, because of the gender imbalance among immigrants, the delay in marriages because of servitude, and the hostile disease environment, the population grew primarily through additional infusions of immigrants. In New England, despite the virtual end to immigration in the early 1640s, the initial population was more balanced by gender, fewer persons delayed marriage because of servitude, and a favorable environment provided conditions in which mortality rates were low and population growth rapid.[12]

Conditions in both the Chesapeake and New England began to change in the eighteenth century, and to some extent, the two regions became more similar.[13] In the Chesapeake the numbers of white immigrants declined. Unencumbered by the restrictions of indentured servitude, creole women married at younger ages, with the prospect of bearing more children than their mothers. Population growth among whites increasingly reflected natural increase rather than immigration. In New England, the expansion of overseas trade and the wars of the eighteenth century facilitated the introduction of diseases, which spread more quickly and with lethal effects among a more densely settled population. In port cities and towns, smallpox was particularly devastating, although the introduction and increasing use of inoculation in the 1720s helped to protect the population; nonetheless, eighteenth-century Boston had "a mortality pattern like that in English or Continental towns."[14] There was little, however, that could be done in the face of dysentery, which "climbed to first position among epidemic diseases afflicting New England,"[15] or the diphtheria epidemic known as the "throat distemper," which ravaged New England in the middle of the eighteenth century, striking particularly at infants and children. As a result, the average size of completed families declined in towns like Andover, and the number of children who lived to age twenty-one declined even more.[16]

In contrast to the Chesapeake and New England, relatively little demographic work has been done on the Middle Colonies, and most of what has been accomplished focuses on Pennsylvania, with particular attention being paid to the Quakers. Pennsylvania appears to have provided a substantially more favorable demographic environment than the Chesapeake colonies well into the eighteenth century, although perhaps a less favorable environment than New England.[17] The major exception was Philadelphia, where patterns of crowdedness, poverty, and disease made its demographic environment similar to other urban areas of North America and, perhaps on a lesser scale, England itself.

Wherever situated, the European inhabitants of colonial America invariably sought to establish and maintain family units, and they made decisions about roughly comparable tasks within the overall cycle of family life from courtship and marriage to death. Patterns and circumstances of courtship in colonial America changed over time and varied across the major regions. Little data survives concerning actual courtships in seventeenth-century Virginia and Maryland, but the scarcity of women, high mortality rates, and relatively high rates of premarital pregnancies suggest that parents and masters had relatively limited power over their children's and even their servants' courtships. Some female servants became pregnant during their years of servitude, thus risking an extension of their contract and the loss of their babies, who might be placed in other families. After the expiration of their indentures, women married quickly, and under the conditions of life and death in the Chesapeake colonies, remarriage was frequent, a pattern that one historian has described as "serial polyandry."[18]

The contrast with the seventeenth-century New England colonies is vivid. In seventeenth- and early eighteenth-century Hingham, Massachusetts, which Daniel Scott Smith has studied for the period between 1635 and 1880, "there existed a stable, parental-run marriage system." This was characterized by: paternal control of property, which affected the timing of marriage for sons; a tendency to favor first sons, which enabled them to marry the daughters of relatively prosperous families; and a culturally sanctioned ordering of marriages by birth order.[19]

Smith notes that "since newly married sons were not incorporated into the paternal economic or living unit, marriage meant a definite transfer of power intergenerationally." With a son's marriage, his father would give up either economic resources (e.g., the land and capital necessary for the newly married son to establish a separate household) or the son's unpaid labor. Among sons who were born to marriages before 1740, those whose fathers died before age sixty were likely to marry at younger ages than those whose fathers lived beyond sixty; in other words, the father's death created conditions under which the son could marry. Among sons born to marriages after 1740, and especially after 1780, the effect of this "paternal power" was significantly reduced.[20]

Smith also notes that birth order affected a son's marital prospects. Intestacy law provided a double share for the eldest son. Fathers could, of course, treat their sons equally, but if the intestacy law reflected prevailing customs, one would expect that favored first sons would marry women from relatively prosperous families. Hingham tax data for 1680, 1779, and 1810 reveal that first sons were more likely than younger sons to have fathers-in-law who were wealthier than their own fathers. "Birth order was thus an important determinant of the economic status of the future spouse and influential in determining the life chances of men during the colonial period." By the mid-nineteenth century, there was a significant change: "Birth order . . . exerted no significant effect on the relationship between the relative wealth of father and father-in-law."[21]

Smith also examines the relationship between birth order and marital timing for Hingham women. He finds "a marked increase in the proportions of daughters who fail to marry in order of sibling position after the middle of the eighteenth century." Another index of parental power over daughters' marriages is wealth. Smith hypothesizes that daughters from wealthier families would be more sought after because of the wealth that they would bring to a marriage and would therefore marry earlier than daughters of poorer families. This in fact was the case for the eighteenth century: "For daughters born to marriages formed in Hingham between 1721 and 1780 there is a perfect inverse relationship between paternal wealth and marriage age."[22]

Patterns of courtship in the Chesapeake and New England colonies changed during the eighteenth century. Among leading planter families, for example, parental control remained weak, but increasingly strong and complex networks of kin and neighbors provided a social context in which courtship took place.[23] In New England weakening parental and community control over courtship is dramatically evidenced in the rising rates of premarital pregnancy.[24] Increasingly, courtship for young New Englanders was controlled by the young rather than by their parents; as Daniel Scott Smith notes, in the nineteenth century there existed "a stable, participant-run system," but this system emerged only after "a period of change and crisis, manifested most notably in the American Revolution itself—a political upheaval not unconnected to the family."[25]

Courtship among Pennsylvania Quakers was deeply influenced by parental and community concerns. The Quaker marriage procedure, which Barry Levy describes as "time-consuming, thorough, intrusive, and delicate," involved parental approval for courtship and marriage as well as investigation by committees of the monthly meetings as to "clearness" and "conversation" of the man and woman.[26] Among the Quaker families that Levy has studied in the Delaware Valley, "an overwhelming majority" of children married other Quakers, a far higher retention rate than had been the case among Quaker households in England. This retention rate appears to have resulted from a combination of the monthly meetings' concern for "holy conversation" and "a carefully constructed social and religious system that shaped the land and its transference between generations." Indeed, despite the Quakers' relative landed abundance, their children tended to marry at later ages than the sons and daughters of families in Andover, Massachusetts, and there were more bachelors and spinsters.[27] Thus, marriages among Quakers reflected a parental- and community-run system. Marriages outside the faith may have reflected participant-run courtships, but the price of success was high. For those who did not marry, no system had worked.

An important dimension of participant-run courtships was the notion of romantic love. As Daniel Blake Smith notes with respect to planter families, "the letters and diaries of young men and women in the middle and upper strata of eighteenth-century Chesapeake society, especially after 1750, clearly reveal a strong belief in romantic love."[28] Jan Lewis is not persuaded that love was as central as Smith suggests: "Pre-Revolutionary gentry relationships lacked—or, more precisely, stifled—emotional intensity. Put another way, love was important, but it was not central. Both within and without the family, other ideals—such as peace and moderation—prevailed, creating the context within which emotion might safely be displayed."[29]

In New England, matters of affection were also increasingly important. New Light minister John Cleaveland advised his daughter in 1769 to "chuse for yourself" a person who would be "most agreable both to your judgment and fancy" as her "nearest and dearest friend." Still, for Cleaveland, three variables—"character, parentage, worldly estate"—remained paramount.[30] The role of affection, which a Cleaveland might acknowledge, assumed increasing importance for the postrevolutionary generation, as Ellen K. Rothman and others have noted. But romantic love was not without its ironies. As Nancy F. Cott points out, "As long as the wife's legal subordination persisted, in combination with romantic love ideals that stressed personal attraction and emotional motivation for both partners, women faced an overwhelming irony: they were to choose their bondage."[31]

Romantic love or no, if a woman was not pregnant at the time of marriage, she was likely to become pregnant in less than a year. While there were seasonal variations in the timing of marriage, conception, and childbirth,[32] the conception of a woman's first child initiated a relentless cycle of pregnancy, childbirth, nursing, and weaning that would dominate her life until menopause or death, whichever came first. In addition, for a woman whose last children were born in her forties, the responsibilities of childrearing would extend through her fifties.

For marriages in which a woman survived her childbearing years, the results of this cycle were large completed families. The average number of children born to completed first-generation families in Andover, Massachusetts, was 8.3; the average number surviving to age twenty-one was 7.2. Comparable figures for the second generation were 8.7 and 7.2 and, for the third generation, 7.6 and 5.5. Completed families in the Delaware Valley were also large, although the average number of children to reach twenty-one was smaller than in Andover: 5.1 in the first generation, 5.5 in the second.[33]

In studying family size, historians have emphasized such variables as women's ages at marriage and mortality rates. While acknowledging the importance of these variables in determining family size, Robert V. Wells has found indirect but compelling evidence of fertility limitation within Quaker marriages toward the end of the eighteenth century. Wells examined three groups of families, including women born before 1730 in the first cohort ("pre-revolutionary"), women born between 1731 and 1755 ("revolutionary"), and women born from 1756 to 1785 ("post-revolutionary"). There was a decline in average size of completed families from 7.51 to 6.23 to 5.12 among the three groups. A slight increase (0.8 of a year) in the age at marriage from the prerevolutionary to the post-revolutionary groups accounts for only about 22 percent in the decline in the average number of children born per couple. Applying criteria from European demographic studies, Wells concludes that by the end of the eighteenth century Quakers were practicing "some form of deliberate family limitation"; this practice was "common among the couples in which the wife was born between 1756 and 1785" and "possible, though less certain," among the women born between 1731 and 1755.[34]

Other studies have found evidence of family limitation in other late eighteenth-century communities. Thus, in Deerfield, Massachusetts, a decline in fertility occurred "not only more than half a century earlier than in most European populations, but also earlier than the general U.S. trend indicates." Part of this resulted from a rising age at marriage, but age-specific fertility rates among older women also declined. "There is no reason to believe that age at menopause was falling or that mortality for women *in older age groups* was increasing with time." Birth intervals and other data lead to the conclusion that "a number of women born between 1741 and 1760 must have begun to practice some form of family limitation." The authors hypothesize that there was a connection between fertility control and the availability of farm land.[35]

The same pattern appeared in Hampton, New Hampshire, for which Lawrence J. Kilbourne has examined data for the years between 1655 and 1840. Dividing the period into seven cohorts, he finds that the mean number of children in completed families dropped by 3.4 births (from 8.44 to 5.00), with the decline starting in the second half of the eighteenth century. The decline reflected both rising female marriage ages and changes in intramarital fertility, the latter a matter of "voluntary choice rather than biological debility." Among women born between 1750 and 1774, those in the most prosperous families had the highest fertility rates, while the poorest women had the lowest fecundity, this pattern stemming from nutritional deficiencies. Among those in the middle range, "fertility fell precipitously after the wife's twenty-fifth year, precisely the expected pattern among couples practicing birth control." Kilbourne suggests that "land pressure provided Hamptonians with the strongest motivation for smaller families."[36]

While couples might decide to limit the number of children that they would have, there was no change in the place where childbirth normally occurred. Births took place in the home, ideally with the assistance of a midwife. There were few doctors until relatively late in the colonial period, and their skills were certainly no better than those of experienced midwives. Catherine M. Scholten summarizes the experience of child-birth for most women in colonial America in the following terms: "Child-bearing had been viewed as the inevitable, even the divinely ordained, occasion of suffering for women; childbirth was an event shared by the female community; and delivery was supervised by a midwife." In the late eighteenth and early nineteenth centuries, according to Scholten, childbirth for upper-class women in urban areas became less a communal event and more private, with the traditional role of the midwife being superseded by a male doctor.[37] For most rural women, and particularly those of modest means, the transition from the communal to the private experience of childbirth would probably not take place until well past the eighteenth century. In rural communities like Martha Ballard's Hol-lowell, Maine, midwives and doctors could work in relative harmony and cooperation. As Laurel Thatcher Ulrich notes, "doctors were not as scientific or midwives as ignorant as older accounts would suggest, nor was there as much friction between the two specialties as more recent literature might lead us to believe."[38]

Women in the colonial period faced greater risks at and after childbirth than women today, with those risks most clearly pronounced in the Chesapeake colonies. In Plymouth Colony, Demos estimates that "a bit less than 20 percent of the deaths among adult women were owing to causes connected with childbirth. Or, to put it another way, something like one birth in thirty resulted in the death of the mother." This estimate of maternal mortality is much higher than the rate of "one maternal death for every 198 living births" among Martha Ballard's patients in the years 1785 to 1812. In Andover, "the likelihood of women dying during their childbearing years was no greater than the likelihood of death for men during the same years, and . . . women's chances of reach-ing advanced ages were as good as those for men, if not somewhat better."[39]

Most children were nursed by their mothers, although there are oc-casional references to wet-nursing and bottle-feeding. Infants were nursed for about twelve to eighteen months, with the decision to wean an infant reflecting the age of the child, the mother's health, convenience, or possibly a husband's desire to resume sexual relations. As Paula A. Treckel points out, "the weaning process was a traumatic one for moth-ers, infants, and husbands, for parental anxiety about their children's well-being was fraught with an underlying sexual tension." Weaning appears often to have been abrupt, with the mother and infant separated from each other.[40]

While evidence on nursing and weaning practices is limited, another dimension of an infant's early life and the values of the wider culture is amply documented: the choice of names that parents made for their children. While historians know relatively little about the actual decision-making process, the results of the decisions are quite apparent. Not surprisingly, most studies have focused on New England, where the extensive records kept by town clerks and published genealogies provide an enormous data base. Daniel Scott Smith's longitudinal study of Hingham, Massachusetts, covering the years 1641 to 1880, has been both the starting point and model for others. As Smith notes, "assigning a 'name' to a child is loaded with fundamental social meaning."[41]

In New England, there were two major changes in child-naming practices, the first occurring early in the settlement of the region, the second in the last decades of the eighteenth century and early nineteenth century. A great variety of naming practices can be discerned in the first generation of settlers: biblical, hortatory, grace, and commemorative names coexisted with traditional English names. By the mid-seventeenth century a pattern emerged that would persist for a century and a half. As David Hackett Fischer's study of Concord, Massachusetts, demonstrates, the Bible became the almost exclusive source of names, but New Englanders' choices were far from random: some biblical names were never used, a few reflected social rank, but the favored names, for boys and girls alike, were associated with moral qualities. In addition to reliance on the Bible, New Englanders' choices of names reflected the desire to maintain family identity, with parents' forenames being given to children in 80 percent of the cases and grandparents' names being passed down through the generations. But there was a bias in this pattern of generational continuity, for the husband's side of the family was more likely to be honored than the wife's: "By these nominal connections, families tied themselves more closely to the paternal line." Finally, so important was the choice of a name that parents commonly gave the name of a dead child to a newborn child.[42]

Naming patterns changed dramatically between roughly 1780 and 1820. Far fewer parents gave their first names to children, and the use of grandparents' names became much less common. A matrilineal pattern of naming emerged, and "the primary (but not the sole) responsibility for naming children passed from the father to the mother." Necronyms largely disappeared, and biblical names became much less important. At the same time, choices of names became more eclectic, and middle names, once rare, became almost universal.[43]

The dominant patterns in naming children in New England may be clear, but New England patterns clearly did not dominate early America. Darrett B. Rutman and Anita H. Rutman provide extensive data from Middlesex County, Virginia, between 1650 and 1750, to show that Virginians, at least, marched to different drummers when it came to naming children. For example, "parents tended to name first sons for the child's paternal grandfather, second sons for the father. Similarly, first daughters tended to be named for their maternal grandmothers, second daughters for their mothers." The strength of this orientation toward family went beyond grandparents. Parents overwhelmingly chose the names of their first and second sons and daughters from a universe of names "defined by the parents' families of origin (their own parents and their parents' siblings)." Among sons this occurred nine out of ten times; among daughters, eight out of ten. Furthermore, the pattern appeared both among parents who began childbearing in the early seventeenth century and among those who became parents after 1720. There were some changes over time. Most interestingly, "brothers and sisters of parents (uncles and aunts of the children) grew in importance as a source of names while parents and grandparents declined, a function perhaps of a growing awareness of the importance of lateral kin in the high-mortality situation of the Chesapeake." These and other differences between Middlesex County and New England prompt the Rutmans to ask whether one or the other region—or possibly both—had departed from English practice, and they offer suggestive evidence that naming patterns in New England were the variant.[44]

The patterns of child naming in New England and in Virginia are all the more tantalizing when one postulates that changes in child-naming patterns over time, as well as regional differences, might serve as proxies for larger dimensions of family life, including childrearing and affective relations between parents and children.[45] At the heart of Edmund S. Morgan's analysis of the Puritan family is the way in which family members felt and expressed their emotions toward one another. Love for the creature was clearly to be subordinate to love for God, and never should one's love for spouse or child become so strong as to usurp or overshadow that higher love. Thus, in one of his most intriguing hypotheses, Morgan suggests that parents sometimes placed children in other families even when there was no clear economic or educational advantage:

The child left home just at the time when parental discipline causes increasing friction, just at the time when a child begins to assert his independence. By allowing a strange master to take over the disciplinary function, the parent could meet the child upon a plane of affection and friendliness. At the same time the child would be taught good behavior by someone who would not forgive him any mischief out of affection for his person.[46]

There was, in other words, an economy of affection: love was appropriate but should never be unbounded. In writing of the Puritans' educational ideas and practices, Morgan concludes:

Here is no disposition to allow the unimpeded development of personality, but at least children were not subjected to a preconceived discipline without reference to their individual needs and capacities. A parent in order to educate his children properly had to know them well, to understand their particular characters, and to treat them accordingly. Granted its purposes and assumptions, Puritan education was intelligently planned, and the relationship between parent and child which it envisaged was not one of harshness and severity but of tenderness and sympathy.

Ultimately, Morgan concludes, the Puritans failed to restrain their affections. They became "tribal," turning inward to a kind of genealogy of salvation in which their children, rather than a wider community, became central to their religious life. They thus "committed the very sin that they so often admonished themselves to avoid: they had allowed their children to usurp a higher place than God in their affections."[47]

More recent studies of Puritan childbearing have evinced less sympathy toward the Puritans' goals and methods. Thus, according to John Demos's psychoanalytically informed study of family life in Plymouth Colony, parents paid special attention to breaking a child's will at about the age of two. This experience, taken in the context of other traumatic events, particularly weaning and the birth of a rival sibling, adversely affected key developmental tasks, thwarting the development of autonomy and rendering the child—and the later adult—particularly vulnerable to shame and doubt.[48]

In his study of *The Protestant Temperament*, Greven posits the existence of three generalized personality types in early America—evangelical, moderate, and genteel—and suggests that breaking the will was crucial to the evangelical type.

With remarkable consistency and persistence, evangelicals through the centuries insisted that parents must control and break the emerging will of children in the first few years of life. The central issue, as they perceived it, was this: the autonomous will and self-assertiveness of the child must be reduced to impotency, be utterly suppressed and contained, or the child ultimately would be damned for eternity.

By contrast, the moderates did not believe that it was necessary to break a child's will; rather, "it could be bent and shaped by parents whose goal was to form characters of piety and virtue in their offspring." Obedience would be obtained through "parental example and reasoning" rather than through the "early conquest" of the child's will. Among the genteel, "fond affection rather than conscientious discipline shaped the relationships between the generations."[49]

While Greven has been criticized for the rather eclectic range of his evidence and the ahistorical character of his classifications,[50] his study does have the effect of both transcending the regional boundaries that are frequently used to classify family values and raising the possibility that class and religious experience, regardless of location, may be central to defining personality types.

If New Englanders emphasized control, discipline, and economy of emotions with respect to their children, considerably different attitudes and practices prevailed in other parts of America. Among the planters of the eighteenth-century Chesapeake, according to Daniel Blake Smith, "parents and kin, at least in middle- and upper-class families, apparently made little effort to stifle childhood willfulness and self-assertion.... Parental indulgence... appears far more frequently in the records than concern for strong discipline." Indeed, by the second half of the eighteenth century, Smith suggests, "what is most striking... is the development of a more openly affectionate, intimate family environment in which emotional attachments were deeply valued, indeed cherished."[51] Jan Lewis finds Smith's general argument unpersuasive. Among the prerevolutionary gentry, she argues,

love was one of the bases of family life; yet pre-Revolutionary gentry relationships lacked—or, more precisely, stifled—emotional intensity. Put another way, love was important, but it was not central. Both within and without the family, other ideals—such as peace and moderation—prevailed, creating the context within which emotion might safely be displayed.[52]

While there is disagreement about the timing of changes in the role of emotional attachments among Chesapeake families, Barry Levy suggests that the Quakers who settled the Delaware Valley brought with them a radical vision of the family, one which was child-centered and presaged wider patterns of value and aspiration of the nineteenth century:

Combining acceptance of pluralism, disciplined privatism, child-centeredness, and wealth, upland Quakers introduced a most enduring form of community into American culture.... The once failed social strategy of poor, clannish, north-western British religious radicals, Quaker domesticity could emerge for many commentators of American life, particularly when stripped of its sectarian peculiarities, as the best, most moral, almost natural, way to develop and tame the lonely North American forests.[53]

John J. Waters makes a somewhat similar point with respect to the smaller number of Quakers in Barnstable: "Both in their testaments and in their lives these plain people, farmers all, affirmed their creedal positions. Without knowing it, these Quaker behavioral patterns spoke for what would become the cultural norms of the nineteenth century."[54]

While the affective relations within families varied among different

groups and over time, it is possible to generalize about the life course
of individuals and families, that is, to delineate the stages of development
that characterized family life. Little is known about the day-to-day care
of infants and small children. This care was probably the almost exclusive
domain of women—mothers, older daughters, and female servants—
although one finds occasional references to boys looking after younger
brothers.[55] By the age of five or six, a child began to be integrated in
the adult world of work responsibilities. This is not to say that children
were in any meaningful sense "miniature adults," for Anglo-American
culture clearly recognized the different developmental stages—physical,
intellectual, and moral—through which a child moved toward full adult
status.[56] In premodern America, whether a child was to become a wife
and mother (the likely role of the overwhelming number of women) or
a farmer or artisan, socialization into those callings began at an early
age. Indeed, with many mouths to feed and much labor-intensive work
to be done, few families could afford not to have their children contribute
such work as their physical stature and mental development might permit. Children's work responsibilities therefore began at an early age and
increased in complexity and responsibility as the children grew in size,
strength, and dexterity.[57]

Demos emphasizes the smooth process of maturation for children in
Plymouth Colony and the absence of any significant stage of development comparable to modern adolescence:

Once the child had begun to assume an adult role and style, around the age of
six or seven, the way ahead was fairly straightforward. Development toward full
maturity could be accomplished in a gradual, piecemeal, and largely automatic
fashion. There were few substantial choices to be made; the boy's own father,
or the girl's own mother, provided relatively clear models for the formation of
a meaningful "identity." Here was no "awkward age"—but rather the steady
lengthening of a young person's shadow, and the whole instinctive process
through which one generation yielded imperceptibly to its successor.[58]

Whatever the case in the relatively undifferentiated society of seventeenth-century Plymouth Colony, other evidence— from contemporary
language, law, religious practice, observation, and behavior—points to
the existence of a period of sometimes difficult transition (difficult to
both young persons and adults) between childhood and full adult
status.[59]

For children and adolescents in the Chesapeake colonies, life was frequently disrupted by the death of parents. With high death rates among
all ages and social groups, the dissolution of primary family units was
frequent, and the likelihood that a child would become an orphan was
quite high. In Middlesex County, Virginia, the Rutmans find that nearly

half the children born between 1690 lost one or both parents by their ninth birthdays, and nearly two-thirds by age thirteen. There were only slight improvements for children born in the years between 1690 and 1709 and between 1710 and 1749.[60]

With the death of one or both parents, a child entered into a new family unit and household. "From the standpoint of children," the Rutmans speculate, "parents were ephemeral. A father might give way to a stepfather, an uncle, a brother, or simply a friend of the deceased father; a mother might well be replaced by an aunt, an elder sister, or a father's 'now-wife,' to use the wording frequently found in conveyances and wills." While such conditions might lead one to conclude that "childhood in this Chesapeake society was a matter of disruption and trauma and that family attachments were consequently weak," the Rutmans emphasize the importance of networks of kin and neighbors: "Stability for children as well as for adults lay not so much in the transitory family of the household but in the permanent network of friends and relations within which the family was embedded. Instability and insecurity lay in being apart from a network."[61]

Under such circumstances in the Chesapeake region, the conditions and duration of adolescence may have differed significantly from adolescence in other regions. In Charles Parish, Virginia, Daniel Blake Smith finds that fathers were likely to die at relatively early ages (most in their early forties), and with relatively few siblings to receive inheritances, "many young men had the wherewithal quite early in life to consider marriage and assert their economic independence."[62] By contrast, for the children of the longer-lived parents of Andover, Massachusetts, and the Delaware Valley of Pennsylvania, marriage and economic independence came considerably later.[63]

As children matured, the families and households of which they were members changed in size, composition, and focus. The concept of the life cycle has been increasingly important in delineating the dynamics and dimensions of family life.[64] The composition of a household was affected by the cyclical growth and decline of the family unit. In New England, a family's need for workers reflected the number, ages, and genders of their children. Early in its development, a family would be relatively dependent on outside workers. As the children matured, more work responsibilities could be entrusted to them. Then, as the children married and moved into separate households, their parents would again become increasingly dependent on outsiders.[65]

As the number and distribution of children changed within a household, so, too, the goals of parents changed in emphasis. In his study of eighteenth-century Concord, Massachusetts, Robert A. Gross notes that families experienced early years of growth, both as the number of children increased and as fathers accumulated property not merely to maintain the family but, perhaps more important, to establish their children's independence. This was followed by years of decline: as children matured, married, and established separate households, the family unit became smaller and its holdings decreased as parents provided land for their sons and dowries for their daughters.[66]

Each family needed to devise a strategy to provide for its children. A family strategy would depend on the number and gender of its children, the size of the family's active and unimproved lands, local opportunities, educational aspirations, the cost of land, and opportunities for migration to new lands. In Andover, Massachusetts, first-generation fathers settled their sons on family land but often withheld title to the land until late in their lives or even until their deaths. Later generations, faced with dwindling resources, provided land for their sons earlier (and increasingly outside Andover), arranged apprenticeships or education, or purchased land outside Andover for their sons, many of whom achieved independence earlier than their predecessors.[67]

Christopher Jedrey traces in fine detail the Cleaveland family's strategies and the preoccupation of fathers with their sons' welfare in the world. The documentation for the Cleaveland family is especially rich, but the kinds of concerns that parents had and their relentless search for successful strategies are found as well in the more prosaic wills and deeds that John J. Waters has examined for seventeenth-century Barnstable, Massachusetts.[68]

The writing of a will marked a father's final statement of his strategy to provide for the future of his family, and historians have turned increasingly to probate records in general, and wills in particular, to study the status of widows and paternal provisions for children, especially sons.[69] Marriages ended most commonly with the death of a spouse.[70] What followed that death reflected a number of variables: the survivor's age and gender, the number of dependents, and economic status, as well as the demographic composition of the area in which the survivor lived. Practical considerations as well as cultural values prompted widows and widowers to remarry if they could—and to do so rather quickly by modern standards. In the seventeenth-century Chesapeake colonies, where marriages were short-lived and men significantly outnumbered women, widows were able to remarry; it is less certain that widowers were as fortunate.[71] But as the balance between men and women shifted, the marital prospects of widows probably deteriorated. For example, in eighteenth-century Middlesex County, Virginia, "adults, largely women, came to dominate the [welfare] rolls,"[72] and in eighteenth-century Lancaster County, Pennsylvania, "when their first husbands died, most women did not remarry."[73]

In eighteenth-century Massachusetts, widows were in an unenviable position. In the town of Woburn in the first half of the century, "probably not more than a fourth of the women whose husbands died found new spouses. Moreover, after the first few years of widowhood had passed, their chances of remarrying were extremely slim." Opportunities for remarriage were clearly affected by the relatively advanced ages at which women became widows and by the sex composition of Woburn and neighboring towns. Like most if not all towns in eastern Massachusetts, Woburn had a surplus of adult women: in 1765 the ratio of adult white males to females was 87.9 to 100.[74]

The age of a widow and the prevailing sex ratio, however, were not the only circumstances that affected the likelihood of remarriage. As Alexander Keyssar points out, as a result of provisions in the law and in wills, "these women, quite simply, did not possess forms of property which would be an incentive to a potential new spouse." They could not sell land that would pass to another generation at death or possibly at remarriage, nor was it likely that land could be profitably rented. In addition, unable to work the land herself, a widow was likely to find herself dependent on family labor and, indeed, living as a dependent in the home of a married son. Dependence on grown children might create tensions between the generations; the explicit provisions for accommodations and support found in many wills suggest that "the older generation sought security, in part, by imposing restraints upon the younger."[75]

The dependence of widows on their adult children frequently resulted in three-generational households, a phenomenon whose frequency remains elusive. While many historians have emphasized the importance of the nuclear family of husband, wife, and children, John J. Waters stresses that "the nature of the family is not static, for in its developmental cycle it may pass through nuclear, stem, and even joint phases." Thus, "the question to ask is not how many households had grandparents, but rather how many grandparents shared households with a son or daughter and their children." In the case of seventeenth-century Barnstable, Massachusetts, "a third and possibly as many as half" of those who wrote wills lived with their grown children.[76]

While death dissolved most marital bonds, there were some divorces during the colonial period, most in Massachusetts and Connecticut, where the laws and customs were least restrictive. Grounds for divorce included adultery, desertion or lengthy absence, and extreme cruelty. In Massachusetts between 1636 and 1786, there were 280 petitions for divorce, 183 of which were successful.[77] Sheldon S. Cohen has studied 839 divorce petitions filed in Connecticut from 1750 through 1797, where, since 1667, divorce could be obtained for adultery, desertion, fraudulent contract, and lengthy absence. The principal cause for divorce, as revealed in the petitions, was desertion, followed by adultery, fraudulent contract, and lengthy absence. In the last quarter of the eighteenth century, the courts' decisions "reflected more understanding toward female plaintiffs." Cohen finds that the American Revolution affected family relations, not only during the war itself but in the postwar period as well. There was an increase in the number of divorce petitions and the emergence of "new attitudes concerning marital relationships and responsibilities." These were reflected in a "post-war acceleration in the number of cases involving desertion and adultery, the growing expectations of emotional fulfillment in marriage, and the tendency of wronged spouses to institute divorce proceedings as soon as legally possible after an alleged indiscretion." Indeed, women "imbibed the revolutionary doctrines of natural rights, liberty and equality," as evidenced in the appearance of the word "tyranny" in petitions. The most pronounced statement of this trend appeared in Abigail Strong's description of herself as "being fully convinced that she is under no obligation to live with him (Charles) [her husband] any longer or submit to his cruelty, for even Kings may forfeit or discharge the allegiance of their Subjects."[78]

Abigail Strong's rhetorical allusion to revolutionary ideology raises a question that transcends her particular circumstances. To what extent were changes in family life and values related to the great political upheaval of the late eighteenth century? While no definitive answers can be given, some observations are in order. The two changes for which there is the broadest base of evidence—shifts in naming patterns and in rates of premarital pregnancy—preceded the Revolution and may both point to significant reorientations or possibly disruptions in family values. The changes in naming patterns indicate a child-centeredness, while the rising rates of premarital pregnancy, perhaps reflecting ideas of romantic love, surely point to a loosening of both parental control and self-control. The persuasive empirical evidence of conscious family limitation similarly indicates changing attitudes, but the changes appear either to coincide with or to follow soon upon, rather than precede, the Revolution. Here Mary Beth Norton's *Liberty's Daughters* suggests an explanation. According to Norton, the Revolution had an empowering effect on those literate women who left diaries and wrote letters. Their self-conception was radically transformed, and with that transformation came new expectations and aspirations with respect to women's roles and to crucial areas of both family and public life, including female education, courtship, marriage, motherhood, and even politics.[79]

Thus, by the early nineteenth century, many aspects of family life in America had been significantly changed from their earliest colonial and European roots. These changes preceded the large-scale economic and political transformations that would take place in the United States in the nineteenth century. As David Hackett Fischer concludes with respect to the change in New Englanders' choices of names for their children:

Behind that change in naming practices is a strong current of secularization, and also of modernization in the special sense of a turning away from tradition. At the same time, there was a radical break in ideas of the family that those naming choices implied. It was not a loss of family consciousness, but the growth of a new ideal that was less patriarchal and more matrifocal, less hierarchical and more egalitarian, less holistic and more individuated.[80]

Values that we associate with the nineteenth century were clearly appearing in eighteenth-century families, thus confirming the importance of studying family history in early America. It is essential to an understanding of the emergence of modern America.

NOTES

1. The most notable exception to this generalization is Edmund S. Morgan, *The Puritan Family: Religion and Domestic Relations in Seventeenth-Century New England* (rev. ed., New York: Harper and Row, Harper Torchbooks, 1966). In reflecting on Morgan's *Puritan Family* and Bernard Bailyn's *Education in the Forming of American Society: Needs and Opportunities for Study* (Chapel Hill: University of North Carolina Press, 1960), David J. Rothman suggests that historians of American family life need to learn more about European family history and American demography. See Rothman, "A Note on the Study of the Colonial Family," *William and Mary Quarterly* 3d ser., 23 (1966): 627–34.

Other studies, some now largely dated, include: Alice Morse Earle, *Child Life in Colonial Days* (New York: Macmillan Co., 1899); idem, *Home Life in Colonial Days* (New York: Macmillan Co., 1898); Arthur W. Calhoun, *A Social History of the American Family from Colonial Times to the Present* (3 vols.; New York: Barnes and Noble, 1917–1919); Sandford Fleming, *Children and Puritanism: The Place of Children in the Life and Thought of the New England Churches, 1620–1847* (New Haven, Conn.: Yale University Press, 1933); Walter Joseph Homan, *Children & Quakerism: A Study of the Place of Children in the Theory and Practice of the Society of Friends, Commonly Called Quakers* (Berkeley, Calif.: Gillick Press, 1939; reprint, New York: Arno Press, 1972).

2. John Demos, *A Little Commonwealth: Family Life in Plymouth Colony* (New York: Oxford University Press, 1970); Philip J. Greven, Jr., *Four Generations: Population, Land, and Family in Colonial Andover, Massachusetts* (Ithaca, N.Y.: Cornell University Press, 1970); Kenneth A. Lockridge, *A New England Town, the First Hundred Years: Dedham, Massachusetts, 1636–1736* (New York: W. W. Norton & Company, 1970).

The importance of these studies can be gauged in part by the number and quality of review essays: James A. Henretta, "The Morphology of New England Society in the Colonial Period," *Journal of Interdisciplinary History* 2 (1971): 379–98; Rhys Isaac, "Order and Growth, Authority and Meaning in Colonial New England," *American Historical Review* 76 (1971): 728–37; Richard S. Dunn, "The Social History of Early New England," *American Quarterly* 24 (1972): 661–79; John M. Murrin, "Review Essay," *History and Theory* 11 (1972): 226–75; and Jack

P. Greene, "Autonomy and Stability: New England and the British Colonial Experience in Early Modern America," *Journal of Social History* 7 (1974): 171–94.

The books by Demos, Greven, and Lockridge were preceded by significant exploratory articles, notably Demos, "Notes on Life in Plymouth Colony," *William and Mary Quarterly* 3d ser., 22 (1965): 264–86; idem, "Families in Colonial Bristol, Rhode Island: An Exercise in Historical Demography," *William and Mary Quarterly* 3d ser., 25 (1968): 40–57; John Demos and Virginia Demos, "Adolescence in Historical Perspective," *Journal of Marriage and the Family* 31 (1969): 632–38; Greven, "Family Structure in Seventeenth-Century Andover, Massachusetts," *William and Mary Quarterly* 3d ser., 23 (1966): 234–66; idem, "Historical Demography and Colonial America: A Review Article," *William and Mary Quarterly* 3d ser., 24 (1967): 438–54; Lockridge, "The Population of Dedham, Massachusetts, 1636–1736," *Economic History Review* 2d ser., 19 (1966): 318–44.

3. For reviews and bibliographies of recent literature, see James Wallace Milden, comp., *The Family in Past Time: A Guide to the Literature* (New York: Garland Publishing, 1977); N. Ray Hiner, "The Child in American Historiography: Accomplishments and Prospect," *Psychohistory Review* 7 (1978): 13–23; idem, "Wars and Rumors of Wars: The Historiography of Colonial Education as a Case Study in Academic Imperialism," *Societas* 8 (1978): 89–114; Daniel Blake Smith, "The Study of the Family in Early America: Trends, Problems, and Prospects," *William and Mary Quarterly* 3d ser., 39 (1982): 3–28; Gerald F. Moran and Maris A. Vinovskis, "The Puritan Family and Religion: A Critical Reappraisal," *William and Mary Quarterly* 3d ser., 39 (1982): 29–63; Joseph M. Hawes and N. Ray Hiner, eds., *American Childhood: A Research Guide and Historical Handbook* (Westport, Conn.: Greenwood Press, 1985); David T. Courtwright, "New England Families in Historical Perspective," in *Families and Children*, ed. Peter Benes (The Dublin Seminar for New England Folklife, *Annual Proceedings 1985*; Boston: Boston University Scholarly Publications, 1987), 11–23; Ross W. Beales, Jr., comp., "Selected Bibliography on Children and Families in New England," in *Families and Children*, 148–57.

Recent attempts at synthesis include Robert V. Wells, *Revolutions in Americans' Lives: A Demographic Perspective on the History of Americans, Their Families, and Their Society* (Westport, Conn.: Greenwood Press, 1982); Steven Mintz and Susan Kellogg, *Domestic Revolutions: A Social History of American Family Life* (New York: The Free Press, 1988); and, on a wider scale, Jack P. Greene, *Pursuits of Happiness: The Social Development of Early Modern British Colonies and the Formation of American Culture* (Chapel Hill: University of North Carolina Press, 1988), and David Hackett Fischer, *Albion's Seed: Four British Folkways in America* (New York: Oxford University Press, 1989).

Documentary collections include Robert H. Bremner et al., eds., *Children and Youth in America: A Documentary History*, Vol. 1: 1600–1865 (Cambridge, Mass.: Harvard University Press, 1970), and Donald M. Scott and Bernard Wishy, eds., *America's Families: A Documentary History* (New York: Harper and Row, 1982).

4. Peter Laslett, *The World We Have Lost: England Before the Industrial Age* (New York: Charles Scribner's Sons, 1965). Keith Wrightson presents a synthesis of recent scholarship in *English Society, 1580–1680* (New Brunswick, N.J.: Rutgers University Press, 1982); on mobility, see pp. 40–44.

5. Greene, *Pursuits of Happiness*, 7–8; see also Bailyn, *The Peopling of British North America: An Introduction* (New York: Alfred A. Knopf, 1986), and David Cressy, *Coming Over: Migration and Communication between England and New England in the Seventeenth Century* (New York: Cambridge University Press, 1987).

The literature on the origins, process, and characteristics of immigration to British colonial America is rich and varied: Nellis M. Crouse, "The Causes of the Great Migration, 1630–1640," *New England Quarterly* 5 (1932): 3–36; Abbot Emerson Smith, *Colonists in Bondage: White Servants and Convict Labor in America, 1607–1776* (Chapel Hill: University of North Carolina Press, 1947); Mildred Campbell, "Social Origins of Some Early Americans," in *Seventeenth-Century America: Essays in Colonial History*, ed. James Morton Smith (Chapel Hill: University of North Carolina Press, 1959), 63–89; Wesley Frank Craven, *White, Red, and Black: The Seventeenth-Century Virginian* (Charlottesville: University Press of Virginia, 1971); Edmund S. Morgan, "Headrights and Headcounts: A Review Article," *Virginia Magazine of History and Biography* 80 (1972): 361–71; T. H. Breen and Stephen Foster, "Moving to the New World: The Character of Early Massachusetts Immigration," *William and Mary Quarterly* 3d ser., 30 (1973): 189–222; Edmund S. Morgan, *American Slavery, American Freedom: The Ordeal of Colonial Virginia* (New York: W. W. Norton & Company, 1975); David Souden, " 'Rogues, Whores and Vagabonds': Indentured Servant Emigrants to North America, and the Case of Mid-Seventeenth-Century Bristol," *Social History* 3 (1978): 23–41; David W. Galenson, " 'Middling People' or 'Common Sort'?: The Social Origins of Some Early Americans Reexamined," *William and Mary Quarterly* 3d ser., 35 (1978): 499–524, with a rebuttal by Mildred Campbell, 525–40; Anthony Salerno, "The Social Background of Seventeenth-Century Emigration to America," *Journal of British Studies* 19 (1979): 31–52; James Horn, "Servant Emigration to the Chesapeake in the Seventeenth Century," in *The Chesapeake in the Seventeenth Century: Essays on Anglo-American Society*, ed. Thad W. Tate and David L. Ammerman (Chapel Hill: University of North Carolina Press, 1979), 51–95; Henry A. Gemery, "Emigration from the British Isles to the New World, 1630–1700: Inferences from Colonial Populations," in *Research in Economic History: A Research Annual* 5 (1980): 179–231; David Grayson Allen, *In English Ways: The Movement of Societies and the Transferal of English Local Law and Custom to Massachusetts Bay in the Seventeenth Century* (Chapel Hill: University of North Carolina Press, 1981); David B. Quinn, "Why They Came," in *Early Maryland in a Wider World*, ed. David B. Quinn (Detroit, Mich.: Wayne State University Press, 1982), 119–48; Virginia DeJohn Anderson, "Migrants and Motives: Religion and the Settlement of New England, 1630–1640," *New England Quarterly* 58 (1985): 339–83; Bernard Bailyn, *Voyagers to the West: A Passage in the Peopling of America on the Eve of the Revolution* (New York: Alfred A. Knopf, 1986); Russell R. Menard, "British Migration to the Chesapeake Colonies in the Seventeenth Century," in *Colonial Chesapeake Society*, ed. Lois Green Carr, Philip D. Morgan, and Jean B. Russo (Chapel Hill: University of North Carolina Press, 1988), 99–132.

6. Earlier scholarship on indentured servants emphasized lowly social origins, but more recent studies have stressed the variety of their social origins and aspirations. See particularly Campbell, "Social Origins of Some Early Americans"; Galenson, " 'Middling People' or 'Common Sort'?," and Campbell's rebuttal.

7. Darrett B. Rutman and Anita H. Rutman, "Of Agues and Fevers: Malaria in the Early Chesapeake," *William and Mary Quarterly* 3d ser., 33 (1976): 31–60; Lois Green Carr and Lorena S. Walsh, "The Planter's Wife: The Experience of White Women in Seventeenth-Century Maryland," *William and Mary Quarterly* 3d ser., 34 (1977): 542–71; Carville V. Earle, "Environment, Disease, and Mortality in Early Virginia," in *Chesapeake in the Seventeenth Century*, ed. Tate and Ammerman, 96–125; Lorena S. Walsh, " 'Till Death Us Do Part': Marriage and Family in Seventeenth-Century Maryland," in *Chesapeake in the Seventeenth Century*, 141–51; Gerald L. Cates, " 'The Seasoning': Disease and Death among the First Colonists of Georgia," *Georgia Historical Quarterly* 64 (1980): 146–58; James M. Gallman, "Mortality among White Males: Colonial North Carolina," *Social Science History* 4 (1980): 295–316; Darrett B. Rutman and Anita H. Rutman, " 'Now-Wives and Sons-in-Law': Parental Death in a Seventeenth-Century Virginia County," in *Chesapeake in the Seventeenth Century*, ed. Thad W. Tate and David L. Ammerman, 153–82.

8. On orphans and orphans' courts, see Lois Green Carr, "The Development of the Maryland Orphans' Court, 1654–1715," in *Law, Society, and Politics in Early Maryland: Proceedings of the First Conference on Maryland History, June 14–15, 1974*, ed. Aubrey C. Land, Lois Green Carr, and Edward C. Papenfuse (Baltimore, Md.: Johns Hopkins University Press, 1977), 141–62.

9. James Axtell has delineated the attraction of native American life for some English people in "The White Indians of Colonial America," *William and Mary Quarterly* 3d ser., 32 (1975): 55–88.

10. Morgan, *American Slavery, American Freedom*, 269–70. For a review of the literature on the origins of slavery in Virginia and the shift from indentured servants to African slaves, see Alden T. Vaughan, "The Origins Debate: Slavery and Racism in Seventeenth-Century Virginia," *Virginia Magazine of History and Biography* 97 (1989): 311–54.

11. Cressy, *Coming Over*, 68–70, 191–212, provides data and suggestions with respect to numbers of immigrants to New England throughout the seventeenth century, including a valuable discussion of "back" or return migration.

12. Susan L. Norton, "Population Growth in Colonial America: A Study of Ipswich, Massachusetts," *Population Studies* 25 (1971): 433–52; Russell R. Menard, "Immigrants and Their Increase: The Process of Population Growth in Early Colonial Maryland," in *Law, Society, and Politics in Early Maryland*, ed. Land et al., 102; Morgan, *American Slavery, American Freedom*, 158–59; Wells, *Revolutions in Americans' Lives*, 29.

13. Jack P. Greene discusses these changes in *Pursuits of Happiness*, 170–206.

14. Gary B. Nash, *The Urban Crucible: Social Change, Political Consciousness, and the Origins of the American Revolution* (Cambridge: Cambridge University Press, 1979), 104.

15. John Duffy, *Epidemics in Colonial America* (Baton Rouge: Louisiana State University Press, 1953), 219.

16. Greven, *Four Generations*, 201.

17. Robert V. Wells, "Family Size and Fertility Control in Eighteenth-Century America: A Study of Quaker Families," *Population Studies* 25 (1971): 73–82; idem, "Quaker Marriage Patterns in a Colonial Perspective," *William and Mary Quarterly* 3d ser., 29 (1972): 415–42; idem, "Family History and Demographic Transition,"

Journal of Social History 9 (1975): 1–19; idem, "Marriage Seasonals in Early America: Comparisons and Comments," *Journal of Interdisciplinary History* 18 (1987): 299–307; idem, "The Demography of a Region: Historical Reality or Historian's Creation," *Proceedings of the American Philosophical Society* 133 (1989): 219–22; J. William Frost, "As the Twig Is Bent: Quaker Ideas of Childhood," *Quaker History* 60 (1971): 67–87; idem, *The Quaker Family in Colonial America: A Portrait of the Society of Friends* (New York: St. Martin's Press, 1973); Barry Levy, " 'Tender Plants': Quaker Farmers and Children in the Delaware Valley, 1681–1735," *Journal of Family History* 3 (1978): 116–35; idem, "The Birth of the 'Modern Family' in Early America: Quaker and Anglican Families in the Delaware Valley, Pennsylvania, 1681–1750," in *Friends and Neighbors: Group Life in America's First Plural Society*, ed. Michael Zuckerman (Philadelphia, Pa.: Temple University Press, 1982), 26–64; idem, "From 'Dark Corners' to American Domesticity: The British Social Context of the Welsh and Cheshire Quakers' Familial Revolution in Pennsylvania, 1657–1685," in *The World of William Penn*, ed. Richard S. Dunn and Mary Maples Dunn (Philadelphia: University of Pennsylvania Press, 1986), 215–39; idem, *Quakers and the American Family: British Settlement in the Delaware Valley* (New York: Oxford University Press, 1988); Rodger C. Henderson, "Demographic Patterns and Family Structure in Eighteenth-Century Lancaster County, Pennsylvania," *Pennsylvania Magazine of History and Biography* 114 (1990): 349–83.

The few studies of demography and family history in New Netherland are summarized in Joyce D. Goodfriend, "The Historiography of the Dutch in Colonial America," in *Colonial Dutch Studies: An Interdisciplinary Approach*, ed. Eric Nooter and Patricia U. Bonomi (New York: New York University Press, 1988), 9–11.

18. Carr and Walsh, "Planter's Wife," 560.

19. Daniel Scott Smith, "Parental Power and Marriage Patterns: An Analysis of Historical Trends in Hingham, Massachusetts," *Journal of Marriage and the Family* 35 (1973): 426.

20. Ibid., 422.

21. Ibid., 424.

22. Ibid., 425. Smith's delineation of this system from the demographic and economic data of Hingham, Massachusetts, finds confirmation in other sources: for example, the case of Michael Wigglesworth's courtship (Morgan, *Puritan Family*, 85–86), and Greven's analysis of the control that fathers exercised over their sons in early Andover, Massachusetts (*Four Generations*, ch. 4).

23. Daniel Blake Smith, *Inside the Great House: Planter Family Life in Eighteenth-Century Chesapeake Society* (Ithaca, N.Y.: Cornell University Press, 1980), 131. On the geographical dimensions of marriage in New England, see Susan L. Norton, "Marital Migration in Essex County, Massachusetts, in the Colonial and Early Federal Periods," *Journal of Marriage and the Family* 35 (1974): 406–18; Doris O'Keefe, "Marriage and Migration in New England: A Study in Historical Population Geography," Department of Geography, Syracuse University, *Discussion Paper Series*, no. 16 (June 1976), and John W. Adams and Alice B. Kasakoff, "Migration at Marriage in Colonial New England: A Comparison of Rates Derived from Genealogies with Rates from Vital Records," in *Genealogical Demog-*

raphy, ed. Bennett Dyke and Warren T. Morrill (New York: Academic Press, 1980), 115–38.

24. Studies of sexuality start with Edmund S. Morgan's now classic "The Puritans and Sex," *New England Quarterly* 15 (1942): 591–607, and include: Lawrence Stone, *The Family, Sex and Marriage in England, 1500–1800* (New York: Harper and Row, 1977); Lyle Koehler, *A Search for Power: The "Weaker Sex" in Seventeenth-Century New England* (Urbana: University of Illinois Press, 1980); Ellen K. Rothman, "Sex and Self-Control: Middle-Class Courtship in America, 1770–1870," *Journal of Social History* 15 (1982): 409–25; Roger Thompson, *Sex in Middlesex: Popular Mores in a Massachusetts County, 1649–1699* (Amherst: University of Massachusetts Press, 1986); idem, "Attitudes towards Homosexuality in the Seventeenth-Century New England Colonies," *Journal of American Studies* 23 (1989): 27–40; John D'Emilio and Estelle B. Freedman, *Intimate Matters: A History of Sexuality in America* (New York: Harper and Row, 1988); Paula A. Treckel, "Breastfeeding and Maternal Sexuality in Colonial America," *Journal of Interdisciplinary History* 20 (1989): 25–51.

25. Smith, "Parental Power and Marriage Patterns," 426–27. On the relationship between family values and the American Revolution, see Melvin Yazawa, *From Colonies to Commonwealth: Familial Ideology and the Beginnings of the American Republic* (Baltimore, Md.: Johns Hopkins University Press, 1985).

Studies of courtship include: Daniel Scott Smith and Michael S. Hindus, "Premarital Pregnancy in America, 1640–1971: An Overview and Interpretation," *Journal of Interdisciplinary History* 5 (1975): 537–70; Robert A. Gross, *The Minutemen and Their World* (New York: Hill & Wang, 1976). Rare data on the participant-run courtships of late eighteenth-century New England appear in Lois K. Stabler, ed., *Very Poor and of a Lo Make: The Journal of Abner Sanger* (Portsmouth, New Hampshire: Historical Society of Cheshire County, 1986), and are analyzed in Laurel Thatcher Ulrich and Stabler, " 'Girling of It' in Eighteenth-Century New Hampshire," in *Families and Children*, ed. Benes, 24–36. See also Chilton L. Powell, "Marriage in Early New England," *New England Quarterly* 1 (1928): 323–34; Edmund S. Morgan, "The Puritan's Marriage with God," *South Atlantic Quarterly* 48 (1949): 107–12; Lorena S. Walsh, " 'Till Death Us Do Part': Marriage and Family in Seventeenth-Century Maryland," in *Chesapeake in the Seventeenth Century*, ed. Tate and Ammerman, 141–51; James M. Gallman, "Determinants of Age at Marriage in Colonial Perquimans County, North Carolina," *William and Mary Quarterly* 3d ser., 39 (1982): 176–91; Ellen K. Rothman, *Hands and Hearts: A History of Courtship in America* (New York: Basic Books, 1984); Patricia Trainor O'Malley, " 'Belovid Wife' and 'Inveigled Affections': Marriage Patterns in Early Rowley, Massachusetts," in *Generations and Change: Genealogical Perspectives in Social History*, ed. Robert M. Taylor, Jr., and Ralph J. Crandall (Macon, Ga.: Mercer University Press, 1986), 181–201; Edith B. Gelles, "Gossip: An Eighteenth-Century Case," *Journal of Social History* 22 (1989): 667–84; J. A. Leo Lemay, ed., *Robert Bolling Woos Anne Miller: Love and Courtship in Colonial Virginia, 1760* (Charlottesville: University Press of Virginia, 1990).

26. Levy, *Quakers and the American Family*, 132.

27. Ibid., 137, 149–50. Levy notes that "while bachelors and spinsters were rare in New England towns, at least 14.4 percent of Chester and Welsh Tract youth did not marry."

28. Smith, *Inside the Great House*, 135.

29. Jan Lewis, *The Pursuit of Happiness: Family and Values in Jefferson's Virginia* (Cambridge: Cambridge University Press, 1983), 30.

30. Christopher M. Jedrey, *The World of John Cleaveland: Family and Community in Eighteenth-Century New England* (New York: W. W. Norton & Company, 1979), 71–72.

31. Nancy F. Cott, *The Bonds of Womanhood: "Woman's Sphere" in New England, 1780–1835* (New Haven, Conn.: Yale University Press, 1977), 77–78.

32. See "Monthly Frequency of Successful Conceptions" in James A. Henretta and Gregory H. Nobles, *Evolution and Revolution: American Society, 1600–1820* (Lexington, Mass.: D. C. Heath, 1987), 37, citing Kenneth A. Lockridge, "The Conception Cycle as a Tool for Historical Analysis," paper presented at the SUNY-Stony Brook Conference on Social History, June 1969; Darrett B. Rutman, Charles Wetherell, and Anita H. Rutman, "Rhythms of Life: Black and White Seasonality in the Early Chesapeake," *Journal of Interdisciplinary History* 11 (1980): 29–53; David Cressy, "The Seasonality of Marriage in Old and New England," *Journal of Interdisciplinary History* 16 (1985): 1–22; Robert V. Wells, "Marriage Seasonals in Early America: Comparisons and Comments," *Journal of Interdisciplinary History* 18 (1987): 299–307.

33. Greven, *Four Generations*, 201; Levy, *Quakers and the American Family*, 237. In Ipswich, Massachusetts, completed families averaged 6.4; Susan L. Norton, "Population Growth in Colonial America: A Study of Ipswich, Massachusetts," *Population Studies* 25 (1971): 444. Demos finds larger families in Plymouth Colony (*Little Commonwealth*, 192), but as Norton points out ("Population Growth in Colonial America," 444), his criteria for inclusion or exclusion of certain families would tend to inflate family size.

34. Wells, "Family Size and Fertility Control in Eighteenth-Century America," 73–82 (quotations from 80–81). Wells tests his data for three patterns, all of which he finds: "The women who married early should have lower age-specific fertility rates at comparable ages, should cease bearing children at an earlier age, and should have a longer interval between the penultimate and the last birth than do women who married late and so achieve their desired family size at a later age"; ibid., 78. Wells offers a wider overview in "Family History and Demographic Transition."

35. H. Temkin-Greener and A. C. Swedlund, "Fertility Transition in the Connecticut Valley: 1740–1850," *Population Studies* 32 (1978): 34, 36, 39.

36. Lawrence J. Kilbourne, "The Fertility Transition in New England: The Case of Hampton, New Hampshire, 1655–1840," in *Generations and Change*, ed. Taylor and Crandall, 209. See also Nancy Osterud and John Fulton, "Family Limitation and Age at Marriage: Fertility Decline in Sturbridge, Massachusetts, 1730–1850," *Population Studies* 30 (1976): 481–94; Edward Byers, "Fertility Transition in a New England Commercial Center: Nantucket, Massachusetts, 1680–1840," *Journal of Interdisciplinary History* 13 (1982): 17–40; Barbara J. Logue, "The Whaling Industry and Fertility Decline: Nantucket, Massachusetts, 1660–1850," *Social Science History* 7 (1983): 427–56.

On other dimensions of fertility decline, see William L. Langer, "Checks on Population Growth: 1750–1850," *Scientific American* 226 (1972): 92–99; Peter T. Marcy, "Factors Affecting the Fecundity and Fertility of Historical Populations,"

Journal of Family History 6 (1981): 309–26; Jane Menken, James Trussell, and Susan Watkins, "The Nutrition Fertility Link: An Evaluation of the Evidence," *Journal of Interdisciplinary History* 11 (1981): 425–41.

37. Catherine M. Scholten, " 'On the Importance of the Obstetrik Art': Changing Customs of Childbirth in America, 1760 to 1825," *William and Mary Quarterly* 3d ser., 34 (1977): 427, 434. There is a growing literature on childbirth and midwifery: Richard W. Wertz and Dorothy C. Wertz, *Lying-In: A History of Childbirth in America* (New York: The Free Press, 1977); Jane Donegan, *Women and Men Midwives: Medicine, Morality and Misogyny in Early America* (Westport, Conn.: Greenwood Press, 1978); Judith Walzer Leavitt, " 'Science' Enters the Birthing Room: Obstetrics in America since the Eighteenth Century," *Journal of American History* 70 (1983): 281–304; idem, *Brought to Bed: Childbearing in America, 1750–1950* (New York: Oxford University Press, 1986); Catherine M. Scholten, *Childbearing in American Society, 1650–1850* (New York: New York University Press, 1985); Laurel Thatcher Ulrich, "Martha Moore Ballard and the Medical Challenge to Midwifery," in *Maine in the Early Republic: From Revolution to Statehood*, ed. Charles E. Clark et al. (Hanover, N.H.: University Press of New England, 1988), 165–83; idem, *A Midwife's Tale: The Life of Martha Ballard, Based on Her Diary, 1785–1812* (New York: Alfred A. Knopf, 1990); Jan Lewis and Kenneth A. Lockridge, " 'Sally Has Been Sick': Pregnancy and Family Limitation among Virginia Gentry Women, 1780–1830," *Journal of Social History* 22 (1988): 5–19. On English practices, see R. V. Schnucker, "The English Puritans and Pregnancy, Delivery and Breast Feeding," *History of Childhood Quarterly* 1 (1974): 637–58, and Stone, *Family, Sex and Marriage in England*.

38. Ulrich, "Martha Moore Ballard and the Medical Challenge to Midwifery," 168.

39. Demos, *Little Commonwealth*, 66; Ulrich, *Midwife's Tale*, 170; Greven, *Four Generations*, 195–96.

40. Treckel, "Breastfeeding and Maternal Sexuality in Colonial America," 35; Ross W. Beales, Jr. "Nursing and Weaning in an Eighteenth-Century New England Household," in *Families and Children*, ed. Benes, 48–63; James Axtell, *The School upon a Hill: Education and Society in Colonial New England* (New Haven, Conn.: Yale University Press, 1974); Joseph E. Illick, "Child-Rearing in Seventeenth-Century England and America," in *The History of Childhood*, ed. Lloyd deMause (New York: Psychohistory Press, 1974), 303–50; John F. Walzer, "A Period of Ambivalence: Eighteenth-Century American Childhood," in *The History of Childhood*, 351–82. For some English and West Indian data, see Schnucker, "English Puritans and Pregnancy, Delivery and Breast Feeding," and Jerome S. Handler and Robert S. Corruccini, "Weaning among West Indian Slaves: Historical and Bioanthropological Evidence from Barbados," *William and Mary Quarterly* 3d ser., 43 (1986): 111–17.

41. Daniel Scott Smith, "Child-Naming Patterns and Family Structure Change: Hingham, Massachusetts, 1640–1880," *The Newberry Papers in Family and Community History*, 76–5 (1977): 3. This working paper, often cited in other studies, set forth ideas which Smith later presented in "Child-Naming Practices, Kinship Ties, and Change in Family Attitudes in Hingham, Massachusetts, 1641 to 1880," *Journal of Social History* 18 (1985): 541–66. See also David Hackett Fischer, "Forenames and the Family in New England: An Exercise in Historical

Onomastics," in *Generations and Change*, ed. Taylor and Crandall, 215–41; John
J. Waters, "Naming and Kinship in New England: Guilford Patterns and Usage,
1693–1759," *New England Historical and Genealogical Register* 138 (1984): 161–
81; David W. Dumas, "The Naming of Children in New England, 1780–1850,"
New England Historical and Genealogical Register 132 (1978): 196–210; and Ross
W. Beales, Jr., "Naming Patterns in Westborough, Massachusetts, 1720–1850"
(unpublished paper, 19th Annual Duquesne History Forum, Pittsburgh, 23 October 1985).

42. Fischer, "Forenames and the Family in New England," 219, 220–24 (quotation from 223).

43. Ibid., 226.

44. Darrett B. Rutman and Anita H. Rutman, " 'In Nomine Avi': Child-
Naming Patterns in a Chesapeake County, 1650–1750," in *Generations and
Change*, ed. Taylor and Crandall, 250–51, 252, 253, 256–57. The Rutmans use
as a test the percentage of first children who shared a name with the same-sex
parent in Middlesex County, Hingham, and among English families who immigrated to New England. The percentages were almost identical for the Middlesex and immigrant samples (27.4 percent and 28.2 percent for sons, 19.2
percent and 19.7 percent for daughters), but were significantly larger for
Hingham in the period 1640–1760 (59.7 percent for sons, 58.6 percent for
daughters).

45. On attitudes toward children and childrearing in colonial America, see
note 3, above, and Ross W. Beales, Jr., "In Search of the Historical Child:
Miniature Adulthood and Youth in Colonial New England," *American Quarterly*
27 (1975): 379–98; idem, "The Child in Seventeenth-Century America," in *American Childhood*, ed. Hawes and Hiner, 15–56; idem, "Anne Bradstreet and Her
Children," in *Regulated Children/Liberated Children: Education in Psychohistorical
Perspective*, ed. Barbara Finkelstein (New York: Psychohistory Press, 1979), 10–
23; Constance B. Schulz, "Children and Childhood in the Eighteenth Century,"
in *American Childhood*, ed. Hawes and Hiner, 57–109; Demos, *Little Commonwealth*;
Morgan, *Puritan Family*; Levy, *Quakers and the American Family*; Smith, *Inside the
Great House*, chs. 2–3; Axtell, *School upon a Hill*; Illick, "Child-Rearing in Sev-
enteenth-Century England and America"; Alice Judson Ryerson, "Medical Ad-
vice on Child Rearing, 1550–1900," *Harvard Educational Review* 31 (1961): 302–
23; N. Ray Hiner, "Cotton Mather and His Children: The Evolution of a Parent
Educator, 1686–1728," in *Regulated Children*, ed. Finkelstein, 24–43; idem, "Cot-
ton Mather and His Female Children: Notes on the Relationship between Private
Experience and Public Thought," *Journal of Psychohistory* 13 (1985): 33–49; idem,
"The Cry of Sodom Enquired into: Educational Analysis in Seventeenth-Century
New England," *History of Education Quarterly* 13 (1973): 3–22; Walzer, "A Period
of Ambivalence: Eighteenth-Century American Childhood"; Philip J. Greven,
Jr., *The Protestant Temperament: Patterns of Child-Rearing, Religious Experience, and
the Self in Early America* (New York: Alfred A. Knopf, 1977).

46. Morgan, *Puritan Family*, 78. On English practice, see Grant McCracken,
"The Exchange of Children in Tudor England: An Anthropological Phenomenon in History Context," *Journal of Family History* 8 (1983): 303–13. While
evidence for this practice and its motives is scattered, parental decisions may
have reflected other circumstances, particularly the evolving size and structure

of the family and household and the need, or perhaps merely the convenience, of alleviating crowded households and disposing of surplus labor. Beales, "Child in Seventeenth-Century America"; idem, "Boys' Work on an Eighteenth Century New England Farm," *Proceedings of the Duquesne University History Forum, 1988* (forthcoming).

47. Morgan, *Puritan Family*, 108, 185. On the comparative and cross-cultural dimensions of "tribalism," see Moran and Vinovskis, "The Puritan Family and Religion," 32–34.

48. Demos, *Little Commonwealth*, 134–39; idem, "Underlying Themes in the Witchcraft of Seventeenth-Century New England," in *Colonial America: Essays in Politics and Social Development*, ed. Stanley N. Katz (Boston: Little, Brown and Company, 1971), 114–33, as revised from the *American Historical Review* 75 (1970): 1311–26; idem, *Entertaining Satan: Witchcraft and the Culture of Early New England* (New York: Oxford University Press, 1982), 207–8.

49. Greven, *Protestant Temperament*, 35, 160, 265.

50. See Edmund S. Morgan's review, *New York Review of Books* 25 February 1978, 13–18.

51. Daniel Blake Smith, *Inside the Great House*, 50–51, 286.

52. Lewis, *Pursuit of Happiness*, 30. See also idem, "Domestic Tranquillity and the Management of Emotions among the Gentry of Pre-Revolutionary Virginia," *William and Mary Quarterly* 3d ser., 39 (1982): 135–49.

53. Levy, *Quakers and the American Family*, 152.

54. John J. Waters, "The Traditional World of the New England Peasants: A View from Seventeenth-Century Barnstable," *New England Historical and Genealogical Register* 130 (1976): 19.

55. See, for example, Ross W. Beales, Jr., "Boys' Work on an Eighteenth Century New England Farm."

56. Beales, "In Search of the Historical Child."

57. Beales, "Boys' Work on an Eighteenth Century New England Farm."

58. Demos, *Little Commonwealth*, 150. See idem, *Entertaining Satan*, 157–65, for an important discussion of the relationship between female adolescence and witchcraft accusations. See also John Demos and Virginia Demos, "Adolescence in Historical Perspective."

59. Beales, "In Search of the Historical Child"; N. Ray Hiner, "Adolescence in Eighteenth-Century America," *History of Childhood Quarterly* 3 (1975): 253–80; Roger Thompson, "Adolescent Culture in Colonial Massachusetts," *Journal of Family History* 9 (1984): 127–44; Vivian C. Fox, "Is Adolescence a Phenomenon of Modern Times?" *Journal of Psychohistory* 5 (1977): 271–90.

60. Rutman and Rutman, *A Place in Time*, 114. Among children born before 1690, 48 percent lost one or both parents by age nine, 61 percent by age thirteen. For the years between 1690 and 1709 and between 1710 and 1749, the comparable percentages are 43 percent and 60 percent, 45 percent and 57 percent.

61. Ibid., 118, 120.

62. Daniel Blake Smith, "Mortality and Family in the Colonial Chesapeake," *Journal of Interdisciplinary History* 8 (1978): 424–25.

63. Greven, *Four Generations*, 35, 120, 206, and Levy, *Quakers and the American Family*, 149. Despite the relatively greater wealth of Quaker families in the Delaware Valley, Levy notes that their sons married later than the sons of Andover

families. A family's land, while allowing the sons of wealthier families to marry earlier than their poorer peers, was less important than family and religious values.

64. See, for example, Thomas C. Thompson, "The Life Course and Labor of a Colonial Farmer," *Historical New Hampshire* 40 (1985): 135–55.

65. Beales, "Boys' Work on an Eighteenth Century New England Farm"; idem, "The Reverend Ebenezer Parkman's Farm Workers, Westborough, Massachusetts, 1726–82," *Proceedings of the American Antiquarian Society* 99 (1989): 121–49. Demos discusses household size in "Families in Colonial Bristol, Rhode Island," and speculates on the psychological dynamics of the presence of large families in relatively small houses in *A Little Commonwealth*, 46–51. On other dimensions of household size, see Peter Benes, "Sleeping Arrangements in Early Massachusetts: The Newbury Household of Henry Lunt, Hatter," in *Early American Probate Inventories*, ed. Peter Benes (The Dublin Seminar for New England Folklife, *Annual Proceedings, 1987*; Boston: Boston University Scholarly Publications, 1989), 140–52; Alan D. Watson, "Household Size and Composition in Pre-Revolutionary North Carolina," *Mississippi Quarterly* 31 (1978): 551–69.

66. Robert A. Gross, *The Minutemen*, 208.

67. Greven, *Four Generations*, 222–58.

68. Jedrey, *The World of John Cleaveland*, 5–16, 74–84, 157–65; Waters, "Traditional World of the New England Peasants, 3–21. See also idem, "Patrimony, Succession, and Social Stability: Guilford, Connecticut, in the Eighteenth Century," *Perspectives in American History* 10 (1976): 129–60, and idem, "Family, Inheritance, and Migration in Colonial New England: The Evidence from Guilford, Connecticut," *William and Mary Quarterly* 3d ser., 39 (1982): 64–86.

69. On patterns of inheritance, see Greven, *Four Generations*, passim; Waters, "Patrimony, Succession, and Social Stability: Guilford, Connecticut, in the Eighteenth Century," and idem, "Family, Inheritance, and Migration in Colonial New England: The Evidence from Guilford, Connecticut"; Linda Auwers, "Fathers, Sons, and Wealth in Colonial Windsor, Connecticut," *Journal of Family History* 3 (1978): 136–49; Carole Shammas, Marylynn Salmon, and Michael Dahlin, *Inheritance in America: From Colonial Times to the Present* (New Brunswick, N.J.: Rutgers University Press, 1987); Daniel Scott Smith, "Inheritance and the Social History of Early American Women," in *Women in the Age of the American Revolution*, ed. Hoffman and Albert, 45–66; Lois Green Carr, "Inheritance in the Colonial Chesapeake," in *Women in the Age of the American Revolution*, 155–208; Susan Grigg, "Women and Family Property: A Review of U.S. Inheritance Studies," *Historical Methods* 22 (1989): 116–22.

70. On old age, see Daniel Scott Smith, "Old Age and the 'Great Transformation': A New England Case Study," in *Aging and the Elderly: Humanistic Perspectives in Gerontology*, ed. Stuart F. Spicker, Kathleen M. Woodward, and David D. Van Tassell (Atlantic Highlands, N.J.: Humanities Press, 1978), 285–302; John Demos, "Old Age in Early New England," in *Turning Points: Historical and Sociological Essays on the Family*, ed. John Demos and Sarane Spence Boocock (Chicago: University of Chicago Press, 1978), 248–87; Gene W. Boyett, "Aging in Seventeenth-Century New England," *New England Historical and Genealogical Register* 134 (1980): 181–93; Tamara K. Hareven and K. J. Adams, eds., *Aging and Life Course Transitions: An Interdisciplinary Perspective* (New York: Guilford

Press, 1982); Carole Haber, *Beyond Sixty-Five: The Dilemma of Old Age in America's Past* (New York: Cambridge University Press, 1983).

On death, see Maris A. Vinovskis, "Angels' Heads and Weeping Willows: Death in Early America," *Proceedings of the American Antiquarian Society* 86 (1976): 273–302; David E. Stannard, *The Puritan Way of Death: A Study in Religion, Culture, and Social Change* (New York: Oxford University Press, 1977); Peter Gregg Slater, *Children in the New England Mind: In Death and in Life* (Hamden, Conn.: Archon Books, 1977); Gordon E. Geddes, *Welcome Joy: Death in Puritan New England* (Ann Arbor, Mich.: UMI Research Press, 1981).

71. Historians have focused their research on the status of widows rather than widowers. What we know about widowers tends to be anecdotal, reflecting the bereavement, courtships, and remarriage of relatively prominent individuals; see, for example, Morgan, *Puritan Family*, 49–50, 55–56, 151–52. Indexes commonly have entries for widows but less often for widowers; see, for example, Greven, *Four Generations*, 328; Demos, *Little Commonwealth*, 201; Smith, *Inside the Great House*, 305.

On other dimensions of widowhood, especially the control and transmission of property and its relationship to the status of women, see Kim Lacy Rogers, "Relicts of the New World: Conditions of Widowhood in Seventeenth-Century New England," in *Women's Being, Women's Place: Female Identity and Vocation in American History*, ed. Mary Kelley (Boston: G. K. Hall & Co., 1979), 26–52; Linda E. Speth, "More than Her 'Thirds': Wives and Widows in Colonial Virginia," in *Women, Family, and Community in Colonial America: Two Perspectives*, ed. Linda E. Speth and Alison Duncan Hirsch (New York: Haworth Press, 1983), 5–41; Lisa Wilson Waciega, "A 'Man of Business': The Widow of Means in Southeastern Pennsylvania," *William and Mary Quarterly* 3d ser., 44 (1987): 40–64; and Gloria L. Main, "Widows in Rural Massachusetts on the Eve of the Revolution," in *Women in the Age of the American Revolution*, ed. Hoffman and Albert, 67–90.

72. Rutman and Rutman, *A Place in Time*, 197.

73. Henderson, "Demographic Patterns and Family Structure in Eighteenth-Century Lancaster County," 368.

74. Alexander Keyssar, "Widowhood in Eighteenth-Century Massachusetts: A Problem in the History of the Family," *Perspectives in American History* 8 (1974): 94, 96. In the first decades of the settlement of Massachusetts, men had outnumbered women by a ratio of about three to two; see Herbert Moller, "Sex Composition and Correlated Culture Patterns of Colonial America," *William and Mary Quarterly* 3d ser., 2 (1945): 115–17.

75. Keyssar, "Widowhood in Eighteenth-Century Massachusetts," 108, 111. Martha Moore Ballard experienced a "pseudo-widowhood" when her husband was imprisoned: "Ephraim's imprisonment now became her imprisonment. She became a lodger in her own house, taking one room as her own, giving over the rest to her son's family." Ulrich, *Midwife's Tale*, 218–82.

76. Waters, "Traditional World of the New England Peasants," 8.

77. Roderick Phillips, *Putting Asunder: A History of Divorce in Western Society* (New York: Cambridge University Press, 1988), 250. Nancy F. Cott examines 229 divorce petitions in Massachusetts between 1692 and 1786, 143 of which were successful; see Cott, "Divorce and the Changing Status of Women in Eighteenth-Century Massachusetts," *William and Mary Quarterly* 3d ser., 33 (1976):

586–614.

78. Sheldon S. Cohen, " 'To Parts of the World Unknown': The Circumstances of Divorce in Connecticut, 1750–1797," *Canadian Review of American Studies* 11 (1980): 284, 288–89. Cott also suggests a connection between the Revolution and increasing numbers of divorce actions; see Cott, "Divorce and the Changing Status of Women," 593.

Other studies that examine divorce in early America include George Elliott Howard, *A History of Matrimonial Institutions Chiefly in England and the United States with an Introductory Analysis of the Literature and the Theories of Primitive Marriage and the Family* (3 vols.; Chicago: University of Chicago Press, 1904; reprint, New York: Humanities Press, 1964); Sheldon S. Cohen, "The Broken Bond: Divorce in Providence County, 1749–1809," *Rhode Island History* 44 (1985): 66–79; idem, "What Man Hath Put Asunder: Divorce in New Hampshire, 1681–1784," *Historical New Hampshire* 41 (1986): 118–41; Henry S. Cohn, "Connecticut's Divorce Mechanism: 1636–1969," *American Journal of Legal History* 14 (1970): 34–54; Nancy F. Cott, "Eighteenth-Century Family and Social Life Revealed in Massachusetts Divorce Records," *Journal of Social History* 10 (1976): 20–43; Alison Duncan Hirsch, "The Thrall Divorce Case: A Family Crisis in Eighteenth-Century Connecticut," in *Women, Family, and Community in Colonial America: Two Perspectives*, ed. Speth and Hirsch, 43–75; D. Kelly Weisberg, " 'Under Greet Temptations Heer': Women and Divorce in Puritan Massachusetts," *Feminist Studies* 2 (1975): 183–94.

79. Mary Beth Norton, *Liberty's Daughters: The Revolutionary Experience of American Women, 1750–1800* (Boston: Little, Brown and Company, 1980), chs. 8–9.

80. Fischer, "Forenames and the Family in New England," 231.

BIBLIOGRAPHY

Adams, John W., and Alice B. Kasakoff. "Migration at Marriage in Colonial New England: A Comparison of Rates Derived from Genealogies with Rates from Vital Records." In *Genealogical Demography*, ed. Bennett Dyke and Warren T. Morrill, 115–38. New York: Academic Press, 1980.

Allen, David Grayson. *In English Ways: The Movement of Societies and the Transferal of English Local Law and Custom to Massachusetts Bay in the Seventeenth Century.* Chapel Hill: University of North Carolina Press, 1981.

Anderson, Terry L., and Robert Paul Thomas. "The Growth of Population and Labor Force in the 17th-Century Chesapeake." *Explorations in Economic History* 15 (1978): 290–312.

Anderson, Virginia DeJohn. "Migrants and Motives: Religion and the Settlement of New England, 1630–1640." *New England Quarterly* 58 (1985): 339–83.

———. "Migration, Kinship, and the Integration of Colonial New England Society: Three Generations of the Danforth Family." In *Generations and Change*, ed. Taylor and Crandall, 269–90.

Auwers, Linda. "Fathers, Sons, and Wealth in Colonial Windsor, Connecticut." *Journal of Family History* 3 (1978): 136–49.

Axtell, James. *The School upon a Hill: Education and Society in Colonial New England.* New Haven, Conn.: Yale University Press, 1974.

Bailyn, Bernard. *Education in the Forming of American Society: Needs and Oppor-*

tunities for Study. Chapel Hill: University of North Carolina Press, 1960.

————. *Voyagers to the West: A Passage in the Peopling of America on the Eve of the Revolution*. New York: Alfred A. Knopf, 1986.

Beales, Ross W., Jr. "Anne Bradstreet and Her Children." In *Regulated Children/ Liberated Children: Education in Psychohistorical Perspective*, ed. Finkelstein, 10–23. New York: Psychohistory Press, 1979.

————. "The Child in Seventeenth-Century America." In *American Childhood: A Research Guide and Historical Handbook*, ed. Hawes and Hiner, 15–56. Westport, Conn.: Greenwood Press, 1985.

————. "In Search of the Historical Child: Miniature Adulthood and Youth in Colonial New England." *American Quarterly* 27 (1975): 379–98.

————. "Nursing and Weaning in an Eighteenth-Century New England Household." In *Families and Children*, ed. Peter Benes, 48–63. The Dublin Seminar for New England Folklife, Annual Proceedings 1985. Boston: Boston University Scholarly Publications, 1987.

————. "Selected Bibliography on Children and Families in New England." In *Families and Children*, ed. Peter Benes, 148–57. The Dublin Seminar for New England Folklife Annual Proceedings 1985. Boston: Boston University Scholarly Publications, 1987.

Benes, Peter. "Sleeping Arrangements in Early Massachusetts: The Newbury Household of Henry Lunt, Hatter." In *Early American Probate Inventories*, ed. Peter Benes, 140–52. The Dublin Seminar for New England Folklife, Annual Proceedings, 1987. Boston: Boston University Scholarly Publications, 1989.

Bloch, Ruth H. "American Feminine Ideals in Transition: The Rise of the Moral Mother, 1785–1815." *Feminist Studies* 4 (1978): 101–26.

Bodle, Wayne, "The 'Myth of the Middle Colonies' Reconsidered: The Process of Regionalization in Early America." *Pennsylvania Magazine of History and Biography* 113 (1989): 527–48.

Boyer, Paul, and Stephen Nissenbaum. *Salem Possessed: The Social Origins of Witchcraft*. Cambridge, Mass.: Harvard University Press, 1974.

Boyett, Gene W. "Aging in Seventeenth-Century New England." *New England Historical and Genealogical Register* 134 (1980): 181–93.

Breen, T. H., and Stephen Foster. "Moving to the New World: The Character of Early Massachusetts Immigration." *William and Mary Quarterly* 3d ser., 30 (1973): 189–222.

Bremner, Robert H., et al., eds. *Children and Youth in America: A Documentary History*. Vol. 1, *1600–1865*. Cambridge, Mass.: Harvard University Press, 1970.

Brobeck, Stephen. "Images of the Family: Portrait Paintings as Indices of American Family Culture, Structure, and Behavior, 1730–1860." *Journal of Psychohistory* 5 (1977): 81–106.

Buel, Joy Day, and Richard Buel, Jr. *The Way of Duty: A Woman and Her Family in Revolutionary America*. New York: W. W. Norton & Company, 1984.

Byers, Edward. "Fertility Transition in a New England Commercial Center: Nantucket, Massachusetts, 1680–1840." *Journal of Interdisciplinary History* 13 (1982): 17–40.

Calhoun, Arthur W. *A Social History of the American Family from Colonial Times to the Present.* 3 vols. Cleveland, Ohio: The Arthur H. Clark Company, 1917–1919. Reprint. New York: Barnes & Noble, 1945.

Calvert, Karin. "Children in American Family Portraiture, 1670 to 1810." *William and Mary Quarterly* 3d ser., 39 (1982): 87–113.

Campbell, Mildred. "Social Origins of Some Early Americans." In *Seventeenth-Century America: Essays in Colonial History*, ed. James Morton Smith, 63–89. Chapel Hill: University of North Carolina Press, 1959.

Carr, Lois Green. "The Development of the Maryland Orphans' Court, 1654–1715." In *Law, Society, and Politics in Early Maryland: Proceedings of the First Conference on Maryland History, June 14–15, 1974*, ed. Land, et al., 41–62. Baltimore, Md.: Johns Hopkins University Press, 1977.

———. "Inheritance in the Colonial Chesapeake." In *Women in the Age of the American Revolution*, ed. Hoffman and Albert, 155–208. Charlottesville: University Press of Virginia, 1989.

Carr, Lois Green, and Russell R. Menard. "Immigration and Opportunity: The Freedman in Early Colonial Maryland." In *The Chesapeake in the Seventeenth Century: Essays on Anglo-American Society*, ed. Tate and Ammerman, 206–42. Chapel Hill: University of North Carolina Press, 1979.

Carr, Lois Green, Philip D. Morgan, and Jean B. Russo, eds. *Colonial Chesapeake Society.* Chapel Hill: University of North Carolina Press, 1988.

Carr, Lois Green, and Lorena S. Walsh. "The Planter's Wife: The Experience of White Women in Seventeenth-Century Maryland." *William and Mary Quarterly* 3d ser., 34 (1977): 542–71.

Cates, Gerald L. " 'The Seasoning': Disease and Death among the First Colonists of Georgia." *Georgia Historical Quarterly* 64 (1980): 146–58.

Chambers-Schiller, Lee Virginia. *Liberty, A Better Husband: Single Women in America, The Generations of 1780–1840.* New Haven, Conn.: Yale University Press, 1984.

Cohen, Sheldon S. "The Broken Bond: Divorce in Providence County, 1749–1809." *Rhode Island History* 44 (1985): 66–79.

———. " 'To Parts of the World Unknown': The Circumstances of Divorce in Connecticut, 1750–1797."

———. "What Man Hath Put Asunder: Divorce in New Hampshire, 1681–1784." *Historical New Hampshire* 41 (1986): 118–41.

Cohn, Henry S. "Connecticut's Divorce Mechanism: 1636–1969." *American Journal of Legal History* 14 (1970): 34–54.

Cole, Thomas R. "Family, Settlement, and Migration in Southeastern Massachusetts, 1650–1805: The Case for Regional Analysis." *New England Historical and Genealogical Register* 132 (1978): 171–85.

Cott, Nancy F. *The Bonds of Womanhood: "Woman's Sphere" in New England, 1780–1835.* New Haven, Conn.: Yale University Press, 1977.

———. "Divorce and the Changing Status of Women in Eighteenth-Century Massachusetts." *William and Mary Quarterly* 3d ser., 33 (1976): 586–614.

———. "Eighteenth-Century Family and Social Life Revealed in Massachusetts Divorce Records." *Journal of Social History* 10 (1976): 20–43.

Courtwright, David T. "New England Families in Historical Perspective." In *Families and Children*, ed. Peter Benes, 11–23. The Dublin Seminar for New England Folklife Annual Proceedings 1985. Boston: Boston University Scholarly Publications, 1987.

Crandall, Ralph J. "Family Types, Social Structure, and Mobility in Early Amer-
ica: Charlestown, Massachusetts, A Case Study." In *Changing Images of the
Family*, ed. Virginia Tufte and Barbara Myerhoff, 61–81. New Haven,
Conn.: Yale University Press, 1979.

Cressy, David. *Coming Over: Migration and Communication between England and
New England in the Seventeenth Century.* New York: Cambridge University
Press, 1987.

———. "The Seasonality of Marriage in Old and New England." *Journal of
Interdisciplinary History* 16 (1985): 1–22.

Crouse, Nellis M. "The Causes of the Great Migration, 1630–1640." *New England
Quarterly* 5 (1932): 3–36.

Degler, Carl N. *At Odds: Women and the Family in America from the Revolution to
the Present.* New York: Oxford University Press, 1980.

D'Emilio, John, and Estelle B. Freedman. *Intimate Matters: A History of Sexuality
in America.* New York: Harper & Row, 1988.

Demos, John. "The American Family in Past Time." *American Scholar* 43 (1974):
422–46.

———. "Demography and Psychology in the Historical Study of Family-Life: A
Personal Report." In *Household and Family in Past Time*, ed. Laslett and
Wall, 561–69. Cambridge: Cambridge University Press, 1972.

———. "Developmental Perspectives on the History of Childhood." *Journal of
Interdisciplinary History* 2 (1971): 315–27.

———. *Entertaining Satan: Witchcraft and the Culture of Early New England.* New
York: Oxford University Press, 1982.

———. "Families in Colonial Bristol, Rhode Island: An Exercise in Historical
Demography." *William and Mary Quarterly* 3d ser., 25 (1968): 40–57.

———. *A Little Commonwealth: Family Life in Plymouth Colony.* New York: Oxford
University Press, 1970.

———. "Notes on Life in Plymouth Colony." *William and Mary Quarterly* 3d ser.,
22 (1965): 264–86.

———. "Old Age in Early New England." In *Turning Points: Historical and Sociological Essays on the Family*, ed. Demos and Boocock, 248–87. Chicago:
University of Chicago Press, 1978. Reprint. In *Aging, Death, and the Completion of Being*, ed. David D. Van Tassel, 115–64. Philadelphia: University
of Pennsylvania Press, 1979. Reprint. In Demos, *Past, Present, and Personal:
The Family and the Life Course in American History*, 139–85. New York:
Oxford University Press, 1986.

———. *Past, Present, and Personal: The Family and the Life Course in American History.*
New York: Oxford University Press, 1986.

———. "Underlying Themes in the Witchcraft of Seventeenth-Century New
England." *American Historical Review* 75 (1970): 1311–26. Reprint. In *Colonial America: Essays in Politics and Social Development*, ed. Stanley Katz,
114–33. Boston: Little, Brown and Company, 1971.

Demos, John, and Sarane Spense Boocook, eds. *Turning Points: Historical and Sociological Essays on the Family.* Chicago: University of Chicago Press, 1978.

Demos, John, and Virginia Demos. "Adolescence in Historical Perspective." *Journal of Marriage and the Family* 31 (1969): 632–38.

Donegan, Jane. *Women and Men Midwives: Medicine, Morality and Misogyny in Early America.* Westport, Conn.: Greenwood Press, 1978.

Dumas, David W. "The Naming of Children in New England, 1780–1850." *New England Historical and Genealogical Register* 132 (1978): 196–210.

Dunn, Richard S. "The Barbados Census of 1680: Profile of the Richest Colony in English America." *William and Mary Quarterly* 3d ser., 26 (1969): 3–30.

———. "The Social History of Early New England." *American Quarterly* 24 (1972): 661–79.

Earle, Alice Morse. *Child Life in Colonial Days.* New York: Macmillan Co., 1899.

———. *Home Life in Colonial Days.* New York: Macmillan Co., 1898.

Earle, Carville V. "Environment, Disease, and Mortality in Early Virginia." In *The Chesapeake in the Seventeenth Century: Essays on Anglo-American Society,* ed. Tate and Ammerman, 96–125. Chapel Hill: University of North Carolina Press, 1979.

Faragher, John. "Old Women and Old Men in Seventeenth-Century Wethersfield, Connecticut." *Women's Studies* 4 (1976): 110–31.

Farber, Bernard. *Guardians of Virtue: Salem Families in 1800.* New York: Basic Books, 1972.

Finkelstein, Barbara, ed. *Regulated Children/Liberated Children: Education in Psychohistorical Perspective.* New York: Psychohistory Press, 1979.

Fischer, David Hackett. *Albion's Seed: Four British Folkways in America.* New York: Oxford University Press, 1989.

———. "Forenames and the Family in New England: An Exercise in Historical Onomastics." *Chronos* 1 (1981): 76–111. Reprint. In *Generations and Change,* ed. Taylor and Crandall, 215–41.

Flaherty, David H. *Privacy in Colonial New England.* Charlottesville: University Press of Virginia, 1972.

Fleming, Sandford. *Children and Puritanism: The Place of Children in the Life and Thought of the New England Churches, 1620–1847.* New Haven, Conn.: Yale University Press, 1933.

Fox, Vivian C. "Is Adolescence a Phenomenon of Modern Times?" *Journal of Psychohistory* 5 (1977): 271–90.

Fox, Vivian C., and Martin H. Quitt, eds. *Loving, Parenting and Dying: The Family Cycle in England and America, Past and Present.* New York: Psychohistory Press, 1980.

Francis, Elizabeth A. "American Children's Literature, 1646–1880." In *American Childhood: A Research Guide and Historical Handbook,* ed. Hawes and Hiner, 185–233. Westport, Conn.: Greenwood Press, 1985.

Frost, J. William. *The Quaker Family in Colonial America: A Portrait of the Society of Friends.* New York: St. Martin's Press, 1973.

Frost, Jerry W. "As the Twig Is Bent: Quaker Ideas of Childhood." *Quaker History* 60 (1971): 67–87.

Galenson, David W. " 'Middling People' or 'Common Sort'?: The Social Origins of Some Early Americans Reexamined." *William and Mary Quarterly* 3d ser., 35 (1978): 499–524; with a rebuttal by Mildred Campbell, 525–40.

Gallman, James M. "Determinants of Age at Marriage in Colonial Perquimans County, North Carolina." *William and Mary Quarterly* 3d ser., 39 (1982): 176–91.

———. "Mortality among White Males: Colonial North Carolina." *Social Science History* 4 (1980): 295–316.

Geddes, Gordon E. *Welcome Joy: Death in Puritan New England*. Ann Arbor, Mich: UMI Research Press, 1981.

Gemery, Henry A. "Disarray in the Historical Record: Estimates of Immigration to the United States, 1700–1860." *Proceedings of the American Philosophical Society* 133 (1989): 123–27.

———. "Emigration from the British Isles to the New World, 1630–1700: Inferences from Colonial Populations." In *Research in Economic History: A Research Annual* 5, ed. Uselding, 179–231. Greenwich, Conn.: JAI Press, 1980.

Greene, Jack P. "Autonomy and Stability: New England and the British Colonial Experience in Early Modern America." *Journal of Social History* 7 (1974): 171–94.

———. *Pursuits of Happiness: The Social Development of Early Modern British Colonies and the Formation of American Culture*. Chapel Hill: University of North Carolina Press, 1988.

Greven, Philip J., Jr. "The Average Size of Families and Households in the Province of Massachusetts in 1764 and in the United States in 1790: An Overview." In *Household and Family in Past Time*, ed. Laslett and Wall, 545–60. Cambridge: Cambridge University Press, 1972.

———. "Family Structure in Seventeenth-Century Andover, Massachusetts." *William and Mary Quarterly* 3d ser., 23 (1966): 234–56.

———. *Four Generations: Population, Land, and Family in Colonial Andover, Massachusetts*. Ithaca, N.Y.: Cornell University Press, 1970.

———. "Historical Demography and Colonial America: A Review Article." *William and Mary Quarterly* 3d ser., 24 (1967): 438–54.

———. *The Protestant Temperament: Patterns of Child-Rearing, Religious Experience, and the Self in Early America*. New York: Alfred A. Knopf, 1977.

———. "Youth, Maturity, and Religious Conversion: A Note on the Ages of Converts in Andover, Massachusetts, 1711–1749." *Essex Institute Historical Collections* 108 (1972): 119–34.

Grigg, Susan. "Women and Family Property: A Review of U.S. Inheritance Studies." *Historical Methods* 22 (1989): 116–22.

Gross, Robert A. *The Minutemen and Their World*. New York: Hill & Wang, 1976.

Grubb, Farley. "Servant Auction Records and Immigration into the Delaware Valley, 1745–1831: The Proportion of Females among Immigrant Servants." *Proceedings of the American Philosophical Society* 133 (1989): 154–69.

Haber, Carole. *Beyond Sixty-Five: The Dilemma of Old Age in America's Past*. Cambridge and New York: Cambridge University Press, 1983.

Hall, Peter Dobkin. "Family Structure and Economic Organization: Massachusetts Merchants, 1700–1850." In *Family and Kin in Urban Communities, 1700–1930*, ed. Tamara K. Hareven, 38–61. New York: New Viewpoints, 1977.

Handler, Jerome S., and Robert S. Corruccini. "Weaning among West Indian Slaves: Historical and Bioanthropological Evidence from Barbados." *William and Mary Quarterly* 3d ser., 43 (1986): 111–17.

Hareven, Tamara K., and K. J. Adams, eds. *Aging and Life Course Transitions: An Interdisciplinary Perspective*. New York: Guilford Press, 1982.

Harris, P.M.G. "The Demographic Development of Colonial Philadelphia in Some Comparative Perspective." *Proceedings of the American Philosophical Society* 133 (1989): 262–304.

Hawes, Joseph M., and N. Ray Hiner, eds. *American Childhood: A Research Guide and Historical Handbook*. Westport, Conn.: Greenwood Press, 1985.

Hecht, Irene W. D. "The Virginia Muster of 1624/5 as a Source for Demographic History." *William and Mary Quarterly* 3d ser., 30 (1973): 65–92.

Henderson, Rodger C. "Demographic Patterns and Family Structure in Eighteenth-Century Lancaster County, Pennsylvania." *Pennsylvania Magazine of History and Biography* 114 (1990): 349–83.

———. "Matters of Life and Death: A Demographic Analysis of 18th-Century Lancaster Reformed Church Records." *Journal of the Lancaster County Historical Society* 91 (1987/88): 43–77.

Henretta, James A. "Families and Farms: *Mentalité* in Pre-Industrial America." *William and Mary Quarterly* 3d ser., 35 (1978): 3–32.

———. "The Morphology of New England Society in the Colonial Period." *Journal of Interdisciplinary History* 2 (1971): 379–98.

Higgs, Robert, and H. Louis Stettler III. "Colonial New England Demography: A Sampling Approach." *William and Mary Quarterly* 3d ser., 27 (1970): 282–94.

Hiner, N. Ray. "Adolescence in Eighteenth-Century America." *History of Childhood Quarterly* 3 (1975): 253–80.

———. "The Child in American Historiography: Accomplishments and Prospect." *Psychohistory Review* 7 (1978): 13–23.

———. "Cotton Mather and His Children: The Evolution of a Parent Educator, 1686–1728." In *Regulated Children/Liberated Children: Education in Psychohistorical Perspective*, ed. Finkelstein, 24–43. New York: Psychohistory Press, 1979.

———. "Cotton Mather and His Female Children: Notes on the Relationship Between Private Experience and Public Thought." *Journal of Psychohistory* 13 (1985): 33–49.

———. "The Cry of Sodom Enquired into: Educational Analysis in Seventeenth-Century New England." *History of Education Quarterly* 13 (1973): 3–22.

———. "Wars and Rumors of Wars: The Historiography of Colonial Education as a Case Study in Academic Imperialism." *Societas* 8 (1978): 89–114.

Hirsch, Alison Duncan. "The Thrall Divorce Case: A Family Crisis in Eighteenth-Century Connecticut." In *Women, Family, and Community in Colonial America: Two Perspectives*, ed. Speth and Hirsch, 43–75. New York: Haworth Press, 1983.

Hoffer, Peter C., and N.E.H. Hull. *Murdering Mothers: Infanticide in England and New England, 1558–1803*. New York: New York University Press, 1981.

Hoffman, Ronald, and Peter J. Albert, eds. *Women in the Age of the American Revolution*. Charlottesville: University Press of Virginia, 1989.

Homan, Walter Joseph. *Children & Quakerism: A Study of the Place of Children in the Theory and Practice of the Society of Friends, Commonly Called Quakers*. Berkeley, Calif.: Gillick Press, 1939. Reprint. New York: Arno Press, 1972.

Horn, James. "Adapting to a New World: A Comparative Study of Local Society in England and Maryland, 1650–1700." In *Colonial Chesapeake Society*, ed. Carr, Morgan, and Russo, 133–75. Chapel Hill: University of North Carolina Press, 1988.

———. "Servant Emigration to the Chesapeake in the Seventeenth Century." In *The Chesapeake in the Seventeenth Century: Essays on Anglo-American Society*, ed. Tate and Ammerman, 51–95. Chapel Hill: University of North Carolina Press, 1988.

Howard, George Elliott. *A History of Matrimonial Institutions Chiefly in England and the United States with an Introductory Analysis of the Literature and the Theories of Primitive Marriage and the Family*. 3 vols. Chicago: University of Chicago Press, 1904. Reprint. New York: Humanities Press, 1964.

Illick, Joseph E. "Child-Rearing in Seventeenth-Century England and America." In *The History of Childhood*, ed. Lloyd deMause, 303–50. New York: Psychohistory Press, 1974.

Innes, Stephen. *Labor in a New Land: Economy and Society in Seventeenth-Century Springfield*. Princeton, N.J.: Princeton University Press, 1983.

Isaac, Rhys. "Order and Growth, Authority and Meaning in Colonial New England." *American Historical Review* 76 (1971): 728–37.

Jedrey, Christopher M. *The World of John Cleaveland: Family and Community in Eighteenth-Century New England*. New York: W. W. Norton & Company, 1979.

Jensen, Joan M. *Loosening the Bonds: Mid-Atlantic Farm Women, 1750–1850*. New Haven, Conn.: Yale University Press, 1986.

Johnson, Paul E. "The Modernization of Mayo Greenleaf Patch: Land, Family, and Marginality in New England, 1766–1818." *New England Quarterly* 55 (1982): 488–516.

Kammen, Michael. "Changing Perceptions of the Life Cycle in American Thought and Culture." *Proceedings of the Massachusetts Historical Society* 91 (1979): 35–66.

Kantrow, Louise. "Life Expectancy of the Gentry in Eighteenth and Nineteenth-Century Philadelphia." *Proceedings of the American Philosophical Society* 133 (1989): 312–27.

Karlsen, Carol F. *The Devil in the Shape of a Woman: Witchcraft in Colonial New England*. New York: W. W. Norton & Company, 1987.

Kerber, Linda K. " 'History Can Do It No Justice': Women and the Reinterpretation of the American Revolution." In *Women in the Age of the American Revolution*, ed. Hoffman and Albert, 3–42. Charlottesville: University Press of Virginia, 1989.

———. *Women of the Republic: Intellect and Ideology in Revolutionary America*. Chapel Hill: University of North Carolina Press, 1980.

Kerber, Linda K., et al. "Beyond Roles, Beyond Spheres: Thinking about Gender in the Early Republic." *William and Mary Quarterly* 3d ser., 46 (1989): 565–85.

Kett, Joseph F. *Rites of Passage: Adolescence in America, 1790 to the Present*. New York: Basic Books, 1977.

Keyssar, Alexander. "Widowhood in Eighteenth-Century Massachusetts: A Problem in the History of the Family." *Perspectives in American History* 8 (1974): 83–119.

Kiefer, Monica. *American Children through Their Books, 1700–1835.* Philadelphia: University of Pennsylvania Press, 1948.

Kierner, Cynthia A. "Family Values, Family Business: Work and Kinship in Colonial New York." *Mid-America* 71 (1989): 55–64.

Kilbourne, Lawrence J. "The Fertility Transition in New England: The Case of Hampton, New Hampshire, 1655–1840." In *Generations and Change: Genealogical Perspectives in Social History,* ed. Taylor and Crandall, 203–14. Macon, Ga.: Mercer University Press, 1986.

Klein, Randolph Shipley. *Portrait of an Early American Family: The Shippens of Pennsylvania Across Five Generations.* Philadelphia: University of Pennsylvania Press, 1975.

Klepp, Susan E. "Demography in Early Philadelphia, 1690–1860." *Proceedings of the American Philosophical Society* 133 (1989): 85–111.

———. "Fragmented Knowledge: Questions in Regional Demographic History." *Proceedings of the American Philosophical Society* 133 (1989): 223–33.

Koehler, Lyle. *A Search for Power: The "Weaker Sex" in Seventeenth-Century New England.* Urbana: University of Illinois Press, 1980.

Lacey, Barbara E. "The World of Hannah Heaton: The Autobiography of an Eighteenth-Century Connecticut Farm Woman." *William and Mary Quarterly* 3d ser., 45 (1988): 280–304.

Land, Aubrey C., Lois Green Carr, and Edward C. Papenfuse, eds. *Law, Society, and Politics in Early Maryland: Proceedings of the First Conference on Maryland History, June 14–15, 1974.* Baltimore, Md.: Johns Hopkins University Press, 1977.

Landsman, Ned C. "Ethnicity and National Origin among British Settlers in the Philadelphia Region: Pennsylvania Immigration in the Wake of *Voyagers to the West.*" *Proceedings of the American Philosophical Society* 133 (1989): 170–74.

Lantz, Herman R., et al. "Pre-Industrial Patterns in the Colonial Family in America: A Content Analysis of Colonial Magazines." *American Sociological Review* 33 (1968): 413–26.

Laslett, Peter. *The World We Have Lost: England Before the Industrial Age.* New York: Charles Scribner's Sons, 1965.

Laslett, Peter, and Richard Wall, eds. *Household and Family in Past Time.* Cambridge: Cambridge University Press, 1972.

Leavitt, Judith Walzer. *Brought to Bed: Childbearing in America, 1750–1950.* New York: Oxford University Press, 1986.

———. " 'Science' Enters the Birthing Room: Obstetrics in America since the Eighteenth Century." *Journal of American History* 70 (1983): 281–304.

Lee, Joan Butenhoff. "Land and Labor: Parental Bequest Practices in Charles County, Maryland, 1732–1783." In *Colonial Chesapeake Society,* ed. Carr, Morgan, and Russo, 306–41. Chapel Hill: University of North Carolina Press, 1988.

Lemay, J. A. Leo, ed. *Robert Bolling Woos Anne Miller: Love and Courtship in Colonial Virginia, 1760.* Charlottesville: University Press of Virginia, 1990.

Lemon, James T. "Spatial Order: Households in Local Communities and Regions." In *Colonial British America: Essays in the New History of the Early Modern Era*, ed. Jack P. Greene and J. R. Pole, 86–122. Baltimore: Johns Hopkins University Press, 1984.

Levy, Barry. "The Birth of the 'Modern Family' in Early America: Quaker and Anglican Families in the Delaware Valley, Pennsylvania, 1681–1750." In *Friends and Neighbors: Group Life in America's First Plural Society*, ed. Michael Zuckerman, 26–64. Philadelphia, Pa.: Temple University Press, 1982.

———. "From 'Dark Corners' to American Domesticity: The British Social Context of the Welsh and Cheshire Quakers' Familial Revolution in Pennsylvania, 1657–1685." In *The World of William Penn*, ed. Richard S. Dunn and Mary Maples Dunn, 215–39. Philadelphia: University of Pennsylvania Press, 1986.

———. *Quakers and the American Family: British Settlement in the Delaware Valley.* New York: Oxford University Press, 1988.

———. " 'Tender Plants': Quaker Farmers and Children in the Delaware Valley, 1681–1735." *Journal of Family History* 3 (1978): 116–35.

Lewis, Jan. "Domestic Tranquillity and the Management of Emotions among the Gentry of Pre-Revolutionary Virginia." *William and Mary Quarterly* 3d ser., 39 (1982): 135–49.

———. *The Pursuit of Happiness: Family and Values in Jefferson's Virginia.* Cambridge: Cambridge University Press, 1983.

———. "The Republican Wife: Virtue and Seduction in the Early Republic." *William and Mary Quarterly* 3d ser., 44 (1987): 689–721.

Lewis, Jan, and Kenneth A. Lockridge. " 'Sally Has Been Sick': Pregnancy and Family Limitation among Virginia Gentry Women, 1780–1830." *Journal of Social History* 22 (1988): 5–19.

Lockridge, Kenneth A. *The Diary and Life of William Byrd II of Virginia, 1674–1744.* Chapel Hill: University of North Carolina Press, 1987.

———. *A New England Town: The First Hundred Years, Dedham, Massachusetts, 1636–1736.* New York: W. W. Norton & Company, 1970.

———. "The Population of Dedham, Massachusetts, 1636–1736." *Economic History Review* 2d ser., 19 (1966): 318–44.

Logue, Barbara J. "The Whaling Industry and Fertility Decline: Nantucket, Massachusetts, 1660–1850." *Social Science History* 7 (1983): 427–56.

Macfarlane, Alan. *The Family Life of Ralph Josselin, a Seventeenth-Century Clergyman: An Essay in Historical Anthropology.* Cambridge: Cambridge University Press, 1970.

Main, Gloria L. "Widows in Rural Massachusetts on the Eve of the Revolution." In *Women in the Age of the American Revolution*, ed. Hoffman and Albert, 67–90. Charlottesville: University Press of Virginia, 1989.

Marcy, Peter T. "Factors Affecting the Fecundity and Fertility of Historical Populations." *Journal of Family History* 6 (1981): 309–26.

Mason, Sally D. "Mama, Rachel, and Molly: Three Generations of Carroll Women." In *Women in the Age of the American Revolution*, ed. Hoffman and Albert, 244–89. Charlottesville: University of Virginia, 1989.

Masters, Ardyce. "Stumbling into the History of Childhood." *Journal of Psychohistory* 16 (1988): 173–75.

McCracken, Grant. "The Exchange of Children in Tudor England: An Anthropological Phenomenon in History Context." *Journal of Family History* 8 (1983): 303–13.

Mechling, Jay. "Advice to Historians on Advice to Mothers." *Journal of Social History* 9 (1975): 44–63.

Mellor, George R. "Emigration from the British Isles to the New World, 1765–1775." *History: The Journal of the Historical Association* 40 (1955): 68–83.

Menard, Russell R. "British Migration to the Chesapeake Colonies in the Seventeenth Century." In *Colonial Chesapeake Society*, ed. Carr, Morgan, and Russo, 99–132. Chapel Hill: University of North Carolina Press, 1988.

———. "From Servant to Freeholder: Status Mobility and Property Accumulation in Seventeenth-Century Maryland." *William and Mary Quarterly* 3d ser., 30 (1973): 37–64.

———. "The Growth of Population in the Chesapeake Colonies: A Comment." *Explorations in Economic History* 18 (1981): 399–410. Reply by Terry L. Anderson. "From the Parts to the Whole: Modeling Chesapeake Population": 411–14.

———. "Immigrants and Their Increase: The Process of Population Growth in Early Colonial Maryland." In *Law, Society, and Politics in Early Maryland: Proceedings of the First Conference on Maryland History, June 14–15, 1974*, ed. Land, Carr, and Papenfuse, 88–110. Baltimore, Md.: Johns Hopkins University Press, 1977.

———. "Was There a 'Middle Colonies Demographic Regime'?" *Proceedings of the American Philosophical Society* 133 (1989): 215–18.

Menken, Jane, James Trussell, and Susan Watkins. "The Nutrition Fertility Link: An Evaluation of the Evidence." *Journal of Interdisciplinary History* 11 (1981): 425–41.

Milden, James Wallace, comp. *The Family in Past Time: A Guide to the Literature.* New York: Garland Publishing, 1977.

Mintz, Steven, and Susan Kellogg. *Domestic Revolutions: A Social History of American Family Life.* New York: The Free Press, 1988.

Molen, Patricia A. "Population and Social Patterns in Barbados in the Early Eighteenth Century." *William and Mary Quarterly* 3d ser., 28 (1971): 287–300.

Moller, Herbert. "Sex Composition and Correlated Culture Patterns of Colonial America." *William and Mary Quarterly* 3d ser., 2 (1945): 113–53.

Moran, Gerald F. "Religious Renewal, Puritan Tribalism, and the Family in Seventeenth-Century Milford, Connecticut." *William and Mary Quarterly* 3d ser., 36 (1979): 236–54.

Moran, Gerald F., and Maris A. Vinovskis. "The Puritan Family and Religion: A Critical Reappraisal." *William and Mary Quarterly* 3d ser., 39 (1982): 29–63.

Morgan, Edmund S. *American Slavery, American Freedom: The Ordeal of Colonial Virginia.* New York: W. W. Norton & Company, 1975.

———. *The Puritan Family: Religion and Domestic Relations in Seventeenth-Century New England.* Revised edition. New York: Harper & Row, 1966.

———. "The Puritans and Sex." *New England Quarterly* 15 (1942): 591–607.

———. "The Puritan's Marriage with God." *South Atlantic Quarterly* 48 (1949): 107–12.

Murrin, John M. "Review Essay." *History and Theory* 11 (1972): 226–75.

Narrett, David E. "Men's Wills and Women's Property Rights in Colonial New York." In *Women in the Age of the American Revolution*, ed. Hoffman and Albert, 91–133. Charlottesville: University Press of Virginia, 1989.

Nooter, Eric, and Patricia U. Bonomi, eds. *Colonial Dutch Studies: An Interdisciplinary Approach*. New York: New York University Press, 1988.

Norton, Mary Beth. "The Evolution of White Women's Experience in Early America." *American Historical Review* 89 (1984): 593–619.

———. "Gender and Defamation in Seventeenth-Century Maryland." *William and Mary Quarterly* 3d ser., 44 (1987): 3–39.

———. *Liberty's Daughters: The Revolutionary Experience of American Women, 1750–1800*. Boston: Little, Brown and Company, 1980.

———. "Reflections on Women in the Age of the American Revolution." In *Women in the Age of the American Revolution*, ed. Hoffman and Albert, 479–93. Charlottesville: University Press of Virginia, 1989.

Norton, Susan L. "Marital Migration in Essex County, Massachusetts, in the Colonial and Early Federal Periods." *Journal of Marriage and the Family* 35 (1973): 406–18.

———. "Population Growth in Colonial America: A Study of Ipswich, Massachusetts." *Population Studies* 25 (1971): 406–18.

O'Keefe, Doris. "Marriage and Migration in New England: A Study in Historical Population Geography." Department of Geography, Syracuse University, *Discussion Papers Series*, no. 16, June 1976.

O'Malley, Patricia Trainor. " 'Belovid Wife' and 'Inveigled Affections': Marriage Patterns in Early Rowley, Massachusetts." In *Generations and Change: Genealogical Perspectives in Social History*, ed. Taylor and Crandall, 181–201. Macon, Ga.: Mercer University Press, 1986.

Osterud, Nancy, and John Fulton. "Family Limitation and Age at Marriage: Fertility Decline in Sturbridge, Massachusetts, 1730–1850." *Population Studies* 30 (1976): 481–94.

Phillips, Roderick. *Putting Asunder: A History of Divorce in Western Society*. New York: Cambridge University Press, 1988.

Potter, J. "The Growth of Population in America, 1700–1860." In *Population in History: Essays in Historical Demography*, ed. D. V. Glass and D. E. C. Eversley, 631–88. Chicago: Aldine Publishing Company, 1965.

Potter, Jim. "Demographic Development and Family Structure." In *Colonial British America: Essays in the New History of the Early Modern Era*, ed. Jack P. Greene and J. R. Pole, 123–56. Baltimore, Md.: Johns Hopkins University Press, 1984.

Powell, Chilton L. "Marriage in Early New England." *New England Quarterly* 1 (1928): 323–34.

Quinn, David B. "Why They Came." In *Early Maryland in a Wider World*, ed. Quinn, 119–48. Detroit, Mich.: Wayne State University Press, 1982.

Rogers, Kim Lacy. "Relicts of the New World: Conditions of Widowhood in Seventeenth-Century New England." In *Women's Being, Women's Place: Female Identity and Vocation in American History*, ed. Mary Kelley, 26–52. Boston: G. K. Hall & Co., 1979.

Rothman, Ellen K. *Hands and Hearts: A History of Courtship in America*. New York:

Basic Books, 1984.

―――. "Sex and Self-Control: Middle-Class Courtship in America, 1770–1870." *Journal of Social History* 15 (1982): 409–25.

Rutman, Darrett B. "People in Process: The New Hampshire Towns of the Eighteenth Century." In *Family and Kin in Urban Communities, 1700–1930.* ed. Tamara K. Hareven, 16–37. New York: New Viewpoints, 1977.

Rutman, Darrett B., and Anita H. Rutman. "Child-Naming Patterns." *A Place in Time: Explicatus*, 83–106. New York: W. W. Norton & Company, 1984. Reprint (in part). " 'In Nomine Avi': Child-Naming Patterns in a Chesapeake County, 1650–1750." In *Generations and Change: Genealogical Perspectives in Social History*, ed. Taylor and Crandall, 243–65.

―――. " 'Now-Wives and Sons-in-Law': Parental Death in a Seventeenth-Century Virginia County." In *Chesapeake in the Seventeenth Century: Essays on Anglo-American Society*, ed. Tate and Ammerman, 153–82. Chapel Hill: University of North Carolina Press, 1979.

―――. "Of Agues and Fevers: Malaria in the Early Chesapeake." *William and Mary Quarterly* 3d ser., 33 (1976): 31–60.

―――. *A Place in Time: Middlesex County, Virginia, 1650–1750.* New York: W. W. Norton & Company, 1984.

Rutman, Darrett B., Charles Wetherell, and Anita H. Rutman. "Rhythms of Life: Black and White Seasonality in the Early Chesapeake." *Journal of Interdisciplinary History* 11 (1980): 29–53.

Ryerson, Alice Judson. "Medical Advice on Child Rearing, 1550–1900." *Harvard Educational Review* 31 (1961): 302–23.

Salerno, Anthony. "The Social Background of Seventeenth-Century Emigration to America." *Journal of British Studies* 19 (1979): 31–52.

Salmon, Marylynn. "Republican Sentiment, Economic Change, and the Property Rights of Women in American Law." In *Women in the Age of the American Revolution*, ed. Hoffman and Albert, 447–75. Charlottesville: University Press of Virginia, 1989.

Saveth, Edward N. "The Problem of American Family History." *American Quarterly* 21 (1969): 311–29.

Schlesinger, Elizabeth Bancroft. "Cotton Mather and His Children." *William and Mary Quarterly* 3d ser., 10 (1953): 181–89.

Schnucker, R. V. "The English Puritans and Pregnancy, Delivery and Breast Feeding." *History of Childhood Quarterly* 1 (1974): 637–58.

Scholten, Catherine M. *Childbearing in American Society, 1650–1850.* New York: New York University Press, 1985.

―――. " 'On the Importance of the Obstetrik Art': Changing Customs of Childbirth in America, 1760 to 1825." *William and Mary Quarterly* 3d ser., 34 (1977): 426–45.

Schulz, Constance B. "Children and Childhood in the Eighteenth Century." In *American Childhood: A Research Guide and Historical Handbook*, ed. Hawes and Hiner, 57–109. Westport, Conn.: Greenwood Press, 1985.

Scott, Donald M., and Bernard Wishy, eds. *America's Families: A Documentary History.* New York: Harper and Row, 1982.

Selig, Robert A. "Emigration, Fraud, Humanitarianism, and the Founding of Londonderry, South Carolina, 1763–1765." *Eighteenth-Century Studies* 23

(1989): 1–23.

Seward, Rudy Ray. *The American Family: A Demographic History.* Beverly Hills, Calif.: Sage Publications, 1978.

———. "The Colonial Family in America: Toward a Socio-Historical Restoration of Its Structure." *Journal of Marriage and the Family* 35 (1973): 58–70.

Shammas, Carole. "The Domestic Environment in Early Modern England and America." *Journal of Social History* 14 (1980): 3–24.

———. "Early American Women and Control over Capital." In *Women in the Age of the American Revolution*, ed Hoffman and Albert, 134–54. Charlottesville: University Press of Virginia, 1989.

Shammas, Carole, Marylynn Salmon, and Michael Dahlin. *Inheritance in America: From Colonial Times to the Present.* New Brunswick, N.J.: Rutgers University Press, 1987.

Shumsky, Neil Larry. "Parents, Children, and the Selection of Mates in Colonial Virginia." *Eighteenth-Century Life* 2 (1976): 83–88.

Simler, Lucy, and Paul G. E. Clemens. "The 'Best Poor Man's Country' in 1783: The Population Structure of Rural Society in Late-Eighteenth-Century Southeastern Pennsylvania." *Proceedings of the American Philosophical Society* 133 (1989): 234–61.

Slater, Peter Gregg. *Children in the New England Mind: In Death and in Life.* Hamden, Conn.: Archon Books, 1977.

———. " 'From the *Cradle* to the *Coffin*': Parental Bereavement and the Shadow of Infant Damnation in Puritan Society." *Psychohistory Review* 6 (1977–78): 4–24.

Smith, Billy G. "The Family Lives of Laboring Philadelphians during the Late Eighteenth Century." *Proceedings of the American Philosophical Society* 133 (1989): 328–32.

Smith, Daniel Blake. "Autonomy and Affection: Parents and Children in Eighteenth-Century Chesapeake Families." *Psychohistory Review* 6 (1977–78): 32–51.

———. *Inside the Great House: Planter Family Life in Eighteenth-Century Chesapeake Society.* Ithaca, N.Y.: Cornell University Press, 1980.

———. "Mortality and Family in the Colonial Chesapeake." *Journal of Interdisciplinary History* 8 (1978): 403–27.

———. "The Study of the Family in Early America: Trends, Problems, and Prospects." *William and Mary Quarterly* 3d ser., 39 (1982): 3–28.

Smith, Daniel Scott. " 'All in Some Degree Related to Each Other': A Demographic and Comparative Resolution of the Anomaly of New England Kinship." *American Historical Review* 94 (1989): 44–49.

———. "Child-Naming Practices, Kinship Ties, and Change in Family Attitudes in Hingham, Massachusetts, 1641 to 1880." *Journal of Social History* 18 (1985): 541–66.

———. "The Demographic History of Colonial New England." *Journal of Economic History* 32 (1972): 165–83.

———. "The Estimates of Early American Historical Demographers: Two Steps Forward, One Step Backward, What Steps in the Future?" *Historical Methods* 12 (1979): 24–38.

———. "Inheritance and the Social History of Early American Women." In

Women in the Age of the American Revolution, ed. Hoffman and Albert, 45–66. Charlottesville: University Press of Virginia, 1989.

———. "Old Age and the 'Great Transformation': A New England Case Study." In *Aging and the Elderly: Humanistic Perspectives in Gerontology*, ed. Stuart F. Spicker, Kathleen M. Woodward, and David D. Van Tassel, 285–302. Atlantic Highlands, N.J.: Humanities Press, 1978.

———. "Parental Power and Marriage Patterns: An Analysis of Historical Trends in Hingham, Massachusetts." *Journal of Marriage and the Family* 35 (1973): 419–28.

———. "A Perspective on Demographic Methods and Effects in Social History." *William and Mary Quarterly* 3d ser., 39 (1982): 442–68.

Smith, Daniel Scott, and Michael S. Hindus. "Premarital Pregnancy in America, 1640–1971: An Overview and Interpretation." *Journal of Interdisciplinary History* 5 (1975): 537–70.

Somerville, James K. "Family Demography and the Published Records: An Analysis of the Vital Statistics of Salem, Massachusetts." *Essex Institute Historical Collections* 106 (1970): 243–51.

Sommerville, C. John. "English Puritans and Children: A Social-Cultural Explanation." *Journal of Psychohistory* 6 (1978): 113–37.

Souden, David. " 'Rogues, Whores and Vagabonds': Indentured Servant Emigrants to North America, and the Case of Mid-Seventeenth-Century Bristol." *Social History* 3 (1978): 23–41.

Speth, Linda E. "More Than Her 'Thirds': Wives and Widows in Colonial Virginia." In *Women, Family, and Community in Colonial America: Two Perspectives*, ed. Speth and Hirsch, 5–41. New York: Haworth Press, 1983.

Speth, Linda E., and Alison Duncan Hirsch, eds. *Women, Family, and Community in Colonial America: Two Perspectives*. New York: Haworth Press, 1983.

Stannard, David E. "Death and the Puritan Child." *American Quarterly* 26 (1974): 456–76.

———. *The Puritan Way of Death: A Study in Religion, Culture, and Social Change*. New York: Oxford University Press, 1977.

Starkey, Marion L. *The Devil in Massachusetts: A Modern Enquiry into the Salem Witch Trials*. New York: Alfred A. Knopf, 1949.

———. "The Easiest Room in Hell." *Essex Institute Historical Collections* 92 (1956): 33–42.

Steffen, Charles G. "The Sewall Children in Colonial New England." *New England Historical and Genealogical Register* 131 (1977): 163–72.

Stettler, H. Louis, III. "The New England Throat Distemper and Family Size." In *Empirical Studies in Health Economics: Proceedings of the Second Conference on the Economics of Health*, ed. Herbert E. Klarman, 17–27. Baltimore: Johns Hopkins University Press, 1970.

Stone, Lawrence. *The Family, Sex and Marriage in England, 1500–1800*. New York: Harper and Row, 1977.

Sutton, John R. *Stubborn Children: Controlling Delinquency in the United States, 1640–1981*. Berkeley: University of California Press, 1989.

———. "Stubborn Children: Law and the Socialization of Deviance in the Puritan Colonies." *Family Law Quarterly* 15 (1981): 31–64.

Tate, Thad W., and David L. Ammerman, eds. *The Chesapeake in the Seventeenth*

Century: Essays on Anglo-American Society. Chapel Hill: University of North Carolina Press, 1979.

Taylor, Karen. "Disciplining the History of Childhood." *Journal of Psychohistory* 16 (1988): 189–90.

Taylor, Robert M., Jr., and Ralph J. Crandall, eds. *Generations and Change: Genealogical Perspectives in Social History.* Macon, Ga.: Mercer University Press, 1986.

Temkin-Greener, H., and A. C. Swedlund. "Fertility Transition in the Connecticut Valley: 1740–1850." *Population Studies* 32 (1978): 27–41.

Thompson, R. "Seventeenth-Century English and Colonial Sex Ratios: A Postscript." *Population Studies* 28 (1974): 153–65.

Thompson, Roger. "Adolescent Culture in Colonial Massachusetts." *Journal of Family History* 9 (1984): 127–44.

———. "Attitudes towards Homosexuality in the Seventeenth-Century New England Colonies." *Journal of American Studies* 23 (1989): 27–40.

———. "Popular Attitudes towards Children in Middlesex County, Massachusetts, 1649–1699." *Journal of Psychohistory* 13 (1985): 145–58.

———. *Sex in Middlesex: Popular Mores in a Massachusetts County, 1649–1699.* Amherst: University of Massachusetts Press, 1986.

Thompson, Thomas C. "The Life Course and Labor of a Colonial Farmer." *Historical New Hampshire* 40 (1985): 135–55.

Tracy, Patricia J. "Re-Considering Migration within Colonial New England." *Journal of Social History* 23 (1989): 93–113.

Treckel, Paula A. "Breastfeeding and Maternal Sexuality in Colonial America." *Journal of Interdisciplinary History* 20 (1989): 25–51.

Ulrich, Laurel Thatcher. " 'Daughters of Liberty': Religious Women in Revolutionary New England." In *Women in the Age of the American Revolution*, ed. Hoffman and Albert, 211–43. Charlottesville: University Press of Virginia, 1989.

———. *Good Wives: Image and Reality in the Lives of Women in Northern New England, 1650–1750.* New York: Alfred A. Knopf, 1982.

———. "Housewife and Gadder: Themes of Self-sufficiency and Community in Eighteenth-Century New England." In *"To Toil the Livelong Day": America's Women at Work, 1780–1980*, ed. Carol Groneman and Mary Beth Norton, 21–34. Ithaca, N.Y.: Cornell University Press, 1987.

———. "Martha Ballard and Her Girls: Women's Work in Eighteenth-Century Maine." In *Work and Labor in Early America*, ed. Stephen Innes, 70–105. Chapel Hill: University of North Carolina Press, 1988.

———. "Martha Moore Ballard and the Medical Challenge to Midwifery." In *Maine in the Early Republic: From Revolution to Statehood*, ed. Charles E. Clark, et al., 165–83. Hanover, N.H.: University Press of New England, 1988.

———. *A Midwife's Tale: The Life of Martha Ballard, Based on Her Diary, 1785–1812.* New York: Alfred A. Knopf, 1990.

Ulrich, Laurel Thatcher, and Lois K. Stabler. " 'Girling of It' in Eighteenth-Century New Hampshire." In *Families and Children*, ed. Peter Benes, 24–36. The Dublin Seminar for New England Folklife, Annual Proceedings, 1985. Boston: Boston University Scholarly Publications, 1987.

Verduin, Kathleen. " 'Our Cursed Natures': Sexuality and the Puritan Con-
    science." *New England Quarterly* 56 (1983): 220–37.
Vinovskis, Maris A. "Angels' Heads and Weeping Willows: Death in Early Amer-
    ica." *Proceedings of the American Antiquarian Society* 86 (1976): 273–302.
———. *Fertility in Massachusetts from the Revolution to the Civil War.* New York:
    Academic Press, 1981.
Waciega, Lisa Wilson. "A 'Man of Business': The Widow of Means in South-
    eastern Pennsylvania." *William and Mary Quarterly* 3d ser., 44 (1987): 40–
    64.
Wagner, Peter. "A Note on Puritans and Children in Early Colonial New En-
    gland." *Amerikastudien* 25 (1980): 47–62.
Walsh, Lorena S. "The Historian as Census Taker: Individual Reconstitution
    and the Reconstruction of Censuses for a Colonial Chesapeake County."
    William and Mary Quarterly 3d ser., 38 (1981): 242–60.
———. "Staying Put or Getting Out: Findings for Charles County, Maryland,
    1650–1720." *William and Mary Quarterly* 3d ser., 44 (1987): 89–103.
———. " 'Till Death Us Do Part': Marriage and Family in Seventeenth-Century
    Maryland." In *The Chesapeake in the Seventeenth Century: Essays on Anglo-
    American Society*, ed. Tate and Ammerman, 126–52. Chapel Hill: Univer-
    sity of North Carolina Press, 1979.
Walsh, Lorena S., and Russell R. Menard. "Death in the Chesapeake: Two Life
    Tables for Men in Early Colonial Maryland." *Maryland Historical Magazine*
    69 (1974): 211–27.
Walzer, John F. "A Period of Ambivalence: Eighteenth-Century American Child-
    hood." In *The History of Childhood*, ed. Lloyd deMause, 351–82. New York:
    Psychohistory Press, 1974.
Waters, John J. "Family, Inheritance, and Migration in Colonial New England:
    The Evidence from Guilford, Connecticut." *William and Mary Quarterly*
    3d ser., 39 (1982): 64–86.
———. "Naming and Kinship in New England: Guilford Patterns and Usage,
    1693–1759." *New England Historical and Genealogical Register* 138 (1984):
    161–81.
———. "Patrimony, Succession, and Social Stability: Guilford, Connecticut, in
    the Eighteenth Century." *Perspectives in American History* 10 (1976): 129–
    60.
———. "The Traditional World of the New England Peasants: A View from
    Seventeenth-Century Barnstable." *New England Historical and Genealogical
    Register* 130 (1976): 3–21.
Watson, Alan D. "Household Size and Composition in Pre-Revolutionary North
    Carolina." *Mississippi Quarterly* 31 (1978): 551–69.
Watters, David H. " 'I Spake as a Child': Authority, Metaphor and *The New
    England Primer*." *Early American Literature* 20 (1985/86): 193–213.
Weisberg, D. Kelly. " 'Under Greet Temptations Heer': Women and Divorce in
    Puritan Massachusetts." *Feminist Studies* 2 (1975): 183–94.
Wells, Robert V. "The Demography of a Region: Historical Reality or Historian's
    Creation." *Proceedings of the American Philosophical Society* 133 (1989): 219–
    22.
———. "Family History and Demographic Transition." *Journal of Social History*

9 (1975): 1–19.

———. "Family Size and Fertility Control in Eighteenth-Century America: A Study of Quaker Families." *Population Studies* 25 (1971): 73–82.

———. "Marriage Seasonals in Early America: Comparisons and Comments." *Journal of Interdisciplinary History* 18 (1987): 299–307.

———. "Population and the American Revolution." In *The American Revolution: Changing Perspectives*, ed. William M. Fowler, Jr., and Wallace Cole, 107–22. Boston: Northeastern University Press, 1979.

———. *The Population of the British Colonies in America before 1776: A Survey of Census Data*. Princeton, N.J.: Princeton University Press, 1975.

———. "Quaker Marriage Patterns in a Colonial Perspective." *William and Mary Quarterly* 3d ser., 29 (1972): 415–42.

———. *Revolutions in Americans' Lives: A Demographic Perspective on the History of Americans, Their Families, and Their Society*. Westport, Conn.: Greenwood Press, 1982.

Wertz, Richard W., and Dorothy C. Wertz. *Lying-In: A History of Childbirth in America*. New York: The Free Press, 1977.

Whitney, Herbert A. "Estimating Precensus Populations: A Method Suggested and Applied to the Towns of Rhode Island and Plymouth Colonies in 1689." *Annals of the Association of American Geographers* 55 (1965): 179–89.

Withey, Lynne E. "Household Structure in Urban and Rural Areas: The Case of Rhode Island, 1774–1800." *Journal of Family History* 3 (1978): 37–50.

Wokeck, Marianne S. "German and Irish Immigration to Colonial Philadelphia." *Proceedings of the American Philosophical Society* 133 (1989): 128–43.

Wolf, Stephanie Grauman. *Urban Village: Population, Community, and Family Structure in Germantown, Pennsylvania, 1683–1800*. Princeton, N.J.: Princeton University Press, 1977.

Zuckerman, Michael. "William Byrd's Family." *Perspectives in American History* 12 (1979): 255–311.

4

The New Model Middle-Class Family (1815–1930)

Marilyn Dell Brady

During the first third of the nineteenth century, middle-class American families developed a new model, one that drew on colonial ideas about proper family life but that adapted them to meet a new set of needs. This model featured strongly differentiated gender roles, a vision of domestic security and harmony, and an emphasis on childrearing. Many Americans soon came to view its dictates as traditional, or even as biologically and theologically ordained. In reality, however, the model contained basic contradictions, and it was not universally or uniformly practiced even among those most committed to it. By the early twentieth century, conflicts had intensified within families, and debates about families had entered the public political arena. Newer models were proposed by the children of the middle class and a new generation of experts. These conflicts and contradictions in the model family of the nineteenth and early twentieth centuries continue to be critical, since the language and values we use when thinking about the family today are still shaped by its ideals.

Historians have amassed a large body of research relating to the models for middle-class American families that were popular in the nineteenth and early twentieth centuries. Significant gaps in the story still exist, however, and preliminary work has not always been confirmed by additional studies. Agreement about how the pieces fit together or the relative importance of various factors remains elusive. Value judgments from the twentieth century about proper roles for men and women have sometimes overshadowed analysis of nineteenth-century families, as historians have focused on different parts of the total picture rather than face the model's inherent contradictions. Although recent surveys of American families have centered on the nineteenth century, the task of synthesis remains hazardous and controversial.[1]

The extensive literature written for and about the antebellum middle-class family was an initial starting place for historians.[2] However, despite careful and meticulous research into the prescriptive writings, the usefulness of such sources has been questioned by scholars like Carl Degler, who pointed out that what "is" often differs significantly from what "ought to be."[3] Urging historians to move beyond the advice literature, Jay Mechling and Nancy Cott have recommended focusing on its authors and the social needs that their writing addressed.[4] Other scholars, aware of the complexity of family issues, are exploring relationships between rhetoric and lived experience. For example, Carroll Smith-Rosenberg, Joan Scott, John D'Emilio and Estelle Freedman, and others are using concepts from symbolic anthropology and literary theory to help interpret nineteenth-century family-related topics. Their approach places language about gender and sexuality in the context of power struggles between social and economic groups and between family members. Instead of assuming that the home was as private and isolated as advocates of the antebellum middle-class family model proclaimed, these historians are investigating the relationships between the allegedly separate spheres of work and home. Rejecting the assumption that values were internally consistent, they are examining tensions embedded within various ideals. Language and lived experience are seen as different, but overlapping realities. Their approach raises important issues in family history as well as for the historical enterprise as a whole.[5]

This chapter will follow the lead of scholars seeking to reconceptualize how we think about language, gender, and society in examining the models of the middle-class family popular in America between 1815 and 1930. The initial sections place the new family model in the social, economic, and political context of the antebellum America out of which it emerged and within which it was popular. Next, individuals who articulated the model family in the 1800s are discussed. The focus of the chapter then shifts to the relationships within the model family in the nineteenth century, as revealed in its definitions of gender roles, marriage, and childrearing. The last section examines, somewhat more briefly, the uses to which the model was put and the challenges that emerged in the late nineteenth and early twentieth centuries as middle-class American families became embroiled in the politics of resisting and promoting a variety of social changes. Regrettably, the entire chapter will focus primarily on the urbanizing areas of the Northeast, because that is where most of the research has been concentrated. The intent here is to draw together new research about the model middle-class American family during the period of its creation and subsequent development, not to offer a definitive new synthesis.

THE PRIVATE FAMILY AND THE PUBLIC WORLD

The family model articulated in the early 1800s sharply divided the public, treacherous world of business and politics from the private, safe world of women and children. Families were to create affectionate and harmonious homes, presided over by self-sacrificing wives and mothers, where children could be properly raised to become virtuous adults, and husbands could refresh themselves after regularly assaulting the vicious world outside. Most scholars agree, however, that the idea of a secure, privatized family was itself a product of the world in which the model emerged, not a practical alternative to it. The new model and the particular families who tried to live by its prescriptions were not isolated from the world but were rather in continual interaction with it. The need for a home to be a haven from the world was a response to frightening changes occurring in the heartless world where the model was being created.[6]

Massive economic changes seem to have had a role in the formation of the new family model in the United States. Although scholars still debate exactly what that role was and when it occurred, awareness of a relationship between family patterns and economic modes of production goes back to Marx and Engels, who argued that the bourgeois or middle-class family was a result of industrialization and marked a "decline" in the family. More conservative twentieth-century scholars, many of them structural-functionalists led by Talcott Parsons, have maintained that as societies "advanced" into industrialism, family roles became more specialized. They confidently claimed that problems created for individuals within the family were more than compensated for by overall social gains. Contemporary historians usually reject such total reliance on economic theory as a valid way to explain nineteenth-century family development and point out both gains and losses for families, but to varying degrees they continue to see economic development as a key element.

Recent scholarship relating U.S. antebellum economic conditions and family history has called into question the role of industrialization. New research makes clear that shifts toward a more private ideal of the family were well underway in the 1700s and widespread, at least in the urban Northeast, in the early 1800s. Since factories first emerged in America around 1800 and only became widespread at the time of the Civil War, industrialism is no longer assumed to have been the cause of changes in the middle-class family. In addition, as Jane Censer and others point out, white plantation families of the unindustrialized South shared some of the values that scholars have attributed to the impact of industrialization in the Northeast.[7]

Scholars who have linked the new family patterns to the rise of mercantile or commercial capitalism, rather than industrialism, have found a better chronological fit with the rise of the new model middle-class family. Before the end of the seventeenth century, commercial capitalism resulted in more and more people being pulled into a cash or market economy of both local and international proportions. Land was declining as a source of wealth in the Northeast, and cities were developing. Opportunities for inheritance and employment were affecting generational bonds. Some households were losing their economic productivity as the father, accompanied by apprentices and relatives who worked under him, pursued wealth outside of the family dwelling. Instead of a shared family economy based in the household and depending on mutual obligations to produce and share wealth, family members were increasingly earning wages as individuals outside of the household. Home and work were in reality becoming more geographically separate for middle-class family members.

Intensive research on limited geographic areas is also contributing to our understanding of factors obscured at the national level. Focusing on Oneida County, New York, between 1790 and 1865, Mary P. Ryan carefully delineated the chronology of events showing the interrelationships of family roles, family status, religion, and economic change. She claims that the middle-class families she studied found the new family model useful in retaining their middle-class status and passing it on to their children. According to Ryan, these families were active agents of change who were neither forced to accept the new model, nor were they docile followers of advice literature.[8]

Relying heavily on Ryan's findings, Stephanie Coontz has attempted her own ambitious and meticulous synthesis of American family history. Although the economy is central to her account, Coontz does not claim that economic changes simply and automatically created a new family model. Her narrative is useful in bringing together new findings, but the danger of generalizing from small, regional samples remains a problem for her and for other scholars.[9]

Economic factors also contributed to the class definitions that were integral to the new definition of the model family. Living by the dictates of the new model became a hallmark of middle-class status, the way in which a family announced to the world its privileged position. The ability of husbands to acquire and preserve wealth in the world outside the home was critical for insuring a family's middle-class status. The new emphasis on the mother as a consumer, evident in the advertisements and shopping advice in women's magazines, also linked the family to the emerging economy. If a family lost its wealth, as frequently happened in the nineteenth century, the family or the remaining women and children were likely to lose their middle-class family life-style. Responding to the rhetoric, some families actually did achieve a degree of seclusion, but they were able to do so because they possessed economic resources not available to other Americans. Those individuals who benefited most from the new model family often did so at a cost to others, a fact forgotten by many who praise the benefits of privatized families today. Wives and servants in middle-class households had to work hard to provide a safe haven for husbands and children. Despite attempts to enforce middle-class values on other groups within society, the model family was fundamentally a way of insuring the status of the middle class and the ability of children of middle-class homes to retain their social position. The model family was never meant to insure an egalitarian society.[10]

Changing ideas and images also contributed to the new family model. New political institutions, new systems of religious belief, greater possibility of failure, and increased geographic mobility of family members increased uncertainty in the daily lives of middle-class Americans. Deliberately seeking stability, they defined the home as secluded and protected, and gender roles as biologically fixed. Their new family model promised that security and emotional fulfillment, difficult to find in the larger society, were possible in private, familial relationships. Kirk Jeffrey has identified similarities between the middle-class families who attempted to follow the model and utopian communities in antebellum America, showing that both withdrew from the mainstream society, consciously structured their lives, and expected perfection from their efforts.[11] Carl Degler, Stephen Mintz, and Susan Kellogg follow the lead of Alexis de Tocqueville in claiming that the political mood of the new nation also created a "democratic family" bonded together by ties of voluntary affection rather than hierarchical authority. Their claims that such a change actually occurred has been challenged, however.[12]

Scholars agree that the political context of a new democracy did lead to the belief that the moral rearing of children was necessary for national survival. As Linda Kerber and Ruth Bloch have demonstrated, the definition of "republican" or "moral" mothers, who would insure that their sons would be the kind of voters needed to preserve the stability of the American nation, gave women a public role while confining them to the privacy of the domestic sphere. Thus the morality of private homes was linked to the success of the American nation, creating a peculiarly American version of middle-class families and a basis for later conflicts over women's public responsibilities.[13] By the end of the 1800s and into the early 1900s, the linkage of specific definitions of domestic virtue with American security also provided a rationale for governmental involvement in family morality.

Throughout the nineteenth century, government's role in the allegedly private world of the family was expanding as laws and judicial decisions gradually carved out a doctrine of individual rights for women and children based on the ideal of voluntary obedience and egalitarian decisions within families. In his careful study of the development of family relations law, Michael Grossberg has documented the steps of legal intervention. He discusses changes in laws regarding courtship, marriage restrictions, abortion, divorce, and custody, and he claims that the defense of the individual rights of children and women allowed male-run governments and male judges to move into the patriarchal role formerly played by individual husbands and fathers.[14] Focusing on the campaign for married women's property rights in the state of New York, Norma Basch has examined another way in which political decisions affected family issues. Basch describes the assumption of a woman's legal death or loss of identity in marriage and the ways men and women found to go around the law to protect their inheritance or other wealth. According to Basch, pressure on the state legislature to simplify property ownership by married women came both from economic groups in which husbands lacked the financial ability to set up separate estates for wives and from the slowly emerging women's rights movement, which used the idea of women's legal death to symbolize what they viewed as women's oppression in marriage.[15]

Changing ideas about religion were also significant in the creation of America's new model family. Because there were many different religious groups in the young nation, religious freedom and voluntary conversion became the norm. In religion, women were again entrusted with the protection of beliefs and moral behavior of family members in a time when more and more middle-class men were turning away from religion and its restraints. Nancy Cott, Mary Ryan, and others have documented the importance of women in the development of new attitudes about religion, class, and domesticity, as well as in the success of the revivals for which Charles Grandison Finney gained fame. Acting as wives and mothers, women linked religion, domesticity, and activity outside the home, and so found ways to be influential in the allegedly male sphere of politics. The sense that they were following God's will sometimes gave them the authority to move beyond the limits that husbands and society imposed on them.[16]

ARTICULATORS OF THE NEW FAMILY MODEL

The particular historical context of nineteenth-century America helped to structure the new model family, but middle-class family members also had a voice in articulating the new values, especially those who wrote about private families in the public media of print. As printing industrialized in the early 1800s, publishers quickly discovered that middle-class families, trying to adapt to the social changes surrounding them, were avid customers for domestic fiction and advice literature.[17]

The authors of the domestic fiction and advice literature popular in the nineteenth century shared middle-class, Protestant identities, which gave them consensus on many issues. Differences of gender, generation, and profession among the authors, however, contributed to disagreements in their messages as well as to recent historians' debates about nineteenth-century family attitudes. Research about female authors explore the motivation behind their writings, especially as it emerged out of the authors' family roles. Margaret Marsh has identified some ways in which men and women stressed different elements in advice on domestic, suburban life. Research on the male authors remains slight, however, generally focusing on their professional roles and seldom considering their family relationships.[18]

Prominent among those offering advice about family matters in the early 1800s were ministers, who had published sermons, obituaries that emphasized proper family roles, and advice to colonial families. After 1800, these men gradually shifted their messages, recognizing mothers as the parent primarily responsible for children's upbringing and stressing the innocence rather than the depravity of children. With the emergence of medicine as a profession, physicians began replacing ministers as the voice of male authority; they wrote about the family and such related issues as childrearing, marriage, and sexuality. Their words often reflected their efforts to increase respect for their profession. But antebellum medical practitioners were a diverse group offering a wide variety of treatment and advice to middle-class readers. Those calling themselves "regular physicians" usually defended "heroic" measures, such as bleeding, while "irregular physicians" advocated procedures meant to help the body heal itself with proper eating, exercise, and clothing. Rather than the dependence on authority stressed by regular physicians, the reformers advocated healthy living within the family. They also tended to be more open about the human body and sexuality. A few women were among the irregular physicians advocating health reform.[19]

Some radicals went even further, withdrawing from the mainstream and challenging whether the middle-class family model was, or should be, the basis of American life and society. According to John Spurlock, some middle-class Americans espoused "free love" as the way in which to create the loving devotion demanded by the model family. In addition, groups such as the Oneida Community, the Shakers, and the Mormons all proposed family models and practices radically different from those advocated and practiced by most Americans. Even the most extreme of these, however, sought to restructure rather than destroy the family and continued to see familylike institutions as an essential part of a good society. Their innovative ideas about sexuality and family structure did little to redefine the gender roles typical of antebellum America.[20]

As home and family became synonymous after 1830, architects also joined the ranks of authors addressing domestic issues. Clifford Clark has researched the ways in which a single family dwelling became one of the hallmarks of middle-class status and morality. As the new ideology spread, middle-class families chose to follow the dictates of Andrew Jackson Downing and other designers who urged them to create homes that literally were to insure the virtue of family members. Suburban homes were to provide seclusion from the distractions of the city. Gothic decorations on homes were said to inspire piety. Public and private areas within houses were carefully separated, and the areas where servants worked were isolated from family areas. Additional bedrooms provided privacy for family members. Yards, gardens, and orchards contributed to the home's idyllic settings. Perhaps architects, like physicians, sought to gain prestige in an emerging profession by addressing domestic concerns.[21]

In addition to these predominantly male groups of authors, nineteenth-century publishers found it profitable to hire women to write stories and articles considered suitable for their growing audiences of women and children. Writing became one of the more lucrative ways for a middle-class woman without income from a male breadwinner to support herself and her children. Women often explicitly expressed their need to earn money for their family as the reason, or perhaps the rationale, for assuming a role as public as that of author.

As allegedly morally superior beings, female authors helped to legitimize fiction as respectable reading matter for women and children. Much of their writing had a heavily didactic tone. Antebellum children's literature, in particular, was meant to be more uplifting than entertaining. Women's contributions to magazines helped establish their popularity in antebellum America. The theme of suffering as "women's lot" ran through women's poetry, essays, and fiction, but female authors seldom explicitly supported political or public rights for women. Instead, they glorified women's place within the home and urged women to use their moral power within the domestic sphere to the utmost.[22]

Recent interest in women's literature has resulted in serious attention being given to the words and lives of nineteenth-century women authors. As early as 1956, Helen Papashvilly noted the thinly veiled anger at men present in much of women's fiction. She observed that men were consistently depicted as wicked, evil, or weak and were usually killed off at the end of the story. Ann Douglas Wood has also noted the female authors' need to write for self-definition and sanity. Nina Baym has identified nineteenth-century women's fiction as an important genre characterized by strong and capable women and their bonds to each other.[23] Other scholars have looked at ways the "cult of domesticity" that nineteenth-century women wrote about related to their opportunities and limitations. Mary Kelley has examined the complexities within the lives and writings of the women she calls "literary domestics" and revealed difficulties they had bridging the contradictions between their roles as public authors and as private women.[24] Kathryn Sklar's biography of Catherine Beecher, which appeared in 1973, helped to define domesticity as a useful concept for scholars examining women's roles in the nineteenth century. Sklar shows how Beecher's family experiences shaped her definition of female domesticity as a means of achieving "womanly" power within the home rather than through seeking public political rights. Explicitly rejecting the emerging women's rights movement, Beecher stressed women's moral superiority as the key to better families and a better nation. Beecher herself, however, remained single; she lectured and taught extensively, and worked to organize schools that would allow other women to remain single and autonomous as teachers. In her depiction of Beecher, her family, and her society, Sklar identified many of the basic problems facing both women in antebellum America and historians of the nineteenth-century family.[25]

Louisa May Alcott has also received attention from scholars interested in how her life and her writing both reflected and shaped nineteenth-century domesticity. Alcott's autonomy rested on her singleness and her ability to support herself and other family members as a writer, possibilities not available to most middle-class women. Both her life and writings exemplify ways a woman could achieve a substantial degree of the power and autonomy that the model family denied her, while retaining allegiance to the values it prescribed. Alcott's popular fiction for children helped sustain the image of the family as a woman-dominated haven well into the twentieth century.[26]

Information about these women authors makes clear that they all sincerely believed in what they were doing and writing, and that they were not deliberately hypocritical or acting in bad faith. Although modern historians are often troubled by their choices and by the contradictions that seem implicit in their writing and their lives, the women themselves believed that the ideology of the model family reconciled those contradictions. In addition, scholarship on these female authors establishes that the family model to which their writing contributed was not one imposed on women by the oppressive restrictions of powerful men. Rather, women authors were active participants in the creation of the new model, shaping it, to some degree, out of their personal experiences and frustrations.

Although nineteenth-century domestic fiction should not be simplistically taken as evidence of women's actual experiences, scholars have found overlap between it and the lives of its female readers. The popularity of female authors indicates that written texts related to the experiences and needs of many women readers. Mary Ryan suggests that the writings about motherhood as a "cult" or "litany" helped women give meaning to what was required of them.[27] Nancy Theriot hypothesizes that what women read and what they actually experienced formed a dialectic, each adapting to and influencing the other.[28] Such theories offer innovative ways of conceptualizing relationships between published documents and private lives and suggest that domestic fiction could have been meaningful for individual women seeking to make sense out of their own experiences, even when their experiences differed from the ones described in the literature.

SEPARATE SPHERES AND GENDERS

The new model family that middle-class Americans espoused in the nineteenth century emphasized a sharp delineation of differences, especially in the mutually exclusive gender roles required of men and women and the mutually exclusive spheres of world and home within which they were expected to operate. Despite claims that these separations were natural and inevitable, the vision of the new model family instructed men and women to bridge the gulfs between their worlds with intimacy and romantic love within marriage. By the end of the nineteenth century, as middle-class women were moving into the allegedly male world of economics and politics, definitions of gender and the call for companionship within marriage intensified, creating conflicting demands for both women and men.

Initially, historians who focused on the ideology of separate spheres argued over whether women gained or lost with the creation of a domestic sphere. Recently, Linda Kerber and others have questioned the validity of the concept of separate spheres. Carroll Smith-Rosenberg has pushed for a complex understanding of nineteenth-century language that recognizes why the concept of spheres was useful and why the concept was popular for so long despite its failure to portray the lived reality of people's lives. Focusing on the nineteenth century's language of genders and spheres has allowed scholars to reconceptualize the relationship of public and private life and to move beyond topics traditionally defined as family history to call for a radical rethinking of how all historians approach the past.[29]

Nineteenth-century writers gave clear definitions of gender roles and separate spheres in both their published and personal writings. Because of the interest of women's historians in this topic, we know much more about the century's expectations for middle-class women than for men. In her classic article "The Cult of True Womanhood," Barbara Welter identified "piety, purity, submissiveness, and domesticity" as the qualities that a middle-class Victorian woman was expected to possess.[30] Moving beyond Welter's formulation, historians have suggested other characteristics demanded of "true women" and how these concepts could legitimate women's power. Nancy Cott argues that many women were not victimized by the denial of their sexual needs, but that they used the concept of "passionlessness" to protect themselves from unwanted pregnancy and to claim their own moral superiority.[31] Frances Cogan maintains that the alternative image of "real womanhood" encouraged women to be strong and self-reliant, not dependent.[32] Nancy Theriot claims that because a woman's fulfillment was to come from her sacrifices for her family, not from individualistic gains for herself, a woman's needs could not be seen to be in conflict with those of other family members. Only by service within her family could a woman achieve fulfillment and happiness. The fact that such definitions of womanhood did not allow for female autonomy raises important questions about the dynamics of nineteenth-century households. If a woman could gain power only by denying her own sexuality and by explicit self-sacrifice, did she really have the significant power over other family members that some historians credit her with having?[33]

Middle-class American men also had problems living up to the roles defined for them in the new model family. According to the ideology, men had those qualities that women did not. Home and family were women's domain, where "womanly qualities" supposedly reigned, but men had to be able to function in both the family and in the public sphere. Undomestic qualities like aggressiveness, anger, and violence were considered valuable and even necessary in order to assure financial support and protection for a family, but they were not acceptable behavior within the family itself. Men were expected to make the transition from the wickedness of the world outside to harmonious family circles, taking care not to contaminate women and children with emotions and behavior that would threaten domestic purity and peace.[34]

Sexuality was another area where men were faced with contradictions. While true women were defined as sexually pure and perhaps lacking sexual responses, men were said to be naturally lustful beings in need of sexual release. Advice manuals and mothers cautioned men against giving in to the evils of sexuality and encouraged them to show sexual restraint within marriage as well as abstinence outside of it. Some authors relied on the concept of the body as a fixed energy system and urged men to limit the waste of sperm in order to have full power to engage in the competitive economy. According to the ideal, men's alternatives were either to control their "natural" sexuality or to hurt their wives. Neither alternative offered much inducement for sexual closeness between husband and wife.[35]

Throughout the nineteenth century, husbands and fathers theoretically retained authority over submissive wives and children, but their leadership role was probably dwindling. As Steven Mintz and Bertram Wyatt-Brown have indicated, in some families the father did retain powerful control, but many men's extensive absence from the household interfered with such a role.[36] Obedience to the male head of household was consistently considered crucial, but women and children were supposed to give it voluntarily and cheerfully. The idea that they were moral individuals with their own rights had the potential for undermining this "unquestioned" power of the husband and father.

In his provocative study of nineteenth-century masculinity, David Pugh suggests other psychological dilemmas facing men and the impact of these dilemmas on women in nineteenth-century America. According to Pugh, after the Revolution had destroyed the authoritarian father figure of the British king, men projected moral authority onto women, whom they came to hate and fear. American men responded by seeking to prove their true manhood outside of the home by conquering the frontier or the world of business. Men, in life and in fiction, rebelled against their own image of women by periodically escaping from women and from family responsibility. According to Pugh, such a psychological scenario increased the difficulties of men and women trying to become emotionally close to each other.[37]

The demands of rigid gender roles made the expectation of an affectionate, loving marriage difficult, but not always impossible to achieve.

MARRIAGE

Affection and intimacy within marriage offered the major hope for transcending the separation of women's and men's spheres and achieving harmony and voluntary devotion. Scholars generally agree that the ideals of companionship in marriage and female moral supremacy were widely voiced among the middle class and gave their women some additional power within the home. Controversy continues, however, about relative power of men and women within marriage and about the realistic possibilities of couples achieving closeness. During the 1970s, women's historians claimed that women lost significant power with the rise of the "cult of domesticity" in the nineteenth century.[38] Opposing their conclusion, Carl Degler argued that individual women's power was rising and was "at odds" with the needs of other family members but that sexual relationships between husbands and wives were pleasurable. In addition, Daniel Scott Smith claimed that the falling birthrate among middle-class Americans was a sign of women's dominance over men.[39]

As the debate continued through the 1980s, scholars began to face the variety of experiences of middle-class couples and the complexities and contradictions inherent in the sexual relations of Victorian husbands and wives. Less extreme positions are now being taken about the presence or absence of sexual repression.[40] Attention has shifted to losses and gains for all family members, although argument continues over whether psychological, economic, or social factors were most important and whether or not marriage continued to be unequal or, to use Suzanne Lebsock's word, "asymmetrical."[41]

Certainly courtship was a time when many women and men sought to find or create the bonds of affection that could bridge the differences between genders. In her study of courtship in the urban Northeast, Ellen Rothman shows how parental influence was replaced by a new commitment to voluntary affection between young people. Choices remained limited, however, by the values internalized from parents and by the social circles within which couples moved, circles that insured that partners would share class and race identification and, preferably, religious affiliation.[42]

Although practicality still required a man to be able to support a wife and a woman to be able to care for the physical and moral needs of a husband and children, Rothman argues that many couples were intent on getting to know each other and on falling in love during courtship, rather than marrying for purely practical considerations. Romance came to be an expected element in their relationship. By the late 1800s, some couples' private letters and diaries reveal a willingness and desire to experience sexual passion with each other. Karen Lystra found a similar pattern when examining letters from a wider geographical range.[43]

Suzanne Lebsock, focusing on Petersburg, Virginia, paints a different picture of courtship. She claims that economic factors continued to be important in the courtship behavior of southern urban women throughout the antebellum period, an analysis that raises interesting questions. Her work may indicate regional variations or it may suggest that historians have overestimated the romantic elements in nineteenth-century marriage choices.[44] More work involving regional comparisons is needed on this and other issues before conclusions can be established.

Both Rothman, focusing on the Northeast, and Lebsock, focusing on the South, do agree that courtship and marriage were experienced differently for men and women. From the beginning of courtship, the choice of a marriage partner was more important for a young woman than a young man because a woman's financial survival rested squarely on her marriage to a responsible and industrious husband. Yet within courtship, women were told to remain passive. They only had the power to say yes or no, while men were expected to pursue a potential mate openly. Inequality during courtship was evident in other areas as well, as Rothman indicates. Privacy and the expression of affection offered temptations, and it was the responsibility of the young woman to insure that the couple practiced self-control and physical restraint. Hers was the major guilt if the man overstepped accepted boundaries.[45]

Rothman also found that while women appeared more willing than men to commit themselves to an engagement, they often sought to postpone the wedding as long as possible, even, in many cases, for several years after the engagement was formalized. A fundamental reason for this delay, Rothman claims, was the young women's unwillingness to leave their families of origin to create homes of their own. A woman's life was radically changed by marriage in ways that a man's was not. She acquired an enormous set of new responsibilities for the physical and moral needs of others. Childbirth, which usually quickly followed marriage, raised realistic fears of death and pain. Men, on the other hand, tended to be slower to decide to marry, but once the decision was made they pushed to have the wedding as soon as possible. For men, marriage meant gaining the respect and authority given to the head of a household. The husband's involvements outside the home continued and even improved as friends and creditors acknowledged his new role.[46]

Affection developed during courtship was supposed to create the foundation for the love and intimacy lauded by the new ideals of companionate marriage. Certainly Degler, Lystra, and others are correct in pointing out that Victorian marriages could be passionate and intimate rather than unhappy, distant, or sexless. Companionate marriages in which both partners had emotional and sexual fulfillment were increasingly held up as a goal in nineteenth-century America. Letters between married couples are often full of affection and explicit physical longing for each other, especially by the late 1800s. Such documents prove that for some couples, at least, marriage could bring a closeness and affection between husbands and wives that bridged the separateness of their spheres and could make for more companionship and intimacy in marriage.[47] In addition, some couples did not strictly follow the dictates of separate spheres. For example, Blanche Hersh's study of marriages between abolitionists reveals ways in which wives and husbands could share an interest in a cause that transcended prescribed gender roles. Within reform circles, her research shows, husbands could be supportive of their wives' public activities, and couples could strive for egalitarian and affectionate marriages.[48]

On the other hand, Victorian marriages faced specific obstacles to achieving voluntary affection and closeness. Sexuality and birth control could be divisive, given husbands' lack of knowledge about women's sexual fulfillment. While some women expressed their physical enjoyment of sexuality in private writings, others seemed to have accepted their husbands' sexual advances as part of the sacrificial female role. Even more fundamental were the risks that sexuality brought to wives. Childbirth was dangerous and adequate birth control could not be guaranteed. Women had good reason to dread pregnancy and the prospect of administering the intensive care they believed each baby needed.[49] Venereal disease was another threat beyond a wife's control. She could become infected and see her infants infected by diseases that her husband had caught.

The steady decline of the middle-class birthrate indicates that these couples were using some means of restricting fertility throughout the 1800s. The options, however, were neither dependable nor conducive to sexual pleasure. Abstinence and coitus interruptus, the most effective means of birth control available, depended on the husband's cooperation. Early forms of diaphragms and condoms had also been introduced, and abortion, legal until midcentury, was also practiced. The numerous advertisements for birth control and abortions in magazines and newspapers indicate that options were available and that some individuals were choosing to take them.[50]

Conflict between a husband and wife could also develop out of the idea that women were morally superior to men and responsible for controlling male sexual behavior. Such dictates contradicted instruction urging women to be submissive to their husbands and never to engage in conflict. During the course of the nineteenth century, domestic power for women rested largely on power over their children rather than their spouses.

Rising divorce rates after the Civil War indicate that for some couples marriage did not bring happiness and intimacy. Looking at divorce records in California in the late nineteenth and early twentieth centuries, Elaine Tyler May and Robert Griswold maintain that the raised expectations that wives had for their husbands' behavior were a major reason women sought divorce. Despite their small and atypical sources, May and Griswold claim that their findings indicate increased power for women within families.[51]

The scholars, like Degler, Scott, Griswold, and May, who argue that women's power over their husbands was increasing to threatening proportions, stress psychological factors and the problems of men. Women's historians like Cott, Smith-Rosenberg, Theriot, Kerber, and Lebsock continue to disagree with their assessment. Looking at the family from the perspective of women, they point out that economic, legal, political, social, and sexual factors all restricted women and made their domestic gains ambiguous. The growing acceptance of the ideal of egalitarian, companionate families developed alongside the wife's continuing financial and legal dependency. As wife, a woman received her legal identity and financial support from her husband. He continued to be the head of the household, a role that he could choose to perform with love and kindness. If he did not, the wife, although considered morally superior, could only seek to persuade him to change.

Just as men's authority within the family rested partially on their participation in the world outside, women also had some more limited contacts outside the nuclear family. Although restricted, these bonds had the potential to increase women's rights as individuals. Carroll Smith-Rosenberg was the first to describe the close emotional ties that sometimes existed between married women, ties that often lasted for decades and sometimes included relationships that twentieth-century readers find surprisingly sensual and sexual.[52] In a study of Michigan women, Marilyn Motz has focused on networks of female relatives rather than friends, but she makes a similar point. Relatives, and the resources they might supply in a crisis, were an essential part of the family as understood by middle-class women. Women exchanged gifts and services with their relatives, sometimes for their husbands' benefit, and sometimes because relatives provided them with an alternative in case of his desertion, failure, or death. Motz claims that female friends and relatives did not necessarily compete with a husband for a woman's loyalty, but practically and emotionally helped to lessen wives' dependence on husbands and eased the restrictions that the private sphere placed on them.[53]

Although the family model did not consider singleness to be a viable option for either young women or men in the nineteenth century, increasing numbers of individuals chose to postpone marriage or not to marry. For example, large numbers of young men left settled portions of the country to go to sea or to pursue their fortunes on various Western frontiers. In the process, they lived temporarily or permanently in predominantly male communities. Increasing numbers of young women were also remaining single or marrying late, causing some Easterners to worry about a "surplus of women." These single women often served supporting roles in the families of others, although Catherine Beecher and others advocated education and teaching as other types of respectable employment for single middle-class women. While the model continued to hold out marriage as the only option for women, increasing numbers of them expressed ambivalence and were pleased to remain in the "blessed state of singleness" in antebellum America. After the Civil War, even more women agreed with Louisa May Alcott that "liberty" was "a better husband" than any actual male spouse. These women found the means to justify their singleness within the ideology of the model family, by stressing their "womanly" qualities, such as purity, and by giving service to others.[54]

Changing expectations and experiences of marriage, however, were only part of a larger picture that included more intensive attention to the rearing of children, especially on the part of mothers.

CHILDREARING

Although scholars continue to debate whether or not wives and husbands experienced the intimacy and companionship idealized in the model family, they agree that a newly intensified bond between mothers and their children was central to both the rhetoric and the reality of middle-class life. Whether nineteenth-century women gained or lost power as wives, they definitely took on new importance as mothers.

By 1815, children were central to the middle-class family to a degree they had seldom been in colonial households. As middle-class birthrates fell, parents had fewer children and focused more intently on each of them. Popular advice books told them to guarantee that children internalized such values as responsibility, thrift, industry, delayed gratification, and sexual restraint. Self-control, learned at their mother's knee, was to insure independence and success.

The changing patterns of childrearing reflected new definitions of childhood. American parents accepted the views of Enlightenment thinkers such as John Locke that children were innocent beings, capable of being influenced by their environment and their early education. Increasingly, however, they rejected Locke's notion that children should be raised only by the dictates of reason: mother's love was just as essential. Theological changes also contributed to the new view of the child. Infants were no longer considered damned but were believed capable of being guided toward salvation. By midcentury, children were even assumed to be capable of assisting in the salvation of other family members.[55]

The theme of child as savior was particularly popular in fiction and articles dealing with the death of a young child, an event that still occurred, although less frequently, in middle-class families. But historians like Sylvia Hoffert have identified troubling contradictions underlying all the sentimental images of dying infants. Could children grow up without losing their innocence and becoming sinful? If so, was their death and sacrifice preferable to life? If children were more pure than parents, what should the parents' role be?[56]

The mother was assumed to be the parent with the time and attention necessary to implement the new intensive childrearing practices. Because women were believed to be more religious and pure, as well as more intuitive and emotional than men, they were said to be particularly capable of educating children. Emotional bonds and dependency on mothers were to insure that sons and daughters internalized the proper values and behavior patterns. The major relationship in the middle-class home shifted from that between spouses to that between mother and child. As mothers, women were to find the power and respect that they lacked as wives, and the domestic sphere became the "empire of the mother."[57]

Fathers generally played a declining role in the day-to-day interactions that came to characterize middle-class childrearing. But occasionally, they too were involved in insuring the emotional dependence of their children. Reverend Francis Wayland's account of locking his fifteen-month-old son in his room and withholding food from him for over a day gives evidence of one father whose duties as a minister allowed him time to devote to his young son. It also indicates some of the emotional pain the goals of the new model family could inflict on children.[58]

But most fathers' duties as breadwinners took them away from the kind of involvement that Reverend Wayland's account describes. Their primary responsibility was to earn the wealth necessary for their prolonged education. Although retaining authority as head of the household, fathers were becoming distant figures in their children's lives. They might step in to punish or to act as the ultimate authority, but some sons and daughters were being raised in almost exclusively female, domestic worlds.[59]

Degler, Mintz, and Kellogg see the new emphasis on children as a mark of the progress of the new American nation. They claim that the new closeness between children and parents, more affection within the family, and more freedom for the young served to "democratize" the family.[60] The concept of the democratization of parent-child relations downplays the fact that parents still required obedience, although it was to be shown in new ways. Cheerful, voluntary obedience could be more difficult for a child than the grudging submission acceptable in an earlier period, as Reverend Wayland's story makes clear.

Nonetheless, some middle-class children certainly were better off than their counterparts in earlier eras. They were more likely to survive, for example, and to have parents and siblings survive with them. They probably had fewer siblings and received more intensive care from their mothers than would have been possible earlier. Because they were middle class, they usually had no need to contribute to the family income and therefore were able to devote time and attention to lessons. Such gains, however, present only part of the picture. As abundant scholarship has shown, Victorians were not the first to love their children, although they may have expressed their affection in ways more recognizable to twentieth-century historians.[61]

An expanding scholarly literature describes how birth and infant care were changing for middle-class American families in the nineteenth century, but it seldom addresses gender differences in childrearing, as Anne Boylan has shown.[62] With Nancy Chodorow and others introducing popular theories on the formation of gender identity in early infancy, the issue became particularly important.[63] Historians must carefully examine whether or not contemporary psychological theories are relevant when discussing previous eras rather than blindly adopting them. In addition, the growing literature on the history of adolescence focuses largely on the activities of youth outside of the family in which they grew up. New research on courtship by Ellen Rothman and Karen Lystra is beginning to tell us about the transition that both young men and women made from their families of origin to their own life in a new family.[64] Anne Boylan makes the point that young women's employment outside the home played an important role in their adolescence, and Joseph Kett's scholarship on young men reveals the importance of nonfamilial influences on them.[65]

Too much of what we know about gender or about the parent-child relations between infants and adolescents, however, continues to be based on advice literature written to mothers, and important questions remain to be answered. In the nineteenth century, no one considered the possibility that either sons or daughters could suffer because of emotional dependence on a parent or from being too closely bound to the domestic sphere. Today, however, some scholars find fault with Victorian childrearing practices, especially with children's intensive ties to their mothers, which could interfere with sons' and daughters' abilities to function as mature adults. An important element in Victorian homes was the extreme closeness between the mother and her children, a closeness that contemporary scholars assume had a strong impact on the development of gender roles.

The nineteenth century seems to have been a time when daughters and mothers retained close ties, with daughters serving as "apprentices" who learned everything from domestic skills to the emotional ties linking women together.[66] The advice literature idealized the mother-daughter relationship, but whether this language actually reflected closeness between mothers and daughters remains unclear. We know that daughters frequently expressed regret at parting with mothers at marriage and sought their presence when they gave birth. Marilyn Dell Brady's research reveals that some women, coming of age at the end of the nineteenth century and writing their autobiographies in the twentieth, emphasized their closeness with their mothers and credited their domestically oriented mothers with having provided them with essential assistance for their own entry into careers in the public sphere. But, as Brady's work also suggests, extreme closeness between mothers and daughters could make it difficult for women to become autonomous.[67] Introducing a generational approach, Nancy Theriot has related the dynamics of the mother-daughter relationship for women to changes in the relationship over time. According to her theory, women conceptualized what it meant to be a wife and mother from their own experience and reading and then passed their understanding on to daughters who modified it, in turn, in light of their own experiences as women.[68] Theriot and Joan Brumberg have both suggested that the eating problems that some adolescent middle-class girls developed resulted from their relations with their mothers and the intense emotional climates of their homes.[69] More historical research on how both mothers and daughters in the past experienced their relationship is needed, however, especially as feminist theorists seek a new understanding of mother-daughter bonds.

Even less has been written about the relations of fathers and daughters than about mother-daughter bonds. Steven Mintz claims that the two American women authors he researched were "pseudo-sons" raised primarily by fathers.[70] Barbara Welter follows the Freudian position that women who became important achievers in the public sphere were close to strong fathers and rejected weak mothers.[71] However, little evidence from the nineteenth century supports such generalizations about the experience of most daughters. In fact, Brady found that fathers were seldom significant figures in the women's autobiographies she examined, whether or not the autobiographers had important nondomestic roles as adults. Even if fathers were described with emotion and pride, they were not always strong, successful men able to lead daughters into the public sphere. Two of the fathers most fondly remembered were financial failures who committed suicide.[72] In addition, issues of incest by fathers have seldom been addressed. It is simply too soon to draw sweeping conclusions here.[73]

Extreme closeness with mothers may have also caused difficulties for sons, some scholars suggest. The dichotomy that the middle class had tried to create between the home and the world complicated a woman's task of raising boys. Excluded from the public sphere herself, the mother was nevertheless to instruct sons how to function in it. Stressing the moral superiority of women, she was to teach sons to be virtuous and self-disciplined men. While making sons emotionally dependent, she required them to succeed in the aggressive, competitive world of business and politics. Such lessons could make it hard for some sons to function as adult men in either the private or the public sphere, much less in both. Bryan Strong has argued that the intense bonding of mothers and sons could also have an erotic element. Although he does not claim that these relations were physically acted out, he does view them as "latently incestuous." If a mother's relationship with her husband was distant and unfulfilling, as at least some women's evidently were, then for mothers to turn to sons for affection is not surprising.[74]

Fathers' relationships with sons have only been sketched in bare outline, with most attention given to the contributions of fathers as breadwinners.[75] Mary Ryan claims that the relations between middle-class sons and both of their parents helped the sons to maintain or achieve a secure economic position. She points out that fathers contributed to childrearing by providing the resources that allowed sons to stay out of the labor market. Family resources gave middle-class sons an advantage over their working-class cohorts in moving into the growing ranks of clerks and managers who made up much of the new middle class by midcentury. In addition, Ryan says mothers guaranteed that their sons internalized self-control and self-discipline and learned habits of thrift and hard work that helped them to protect wealth already acquired. Perhaps these values also helped sons to sublimate sexual urges until they had acquired enough financial resources to marry. Ryan notes the irony of calling sons who profited by such measures "self-made men."[76]

Children, like women, received more favorable attention in the middle-class families of the nineteenth century, but whether or not they profited from that attention remains debatable. Perhaps the economic advantages balanced the emotional scars in antebellum America. By the post–Civil War period, however, difficulties were intensifying for those who espoused the nineteenth-century model family.

THE MODEL FAMILY AND THE POLITICS OF CHANGE

Contradictions in and around the new family model of the early 1800s erupted into conflicts by the end of the century. Some middle-class reformers anxiously intervened in families whose values differed from their own, and generational conflicts as well as conflicts between regions and classes broke out. Pressures within middle-class families and new opportunities for sons and daughters also contributed to disturbing changes in the sphere defined as private. Some young, urban, middle-class men and women, who wanted to expand the nineteenth-century family model's ideals of individual rights, protested against the limitations the model contained. Their challenges were met by conservative defenders of the same family model who stressed a stricter allegiance to the ideals of obedience and female subordination and domesticity. To complicate matters, various groups turned to the state to enforce their own version of family virtues. By the first decades of the twentieth century, new experts were defining proper family behavior, and governmental involvement in the "private sphere" was reaching a new high. By the 1920s, no one family model was shared even among middle-class Americans, and public debates about the family took for granted the involvement of outside authorities.

Overlapping groups, contradictory demands, and unlikely alliances make the story of the model middle-class family in post–Civil War America extremely complex. Historians have barely begun to sort out the contradictions and the relationships between the various pieces. Even more than for earlier periods, the research relevant for family history has focused on women, children, or men, or rested heavily on economic or ideological theory. Although attention has been paid to the role of the state and the experts, few scholars have examined the relationship of different factors in the lives of identifiable groups. In addition, information is regrettably sparse on groups that were not on the cutting edge of change and that opposed new family practices.

The economic development of America during the post–Civil War period provided the context for the conflicts over the family.[77] As the nation entered an era of cities and factories, of national advertising and international markets, conflicts between social groups often included, or were couched in, familial language. Middle-class Americans felt caught between the increasing wealth of the "captains of industry" and the increasing poverty of the urban, often immigrant, working class. As change moved irregularly across the nation and through families, small businessmen and farmers lost their claims to self-sufficiency and their ability to insure the security and status of their children. Wives and youths no longer automatically accepted the authority of husbands and fathers. Victorian gender roles, and their exclusion of women from the world of business and politics, began to break down. The sons of the middle class who moved into managerial and bureaucratic positions in cities and the nationalizing industries by the 1890s were followed by middle-class daughters demanding and receiving college educations and finding white-collar careers of their own. Wives and mothers of the middle class were seldom drawn into employment, but in increasing numbers they were also moving outside domestic circles, bringing their alleged moral superiority to bear on the needs of urban America.

Women who moved into new public roles were rejecting parts of the definition of womanhood that had been popular in antebellum America. Nancy Theriot claims that with more ability to control their own lives, daughters were less willing to accept self-sacrifice as an essentially female trait.[78] Pursuing college educations and entering careers, daughters could experience a degree of autonomy beyond any their mothers could have imagined. By the 1890s, a small but highly visible group of "new women" caught the attention of society with their sensible dress and desire for independence. Rejecting the ideal of wifely subordination, some women rejected marriage and service to family for lives of service to society. A few formed long-term, loving partnerships with other women or lived in the familylike environments of settlement houses. Adapting "motherly" qualities of nurturance, and expanding their familial roles into ways of making a living and exerting power in the public sphere, women supported a wide range of causes with the validating claim of being "social housekeepers."[79]

Reform movements of the Progressive era depended heavily on such women and their domestic language. Stable wives and matrons of middle-class families, as well as single women, were extending their power into the public sphere as they sought to "clean up society." Angrily, they often attacked men, whom they blamed for many of society's ills. Homeless, orphaned, and neglected children caught their attention. Inspired by images of family life gone awry, these reformers joined the temperance movement, campaigned for "moral purity," and promoted "voluntary motherhood." The drunkard and his family, the seducer of the prostitute, and the parents who sent their children into factories to work all seemed to require government intervention. Some reformers believed that the government should step in to enforce the rights of wives and children and protect them from abuse by husbands and fathers.

The ideology of the family that had originally been useful for teaching middle-class sons and daughters self-control and self-discipline was applied, with the help of the government, to control and discipline other social groups. This governmental intervention was supported by the rationale that families who did not adhere to middle-class definitions of domesticity and virtue were a threat to the American nation.

But all women who sought public power and the expansion of the government's role in families did not necessarily seek the vote or other public expansion of women's roles. Paradoxically, some women continued to defend a doctrine of separate spheres and the privacy of the family while demanding local, state, and national intervention into areas the new model family had once defined as private.[80]

As middle-class women began to expand their activities, middle-class men also faced a new set of problems. At one level, major industrial expansion was displacing them from familiar niches, and the presence of immigrants and blacks was breaking up their homogeneous communities. According to some scholars, middle-class men were facing a "crisis of masculinity," as they moved from running small businesses to being a part of large corporate structures. Increasing numbers of women were competing with them for entry-level white-collar jobs as salesclerks and secretaries. In the Progressive movement, women were assuming some leadership positions. Perhaps, as some scholars argue, Progressive men like Teddy Roosevelt, William Allen White, and David Graham Phillips were intent on proving their manhood in the face of increased female involvement in the public sphere. Peter Filene argues that World War I also served this function.[81]

Changes in gender roles in the public world were accompanied by increased challenges to the ideas of home land family inherited from the early 1800s. Middle-class wives were choosing birth control or abortion instead of repeated pregnancies. More women were remaining single or marrying late. More divorces were occurring, despite stricter divorce laws. Even before World War I, men and women in Greenwich Village were discarding the dictates of the model family. A few radicals openly advocated the enjoyment of sexuality and claimed safe and simple birth control as the most fundamental right for women.[82]

Other groups of middle-class men and women were appalled at what they saw happening and at the radical suggestions being publicly discussed. From mid-nineteenth century on, the medical profession sided with those who wanted to control sexuality and stop the declining birthrate among the middle class. Using Darwinism and new scientific findings, they came up with new "proofs" of why women should not be

allowed to pursue higher education or careers. They pronounced that
women who chose not to devote all their energies to frequent childbirth
were shirking their responsibilities and failing their "race."[83] Declaring
a crisis in the American family and a threat to national greatness, some
reformers sought to insure that couples would continue to get married,
to stay married, and to have as many children as had the couples of a
generation earlier. They supported legislation to tie women more closely
to the home. In their view, the government needed to step in to save
the family from sons and daughters unwilling to duplicate their parents'
lives and from those who had always lived outside the middle class. New
legislation outlawed abortions and made it more difficult to get a divorce.
In the 1870s, Anthony Comstock led those who obtained passage of
national laws forbidding any materials on sexual matters to be sent
through the U.S. mail. The strict enforcement of the Comstock Laws,
by Comstock himself, not only stopped the spread of pornography but
also effectively halted the spread of information about birth control and
the availability of birth control devices. Demanding constitutional protection of free speech, opponents of Comstock were jailed. But the active
intervention of the state could not stop the declining marriage and birthrates, or slow the pace of divorce.[84]

Although change and conflict over family practices had begun before
World War I, the 1920s witnessed intensified public challenges to the
earlier family model. The twenties are often characterized by the image
of the flapper, perhaps the most shocking, but hardly the most significant, of these challenges. Some small groups of urban middle-class men
and women were increasingly rebellious against the family virtues that
had guided their parents. Youth no longer listened to, obeyed, or followed the examples of their elders. Pleasure replaced thrift, industry,
social service, and reform in some middle-class circles. Sexuality was
becoming more open, especially in urban settings where young working-
class men and women refused to follow middle-class norms during their
leisure time. Rather than repressing sexuality, some claimed that it
should be enjoyed, at least with a spouse or a probable marriage partner.
Women were openly provocative, if stylishly boyish. Procreation was no
longer the sole or primary goal of sexuality, and middle-class wives
turned to physicians for birth control devices.

"Traditional" values seemed to have totally disappeared from some
sections of the population, as middle-class Americans moved into an
economic era characterized by abundance and advertising. Pleasure grew
in importance, and the nation swung back from the optimistic radicalism
and reform of the Progressive era. Freedom came to mean privatized,
emotional, and sexual pleasure, rather than significant autonomy for
either middle-class women or men.[85] Those most affected by these
changes were urban, educated, middle-class youth whose life-styles and

values were diverging from their rural counterparts in a wide variety of ways. Much of what we know about family history in the early 1900s has focused on this group, distorting our knowledge and ignoring the family views and practices of more conservative Americans. Although historians have looked at conflicts over religion, politics, and even women's roles, more information about the groups that remained committed to the nineteenth-century family definitions and practices might offer clues about the resurgence of conservative family attitudes that has occurred since the 1920s.

As Americans sought to cope with changing social patterns, a new generation of experts established themselves as the arbitrators of such family matters as sexual behavior and childrearing. Sexuality became controversial as a segment of the American population accepted the views of Europeans such as Havelock Ellis and Sigmund Freud, who held that both men and women had sexual desires that should not be continually repressed. Popularizers of such views encouraged middle-class Americans to push aside the generally restrictive sexual attitudes of the Victorian era. Companionship, which had long been a part of the ideal family, came to demand sexual compatibility, or even mutual orgasm. Relations between husband and wife pushed aside the primacy of the mother-child relationship. Christina Simmons argues that the new attitudes took away the power that women had had as mothers while continuing and intensifying their dependence on men. The new experts also retained the idea that women received their fulfillment as wives and mothers, roles that they defined as excluding a career.[86] In fact, a new emphasis on heterosexual love and the rigid definition of homosexual attraction as deviant probably encouraged the widespread return of the idea that marriage was the only acceptable alternative.[87]

Meanwhile, reformers of the late nineteenth and early twentieth centuries had established roles for experts on children and for the national government in the lives of families. Progressives, many of them women, had been deeply committed to various plans to "save the children." Child abuse, child labor, children's food and recreational needs, and schools all received attention.[88] The establishment of the U.S. Children's Bureau in 1912 climaxed an important drive by activists and gave the national government a formal role within families. The women who led the Children's Bureau were particularly concerned about the nation's high infant mortality rate and undertook campaigns to insure prenatal care and proper care of babies. They founded well-baby clinics and provided clean, tested milk for infants, distributed leaflets giving mothers the latest advice on childrearing, and carried on extensive correspondence with women who asked their advice about children.[89]

The professionalization of motherhood and the development of child study and domestic science as academic fields within universities produced a group of experts ready to advise women with children. In the early 1900s, child care was supposed to emphasize rigid, orderly practices. Soon, however, experts began to disagree with these highly structured demands and began to instruct mothers to be more permissive with their children. By 1930 John Watson was again telling mothers that emotional distance and structured patterns of reenforcement were necessary in raising children. Despite the contradictory advice, many mothers seemed willing to try and do what they were told rather than to follow their own best judgment.[90]

Ironically, the model family of the 1920s bore a striking resemblance to the one that had emerged a century earlier. Following the lead of the experts, families were again encouraged to turn inward, focusing their attention on pleasure and fulfilling each others' emotional needs. Some American middle-class families, especially those in rural areas, even retained Victorian attitudes toward sexuality and obedience. But some things had changed. Experts were becoming even more authoritative and, more often than in the early nineteenth century, were male. The emphasis on individual pleasure that was developing had the potential for destroying ideas about both parents having responsibility for children. The individuality being stressed rested more on peer activities and consumerism than on personal or social radicalism. And finally, the role of the government in family matters had increased significantly and would continue to do so after 1930.

The new model family of the 1920s had adapted to the industrial age, but the new experts had only partially and temporarily achieved a public consensus about the American family. Some groups within American society did not follow the newest model. Deeper gulfs between classes, races, and generations were developing. Contradictions within the family model, between authority and individual rights, remained unresolved. As the country entered the Great Depression, the new middle-class model family lauded in the early 1800s and adapted with the help of experts and government in the early 1900s became increasingly difficult to sustain. Individuals were not able to resolve its conflicts or meet the new psychological demands being placed on them. And yet, the language of the new model middle-class family of the early nineteenth century continues to structure public debates about social power even in the present, limiting the choices of families as they move into the twenty-first century.

NOTES

1. Carl Degler, *At Odds: Women and the Family in America from the Revolution to the Present* (New York: Oxford University Press, 1980); Stephanie Coontz, *The Social Origins of Private Life: A History of American Families* (New York: Verso,

1988); and Steven Mintz and Susan Kellogg, *Domestic Revolutions: A Social History of American Family Life* (New York: The Free Press, 1988).

2. Anne Kuhn, *The Mother's Role in Childhood Education: New England Concepts, 1830–1860* (New Haven, Conn.: Yale University Press, 1947); Monica Kiefer, *American Children through Their Books, 1700–1835* (Philadelphia: University of Pennsylvania Press, 1948); Bernard Wishy, *The Child and the Republic: The Dawn of Modern Child Nurture* (Philadelphia: University of Pennsylvania Press, 1968); and R. Gordon Kelly, *Mother Was a Lady: Self and Society in Selected American Children's Periodicals, 1865–1890* (Westport, Conn.: Greenwood Press, 1974).

3. Carl Degler, "What Ought to Be and What Was: Women's Sexuality in the Nineteenth Century," in *The American Family in Social-Historical Perspective*, ed. Michael Gordon, 2d ed. (New York: St. Martin's Press, 1978), 403–25.

4. Jay Mechling, "Advice to Historians on Advice to Mothers," *Journal of Social History* 9 (1975): 44–63. See also Nancy Cott, "Notes toward an Interpretation of Antebellum Childrearing," *The Psychohistorical Review* 6 (Spring 1978): 4–20. See also Glen Elder, Jr., "History and the Family: The Discovery of Complexity," *Journal of Marriage and the Family* 43 (1981): 439–519.

5. For a discussion of this approach, see Carroll Smith-Rosenberg, "Hearing Women's Words: A Feminist Reconstruction of History," in her *Disorderly Conduct: Visions of Gender in Victorian America* (New York: Oxford University Press, 1985), 11–52; Joan W. Scott, "Gender: A Useful Category of Historical Analysis," in her *Gender and the Politics of History* (New York: Columbia University Press, 1988), 28–50; and John D'Emilio and Estelle B. Freedman, *Intimate Matters: A History of Sexuality in America* (New York: Basic Books, 1988), xv–xix.

6. The phrase "haven in a heartless world" was introduced by Christopher Lasch, *Haven in a Heartless World: The Family Besieged* (New York: Basic Books, 1977).

7. Jane Turner Censer, *North Carolina Planters and Their Children, 1800–1860* (Baton Rouge: Louisiana University Press, 1984). For additional research on Southern families, see also Bertram Wyatt-Brown, *Southern Honor: Ethics and Behavior in the Old South* (New York: Oxford University Press, 1982); Steven Stowe, *Intimacy and Power in the Old South: Ritual in the Lives of the Planters* (Baltimore, Md.: Johns Hopkins University Press, 1987); Daniel Blake Smith, *Inside the Great House: Planter Family Life in Eighteenth-Century Chesapeake Society* (Ithaca, N.Y.: Cornell University Press, 1980); and Suzanne Lebsock, *The Free Women of Petersburg: Status and Culture in a Southern Town, 1784–1860* (New York: W. W. Norton & Company, 1984). For a discussion of the regional differences and the challenge of existing conceptual models based on the urban Northeast, see Jacquelyn Dowd Hall, "Partial Truths," *Signs* 14 (1989): 902–11.

8. Mary P. Ryan, *Cradle of the Middle Class: The Family in Oneida County, New York, 1790–1865* (Cambridge: Cambridge University Press, 1981).

9. Coontz, *Social Origins*.

10. For discussion of the impact of family ideology on the formation of the English middle class see Leonore Davidoff and Catherine Hall, *Family Fortunes: Men and Women of the English Middle Class, 1780–1850* (London: Hutchinson, 1987).

11. Kirk Jeffrey, "The Family as Utopian Retreat from the City," *Soundings* 55 (1972): 21–41.

12. Degler, *At Odds*, and Mintz and Kellogg, *Domestic Revolutions*; Steven Mintz, *A Prison of Expectations: The Family in Victorian Culture* (New York: New York University Press, 1983), plays down the idea of haven and emphasizes issues of authority in both family and society in the writings of British and American literary figures.

13. Linda Kerber, *Women of the Republic: Intellect and Ideology in Revolutionary America* (Chapel Hill: University of North Carolina Press, 1980), and "The Republican Mother: Women and the Enlightenment, An American Perspective," *American Quarterly* 28 (1976): 187–205; Ruth Bloch, "American Feminine Ideals in Transition: The Rise of the Moral Mother, 1785–1815," *Feminist Studies* 4 (1978): 100–126; and Ellen DuBois, et al., "Politics and Culture in Women's History: A Symposium," *Feminist Studies* 6 (1980): 26–64.

14. Michael Grossberg, *Governing the Hearth: Law and Family in Nineteenth-Century America* (Chapel Hill: University of North Carolina Press, 1985).

15. Norma Basch, *In the Eyes of the Law: Women, Marriage and Property in Nineteenth-Century New York* (Ithaca, N.Y.: Cornell University Press, 1982).

16. Nancy Cott, "Young Women in the Second Great Awakening in New England," *Feminist Studies* 3 (Fall 1975): 15–29, and *The Bonds of Womanhood: "Woman's Sphere" in New England, 1780–1835* (New Haven, Conn.: Yale University Press, 1977); Mary P. Ryan, *Cradle of the Middle Class*; Barbara Epstein, *The Politics of Domesticity: Women, Evangelism, and Temperance in Nineteenth-Century America* (Middletown, Conn.: Wesleyan University Press, 1981); and Carroll Smith-Rosenberg, "The Cross and the Pedestal," in *Disorderly Conduct*, 129–64. Ann Douglas, *Feminization of American Culture* (New York: Alfred A. Knopf, 1977) is more negative about women's impact on religion.

17. For a thorough discussion of this process, see Mary P. Ryan, *The Empire of the Mother: American Writing about Domesticity, 1830–1860* (New York: Haworth Press, 1982), 19–20.

18. Margaret Marsh, *Suburban Lives* (New Brunswick, N.J.: Rutgers University Press, 1990). Steven Mintz, *A Prison of Expectations*, discusses British male authors popular in America, but he examines literary figures, not the men who wrote advice books.

19. Sylvia Hoffert, *Private Matters: American Attitudes toward Childbearing and Infant Nurture in the Urban North, 1800–1860* (Urbana: University of Illinois Press, 1989); Regina Markell Morantz-Sanchez, *Sympathy and Science: Women Physicians in American Medicine* (New York: Oxford University Press, 1985), 28–46; John S. Haller, Jr., and Robin M. Haller, *The Physician and Sexuality in Victorian America* (Urbana: University of Illinois Press, 1974); and Michael Gordon, "From an Unfortunate Necessity to a Cult of Mutual Orgasm: Sex in American Marital Educational Literature, 1830–1940," in *Studies in the Sociology of Sex*, ed. James Henslin (New York: Appleton-Century Crofts, 1971), 53–80.

20. John Spurlock, *Free Love: Marriage and Middle-Class Radicalism in America, 1825–1860* (New York: New York University Press, 1988); and Louis Kern, *An Ordered Love: Sex Roles and Sexuality in Victorian America* (Chapel Hill: University of North Carolina Press, 1977).

21. Clifford Edward Clark, "Domestic Architecture as an Index to Social History: The Romantic Revival and the Cult of Domesticity in America, 1840–1870," *Journal of Interdisciplinary History* 7 (1976): 33–56, and *The American Family*

Home, 1800–1960 (Chapel Hill: University of North Carolina Press, 1986); Margaret Marsh, *Suburban Lives* (New Brunswick, N.J.: Rutgers University Press, 1990); Gwendolyn Wright, *Building the Dream: A Social History of Housing in America* (Cambridge, Mass.: MIT Press, 1983). Wright's *Moralism and the Model Home: Domestic Architecture and Cultural Conflict in Chicago, 1873–1913* (Chicago: University of Chicago Press, 1980) makes similar points, but focuses on the period after the Civil War.

22. Nancy Woloch, *Women and the American Experience* (New York: Alfred A. Knopf, 1984), 97–150; Nina Baym, *Women's Fiction: A Guide to Novels by and about Women in America, 1820–1870* (Ithaca, N.Y.: Cornell University Press, 1978); and Mary Kelley, *Private Women, Public Stage: Literary Domesticity in Nineteenth-Century America* (New York: Oxford University Press, 1984).

23. Helen Papashvily, *All the Happy Endings* (New York: Harper and Row, 1956); Ann Douglas Wood, "The 'Scribbling Women' and Fanny Fern: Why Women Wrote," *American Quarterly* 28 (1971): 3–24; and Baym, *Women's Fiction*.

24. Kelley, *Private Women*.

25. Kathryn Kish Sklar, *Catharine Beecher: A Study in American Domesticity* (New Haven, Conn.: Yale University Press, 1973). See Linda Kerber, "Separate Spheres, Female Worlds, Woman's Place: The Rhetoric of Women's History," *Journal of American History* 75 (1988): 9–39, on the need for scholars to move beyond this concept.

26. Sarah Elbert, *A Hunger for Home: Louisa May Alcott's Place in American Literature* (New Brunswick, N.J.: Rutgers University Press, 1987); Charles Strickland, *Victorian Domesticity: Families in the Life and Art of Louisa May Alcott* (University: University of Alabama Press, 1985). See also Kirk Jeffrey, "Marriage, Career, and Feminine Ideology in Nineteenth-Century America: Reconstructing the Marital Experience of Lydia Maria Child, 1828–1874," *Feminist Studies* 7 (1981): 113–30. Mintz, *A Prison of Expectations*, focuses on the struggles that Harriet Beecher Stowe and Catherine Sedgewick had against strong fathers, rather than on their experiences and values as women.

27. Ryan, *Empire of the Mother*, 143.

28. Nancy Theriot, *The Biosocial Construction of Femininity: Mothers and Daughters in Nineteenth-Century America* (Westport, Conn.: Greenwood Press, 1988).

29. Kerber, "Separate Spheres" and Smith-Rosenberg, "Hearing Women's Words," in her *Disorderly Conduct*, 11–52. See also Joan Scott, "Gender" in her *Gender and the Politics of History*, 28–50; and DuBois, et al., "Politics and Culture in Women's History." Mary P. Ryan challenges the concept of separate spheres by pointing out the activities of middle-class women in the public sphere in the nineteenth century. See her *Women in Public: Between Banners and Ballots* (Baltimore, Md.: Johns Hopkins University Press, 1990).

30. Barbara Welter, "The Cult of True Womanhood: 1800–1860," *American Quarterly* 18 (1966): 151–75. Reprinted in her *Dimity Conventions: The American Woman in the Nineteenth Century* (Athens: Ohio University Press, 1976).

31. Nancy Cott, "Passionlessness: An Interpretation of Victorian Sexual Ideology, 1790–1850," in *Heritage of Her Own*, ed. Nancy Cott and Elizabeth Pleck (New York: Simon and Schuster, 1974), 162–81.

32. Frances Cogan, *All-American Girl: The Ideal of Real Womanhood in Mid-Nineteenth-Century America* (Athens: University of Georgia Press, 1989).

33. Theriot, *The Biosocial Construction of Femininity*, claims that by the end of the 1880s, daughters were rejecting their mothers' emphasis on sacrifice. Debates among historians, as well as among activists on family issues, over conflicts between women's familial and nonfamilial roles reveal ongoing tensions over this point.

34. Peter N. Stearns, *Be a Man! Males in Modern Society* (New York: Holmes & Meier Publishers, 1979), 79–112.

35. G. J. Barker-Benfield, "The Spermatic Economy: A Nineteenth-Century View," in *The American Family in Social-Historical Perspective*, 2d ed., ed. Michael Gordon (New York: St. Martin's Press, 1978), 374–402; and Peter Stearns, *Be a Man!*, 79–112.

36. Mintz, *Prison*; and Bertram Wyatt-Brown, "Three Generations of Yankee Parenthood: The Tappen Family, a Case Study of Antebellum Nurture," *Illinois Quarterly* 38 (Fall 1975): 12–28.

37. David Pugh, *Sons of Liberty: The Masculine Mind in Nineteenth-Century America* (Westport, Conn.: Greenwood Press, 1983).

38. Cott, *Bonds of Womanhood*; Smith-Rosenberg, "The World of Love and Ritual," in *Disorderly Conduct*; and Ryan, *Womanhood in America*.

39. Degler, *At Odds*; Daniel Scott Smith, "Family Limitation, Sexual Control, and Domestic Feminism in Victorian America," *Feminist Studies* 1 (1973): 40–58. Smith has received major criticism for this stance from scholars who show more concrete reasons for declining middle-class birthrates and who oppose Smith's use of the term "feminism" to refer to a nonideological power strictly limited to the domestic sphere. For a careful rebuttal of Degler and Smith, see Lebsock, *Free Women*, 48–53.

40. Estelle Freedman, "Sexuality in Nineteenth-Century America: Behavior, Ideology and Politics," *Reviews in American History* 10 (1982): 196–215; Christina Simmons, "Modern Sexuality and the Myth of Victorian Repression," in *Passion and Power: Sexuality in History*, ed. Kathy Peiss and Christina Simmons (Philadelphia, Pa.: Temple University Press, 1989), 157–77; and Carol Z. Stearns and Peter Stearns, "Victorian Sexuality: Can Historians Do It Better?" *Journal of Social History* 18 (1985): 625–34.

41. Lebsock, *Free Women*, p. 18.

42. Ellen K. Rothman, *Hands and Hearts: A History of Courtship in America* (Cambridge, Mass.: Harvard University Press, 1984): 17–55.

43. Karen Lystra, *Searching the Heart: Women, Men, and Romantic Love in Nineteenth-Century America* (New York: Oxford University Press, 1989), 28–56 and 157–91.

44. Lebsock, *Free Women*, 15–54.

45. Rothman, *Hands and Hearts*, 17–84.

46. Rothman, *Hands and Hearts*, 87–176. Additional support for this point can be found in Ethel Peal, "The Atrophied Rib: Urban Middle-Class Women in Jacksonian America" (Ph.D. diss., University of Pittsburgh, 1970).

47. Degler, *At Odds*; and Lystra, *Searching the Heart*.

48. Blanche Glassman Hersh, *The Slavery of Sex: Feminist-Abolitionists in America* (Urbana: University of Illinois Press, 1978). Abolitionist couples were rare, however, and had strong common commitments that were lacking in most middle-class marriages.

49. Nancy Theriot, *Biosocial Construction*, 51–68, maintains that fear of child-birth and problems with birth control methods cut down on the probability of wives' sexual enjoyment.

50. Linda Gordon, *Woman's Body, Woman's Right: A Social History of Birth Control in America* (New York: Penguin Books, 1977); and D'Emilio and Freedman, *Intimate Matters*, 55–82.

51. Robert Griswold, *Family and Divorce in California, 1850–1890: Victorian Illusions and Everyday Realities* (Albany: State University of New York Press, 1982); and Elaine Tyler May, *Great Expectations: Marriage and Divorce in Post-Victorian America* (Chicago: University of Chicago Press, 1980).

52. Smith-Rosenberg, "The Female World of Love and Ritual," in her *Disorderly Conduct*, 53–76. Degler argues that Smith-Rosenberg's findings are invalid because of her reliance on letters, which were seldom the way husbands and wives communicated. Degler's position has been attacked in turn for presenting too rosy a picture of relationships between spouses.

53. Marilyn Motz, *The True Sisterhood: Michigan Women and Their Kin, 1820–1920* (Albany: State University of New York Press, 1983).

54. Virginia Chambers-Schiller, *Liberty, a Better Husband: Single Women in America, The Generations of 1780–1840* (New Haven, Conn.: Yale University Press, 1984); quote from Alcott, xi.

55. Kerber, "The Republican Mother"; Bloch, "American Feminine Ideals in Transition," 34–48; and Wishy, *The Child and the Republic*.

56. Hoffert, *Private Matters*, 170–85; and Nancy Schrom Dye and Daniel Blake Smith, "Mother Love and Infant Death, 1750–1920," *Journal of American History* 73 (1986): 329–53.

57. Ryan, *Empire of the Mother*; Bloch, "Moral Mother"; and Kerber, "The Republican Mother."

58. William McLoughlin, "Evangelical Child Rearing in the Age of Jackson: Francis Wayland's Views on When and How to Subdue Willfulness of Children," in *Growing Up in America: Children in Historical Perspective*, ed. N. Ray Hiner and Joseph M. Hawes (Urbana: University of Illinois Press, 1985), 86–107.

59. John Demos and Anthony Rotundo have begun to address the history of fatherhood, but it remains an important and little explored area of research. See John Demos, "The Changing Faces of Fatherhood," in his *Past, Present, and Personal: The Family and the Life Course in American History* (New York: Oxford University Press, 1986), 41–67; and E. Anthony Rotundo, "American Fatherhood: A Historical Perspective," *American Behavioral Scientist* 29 (1985): 7–25.

60. Degler, *At Odds*, 86–110; and Mintz and Kellogg, *Domestic Revolutions*, 43–65.

61. See for example Ross W. Beales, Jr., "In Search of the Historical Child: Miniature Adulthood and Youth in Colonial New England," in *Growing Up in America: Children in Historical Perspective*, ed. Hiner and Hawes, 6–24.

62. Anne Boylan, "Growing Up Female in Young America, 1800–1860," in *American Childhood: A Research Guide and Historical Handbook*, ed. Joseph M. Hawes and N. Ray Hiner (Westport, Conn.: Greenwood Press, 1985), 153–84.

63. Nancy Chodorow, *Reproduction of Mothering: Psychoanalysis and the Sociology of Gender* (Berkeley: University of California Press, 1978).

64. Rothman, *Hands and Hearts*; Lystra, *Searching the Heart*.

65. Boylan, "Growing Up Female," 164–71; and Joseph Kett, *Rites of Passage: Adolescence in America, 1790 to the Present* (New York: Basic Books, 1977).

66. Smith-Rosenberg, "Female World," in *Disorderly Conduct*, 60; Theriot, *Biosocial Construction*, 75–90; and Barbara Welter, "Coming of Age in America: The American Girl in the Nineteenth-Century" in her *Dimity Conventions*, 3–20.

67. Marilyn Dell Brady, "Their Mothers' Daughters: Perceptions of Motherhood in Autobiographies by Selected American Women, 1920–1940" (Ph.D. diss., University of Kansas, 1987).

68. Theriot, *Biosocial Construction*, 75–106.

69. Theriot, *Biosocial Construction*, 119–32; and Joan Jacobs Brumberg, *Fasting Girls: The Emergence of Anorexia Nervosa as a Modern Disease* (Cambridge, Mass.: Harvard University Press, 1988), 126–40.

70. Mintz, *Prison of Expectations*.

71. Welter, "Coming of Age," *Dimity Conventions*, 3–20.

72. Brady, "Their Mothers' Daughters," 255–64.

73. Linda Gordon, *Heroes of Their Own Lives: The Politics and History of Family Violence, Boston, 1880–1960* (New York: The Viking Press, 1988), discusses incest and other types of domestic violence, but not in explicitly middle-class families.

74. Bryan Strong, "Toward a History of the Experiential Family: Sex and Incest in the Nineteenth Century Family," *Journal of Marriage and Family* 35 (1973): 457–66. See also Ryan, *Empire of the Mother*, 45–58. Before labeling mothers and sons as deviant, however, it is necessary to examine differing definitions of sexuality, as Smith-Rosenberg suggests in regard to her findings on women's bonds in *Disorderly Conduct*, 74–76.

75. Rotundo, "American Fatherhood"; and Demos, "The Changing Faces of Fatherhood."

76. Ryan, *Cradle of the Middle Class*, 145–85.

77. Lasch, *Haven in a Heartless World*.

78. Theriot, *Biosocial Construction*, 93–97.

79. The phrase is Jane Adams's, but it was widely used by others. For an overall picture of women's changing roles see Sheila Rothman, *Woman's Proper Place: A History of Changing Ideals and Practices: 1870 to the Present* (New York: Basic Books, 1978), 13–93; Barbara Solomon, *In the Company of Educated Women: A History of Women and Higher Education in America* (New Haven, Conn.: Yale University Press, 1985), 1–93; Peter Gabriel Filene, *Him/Her/Self: Sex Roles in Modern America* (Baltimore, Md.: Johns Hopkins University Press, 1986), 6–38; Lillian Faderman, *Surpassing the Love of Men: Romantic Friendships and Love between Women from the Renaissance to the Present* (New York: William Morrow & Co., 1981), 145–230; D'Emilio and Freedman, *Intimate Matters*, 188–94; Kathryn Kish Sklar, "Hull House in the 1890s: A Community of Women Reformers," *Signs* 10 (1985): 658–77; Maureen Fastenau, "Maternal Government: The Settlement Houses and the Politicalization of Women's Sphere, 1889–1920" (Ph.D. diss., Duke University, 1982); Wayne Roberts, " 'Rocking the Cradle for the World': The New Woman and Maternal Feminism, Toronto, 1877–1914," in *A Not Unreasonable Claim: Women and Reform in Canada, 1880s–1920s*, ed. Linda Kealey (Toronto: The Woman's Press, 1979), 15–45; and Paula Baker, "Domestication of American Politics," *American Historical Review* 89 (1984): 620–49.

80. D'Emilio and Freedman, *Intimate Matters*, 202–21; Epstein, *The Politics of*

Domesticity; Joseph Hawes, *Children in Urban Society: Juvenile Delinquency in Nine-teenth-Century America* (New York: Oxford University Press, 1971); Ronald Cohen, "Child Saving and Progressivism, 1885–1915," in *American Childhood*, 273–309; Anthony Platt, *The Child Savers: The Invention of Delinquency* (Chicago: University of Chicago Press, 1969); David Pivar, *Purity Crusade: Sexual Morality and Social Control, 1868–1900* (Westport, Conn.: Greenwood Press, 1973); Pleck, *Domestic Tyranny*, 43–144; and Gordon, *Heroes of Their Own Lives*, 27–81. Current scholarship on the Progressive movement emphasizes the variety and contra-dictions among different groups labeled as "Progressives."

81. James McGovern, "David Graham Phillips and the Virility Impulse of Progressives," *New England Quarterly* 34 (1966): 333–48; Joe L. Duberman, "Pro-gressivism and the Masculinity Crisis," in *The American Man*, ed. Elizabeth H. Pleck and Joseph H. Pleck (Englewood Cliffs, N.J.: Prentice-Hall, 1980), 303–20; Jeffrey P. Hantover, "The Boy Scouts and the Validation of Masculinity," in *The American Man*, 285–301; and Filene, *Him/Her/Self*, 69–112.

82. James R. McGovern, "The American Woman's Pre-World-War Manners and Morals," *Journal of American History* 55 (1968): 315–33; D'Emilio and Freed-man, *Intimate Matters*, 177–255; and Mintz and Kellogg, *Domestic Revolutions*, 107–31.

83. Cynthia Russett, *Sexual Science: The Victorian Construct of Womanhood* (Cam-bridge: Cambridge University Press, 1989); Kathleen W. Jones, "Sentiment and Science: The Late Nineteenth Century Pediatrician as Mother's Advisor," *Journal of Social History* 17 (1983): 79–96; Smith-Rosenberg, "The Hysterical Woman" and "The Abortion Movement," in her *Disorderly Conduct*, 197–244; and Anita Clair Fellman and Michael Fellman, *Making Sense of Self: Medical Advice Literature in Late Nineteenth-Century America* (Philadelphia: University of Pennsylvania Press, 1981).

84. Linda Gordon, *Woman's Body, Woman's Right*; James Mohr, *Abortion in America: The Origins and Evolution of National Policy, 1800–1900* (New York: Ox-ford University Press, 1978); May, *Great Expectations*; and Mintz and Kellogg, *Domestic Revolutions*, 109–20.

85. Paula Fass, *The Damned and the Beautiful: American Youth in the 1920's* (New York: Oxford University Press, 1977); Smith-Rosenberg, "The New Woman as Androgyne," in her *Disorderly Conduct*, 245–96; Filene, *Him/Her/Self*, 123–47; Gordon, "From an Unfortunate Necessity to a Cult of Mutual Orgasm"; and Rothman, *Woman's Proper Place*, 177–218.

86. Christina Simmons, "Modern Sexuality and the Myth of Victorian Repres-sion," in *Passion and Power: Sexuality in History*, 157–77, ed. Kathy Peiss and Christina Simmons (Philadelphia, Pa.: Temple University Press, 1989); Nathan Hale, *Freud and the Americans: The Beginnings of Psychoanalysis in the United States, 1876–1917* (New York: Oxford University Press, 1971); and Paul Robinson, *The Modernization of Sex: Havelock Ellis, Alfred Kinsey, William Masters, and Virginia Johnson* (New York: Harper and Row, 1976).

87. Lillian Faderman, *Surpassing*, 233–37; and Christina Simmons, "Compa-nionate Marriage and the Lesbian Threat," *Frontiers* 4 (1979): 54–59.

88. Barbara Ehrenreich and Deirdre English, *For Her Own Good: 150 Years of the Experts' Advice to Women* (Garden City, N.J.: Anchor/Doubleday, 1978), 183–210; Nancy Pottishman Weiss, "Mother, the Invention of Necessity: Dr. Ben-

jamin Spock's *Baby and Child Care*," in *Growing Up in America*, 283–303; Susan Tiffin, *In Whose Best Interests? Child Welfare Reform in the Progressive Era* (Westport, Conn.: Greenwood Press, 1982); and Margaret Steinfels O'Brien, *Who's Minding the Children? The History and Politics of Day Care in America* (New York: Simon and Schuster, 1973), 34–63.

89. Barbara Finkelstein, "Uncle Sam and the Children: History of Government Involvement in Child Rearing," in *Growing Up in America*, 255–68; Weiss, "Mother, the Invention of Necessity"; Molly Ladd-Taylor, *Raising a Baby the Government Way: Mothers' Letters to the Children's Bureau* (New Brunswick, N.J.: Rutgers University Press, 1986).

90. Hamilton Cravens, "Child-Saving in the Age of Professionalism, 1915–1930," in *American Childhood*, 415–88.

REFERENCES

Baker, Paula. "Domestication of American Politics." *American Historical Review* 89 (1984): 620–49.

Barker-Benfield, G. J. "The Spermatic Economy: A Nineteenth-Century View." In *The American Family in Social-Historical Perspective*, 2d ed., ed. Michael Gordon, 374–402. New York: St. Martin's Press, 1978.

Basch, Norma. *In the Eyes of the Law: Women, Marriage and Property in Nineteenth-Century New York*. Ithaca, N.Y.: Cornell University Press, 1982.

Baym, Nina. *Women's Fiction: A Guide to Novels by and about Women in America, 1820–1870*. Ithaca, N.Y.: Cornell University Press, 1978.

Bloch, Ruth H. "American Feminine Ideals in Transition: The Rise of the Moral Mother, 1785–1815." *Feminist Studies* 4 (1978): 101–26.

Boylan, Anne. "Growing Up Female in Young America, 1800–1860." In *American Childhood: A Research Guide and Historical Handbook*, ed. Joseph M. Hawes and N. Ray Hiner, 153–84. Westport, Conn.: Greenwood Press, 1985.

Brady, Marilyn Dell. "Their Mothers' Daughters: Perceptions of Motherhood in Autobiographies by Selected American Women, 1920–1940." Ph.D. diss., University of Kansas, 1987.

Brumberg, Joan Jacobs. *Fasting Girls: The Emergence of Anorexia Nervosa as a Modern Disease*. Cambridge, Mass.: Harvard University Press, 1988.

Burnham, John. *Paths into American Culture: Psychology, Medicine, and Morals*. Philadelphia, Pa.: Temple University Press, 1988.

Bushman, Richard. "Family Security in the Transition from Farm to City, 1750–1850." *Journal of Family History* 6 (Fall 1981): 238–56.

Censer, Jane Turner. *North Carolina Planters and Their Children, 1800–1860*. Baton Rouge: Louisiana State University Press, 1984.

Chambers-Schiller, Virginia. *Liberty, A Better Husband: Single Women in America, The Generations of 1780–1840*. New Haven, Conn.: Yale University Press, 1984.

Chodorow, Nancy. *Reproduction of Mothering: Psychoanalysis and the Sociology of Gender*. Berkeley: University of California Press, 1978.

Clark, Clifford Edward. *The American Family Home, 1800–1960*. Chapel Hill: University of North Carolina Press, 1986.

———. "Domestic Architecture as an Index to Social History: The Romantic

Revival and the Cult of Domesticity in America, 1840–1870." *Journal of Interdisciplinary History* 7 (1976): 33–56.

Cogan, Frances. *All-American Girl: The Ideal of Real Womanhood in Mid-Nineteenth-Century America.* Athens: University of Georgia Press, 1989.

Cohen, Ronald. "Child Saving and Progressivism, 1885–1915." In *American Childhood: A Research Guide and Historical Handbook,* ed. Joseph M. Hawes and N. Ray Hiner, 273–310. Westport, Conn.: Greenwood Press, 1985.

Coontz, Stephanie. *The Social Origins of Private Life: A History of American Families.* New York: Verso, 1988.

Cott, Nancy F. *The Bonds of Womanhood: "Woman's Sphere" in New England, 1780–1835.* New Haven, Conn.: Yale University Press, 1977.

———. "Notes toward an Interpretation of Antebellum Childrearing." *The Psychohistorical Review* 6 (Spring 1978): 4–20.

———. "Passionlessness: An Interpretation of Victorian Sexual Ideology, 1790–1850." In *A Heritage of Her Own,* edited by Nancy F. Cott and Elizabeth H. Pleck, 162–81. New York: Simon and Schuster, 1979.

———. "Young Women in the Second Great Awakening in New England." *Feminist Studies* 3 (Fall 1975): 15–29.

Cowan, Ruth Schwartz. *More Work for Mother: The Ironies of Household Technology from the Open Hearth to the Microwave.* New York: Basic Books, 1983.

Crandall, John C. "Patriotism and Humanitarian Reform in Children's Literature, 1825–1860." *American Quarterly* 21 (1969): 3–22.

Cravens, Hamilton. "Child-Saving in the Age of Professionalism, 1915–1930." In *American Childhood: A Research Guide and Historical Handbook,* ed. Joseph M. Hawes and N. Ray Hiner, 415–88. Westport, Conn.: Greenwood Press, 1985.

Davidoff, Leonore, and Catherine Hall. *Family Fortunes: Men and Women of the English Middle Class, 1780–1850.* London: Hutchinson, 1987.

Degler, Carl N. *At Odds: Women and the Family in America from the Revolution to the Present.* New York: Oxford University Press, 1980.

———. "What Ought to Be and What Was: Women's Sexuality in the Nineteenth Century." In *The American Family in Social-Historical Perspective,* 2d ed., ed. Michael Gordon, 403–25. New York: St. Martin's Press, 1978.

D'Emilio, John, and Estelle B. Freedman. *Intimate Matters: A History of Sexuality in America.* New York: Basic Books, 1988.

Demos, John. *Past, Present, and Personal: The Family and the Life Course in American History.* New York: Oxford University Press, 1986.

Douglas, Ann. *The Feminization of American Culture.* New York: Alfred A. Knopf, 1977.

Duberman, Joe L. "Progressivism and the Masculinity Crisis." In *The American Man,* ed. Elizabeth H. Pleck and Joseph H. Pleck, 303–20. Englewood Cliffs, N.J.: Prentice-Hall, 1980.

DuBois, Ellen. *Feminism and Suffrage: The Emergence of an Independent Women's Movement in America.* Ithaca, N.Y.: Cornell University Press, 1978.

DuBois, Ellen, et al. "Politics and Culture in Women's History: A Symposium." *Feminist Studies* 6 (1980): 26–64.

Dye, Nancy Schrom, and Daniel Blake Smith. "Mother Love and Infant Death, 1750–1920." *Journal of American History* 73 (1986): 329–53.

Ehrenreich, Barbara, and Deirdre English. *For Her Own Good: 150 Years of the Experts' Advice to Women.* Garden City, N.J.: Anchor/Doubleday, 1978.

Elbert, Sarah. *A Hunger for Home: Louisa May Alcott's Place in American Literature.* New Brunswick, N.J.: Rutgers University Press, 1987.

Elder, Glen H., Jr. "History and the Family: The Discovery of Complexity." *Journal of Marriage and the Family* 43 (1981): 439–519.

Epstein, Barbara. *The Politics of Domesticity: Women, Evangelism, and Temperance in Nineteenth-Century America.* Middletown, Conn.: Wesleyan University Press, 1981.

Faderman, Lillian. *Surpassing the Love of Men: Romantic Friendships and Love between Women from the Renaissance to the Present.* New York: Wiliam Morrow & Co., 1981.

Fass, Paula. *The Damned and the Beautiful: American Youth in the 1920's.* New York: Oxford University Press, 1977.

Fastenau, Maureen. "Maternal Government: The Settlement Houses and the Politicalization of Women's Sphere, 1889–1920." Ph.D. diss., Duke University, 1982.

Fellman, Anita Clair, and Michael Fellman. *Making Sense of Self: Medical Advice Literature in Late Nineteenth-Century America.* Philadelphia: University of Pennsylvania Press, 1981.

Filene, Peter Gabriel. *Him/Her/Self: Sex Roles in Modern America.* 2d ed. Baltimore, Md.: Johns Hopkins University Press, 1986.

Finkelstein, Barbara. "Casting Networks of Good Influence: The Reconstruction of Childhood in the United States, 1790–1870." In *American Childhood: A Research Guide and Historical Handbook,* ed. Joseph M. Hawes and N. Ray Hiner, 111–52. Westport, Conn.: Greenwood Press, 1985.

———. "Uncle Sam and the Children: History of Government Involvement in Child Rearing." In *Growing Up in America: Children in Historical Perspective,* ed. N. Ray Hiner and Joseph M. Hawes, 255–68. Urbana: University of Illinois Press, 1985.

Freedman, Estelle. "The New Woman: Changing Views of Women in the 1920's." *Journal of American History* 61 (1974): 372–93.

———. "Sexuality in Nineteenth-Century America: Behavior, Ideology and Politics." *Reviews in American History* 10 (1982): 196–215.

Gordon, Jean, and Jan MacArthur. "American Women and Domestic Consumption, 1800–1920." In *Making the American Home: Middle-Class Women and Domestic Material Culture, 1840–1940,* ed. Marilyn Ferris Motz and Pat Browne, 27–47. Bowling Green, Ohio: Bowling Green University, 1988.

Gordon, Linda. *Heroes of Their Own Lives: The Politics and History of Family Violence, Boston, 1880–1960.* New York: The Viking Press, 1988.

———. *Woman's Body, Woman's Rights: A Social History of Birth Control in America.* New York: Penguin Books, 1976.

Gordon, Michael. "From an Unfortunate Necessity to a Cult of Mutual Orgasm: Sex in American Marital Educational Literature, 1830–1940." In *Studies in the Sociology of Sex,* ed. James Henslin, 53–80. New York: Appleton-Century Crofts, 1971.

Gordon, Michael, and M. Charles Bernstein. "Mate Choice and Domestic Life in the Nineteenth-Century Marriage Manual." *Journal of Marriage and the*

Family 32 (1970): 665–74.

Griswold, Robert. *Family and Divorce in California, 1850–1890: Victorian Illusions and Everyday Realities.* Albany: State University of New York Press, 1982.

Grossberg, Michael. *Governing the Hearth: Law and Family in Nineteenth-Century America.* Chapel Hill: University of North Carolina Press, 1985.

Hale, Nathan. *Freud and the Americans: The Beginnings of Psychoanalysis in the United States, 1876–1917.* New York: Oxford University Press, 1971.

Hall, Jacquelyn Dowd. "Partial Truths." *Signs: Journal of Women in Culture and Society* 14 (1989): 902–11.

Haller, John S., Jr., and Robin M. Haller. *The Physician and Sexuality in Victorian America.* Urbana: University of Illinois Press, 1974.

Hantover, Jeffrey P. "The Boy Scouts and the Validation of Masculinity." In *The American Man,* ed. Elizabeth H. Pleck and Joseph H. Pleck, 285–301. Englewood Cliffs, N.J.: Prentice-Hall, 1980.

Hareven, Tamara K. *Anonymous Americans: Explorations in Nineteenth-Century Social History.* Englewood Cliffs, N.J.: Prentice-Hall, 1971.

Hawes, Joseph. *Children in Urban Society: Juvenile Delinquency in Nineteenth-Century America.* New York: Oxford University Press, 1971.

Hawes, Joseph M., and N. Ray Hiner, eds. *American Childhood: A Research Guide and Historical Handbook.* Westport, Conn.: Greenwood Press, 1985.

Hayden, Dolores. *The Grand Domestic Revolution: A History of Feminist Designs for American Homes, Neighborhoods, and Cities.* Cambridge, Mass.: MIT Press, 1981.

Hersh, Blanche Glassman. *The Slavery of Sex: Feminist-Abolitionists in America.* Urbana: University of Illinois Press, 1978.

Hiner, N. Ray, and Joseph M. Hawes, eds. *Growing Up in America: Children in Historical Perspective.* Urbana: University of Illinois Press, 1985.

Hoffert, Sylvia. *Private Matters: American Attitudes toward Childbearing and Infant Nurture in the Urban North, 1800–1860.* Urbana: University of Illinois Press, 1989.

Jeffrey, Kirk. "The Family as Utopian Retreat from the City." *Soundings* 55 (1972): 21–41.

———. "Marriage, Career, and Feminine Ideology in Nineteenth-Century America: Reconstructing the Marital Experience of Lydia Maria Child, 1828–1874." *Feminist Studies* 7 (1981): 113–30.

Jones, Kathleen W. "Sentiment and Science: The Late Nineteenth Century Pediatrician as Mother's Advisor." *Journal of Social History* 17 (1983): 79–96.

Kelley, Mary. *Private Women, Public Stage: Literary Domesticity in Nineteenth-Century America.* New York: Oxford University Press, 1984.

Kelly, R. Gordon. *Mother Was a Lady: Self and Society in Selected American Children's Periodicals, 1865–1890.* Westport, Conn.: Greenwood Press, 1974.

Kerber, Linda. "The Republican Mother: Women and the Enlightenment, An American Perspective." *American Quarterly* 28 (1976): 187–205.

———. "Separate Spheres, Female Worlds, Woman's Place." *Journal of American History* 75 (1988): 9–39.

———. *Women of the Republic: Intellect and Ideology in Revolutionary America.* Chapel Hill: University of North Carolina Press, 1980.

Kern, Louis. *An Ordered Love: Sex Roles and Sexuality in Victorian America.* Chapel

Hill: University of North Carolina Press, 1977.

Kett, Joseph. *Rites of Passage: Adolescence in America, 1790 to the Present.* New York: Basic Books, 1977.

Kiefer, Monica. *American Children through Their Books, 1700–1835.* Philadelphia: University of Pennsylvania Press, 1948.

Kuhn, Anne. *The Mother's Role in Childhood Education: New England Concepts, 1830–1860.* New Haven, Conn.: Yale University Press, 1947.

Ladd-Taylor, Molly. *Raising a Baby the Government Way: Mothers' Letters to the Children's Bureau, 1915–1932.* New Brunswick, N.J.: Rutgers University Press, 1986.

Lasch, Christopher. *Haven in a Heartless World: The Family Besieged.* New York: Basic Books, 1977.

Lebsock, Suzanne. *The Free Women of Petersburg: Status and Culture in a Southern Town, 1784–1860.* New York: W. W. Norton & Company, 1984.

Lewis, Jan. *The Pursuit of Happiness: Family and Values in Jefferson's Virginia.* Cambridge: Cambridge University Press, 1983.

Lystra, Karen. *Searching the Heart: Women, Men, and Romantic Love in Nineteenth-Century America.* New York: Oxford University Press, 1989.

McDannell, Colleen. *The Christian Home in Victorian America, 1840–1900.* Bloomington: Indiana University Press, 1986.

McGlone, Robert Elno. "Suffer the Children: The Emergence of Middle-Class Family Life in America, 1820–1870." Ph.D. diss., UCLA, 1971.

McGovern, James R. "The American Woman's Pre-World-War Manners and Morals." *Journal of American History* 55 (1968): 315–33.

———. "David Graham Phillips and the Virility Impulse of Progressives." *New England Quarterly* 34 (1966): 333–48.

MacLeod, Anne. *A Moral Tale: Children's Fiction and American Culture, 1820–1860.* Hartford, Conn.: Anchor Books, 1975.

McLoughlin, William. "Evangelical Child Rearing in the Age of Jackson: Francis Wayland's Views on When and How to Subdue Willfulness of Children." In *Growing Up in America: Children in Historical Perspective,* ed. N. Ray Hiner and Joseph M. Hawes, 86–107. Urbana: University of Illinois Press, 1985.

McNall, Sally Allen. *Who Is in the House: A Psychological Study of Two Centuries of Women's Fiction in America, 1795 to the Present.* New York: Elsevier, 1981.

Marsh, Margaret. *Suburban Lives.* New Brunswick, N.J.: Rutgers University Press, 1990.

May, Elaine Taylor. *Great Expectations: Marriage and Divorce in Post-Victorian America.* Chicago: University of Chicago Press, 1980.

Mechling, Jay. "Advice to Historians on Advice to Mothers." *Journal of Social History* 9 (1975): 44–63.

Milden, James Wallace. "The Sacred Sanctuary: Family Life in 19th-Century America." Ph.D. diss., University of Maryland, 1974.

Mintz, Steven. *A Prison of Expectations: The Family in Victorian Culture.* New York: New York University Press, 1983.

Mintz, Steven, and Susan Kellogg. *Domestic Revolutions: A Social History of American Family Life.* New York: The Free Press, 1988.

Mohr, James. *Abortion in America: The Origins and Evolution of National Policy, 1800–1900.* New York: Oxford University Press, 1978.

Morantz-Sanchez, Regina Markell. *Sympathy and Science: Women Physicians in American Medicine*. New York: Oxford University Press, 1985.

Motz, Marilyn Ferris. *The True Sisterhood: Michigan Women and Their Kin, 1820–1920*. Albany: State University of New York Press, 1983.

O'Brien, Margaret Steinfels. *Who's Minding the Children? The History and Politics of Day Care in America*. New York: Simon and Schuster, 1973.

Papashvily, Helen. *All the Happy Endings*. New York: Harper and Row, 1956.

Peal, Ethel. "The Atrophied Rib: Urban Middle-Class Women in Jacksonian America." Ph.D. diss., University of Pittsburgh, 1970.

Pivar, David. *Purity Crusade: Sexual Morality and Social Control, 1868–1900*. Westport, Conn.: Greenwood Press, 1973.

Platt, Anthony. *The Child Savers: The Invention of Delinquency*. Chicago: University of Chicago Press, 1969.

Pleck, Elizabeth. *Domestic Tyranny: The Making of American Social Policy against Family Violence from Colonial Times to the Present*. New York: Oxford University Press, 1987.

Pleck, Elizabeth H., and Joseph H. Pleck, eds. *The American Man*. Englewood Cliffs, N.J.: Prentice-Hall, 1980.

Pugh, David. *Sons of Liberty: The Masculine Mind in Nineteenth-Century America*. Westport, Conn.: Greenwood Press, 1983.

Reed, James. *Private Vice to Public Virtue: The Birth Control Movement and American Society since 1830*. New York: Basic Books, 1978.

Roberts, Wayne. " 'Rocking the Cradle for the World': The New Woman and Maternal Feminism, Toronto, 1877–1914." In *A Not Unreasonable Claim: Women and Reform in Canada, 1880–1920*, ed. Linda Kealey. Toronto: The Woman's Press, 1979.

Robinson, Paul H. *The Modernization of Sex: Havelock Ellis, Alfred Kinsey, William Masters, and Virginia Johnson*. New York: Harper and Row, 1976.

Rosenberg, Charles E. "Sexuality, Class, and Role in Nineteenth-Century America." *American Quarterly* 25 (May 1973): 131–53.

Rothman, Ellen K. *Hands and Hearts: A History of Courtship in America*. New York: Basic Books, 1984.

Rothman, Sheila M. *Woman's Proper Place: A History of Changing Ideals and Practices: 1870 to the Present*. New York: Basic Books, 1978.

Rotundo, E. Anthony. "American Fatherhood: A Historical Perspective." *American Behavioral Scientist* 29 (1985): 7–25.

———. "Manhood in America: The Northern Middle Class, 1770–1920." Ph.D. diss., Brandeis University, 1982.

Russett, Cynthia. *Sexual Science: The Victorian Construct of Womanhood*. Cambridge: Cambridge University Press, 1989.

Ryan, Mary P. *Cradle of the Middle Class: The Family in Oneida County, New York, 1790–1865*. Cambridge: Cambridge University Press, 1981.

———. *The Empire of the Mother: American Writing about Domesticity, 1830–1860*. New York: Haworth Press, 1982.

———. *Womanhood in America*. New York: New Viewpoints, 1979.

———. *Women in Public: Between Banners and Ballots*. Baltimore, Md.: Johns Hopkins University Press, 1990.

Scott, Joan Wallach. *Gender and the Politics of History*. New York: Columbia University Press, 1988.

Simmons, Christina. "Companionate Marriage and the Lesbian Threat." *Frontiers* 4 (1979): 54–59.

———. "Modern Sexuality and the Myth of Victorian Repression." In *Passion and Power: Sexuality in History*, ed. Kathy Peiss and Christina Simmons, 157–77. Philadelphia, Pa.: Temple University Press, 1989.

Sklar, Kathryn Kish. *Catharine Beecher: A Study in American Domesticity*. New Haven, Conn.: Yale University Press, 1973.

———. "Hull House in the 1890s: A Community of Women Reformers." *Signs: Journal of Women in Culture and Society* 10 (1985): 658–77.

Smith, Daniel Blake. *Inside the Great House: Planter Family Life in Eighteenth-Century Chesapeake Society*. Ithaca, N.Y.: Cornell University Press, 1980.

Smith, Daniel Scott. "Family Limitation, Sexual Control, and Domestic Feminism in Victorian America." *Feminist Studies* 1 (1973): 40–58.

Smith-Rosenberg, Carroll. *Disorderly Conduct: Visions of Gender in Victorian America*. New York: Oxford University Press, 1985.

Smith-Rosenberg, Carroll, and Charles Rosenberg. "The Female Animal: Medical Views of Woman and Her Role in Nineteenth-Century America." *Journal of American History* 60 (1973): 332–56.

Solomon, Barbara. *In the Company of Educated Women: A History of Women and Higher Education in America*. New Haven, Conn.: Yale University Press, 1985.

Spurlock, John. *Free Love: Marriage and Middle-Class Radicalism in America, 1825–1860*. New York: New York University Press, 1988.

Stearns, Carol Z., and Peter Stearns. "Victorian Sexuality: Can Historians Do It Better?" *Journal of Social History* 18 (1985): 625–34.

Stearns, Peter N. *Be a Man! Males in Modern Society*. New York: Holmes & Meier Publishers, 1979.

Stowe, Steven. *Intimacy and Power in the Old South: Ritual in the Lives of the Planters*. Baltimore, Md.: Johns Hopkins University Press, 1987.

Strickland, Charles. "A Transcendental Father: The Childrearing Practices of Bronson Alcott." *Perspectives in American History* 3 (1969): 5–73.

———. *Victorian Domesticity: Families in the Life and Art of Louisa May Alcott*. University: University of Alabama Press, 1985.

Strong, Bryan. "Toward a History of the Experiential Family: Sex and Incest in the Nineteenth Century Family." *Journal of Marriage and the Family* 35 (1973): 457–66.

Theriot, Nancy. *The Biosocial Construction of Femininity: Mothers and Daughters in Nineteenth-Century America*. Westport, Conn.: Greenwood Press, 1988.

Tiffin, Susan. *In Whose Best Interests? Child Welfare Reform in the Progressive Era*. Westport, Conn.: Greenwood Press, 1982.

Walters, Ronald. "The Family and Antebellum Reform." *Societas* 3 (1973): 221–32.

Weiss, Nancy Pottishman. "Mother, the Invention of Necessity: Dr. Benjamin Spock's *Baby and Child Care*." In *Growing Up in America: Children in Historical Perspective*, ed. N. Ray Hiner and Joseph M. Hawes, 283–303. Urbana: University of Illinois Press, 1985.

Wells, Robert V. "Women's Lives Transformed: Demographic and Family Patterns in America, 1600–1970." In *Women's America*, ed. Linda Kerber and Jane de Hart Matthews, 16–36. New York: Oxford University Press, 1982.

Welter, Barbara. "The Cult of True Womanhood: 1800–1860." *American Quarterly* 18 (1966): 151–75.

———. *Dimity Conventions: The American Woman in the Nineteenth Century.* Athens: Ohio University Press, 1976.

Wishy, Bernard. *The Child and the Republic: The Dawn of Modern Child Nurture.* Philadelphia: University of Pennsylvania Press, 1968.

Woloch, Nancy. *Women and the American Experience.* New York: Alfred A. Knopf, 1984.

Wood, Ann Douglas. "The 'Scribbling Women' and Fanny Fern: Why Women Wrote." *American Quarterly* 28 (1971): 3–24.

Wright, Gwendolyn. *Building the Dream: A Social History of Housing in America*, 2d ed. Cambridge, Mass.: MIT Press, 1983.

———. *Moralism and the Model Home: Domestic Architecture and Cultural Conflict in Chicago, 1873–1913.* Chicago: University of Chicago Press, 1980.

Wyatt-Brown, Bertram. "Conscience and Career: Young Abolitionists and Missionaries Compared." In *Yankee Saints and Southern Sinners*, ed. Bertram Wyatt-Brown, 42–75. Baton Rouge: Louisiana State University Press, 1985.

———. *Southern Honor: Ethics and Behavior in the Old South.* New York: Oxford University Press, 1982.

———. "Three Generations of Yankee Parenthood: The Tappen Family, a Case Study of Antebellum Nurture." *Illinois Quarterly* 38 (Fall 1975): 12–28.

Zaretsky, Eli. *Capitalism, The Family, and Personal Life.* New York: Harper and Row, 1973.

5

Families Face the Great Depression (1930–1940)

Winifred D. Wandersee

The Great Depression of the 1930s has been the subject of literary accounts ranging from autobiography and biography to novels, essays, documentaries, and short stories. The pathos of the period has been captured in tragic, humorous, and heroic terms through film and literature. Nearly anyone growing up in the mid-to-late twentieth century has heard Depression-era stories from older family members, schoolteachers, and television commentators. With the possible exception of World War II, the Great Depression stands out as perhaps the most important generational experience of the twentieth century. It is part of our America folklore and clearly a formative event in our sociopolitical coming of age. Along with World War I, it forms a watershed of family change in the twentieth century.

And yet for all of its importance, for all of the romance and the reality, and finally, for all of the availability of primary sources, there have been few historical interpretations of the family in the Great Depression. The several works of scholarly interest that appeared in the early eighties had a focus upon particular social categories—women, blacks, ethnic groups, workers—rather than upon the overall changes that occurred as a direct outgrowth of the Depression.[1] There is a certain logic to this tendency, since one of the hallmarks of the Great Depression is the variation in its impact. Although the economic crisis may have provided a generational experience, the burdens of this experience were not equally shared. Thus interpreting the 1930s requires a sensitivity to the history of a diverse, socially segregated experience, influenced by class, race, and ethnicity, as well as a recognition of a certain commonality of experience.

But in addition, the social historian cannot help but be aware of the concerns of contemporaries who were involved in analyzing what they

saw as the crisis of the modern American family, which went beyond
the exigencies of unemployment to affect the whole direction of modern
family life.[2] The contemporary literature on the family of the 1930s was
immense, and it reflected the growth of the social sciences—in particular,
sociology and psychology—as well as a growing concern about family
breakdown under the pressure of changing values. The issues raised
had been emerging for several decades, but until the Great Depression
they were couched in terms of a "culture of abundance," as Warren
Susman has pointed out in his interpretation of American culture in the
twentieth century. Indeed, Susman argues that even in 1933, in the
depths of the Depression, Franklin Roosevelt's speeches argued for a
world of abundance; only some technical difficulties with distribution
kept the American people from their rightful share of that abundance.[3]

This culture of abundance is a critical underlying theme of twentieth-
century American family life. The economic transformation that occurred in the early decades of the century, as America went from an
industrial society to a service and consumer society, had an impact upon
American families that greatly affected their response to the Great
Depression. What made the depression of the thirties different from
earlier depressions was not merely the fact that it was worldwide and of
greater intensity and length than any previous depression: it also came
at the culmination of several decades of unprecedented prosperity—
decades in which many families were making the important and nearly
irreversible adaptation to a mass consumption society.[4]

The changes that were occurring within the context of American family life in the 1930s were in part the consequence of economic crisis, but
to a larger extent, part of the long-term change in social and economic
values affecting family life. Thus, the twentieth-century family was
clearly viewed as "the family under pressure" by sociologists, psychologists, social reformers, and caseworkers. But the burgeoning interest in
family studies was no doubt also reflective of a general interest in defining
the nature of American civilization—a pastime that particularly occupied
intellectuals of the 1920s.

Warren Susman has explored this topic in his essay, "Culture and
Civilization: The Nineteen-Twenties." By 1922, many American intellectuals believed that the structure of their world—natural, technological, social, personal, and moral—was rapidly changing.

One of the more striking observed results of the structural changes in the social
order was that a larger proportion of it was increasingly engaged in professionals
seeking to understand it, with a special calling to "know" the world as writers,
artists, intellectuals, journalists, scientists, social scientists, philosophers,
teachers.[5]

The professionalization of social inquiry had a particularly strong impact upon studies of family life and childrearing. Christopher Lasch has analyzed this development and scrutinized its impact in his controversial critique of twentieth-century family policy. He argues that the "so-called helping professions," in their attempts to "save" the family, actually contributed to the deterioration of domestic life. "The family did not simply evolve in response to social and economic influences; it was deliberately transformed by the intervention of planners and policymakers."[6]

Lasch is critical of the sociological theory of the modern family that emerged in the 1920s and 1930s. Its central tenet was an abstract and impersonal evolutionary process known as "the transfer of functions." Agencies outside of the family, such as schools, welfare agencies, hospitals, and social workers, had expropriated the functions of the family, especially its parental functions. Lasch calls this process "the socialization of reproduction." He argues that the social experts of this era were convinced that the family was in the midst of a painful but necessary transition, and that it would adapt only by emphasizing its affectional and companionship functions. Meanwhile, the community would take on the functions that the family could no longer do for itself.[7]

What the experts saw as a positive adaptation, Lasch saw as a destructive force undermining the stability of family, the authority of parents, and the security of children within the family. As a consequence, the individual in modern society has lost his or her "haven in a heartless world" and is subjected to the pressures of the state and the marketplace. The gradual erosion of the authoritarian family led to the reestablishment of political despotism in a form based on the dissolution of the family. "Instead of liberating the individual from external coercion, the decay of family life subjects him to new forms of domination, while at the same time weakening his ability to resist them.[8] What Lasch does not do, at least not directly, is to consider to what extent the Great Depression, and in particular the reforms of the New Deal, contributed to this transfer of functions. In fact, his interpretation seems peculiarly detached from the reality of the Depression and the extreme conditions of economic deprivation that affected so many families. But interestingly enough, many of the family studies of the 1930s treated the Depression as a sideshow to the main event.

The Lynds' famous studies of Middletown revealed the transformation in values that had occurred since the late nineteenth century and the sense that the residents lacked control over those changes within their own families.[9] The new material culture, the automobile, the freedom of youth, the intrusion of school and community into the life of the family—these were all factors that Middletown residents observed, almost passively, with little or no sense of their ability to protect themselves or their children from the consequences.

For instance, parental concern for their children was mirrored by increased community involvement through the child welfare movement, health centers, playgrounds, youth organizations, camps, and religious agencies. Thus, the Middletown mother saw less of her children because of their involvement in school and community, and she probably had access to many resources for information on and assistance with child raising. But she was also under a great deal of pressure to produce happy and well-adjusted children under complicated conditions. A Middletown mother expressed her confusion: "Life was simpler for my mother.... In those days one did not realize that there was so much to be known about the care of children. I realize that I ought to be half a dozen experts, but I'm afraid of making mistakes and usually do not know where to go for advice."[10]

This confusion was probably exacerbated rather than alleviated by the profusion of expertise in the newly emergent field of child studies. The child-saving movement had emerged at the turn of the century as an underlying theme of the Progressive era. In its early stages, it was primarily a reaction to the social chaos that accompanied the rapid urbanization and industrialization of America, contributing to broken families, inadequate schools, juvenile delinquency, dangers to health and morality, poverty and dependency. Reformers wanted to "save" the children from these dire conditions, but as some historians have argued, they also wanted to control them.[11]

The early efforts at child saving emphasized reform of the child's life circumstances through public policy, but from about 1915 to the 1930s the emphasis changed to professional activities: "to the use of the human sciences and technologies to investigate children, or, more precisely, the so-called normal child, as the necessary precondition of further public action." The professional child savers strongly believed that research must precede social intervention and application. They were more conscious than their predecessors of the Progressive era that the scientific and medical conceptions of children were beginning to change. By the early 1930s, the professionalization of organized child saving was well entrenched within the academic culture, aided by philanthropy, primarily because the federal and state governments still played a very limited role in this realm. The professionalized, academic approach to child saving paralleled the "search for culture" that also occupied the intellectual elite of the 1930s. The sense that there existed an American national and cultural identity meant that there was also a "normal child" within that identity. It was the task of the modern parent to assure that her child measured up to the normal child that was the creation of the experts.[12]

The changing character of childhood was a concern of relatively long duration that preceded the Great Depression and continued to create anxiety in the midst of economic deprivation. Closely related was the changing status of women. The new morality, women's position in the work force, in high schools, colleges and universities, and in the speak-easies and dance halls of America excited comment that probably over-stated the reality of any actual transformation of gender roles. But historian Dorothy M. Brown has observed that the "new woman" entered the decade of the twenties in many guises. Her numbers "included vet-eran reformers, victorious suffragists, powerful athletes, pioneering sci-entists, Marxists, bohemians, and aviators.... The magazines of the decade were filled with attempts to cut through the variety, to predict her course and the implications for American society, and to sort out just who this new woman was."[13]

Alice Kessler-Harris supports this colorful interpretation when she notes that the crash of 1929 came at the end of a decade of seemingly unlimited material affluence, during which time new forms of compan-ionship were tested and new sexual relationships developed. "The depression turned what had been the previous decade's joyous discovery of freedom to work into a bitter defense of the right to a job; it buried the options and choices for which women had struggled beneath the relentless pressure of family need."[14]

The Great Depression changed the roles of women in several different ways: through economic deprivation within the family; through chang-ing economic roles, in particular entry into the work force; and through direct involvement with governmental programs, especially work relief or direct relief. In addition, marital relationships were likely to change during the Depression as men faced the humiliation of unemployment and women took on new and expanded responsibilities.

The first of these factors was the most obvious and one that cut across classes. Nearly everyone felt *some* degree of deprivation as a result of the Depression. Family expectations with respect to standard of living were high, partly because of the growing array of goods and services that had characterized the 1920s, but also because of increasing individ-ualism on the part of family members. The utilization of goods and services was passing from total-family consumption to consumption by individuals—men, women, boys and girls of different ages and needs. Family members, as their status and roles became more a matter of personality rights of the individual, constituted less of a unit than in any previous period in American history. American culture, with its emphasis on the health of business rather than the quality of family life, encour-aged irrationality of consumption through advertising, thereby contrib-uting to family conflict and even disintegration. Robert Lynd noted that "the tradition that rigorous saving and paying each are the marks of sound family economy and personal self-respect" often clashed with "the new gospel which encourages liberal spending to make the wheels of industry turn as a duty of a citizen."[15]

My own work, *Women's Work and Family Values, 1920–1940* (1981), is based upon the premise that by the 1920s American economic and social life reflected what was commonly referred to as "the American Standard of Living," a standard that varied according to social class and regional differences but that essentially meant that family members set their aspirations beyond their means. "A family defined its standard of living in terms of an income that it hoped to achieve rather than by the reality of the paycheck." The American standard of living gave the term "economic need" a new definition. Instead of referring merely to food, clothing, and shelter, economic need came to mean "anything that a particular family was unwilling to go without."[16]

The economic complexities of family life became greatly intensified during the 1930s. Family expectations with respect to standard of living remained high, but the means to maintain these expectations declined. There was a variety of ways to meet the crunch. Some families borrowed, while others simply did not pay their bills. Some moved in with relatives, and some went on relief. None of these responses was exclusive of the others, and all of them were particularly characteristic of low-income families living on the earnings of marginal workers who experienced frequent unemployment. These various strategies are described in some detail in *Women's Work and Family Values.*

The most logical way for a family to adapt to Depression conditions was to adopt a lower standard of living. This remedy was accepted with varying degrees of success by nearly all classes in America except the well-to-do. The extent to which families were successful depended upon several factors, some of them beyond their control. These included the cost of living, the family income, the family's material needs and expectations, and the budgeting skill of the family's consumer manager, usually the woman.[17]

Many families met the economic crisis by placing "additional workers" in the labor force. Ironically, although the man of the family was often unable to find work, other family members—wife and children—were apt to be more successful. Even in families where the father held on to his job, there was almost certain to be a cut in pay or hours or both. Of course, additional wage earners have always been important to the American family, and with the decline of child labor in the 1920s and 1930s this responsibility often fell upon the married woman. The paid employment of the married woman almost always reflected the primacy of her home life. In the case of the "middle-income" family, she was probably working to pay for a home, keep her children in school, help her husband with his business, or pay for the "extras."[18]

It would be a mistake, however, to assume that the home life of the married working woman remained unchanged. The changing pattern of family relations under the impact of the Depression was the subject of several studies during those years. Samuel A. Stouffer and Paul E. Lazarsfeld, in their work for the Social Science Research Council, advanced the hypothesis that women probably increased their authority within the family because they fared better than men with respect to employment, at least in the early years of the Depression. Thus, some married women may have increased their contributions to the support of the family at the same time that their husbands were experiencing unemployment or a decline in earnings.[19]

Although the unemployment of the husband did not always result in the employment of the wife, it usually brought about a change in family relationships. The causes of the change were often complex and were not necessarily economic alone. Mirra Komarovsky found that the unemployed husband lost status in thirteen out of the fifty-eight families she studied in the 1930s. The decline was usually related to the fact of unemployment, but deterioration in the man's personality and his continual presence in the home also contributed to his loss of status.[20]

Komarovsky also observed the effects of different family authority patterns upon the husband's status during unemployment. When the husband's authority was primary rather than instrumental, that is, when it was based upon love and respect rather than upon his provider role, the family showed a remarkable stability in the face of unemployment. In the patriarchal family, subordination to the unemployed husband might continue through habit, but if the role of provider was important to the patriarchal structure, the loss of that role could disrupt the whole concept of the husband's prerogatives.[21]

Thus, the unemployed man's status in the family depended upon factors beyond the loss of his provider role. His own adaptation to his loss was important, including his attitude toward the family, his willingness to help them in various ways, and the maintenance of his morale. But his wife's attitude toward him, both before and during his unemployment, was also an important factor. If the father was to maintain his position with his children, he had to maintain it with his wife: "Apparently the father does not rule alone. His prestige needs the mother's endorsement."[22]

Komarovsky's observation points to a shift in the basis of marital authority, which was becoming increasingly obvious during the twentieth century. One of the most common ways of explaining this shift is to note the emergence of the "companionship" marriage, in contrast to the patriarchal system of the nineteenth century. Marriage is by its very nature a partnership, but companionship marriage moves beyond a functional partnership with a sharp division of spheres and an emphasis on the man as patriarch to sharing of activities and mutual interests that includes not only work and domestic chores but also recreational and leisure-time concerns. The companionship marriage is not necessarily egalitarian. There may be a dominant partner, but this arrangement is basically satisfactory to both because the dominance is defined by them as part of the relationship, rather than forced upon them by tradition.

During the Depression, an unemployed man may have lost power based on his occupational role, but unless he failed to function as a family member, he could still hope for love and respect, especially if he was the head of a family with strong primary attitudes rather than instrumental ones. This point was supported by several studies done during the 1930s. Ruth S. Cavan and Katherine H. Ranck, in *The Family and the Depression* (1938), reported that well-organized families, even when greatly affected by the Depression, continued to be well organized, whereas initially disorganized families became further disorganized. They argued that adjustment to the crisis was as much or more an attribute of family organization as it was external pressure exerted by the Depression.[23]

Likewise, Robert C. Angell argued that the vulnerability of the family to the Depression varied inversely with the family's integration and adaptation. By integration he meant a family unity based upon kindly feelings, common activities, mutuality of interests, and family ambition and pride. The pride had to derive from the qualities of the family members themselves and from the community recognition they had received, rather than from material possessions. But Angell stressed flexibility as much as family integration in adjusting to Depression conditions. Accordingly, if the wife became the chief breadwinner, an adaptable family would be able to rationalize the change through new concepts of member roles. Similarly, the adaptable family would be able to accept a lower standard of living in the face of necessity without losing its coherence. Conditions that produced rigidity rather than flexibility in family structure included a materialistic philosophy of life, traditionalism in family mores, and irresponsibility of one or both parents.[24]

Thus, the Depression itself had little disorganizing effect upon successful families, even though it may have caused a considerable decline in their standard of living and a readjustment to new member roles. The wife in such a family probably already had a voice in family matters, although in most cases she recognized her husband as head of the household. If she was forced to work, owing to her husband's unemployment, her position might be strengthened somewhat, but basically her work was recognized as a temporary expedient, and the traditional authority pattern was sustained.

Sydney Stahl Weinberg's study of immigrant Jewish women, *The World of Our Mothers* (1988), picks up on a similar relationship between work and family. Weinberg's work, which is based upon oral history, indicates that some women were forced into the labor market and others were not, but as in other working-class families, "a wife's employment was a symbol of defeat." A successful husband was one who could support his family while his wife stayed at home with the children, and the Depression certainly frustrated that possibility for many first- and second-generation Jewish families.[25]

In general, the strong family values that the Jews brought with them meant that there was only one avenue of work that was automatically acceptable for married women, and that was working in a family enterprise—a logical extension of the wife's proper role as her husband's helpmeet. However, for those women who did work at some time during the Depression, their new economic roles sometimes affected their roles within the family. Frequently they became more assertive in handling money or making economic decisions. And there were clear indications of an emerging companionship marriage: "a strong bond of affection and mutual understanding in marriage often cushioned the effects of adversity, and these were precisely the traits that many Jewish women had sought and found in their husbands."[26]

But many families had weaknesses before the Depression, with respect to either their material values, their inflexibility in the face of changing roles, or their internal structure. There is general agreement among students of the Depression family that men tended to be less flexible than women in meeting the crisis. Angell suggested that the loss of economic security weighed most heavily upon the man, whereas the woman had her household routine to distract and sustain her. Cavan and Ranck noted that men felt more keenly the personal loss of status as well as the loss of accustomed activity. Komarovsky felt that the man's loss was threefold: he lost his provider role, his prestige, and his daily work routine. Although men varied in their reactions to these losses, there is no doubt that most of them had a difficult time adjusting, and many of them stubbornly resisted role change or a new concept of family patterns.[27]

When a man lost his job, the woman often bore the entire burden of family responsibility: she faced a double task of maintaining it both economically and emotionally. But she was seldom openly acknowledged to be head of the household, except in cases where the husband deserted the family and the children were too small to challenge their mother's authority. When the husband remained with the family, and when there were older children present, the woman found it difficult to establish her authority in any clear-cut fashion because the economic system and societal pressure worked against her potential leadership. Even as a gainful worker, she had a low economic status in the community. But more important, custom and tradition made it almost impossible for most families to accept a radical change in family structure while the husband was present. Most wives were themselves reluctant to usurp their husband's authority and to assert their own.

Attitudes toward the long-term arrangements of power within the marriage relationship changed little as a result of the Depression. But there was a change in attitudes toward working wives and mothers. It was probably experienced by the children of the Depression rather than by the adult generation, and it had its greatest impact upon families of the 1950s and 1960s. E. E. LeMasters, in a study of life-styles among blue-collar workers in the early 1970s, pointed out that although his subjects overwhelmingly favored traditional male-dominant roles, over 90 percent of them were willing to have their wives work outside of the home. For some of the older men, this attitude dated back to the Depression; for others, World War II was the formative event. But for these men, a working wife did not necessarily change her family status. Work was an added responsibility, which might or might not result in more prestige or privilege. Whether it did usually depended upon the personal resources of the individual marriage partners rather than upon their economic contributions.[28]

Nonetheless, most of the social trends affecting family life appeared to be favorable to women. The gradual emergence of the companionship marriage among middle-class families certainly reflected a new understanding of family power relations, even if the basic husband-dominant structure remained the norm. Also, the family assumed a new importance during a time of crisis, as more people found their entertainment at home, listening to the radio and sharing in the labor-intensive activities that characterized a lower standard of living.[29]

But the stress of economic hardship and continual insecurity may also have had a detrimental effect upon family relations. Glen Elder has suggested that the economic crisis had a negative impact upon the trend toward companionship marriage. "These conditions often brought instrumental values to the fore and severely strained the fabric of companionship . . . the evidence suggests that social and economic security favors the emergence of companionship values and their expression in family relationships."[30]

Elder also suggested that the Depression had an impact upon women's roles that carried into the postwar years and that strongly affected the familism of the 1950s. For instance, the example of working mothers influenced young people to accept that role in their own family lives. But although women's activities changed, the behavioral development far exceeded any corresponding value change; that is, young people who grew up during the Depression viewed working wives and mothers not as the norm but as a response to unusual circumstances. In particular, Elder stressed the strong domestic orientation of girls who were the products of economically deprived households. The family strain in such a home could result in emotional estrangement from the father, centrality for the mother's role, an early involvement of the daughter in household work, and a lack of parental support for the daughter's higher education.[31]

According to Elder, the deprived household created a conducive environment for traditional sex roles and an accelerated movement toward adulthood. Children took on adultlike responsibilities at an early age. Girls were drawn into the household operation and were oriented toward a domestic future. They developed family-centered values and a view of life that emphasized responsibility rather than self-fulfillment. Traditional male roles were also reinforced, but boys were liberated from parental control as they were forced to take upon themselves economic responsibilities at an early age. Unlike their sisters, boys were oriented toward the world beyond the family through their work roles.[32]

Thus, children were socialized to adapt to the economic and functional needs of the family, and there was little concern with preparing them for the future. Elder argues that the Depression performed perhaps the greatest disservice for young people by causing many of them to lose that vision of their own potential that is essential to achievement beyond the ordinary routine of work and family.[33] What Elder did not address was the fact that many young Americans were born into families that could offer them no hope or vision of their own future potential, regardless of the particular economic conditions that beset the nation as a whole.

One of the problems facing the historian who is trying to evaluate the impact of the Depression on families is the fact that generalities offer only a limited view. Class and ethnicity, as well as regional variation, resulted in a diversified experience of economic deprivation. There are two kinds of literature that directly confront the issue of the vast underclass of Americans who were poor before the Depression and who had never experienced firsthand the "culture of abundance." The Depression-era documentaries are one kind; the new "women's history" of the 1970s and 1980s is another.

Julia Kirk Blackwelder's study of women in San Antonio, Texas, *Women of the Depression: Caste and Culture in San Antonio, 1929–1939*, focuses upon women as members of particular economic and ethnic groups whose circumstances determined the impact of the Depression upon their lives. Blackwelder used the concept of caste in her attempt to understand and explain ethnic discrimination and the social structure of early twentieth-century San Antonio. Both blacks and Hispanics suffered the occupational and social distinctions of caste, although in different ways, at the hands of the oppressor race, the Anglos.[34]

Blackwelder stresses the physical and economic deterioration suffered by San Antonio women during the Depression. Twin themes run through their stories: ethnicity and family.

Ethnic prejudices divided women into what were virtually three separate worlds. Women understood the Depression largely in the context of the collective experiences of Anglos, blacks, and Mexican Americans. Ethnicity was the most important single indicator of socioeconomic status in San Antonio, and the Depression reinforced the pattern of segregation.

If ethnicity was a primary factor affecting economic status in San Antonio, family was a close second. Women's experiences during the Depression were not individual or solitary. Women were almost always part of a family unit, and were usually dependent on male wage earners. Although family composition might change for individual women as they passed through the decade, for most women family concerns were ever present. Family considerations rather than individual ambition determined whether or not a woman sought work outside of the home. This had been true before the Depression, and it was intensified by economic need during the Depression.[35]

Blackwelder argues that the histories of San Antonio women reveal the degree to which generalizations about the Depression experience camouflage the realities for individual groups. Although a privileged few may have passed through the Depression with ease, overall San Antonians suffered more than did most city dwellers in other parts of the country. In addition, women adapted differently from men; and Anglo, black, and Hispanic women faced very different circumstances of employment, living conditions, and family life. Finally, San Antonio women adopted many survival strategies—sharing housing, taking in lodgers, seeking employment, applying for relief, striking against wage cuts, and engaging in criminal acts—but they did not choose freely from among their options. Family status and caste determined which options a woman might pursue.[36]

The experience of minority women is also the subject of two articles that appear in an anthology edited by Lois Scharf and Joan M. Jensen, *Decades of Discontent* (1983). Rosalinda M. Gonzalez argues that the patriarchal family pattern was very strong among the Mexican families that did much of the agricultural labor of the Southwest during the early decades of the twentieth century. Childbearing was a major way in which a rural woman contributed economically to her family because large families provided a cheap and stable labor force for tenant landlords and other employers. Family and child labor was especially important in Texas cotton production and in beet production in Colorado. Gonzalez notes that "the patriarchal bondage of women" was perpetuated by the family labor contract, the family wage paid to the male head of the family, and the isolation of Mexican peon families in labor camps. Even in urban areas, the Mexican family retained its importance as a patriarchal social institution.[37]

But changes began to occur in the 1920s and 1930s, as women were drawn into industrial production and as family life became disorganized under the pressure of economic hardship. The loosening of patriarchal authority was most likely to occur in urban areas, where women had access to independent employment. Also, the inability of fathers to support their families sometimes resulted in abandonment, thus forcing the female head of the household to support the family.[38]

Perhaps the major impact that the Depression had upon Mexican immigrant families was that it forced them to leave the country when their labor was no longer needed. They had to return to Mexico to face even more miserable conditions than those they experienced in the United States. According to Gonzalez, the Mexican population in the United States in 1940 was almost half what it had been in 1930. This decrease was due to repatriations and immigration restrictions. By 1940 most of the Mexican population was urban, and a larger number of Mexican women than men lived in urban areas, thus contributing further to a deterioration of the patriarchal family.[39]

Dolores Janiewski's work on black and white women tobacco and textile workers in Durham, North Carolina, reinforces the sense of a socially segregated Depression experience. The residents of Durham lived and worked in racial-, class-, and sex-ordered categories. Many of the women workers were young migrants from rural areas, and they came equipped with deeply ingrained ideas about the proper occupations for men and women, blacks and whites. "White women, for the most part, never questioned the justice of the racially stratified system. If they considered the black woman's situation at all, white women preferred to think that blacks were as satisfied with race relations as whites desired them to be."[40]

Janiewski notes that by the 1930s the women who worked in the Durham mills and factories represented a new type of woman worker who, like most black women, began to see themselves as permanent workers. These women were mature workers whose families needed their wages, rather than the young single girls who dominated the labor force in the early years of the twentieth century. Thus, they faced the burden of combining child care, housework, and wage earning. The absence of household conveniences made domestic chores even more burdensome.

Clothes often had to be washed in pots in the yard. Food had to be cooked on a wood- or oil-burning stove. The poorest people continued to eat the filling but nutritionally limited characteristic rural diet of meal, molasses, and salt pork because their budgets and culinary training perpetuated that routine. Bathing had to be done in a basin or a tin tub because many homes lacked bathrooms. Indoor toilets were a rarity in black tobacco households, making sanitation and personal cleanliness still more difficult to achieve.[41]

The burden of inadequate housing and living conditions was not equally distributed. Conveniences such as electricity, indoor toilets, and bathtubs were much more accessible to white families than to black families, and yet black workers paid much more for their housing than did white workers. Janiewski points out that this racial inequity was more than simply a matter of inconvenience: it cost the lives of black women and their children. Black women in Durham in the early 1930s died in childbirth at almost twice the rate of white women, and their children were more than twice as likely to die before reaching one year of age than were those of whites.[42]

Racial minorities were systematically marginalized and eliminated from the American dream, the culture of abundance, in such an absolute way that the Great Depression seemed, in a way, irrelevant to their basic problems. But there were whites who suffered similarly—in particular the rural population, especially in the Southeast. Much of the documentary literature of the era focused on the rural poor who seemed to be stuck in some kind of a time warp that had little to do with the stock market crash of 1929 and everything to do with the long-term, historical trends of economic and human stagnation.

The documentaries of the period captured the continuity of human misery in the midst of deprivation that seemed to have no specific cause and no specific cure. Social documentary, or what William Stott has called the "genre of actuality," the communication of "real things only," was the primary expression of America in the thirties. It was a diverse literature that included caseworkers' reports, angry exposés, worker narratives, first-person quests for reality, and photography. The intent was to "increase our knowledge of public facts, but sharpen it with feeling; put us in touch with the perennial human spirit, but show it struggling in a particular social context at a specific historical moment."[43]

Like the muckrakers of the Progressive era, those who created these works strove to expose evil, educate the middle class, and achieve reform. But their descriptions of the living standards and the lot of the poor—especially the rural southern poor—seemed to suggest that agencies such as the Works Progress Administration (WPA), the National Youth Administration (NYA), and the Farm Security Administration (FSA) could only begin to touch the lives of the people.

But the New Deal agencies did provide the means to explore these lives. The rural South became a symbol of the Depression, and southerners employed by the Federal Writers Project (FWP), a New Deal program under the WPA, collected over one thousand stories, thirty-five of which were published in the critically acclaimed work *These Are Our Lives* (1939). These life histories provided a view of the world, the work, and the family life of a rural, impoverished people, most of whom were poor before the Great Depression; then things got worse. "We seem to move around in circles like the mule that pulls the syrup mill. We are never still, but we never get anywhere. For twenty-three long years we have begun each year with nothing and when we settled in November we had the same.[44]

The stories, some of them appearing in an anthology edited by Tom E. Terrill and Jerrold Hirsch, *Such as Us* (1978), illuminate the region's agricultural history and reflect the importance of farming in the South. The evolution of a one-crop agriculture and tenant farming had little to do with the stock market crash and the ensuing collapse of capitalism. It must be understood as a problem in regional economic development, as a labor system, and as a form of social control.[45]

One of the writers who captured most eloquently the intense deprivation of family life in the rural South was James Agee. His *Let Us Now Praise Famous Men* was turned down for publication—first by *Fortune* magazine, one of the most liberal magazines of the decade. *Fortune* had originally assigned Agee and the photographer, Walker Evans, to collaborate on a series of documentary articles on cotton tenancy in the deep South, but found the work to be too long, too rhetorical, philosophical, and artsy. Harper and Brothers contracted for an expanded version but turned it down, judging the work to be unfit to print. The material was finally published in 1941 by Houghton Mifflin, and by 1960, when a new edition came out, it had become an American classic.[46]

Agee and Evans played the role of participant observers, an approach that characterizes much of the documentary literature of the 1930s. For a period of about six weeks, the two men lived with three families in rural Alabama, sharing their food and sleeping in their cabins. They did not see their subjects as "social problems." Instead, with great respect for their human dignity, they set out to confront the reader with the actuality of these people's lives. James Agee speaks of a very particular people, treating each one as an individual rather than a "case."[47]

But Agee also speaks to the universality of those who "all over the whole round earth...are drawn inward within their little shells of rooms."[48] He illuminates the family lives of those who are caught in despair. *Let Us Now Praise Famous Men*, as much as any document of the 1930s, projected itself into the privacy of everyday family life and articulated the helplessness of poverty-stricken childhood, the lack of basic human needs, the grueling labor necessary for subsistence. Agee included long passages describing the homes, which were no more than shacks, with nails on the walls of shallow closets, a few garments hung on them; had homemade pallets for the children to sleep on; and had

rat turds on the floor. Four rooms was a large tenant home; they were
more likely to have three or two rooms, and there were more with only
one than with four.[49]

They live in a steady shame and insult of discomforts, insecurities, and inferi-
orities, piecing these together into whatever semblance of comfortable living
they can, and the whole of it is a stark nakedness of makeshifts and the lack of
means: yet they are also, of course, profoundly anesthetized.[50]

By "anesthetized" Agee meant, of course, apathetic. But he did not see
apathy as ameliorative, since he felt that it was more unfortunate to be
unaware of an ill than to be conscious of it. And he was critical of the
rationalizations of those middle-class southerners who deeply believed
that the poor were "used to it."

Agee went beyond his contemporaries in exposing the unacknowl-
edged sexuality of everyday experience, or what Stott has called the
"random small liaisons that happen all the time but that one doesn't talk
about nor even, sometimes, realize." Stott argues that Agee, by revealing
his own physical awareness of the tenant women, has bridged the social
and economic gulf between the social "victim" and the reporter documenting her life. This bridging of the gulf tended to "severely weaken
the idea that hardship is the basic fact of the victim's life."[51]

Stott sees this self-conscious frankness as one of the book's real
triumphs, but it was the rawness of the material, as well as its length and
its highly personal tone, that contributed to the difficulties in getting it
published. Agee's self-revelation was intended to confront middle-class
sensibilities and to shock his readers into awareness, so he spared them
nothing in his crudity and in his emotional intrusion into the data.

Agee's material departs significantly from the casework studies done
on family life by sociologists like Komarovsky, Angell, Bakke, Cavan,
and Ranck. The Ricketts, Woods, and Gudger families were not supposed to be "representative," nor were they moving toward a mid-
twentieth-century version of the "companionship" marriage. And certainly they were not unduly subjected to the paternalistic control of social
workers and others in the helping professions that are a source of concern to Christopher Lasch. Indeed, they may have welcomed a little
paternalistic intervention.

The New Deal programs seemed to have made little impression on
their lives. Agee pointed out, for instance, that WPA work was available
to very few tenants, because they were technically employed and therefore did not qualify. If, by some fluke, a tenant farmer was able to get
a WPA job, the landlord was likely to intervene, feeling that wages spoiled
the tenant farmer, even for a little while. A tenant who so much as tried
to get that kind of work was under disapproval.[52] Perhaps Agee's position

on the limitations of the WPA—he was also unimpressed by rural electrification, although his objections here seemed like rather ill-founded romanticism—were a reflection of his basically pessimistic perspective. Although Agee called himself "a Communist by sympathy and conviction," as Stott points out the message contained in his work was not radical, nor was it reformist or even socially constructive. Agee did not feel that the evils of the tenant system were rectifiable; he did not see it as a problem that could be attacked or solved, especially if the solution was sought on its own terms.[53]

Yet the "farm problem," in its broadest sense, was very much the target of New Deal reforms, and although the tenant farm family was hardly the largest beneficiary, many of them did, in fact, benefit from various programs ranging from work relief to the Civilian Conservation Corps (CCC), to direct relief, and to various loan programs under the Farm Security Administration (FSA). But those who benefited the most from New Deal agricultural programs were the landowners. Large farmers got federal bonus payments and higher farm prices—virtually guaranteed income maintenance—whereas the small farmers, tenants, and sharecroppers were either forced off the land or remained to eke out a miserable existence.[54]

Ironically, it is the particularistic studies such as Agee's that reveal the dimensions of what was a condition of "universal" misery and deprivation. And they also reveal the difficulty facing the historian who is attempting to evaluate the impact of the Depression upon the structure and the texture of family life, whether it be in economic, social, or moral terms. The impact of New Deal policies was very particularistic. Certainly in some cases it represented so little, and the family was so destitute, that a few dollars from "relief" was little more than a sop. Also, the application of relief policies varied tremendously both in generosity and in administration from state to state and locale to locale.

During the first two years of the New Deal, 1933 and 1934, Lorena Hickok, an experienced newspaperwoman and a friend of Eleanor Roosevelt was sent by Harry Hopkins out into the countryside to report on Depression conditions. Hickok's correspondence with Hopkins, and to a lesser extent with Eleanor Roosevelt, created a firsthand record of the living conditions of the American people, as well as the politics, and the efficiency and functionality of relief in the various cities and states across the nation.[55]

Harry Hopkins was responsible for the Federal Emergency Relief Administration (FERA), the greatest organized effort ever made in the United States to relieve nationwide distress. The FERA had $500 million allocated by Congress to help the states combat the problems of unemployment and relief. Half of this sum was available to the states on a matching funds basis of three to one. The remaining $250 million was a discretionary fund that Hopkins could allocate to states that could not meet the matching provisions. In 1934, Hopkins was also made administrator of the Surplus Relief Corporation, which provided material subsistence to the needy in the form of surplus foodstuffs. He also became head of the Civil Works Administration (CWA), and in 1935 he became director of the WPA. Both of the latter agencies were intended to create jobs that would provide workers with wages and remove the stigma of being on relief.[56]

Obviously these were programs that had a direct impact on the family life of millions of Americans. But Hopkins's activities extended even further. For instance, within the FERA he established a Division of Transient Activities, which assisted almost 300,000 homeless transients—families, as well as individuals—by providing them with various kinds of support programs. Finally, Hopkins set up a Rural Rehabilitation Division, also under the FERA, to help farmers in distress. One objective of rural rehabilitation was to help farm families become self-supporting, especially by loaning them money to buy their farms or to avoid bankruptcy.[57]

Hopkins's concerns penetrated every community, city, and county in the United States. He had to provide data to the public, the president, and Congress, and he had to be aware of the activities of other New Dealers, governors, and citizens. His problem was not a lack of data— he had more than enough data. But he had little information as to the human dimensions of the situation. Thus, in the summer of 1933 he decided to send investigators out into the field to report directly to him the conditions that they found. The first and most important of these investigators was Lorena Hickok. During the fall of 1933 and all through 1934, Hickok visited some of the worst areas in the country, reporting on what she saw through her daily letters to Hopkins, which proved an invaluable source of information on that "one-third of a nation" that concerned Franklin D. Roosevelt.[58]

Hickok's approach was very different from Agee's. She had to tell Hopkins how the machinery of federal relief was working in an area that had previously been regarded as the domain of the state and local agencies. So her observations were political as well as humane, and they were nationwide rather than geographically restricted.[59]

For instance, New York State was far ahead of other states with respect to administration and adequacy of relief. Indeed, according to Hickok, New York State's Temporary Emergency Relief Administration (TERA) had just about achieved the standards that the FERA wanted for the rest of the country. Families could get up to sixteen dollars a month for rent. Medicine and medical care in the home were provided, as well as hospitalization. Clothing needs were met at a sufficient level, at least in comparison to other states, such as Pennsylvania. In some cases, families were even helped with their insurance payments and house payments. Food allowances were generous and work projects extensive, carefully planned, and carried out with a good deal of imagination. "An attempt is made—particularly in Syracuse and in Rochester—to meet the needs of the individual families. As a result, a man with a large family may earn, on work relief, as much as $16 a week."[60]

On the other hand, Hickok found a situation in the state of Maine that was "almost medieval in its stinginess and stupidity." The great majority of the communities simply would not turn to the federal government for help. As Hickok put it, they preferred to "get along somehow." The relief problem in Maine was exacerbated by an intensely conservative value system—"A 'Maine-ite' being the type of person he is, would almost starve rather than ask for help." This was the expected behavior. It was considered a disgrace to be "on the town," and that feeling was reflected in the attitude toward those who did ask for relief—especially if they were French Canadians. After all, "there must be something wrong with a fellow if he can't get a job." Finally, the unemployed and poverty-stricken in Maine faced a special problem that did not affect southern farm families, and that was the climate. The family allotment needed to be higher in order to pay for more clothing, more food, fuel, and warmer houses.[61]

Hickok's accounts are convincing, but in a different way than the intense and emotional, almost confessional descriptions of James Agee. Hickok gives a sense of the range and the diversity of the Great Depression, geographically and also socially. To be unemployed and poverty-stricken in Maine was very different than it was in New York, and still different from the situation of the poverty-stricken and unemployed in Alabama or West Virginia or Colorado. It was also different to be black or French Canadian. Furthermore, many families really did benefit from the direct-relief and work-relief programs of the New Deal, but some benefited much more than others. Hickok offers a special insight into the human reality that the federal government was trying to confront. Her style is simple, direct, and honest—sometimes so honest that her own racial biases are exposed. Thus, the following account of unemployed blacks in Savannah, Georgia, getting twelve dollars a week on the CWA payroll:

—Northerner that I am, raised in the sentimental tradition that all men are created equal—I'm not so sure these Southerners aren't right. What makes it tougher for the Savannians . . . is that while these illiterate creatures, whom they regard as animals, are getting more money than they ever had in their lives before, hundreds of white workingmen are unable to get CWA jobs, and their families are hungry.[62]

Hickok's accounts, impressionistic as they are, offer one kind of insight into the impact of the Depression upon family life and the extent to which the federal government, working through the states and local agencies, was able to ameliorate the situation. But there were also a number of scholarly attempts to confront similar issues.

In 1939 the University of North Carolina Press published *Mothers of the South: Portraiture of the White Tenant Farm Woman*, written by a sociologist, Margaret Jarman Hagood. Hagood had earned her doctoral degree at the University of North Carolina in 1937 with a detailed statistical analysis of the fertility patterns of native white women of childbearing age in the Southeast. Her work was part of a regional study carried out by scholars at the university and inspired by President Roosevelt's observation that the South was the nation's number one economic problem. The Southeast was the least urbanized section of the country, and it had the highest birthrate of any region. Hagood had presented the statistical data in her thesis, but she wanted to move beyond the statistics to look at social context. The tenant farm family was not only a problem for the agricultural economist, but also it was a problem for those concerned with the human resources of the country.[63]

Hagood was a social scientist whose research had a purpose, not unlike those Progressive social scientists who collected data on family life in the burgeoning cities of the new industrial era. She saw the possibility of a "scientific" solution, and she also saw evidence of at least individual families who benefited from New Deal programs. For instance, she described a tenant farmer who had an opportunity to buy his farm if he could secure a loan with the Farm Society Administration. The tenant had already secured a government loan for $105 that had enabled him to buy a mule, a buggy, and a plow, and have enough money left over to live until his tobacco crop sold. Within one year he and his wife gained considerable favorable attention in the community, and he was able to move to a better piece of land—one which three years later they had an opportunity to buy. Hagood noted that "this couple faces the year hopefully.... They are rather confidently now waiting on Washington."[64]

Hagood's primary interest was not the New Deal or even the Great Depression, but what she perceived to be a larger social issue—the plight of the southern tenant farm mothers, a group that epitomized the results of the waste and stagnation of the South. They were the victims of the cash-crop economy and the lack and unequal distribution of institutional services. They also bore the brunt of a regional tradition of class and sex discrimination. But as Hagood pointed out, they exacerbated these conditions through their own family and reproductive roles. Children might have provided labor, but a large family required that even marginal land be cultivated to raise the cotton and tobacco necessary to sustain it. Children were both the greatest asset and the most crucial problem of the region.[65]

The women in Hagood's study were much more affected by the occupations of their husbands within this cash-crop economy than they were by the Great Depression. First of all, they shared the occupation in the most literal sense; that is, they spent a good part of each year in chopping, hoeing, and picking cotton, or in planting, suckering, worming, "saving," and "stripping" tobacco. Then the farm provided the locale and the physical plant for homemaking, and, of course, it determined the family income as well as the landlord-tenant relations. Thus, knowledge about the farms was essential to an understanding of the women who lived and worked on them. Hagood's study explores all aspects of farm life—the economics of farming in the Piedmont South, the standard of living, and the relative lack of opportunity to rise on the economic scale.[66]

In assessing the impact of these factors upon the women themselves, Hagood observed some common personality traits. Most striking was the utilitarian, "no frills" approach to life and work, but even more important was "the emotional maturity evidenced in their acceptance of economic hardship." Hagood argued that this was not simply passive acceptance, because it involved a constant output of labor. "It is mature in the sense that activities are directed toward the objective factors of the situation— toward farm, children, home—rather than toward inner goals demanded by inferiority feelings or other internal maladjustments.[67]

This was an interesting observation, given the findings of those who were investigating urban family life during the same period. Apparently these farm families were living in a kind of nineteenth-century "time warp," unaffected by consumerism, Freudian psychology, and "alienation"—the curse of twentieth-century humankind. Warren Susman has contrasted the twentieth-century "personality" with the nineteenth-century "character," arguing that as Americans moved through the twentieth century, appearances became more important than internal integrity. Clearly the extent to which such a transformation was occurring varied by region, class, and occupation.[68]

Hagood found widespread interest and knowledge in farming among the tenant farm women, and indeed, the overwhelming majority liked field work, including work in tobacco barns, better than housework. There was pride in the ability to work like a man and an enjoyment of companionship in field and barn. But the matter of preference was not so simple. Given the triple role of childbearing and rearing, homemaking, and fieldwork, most women found it easier to concentrate on home and children, at least when the children were young. And, of course, although the women worked in both the field and the home, the men did not help with the housework. Also, as the women got older, they lost their strength and energy and tended to stay with their housework—especially if they had older children to take their place in the field.[69]

The role that was of the most interest to Hagood was the childbearing and rearing role, because the high fertility of these women seemed to her to be an important factor in the total equation of economic and social lag. In the group that she studied, the mean number of children born per woman was 6.3, but because of the weighting effect of large families, over two-thirds of the children were in families where there were seven or more children. Childbirth was regarded as an achievement—a matter of great importance both to the mother and to society. In fact, large numbers of children were a source of great pride, although most women expressed the attitude, "I hope this is the last one." In other words, there was a certain amount of ambivalence toward childbearing, yet the children kept arriving.[70]

Hagood was interested in the attitudes toward childbearing, "for it is the psychological reaction to external factors, such as traditional economic pressures, which finally translates these societal forces into effects on the birth rate." A combination of factors—inertia, insufficient knowledge of contraceptive methods, expense, lack of cooperation on the part of the husband, and religious values—all operated against the widespread use of contraceptives. Only two of these—insufficient information and cost of contraceptives—could be dealt with directly by public intervention. The others could be removed only gradually by emphasizing the advantages of small families through education and economic opportunity.[71]

Those who read *Mothers of the South* saw it as a kind of call to action. The problem of farm tenancy was a national issue that had to be resolved. But in fact, over the next thirty years the problems of southern agriculture were dramatically transformed. The agricultural reforms of the New Deal, mechanization, new crops, and the stimulus of World War II depleted the tenant farm population. The war, in particular, attracted the farmers, their wives, and children into the war-related industry of the 1940s. After the war, machinery replaced people all across the South, and the exodus to the towns and cities continued. Poverty still exists in the rural Southeast, but the structure of agriculture has changed dramatically, and there are very few sharecroppers and tenant farm families who live their lives as Hagood described them.[72]

The 1930s was an important turning point for the nation politically, socially, and economically. But it is difficult to pinpoint the Great Depression as the transforming event. It was only one of several events, and since its impact was so varied, the consequences cannot be measured. Many of the changes that were occurring within the family—the focus upon childhood, the "new morality," the "companionship marriage," and the absorption with consumerism—had been emerging for several decades. The Depression, if anything, acted as a brake on these steps toward modernity.

The most significant change to come out of the Depression era was the new reliance upon the federal government as a safety net for the "deserving poor." But even the reforms contributed mixed results as far as their impact upon the family. Michael Katz, in his critical assessment of the New Deal, notes that "the limits of the early American welfare state glare so brightly they deflect attention away from the magnitude of the New Deal's achievements."[73]

There is no question that government at all levels greatly expanded its activities in the area of public assistance. For instance, in the fiscal year 1913, all levels of government spent about $21 million in public aid. By 1932, the amount had increased to $208 million. In 1939, it jumped to $4.9 billion. In both 1913 and 1923 public aid consumed only 1 percent of all government expenses; by 1933 it took 6.5 percent; and by 1939, 27.1 percent. The New Deal legislation forced the states to expand their commitment to public welfare. The Social Security Act, in particular, forced states to develop systems of unemployment insurance and improve the quality of their administration and professionalize their staffs.[74]

The actual impact of these expenditures upon American families has not been adequately addressed except in very general terms. In the late 1940s Eveline Burns, a leading authority on social insurance, noted that the system was a sprawling, inadequate, incoherent series of programs that left many people in need. "Needy people are denied access to any form of public aid largely as a result of the accident of where they live or the length of time they have lived in a particular area, or their possession of certain characteristics, such as age, that are irrelevant to the question of need."[75]

According to Katz, although the New Deal had vastly expanded the role of the federal government and had assumed a degree of responsibility for economic security, it erected a new structure on an old foundation. It compromised with the local basis of relief and modified without erasing the distinction between the worthy and unworthy poor. It created two distinct kinds of public aid—social insurance and public assistance—which reinforced the stigma attached to relief or welfare. It did not attempt to redistribute income or interfere with welfare's role in the regulation of the labor market and the preservation of social order.[76]

Other scholars have also been critical of New Deal reforms, especially with respect to family policy. James T. Patterson observed that the limitations on Aid to Dependent Children (ADC) seemed designed to encourage family breakup. The grants were so low in most states, especially in the South, that they forced mothers out of the home and into the cheap labor market. There were also "absent father" clauses which meant that the father, or any other male, could not live with the family receiving ADC. Also, localism resulted in wide interstate variations.[77]

Nonetheless, the 1930s must be seen as a break from the past with respect to the government's role in the lives of American families. In other ways, family life continued on the same general path toward greater equality within marriage and between parents and children. Although consumerism suffered a temporary setback during the Great Depression, it cannot be said that the American people gave up on the dream of material abundance. Rather, they carried into the postwar era a renewed faith in the capitalist system and the consumer society, which was reflected in family life-styles and expenditures for the next several decades. And for a time—nearly twenty-five years—the American people and their government forgot about the culture of poverty, inhabited by those who had never really felt the Depression in quite the same way as the middle class, and had never quite moved beyond it. It took a modern "muckraker," Michael Harrington, to call attention to that "Other America" of families who were still unable to share in the American dream.[78]

NOTES

1. See especially Glen H. Elder, Jr., *Children of the Great Depression* (Chicago: University of Chicago Press, 1974); Winifred D. Wandersee, *Women's Work and Family Values, 1920–1940* (Cambridge, Mass.: Harvard University Press, 1981); Lois Scharf, *To Work and to Wed: Female Employment, Feminism, and the Great Depression* (Westport, Conn.: Greenwood Press, 1980); and Julia Kirk Blackwelder, *Women of the Depression: Caste and Culture in San Antonio, 1929–1939* (College Station: Texas A & M University Press, 1984).

2. Alice Kessler-Harris, in *Out to Work: A History of Wage-Earning Women in the United States* (New York: Oxford University Press, 1982), 252, notes the fears of contemporaries, who saw the family "crisis" reflected in moral laxity, a tendency to postpone marriage, families doubling up in a single household, and a decline in the birthrate.

3. Warren Susman, *Culture as History: The Transformation of American Society in the Twentieth Century* (New York: Pantheon Books, 1984), xxiv.

4. My own work, *Women's Work and Family Values*, argues this point. See also, Winifred D. Wandersee Bolin, "The Economics of Middle-Income Family Life: Working Women during the Great Depression," *Journal of American History* 65 (June 1978): 60–74; and Shelia K. Bennett and Glen Elder, Jr., "Women's Work in the Family Economy: A Study of Depression Hardship in Women's Lives," *Journal of Family History* 4 (Summer 1979): 153–76.

5. Susman, *Culture as History*, 106–7. See especially his discussion of Harold Stearns, *Civilization in the United States* (1922).

6. Christopher Lasch, *Haven in a Heartless World: The Family Besieged* (New York: Basic Books, 1977), 13.

7. Ibid., ch. 2.

8. Ibid., 91.

9. Robert S. and Helen M. Lynd, *Middletown: A Study in Modern American Culture* (New York: Harcourt, Brace & World, 1929); and idem., *Middletown in Transition: A Study in Cultural Conflicts* (New York: Harcourt, Brace & World, 1937).

10. Joseph F. Kett, *Rites of Passage: Adolescence in America, 1790 to the Present* (New York: Basic Books, 1977), chs. 7 and 8; and Lynd, *Middletown* (1929), 151, quoted in Wandersee, 57–58.

11. See Ronald D. Cohen, "Child-Saving and Progressivism, 1885–1915," in *American Childhood: A Research Guide and Historical Handbook*, ed. Joseph M. Hawes and N. Ray Hiner (Westport, Conn.: Greenwood Press, 1985), 273–310, for an excellent study of the relationship between progressivism and child saving. Obviously this concept fits within Lasch's interpretation of social reform as an intrusion on family life. Others who have interpreted the progressives in this light are Anthony Platt, *The Child-Savers: The Invention of Delinquency* (Chicago: University of Chicago Press, 1969); David Rothman, *Conscience and Convenience: The Asylum and Its Alternatives in Progressive America* (Boston: Little, Brown and Company, 1980); David Rothman, "The State as Parent," in *Doing Good: The Limits of Benevolence*, ed. Willard Gaylin, et al. (New York: Random House, 1978), 67–96; and Steven L. Schlossman, *Love and the American Delinquent: The Theory and Practice of "Progressive" Juvenile Justice, 1825–1920* (Chicago: University of Chicago Press, 1977). For a good discussion of this literature, see Cohen, "Child-Saving," 275–81.

12. Hamilton Cravens, "Child-Saving in the Age of Professionalism, 1915–1930," in Hawes and Hiner, *American Childhood*, 417, 419, 462–67.

13. Dorothy M. Brown, *Setting a Course: American Women in the 1920s* (Boston: Twayne Publishers, 1987), 29.

14. Kessler-Harris, *Out to Work*, 250.

15. Robert S. Lynd, "The People as Consumers," in *Recent Social Trends*, President's Research Committee on Social Trends, (New York: McGraw-Hill, 1933), 2:867, quoted in Wandersee, *Women's Work*, 15. See also Lynd, "Family Members as Consumers," *Annals of the American Academy of Political and Social Science* (1932), 86–93; and Wandersee, *Women's Work and Family Values*, 16–18.

16. Winifred D. Wandersee Bolin, "The Economics of Middle-Income Family Life: Working Women During the Great Depression," *Journal of American History* 65 (June 1978): 64.

17. Wandersee, *Women's Work and Family Values*, 27.

18. Ibid., 71–77, 102.

19. Samuel A. Stouffer and Paul E. Lazarsfeld, *Research Memorandum on the Family in the Depression*, Bulletin no. 29 (New York: Social Science Research Council, 1937), 28, 36. See also Lynd, *Middletown in Transition*, 178–79.

20. Mirra Komarovsky, *The Unemployed Man and His Family: The Effect of Unemployment upon the Status of the Man in Fifty-Nine Families* (New York: Dryden Press, 1940), 42.

21. Ibid., 55–61.

22. Ibid., 114–15.

23. Ruth S. Cavan and Katherine H. Ranck, *The Family and the Depression: A*

Study of One Hundred Chicago Families (Chicago: University of Chicago Press, 1938), 1–8, 29–35.

24. Robert C. Angell, *The Family Encounters the Depression* (New York: Charles Scribner's Sons, 1936), 17, 84.

25. Sydney Stahl Weinberg, *The World of Our Mothers: The Lives of Jewish Immigrant Women* (Chapel Hill: University of North Carolina Press, 1988). See especially ch. 12.

26. Ibid., 234.

27. Ibid., 254; Angell, 254; Cavan and Ranck, *The Family and the Depression*, 72–73; Komarovsky, *The Unemployed Man and His Family*, 43–47, 78–82. See also E. Wight Bakke, *Citizens without Work: A Study of the Effects of Unemployment upon the Workers' Social Relations and Practices* (New Haven, Conn.: Yale University Press, 1940), 135–40, 182–84.

28. E. E. LeMasters, *Blue-Collar Aristocrats: Life-Styles at a Working-Class Tavern* (Madison: University of Wisconsin Press, 1975), 84–85.

29. Bolin, 115.

30. Elder, *Children of the Great Depression*, 290, quoted in Wandersee, 115.

31. Ibid., 291, quoted in Wandersee, 13.

32. Ibid., 279.

33. Ibid., 222.

34. Blackwelder, *Women of the Depression*, xvii–xviii.

35. Ibid., 8, 26.

36. Ibid., 168.

37. Rosalinda M. Gonzalez, "Chicanos and Mexican Immigrant Families, 1920–1940: Women's Subordination and Family Exploitation," in *Decades of Discontent: The Women's Movement, 1920–1940*, ed. Lois Scharf and Joan M. Jensen (Westport, Conn.: Greenwood Press, 1983), 72–73.

38. Ibid., 74.

39. Ibid., 71.

40. Dolores Janiewski, "Flawed Victories: The Experiences of Black and White Women Workers in Durham during the 1930s," in Scharf and Jensen, *Decades of Discontent*, 90, 94.

41. Ibid., 93.

42. Ibid., 93–94.

43. William Stott, *Documentary Expression and Thirties America* (New York: Oxford University Press, 1973), xi, 4, 18.

44. A woman tenant farmer, quoted in Tom E. Terrill and Jerrold Hirsch, eds., *Such as Us: Southern Voices of the Thirties* (New York: W. W. Norton & Company, 1978), xiii.

45. Ibid., xi–xiii.

46. James Agee and Walker Evans, *Let Us Now Praise Famous Men* (Boston: Houghton Mifflin, 1941). For a publication history of the book, see Stott, *Documentary Expression*, 461.

47. Stott, *Documentary Expression*, 291.

48. Agee, *Let Us Now*, 52.

49. See ibid., 115–97, for detailed and graphic descriptions of the insides of the family homes.

50. Ibid., 188.

51. Stott, *Documentary Expression*, 302.

52. Agee, *Let Us Now*, 110.

53. Stott, *Documentary Expression*, 294.

54. James T. Patterson, *America's Struggle against Poverty, 1900–1980* (Cambridge, Mass.: Harvard University Press, 1981), 61.

55. Richard Lowitt and Maurine Beasley, eds., *One Third of a Nation: Lorena Hickok Reports on the Great Depression* (Chicago: University of Illinois Press, 1983).

56. Ibid., viii–xx.

57. Ibid., xxi–xxii. See also, Joan M. Crouse, *The Homeless Transient in the Depression: New York State, 1929–1941* (Albany: State University of New York Press, 1986).

58. Lowitt and Beasley, *One Third of a Nation*, xxiii–xxv.

59. Ibid., xviii–xix. See Jo Ann E. Argersinger, *Toward a New Deal in Baltimore: People and Government in the Great Depression* (Chapel Hill: University of North Carolina Press, 1988), for an example of the impact of federal programs upon a particular state; also, Charles H. Trout, *Boston, the Great Depression and the New Deal* (New York: Oxford University Press, 1977), and James F. Wickens, *Colorado in the Great Depression* (New York: Garland, 1979).

60. Lowitt and Beasley, *One Third of a Nation*, 28–29.

61. Ibid., 35–37.

62. Ibid., 152.

63. Anne Firor Scott, Introduction to Margaret Jarman Hagood, *Mothers of the South: Portraiture of the White Tenant Farm Woman* (New York: W. W. Norton & Company, 1977), iv–v.

64. Hagood, *Mothers of the South*, 44–46.

65. Ibid., 4.

66. Ibid., 5–6.

67. Ibid., 75–76.

68. See Susman, " 'Personality' and the Making of Twentieth-Century Culture," in *Culture as History*, 271–85.

69. Hagood, *Mothers of the South*, 89–91.

70. Ibid., 108–10, 120–22.

71. Ibid., 120–26.

72. Scott, Introduction to Hagood, *Mothers of the South*, vii–viii.

73. Michael B. Katz, *In the Shadow of the Poorhouse: A Social History of Welfare in America* (New York: Basic Books, 1986), 246.

74. Ibid.

75. Quoted in ibid., 246–47.

76. Ibid., 247.

77. Patterson, *America's Struggle*, 67–69. See also Scharf, *To Work and to Wed*, 127–29, for a critique of social security, especially in terms of its impact upon women.

78. Michael Harrington, *The Other America: Poverty in the United States* (New York: Macmillan Co., 1963).

REFERENCES

Aaron, Daniel, and Robert Bendiner, eds. *The Strenuous Decade: A Social and Intellectual Record of the Nineteen-Thirties.* New York: Anchor Books, 1970.

Adamic, Louis. *My America, 1928–1938.* New York: Harper and Brothers, 1938.

Agee, James, and Walker Evans. *Let Us Now Praise Famous Men.* Boston: Houghton Mifflin Co., 1941; New York: Ballantine Books, 1966.

Angell, Robert C. *The Family Encounters the Depression.* New York: Charles Scribner's Sons, 1936.

Angelou, Maya. *I Know Why the Caged Bird Sings.* New York: Random House, 1969.

Argersinger, Jo Ann E. *Toward a New Deal in Baltimore: People and Government in the Great Depression.* Chapel Hill: University of North Carolina Press, 1988.

Ashby, Leroy. "Partial Promises and Semi-Visible Youths: The Depression and World War II." In *American Childhood: A Research Guide and Historical Handbook,* ed. Joseph M. Hawes and N. Ray Hiner, 489–532. Wesport, Conn.: Greenwood Press, 1985.

Baker, Russell. *Growing Up.* New York: Congdon & Weed, 1982.

Bakke, E. Wight. *Citizens without Work: A Study of the Effects of Unemployment upon the Workers' Social Relations and Practices.* New Haven, Conn.: Yale University Press, 1940.

Bennett, Shelia K., and Glen H. Elder, Jr. "Women's Work in the Family Economy: A Study of Depression Hardship in Women's Lives." *Journal of Family History* 4 (Summer 1979): 153–76.

Bernstein, Irving. *A Caring Society: The New Deal, the Worker, and the Great Depression.* Boston: Houghton Mifflin Co., 1985.

———— *The Lean Years: A History of the American Worker, 1920–1933.* Boston: Houghton Mifflin Co., 1966.

Bird, Caroline. *The Invisible Scar.* New York: David McKay, 1966.

Blackwelder, Julia Kirk. "Letters from the Great Depression." *Southern Exposure* 6 (Fall 1978): 73–77.

————. "Quiet Suffering: Atlanta Women in the 1930s." *Georgia Historical Quarterly* 61 (Summer 1977): 112–24.

————. *Women of the Depression: Caste and Culture in San Antonio, 1929–1939.* College Station: Texas A & M University Press, 1984.

Bolin, Winifred D. Wandersee. "The Economics of Middle-Income Family Life: Working Women During the Great Depression." *Journal of American History* 65 (June 1978): 60–74.

Brandt, Lillian. *An Impressionistic View of the Winter of 1930–1931 in New York City.* New York: Welfare Council of New York City, 1932.

Bremer, William W. "Along the 'American Way': The New Deal's Work Relief Programs for the Unemployed." *Journal of American History* 62 (December 1975): 636–52.

————. *Depression Winters: New York Social Workers and the New Deal.* Philadelphia, Pa.: Temple University Press, 1984.

Bremner, Robert H., and Gary W. Reichard, eds. "Families, Children, and the State." In *Reshaping America: Society and Institutions, 1945–1960,* 3–32. Columbus: Ohio University Press, 1982.

Brown, Dorothy M. *Setting a Course: American Women in the 1920s.* Boston: Twayne Publishers, 1987.

Byrne, Harriet A. *The Effects of the Depression on Wage Earners' Families.* Women's Bureau, Bulletin no. 108. Washington, D.C.: Government Printing Office,

1933.

Calverton, Victor F., and Samuel D. Schmalhausen, eds. *The New Generation: The Intimate Problems of Modern Parents and Children*. New York: Macaulay, 1930.

Caplow, Theodore, et al., *Middletown Families: Fifty Years of Continuity and Change*. Minneapolis: University of Minnesota Press, 1982.

Cavan, Ruth S., and Katherine H. Ranck. *The Family and the Depression: A Study of One Hundred Chicago Families*. Chicago: University of Chicago Press, 1938.

Charles, Searle F. *Minister of Relief: Harry Hopkins and the Depression*. Syracuse, N.Y.: Syracuse University Press, 1963.

Clague, Ewan, and Powell Webster. *Ten Thousand Out of Work*. Philadelphia: University of Pennsylvania Press, 1931.

Conrad, Laetitia M. "Some Effects of the Depression on Family Life." *Social Forces* 15 (1936–1937): 76–81.

Cowan, Ruth Schwartz. "Two Washes in the Morning and a Bridge Party at Night: The American Housewife between the Wars." In *Decades of Discontent: The Women's Movement, 1920–1940*, ed. Lois Scharf and Joan M. Jensen, 177–96. Westport, Conn.: Greenwood Press, 1983.

Crouse, Joan M. *The Homeless Transient in the Great Depression: New York State, 1929–1941*. Albany: State University of New York Press, 1986.

Elder, Glen H., Jr. *Children of the Great Depression: Social Change in Life Experience*. Chicago: University of Chicago Press, 1974.

———. "History and the Family: The Discovery of Complexity." *Journal of Marriage and the Family* 43 (August 1981): 489–519.

Federal Writers Project. *These Are Our Lives*. 2d ed. Chapel Hill: University of North Carolina Press, 1969.

Gaylin, Willard, et al., eds. *Doing Good: The Limits of Benevolence*. New York: Random House, 1978.

Gonzalez, Rosalinda M. "Chicanos and Mexican Immigrant Families, 1920–1940: Women's Subordination and Family Exploitation." In *Decades of Discontent: The Women's Movement, 1920–1940*, ed. Lois Scharf and Joan M. Jensen, 59–84. Westport, Conn.: Greenwood Press, 1983.

Hagood, Margaret Jarman. *Mothers of the South: Portraiture of the White Tenant Farm Woman*. 1939. Reprint. New York: W. W. Norton & Company, 1977.

Hargreaves, Mary W. M. "Darkness Before Dawn: The Status of Women in the Depression Years." In *Clio Was a Woman*, ed. Mabel E. Deutrich and Virginia C. Purdy. Washington, D.C.: Howard University Press, 1980.

Harrington, Michael. *The Other America: Poverty in the United States*. New York: Macmillan Co., 1963.

Hasting, Robert J. *A Nickel's Worth of Skim Milk, A Boy's View of the Great Depression*. Carbondale: Southern Illinois University Press, 1972.

Hawes, Joseph M., and N. Ray Hiner, eds. *American Childhood: A Research Guide and Historical Handbook*. Westport, Conn.: Greenwood Press, 1985.

Hogg, Margaret H. *The Incidence of Work Shortage: Report of a Survey by Sample of Families Made in New Haven, Connecticut, in May–June, 1931*. New York: Russell Sage Foundation, 1932.

Humphries, Jane. "Women, Scapegoats and Safety Valves in the Great Depression." *Review of Radical Economics* 8 (Spring 1976): 98–121.

Janiewski, Dolores. "Flawed Victories: The Experiences of Black and White Women Workers in Durham during the 1930s." In *Decades of Discontent: The Women's Movement, 1920–1940,* ed. Lois Scharf and Joan M. Jensen, 85–109. Westport, Conn.: Greenwood Press, 1983.

Johnson, Charles S. *Shadow of the Plantation.* Chicago: University of Chicago Press, 1934.

Katz, Michael B. *In the Shadow of the Poorhouse: A Social History of Welfare in America.* New York: Basic Books, 1986.

Kessler-Harris, Alice. *Out to Work: A History of Wage-Earning Women in the United States.* New York: Oxford University Press, 1982.

Kett, Joseph F. *Rites of Passage: Adolescence in America, 1790 to the Present.* New York: Basic Books, 1977.

Komarovsky, Mirra. *The Unemployed Man and His Family: The Effects of Unemployment upon the Status of the Man in Fifty-Nine Families.* New York: Dryden Press, 1940.

Ladd-Taylor, Molly. *Raising a Baby the Government Way: Mothers' Letters to the Children's Bureau, 1915–1932.* New Brunswick, N.J.: Rutgers University Press, 1986.

Lasch, Christopher. *Haven in a Heartless World: The Family Besieged.* New York: Basic Books, 1977.

LeMasters, E. E. *Blue-Collar Aristocrats: Life-Styles at a Working-Class Tavern.* Madison: University of Wisconsin Press, 1975.

Lowitt, Richard, and Maurine Beasley, eds. *One Third of a Nation: Lorena Hickok Reports on the Great Depression.* Chicago: University of Illinois Press, 1983.

Lynd, Robert S. "Family Members as Consumers." *Annals of the American Academy of Political and Social Sciences* (1932): 86–93.

———. "The People as Consumers." In *Recent Social Trends,* President's Research Committee on Social Trends, 2:857–911. New York: McGraw-Hill, 1933.

Lynd, Robert S., and Helen Merrell Lynd. *Middletown: A Study in Modern American Culture.* New York: Harcourt, Brace & World, 1929.

———. *Middletown in Transition: A Study in Cultural Conflicts.* New York: Harcourt, Brace & World, 1937.

McElvaine, Robert S. *Down and Out in the Great Depression: Letters from the "Forgotten Man."* Chapel Hill: University of North Carolina Press, 1983.

Milkman, Ruth. "Women's Work and the Economic Crisis: Some Lessons From the Great Depression." *Review of Radical Political Economics* 8 (Spring 1976): 73–97.

Mintz, Steven, and Susan Kellogg. *Domestic Revolutions: A Social History of American Family Life.* New York: The Free Press, 1988.

Monroe, Day. *Chicago Families: A Study of Unpublished Data.* Chicago: University of Chicago Press, 1932.

Morgan, Winona L. *The Family Meets the Depression.* Minneapolis: University of Minnesota Press, 1939.

Mowrer, Ernest. *Family Disorganization: An Introduction to a Sociological Analysis.* Chicago: University of Chicago Press, 1932.

Ogburn, William F. "The Changing Family." *The Family* 19 (July 1938): 139–43.

———. "The Family and Its Functions." In *Recent Social Trends*, President's Research Committee on Social Trends, 661–708. New York: McGraw-Hill, 1933.

———. "Recent Changes in Marriage." *American Journal of Sociology* 41 (November 1935): 285–98.

Patterson, James T. *America's Struggle against Poverty, 1900–1980*. Cambridge, Mass.: Harvard University Press, 1981.

Platt, Anthony. *The Child-Savers: The Invention of Delinquency*. Chicago: University of Chicago Press, 1969.

Pleck, Elizabeth H. "Two Worlds in One: Work and Family." *Journal of Social History* 9 (Winter 1976): 178–95.

Pruette, Lorine. *Women Workers through the Depression*. New York: Macmillan Co., 1934.

Rothman, David. *Conscience and Convenience: The Asylum and Its Alternatives in Progressive America*. Boston: Little, Brown and Company, 1980.

Scharf, Lois. *To Work and to Wed: Female Employment, Feminism, and the Great Depression*. Westport, Conn.: Greenwood Press, 1980.

Schlossman, Steven L. *Love and the American Delinquent: The Theory and Practice of "Progressive" Juvenile Justice, 1825–1920*. Chicago: University of Chicago Press, 1977.

Seward, Ruby Ray. *The American Family: A Demographic History*. Beverly Hills, Calif.: Sage Publications, 1978.

Stott, William. *Documentary Expression and Thirties America*. New York: Oxford University Press, 1973.

Stouffer, Samuel A., and Paul E. Lazarsfeld. *Research Memorandum on the Family in the Depression*. Bulletin no. 29. New York: Social Science Research Council, 1937.

Susman, Warren I. *Culture as History: The Transformation of American Society in the Twentieth Century*. New York: Pantheon Books, 1984.

Terkel, Studs. *Hard Times: An Oral History of the Depression*. New York: Avon Books, 1970.

Terrill, Tom E., and Jerrold Hirsch. *Such as Us: Southern Voices of the Thirties*. New York: W. W. Norton & Company, 1978.

Thurston, Flora M. *A Bibliography of Family Relationships*. New York: National Council of Parent Education, 1932.

Trout, Charles H. *Boston, the Great Depression and the New Deal*. New York: Oxford University Press, 1977.

Vaile, Roland S. *Research Memorandum on Social Aspects of Consumption in the Depression*. New York: Social Science Research Council, 1937.

Wandersee, Winifred D. *Women's Work and Family Values, 1920–1940*. Cambridge, Mass.: Harvard University Press, 1981.

Ware, Susan. *Holding Their Own: American Women in the 1930s*. Boston: G. K. Hall & Co., 1982.

Weinberg, Sydney Stahl. *The World of Our Mothers: The Lives of Jewish Immigrant Women*. Chapel Hill: University of North Carolina Press, 1988.

Westin, Jeane. *Making Do: How Women Survived the '30s*. Chicago: Follett Pub-

lishing Company, 1976.
White, R. Clyde, and Mary K. White. *Research Memorandum on Social Aspects of Relief Policies in the Depression.* New York: Social Science Research Council, 1937.
Wickens, James F. *Colorado in the Great Depression.* New York: Garland, 1979.
Williams, J. M. *Human Aspects of Unemployment and Relief.* Chapel Hill: University of North Carolina Press, 1933.
Young, Pauline V. "Human Cost of Unemployment." *Sociology and Social Research* 17 (March-April 1933): 361–69.
———. "The New Poor." *Sociology and Social Research* 17 (January-February 1933): 234–42.
Zawadzki, Bohan, and Paul Lazarsfeld. "The Psychological Consequences of Unemployment." *Journal of Social Psychology* 6 (May 1935): 224–51.

6

Families, World War II, and the Baby Boom (1940–1955)

Judith Sealander

By World War II, reading comic strips had become an immensely popular activity shared by tens of millions of American families. They turned to their newspapers daily to devour the already familiar adventures of Dick Tracy, Buck Rogers, and Flash Gordon, as well as new ones featuring Amazonian women. Wonder Woman, for instance, who appeared in national newspapers for the first time in 1941, had "a hundred times the strength of the strongest male wrestler."[1] She bested men at their own strategies and symbolized the possibilities of what dramatic cultural transformations could result from warfare.

Serious examination of the American family in the 1940s and 1950s for a similar transformation has occupied scholars only since the early 1970s. Nonetheless, despite this relatively brief period of study, numerous debates among economists, demographers, historians, and sociologists have erupted. This chapter will attempt to identify the key issues raised and summarize patterns and trends in this new literature. In general, a view that World War II transformed the American family, as Wonder Woman challenged all traditional roles for women, has been replaced with a more skeptical and complicated interpretation. It demands that family life during the war be linked with subsequent events in the fifties and judges the period as one during which crucial, but more subtle and long-term change altered roles and expectations of both adults and children in American families. Central to many questions were the roles played by wives. American society's welter of often irreconcilable economic and cultural demands analyzed together with women's ambiguous responses help in many of the most recent interpretations to explain change as well as continuity in the American family during time of war and periods of baby boom.

This chapter, too, will see the status of women as a key factor influencing developments in the American family during this period. But the focus throughout will be on the history of the family, not on all the myriad issues that an examination of a topic like the status of women could encompass. In similar fashion, discussion of the consequences of World War II and the baby boom will be confined to their impact on the nature and status of the family.

The major shifts in American family life since the Depression routinely took contemporary experts by surprise. The terrible employment prospects of the 1930s forced engaged couples to delay marriage and married couples to delay starting their families. American fertility rates collapsed. During the entire decade, the U.S. population grew by only 9 million, the smallest percentage increase in American history. Almost a quarter of women in their midtwenties, those at the most risk of pregnancy, had no children at all. Eminent demographers saw evidence everywhere of population stagnation and the decline of the American family. By 1938, such worries had become official creed. The final report of President Roosevelt's National Resources Committee concluded that fewer Americans would marry; more adults would live outside marriages for longer periods of their lives; and the birthrate would steadily decline.[2]

World War II provided planners with additional reasons for pessimism. As more than six million women entered the labor force for the first time, pundits worried that the war would accelerate trends begun in the Depression: as late as 1944, most prominent demographers stuck to their predictions of long-term population decreases and declines in overall marriage rates. Other experts warned that new patterns of female employment would encourage divorce and smaller families.[3]

Even as birth and marriage rates soared during the war, analysts remained gloomy. At most, the increases would be temporary, a phenomenon to be explained by the efforts of couples to remedy the postponements of the Depression. As late as 1947, the editors of the highly respected *Population Index* assured: "No one anticipates the restoration of levels of fertility that could be regarded as high in a world setting."[4]

Needless to say, society's analysts did not anticipate the baby boom. Instead of the expected decline in numbers, the American population exploded between 1946 and 1964. More than 76 million children, a third of the present U.S. total population, arrived. Chastened social scientists at the Census Bureau and elsewhere stopped predicting the imminent extinction of the American family. Instead, by the mid–1960s they began to issue revised reports that warned of "new tidal waves of births" to come.[5] Paralleling the appearance of such documents, the national birthrate plunged. Contrary to most expert predictions, the baby boom generation reached adulthood without even replacing itself, much less stimulating repeated cycles of greatly increased birthrates. Instead, the kinds of decisions millions of "boomers" made about marriage, divorce, and parenting once again led to unanticipated changes in American family structure.

Contemporary experts were repeatedly forced to abandon practically every judgment they made about the American family since the Depression. Any survey of writings on the family during time of war and baby boom, then, will include much currently accepted scholarship that will be questioned in the future.

With that caveat issued, this chapter will focus on three issues that dominate the scholarly literature: the economics of family life, relationships between husbands and wives, and roles played by children. These issues focus discussion about World War II and the immensely procreative decade that followed.

The first group of scholars writing about economic issues and the family during World War II saw the growth of opportunity for paid employment among married women as an important spur to change in the family. William Chafe, for instance, the first historian to look carefully at women's status, analyzed World War II as a watershed for the family. Women war workers played a crucial role in maintaining the home-front economy. Moreover, their wages provided essentials for families where a husband was often absent, as well as a pool of savings allowing postwar purchases of previously unattainable items: homes, cars, washing machines, and televisions. Before the war, single women from working-class backgrounds predominated in the female labor force. Beginning in 1942, however, married women who were in or entering the middle class composed the group with the fastest rates of percentage increase among women workers. By the end of the war, a revolution in family economic structure had been launched. While her wages were almost always inferior to her husband's, and chances at high-paying untraditional work were confined only to the wartime emergency, a working wife was indispensable to a family's achievement of middle-class status.[6]

Interestingly, subsequent scholarship has not really challenged this basic premise. Most analysts continue to identify the birth of the two-income, middle-class family with World War II. However, the most current literature, while also locating the roots of long-term change in family economics during this period, makes two significant correctives. While not denying the great number of burdens imposed by wartime shortages, several new works emphasize improvements in family living standards that began during the war. In addition, they argue that the working wife, while undoubtedly a harbinger of major postwar shifts in a family's earning patterns, was not the average wife. To focus such attention on her life and on the changes brought to her family is to neglect the fact that the majority of wives and the overwhelming majority of mothers stayed home between 1942 and 1945.[7]

As the historian D'Ann Campbell has noted, inflation, rationing, poor-quality goods, and shortages of all kinds prompted American families to deny that they were better off economically during the war. And scholars who first examined family life during wartime emphasized, along with those families, the privations. But Campbell and others persuasively argue that such an emphasis needs modification.[8]

They do not discount the immense frustration families often felt in trying to satisfy even basic needs. Especially in war production centers, housing problems were acute. Families, even those where one or more members was earning a decent wage, sometimes lived in tool sheds, tents, or cellars. Moreover, families with children in these crowded areas faced special problems. Landlords enjoyed the benefits of a sellers' market and often refused to allow children in their buildings. Shortages of almost all household equipment made basic family routines difficult, even for those fortunate enough to have adequate housing. Stoves, refrigerators, metal kitchenware, water heaters, lawn mowers, and radios, to name only some items, became virtually impossible to find at any price. Families lucky enough already to own these items discovered that they were usually not lucky enough to locate replacement parts or repairmen should they break.[9]

Families that might not have been able to afford shoes for their growing children during the Depression still often lacked these essentials, even though they now had the money for the purchase. Sweaters and blankets disappeared from stores as military needs absorbed almost the entire national wool supply. After 1942, the federal government began an elaborate food-rationing system. Gasoline rations of three gallons a week forced most families to forgo many kinds of leisure activities.[10]

Given all these difficulties, it is not surprising that wartime families focused on the irritations of trying to run a household. But several recent works note that in some important ways a better standard of living for the average American family began during the war, not only, as has previously been argued, with the postwar economic boom. For one thing, despite rationing families were better nourished than ever. Most families groused about the lack of some favorite foods, but their diets improved during the war. And for the first time in American history, high nutritional standards became an achievable goal for the average family. The difference between the quantity of calories, proteins, and vitamins consumed by the richest and poorest American families shrank drastically during the war. Spurred by rationing, families of all incomes ate new, and often more healthful foods. Eggplant, for instance, appeared on tables outside Greek and Italian neighborhoods. The federal government began to require that basic foods like bread, milk, and margarine be fortified with iron and vitamins.[11]

Moreover, during the war years the proportion of poor families declined dramatically. Rather than poverty, many families experienced, for the first time since the onset of the Depression, the chance to plan for the future with confidence. Burdened by shortages and frustrations, nonetheless they were becoming more prosperous. The number of families with savings accounts skyrocketed, and liquid assets held by individuals increased from $50 billion to over $140 billion.[12]

Recent scholarship also argues that if the grief of rationing has to be put into a more complex perspective, so too does the role of the working wife. At all times during the war most adult American women were housewives, even though the number of employed women increased from 12 million to 18 million by 1945. The war certainly accelerated trends toward paid work by wives, but the great majority of wives who worked did not, at any one time, hold full-time jobs. And wives, far more than unmarried women, shifted in and out of the work force, often on a month-by-month basis. Many scholars now argue that while the war caused increases in the average number of women employed, it did not mark a drastic break with traditional patterns of American household economics, in which the wages of married women were not a component of the regular budget of the average family. Moreover, these analysts say it is important to note that while divorces increased, and several million husbands went off to military service, unbroken families were still the norm for Americans. The most common family arrangement was one in which husband, wife, and any children lived for the duration of the war by themselves in their own household. Only 5 percent of married couples had to double up with relatives or live in some other kind of nonnuclear situation, such as boarding with friends or strangers.[13]

In fact much recent literature on the family in World War II emphasizes continuity, not just in family economic planning but in relationships between husbands and wives as well. In that sense this literature challenges the earlier work of scholars such as William Chafe and Valerie Oppenheimer, who saw in World War II the origins of a sex-roles revolution within the family. Chafe, for instance, has argued that married women, given more crucial roles in the national economy and in the physical functioning of their own families, began to reevaluate domesticity and lives centered on home and husband.[14]

More recent literature, published since the early 1980s, emphasizes that even though millions of women held unusual jobs during the war, neither they nor society saw that as reason to challenge basic beliefs about women's roles. And women still wanted most of all to be wives and mothers. Historians Susan Hartmann, Leila Rupp, and Karen Anderson argue that the strength of male control and sex-role socialization helps explain why, at war's end, no revolution in female expectations about marriage and family occurred. Businessmen, labor leaders, and government officials all participated in major efforts at social control aimed at buttressing traditional values. Repeatedly women heard that they should relinquish their jobs at war's end and refocus their lives on families. Magazines, radio shows, and celebrities all told them that the housewife and mother were still the most admired of American women, that women's true place remained in the home.[15] However, D'Ann Campbell, author of the most comprehensive examination of American women and World War II, *Women at War with America: Private Lives in a Patriotic Era*, discounts the need for any elaborate campaign to keep women circled around the family hearth. Women, she argues, in large part genuinely preferred private, domestic lives. Most American women, Campbell concludes, saw their lives centered in responsibility to husbands and children, enjoyed that responsibility, and viewed the preservation of the American family as the primary purpose of the war.[16]

These and other scholars persuasively warn against reading family values of the 1980s back into the 1940s. Few women, they argue, idealized equality between husband and wife. In fact, the war may even have reinforced traditional sex roles within families. Fewer than 2 percent of the nation's 16 million soldiers and sailors were women. Most of the WACs, WAVEs, SPARs, and women marines worked as clerks. Almost all suffered severe restrictions and discrimination as members of a military system determined to keep women subordinate. Certainly, with some 99 percent of the American female population uninvolved with military service, it remained easy for society to view warfare as a man's domain. Men, not women, were the sex far more likely to be lionized as heroes. Husbands and husbands-to-be emerged from the war idealized as women's protectors, not as their equals.[17]

It is important to note that while the current pattern in scholarly analysis of World War II family relations emphasizes continuity in sex roles and expectations, no one completely denies or, in most cases, even seeks to discount the monumental impact that the war had on the lives of great numbers of individual women and families. If scholars now emphasize the factors that undermined the war's potential for challenging sex-role behavior in families, they do not disprove the thesis first stated by William Chafe that wartime economic changes may have stimulated future changes in society's attitudes about ideal roles to be played by husband and wife within the family.

Scholars debate the ways World War II may have affected sex-role behavior and attitudes within marriages. However, they generally agree that the decade of the forties witnessed new roles played by children within families and new social expectations of parents. The marriage rate, and with it the birthrate, rose dramatically during the war. By 1943, the government reported a million more marriages than would have been expected in normal times. And most of those new households quickly added children. In 1941, the Census Bureau announced the highest birthrate since the late 1920s. By 1943, total American births exceeded three million a year for the first time in U.S. history. *Life* magazine exulted that the United States was "winning the baby war against Hitler."[18]

Not only were American families during the war producing millions more children, but also they were becoming child centered. The kind of advice experts gave parents experienced a significant shift. Since the turn of the century most literature available on child care had stressed the importance of discipline and denial. In the 1920s leaders of this behaviorist approach, like John Watson, emphasized that parents had to establish strict rules. They had to construct regular, even stringent, regimes for almost all aspects of child raising. Mealtimes, bedtimes, playtimes, and certainly toilet training should be carefully scheduled. Watson's influential *The Psychological Care of Infant and Child* warned parents not to hug and kiss their offspring or allow toddlers to sit in adult laps. Children were, above all, "not to be coddled." The key word was control.[19]

During the war, however, and beginning with the middle class, methods for rearing children began to change. Strict scheduling by parents of every aspect of their offspring's lives gave way to permissiveness. A different group of experts, led by pediatricians Arnold Gesell and Benjamin Spock, told parents to let their children take the lead in numerous activities. The ideal parent would create an environment in which children could discover appropriate behavior on their own. In practical terms rigid schedules and rules were discouraged. Children, for instance, should be able to choose more of their own foods. Isolation techniques, such as standing a child in a corner, should replace physical punishments like spanking. Parents would be better advised to cuddle their children than to shake hands with them in the morning, as early twentieth-century experts commonly suggested. Dr. Spock's *Baby and Child Care*, first published in 1946, emphasized that a child's chance to develop its fullest potential depended on its freedom to explore and experiment. The child-centered American family had made its debut.[20]

An overview of literature about the family during the 1940s and 1950s shows that patterns of trends linking rather than dividing the entire period emerge from even a cursory reading of the many books and articles available for review. Interestingly, the same three topics—family economics, sex roles between husband and wife, and the place of children—unify the literature on the family and the baby boom. However, no author interested in either the general topic of the American family or in its specialized aspects, like child-care advice, women's status, or patterns of juvenile delinquency, has in fact linked the two decades completely. Discussions of the family during World War II appear most often in social histories or histories of women focused on the war or on the forties. While historians most commonly are authors of these studies, demographers and sociologists dominate studies of the baby boom. No comprehensive analytic review of the American family between 1940 and 1960 exists.

If it did, it might note that most discussions of the family in the baby boom era begin with discussions of family economics. The period, usually defined as spanning the years of truly dramatic national fertility, 1947 to 1964, was also an era of economic boom. The gross national product increased more than 250 percent between 1945 and 1960. By 1960, more than 65 percent of American families had achieved what the Census Bureau defined as a middle-class standard of living, in contrast to only 30 percent in 1929. Seventy-five percent of American families owned their own car; in fact, between 1945 and 1960 the number of automobiles in the country soared by 133 percent. And American families used these millions of new cars to indulge in another new mass phenomenon, the family vacation. A whole new leisure industry thrived; profits from road-side hotels and motels increased over 2,000 percent during the decade. Almost 90 percent of families possessed a television by 1960. A luxury item unfamiliar to most people at war's end had become a household commonplace. Family purchases of all sorts of other appliances and new furniture also increased dramatically. Most important, many more families had a home of their own in which to cram all of their newly acquired material assets.[21]

During the decade some 13.5 million homes were built, 11 million of them in new residential communities that circled the edges of most of the nation's cities. The great American suburb had come spectacularly into its own within less than a fifteen-year period. By 1960 more than a quarter of all American families lived there. During years of great national prosperity even families in the lower middle class could leave cramped urban apartments for homes of their own on city outskirts. The American family ideal became a suburban house with several bedrooms and its own backyard.[22]

All of this prosperity, the earliest literature on the family in the fifties argued, encouraged the retention of traditional sex-role relationships between husband and wife. The man would bring wages home from his good job to a wife more than ever occupied with her feminine duties of household management and child care. In 1956 sociologist David Reisman conducted 183 extensive interviews with college seniors in a study commissioned by *Time* magazine. In most he found remarkable confidence and strong intentions to establish a conventional husband-wife relationship. One Harvard senior said of his prospective wife: "She shouldn't be submissive, she can be independent on the little things, but the big decisions will have to go my way." A Princeton graduate had a clear idea of his future life. It would be centered on: "wife and family— remember I hope for five children. . . . Although an Ivy League type [my wife] will also be centered in the home, a housewife. Perhaps at forty-five, with the children grown up, she will go in for hospital work and so on."[23]

The first group of sociologists to examine the American family during the baby boom era echoed these self-assessments. It was a time, they said, obsessed with marriage, family togetherness, and maintenance of conventional sex roles. These analysts argued that couples took seriously the advice of experts who warned that women who did not want to be wives and mothers were neurotic. In their very popular book, *Modern Woman: The Lost Sex*, psychiatrists Marynia Farnham and Ferdinand Lundberg urged wives to center themselves on their homes, to learn for instance to make jelly, or can vegetables, or reupholster furniture in their spare moments. The fifties family, then, was one that glorified old-fashioned values. In an ideal marriage, a suburban wife supported her upwardly mobile husband.[24]

Recent literature challenges this early view of the family in the fifties by noting the existence of ambiguities and tension. Instead of contented exponents of tradition, couples in the baby boom decade were people in the midst of a tug-of-war between conventional and new sex roles. They were more confused and uncertain than earlier analyses have suggested. Current scholarship focuses on changing work patterns for married women as a key to understanding sex roles during the period. More and more, several authors argue, the employment of a wife meant the difference between a middle-class and a working-class life-style for American families. Indeed, although the number of single women in the labor force experienced a gradual twenty-year decline between 1940 and 1960, the number of wives and mothers at work soared over 400 percent—from 1.5 million to 6.6 million. By 1960, both husband and wife worked in over 10 million households, an increase of 333 percent over 1940. Most of the new working wives held low-paying jobs in the clerical and service sector. Most who answered surveys about their attitudes about paid work justified their activities as a way to help their husbands or families and denied they were competing with men for careers. Nonetheless, as the historian Eugenia Kaledin and others have noted, the situation almost guaranteed moments of conflict and tension. The stereotypes of relations between baby boom couples, they argue, demand further investigation. While the culture and couples themselves extolled families where a woman stayed home and a husband left home to work, in fact a very significant minority of American families did not fit that pattern.[25]

One pattern that almost all scholars agree characterized the American family during this period was a significantly increased chance that it would include young children. The baby boom was an undeniable demographic fact. Most scholars of the phenomenon define it as a dramatic increase in the American birthrate occurring between the end of World War II and 1964. A few include the years since 1941, because of the rising birthrates that began during the war.[26]

At least 4 million babies were born every year between 1954 and 1964, the decade of highest fertility. Before the boom ended American couples produced 76,441,000 children, one-third of the present U.S. population. Scholars generally agree that three major demographic trends powered this tremendous increase in American fertility.

First, a generation of older women who normally would have had their children during the Depression and World War II postponed their families during these twin emergencies and then, with biological clocks ticking, gave birth in their late thirties and early forties. So, a first group of American mothers over age thirty-five had an abnormally large number of children late in life.

Second, the age of first marriage fell, and the median age at which American women first became mothers declined. Americans during this decade married younger and faster than did any other cohort in the country's history. As recently as 1940, some 15 percent of all women who reached age thirty-two had not yet married. By 1960, fewer than 3 percent were still single. Altogether, some 95 percent of all Americans of marriageable age were getting married. The median age that women married dropped significantly. By the midfifties one of every two first-time brides in the United States was still in her teens. And, once married, these women began almost immediately to start their families. So, a second group of American mothers under age twenty-five was having an abnormally large number of children early in life.

Third, there was an overall increase in the number of children women actually had during the boom years. The average American family expanded by one child. Key to understanding the baby boom is the realization that this addition did not lead to great increases in large families. To reach a new national average of 3.2 children per family by 1958, millions of families decided that they should move from one child to at least two. By 1958, the number of families with at least two children still at home had jumped to 16.2 million, an increase of 46 percent over the previous decade. The baby boom, then, was not the establishment of many large families, but a national movement away from one-child families or childless marriages. In fact families with more than five children at home dropped steadily throughout the period. So, finally, the baby boom was a kind of mass movement, involving all races and classes, to a two- and three-child family. In fact, the range of family sizes narrowed strikingly at both ends: there were few very large or very small families. The baby boom was a boom in what were, by nineteenth-century standards, small families.[27]

While scholars generally agree on these three demographic forces powering the baby boom, they debate the explanations for it. Why did women at all points on the fertility spectrum, including women in much older and much younger cohorts than would usually be considered typical for childbearing, have so many babies? Why did so many fewer one-child families exist in the United States by the end of the era? Why, in fact, did American families, which had for much of the nineteenth century distributed children evenly along a range from zero to six, conform to what became in the fifties a near-universal norm of 3.5 children? On one end of the spectrum, unmarried people, childless couples, and families with only one child just about vanished. On the other, the chances that a family would include five or more children plummeted. Why did the usual factors that demographers identify as key determinants of family size, like education, income, race, and religion, play so little a role during an era when one of the truly remarkable aspects of the baby boom was its universality? Rich couples, poor couples, urban couples, rural couples, people with college degrees and without, Catholics, Protestants, Jews, blacks, whites, and Hispanics all created families of two or three children.

No absolutely conclusive answers to these questions exist in the scholarly literature about the baby boom, but three categories of explanations predominate. Sociocultural, economic, and psychological theories all appear repeatedly in discussions of the causes of the baby boom. The most persuasive authors combine elements of more than one explanation. Many accounts of the baby boom argue that it resulted from postwar economic prosperity. Economists like W. P. Butz and M. P. Ward, as well as demographers led by Richard Easterlin and Norman Ryder, identify the good job prospects and low unemployment rates of the era as major stimulants to early marriages in which couples, confident about their futures, almost immediately became parents. However, were economic factors the only ones, it would stand to reason that rich and middle-class couples would have the largest families. Instead the baby boom cut across income and class groups. Of course, it could be argued that the great national wealth of the period induced optimism about their future prospects among even the poor, but none of the series of fertility surveys social scientists have conducted as they have examined the baby boom provides clear proof that some kind of universal national optimism rooted in American wealth ever existed.[28]

Led by sociologist Landon Jones, other analysts of the boom phenomenon have identified an American "procreation ethic." Its chief characteristics, according to Jones, were:

1. Strong social pressure at all levels of society to marry. Single persons, by their midtwenties, had to explain themselves.
2. Strong social pressure on all married couples to have children. Again those without children had to provide excuses.
3. Finally, a cultural ethic that argued that an only child was likely to be troubled and pitied.

Parents without medical or financial excuses needed to realize the great advantages siblings provided each other. To have an only child was to place that child in emotional and cultural jeopardy.[29] Jones and other social scientists, such as Prithwis das Gupta, Judith Blake, and Larry Bumpass provide a great deal of evidence from the era demonstrating that paeans to marriage and children were almost omnipresent.[30] It is important to note, however, that these sociocultural arguments often beg the question of the origins of such apparently pervasive social norms affecting fertility. To use the high fertility and marriage rates of the baby boom era as proof that the culture placed immense value on children and wedded bliss is, of course, to make a circular argument.

Finally, a group of sociologists led by Glen Elder has explained the baby boom as a sociopsychological phenomenon. Elder, for instance, has examined the long-term psychological impact of growing up during the Depression on a case-study cohort of Californians. So many families experienced hard times during these years, he argues, that the Depression at once diminished the role of the father as breadwinner while enhancing the economic roles of children, who could often supply urgently needed cash through part-time or occasional work. As a result those who grew up during the Depression entered adulthood with an enhanced appreciation of the value of children in families. Such judgments led to a postwar increase in family size.[31] There are several problems with an emphasis on psychological factors when attempting to explain the baby boom, however. As sociologist Frank Bean has noted, such research usually focuses on the intense psychological pressures faced by the working class during the Depression. Such pressures might have influenced those who were poor children during the thirties to have larger families after the war. In fact, however, all classes participated in creating the huge increases in national fertility rates, and the baby boom, while near universal, happened earliest among the middle class and rich and among those who suffered relatively little as children during the Depression. Moreover, those who did the most to cause the baby boom were not impressionable adolescents during the thirties but very small children. Most baby boom mothers and fathers were under the age of ten during the Depression, too young to have been able to help support their own families and to have gained from that experience a great appreciation of the economic value of children.[32]

If few sociologists accept the idea that the baby boom had its origins in a national psychology rooted in the absolute deprivation of the Depression, several emphasize some psychological factors, especially when in conjunction with cultural and economic explanations. Richard Easterlin, for instance, has argued that growing up during the Depression not only meant that people came to expect fewer material goods, but also because of the low national fertility during the decade, they entered the labor force as adults after the war as members of a small cohort. They experienced less competition from each other just at a time when great postwar prosperity drove up salaries and created all kinds of opportunities for job improvement. Since their economic expectations had been diminished by a Depression childhood, young adults after the war had more children as an outlet for their new prosperity. Easterlin, then, argues that relative economic status (income opposed to material expectations) helps explain the readiness with which couples after the war took on the responsibilities of marriage and family. They felt that they had more than enough money for themselves and could afford more children.[33]

Frank Bean adds an interesting postscript to arguments about national psychology and causes for the baby boom. He cites surveys by Norman Ryder, Andrew Cherlin, and others that discuss the probability of a good deal of unwanted as well as wanted fertility during the baby boom years. The 1965 National Fertility Study, for instance, showed that one out of every three mothers who gave birth during the baby boom admitted to having at least one unwanted child in her life. Falling ages of marriages certainly put couples at risk of pregnancy for a longer period of time. The conventional explanation for increases in unplanned pregnancies, especially among couples who already had two children, has emphasized the lower economic cost of carelessness during an era of great prosperity. Husbands and wives may not have actively wanted another baby, but unlike Depression partners they could afford one. As a result, scholars like Ryder argue, people in fifties marriages may not have been very diligent in practicing effective contraception. Bean does not challenge the results of surveys that indicate increasing rates for unwanted pregnancies after two children. However, he emphasizes the significant contradictions in messages society sent women during the postwar period as a possible cause of contraceptive failure and further rises in national fertility rates. Given changes in patterns of paid work for wives and mothers during the fifties, women increasingly had to cope with cultural ideals that glorified motherhood at the same time that they confronted the day-to-day realities of a job. Both they and their husbands might have felt ambivalent about their working. One escape from the resultant tension might have been another pregnancy. In an era that experienced tremendous conflict between attitudes and realities describing sex roles in families, more babies may have been an inevitable result.[34]

If the causes of the baby boom are subject to debate, so are its effects. The boomers are one of the most analyzed of subpopulations. They have been described as a "generational tyranny," exercising by virtue of sheer size enormous power over national political, economic, and social trends.[35] But they have also been labeled a "lost generation," doomed, again by size, to endless and bitter struggles among themselves for adequate education, employment, housing, and medical care.[36]

The range of discussion about the ways in which the boom generation changed American society has been enormously varied, including analyses of the economy, educational structures, housing stock, and patterns in hospitalization. This chapter, however, will confine itself to one aspect of that discussion: the baby boom and the reshaping of the family.

Most scholars agree that the American family between the late forties and early sixties became even more child centered. In fact, some argue that the emphasis on the intense satisfactions children could bring began with pregnancy and delivery. Grantly Dick-Read's *Childbirth without Fear* became an enormously popular guide to "natural" childbirth. Dick-Read, an English obstetrician, exultantly described delivery as an ecstatic, clearly sexual kind of experience. A widely reprinted section of *Childbirth without Fear* entitled "Birth Orgasm" provided quotations from women remembering their labor. One, for instance, recalled that: "There was no pain whatsoever, only a primitive sexual elation. . . . I felt as if I had enough strength to pull the world apart—everything was bright, illuminated. In between contractions, I shouted deliriously, 'This is wonderful! My husband only wants two babies, but I want a thousand.' "[37]

Such accounts, of course, were a dramatic challenge to traditional notions of pregnancy and childbirth as a pain-filled female curse. Dick-Read and other experts urged women to continue the joyful bonding begun in the delivery room with breast-feeding and close physical contact with their children. Fathers, although at a biological disadvantage, could also enjoy relationships of warm intimacy with their offspring. Experts urged them to spend their free time with their youngsters, especially with boys. The fifties idealized itself as a nation of fathers spending free evenings coaching sons at Little League baseball practice. While romanticized, the self-image had substance. The typical American family during the baby boom era did spend more time on child-oriented activities. And, for the first time, even little children prompted national fads. The country had always been prone to popular crazes, from goldfish eating to marathon dancing to miniature golf. But only during the boom decade did children under the age of ten act as primary participants. In 1955, for instance, millions of second and third graders successfully pestered their parents to buy them Davy Crockett coonskin caps, sweatshirts, toothbrushes, and lunch boxes. Between January and September the Crockett craze, spurred by Fess Parker's enormously popular Wednesday-night television portrayals of the folk hero on *Disneyland*, exceeded $100 million in retail sales.[38]

Some contemporaries worried that parents had become too obsessed with their children. Writers talked about children as the new American religion, worshiped with too many toys, too much attention. Historian Richard Hofstadter fretted that the country was becoming the "land of the overvalued child."[39]

If the era when the boom generation were children was one in which society glorified the traditional family, the era now shaped by boomers' decisions as adults has done just the opposite. Baby boomers as adults have created anything but the child-centered family. In fact, they have put their signatures on many strikingly new definitions of family life. The generation born between 1946 and 1964 has established new norms in fertility patterns. The lowest birthrate in U.S. history was recorded in 1978. No really significant change has occurred since then. The baby boom has been responsible for a baby bust. It has been a generation characterized by distinctive characteristics: trends toward both childless marriages and delayed childbearing, with more women having a first child after age thirty-five.

Contributing to such patterns is another trend of great importance to the family. The boom generation now includes lifetime paid work for women as a general expectation. Over 70 percent of baby boom women between the ages of nineteen and forty are in the labor force. Included in this figure are unprecedentedly large numbers of wives and mothers. Over 40 percent of mothers in this cohort, whose children were still infants under one year of age, were at work. For the baby boom, the most common family structure is one in which there are two wage-earning parents and two children, cared for outside the home during the day.[40]

Not only does this "typical" family structure have no precedent in American history, this generation has greatly widened the variety of socially acceptable alternative family living arrangements. While not preferred by many living within them, these arrangements are becoming increasingly common and include separated families, families in which parents were divorced, and families headed by never-married women. Born in an era that idealized family togetherness and stability, baby boomers themselves experienced record levels of separation and divorce. Almost 60 percent of American men and women born between 1951 and 1962 already have ended or, according to social science predictions, will end their first marriages with a divorce. Experts have come up with a long list of reasons for the greatly increased baby boom divorce rate, currently the highest divorce rate in the world. Any extensive analysis is beyond the scope of this chapter but they include: increased paid work for married women, a general cultural expectation emphasizing an individual's right to personal happiness, and lessened stigmata for divorce, coupled with legislative changes such as no-fault divorce.[41] American children in previous generations raised by one parent were usually the victims of an adult death. But typically, the single parents of the baby boom were divorced or separated, not widowed. Indeed, in 1982 only 2 percent of such families existed because of the death of a spouse.[42]

Baby boomers departed in striking ways from previous generations in establishing three additional, and unique, types of family compositions: never-married women with dependent children; "nonfamily households" of men and women living alone or with other unrelated adults; and remarried households of adults with one or more previous divorces, along with children from one or more previous marriages.[43]

The ramifications of all of these changes for the future of the American family could be tremendous. Just a few questions provide hints of the possible conundrums. How, in the future, will marital assets be defined and, if necessary, divided? Who will be responsible for care and support of children, and who will enforce these responsibilities? In 1986, more than one in six American children was born to an unmarried woman. If that trend continues or accelerates, will it signal dramatic changes in roles played by fathers? In what ways should society intervene, if at all, to provide care for this group of children, statistically the most likely to live in poverty? What should be the responsibilities of unmarried cohabitating adults to each other and to any dependent children living with them?

All of these questions are beyond the scope of this chapter. The fact that it ends with them, however, is an indication of the need to continue to study the family during World War II and the baby boom. In these years probably lie the roots of future trends. Although scholars are no more likely than contemporaries to be wise prophets, their analyses of the family during recently past decades may help provide lessons for the ones to come.

NOTES

1. Quoted in Susan Hartmann, *The Home Front and Beyond: American Women in the 1940's* (Boston: Twayne, 1982): 189–90.

2. Landon Y. Jones, *Great Expectations: America and the Baby Boom Generation* (New York: Ballantine Books, 1980): 14–18.

3. See, for instance, discussions in Charles Westoff, "Baby Boom Critic: Theory a Bust," *The Wharton Magazine* (1979): 66–67; idem., "Some Speculations

on the Future of Marriage and Fertility," *Family Planning Perspectives* 10 (1978): 79–83; Thomas Espenshade and William Serow, eds., *The Economic Consequences of Slowing Population Growth* (New York: Academic Press, 1978), 12–89.

4. Quoted in Jones, *Great Expectations*, 19.

5. Philip Hauser, "A New Tidal Wave of Births," *New York Times*, 25 February 1971.

6. William Chafe, *The American Woman: Her Changing Social, Economic, and Political Roles, 1920–1970* (New York: Oxford University Press, 1972); see also Chafe's *Women and Equality: Changing Patterns in American Culture* (New York: Oxford University Press, 1977). Some of these arguments also appear in Valerie Oppenheimer, *The Female Labor Force in the United States* (Berkeley: University of California Press, 1970), and Glen Cain, *Married Women in the Labor Force: An Economic Analysis* (Chicago: University of Chicago Press, 1966).

7. Important among these works are the following: Hartmann, *The Home Front and Beyond*; Leila Rupp, *Mobilizing Women for War: German and American Propaganda, 1939–1945* (Princeton, N.J.: Princeton University Press, 1978); Karen Anderson, *Wartime Women: Sex Roles, Family Relations, and the Status of Women during World War II* (Westport, Conn.: Greenwood Press, 1981); D'Ann Campbell, *Women at War with America: Private Lives in a Patriotic Era* (Cambridge, Mass.: Harvard University Press, 1984); Margaret Allen, "The Domestic Ideal and the Mobilization of Womanpower in World War II," *Women's Studies International Forum* 6 (1983): 401–12; Nancy Loring Goldman, ed., *Female Soldiers: Combatants or Noncombatants? Historical and Contemporary Perspectives* (Westport, Conn.: Greenwood Press, 1982).

8. See, for instance, Campbell, *Women at War with America*, 169–75; Hartmann, *The Home Front and Beyond*; William Chafe, *The Unfinished Journey: America Since World War II* (New York: Oxford University Press, 1986).

9. Ibid, 169–80.

10. Ibid; see also Hartmann, *The Home Front and Beyond*, 174–81.

11. Campbell, *Women at War with America*, 182–85.

12. A good summary of the economic changes brought to families by the war years can be found in John Blum, *V was for Victory: Politics and American Culture during World War II* (New York: Harcourt, Brace, Jovanovich, 1976), 25–68. See also William Chafe, *The Unfinished Journey*, 112–20.

13. See Campbell, *Women at War with America*, 167.

14. Chafe, *The American Woman* and Oppenheimer, *The Female Labor Force*. See also Valerie Oppenheimer, "The Sociology of Women's Economic Role in the Family," *American Sociological Review* 42 (1977): 387–406.

15. Hartmann, *The Homefront and Beyond*; Rupp, *Mobilizing Women for War*; Anderson, *Wartime Women*. Ruth Milkman buttresses these arguments in "Organizing the Sexual Division of Labor: Historical Perspectives on 'Women's Work' and the American Labor Movement," *Socialist Review* 49 (1980): 95–150.

16. Campbell, *Women at War with America*, 8–14.

17. Ibid, 21–33.

18. Quoted in Jones, *Great Expectations*, 18.

19. John Watson's theories are discussed in Hartmann, *The Home Front and Beyond*, 176–86. See also Margaret Steinfels O'Brien, *Who's Minding the Children?*

The History and Politics of Day Care in America (New York: Simon and Schuster, 1973).

20. See Martha Wolfstein, "Fun Morality: An Analysis of Recent American Child Training Literature," *Journal of Social Issues* 7 (1951): 15–21.

21. The best discussion to date of the impact of the suburb on American life is Kenneth Jackson, *Crabgrass Frontier: The Suburbanization of the United States* (New York: Oxford University Press, 1984).

22. Ibid. See esp. 118–40.

23. Quoted in David Reisman, *Abundance for What? and Other Essays* (New York: Doubleday, 1964), 318–19.

24. Ferdinand Lunberg and Marynia Farnum, *Modern Woman: The Lost Sex* (New York: Harper and Brothers, 1947). For a good summary of the work of these sociologists see Eugenia Kaledin, *Mothers and More: American Women in the 1950's* (Boston: Twayne, 1984), 173–91.

25. The best summary of this new literature is in ibid., 61–83.

26. The definition of the baby boom in Jones, *Great Expectations*, 2–10, is the most commonly accepted.

27. For an interesting summary of the demographics of the baby boom see Frank Bean, "The Baby Boom and Its Explanations," *Sociological Quarterly* 24 (1983): 353–65. This literature is introduced in Juanita Kreps, ed., *Women and the American Economy* (Englewood Cliffs, N.J.: Prentice-Hall, 1976). See also Charles Westoff, et al., *Toward the End of Growth: Population in America* (Englewood Cliffs, N.J.: Prentice-Hall, 1973).

28. See, for instance, W. P. Butz and M. P. Ward, "The Emergence of Countercyclical U.S. Fertility," *American Economic Review* 69 (1979): 318–28; Richard Easterlin, *Birth and Fortune: The Impact of Numbers on Personal Welfare* (New York: Basic Books, 1980); Norman Ryder, "Where do Babies Come From?" in *Sociological Theory and Research: A Critical Appraisal*, ed. H. Blalock, Jr. (New York: Free Press, 1980), 189–202; "Fertility Trends," in *International Encyclopedia of Population*, ed. John A. Ross (New York: Macmillan, 1982), 286–92.

29. Jones, *Great Expectations*, 28–31.

30. Charles Westoff and Larry Bumpass, *The Later Years of Chilbearing* (Princeton, N.J.: Princeton University Press, 1970); Judith Blake and Prithwis das Gupta, "Reply to: Reproductive Motivation versus Contraceptive Technology: Is Recent American Experience an Exception?" *Population and Development Review* 4 (1978): 326–29.

31. Glen H. Elder, Jr., *Children of the Great Depression: Social Change in Life Experience* (Chicago: University of Chicago Press, 1974).

32. The best summary of these criticisms is in Bean, "The Baby Boom and Its Explanations."

33. Easterlin has written extensively on the boom. Among the most cited of his works is "Demographic Influences on Economic Stability: The United States Experience," *Population and Development Review* 4 (1978): 1–22. See also Deborah Freedman, "Fertility, Aspirations, and Resources: A Symposium on the Easterlin Hypothesis," *Population and Development Review* 2 (1976): 411–15.

34. Bean, "The Baby Boom and Its Explanations," 360–61.

35. Jones, *Great Expectations*, 61.

36. Ira S. Steinberg, *The New Lost Generation: The Population Boom and Public Policy* (New York: St. Martin's Press, 1982).

37. Quoted in Richard Wertz and Dorothy Wertz, *Lying-In: A History of Childbirth in America* (New York: The Free Press, 1979), 190.

38. Jones, *Great Expectations*, 44–45.

39. Quoted in ibid., 47.

40. One of the best summaries of these trends is in Esther Wattenberg, 'The Fate of Baby Boomers and Their Children," *Social Work* 31 (1986): 20–28.

41. See U.S. Department of Labor, Bureau of Labor Statistics, *Employment in Perspective: Working Women* (Washington, D.C.: Government Printing Office, 1982), 2–44; M. O. Cannel, A. C. Orr, and M. Lueck, "Children of Working Mothers," *American Demographics* 5 (1982): 6–12; A. J. Norton and P. C. Glick, "What's Happening to Households?" *American Demographics* 1 (1979): 21–22.

42. Norton and Glick, "What's Happening to Households?," 21.

43. Wattenberg, "The Fate of Baby Boomers and Their Children," 20–22.

REFERENCES

"ACLI. Analysis Shows Effect of Maturing Members of Baby Boom." *The National Underwriter: Life and Health Insurance Edition* 85 (1981): 5.

Allen, Margaret, "The Domestic Ideal and the Mobilization of Woman Power in World War II." *Women's Studies International Forum* 6 (1983): 401–12.

Anderson, Joseph M. *Population Change and the American Labor Market: 1950–2000.* U.S. Congress. House. Select Committee on Population, Hearings on the Consequences of Changing U.S. Population: Baby Boom and Bust. 95th Cong. 2d Sess., 2 June 1978, 781–804.

Anderson, Karen. *Wartime Women: Sex Roles, Family Relations, and the Status of Women during World War II.* Westport, Conn.: Greenwood Press, 1981.

"Babies Bottom Out: A 'Maybe Boom'." *Science News* 112 (1977): 101.

"Baby Boom Families." *American Demographics* 4 (1982): 46–47.

Barabba, Vincent P. *Effects of Population Change on Voting Behavior and Other Aspects of Lifestyle.* U.S. Congress. House. Select Committee on Population, Hearings on the Consequences of Changing U.S. Population: Baby Boom and Bust. 95th Cong. 2d Sess., 23 May 1978, 369–83.

Bean, Frank D. "The Baby Boom and Its Explanations." *Sociological Quarterly* 24 (1983): 353–65.

Bean, Frank D., and Linda Aiken. "Intermarriage and Unwanted Fertility in United States." *Journal of Marriage and the Family* 38 (1976): 61–72.

Behrman, S. J., Leslie Corsa, Jr., and Ronald Frudman, eds. *Fertility and Family Planning.* Ann Arbor: University of Michigan Press, 1969.

Berger, Bennett M. *Looking for America: Essays on Youth, Suburbia, and Other American Obsessions.* Englewood Cliffs, N.J.: Prentice-Hall, 1971.

———. *Working Class Suburb.* Berkeley: University of California Press, 1971.

Berkin, Carol, and Clara Lovett, eds. *Women, War, and Revolution.* New York: Holmes and Meier, 1980.

Blake, Judith, and Prithwis das Gupta. "Reproduction Motivation Versus Contraceptive Technology: Is Recent American Experience an Exception?" *Population and Development Review* 1 (1975): 229–49.

Blake, Judith, and Prithwis das Gupta. "Reply to: Reproductive Motivation versus Contraceptive Technology: Is Recent American Experience an Exception?" *Population and Development Review* 4 (1978): 326–29.

Blalock, Herbert M., Jr., ed. *Sociological Theory and Research: A Critical Appraisal.* New York: Free Press, 1980.

Blum, John. *V Was for Victory: Politics and American Culture During World War II.* New York: Harcourt, Brace, Jovanovich, 1976.

Breines, Wini. "Domineering Mothers in the 1950s: Image and Reality." *Women Studies International Forum* 8 (1985): 601–8.

Bumpass, Larry L., and James A. Sweet. "Differentials in Marital Instability: 1970." *American Sociological Review* 37 (1972): 754–66.

Butz, William P., and Michael P. Ward. "Baby Boom and Baby Bust: A New View." *American Demographics* 1 (1979); 11–17.

———. "The Emergence of Countercyclical U.S. Fertility." *American Economic Review* 69 (1979): 318–28.

Cable, Mary. *The Little Darlings: A History of Child Rearing in America.* New York: Charles Scribner's Sons, 1975.

Cain, Glen. *Married Women in the Labor Force: An Economic Analysis.* Chicago: University of Chicago Press, 1966.

Campbell, D'Ann. *Women at War with America: Private Lives in a Patriotic Era.* Cambridge, Mass.: Harvard University Press, 1984.

Cannell, M. O., A. C. Orr, and M. Leuck. "Children of Working Mothers." *American Demographics* 5 (1982): 6–12.

Chafe, William H. *The American Woman: Her Changing Social, Economic, and Political Roles, 1920–1970.* New York: Oxford University Press, 1972.

———. *The Unfinished Journey: America Since World War II.* New York: Oxford University Press, 1986.

———. *Women and Equality: Changing Patterns in American Culture.* New York: Oxford University Press, 1977.

Cherlin, Andrew. *Marriage, Divorce, Remarriage.* Cambridge, Mass.: Harvard University Press, 1981.

Clayton, Richard R., and Harwin L. Vocc. "Shacking Up: Cohabitation in the 1970s." *Journal of Marriage and the Family* 39 (1977): 273–83.

Clive, Alan. "Women Workers in World War II: Michigan as a Test Case." *Labor History* 20 (1979): 44–72.

Coale, Ansley. *The Growth and Structure of Human Populations.* Princeton, N.J.: Princeton University Press, 1972.

Coale, Ansley J., and Melvin Zelnik. *New Estimates of Fertility and Population in the U.S.: A Study of Annual White Births from 1855 to 1960 and of Completeness of Enumeration in the Censuses from 1880 to 1960.* Princeton, N.J.: Princeton University Press, 1963.

Cohen, Wilbur J., and Charles F. Westoff. *Demographic Dynamics in America.* New York: The Free Press, 1977.

Cottle, Thomas J. *Time's Children: Impressions of Youth.* Boston: Little, Brown and Company, 1971.

Cowan, Ruth Schwartz. "The 'Industrial Revolution' in the Home: Household Technology and Social Change in the 20th Century." *Technology and Culture* 17 (1976): 1–23.

Davis, Kingsley, *The American Family in Relation to Demographic Change.* Commission on Population Growth and the American Future, Research Reports, 1, Demographic and Social Aspects of Population Growth. Washington, D.C.: Government Printing Office, 1972.

Degler, Carl N. *At Odds: Women and the Family in America from the Revolution to the Present.* New York: Oxford University Press, 1980.

Dorn, Harold F. "Pitfalls in Population Forecasts and Projections." *Journal of the American Statistical Association* 45 (1950): 311–34.

Easterlin, Richard Ainley. *The American Baby Boom in Historical Perspective.* New York: National Bureau of Economic Research, 1962.

————. *Birth and Fortune: The Impact of Numbers on Personal Welfare.* New York: Basic Books, 1980.

————. "Demographic Influences on Economic Stability: The United States Experience." *Population and Development Review* 4 (1978): 1–22.

————. "Here Comes Another Baby Boom." *The Wharton Magazine* (Summer 1979): 29–33.

————. *Population, Labor Force, and Long Swings in Economic Growth.* New York: National Bureau of Economic Research, 1968.

————. "What Will 1984 Be Like? Socioeconomic Implications of Recent Twists in the Age Structure." *Demography* 15 (1978): 397–432.

Elder, Glen H., Jr. *Children of the Great Depression: Social Change in Life Experience.* Chicago: University of Chicago Press, 1974.

Espenshade, Thomas, and William Serow, eds. *The Economic Consequences of Slowing Population Growth.* New York: Academic Press, 1978.

"Fertility Trends." In *International Encyclopedia of Population*, ed. J. A. Ross, 286–92. New York: Macmillan, 1982.

Freedman, Deborah. "Fertility, Aspirations, and Resources: A Symposium on the Easterlin Hypothesis." *Population and Development Review* 2 (1976): 411–15.

Freedman, Ronald, Deborah Freedman, and Arland Thornton. "Changes in Fertility Expectations and Preferences between 1962 and 1977: Their Relation to Final Parity." *Demography* 17 (1980): 365–78.

Gabin, Nancy. "Women Workers and the UAW in the Post-World War II Period: 1945–1954." *Labor History* 21 (1979–80): 5–30.

Gans, Herbert J. *The Levittowners.* New York: Columbia University Press, 1967.

Goldman, Eric F. "The Emerging Upper American." *American Demographics* 3 (1981): 20–23.

Goldman, Nancy, ed. *Female Soldiers: Combatants or Noncombatants? Historical and Contemporary Perspectives.* Westport, Conn.: Greenwood Press, 1982.

"Go West Small Fry." *American Demographics* 4 (November 1982): 12.

Greider, William. "The Unlucky Cohort." *American Demographics* 1 (1979): 2–3.

Grier, George. *The Baby Bust.* Washington, D.C.: Center for Metropolitan Studies, 1971.

Handlin, Oscar, and Mary F. Handlin. *Facing Life: Youth in the Family in American History.* Boston: Little, Brown and Company, 1971.

Hardin, Garrett, ed. *Population, Evolution and Birth Control.* San Francisco: W. H. Freeman Co., 1969.

Hareven, Tamara K. "Origins of the 'Modern Family' in the United States." *Journal of Social History* 17 (1983): 338–44.

Hartmann, Susan. *The Home Front and Beyond: American Women in the 1940's.* Boston: Twayne, 1982.

Hauser, Philip. "A New Tidal Wave of Births." *New York Times*, 25 February 1971.

Jackson, Kenneth. *Crabgrass Frontier: The Suburbanization of the United States.* New York: Oxford University Press, 1984.

Jacobs, Rita P. "Making Sense of the Recent Past." *American Quarterly* 36 (1984): 581–86.

Johnston, Denis Foster. "The Aging of the Baby Boom Cohorts." *Statistical Reporter* 76 (1976): 161–65.

———. "Population and Labor Force Projections." *Monthly Labor Review* 96 (1973): 8–17.

Jones, Landon Y. "The Emerging Superclass." *American Demographics* 3 (1981): 30–35.

———. *Great Expectations: America and the Baby Boom Generation.* New York: Ballantine Books, 1980.

———. "My Son, The Doctor of Cab Driving." *American Demographics* 2 (1980): 20.

Kaledin, Eugenia. *Mothers and More: American Women in the 1950's.* Boston: Twayne, 1984.

Kelly, William R., and Phillips Cutright. "Economic and Other Determinants of Annual Change in U.S. Fertility: 1917–1976." *Social Science Research* 13 (1984): 250–67.

Keyfitz, Nathan. "The Baby Boom Meets the Computer Revolution." *American Demographics* 6 (1984): 22.

Kiser, Clyde, et al. *Trends and Variations in Fertility in the United States.* Cambridge, Mass.: Harvard University Press, 1968.

Krebs, Juanita, ed. *Women and the American Economy.* Englewood Cliffs, N.J.: Prentice-Hall, 1976.

Leasure, J. William. "United States Demographic and Family History." *Historical Methods* 16 (1983): 163–68.

Lee, R. D. "Aiming at a Moving Target: Period Fertility and Changing Reproductive Goals." *Population Studies* 34 (1980): 205–26.

Lingeman, Richard R. *Don't You Know There's a War On? The American Home Front, 1941–1945.* New York: G. P. Putnam's Sons, 1970.

Lundberg, Ferdinand, and Marynia Farnham. *Modern Woman: The Lost Sex.* New York: Harper and Brothers, 1947.

McCarthy, James. "A Comparison of the Probability of the Dissolution of First and Second Marriages." *Demography* 15 (1978): 345–59.

McCue, Julia. "Baby Boom's New Echo." *Editorial Research Reports* 26 (1981): 471–88.

MacDonald, Maurice, and Ronald Rindfuss. "Earnings, Relative Income, and Family Formation." *Demography* 18 (1981): 123–36.

Mack, Raymond W. *Transforming America: Patterns of Social Change.* New York: Random House, 1967.

Macklin, Eleanor D. "Nonmarital Heterosexual Cohabitation." *Marriage and Family Review* 1 (1978): 1–12.

Masnick, George S., and Joseph A. McMalls, Jr. "Those Perplexing U.S. Fertility Swings: A New Perspective on a 20th Century Puzzle." *PRB Report* (1978): 1–10.

Mason, Karen Oppenheimer, John L. Czajka, and Sara Arber. "Change in U.S. Women's Sex-Role Attitudes, 1964–1974." *American Sociological Review* 41 (1976): 573–96.

Michaels, Joanne. *Living Contradictions: The Women of the Baby Boom Come of Age.* New York: Simon and Schuster, 1982.

Milkman, Ruth. "Organizing the Sexual Division of Labor: Historical Perspectives on 'Women's Work' and the American Labor Movement." *Socialist Review* 49 (1980): 95–150.

———. "Women's Work and the Economic Crisis: Some Lessons from the Great Depression." *Review of Radical Economics* 8 (1976): 73–97.

Miller, Marc. "Working Women and World War II." *New England Quarterly* 53 (1980): 52–61.

Modell, John. "Normative Aspects of American Marriage Timing since World War II." *Journal of Family History* 5 (1980): 210–34.

Moore, Charles Guy. *Baby Boom Equals Career Bust.* U.S. Department of Health, Education and Welfare. Office of Education. Washington, D.C.: 1977. 18 pp; Arlington, Va., *ERIC Document Reproduction Service*, ED 145411, 1971.

Morrison, Peter A. "Demographic Trends That Will Shape Future Housing Demand." *The Rand Paper Series P–5596* (1978).

———. "The Future Demographic Context of the Health Care Delivery System." *Rand Publication Series: N–1347–NICHD* (1979).

Norton, A. J. "Keeping Up with Households." *American Demographics* 5 (February 1983): 17–21.

O'Brien, Margaret Steinfels. *Who's Minding the Children? The History and Politics of Day Care in America.* New York: Simon and Schuster, 1973.

"Openers: Job Jumping." *American Demographics* 2 (June 1980): 10.

Oppenheimer, Valerie Kincade. "The Easterlin Hypothesis: Another Aspect of the Echo to Consider." *Population and Development Review* 2 (1976): 433–57.

———. *The Female Labor Force in the United States.* Berkeley: University of California Press, 1970.

———. "The Sociology of Women's Economic Role in the Family." *American Sociological Review* 42 (1977): 387–406.

Peck, Ellen, and Judith Senderowitz, eds. *Pronatalism: The Myth of Moms and Apple Pie.* New York: Crowell, 1974.

Plane, David A. "A Systemic Demographic Efficiency Analysis of United States Interstate Population Exchange, 1935–1980." *Economic Geography* 60 (1984): 294–312.

Reisman, David. *Abundance for What? and Other Essays.* New York: Doubleday, 1964.

Robey, Bryant. "Baby Boom Economics." *American Demographics* 5 (1983): 38–41.

Robey, Bryant, and Cheryl Russell. "Trends: A Portrait of the American

Worker." *American Demographics* 6 (1984): 17–21.

Ross, Heather, and Isabel B. Sawhill. *Time of Transition: The Growth of Families Headed by Women.* Washington, D.C.: Urban Institute, 1975.

Ross, John A., ed. *International Encyclopedia of Population.* New York: Macmillan, 1982.

Rupp, Leila. *Mobilizing Women for War: German and American Propaganda, 1939–1945.* Princeton, N.J.: Princeton University Press, 1978.

Russell, Louise B. *The Baby Boom Generation and the Economy.* Washington, D.C.: Brookings Institute, 1982.

———. "The Baby Boom Generation and the Labor Market in the Next Decade." *World Future Society Bulletin* 17 (1983): 20–22.

Ryder, Norman B. "The Cohort as a Concept in the Study of Social Change." *American Sociological Review* 30 (1965): 843–61.

———. "The Future of American Fertility." *Social Problems* 26 (1979): 359–69.

———. "Where do Babies Come From?" in *Sociological Theory and Research: A Critical Approach*, ed. H. Blalock, 189–202. New York: Free Press, 1980.

Ryder, Norman B., and Charles F. Westoff. *Reproduction in the United States.* Princeton, N.J.: Princeton University Press, 1971.

———. "Wanted and Unwanted Fertility in the United States: 1965 and 1970." In *Demographic and Social Aspects of Population Growth.* ed. Charles Westoff and R. Parke. Vol. 1. Commission on Population Growth and the American Future, Research Reports. Washington, D.C.: Government Printing Office, 1972.

Samuelson, Robert J. "Baby Boom Talk." *National Journal* (1979): 191.

———. "Look Closely, and the Recovery Starts to Make Some Sense." *American Banker* 149 (1984): 8–10.

Scharf, Lois. *To Work and to Wed: Female Employment, Feminism, and the Great Depression.* Westport, Conn.: Greenwood Press, 1980.

Schofield, Roger. "Historical Demography in the 1980s." *Historical Methods* 18 (1985): 71–75.

Scott, Loren C. "Demographic Shifts and the Economy of the 1980's." *Louisiana Business Review* 44 (1980): 2–5.

Singell, Larry D. "Some Private and Social Aspects of Labor Mobility of Young Workers." *Quarterly Review of Economics and Business* 6 (1966): 19–28.

Smith, James P., and Finis Welch. "No Time to Be Young: The Economic Prospects for Large Cohorts in the United States." *Population and Development Review* 7 (1981): 71–83.

Spain, Daphne, and Suzanne M. Bianchi. "How Women Have Changed." *American Demographics* 5 (1983): 18–25.

Stanley, Thomas J., and George P. Moschis. "American Affluence." *American Demographics* 6 (1984): 28–33.

Steinberg, Ira S. *The New Lost Generation: The Population Boom and Public Policy.* New York: St. Martin's Press, 1982.

Sternlieb, George, and James W. Hughes. "Running Faster to Stay in Place—Family Income and the Baby Boom." *American Demographics* 4 (1982): 16–19.

Stockwell, Edward G. *Population and People.* Chicago: 1968.

Straub, Eleanor. "United States Government Policy toward Civilian Women during World War II." *Prologue* 5 (1973): 240–54.

Sweezy, A. "The Economic Explanation of Fertility Changes in the United States." *Population Studies* 25 (1971): 255–67.

Tarter, Jeffrey. "The Baby Boom: Where Have All the Children Gone." *Inc.* 2 (1980): 78–80.

U.S. Department of Labor, Bureau of Labor Statistics. *Employment in Perspective: Working Women.* Washington, D.C.: Government Printing Office, 1982.

Vaughan, Jerry L. "The Major Impacts of the Baby Boom upon American Life, 1945–2050." Arlington, Va.: *ERIC Document Reproduction Service*, ED 230478, 1983.

Wandersee, Winifred F. *Women's Work and Family Values, 1920–1940.* Cambridge, Mass.: Harvard University Press, 1981.

Wattenberg, Esther. "The Fate of Baby Boomers and Their Children." *Social Work* 31 (1986): 20–28.

Weiner, Nella Fermi. "Baby Bust and Baby Boom: A Study of Family Size in a Group of University of Chicago Faculty Wives Born 1900–1934." *Journal of Family History* 8 (1983): 279–91.

Welch, Finis. "Effects of Cohort Size on Earnings: The Baby Boom Babies Financial Bust." *Journal of Political Economy* 87 (1979): 565–97.

Wertz, Richard, and Dorothy Wertz. *Lying-In: A History of Childbirth in America.* New York: The Free Press, 1977.

Westoff, Charles. "Baby Boom Critic: Theory a Bust." *The Wharton Magazine* (1979) 66–67.

———. "The Decline of Fertility." *American Demographics* 1 (1979): 16–19.

———. "The Decline of Unplanned Births in the United States." *Science* 191 (1976): 38–41.

———. "Some Speculations on the Future of Marriage and Fertility." *Family Planning Perspectives* 10 (1978): 79–83.

Westoff, Charles F., et al. *Toward the End of Growth: Population in America.* Englewood Cliffs, N.J.: Prentice-Hall, 1973.

Westoff, Charles, and Larry Bumpass. *The Later Years of Childbearing.* Princeton, N.J.: Princeton University Press, 1970.

Westoff, Charles F., Robert Potter, and Philip Sagi. *The Third Child.* Princeton, N.J.: Princeton University Press, 1963.

Whaley, Charles E. "The Major Impacts of the Baby Boom Cohort upon American Life, Past, Present and Future." Arlington, Va.: *ERIC Document Reproduction Service*, ED 231–709, 1983.

Wolfstein, Martha. "Fun Morality: An Analysis of Recent American Child Training Literature." *Journal of Social Issues* 7 (1951): 15–21.

7

New Rules: Postwar Families (1955–Present)

Steven Mintz

To understand the changes that have taken place in American family life since the early 1950s, one would do well to start by looking at television. Television is not a mere pastime; it is also a powerful cultural medium that communicates values and conveys messages about how adults and children are expected to behave.

During the 1950s, the most popular television shows were family comedies such as "The Adventures of Ozzie and Harriet," "Father Knows Best," and "Leave It to Beaver" that gave expression to the prevailing American dream. Situated in neat tree-lined suburbs, in spacious homes featuring gleaming kitchens and carefully appointed living rooms, these shows depicted a world in which "Dad presided over the dinner table in a suit and tie; Mom—trim, prim and loyal—stood by in a well-starched apron; pesky sons like Bud and Beaver made mild stabs at independence; and daughters were 'Princess' and 'Kitten,' ever Daddy's little girls."[1]

Three decades later, domestic comedies remain a staple of prime-time television. Yet television's images of family life have radically shifted. Diversity—not uniformity—characterizes today's television families. They run the gamut from traditional families like "The Waltons" to two-career families like the Huxtables on "The Cosby Show" or the Keatons on "Family Ties"; "blended" families like the Bradys on "The Brady Bunch," with children from previous marriages; motherless families on "My Two Dads" and "Full House"; two single mothers and their children on "Kate and Allie"; a homosexual who serves as a surrogate father on "Love, Sidney"; an unmarried couple who cohabit in the same house on "Who's the Boss?"; and a circle of friends who think of themselves as a family, congregating at a Boston bar on "Cheers."[2]

Not only has family structure grown more diverse, but the emotional and psychological dynamics of television family life have also undergone profound changes. Family roles have been inverted. The children, on such current television shows as "Full House" or "My Two Dads" are portrayed as knowledgeable and independent, indeed as wiser and more sensible than their parents, who appear to be confused and guilt-ridden about how to rear their own children properly.[3]

The changes that have occurred in television's images of the family mirror a much broader transformation of American family patterns. Over the past three decades, American family life has undergone a historical transformation as radical as any that has taken place in the last 150 years. As recently as 1960, 70 percent of all American households consisted of a breadwinner father, a housewife mother, and their children. Today, fewer than 15 percent of American households consist of a go-to-work dad, a stay-at-home wife, and the kids.[4]

In the space of a decade, divorce rates doubled from 2.5 divorces per thousand people in 1966 to 5 per thousand a decade later. The number of divorces today is twice as high as in 1966 and three times higher than in 1950. As the divorce rate climbed, the stigma attached to divorce declined. In the 1960s, a divorce shattered Nelson Rockefeller's presidential aspirations, but in 1980 when Ronald W. Reagan became the first divorced president, attitudes had clearly shifted.[5]

Climbing divorce rates contributed to the rapid growth of stepfamilies—or what are now called "reconstituted" or "blended" families. Today there are 11 million families in which at least one spouse has been married before, an increase from 8.9 million in 1970. About 5 million stepfamilies have children under the age of eighteen. Recent census statistics suggest that one child in four will become a stepchild before reaching age eighteen.[6]

The rapid upsurge in the divorce rate also contributed to a dramatic increase in the number of single-parent households, or what used to be known as "broken homes." The number of households consisting of a woman and her children has tripled since 1960. A shattering of traditional family norms was, in the eyes of many Americans, also evident in a declining marriage rate, delayed marriage, a falling birthrate, and a proliferation of individuals living alone or cohabiting outside of marriage. The marriage rate dropped sharply after 1970, reaching a low of ten marriages per thousand people in 1976, and young people began to delay marriage and childbearing. By 1980, women married on average a year later than in 1975 and two years later than in the 1950s, and the number of women thirty-five or over who are giving birth for the first time quadrupled over the past decade. At the same time the birthrate fell sharply (from 18.4 per thousand in 1970 to just 14.8 per thousand in 1975), and the ratio of children per mother declined by 50 percent, from nearly 3.5 children during the 1950s to 1.8, which was below the natural population replacement level.[7]

Living arrangements changed drastically. The number of people living alone grew by 60 percent during the 1970s, and by 1980 nearly a quarter of all American households consisted of a single member. Although this was mainly the product of a growing elderly population, it also reflected a sharp increase in the number of "swinging singles"—single adults who had never married or who had once married and were now divorced. At the same time, the number of unmarried couples cohabiting climbed steeply. Since 1960, the number of unmarried couples living together has quadrupled.[8]

American sexual behavior has also changed radically. In 1960 nearly half of all women waited until marriage to become sexually active; today the proportion has declined to one in five. Meanwhile, the proportion of births among unmarried women has quadrupled. In 1965 just 5 percent of births took place out of wedlock; by 1986 the figure had climbed to 23 percent—suggesting that out-of-wedlock births would soon overtake divorce as the primary cause of families headed by single mothers. The female adultery rate has risen since the 1950s by about a third. At the same time, rates of abortion have also risen. Each year, for the past decade, 3 percent of women between the ages of fifteen and forty-four have an abortion. Perhaps the most dramatic change lies in the number of Americans who lived with someone of the opposite sex before marriage. Nearly half of all Americans who married between 1980 and 1984 cohabited with a member of the opposite sex while they were single, compared to just one in nine Americans married between 1965 and 1974.[9]

The old stereotype of the housewife mother and breadwinner father has broken down as millions of married women joined the paid labor force. In 1950, 25 percent of married women living with their husbands worked outside the home; in the late 1980s, the figure has climbed to nearly 60 percent. The increase in working mothers was particularly rapid among mothers of young children. Now more than half of all mothers of school-age children hold jobs. What Americans have witnessed since 1960 is a fundamental challenge to the forms, ideals, and role expectations that defined the family for the last century and a half.[10]

These dramatic changes have evoked anxiety, apprehension, and alarm. Pessimists fear that the structure of American family life has eroded as the divorce rate has soared, out-of-wedlock births have increased, rising numbers of children grow up in poverty, and the number of female-headed families has grown. They worry that falling birthrates mean that individuals have grown too self-centered to have children, that increasing numbers of working mothers mean that more and more children fail to get sufficient attention to their needs, that soaring rates of unmarried teenage mothers consign growing numbers of women and their offspring to lives of poverty, unemployment, and dependence, and that high divorce rates and the trend toward delayed marriage spell the impending demise of the family as an institution.[11]

Other more optimistic observers respond that these prophecies of doom are exaggerated, that commitment to marriage is still strong, that the proportion of young people marrying remains very high, and that most women want to have children. They note, for example, that high divorce rates simply indicate people will no longer tolerate loveless marriages that previous generations put up with, that declining birthrates mean parents are having fewer unwanted children, and that middle-class fathers are far more involved in childrearing than were their counterparts of a generation ago. Yet despite many upbeat commentaries, a majority of the public believes that the family is in worse shape today than it was a generation ago.[12]

THE POSTWAR FAMILY

During the 1950s, many American men and women reacted against the poverty of the Depression and the upheavals of World War II by placing renewed emphasis upon family life. The divorce rate slowed and young women married earlier than their mothers had, and had more children and bore them faster. The average marriage age of American women dropped to twenty, a record low. The fertility rate rose 50 percent between 1940 and 1950—producing a population growth rate approaching that of India. Growing numbers of women decided to forsake higher education or a full-time career and achieve emotional fulfillment as wives and mothers. A 1952 advertisement for Gimbel's department store expressed the prevailing point of view. "What's college?" the ad asked. "That's where girls who are above cooking and sewing go to meet a man so they can spend their lives cooking and sewing." By "marrying at an earlier age, rearing larger families," and purchasing a house in the suburbs, young Americans believed, in the words of *McCall's* magazine, that they could find their "deepest satisfaction."[13]

Politicians, educators, psychologists, and the mass media all echoed the view that women would find their highest fulfillment managing a house and caring for children. Many educators agreed with the president of Barnard College, who argued that women could not compete with men in the workplace because they "had less physical strength, a lower fatigue point, and a less stable nervous system." Women's magazines pictured housewives as happy with their tasks and depicted career women as neurotic, unhappy, and dissatisfied.[14]

THE GREAT EXCEPTION

Although many Americans think of the 1950s family as a kind of ideal, it was in fact an historical anomaly, unlike other families in this century.

During the preceding decades, couples married in their mid- or late twenties, the birthrate was declining, and the divorce rate was steadily rising. During the 1950s, in contrast, the marriage age dropped to an historic low, the birthrate rose sharply, and the divorce rate stabilized. Since the 1950s, the marriage age returned to its historic norms, the birthrate resumed its downward drift, and the divorce rate resumed its upward climb.[15]

Yet even in the 1950s, a series of dramatic social changes was under way that would contribute to major transformations in American family life during the 1960s and 1970s. A dramatic upsurge took place during the 1950s in women's employment. More and more married women entered the labor force, and by 1960 the proportion of married women working outside the home was one in three. The number of women receiving college degrees also rose. The proportion of bachelor's and master's degrees received by women rose from just 24 percent in 1950 to over 35 percent a decade later. Meanwhile, beginning in 1957 the birthrate began to drop as women elected to have fewer children.[16]

At the same time that women were breaking away from a single identity as wife and mother, youths were becoming a group more separate and distinct from children and adults. For the first time in recent American history, a large proportion of young people from their teens into their twenties developed a separate existence, relatively free of the demands of adulthood and more independent of parental supervision than children, in a culture marked by distinctive dress, music, and life-styles. During the 1950s, youth culture evolved its own language, employing such terms as "cool," "with it," and "hip." It developed its own distinctive social roles, such as the "greaser," and "beatnik," the "frat rat," and the "hood." It created its own form of music, rock and roll. And in such figures as Holden Caulfield of *The Catcher in the Rye* and actor James Dean, it had its own heroes and archetypes.[17]

During the 1960s and 1970s, these dramatic social transformations in women's and young peoples' lives would undermine the patterns of early marriage, large families, and stable divorce rates characteristic of the early postwar era.

A SHIFT IN VALUES

What are the causes of the dramatic transformations that have taken place in American family life since the late 1950s, such as the sharp increase in divorce and single parenting, in working mothers and two-career families? The driving force behind these transformations lies in a far-reaching shift in values. Three decades ago, an overwhelming majority of Americans endorsed marriage as a prerequisite of well-being, social adjustment, and maturity. Men and women who failed to marry

were denigrated as "sick," "neurotic," or "immoral," and couples who
did not have children were deemed "selfish." A large majority of the
public believed that an unhappily married couple should stay together
for the sake of their children; that a woman should not work if she had
a husband who could support her; that premarital sex was always wrong;
and that an unmarried couple had to get married if they were expecting
a baby.[18]

During the 1960s and 1970s, popular attitudes toward marriage, sex,
and divorce underwent a dramatic change. Cultural biases against divorce, working mothers, premarital sex, and out-of-wedlock births
eroded, encouraged by a sexual revolution, expanding job opportunities for women, women's liberation, and the growing popularity of
psychological therapies stressing "growth," "self-realization," and
"fulfillment."[19]

Economic affluence played a major role in the emergence of a new
outlook. Individuals who came of age during the 1960s and 1970s spent
their childhoods during an era of unprecedented affluence. Between
1950 and 1970, median family income tripled. Increased affluence increased opportunities for education, travel, and leisure, all of which
helped to heighten expectations for fulfillment and personal happiness.[20]

In keeping with the mood of an era of increasing affluence, new
philosophies and psychological therapies stressing individual self-
realization flourished. Beginning in the 1950s, humanistic psychologies
stressing growth and self-actualization triumphed over earlier theories
that had emphasized adjustment as the solution to individual problems.
The underlying assumptions of these new "third force" psychologies (a
name chosen to distinguish them from the more pessimistic psychoan-
alytic and behaviorist psychologies) were that a person's spontaneous
impulses were intrinsically good and that maturity is not a process of
"settling down" and suppressing instinctual needs but of achieving one's
potential. Unlike the earlier psychology of adjustment associated with
Alfred Adler and Dale Carnegie that had counseled compromise,
suppression of instinctual impulses, avoidance of confrontations, and
the desirability of acceding to the wishes of others, the new humanistic
psychologies of Abraham Maslow, Carl Rogers, and Erich Fromm advised individuals to "get in touch" with their feelings and freely voice
their opinions, even if this generated feelings of guilt. A similar impulse
toward self-fulfillment and liberation could also be found in the coun-
terculture and New Left, both of which strongly criticized repression of
an individual's instinctual needs.[21]

Another far-reaching force for change in the family was the sexual
revolution. Contemporary Americans are much more likely than their
predecessors to postpone marriage, to live alone, and to engage in sexual
intercourse outside of marriage. Today, over 80 percent of all women

say they were not virgins when they married, compared to less than 20 percent a generation ago. Simultaneously, rates of adultery soared. Philip Blumstein and Pepper Schwartz, in their 1983 study *American Couples*, reported an adultery rate of 21 percent for women after two years of marriage; Morton Hunt in his *Sexual Behavior in the 1970s* cited a 1974 overall rate of 30 percent.[22]

The roots of these developments were planted in the early 1960s, when a new openness about sexuality swept the nation's literature, movies, theater, advertising, and fashion. In 1960, the birth control pill was introduced, offering a highly effective method of contraception. Two years later, Grossinger's resort in New York State's Catskill mountains introduced the first singles-only weekend, thereby acknowledging couples outside marriage. In 1964 the first singles bar opened in New York City; the musical "Hair" introduced nudity to the Broadway stage; California designer Rudi Gernreich created the first topless bathing suit; and bars began to feature topless waitresses and dancers. Sexually oriented magazines began to display full frontal nudity, and filmmakers began to show simulated sexual acts on the screen. A new era of public sexuality was ushered in, and as a result it became far easier and more acceptable to have an active social life and sex life outside of marriage.[23]

At the same time, the nation's courts and state legislatures liberalized laws governing sex and contraception. In 1957, the Supreme Court narrowed the legal definition of obscenity, ruling that the portrayal of sex in art, literature, and film was entitled to constitutional protections of free speech, unless the work was utterly without redeeming social value. In 1962, Illinois became the first state to decriminalize all forms of private sexual conduct between consenting adults. In succeeding years, the Supreme Court struck down a series of state statutes that prohibited the prescription or distribution of contraceptives, and in 1973, in the case of *Roe* v. *Wade*, the high court decriminalized abortion. Perhaps the most striking changes of all took place in a number of public schools that, beginning in the late 1970s, established birth control clinics and began to encourage unwed mothers to stay in school instead of expelling them. These decisions, to a large extent, took government out of the business of regulating private sexual behavior and defining the sexual norms according to which citizens were supposed to live.[24]

Another factor reshaping family life has been a massive influx of mothers into the work force. As late as 1940, less than 12 percent of white married women were in the work force; today the figure is nearly 60 percent, and over half of all mothers of preschoolers work outside the home. The major forces that have propelled women into the work force include: a rising cost of living, which spurred many families to seek a second source of income; increased control over fertility through contraception and abortion, which allowed women to work without interruption; and rising educational levels, which led many women to seek employment for intellectual stimulation and fulfillment.[25]

As wives assumed a larger role in their family's financial support, they felt justified in demanding that husbands perform more child care and housework. At the same time, fewer children had a full-time mother, and an increasing number were cared for during the day by adults other than their own mother. Today, over two-thirds of all three-to-five year olds take part in a day-care, nursery school, or prekindergarten program, compared to one-fifth in 1970.[26]

Feminism has been another major force that has transformed American family life. The women's liberation movement attacked the societal expectation that women defer to the needs of spouses and children as part of their roles as wives and mothers. Militant feminist activists like Ti-Grace Atkinson denounced marriage as "slavery" and "legalized rape." The larger mainstream of the women's movement articulated a powerful critique of the idea that child care and housework were the apex of a woman's accomplishments or her sole means of fulfillment. As a result of feminism, a substantial majority of women now believe that both husband and wife should have jobs, do housework, and take care of children.[27]

During the 1960s and 1970s, economic affluence, humanistic psychologies, the sexual revolution, the influx of married women into the labor force, and the women's liberation movement combined to produce a heightened spirit of individualism, a preoccupation with self, and a growing commitment to personal freedom, that, in the eyes of a number of recent social critics including Daniel Yankelovich, Peter and Brigitte Berger, Christopher Lasch, and Robert Bellah, is inconsistent with a strong commitment to the family. They fear that today's ideals of love and marital and family relationships, based on therapeutic ideals of openness, emotional honesty, and communication of intimate feelings have proven incapable, in many instances, of sustaining anything stronger than undemanding, short-term, narcissistic sexual relationships.[28]

A REVOLUTION IN FAMILY LAW

The triumph of extreme individualistic values and a therapeutic mindset has been especially evident in the realm of family law. Today, some 50 percent of all court business involves domestic relations. In addressing these cases, traditional views of morality and authority have been thrown into question, and jurists and legislators have become increasingly hesitant about discussing family issues in moral terms.[29]

Older legal definitions of what constitutes a family have been overturned. In cases involving zoning and public welfare, the courts have declared that local, state, and federal authorities cannot define family too restrictively, holding that common-law marriages, cohabitation outside of marriage, and large extended households occupying the same living quarters are entitled to protection against hostile regulation. The Supreme Court has held that government cannot discriminate against groups of nonrelated individuals living together (such as hippie communes), in providing food stamps (while upholding zoning ordinances that limit occupancy of homes to members of families related by blood, marriage, and adoption), and that state legislatures cannot designate one form of the family as a preferred form.[30]

Nineteenth-century legal presumptions about the proper roles of husband and wife have also been called into question. Until recently, the law considered the husband to be "head and master" of his family. His surname became his children's surname, his residence was the family's legal residence, he was immune from lawsuits initiated by his wife, and he was entitled to sexual relations with his spouse. Since the 1970s several state supreme courts have ruled that husbands and wives can sue each other, that a husband cannot give his children his surname without his wife's agreement, and that husbands can be prosecuted for raping their wives.[31]

In addressing questions of divorce or child custody, courts today tend to avoid issues of fault or moral fitness. State legislatures responded to the sharp upsurge in divorce rates in th late 1960s and 1970s by radically liberalizing divorce statutes, making it possible to end a marriage without establishing specific grounds and, in many states, allowing one spouse to terminate a marriage without the consent of the other.[32]

Before California adopted the nation's first no-fault divorce law in 1970, a basic legal assumption was that marital relationships could only be ended for serious causes. California's no-fault divorce legislation abolished the need to demonstrate any moral wrongdoing on the part of one of the spouses in order to dissolve a marriage. Between 1970 and 1975, all but five states adopted the principle of no-fault divorce. Today, every state except South Dakota has enacted some kind of no-fault statute. Rather than sue the other partner, a husband or wife can obtain a divorce by mutual consent or on such grounds as "incompatibility," living apart for a specified period, or "irretrievable breakdown" of the marriage. In an effort to reduce the bitterness associated with divorce, many states changed the terminology used in divorce proceedings, substituting the term "dissolution" for the word "divorce" and eliminating any terms denoting fault or guilt.[33]

In recent years, courts have tended to abandon the so-called "tender years" doctrine that a young child is better off with the mother unless she is proved to be unfit. The current trend is for the courts not to presume in favor of mothers in custody disputes over young children. Most judges now only make custody awards after considering psychological reports and the wishes of the children. To spare children the trauma of custody conflict, a number of jurisdictions now allow judges to award divorced parents joint custody, in which both parents have equal legal rights and responsibilities in decisions affecting the child's welfare.[34]

Likewise, courts have moved away from the concept of alimony and replaced it with a new concept called "spousal support" or "maintenance." In the past, courts regarded marriage as a lifelong commitment and, in cases in which the husband was found guilty of marital misconduct, held that the wife was entitled to lifelong support. Now maintenance can be awarded for a limited period of time to either the husband or wife.[35]

Another dramatic change in the field of family law is the courts' tendency to grant legal rights to minor children. In the past, parents enjoyed wide discretionary authority over the details of their children's upbringing. More recently the nation's courts have held that minors do have independent rights that can override parental authority. The U.S. Supreme Court has struck down state laws that give parents an absolute veto over whether a minor girl can obtain an abortion (while upholding a Utah statute requiring doctors to notify parents before performing an abortion). Two states—Iowa and Utah—have enacted laws greatly expanding minors' rights. These states permit children to seek temporary placement in another home if serious conflict exists between them and their parents, even if the parents are not guilty of abuse or neglect. In one of the most important decisions involving juvenile offenders and the juvenile courts, the 1967 case *In re Gault*, the Supreme Court ruled that juveniles who are subject to commitment to a state institution are entitled to advance notice of the charges against them, as well as the right to legal counsel, the right to confront witnesses, and protections against self-incrimination.[36]

Recent transformations in family law have been characterized by two seemingly contradictory trends. On the one hand, courts have modified or struck down many traditional infringements on the right to privacy. On the other hand, courts have permitted government intrusion into areas traditionally regarded as bastions of family autonomy. Shocked by reports of abuse against children, wives, and the elderly, state legislatures have strengthened penalties for domestic violence and sexual abuse. Courts have reversed traditional precedents and ruled that husbands can be prosecuted for raping their wives. A 1984 federal law gave states new authority to seize property, wages, dividends, and tax refunds from parents who fail to make court-ordered child support payments.[37]

What links these two apparently contradictory trends is a growing sensitivity on the part of the courts and state legislatures toward the individual even when family privacy is at stake. Thus, in recent cases, the courts have held that a husband cannot legally prevent his wife from having an abortion, since it is she who must bear the burden of pregnancy. Court decisions on marital rape reflect a growing recognition that a wife is not her husband's property.[38]

One ironic effect of these legal decisions has been a gradual erosion of the traditional conception of the family as a legal entity. In the collision between two sets of conflicting values—individualism and the family— the courts have tended to stress individual rights. Earlier in time the law was used to reinforce relationships between spouses and parents and children, but the current trend is to emphasize the separateness and autonomy of family members. The Supreme Court has repeatedly overturned state laws that require minor children to receive parental consent before obtaining contraceptive information or an abortion, and lower courts have been unwilling to grant parents immunity from testifying against their own children. Similarly, state legislatures have weakened or abolished earlier laws that made children legally responsible for the support of indigent parents, while laws in states that hold parents accountable for crimes committed by their minor children have been ruled unconstitutional.[39]

Ironically, a heightened judicial concern with protecting individual privacy has not meant a withdrawal from private affairs by the courts. Courts, in recent years, have become more willing to mediate disputes between family members. In the past, judges tended to subscribe to a tradition of noninterference in the family's internal functioning except in extreme circumstances, on the grounds that intervention would embroil the courts in endless disputes and that legal intervention would be futile or counterproductive. In recent years, this tradition of noninterference has broken down as courts have taken on the role of defining and enforcing the rights of wives and mothers, fathers of illegitimate children, grandparents, cohabiting couples, handicapped children, and surrogate mothers. As courts have reconceptualized family life in terms of individual rights, autonomy, and equality, judges have necessarily assumed the role of legal referee.[40]

State involvement in nonmarital relations has increased noticeably. Courts in many states have begun enforcing oral contracts and implied contracts between couples cohabiting outside of marriage, reversing the legal tradition of not enforcing a "contract founded upon an illegal or immoral consideration." Similarly, government has grown increasingly concerned about such issues as enforcement of child support duties, supervision of pre- and postnuptial agreements, and domestic violence.[41]

Judicial intervention in the lives of children has undergone certain important changes. While the legal system has surrendered some of its powers of *parens patriae*, it has gained the legal means to treat older juveniles as adults, fully responsible for their actions. Although it has grown more difficult to strip natural parents of their parental rights and remove children permanently from their custody, temporary foster care services have expanded. Today, approximately 500,000 children are in foster care. In cases of child abuse, legislatures have mandated reporting from professionals working with children and have attempted to abrogate professional-client privilege to make reporting more effective.[42]

To say that the drift in family law is away from explicit moral judgments is not to suggest that the law does not make implicit moral judgments. Prior to the adoption of no-fault divorce statutes, the law of marriage implicitly upheld a marital ideal involving lifelong support and marital fidelity. Since divorce was available only on fault grounds, the spouse who was opposed to a divorce had an advantage in negotiating a property settlement. The tendency now is to avoid questions of fault or responsibility in dividing marital assets. Among the messages conveyed by current divorce laws are that either spouse is free to terminate a marriage at will; that after a divorce each spouse is expected to be economically self-sufficient; and that termination of a marriage frees individuals from most economic responsibilities to their former dependents.[43]

In practice, the shift toward family laws emphasizing equality and individual rights has come at the expense of certain other values. Our current no-fault divorce system, for example, does a poor job of protecting the welfare of children, who are involved in about two-thirds of all divorces. Compared to the divorce laws in Western European countries, American divorce laws make it relatively easy for noncustodial divorced parents to shed financial responsibility to their ex-spouses and minor children. Child support payments are generally low (and are not adjusted for inflation), and spouses have great leeway in negotiating financial arrangements, including child support (in over 90 percent of all divorce cases, the parties themselves negotiate custody, child support, and division of marital property without court supervision). In addition, feminist legal scholars maintain that under present law, divorced women are deprived of the financial support they need. Under no-fault laws many older women, who would have been entitled to lifelong alimony or substantial child support payments under the old fault statutes, find it extremely difficult to support their families. Courts, following the principle of equality, generally require ex-husbands to pay only half of what is needed to raise children, on the assumption that the wife will provide the remainder. Furthermore, the shift toward gender-blind custody standards has led courts to move away from standards that favored the mother—by stressing day-to-day caretaking responsibilities, such as feeding, bathing, dressing, and attending to the health-care needs of the child—and to attach more emphasis on standards that favor the father, such as emphasis on the child's economic well-being.[44]

Earlier in American history, one of the basic functions of family law was to articulate and reinforce certain standards and norms about the family. In recent years, jurists and legislators have tended to back away from using law to enunciate family standards. Yet value judgments remain implicit in the law, and the values that the law tends to emphasize today, such as the terminability of family relationships and obligations, tend to reinforce broader individualistic and therapeutic ideals, stressing self-fulfillment and individual happiness as ultimate values.[45]

SOURCES OF ANXIETY

As America's families have changed, public anxiety about the family's future has mounted. Many Americans fear that traditional norms about marriage, divorce, and illegitimacy have broken down, that unwed teenage motherhood has become epidemic, that black families are disintegrating, and that the well-being of the nation's children is declining. How justified are these fears? And what are the social consequences of the upheavals that have taken place in American family life?

The Changing World of Children

When Americans worry about the future of the family, much of their anxiety centers on children. For the past decade, over a million children have been involved annually in divorces. Today, one child in four lives with only one parent, and a higher proportion of children live in poverty today than in 1975. Educational achievement scores have fallen and today a quarter of all students drop out of high school before graduation. The teenage suicide rate has tripled since 1960, juvenile delinquency has jumped 130 percent, and childhood obesity, drug and alcohol use, eating disorders, and teenage pregnancy rates all are at alarming levels.[46]

Many Americans believe that the lot of children has declined sharply since 1960. They worry about the deleterious effects of divorce, day care, and overexposure—through television, movies, music, and advertisements—to drugs, violence, and sex. They are concerned that parents have absorbed a far too egalitarian view of their relationship with their children and have become incapable of exercising authority and discipline. Above all, they fear that recent social transformations have eroded an earlier conception of childhood as a special protected state—a carefree period of innocence—and that today's permissive culture encourages a "new precocity" that thrusts children into the adult world before they are mature enough to deal with it.[47]

What are the consequences for children, many Americans ask, of increasing divorce rates and single-parent households, of working mothers and day care?

The Impact of Television

Among the most potent forces that have altered relations between parents and children since 1960 is television. The single most important caretaker of children in the United States today is not a child's mother or a baby-sitter or even a day-care center but the television set in each child's home. Young children spend more time watching television than they do in any other activity besides sleep. The typical child between the ages of two and five spends about thirty hours a week viewing television, nearly a third of the child's waking time. Older children spend almost as much time in front of the television. Since 1960 the tendency has been for children to become heavier and heavier television viewers.[48]

The debate about television's impact on children has raged furiously since the early 1950s. Critics are worried about parents' use of the television set as a baby-sitter and pacifier and as a substitute for an active parental role in socialization. They argue that excessive television viewing is detrimental because it encourages passivity and inhibits communication among family members. They express concern that children who watch large amounts of television tend to develop poor language skills, an inability to concentrate, and a disinclination to read. Moreover, they feel that television viewing tends to replace hours previously devoted to playtime, either alone or with others. And, most worrisome, they believe that violence on television provokes children to emulate aggressive behavior and acquire distorted views of adult relationships and communication.[49]

Research into the impact of television on children has substantiated some of these concerns and invalidated others. Television does appear to be a cause of cognitive and behavioral disturbances. Heavy television viewing is associated with reduced reading skills, less verbal fluency, and lower academic effort. Exposure to violence on television tends to make children more willing to hurt people and more aggressive in their play and in their methods of resolving conflicts. Time spent in front of the television set does displace time previously spent on other activities, and as a result, many games and activities—marbles, jacks, and trading cards, for example—are rapidly disappearing from American childhood.[50]

However, television also introduces children to new experiences easily and painlessly and stimulates interest in issues to which they might not otherwise be exposed. For many disadvantaged children, it provides a form of intellectual enhancement that deprived homes lacking books and newspapers could not afford. And, for many children, television programs provide a semblance of extended kinship attachments and outlets for their fantasies and unexpressed emotions. On balance it seems clear, however, that television cannot adequately take the place of parental or adult involvement and supervision of children and that the tendency for it to do so is a justifiable reason for increased public concern.[51]

Working Mothers

The single most profound change that has taken place in children's lives since 1960 is the rapid movement of millions of their mothers into the paid labor force. Between 1975 and 1986, the proportion of mothers who are in the work force and have preschool children jumped by half, from 38 percent to 57 percent. One-quarter of these mothers work full time year-round; the remainder work part time, or full time for part of the year. As a result, half of all infants—and a higher proportion of older preschoolers—are regularly cared for by someone other than their parents.[52]

Who minds these children while their mothers work? Since licensed day-care centers have room for fewer than 3 million youngsters, most children have been cared for in less formal settings. The largest share—37 percent—were cared for in another mother's home. Another 31 percent of preschoolers were cared for in their own homes while their mothers worked, with nearly half watched by their father. Some 22.3 percent were cared for by a nonrelative, 10.2 percent by a grandparent, and 4.5 percent by some other relative. Altogether, there are around 60,000 professional day-care centers in the country, half nonprofit, the other half for profit. Despite widespread demand for day care, relatively few businesses provide child care for their employees' children. Of the nation's 6 million employers in 1987, only about 3,000 provided child-care assistance, and just 150 provide on-site or near-site care.[53]

Although only about 22 percent of preschool children are cared for in organized day-care centers or preschools, this represents the fastest growing form of child care, and public debate has centered on the effects of these institutions on children's psychological well-being, children's social and psychological growth, their intellectual development, and their emotional bond with their mothers. The first shot in this debate was fired four decades ago, when English psychiatrist John Bowlby, who studied orphans in British institutions following World War II, argued that children deprived of an intense maternal relationship exhibited antisocial behavior and an inability to form intense relationships with significant others. Later commentators interpreted Bowlby's scholarship to mean that children needed a full-time mother in order to develop normally and that the family was superior to any other institution in raising well-adjusted young children.[54]

By the early 1970s, expert opinion had shifted. Studies of the federal government's Head Start early education program found that children enrolled in the program were more likely to finish high school, stay off welfare, and avoid crime and teenage pregnancy. Other research emphasized the psychologically beneficial effects of a stimulating peer environment and the fact that children could assimilate information earlier than previously thought.[55]

Today, debate rages anew over the effects of day care on children, particularly upon infants. One highly controversial 1987 review of the scholarly literature by Jay Belsky, a professor of human development at Pennsylvania State University, suggested that infants who are cared for more than twenty hours a week by a surrogate are at risk for future psychological and behavioral difficulties. Belsky argued that extensive infant care is associated with elevated rates of insecurity, less competent functioning at older ages, and heightened aggression and noncompliance—points hotly contested by Belsky's critics. The effects on extensive day care on older children are as yet unknown. Preliminary scholarship appears to suggest that quality day care has "neither salutary nor adverse effects on the intellectual development of most children"; that early entry into full-time care may interfere with "the formation of a close attachment to the parents"; and that children in group day care are somewhat more aggressive, more independent, more involved with other children, more physically active, and less cooperative with adults than mother-raised children.[56]

The most pressing problem for parents is an inadequate supply of quality day care. Child care in the United States today is costly (with high quality care costing upwards of $70 a week), often of low quality, and difficult to find, especially for infants, for older children who need care before or after school, and for children who are ill. Low-income children have a particularly difficult time enrolling in child-care programs, even though studies have suggested that such programs promote intellectual growth in children from underprivileged homes. Seventy-five percent of all children from families with incomes of more than $25,000 a year participate in day-care or preschool programs by the age of six, compared to just a third of children from families with incomes of less than $15,000.[57]

The quality of day-care centers varies widely. High-quality centers, which can charge more than $500 a month, usually enroll only a small group of children and provide a great deal of individual attention. Low-quality centers, in contrast, tend to have a high ratio of children to caretakers, a high level of staff turnover, inadequate supervision of children, a reliance on untrained, underpaid personnel, a low level of parental involvement, and a high noise level.[58]

Single-Parent Households

For a growing number of American children, especially for black children, the two-parent family is not a part of their everyday experience.

Between 1970 and 1985, the proportion of white children living with one parent rose from 9 percent to 18 percent; for black children, from 32 percent to 54 percent. Three decades ago, 19 percent of white children and 48 percent of black children spent a portion of their childhood in a single-parent household. Demographers project that nearly 70 percent of white children and 94 percent of black children born in 1980 will live with only one parent for part of their childhood. Not only do more children spend a portion of their childhood with only one parent, they also spend an increasing proportion of their childhood in a one-parent home. White children born in the early 1950s spent on average about 8 percent of their childhood in a single-parent home; black children, about 22 percent. Demographers project that white children born in 1980 will spend an average of 31 percent of their childhood in a one-parent household, while black children will spend 59 percent of their childhood with one parent.[59]

The major reason for the growth of single-parent households is the rising rate of divorce and separation. Two-thirds of the children living in single-parent homes are in that situation because of divorce or separation; the remainder, because of the death of a parent or an out-of-wedlock birth.[60]

What are the effects of living with only one parent? And what are the emotional consequences of divorce for children? Back in the 1920s authorities on the family, using the case-study method, concluded that children experienced the divorce of their parents as a devastating blow that stunted their psychological and emotional growth and caused maladjustments that persisted for years. Beginning in the late 1950s and continuing into the early 1970s, a new generation of researchers argued that children were better off when their parents divorced than when they had an unstable marriage; that divorce disrupted children's lives no more painfully than the death of a parent, which used to break up families just as frequently; and that the adverse effects of divorce were generally of short duration.[61]

Recent research has thrown both points of view into question. On the one hand, it appears that conflict-laden, tension-filled marriages have more adverse effects on children than divorce. Children from discordant homes permeated by tension and instability are more likely to suffer psychosomatic illnesses, suicide attempts, delinquency, and other social maladjustments than are children whose parents divorce. There is no empirical evidence to suggest that children from "broken" homes suffer more health or mental problems, personality disorders, or lower school grades than children from "intact" homes.[62]

On the other hand, it is clear that divorce is severely disruptive, at least initially, for a majority of children and that a minority of children continue to suffer from the economic and psychological repercussions of divorce for many years after the breakup of their parents' marriage. It is also apparent that children respond very differently to a divorce than to a parent's death. When a father dies children are often moody and despairing; during a divorce many children, and especially sons, exhibit anger, hostility, and conflicting loyalties.[63]

Children's reaction to divorce varies enormously, depending on their age, sex, the amicability or the bitterness of their parents, custody arrangements, and above all, their perception of their parents' marriage. Preadolescent boys, who tend to be less emotionally mature and socially competent than girls of the same age, sometimes exhibit anger, hostility, sadness, withdrawal, and regressive behavior such as bed-wetting following a divorce. Some preadolescent girls grow subdued and depressed. In adolescence, a number of studies have suggested, girls from divorced families are somewhat more likely than girls from two-parent families to use illegal drugs and to become sexually active at an earlier age. Boys sometimes exhibit aggression and hostility.[64]

How well children deal with the stress of divorce appears to be related to the bitterness of the divorce and postdivorce custody arrangements. Children whose parents have gone though a bitter divorce tend to suffer more emotional turmoil than children whose parents remain on amicable terms, and children who are shifted between hostile parents tend to suffer more problems than children who remain in the custody of one parent. Children's perceptions of their parents' marriage also appear to influence how successfully children handle divorce. Children who viewed their parents' marriage as unhappy tend to adjust more easily to divorce than those who regarded their home life as basically happy.[65]

For many children, the most disruptive consequence of divorce is economic. In the immediate aftermath of a divorce, the income of the divorced woman and her children falls sharply by 73 percent in the year following divorce, while the father's income rises by 42 percent. Adding to the financial pressures facing children of divorce is the fact that a majority of divorced men evade court orders to support their children. Other sources of stress result from the mother's new financial responsibilities as her family's breadwinner, additional demands on her time as she tries to balance economic and childrearing responsibilities and frequently, adjustment to unfamiliar and less comfortable living arrangements.[66]

The emotional, economic, and psychological upheavals caused by divorce are often aggravated by a series of readjustments children must deal with, such as loss of contact with the noncustodial parent. More than nine of every ten children are placed in their mother's custody, and recent studies have found that two months following a divorce fewer than half the fathers see their children as often as once a week, and after three years, half the fathers do not visit their children at all.[67]

Further complicating children's adjustment to their parents' divorce is the impact of remarriage. Roughly half of all mothers remarry within approximately two years of their divorce. These reconstituted families often confront jealousies and conflicts of loyalty not found in families untouched by divorce; at the same time, a number of researchers have found that most children of divorce favored remarriage.[68]

Teenage Pregnancy

Few social issues generated a more profound sense of urgency and crisis during the 1970s and 1980s than teenage pregnancy. Between 1960 and 1977, the number of out-of-wedlock births among teenage women age fifteen to nineteen doubled and then rose another 13 percent between 1977 and 1983. Arousing particular concern was a sharp increase in the number of out-of-wedlock births among very young girls. Between 1966 and 1977, the birthrate among girls ten to fourteen rose by a third.[69]

The number of out-of-wedlock teenage births rose for two fundamental reasons: a sharp increase in premarital adolescent sexual activity and a decrease in the teenage marriage rate. Adolescent premarital sexual activity increased dramatically during the 1970s. The proportion of unmarried teenage women fifteen to nineteen who had experienced sexual intercourse climbed from 27.6 percent in 1971 to 46 percent in 1979 (it declined to 42.2 percent in 1982). Today, nearly a million teenagers become pregnant each year and almost half a million have babies. Altogether, 40 percent of all teenage girls become pregnant as adolescents.[70]

During the 1970s, teenagers who became pregnant grew increasingly unwilling to put the child up for adoption or to enter an unwanted marriage. In the early 1970s, as many as 50 percent of out-of-wedlock children were put up for adoption; today, the figure is around 10 percent. At the same time, the proportion of unwed pregnant teenagers who married before their child's birth declined from almost one-half in the early 1950s to less than a third by the early 1980s.[71]

Many Americans fear that these unmarried teenage mothers and their children are doomed to lives of welfare dependence and poverty. The findings of a recent study conducted by Frank Furstenberg, Jr., J. Brooks-Gunn, and S. Philip Morgan contradict the stereotype. After studying some three hundred predominantly black pregnant teenagers in Baltimore from the time of their pregnancy in the late 1960s until the mid-1980s, these researchers found that only about a quarter were still on welfare when they reached their early thirties and that just 13 percent of the women were continuously on the welfare rolls for the preceding five years. A striking number of the unwed adolescent mothers had succeeded in pulling themselves and their families out of poverty. A third of the mothers had received some postsecondary education, and a quarter of the women earned enough to place themselves in the middle class.[72]

Although teenage pregnancy remains a serious social problems, it is important not to exaggerate its severity. Neither the rate nor actual number of teenage births has increased markedly since 1960. Back in 1960, women ages fifteen to nineteen had 586,966 births; in 1977, the number was 559,154. One reason why the number of teenage pregnancies has not increased faster, despite an increase in sexually active teenagers, is because use of contraceptives has increased. In 1971, just 45.4 percent of teenagers had used contraception the last time they had intercourse; by 1976, the figure was 63.5 percent; since then, contraception use has continued to rise.[73]

Domestic Violence

One source of anxiety about the family lies in the fear that changes in young peoples' lives have placed increasing stress on youth—evident in rising rates of suicide, drug use, teenage births, and a deterioration of educational achievement. Another major source of anxiety can be found in widely publicized reports of domestic violence, child abuse, and child abandonment.

In the mid-1950s, the television show "The Honeymooners" poked fun at the issue of domestic violence. Ralph Kramden would raise his fist and shout at his wife, "One of these days, Alice—Pow! Right in the kisser!" Twenty-five years later, domestic violence is not a laughing matter.[74]

As many as two million to four million women each year suffer serious injury at the hands of husbands or boyfriends, more than are hurt in auto accidents, rapes, or muggings. The FBI says that every four days a woman is beaten to death by a man she knows well. Abusive behavior also extends to children. According to the American Association for Protecting Children's data from child protective services around the nation, the number of reports of sexual abuse of children has risen from fewer than 1 in 10,000 children in 1976 to 18 in 10,000 in 1985. In three-quarters of the cases, the abuser was a close relative, most often a father or stepfather.[75]

Domestic violence can be found in homes of all races and social classes. Two of the most highly publicized recent cases involved Joel Steinberg, a New York lawyer, and Hedda Nussbaum, a New York editor, charged with beating to death six-year-old Elizabeth Steinberg; and John Fedders, a former head of the Securities and Exchange Commission, accused of battering his wife. It does appear, however, that domestic violence ending in death is more common in poor and less educated households. New York City statistics for 1984 found that 67 percent of fatal child abuse cases occurred in black families; 21 percent in Hispanic families; and 6 percent in white families. Families on welfare accounted for 71 percent of fatal child abuse cases.[76]

Professional concern about child abuse and family violence first emerged during the mid-1950s. In 1954, the Children's Division of the American Humane Association conducted the first national survey of child neglect, abuse, and exploitation. Three years later the U.S. Children's Bureau launched the first major federal study of child neglect, abuse, and abandonment. By the early 1960s, child cruelty had captured the attention of a growing number of radiologists and pediatricians who found bone fractures and physical trauma in children, suggesting deliberate injury. After C. Henry Kempe, a pediatrician at the University of Colorado Medical School, published a famous essay on the "battered child syndrome" in the *Journal of the American Medical Association* in 1962, legal, medical, psychological, and educational journals began to focus attention on family violence. Growing professional concern about child abuse led to calls for greater state protection and services for abused and neglected children and their parents. At the end of the 1960s, women's groups established the first shelters for battered women and their children.[77]

Black Families in Poverty

Of all the issues that have aroused concern about the family, none has generated more heated controversy than the problems besetting black families living in poverty. The issue first came to public attention in 1965 when the federal government released a confidential report by an obscure assistant secretary of labor named Daniel Patrick Moynihan entitled *The Negro Family: The Case for National Action*. In his report, Moynihan argued that the major obstacle to black advancement was the breakdown of the black family. The black middle class had managed to create stable families, "but for the vast numbers of the unskilled, poorly educated city working class, the fabric of conventional social relationships has all but disintegrated."[78]

Moynihan supported his thesis with startling statistics. Nearly 25 percent of all black women were divorced, separated, or living apart from their husbands, three times the rate for whites. Illegitimacy among blacks had climbed from 16.8 percent in 1940 to 23.6 percent in 1963, while the white rate had only risen from 2 to 3 percent. The breakdown of the black family, Moynihan contended, had led to a sharp increase in welfare dependency, delinquency, unemployment, drug addiction, and failure in school.[79]

The Moynihan Report attributed the instability of the black family to the effects of slavery, Reconstruction, poor education, rapid urbanization, and three to five years of unemployment rates twice those of whites and wages half those of white Americans. The report concluded with a call for national action to strengthen the black family through programs of jobs, family allowances, and birth control.[80]

The Moynihan Report was greeted with a barrage of criticism. Critics charged Moynihan with ignoring the strengths of the black family, exaggerating the problems of illegitimacy and absent fathers, and overestimating the differences between black and white families. Contrary to the impression conveyed by the report, the overwhelming majority of black families during the 1960s, 1970s, and 1980s were composed of two spouses. In 1960, 75 percent of black children lived with two parents; a decade later, 67 percent did. The report's discussion of illegitimacy also distorted the facts. Far from increasing, the black illegitimacy rate was actually declining. In 1960, 98 out of every 1,000 single black women gave birth to a baby. In 1980, only 77 did. By focusing on instability, weakness, and pathology, critics charged, the Moynihan Report ignored the strength and durability of the lower-class black kinship system—an extensive network of kin and friends supporting and reinforcing the lower-class black family.[81]

Over the past quarter century, black Americans have made impressive social and economic gains. The percentage of blacks earning more than $35,000 a year, in constant dollars, nearly doubled between 1970 and 1988. Yet despite civil rights victories, enactment of Great Society programs, and establishment of affirmative action programs, many of the issues identified in the Moynihan Report have intensified. The income gap between black and white families has widened over the last fifteen years; three times as many blacks as whites live in poverty; fewer black Americans live in two-parent families today than in the 1950s; and the proportion of black children born to single women has grown. Today, most black children spend at least a portion of their childhood in a female-headed household, at or near the poverty level, having impermanent relationships with their father or father surrogates. In 1960, just 20 percent of all black children lived in fatherless families; by 1985, the figure was 51 percent. In 1960, 75 percent of all black children were born to a married black woman; in 1985, the figure was less than 40 percent. Why?[82]

Conservative social analysts such as Charles Murray have taken the position that state and federal social welfare policies encouraged family dissolution and out-of-wedlock births. President Ronald Reagan voiced a common conservative viewpoint when he declared, "There is no question that many well-intentioned Great Society-type programs contributed to family breakups, welfare dependency, and a large increase in births out of wedlock." Murray argued that government welfare policies provided poor women with more purchasing power than a minimum-wage job while encouraging nonmarriage, illegitimate births, and nonwork. The belief that government welfare expenditures caused family breakdown rests on close chronological correlations between rising welfare spending and dramatic increases in female-headed households and illegitimacy among the poor. Back in 1959, just 10 percent of low-income black Americans lived in a single parent household. By 1980 the figure had climbed to 44 percent. Had the number of single-parent families remained at the 1970 level, the number of poor families in 1980 would have been 32 percent lower than it was.[83]

Did the expansion of state services contribute to rising rates of illegitimacy and single-parent families? The answer appears to be no. Recent studies by David Ellwood and Mary Jo Bane have found no correlation between the level of welfare payments and the incidence of out-of-wedlock births (although states with higher welfare benefits do tend to have slightly higher divorce rates and lower rates of remarriage). Between 1972 and 1980, for example, the number of black children in single-parent families jumped 20 percent, even though the number of black children on welfare declined. And even though welfare benefits fell in real terms during the 1970s, the number of black female-headed families continued to climb.[84]

The influential sociologist William Julius Wilson has offered an alternate explanation emphasizing structural changes in the American economy. He argues that increases in joblessness among poor black men have made marriage a less attractive option for poor black women. He contends that the number of marriageable black men capable of supporting a family fell after 1970, as the number of jobs in central cities requiring less than a high school education, particularly in manufacturing, decreased. In 1960, there were 70 employed black men ages twenty to twenty-four for every 100 black women in the same age group. By the early 1980s, the number of employed men had fallen to less than 50. In New York City alone, 492,000 low-skill jobs disappeared between 1970 and 1984.[85]

Is male joblessness the primary cause of high rates of divorce and single parenthood in poor black communities? Apparently not. The ratio of marriageable nonwhite men to nonwhite women during the prime years of marriage (ages 25 to 44) did not change markedly between the 1950s and 1960s and the 1980s, dropping from 70 employed black men per 100 black women to 63 per 100 black women in 1982. In fact, the marriage rate among black men with steady jobs declined nearly as much as the rate among all black men, suggesting that noneconomic factors contributed significantly to the decline in black marriage rates.[86]

The fact that needs to be emphasized is that divorce rates, single parenthood, and out-of-wedlock births have increased throughout American society since the 1960s. The trend has affected affluent whites as well as poorer blacks, and middle-class suburbs as well as inner-city ghettos. Increases in single parenthood, divorce, and illegitimacy, however, have posed particular problems for poorer black communities, where rates of divorce, desertion, and single parenthood historically have been much higher than among other groups. In these neighborhoods, a majority of children now grow up without the support of an adult male's earnings.[87]

In an attempt to address problems of poverty, illegitimacy, and single parenthood, Congress in 1988 enacted the first major overhaul of federal welfare laws in half a century. The new law requires states to set up educational, training, work, and child-care programs to help move welfare recipients into private jobs. It also requires absent fathers to contribute to the financial support of their children.

Artificial Reproduction

Of all the transformations that have taken place in the family in recent years, the most unprecedented development lies in the emergence of new reproductive technologies that enable people who could not otherwise have babies to have them. These artificial birth technologies include *in vitro* (literally "in glass") fertilization, artificial insemination, ovum donation (where a third-party female is fertilized with a husband's sperm and the embryo is implanted in the wife), embryo freezing for future use, embryo transfer, and surrogate mothering (in which a woman is artificially inseminated with the semen of another woman's husband or has the couple's embryo implanted in her uterus).[88]

The issue captured public attention in July 1979 when Lesley Brown, a thirty-year-old English woman gave birth to the world's first "test-tube" baby. Since Mrs. Brown was unable to bear children naturally due to an obstruction in her fallopian tubes, surgeons removed an egg from her ovary, fertilized it in a culture dish in a suspension of sperm, and several days later, placed the fertilized egg in her uterus. A five-pound, twelve-ounce girl, Louise Brown, was born almost nine months later. Supporters of in vitro fertilization defend it as a way for infertile couples to have children, noting that one of every six couples of childbearing age is unable to conceive. Many critics expressed fear about the possibilities of discarding of spare embryos, experimentation on or genetic manipulation of the embryo, and growing fetuses on organ farms for transplant into adult patients suffering from such ailments as Alzheimer's or Parkinson's disease. Between 1981 and 1987, about eight hundred test-tube babies were born in the United States.[89]

Controversy erupted anew in 1986 and 1987, when a bitter New Jersey court battle broke out between a surrogate mother, Mary Beth White-head, and a biological father, William Stern, over custody of their infant daughter. Under a surrogacy agreement, Whitehead was artificially im-pregnated by Stern, and she carried their child to term. At issue in the court case was the legality and enforceability of surrogate motherhood contracts, whether such contracts violated state laws against baby selling, and whether a mother should have an opportunity to change her mind about surrendering the baby. The case also provoked debate over whether surrogate motherhood involved class exploitation, since such mothers tended to be less educated and poorer than the couples who hired them. Altogether, about six hundred children had been born to surrogate mothers by 1987, and five surrogate mothers had refused to surrender custody.[90]

With infertility increasing—as a result of venereal disease, exposure to dangerous chemicals, use of intrauterine birth control devices, and the growing number of couples waiting until their thirties or later to start a family—and adoption growing more difficult as the number of the most-desired babies has dropped, many prospective parents have turned to artificial techniques of reproduction. These techniques present a wide range of perplexing ethical and moral dilemmas, including the question of which individuals will be allowed to create children artificially (for example, should artificial reproduction be limited to married cou-ples?); the right of children to know their biological parents; and the question of responsibility if a child is born with a handicap. Surrogate mothering has aroused particularly bitter controversy. Among the issues it has raised are the right of a surrogate mother to change her mind about relinquishing a child and the question of whether women should be encouraged to carry a child for financial gain.[91]

PUBLIC POLICY AND THE FAMILY

Should the federal government help working parents take care of their children? Should parents have the right to take unpaid leave after the birth or adoption of a child? Should the federal government establish national standards governing staff qualifications, child-teacher ratios, and health and safety requirements in child-care centers? These are among the questions that the nation's legislatures have wrestled with as the nature of American family life has, in the course of a generation, been revolutionized.

The changes that have taken place in American family life since 1960 have been disruptive and troubling and have transformed the family into a major political battleground. Conservative activists, fearful that climbing rates of divorce, single parenthood, and working mothers rep-resented a breakdown of family values, launched a politically influential "pro-family" movement during the 1970s. They sought to restrict access to abortion, block ratification of proposed Equal Rights Amendment to the Constitution, restrict eroticism on television, and limit teenagers' access to contraceptives. They have tended to take the position that government has a positive duty to define and enforce family norms and values.[92]

Liberals have approached family issues from a different tack. Unlike conservatives, they are more willing to use government social policies to try to help individual families. Some of the proposals they have made to assist families include expanded nutritional and health programs for pregnant women, federal subsidies for day-care services for low-income families, uniform national standards for child-care centers, and a requirement that employers give parents unpaid leave to take care of a newborn or seriously ill child.[93]

Today, the United States is a society deeply divided over the meaning of what constitutes a family and what role government should take in strengthening American families. Given this deep sense of division, it appears likely that the family will remain a major political battleground.

NOTES

1. The quotation is from Joanmarie Kalter, "Television as Value Setter: Family," *TV Guide*, 23–29 July 1988, 6. On portrayals of the family on television during the 1950s, see Steven Mintz and Susan Kellogg, *Domestic Revolutions: A Social History of American Family Life* (New York: The Free Press, 1988), 190–94; James West Davidson and Mark Hamilton Lytle, "From Rosie to Lucy," in *After the Fact: The Art of Historical Detection* (2d ed.; New York: Alfred A. Knopf, 1986), 364–94.

2. Mintz and Kellogg, *Domestic Revolutions*, 203.

3. Kalter, "Television as Value Setter: Family," 6–11. Also see Alice Hoffman, "Move Over, Ozzie and Harriet," *New York Times*, 14 February 1988, 2:1.

4. Mintz and Kellogg, *Domestic Revolutions*, 203.

5. Peter N. Carroll, *It Seemed Like Nothing Happened: The Tragedy and Promise of America in the 1970's* (New York: Holt, Rinehart, and Winston, 1982), 278–79.

6. *New York Times*, 24 September 1988, 21.

7. Mintz and Kellogg, *Domestic Revolutions*, 203–4; Carroll, *It Seemed Like Nothing Happened*, 279.

8. Mintz and Kellogg, *Domestic Revolutions*, 204; Carroll, *It Seemed Like Nothing Happened*, 280–81.

9. Mintz and Kellogg, *Domestic Revolutions*, 204. On cohabitation, see *Houston Post* 23 April 1988, 14D.

10. Mintz and Kellogg, *Domestic Revolutions*, 204.

11. Stephen L. Klineberg discussed similar themes in a public lecture, "American Families in Transition: Challenges and Opportunities in a Revolutionary Time," delivered at Rice University, 15 February 1983.

12. Mary Jo Bane, *Here to Stay: American Families in the Twentieth Century* (New York: Basic Books, 1976), 12–13, 30; Sar A. Levitan and Richard S. Belous, *What's Happening to the American Family?* (Baltimore, Md.: Johns Hopkins University Press, 1981), 21, 63; Mary Jo Bane et al., "Child Care Settings in the United States," in *Child Care and Mediating Structures*, ed. Brigitte Berger and Sidney Callahan (Washington, D.C.: American Enterprise Institute for Public Policy Research, 1979), 19; Carol Tavris and Carole Offir, *The Longest War: Sex Differences in Perspective* (New York: Harcourt Brace Jovanovich, 1977); Stephen L. Klineberg, "Age of Vicarious Parenting Now Fading," *Houston Post* 25 June 1987, 3B.

13. Mintz and Kellogg, *Domestic Revolutions*, 177–82; Elaine Tyler May, *Homeward Bound: American Families in the Cold War* (New York: Basic Books, 1988); Betty Friedan, *The Feminine Mystique* (New York: W. W. Norton & Company, 1963), 12, 41–42; Andrew J. Cherlin, "The 50's Family and Today's," *New York Times*, 18 November 1981, 1:31; idem., "Changing Family and Household: Contemporary Lessons from Historical Research," *Annual Review of Sociology* 9 (1983): 58–60; idem., *Marriage, Divorce, Remarriage* (Cambridge, Mass.: Harvard University Press, 1981); William H. Chafe, *The Unfinished Journey: America since World War II* (New York: Oxford University Press, 1986), 123–24; idem., *The American Woman: Her Changing Social, Economic, and Political Roles, 1920–1970* (New York: Oxford University Press, 1972), 177, 199–210; Godfrey Hodgson, *America in Our Time* (Garden City, N.Y.: Doubleday and Co., 1976), 50–51; Douglas T. Miller and Marion Nowak, *The Fifties: The Way We Really Were* (Garden City, N.Y.: Doubleday and Co., 1977), 147, 160.

14. See note 13.

15. Mintz and Kellogg, *Domestic Revolutions*, 178–79; Cherlin, "Changing Family and Household," 58–60; Cherlin, "The 50's Family," 1:31; Chafe, *Unfinished Journey*, 123; Hodgson, *America in Our Time*, 50–51.

16. Mintz and Kellogg, *Domestic Revolutions*, 198–99; Chafe, *Unfinished Journey*, 126–28; Jo Freeman, *The Politics of Women's Liberation* (New York: David McKay, 1975), 28–31; Friedan, *Feminine Mystique*, 17–20, 59.

17. Mintz and Kellogg, *Domestic Revolutions*, 199–200; Jeffrey Hart, *When the Going Was Good! American Life in the Fifties* (New York: Crown, 1982), 130–36; Kenneth Keniston, *The Uncommitted: Alienated Youth in American Society* (New York: Harcourt, Brace & World, 1965), 394–406.

18. Mintz and Kellogg, *Domestic Revolutions*, 205–6; Joseph Veroff, Elizabeth Douan, and Richard A. Kulka, *The Inner America: A Self Portrait from 1957 to 1976* (New York: Basic Books, 1981), 191–96; Daniel Yankelovich, *New Rules: Search for Self-Fulfillment in a World Turned Upside Down* (New York: Random House, 1981), 5, 68, 97, 99.

19. Mintz and Kellogg, *Domestic Revolutions*, 205–6; Veroff, Douan, and Kulka, *The Inner America*, 191–96; Yankelovich, *New Rules*, 5, 68, 97, 99.

20. Richard A. Easterlin, "The American Baby Boom in Historical Perspective," Occasional Paper no. 79 (Washington, D.C.: National Bureau of Economic Research, 1962); idem., "The Conflict between Aspirations and Resources," *Population and Development Review* 2 (September/December 1972), 417–26; idem., *Birth and Fortune: The Impact of Numbers on Personal Welfare* (New York: Basic Books, 1980); Arthur A. Campbell, "Baby Boom to Birth Dearth and Beyond,"

Annals of the American Academy of Political and Social Science, 435 (January 1978): 52–53.

21. Mintz and Kellogg, *Domestic Revolutions*, 206; Russell Jacoby, *Social Amnesia: A Critique of Conformist Psychology from Adler to Laing* (Boston: Beacon Press, 1975); Barbra Ehrenreich, *Hearts of Men: American Dreams and the Flight from Commitment* (Garden City, N.Y.: Doubleday and Co., 1983), 89–98, 122, 147, 164–65; Yankelovich, *New Rules*, 235.

22. Mintz and Kellogg, *Domestic Revolutions*, 204; Arlie Russell Hochschild, review of *Women and Love: A Cultural Revolution in Progress*, Shere Hite, *New York Times Book Review*, 15 November 1987, 34; Morton M. Hunt, *Sexual Behavior in the 1970s* (Chicago: Playboy Press, 1974), 235–40, 253–90; Philip Blumstein and Pepper Schwartz, *American Couples: Money, Work, Sex* (New York: William Morrow, 1983), 267–302.

23. Mintz and Kellogg, *Domestic Revolutions*, 208–9; William Manchester, *Glory and the Dream* (Boston: Little, Brown, and Company, 1974), 1035–36; Edward Sagarin, ed., "Sex and the Contemporary American Scene," *Annals of the American Academy of Political and Social Science* 376 (March 1968); Mintz and Kellogg, "Recent Trends in American Family History: Dimensions of Demographic and Cultural Change," *Houston Law Review* 21 (1984): 792–93.

24. Mintz and Kellogg, *Domestic Revolutions*, 208–9; Manchester, *Glory and the Dream*, 1035–36; Mintz and Kellogg, "Recent Trends in American Family History," 792–93.

25. Mintz and Kellogg, "Recent Trends in American Family History," 790–91.

26. Mintz and Kellogg, *Domestic Revolutions*, 223.

27. Ibid., 207–8.

28. Robert Bellah, et al. *Habits of the Heart: Individualism and Commitment in American Life* (Berkeley: University of California Press, 1985); Christopher Lasch, *Haven in a Heartless World: The Family Besieged* (New York: Basic Books, 1977); Yankelovich, *New Rules*; Brigitte and Peter Berger, *The War Over the Family: Capturing the Middle Ground* (Garden City, New York: Doubleday and Co., 1983).

29. Mintz and Kellogg, *Domestic Revolutions*, 228.

30. On shifting legal definitions of family, see Stephen J. Morse, "Family Law in Transition: From Traditional Families to Individual Liberty," in *Changing Images of the Family*, ed. Virginia Tufte and Barbara Myerhoff (New Haven, Conn.: Yale University Press, 1979), 322–25; Eva R. Rubin, *The Supreme Court and the American Family: Ideology and Issues* (Westport, Conn.: Greenwood Press, 1986), 143–61.

31. Mintz and Kellogg, *Domestic Revolutions*, 230–31.

32. Lee E. Teitelbaum, "Moral Discourse and Family Law," *Michigan Law Review* (1985): 430–34.

33. Lenore J. Weitzman and Ruth B. Dixon, "The Transformation of Legal Marriage through No-Fault Divorce: The Case of the United States," in *Marriage and Cohabitation in Contemporary Societies: Areas of Legal, Social, and Ethical Change*, ed. John M. Eekelaar and Sanford N. Katz (Toronto: Buttersworth, 1979), 143–53; Lynne Carol Halem, *Divorce Reform: Changing Legal and Social Perspectives* (New York: The Free Press, 1980), 233–83.

34. Weitzman and Dixon, "The Transformation of Legal Marriage through

No-Fault Divorce," 143–53; Lenore J. Weitzman, *The Divorce Revolution: The Unexpected Social and Economic Consequences for Women and Children* (New York: The Free Press, 1985).

35. *New York Times*, 7 February 1983, A14; 18 April 1982, C1.

36. *New York Times*, 11 October 1980, 1:21; 3 May 1981, 4:9; 6 October 1980, 2:8; 15 January 1975, 1:71.

37. Mary Ann Glendon, *The New Family and the New Property* (Toronto: Buttersworth, 1981), 43.

38. Ibid., 11, 38, 49, 71–73.

39. Ibid., 61; *New York Times*, 7 February 1983, 1:4. As recently as 1956, thirty-eight states had filial responsibility statutes. See Carl E. Schneider, "Moral Discourse and the Transformation of American Family Law," *Michigan Law Review* (1985): 1813. Enforcement of such statutes was difficult because a child who was financially able to support a parent could claim that the parent's need had not been judicially determined, that the parent was unworthy of support, or that liability was shared by a number of children. See W. Walton Garrett, "Filial Responsibility Laws," *Journal of Family Law* 18 (1979–80): 804–8.

40. Schneider, "Moral Discourse and the Transformation of American Family Law," 1835–39.

41. Ibid., 1814–19.

42. On the changing legal treatment of children and adolescents, see Walter O. Weyrauch and Sanford N. Katz, *American Family Law in Transition* (Washington, D.C.: Bureau of National Affairs, 1983), 496–98. On foster care, see Rubin, *Supreme Court and the American Family*, 156.

43. Mary Ann Glendon, *Abortion and Divorce in Western Law* (Cambridge, Mass.: Harvard University Press, 1987), 108–11. In the 1977 case of *Zablocki* v. *Redhail*, the Supreme Court struck down a Wisconsin statute that prohibited divorced parents from remarrying unless they provided proof that they were in compliance with child support orders, ruling that the law violated the individual's right to marry. See Morse, "Family Law in Transition," 333.

44. Glendon, *Abortion and Divorce in Western Law*, 86–104. Glendon maintains that European divorce laws, in sharp contrast to American no-fault divorce laws, require noncustodial fathers to maintain economic responsibility for their children. European governments have established strict formulas that realistically calculate the costs of raising children and have created bureaucratic mechanisms to compel fathers to pay support costs. When paternal support is inadequate, the state steps in to ensure adequate support.

45. Glendon, *Abortion and Divorce in Western Law*, 86–104.

46. Trends in the well-being of American youth are quantified in Office of Educational Research and Improvement, *Youth Indicators 1988* (Washington, D.C.: Government Printing Office, 1988). On youth employment, see Ellen Greenberger and Laurence Steinberg, *When Teenagers Work: The Psychological and Social Costs of Adolescent Employment* (New York: Basic Books, 1986), 3–46. It is true that the suicide rate for white male adolescents increased 260 percent between 1950 and 1976, the illegitimacy rate among white adolescent females increased 143 percent over the same period, and the rate of death by homicide among white adolescent males increased 177 percent between 1959 and 1976. Yet, in spite of these percentage increases, the numbers remained at low levels.

The white male adolescent homicide rate rose from 3 per 100,000 in 1959 to 8 per 100,000 in 1976; the white male adolescent suicide rate climbed from 4 per 100,000 in 1950 to 13 per 100,000 in 1976; and illegitimacy among white teenage women rose from 5.1 per 1,000 to 12.4 per 1,000. It is also easy to exaggerate drug use. Seventeen percent of all high school seniors have tried cocaine once in their lives; 54 percent have tried marijuana at least once. See Ira S. Steinberg, *The New Lost Generation: The Population Boom and Public Policy* (New York: St. Martin's Press, 1982), 7–19; Adam Paul Weisman, "I was a Drug-Hype Junkie," *New Republic*, 6 October 1986, 14–17.

47. Joan Beck, "Growing Up in America Is Tough, *Houston Chronicle*, 2 April 1986, A10; Marie Winn, *Children without Childhood* (New York: Pantheon, 1983); David Elkind, *The Hurried Child: Growing Up Too Soon* (Reading, Mass.: Addison-Wesley, 1981); Vance Packard, *Our Endangered Children: Growing Up in a Changing World* (Boston: Little, Brown and Company, 1983); Eda LeShan, *The Conspiracy against Childhood* (New York: Atheneum, 1967); Peter Uhlenberg and David Eggebeen, "The Declining Well-Being of American Adolescents," *Public Interest* 85 (Winter 1986): 25–38.

48. Mintz and Kellogg, *Domestic Revolutions*, 221; Victor R. Fuchs, *How We Live* (Cambridge, Mass.: Harvard University Press, 1983), 51, 55–56; 69–71; Bane, *Here to Stay*, 15; John P. Murray, *Television and Youth: 25 Years of Research and Controversy* (Stanford, Wash.: Boys Town Center, 1980), 67.

49. Mintz and Kellogg, *Domestic Revolutions*, 221; Marie Winn, *The Plug-In Drug* (New York: The Viking Press, 1977); Murray, *Television and Youth*, 18–57.

50. Mintz and Kellogg, *Domestic Revolutions*, 221; Murray, *Television and Youth*, 18–57.

51. Mintz and Kellogg, *Domestic Revolutions*, 221–22.

52. On the increasing numbers of working mothers, see Office of Educational Research and Improvement, *Youth Indicators 1988*, 38–41; Douglas J. Besharov, "Child Care Another Make-believe Crisis," *Houston Chronicle*, 28 August 1988, 1F.

53. U.S. Bureau of the Census, *Who's Minding the Kids?* (Washington, D.C.: Government Printing Office, 1987); *New York Times*, 11 May 1987, 18.

54. Mintz and Kellogg, *Domestic Revolutions*, 162; Claudia Wallis, "The Child Care Dilemma," *Time*, 22 June 1987, 63; Ellen Ruppel Shell, "Babes in Day Care," *Atlantic* (August 1988), 73–74.

55. See note 54.

56. See note 54.

57. Mintz and Kellogg, *Domestic Revolutions*, 225.

58. Ibid., 224–25.

59. Ann Milne, "Family Structure and the Achievement of Children," 5–41. Paper presented at the Conference on Education and the Family, Office of Educational Research and Improvement, U.S. Office of Education, Washington, D.C., 17–18 June 1988; *New York Times*, 7 April 1988, 24.

60. Milne, "Family Structure and the Achievement of Children," 6–7; *New York Times*, 7 April 1988, 24.

61. Mintz and Kellogg, *Domestic Revolutions*, 225–26; Levitan and Belous, *What's Happening to the American Family?*, 69–72; Halem, *Divorce Reform*, 191–93.

62. Packard, *Our Endangered Children*, 189–201; Halem, *Divorce Reform*, 174–

81; Levitan and Belous, *What's Happening to the American Family?*, 69–72; Judith S. Wallerstein and Joan B. Kelley, *Surviving the Breakup: How Children and Parents Cope with Divorce* (New York: Basic Books, 1980); Cynthia Longfellow, "Divorce in Context: Its Impact on Children," in *Divorce and Separation: Conditions, Causes, and Consequences*, ed. George Levinger et al. (New York: Basic Books, 1979), 287–306.

63. See note 52.

64. Mintz and Kellogg, *Domestic Revolutions*, 226–27; *New York Times*, 7 April 1988, 24.

65. See note 64.

66. Mintz and Kellogg, *Domestic Revolutions*, 227; Fuchs, *How We Live*, 73–75, 149–50, 214; Levitan and Belous, *What's Happening to the American Family?*, 72–75; *New York Times*, 2 April 1974, 1:34; Weitzman, *Divorce Revolution*.

67. See note 66.

68. See note 66.

69. Maris A. Vinovskis, *An "Epidemic" of Adolescent Pregnancy?: Some Historical and Policy Considerations* (New York: Oxford University Press, 1988), 25–28.

70. Vinovskis, *An "Epidemic" of Adolescent Pregnancy?*, 28–31, 34–36.

71. Ibid., 29–31.

72. Frank Furstenberg et al., *Adolescent Mothers in Later Life* (New York: Cambridge University Press, 1987); *Houston Chronicle*, 7 September 1987, 1:7.

73. Vinovskis, *An "Epidemic" of Adolescent Pregnancy?*, 25–46.

74. *New York Times*, 14 November 1987, 14.

75. *Time*, 21 December 1987, 68.

76. *New York Times*, 15 November 1987, A17, E9; 14 November 1987, 14.

77. Elizabeth Pleck, *Domestic Tyranny: The Making of American Social Policy Against Family Violence from Colonial Times to the Present* (New York: Oxford University Press, 1987), 164–200.

78. Mintz and Kellogg, *Domestic Revolutions*, 210. Lee Rainwater and William L. Yancey, *The Moynihan Report and the Politics of Controversy* (Cambridge, Mass.: MIT Press, 1967), includes the full text of *The Negro Family: The Case for National Action* as well as responses to the report by government policymakers, journalists, civil rights leaders, and academic social scientists.

79. Mintz and Kellogg, *Domestic Revolutions*, 210; Rainwater and Yancey, *Moynihan Report and the Politics of Controversy*, 51–60, 75–91.

80. Mintz and Kellogg, *Domestic Revolutions*, 210–11.

81. Ibid., 211–13; Yancey and Rainwater, *Moynihan Report and the Politics of Controversy*, 133–215; Andrew Billingsley, *Black Families in White America* (New York: Prentice-Hall, 1968); R. Farley and A. I. Hermalin, "Family Stability: A Comparison of Trends between Blacks and Whites," *American Sociological Review*, 36 (1971): 1–17; J. Heiss, "On the Transmission of Marital Instability in Black Families," *American Sociological Review* 37 (1972): 82–92; Robert B. Hill, *Strengths of Black Families* (New York: Emerson Hall, 1971); Joyce Ladner, *Tomorrow's Tomorrow* (Garden City, N.Y.: Doubleday and Co., 1972); R. Staples, "Toward a Sociology of the Black Family: A Theoretical and Methodological Assessment," *Journal of Marriage and the Family* 33 (1971): 119–38; Sar A. Levitan, William B. Johnston, and Robert Taggart, *Minorities in the United States: Problems, Progress, and Prospects* (Washington, D.C.: Public Affairs Press, 1975), 38; Carol B. Stack,

All Our Kin: Strategies for Survival in a Black Community (New York: Harper and Row, 1974); Demitri B. Shimkin, Edith M. Shimkin, and Dennis A. Frate, eds., *The Extended Family in Black Societies* (Chicago: University of Chicago Press, 1978).

82. Mintz and Kellogg, *Domestic Revolutions*, 215; *New York Times* 29 February 1988, 1:13.

83. Charles Murray, *Losing Ground: American Social Policy, 1950–1980* (New York: Basic Books, 1984), 129–33; idem., "No, Welfare Isn't Really the Problem," *Public Interest* no. 84 (Summer 1986): 5–6.

84. David Ellwood and Mary Jo Bane, "Household Composition and Poverty," in Sheldon H. Danziger and Daniel H. Weinberg, eds., *Fighting Poverty: What Works and What Doesn't* (Cambridge, Mass.: Harvard University Press, 1986), 209–31; Mintz and Kellogg, *Domestic Revolutions*, 215–16; Robert Greenstein, "Prisoners of the Economy," *New York Times Book Review*, 25 October 1987, 46; Sar A. Levitan and Clifford M. Johnson, *Beyond the Safety Net: Reviving the Promise of Opportunity in America* (Cambridge, Mass.: Ballinger, 1984), 64; Robert Lerman, "The Family, Poverty, and Welfare Programs: An Introductory Essay on Problems of Analysis and Policy," in U.S. Congress, Joint Economic Committee, *Studies in Public Welfare* (Washington, D.C.: Government Printing Office, 1974), 18–19; Marjorie Honig, "The Impact of Welfare Payment Levels on Family Stability," in U.S. Congress, *Studies in Pubic Welfare*, 37–53; Danziger and Weinberg, eds., *Fighting Poverty*.

85. William Julius Wilson, *The Truly Disadvantaged: The Inner City, the Underclass, and Public Policy* (Chicago: University of Chicago Press, 1987); *New York Times*, 16 November 1987, 18.

86. Christopher Jencks, "Deadly Neighborhoods," *New Republic*, 13 June 1988, 24–26.

87. Ibid., 28–30.

88. On new reproductive technologies, see E. Peter Volpe, *Test-Tube Conception: A Blend of Love and Science* (Macon, Ga.: Mercer University Press, 1987); Charles Krauthammer, "The Ethics of Human Manufacture," *New Republic*, 4 May 1987, 17–21; *New York Times*, 17 May 1987, 3:6; R. Snowden, G. D. Mitchell, and E. M. Snowden, *Artificial Reproduction: A Social Investigation* (London: George Allen and Unwin, 1983).

89. On Lesley Brown see Volpe, *Test-Tube Conception*, 1–13.

90. On Mary Beth Whitehead, William Stern, and the Baby M. controversy, see *New York Times*, 4 February 1988, 1:1; 2 April 1987, 1:1, 1 April 1987, 1:1; 18 January 1987, 1:3; 15 February 1987, 4:22.

91. The ethical and moral challenges posed by new reproductive technologies are examined in Krauthammer, "The Ethics of Human Manufacture," 17–21; Snowden, Mitchell, and Snowden, *Artificial Reproduction*, 147–65; Leroy Walters, "Human in Vitro Fertilization: A Review of the Ethical Literature," *The Hastings Center Report* 9 (1979): 23–43; The Ethics Committee of the American Fertility Society, "Ethical Considerations of the New Reproductive Technologies," *Fertility and Sterility* 46, Supplement 1 (1986): 1–94; C. Grobstein, M. Flower, and J. Mendeloff, "Frozen Embryos: Policy Issues," *New England Journal of Medicine* 312 (1985): 1584–1588.

92. Mintz and Kellogg, *Domestic Revolutions*, 233–35, 240–41; Gilbert Y. Steiner, *The Futility of Family Policy* (Washington, D.C.: Brookings Institution, 1981);

Kristin Luker, *Abortion and the Politics of Motherhood* (Berkeley: University of California Press, 1984).

93. Mintz and Kellogg, *Domestic Revolutions*, 237, 240–41; Kenneth Keniston and the Carnegie Council on Children, *All Our Children: The American Family under Pressure* (New York: Harcourt Brace Jovanovich, 1977), 216–21; Packard, *Our Endangered Children*, 343–63.

REFERENCES

Bane, Mary Jo. *Here to Stay: American Families in the Twentieth Century*. New York: Basic Books, 1976.

Beck, Joan. "Growing Up in America Is Tough." *Houston Chronicle*, 2 April 1986: A10.

Bellah, Robert, et al. *Habits of the Heart: Individualism and Commitment in American Life*. Berkeley: University of California Press, 1985.

Berger, Brigitte, and Peter Berger. *The War Over the Family: Capturing the Middle Ground*. Garden City, N.Y.: Doubleday and Co., 1983.

Berger, Brigitte, and Sidney Callahan, eds. *Child Care and Mediating Structures*. Washington, D.C.: American Enterprise Institute for Public Policy Research, 1979.

Bernard, Jessie. *The Future of Marriage*. New York: Bantam Books, 1972.

———. *The Future of Motherhood*. New York: The Dial Press, 1974.

Besharov, Douglas J. "Child Care: Another Make-Believe Crisis." *Houston Chronicle*, 28 August 1988: 1F.

Billingsley, Andrew. *Black Families in White America*. Englewood Cliffs, N.J.: Prentice-Hall, 1968.

Blumstein, Philip, and Pepper Schwartz. *American Couples: Money, Work, Sex*. New York: William Morrow, 1983.

Bronfenbrenner, Urie. "Socialization and Social Class through Time and Space." In *Readings in Social Psychology*, ed. Eleanor Maccoby, Theodore Newcomer, and Eugene Hartley, 400–25. New York: Holt, Rinehart, and Winston, 1958.

Campbell, Arthur A. "Baby Boom to Birth Dearth and Beyond." *Annals of the American Academy of Political and Social Science* 435 (January 1978): 40–59.

Caplow, Theodore, et al. *Middletown Families: Fifty Years of Continuity and Change*. Minneapolis: University of Minnesota Press, 1982.

Carroll, Peter N. *It Seemed Like Nothing Happened: The Tragedy and Promise of America in the 1970's*. New York: Holt, Rinehart, and Winston, 1982.

Carter, Hugh, and Paul Glick. *Marriage and Divorce: A Social and Economic Study*. Cambridge, Mass.: Harvard University Press, 1976.

Castleman, Harry. *Watching TV—Four Decades of American Television*. New York: McGraw-Hill, 1982.

Chafe, William H. *The American Woman: Her Changing Social, Economic, and Political Roles, 1920–1970*. New York: Oxford University Press, 1972.

———. *The Unfinished Journey: America since World War II*. New York: Oxford University Press, 1986.

Cherlin, Andrew J. "Changing Family and Household: Contemporary Lessons from Historical Research." *Annual Review of Sociology* 9 (1983): 51–66.

————. "The 50's Family and Today's," *New York Times* 18 November 1981, 1:31.
————. *Marriage, Divorce, Remarriage.* Cambridge, Mass.: Harvard University Press, 1981.
Chilman, Catherine. *Adolescent Sexuality in a Changing American Society.* New York: John Wiley and Sons, 1983.
Danziger, Sheldon H., and Daniel H. Weinberg, eds. *Fighting Poverty: What Works and What Doesn't.* Cambridge, Mass.: Harvard University Press, 1986.
Davidson, James West, and Mark Hamilton Lytle, eds. "From Rosie to Lucy." In *After the Fact: The Art of Historical Detection.* 2d ed., 364–94. New York: Alfred A. Knopf, 1986.
Degler, Carl N. *At Odds: Women and the Family in America from the Revolution to the Present.* New York: Oxford University Press, 1980.
Easterlin, Richard A. "The American Baby Boom in Historical Perspective." Occasional Paper no. 79. Washington, D.C.: National Bureau of Economic Research, 1962.
————. *Birth and the Fortune: The Impact of Numbers on Personal Welfare.* New York: Basic Books, 1980.
————. "The Conflict between Aspirations and Resources." *Population and Development Review* 2 (September/December 1972): 417–26.
Ehrenreich, Barbara. *Hearts of Men: American Dreams and the Flight from Commitment.* Garden City, N.Y.: Doubleday and Co., 1983.
Elkind, David. *The Hurried Child: Growing Up Too Soon.* Reading, Mass.: Addison-Wesley, 1981.
The Ethics Committee of the American Fertility Society. "Ethical Considerations of the New Reproductive Technologies." *Fertility and Sterility* 46, Supplement 1 (1986): 1–94.
Farley, Reynolds, and Albert I. Hermalin. "Family Stability: A Comparison of Trends between Blacks and Whites." *American Sociological Review* 36 (1971): 1–17.
Freeman, Jo. *The Politics of Women's Liberation.* New York: David McKay, 1975.
Friedan, Betty. *The Feminine Mystique.* New York: W. W. Norton & Company, 1963.
Fuchs, Victor R. *How We Live.* Cambridge, Mass.: Harvard University Press, 1983.
Furstenberg, Frank, et al., *Adolescent Mothers in Later Life.* New York: Cambridge University Press, 1987.
Garrett, W. Walton. "Filial Responsibility Laws." *Journal of Family Law* 18 (1979–80): 804–8.
Glendon, Mary Ann. *Abortion and Divorce in Western Law.* Cambridge, Mass.: Harvard University Press, 1987.
————. *The New Family and the New Property.* Toronto: Butterworths, 1981.
Greenberger, Ellen, and Laurence Steinberg. *When Teenagers Work: The Psychological and Social Costs of Adolescent Employment.* New York: Basic Books, 1986.
Greenstein, Robert, "Prisoners of the Economy." *New York Times Book Review*, 25 October 1987, 46.
Grobstein, C., M. Flower, and J. Mendeloff. "Frozen Embryos: Policy Issues." *New England Journal of Medicine* 312 (1985): 1584–1588.

Halem, Lynne Carol. *Divorce Reform: Changing Legal and Social Perspectives.* New York: The Free Press, 1980.

Hart, Jeffrey. *When the Going Was Good! American Life in the Fifties.* New York: Crown, 1982.

Heiss, J. "On The Transmission of Marital Instability in Black Families." *American Sociological Review* 37 (1972): 82–92.

Hetherington, Mavis. "Effects of Father Absence on Personality Development in Adolescent Daughters." *Developmental Psychology* 7 (1972): 313–26.

Hill, Robert B. *Strengths of Black Families.* New York: Emerson Hall, 1971.

Hochschild, Arlie Russell. A review of *Women and Love: A Cultural Revolution in Progress* by Shere Hite. *New York Times Book Review*, 15 November 1987: 34.

Hodgson, Godfrey. *America in Our Time.* Garden City, N.Y.: Doubleday and Co., 1976.

Hoffman, Alice. "Move Over, Ozzie and Harriet." *New York Times*, 14 February 1988, 2:1.

Hunt, Morton M. *Sexual Behavior in the 1970s.* Chicago: Playboy Press, 1974.

Jacoby, Russell. *Social Amnesia: A Critique of Conformist Psychology from Adler to Laing.* Boston: Beacon Press, 1975.

Jencks, Christopher. "Deadly Neighbors." *New Republic*, 13 June 1988: 24–26.

Kalter, Joanmarie. "Television as Value Setter: Family," *TV Guide*, 23–29 July 1988, 5–15.

Keniston, Kenneth. *The Uncommitted: Alienated Youth in American Society.* New York: Harcourt, Brace & World, 1965.

Keniston, Kenneth, and the Carnegie Council on Children. *All Our Children: The American Family under Pressure.* New York: Harcourt Brace Jovanovich, 1977.

Klineberg, Stephen L. "Age of Vicarious Parenting Now Fading." *Houston Post*, 25 June 1987, 3B.

Klineberg, Stephen L. "American Families in Transition: Challenges and Opportunities in a Revolutionary Time." Public Lecture delivered at Rice University, 15 February 1983.

Kramer, Rita. *In Defense of the Family: Raising Children in America Today.* New York: Basic Books, 1983.

Krauthammer, Charles. "The Ethics of Human Manufacture." *New Republic*, 4 May 1987: 17–21.

Ladner, Joyce. *Tomorrow's Tomorrow: The Black Woman.* Garden City, N.Y.: Doubleday and Co., 1972.

Lasch, Christopher. *Haven in a Heartless World: The Family Besieged.* New York: Basic Books, 1977.

LeShan, Eda. *The Conspiracy against Childhood.* New York: Atheneum, 1967.

Levitan, Sar A., and Richard S. Belous. *What's Happening to the American Family?.* Baltimore, Md.: Johns Hopkins University Press, 1981.

Levitan, Sar A., and Clifford M. Johnson. *Beyond the Safety Net: Reviving the Promise of Opportunity in America.* Cambridge, Mass.: Ballinger, 1984.

Levitan, Sar A., William B. Johnston, and Robert Taggart. *Minorities in the United States: Problems, Progress, and Prospects.* Washington, D.C.: Public Affairs Press, 1975.

Longfellow, Cynthia. "Divorce in Context: Its Impact on Children." In *Divorce and Separation: Conditions, Causes, and Consequences*, ed. George Levinger, et al., 287–306. New York: Basic Books, 1979.

Luker, Kristin. *Abortion and the Politics of Motherhood*. Berkeley: University of California Press, 1984.

McAdoo, Harriette Pipes, ed. *Black Families*. Beverly Hills, Calif.: Sage Publications, 1981.

Manchester, William. *Glory and the Dream: A Narrative History of America, 1932– 1972*. Boston: Little, Brown and Company, 1974.

May, Elaine Tyler. *Homeward Bound: American Families in the Cold War*. New York: Basic Books, 1988.

Miller, Douglas T., and Marion Nowak. *The Fifties: The Way We Really Were*. Garden City, N.Y.: Doubleday and Co., 1977.

Milne, Ann. "Family Structure and the Achievement of Children." Paper presented at the Conference on Education and the Family, Office of Educational Research and Improvement, U.S. Office of Education, Washington, D.C., 17–18 June 1988.

Mintz, Steven, and Susan Kellogg. *Domestic Revolutions: A Social History of American Family Life*. New York: The Free Press, 1988.

———. "Recent Trends in American Family History: Dimensions of Demographic and Cultural Change." *Houston Law Review* 21 (1984): 792–93.

Morse, Stephen J. "Family Law in Transition: From Traditional Families to Individual Liberty." In *Changing Images of the Family*, ed. Virginia Tufte and Barbara Myerhoff, 318–360. New Haven, Conn.: Yale University Press, 1979.

Murray, Charles. *Losing Ground: American Social Policy, 1950–1980*. New York: Basic Books 1984.

Murray, Charles. "No, Welfare Isn't Really the Problem." *Public Interest* 84 (Summer 1986): 3–11.

Murray, John P. *Television and Youth: 25 Years of Research and Controversy*. Stanford, Wash.: Boys Town Center, 1980.

Office of Educational Research and Improvement, U.S. Department of Education. *Youth Indicators 1988*. Washington, D.C.: Government Printing Office, 1988.

Packard, Vance. *Our Endangered Children: Growing Up in a Changing World*. Boston: Little, Brown and Company, 1983.

Pleck, Elizabeth. *Domestic Tyranny: The Making of American Social Policy against Family Violence from Colonial Times to the Present*. New York: Oxford University Press, 1987.

Rainwater, Lee, and William L. Yancey. *The Moynihan Report and the Politics of Controversy*. Cambridge, Mass.: MIT Press, 1967.

Rubin, Eva R. *The Supreme Court and the American Family: Ideology and Issues*. Westport, Conn.: Greenwood Press, 1986.

Sagarin, Edward, ed. "Sex and the Contemporary American Scene." *Annals of the American Academy of Political and Social Science* 376 (March 1968).

Schneider, Carl E. "Moral Discourse and the Transformation of American Family Law." *Michigan Law Review* (1985): 1803–79.

Shell, Ellen Ruppel. "Babes in Day Care." *Atlantic* (August 1988): 73–74.

Shimkin, Demitri B., Edith M. Shimkin, and Dennis A. Frate, eds. *The Extended Family in Black Societies.* Chicago: University of Chicago Press, 1978.

Snowden, R., G. D. Mitchell, and E. M. Snowden. *Artificial Reproduction: A Social Investigation.* London: George Allen and Unwin, 1983.

Stack, Carol B. *All Our Kin: Strategies for Survival in a Black Community.* New York: Harper and Row, 1974.

Staples, R. "Toward a Sociology of the Black Family: A Theoretical and Methodological Assessment." *Journal of Marriage and the Family* 33 (1971): 119–38.

Steinberg, Ira S. *The New Lost Generation: The Population Boom and Public Policy.* New York: St. Martin's Press, 1982.

Steiner, Gilbert Y. *The Futility of Family Policy.* Washington, D.C.: Brookings Institution, 1981.

Tavris, Carol, and Carole Offir. *The Longest War: Sex Differences in Perspective.* New York: Harcourt Brace Jovanovich, 1977.

Teitelbaum, Lee E. "Moral Discourse and Family Law." *Michigan Law Review* (1985): 430–34.

Uhlenberg, Peter, and David Eggebeen. "The Declining Well-Being of American Adolescents." *Public Interest* 85 (Winter 1986): 25–38.

U.S. Bureau of the Census. *Who's Minding the Kids?* Washington, D.C.: Government Printing Office, 1987.

U.S. Congress. Joint Economic Committee. *Studies in Public Welfare.* Washington, D.C.: Government Printing Office, 1974.

Veroff, Joseph, Elizabeth Douan, and Richard A. Kulka. *The Inner America: A Self Portrait from 1957 to 1976.* New York: Basic Books, 1981.

Vinovskis, Maris A. *An "Epidemic" of Adolescent Pregnancy?: Some Historical and Policy Considerations.* New York: Oxford University Press, 1988.

Volpe, E. Peter. *Test-Tube Conception: A Blend of Love and Science.* Macon, Ga.: Mercer University Press, 1987.

Wallerstein, Judith S., and Joan B. Kelley. *Surviving the Breakup: How Children and Parents Cope with Divorce.* New York: Basic Books, 1980.

Wallis, Claudia. "The Child Care Dilemma." *Time,* 22 June 1987: 54–63.

Walters, Leroy. "Human in Vitro Fertilization: A Review of the Ethical Literature." *The Hastings Center Report* 9 (1979): 23–43.

Weisman, Adam Paul. "I was a Drug-Hype Junkie." *New Republic,* 6 October 1986: 14–17.

Weiss, Robert. *Going It Alone: The Family Life and Social Situation of the Single Parent.* New York: Basic Books, 1979.

Weitzman, Lenore J. *The Divorce Revolution: The Unexpected Social and Economic Consequences of Women and Children.* New York: The Free Press, 1985.

Weitzman, Lenore J., and Ruth B. Dixon. "The Transformation of Legal Marriage through No-Fault Divorce: The Case of the United States." In *Marriage and Cohabitation in Contemporary Societies: Areas of Legal, Social, and Ethical Change,* ed. John M. Eekelaar and Sanford N. Katz, 143–53. Toronto: Butterworths, 1979.

Weyrauch, Walter O., and Sanford N. Katz. *American Family Law in Transition.* Washington, D.C.: Bureau of National Affairs, 1983.

Wilson, William Julius. *The Truly Disadvantaged: The Inner City, The Underclass,*

    and Public Policy. Chicago: University of Chicago Press, 1987.
Winn, Marie. *Children without Childhood*. New York: Pantheon Books, 1983.
————. *The Plug-In Drug*. New York: The Viking Press, 1977.
Yankelovich, Daniel. *New Rules: Search for Self-Fulfillment in a World Turned Upside Down*. New York: Random House, 1981.

III

Topics in the History of the American Family

8

Women and Families

Margaret M. Caffrey

As both women and the family have become legitimate areas of historical study since the early 1970s, an ongoing debate has developed concerning the amount of overlap shared by these two new fields. That there is overlap is unquestionable, because women cannot be understood historically minus the context of their roles and relationships within families, nor can families be more than abstract formulations without knowledge of the men, women, and children who give them life. But historians of women and the family have from the first emphasized their differences from each other rather than their similarities, and these differences have been substantial.

Family history began by dealing with the family as an institution that itself changes over time. Its various parts—men, women, and children— were subsumed under the general definition and not considered as individual actors in the historical narrative. Modern versus premodern, industrial versus preindustrial, extended, nuclear, and augmented families were all categories that could be studied outside gender categorizations. This use of the idea of the family still remains a major element. Also, like the larger history of which it was a part, when gender appeared in studies in the early 1970s it often only referred to the roles and activities of men within familial structures, leaving women invisible. Women's history, in contrast, has worked hard to separate women from their *femes covert* role in the family as well as society and to deal with them as individuals outside the family scene.

The study of the family made its way into history from the social sciences, especially sociology, demographics, and economics, and historians initially borrowed methodologies from these and other social sciences and adapted them to the study of past times. This resulted in an emphasis on quantitative studies using population figures and various

kinds of formal statistical analysis and normative techniques. Articles on
the family usually contained lists of averages, means, and percentages
plus comparative graphs, and spoke of such things as regression analysis
and parity progression ratios. This also has been a continuing trend. If
one looks at the *Journal of Family History* one finds this same type of article
to be the norm. But the study of women came from within history itself,
embracing traditional history methodologies in the service of gender.
Thus the study of women originally emphasized more personal, qualitative evidence, such as the diaries and journals of women and the didactic and prescriptive literature on women from a given period.

Periodization itself marked another difference. Women's history initially accepted the traditional periods used in American history, such as
the age of Jackson or the Progressive era, seeking to make women visible
within the accepted frameworks. But the development of the family as
an institution over time did not fit into the traditional periodic scheme,
a scheme that in fact had arisen out of an unquestioned emphasis on
political history as the central core of the study of America. This lack
of traditional political focus has identified family history from its beginnings with social history, the study of ordinary people's lives and doings,
while women's historians have woven a path between political, social,
and cultural history, at times concentrating on exceptional individuals
and political events, at times on ordinary women, and at times on the
ideas and beliefs that shaped women's lives.

Finally, each discipline arose out of a different social context of knowledge in the 1960s and 1970s. Family history grew out of troubled analyses
of the seeming breakdown of family structure during this period that
led scholars to examine the family in historical context to see if a crisis
was indeed occurring and how family change had taken place in the
past. Women were studied in light of the ferment for women's rights
which occurred in the 1960s and 1970s, which renewed interest in wom-
en's rights struggles of the past. The revival of the women's movement
also generated troubled reflection on the crises of contemporary women,
which led to research on how women of the past handled problems of
work and family, sexual issues, creativity, and stereotyping. These studies
both compared past positions with contemporary ones and attempted
to trace the roots of contemporary social organization and roles in order
to understand them. These different views of the historical universe led
women's and family historians to ask different questions of the past and
to view it from a differing conceptual framework.[1]

A rapprochement between the two disciplines occurred around 1980
with two important publications: *A Heritage of Her Own: Toward a New
Social History of American Women* (1979), edited by Nancy Cott and Elizabeth Pleck, and *At Odds: Women and the Family from the Revolution to the
Present* (1980) by Carl Degler. Both books recognized that by then family

historians had modified their identification with quantification, while women's historians had learned to value it as a useful tool. Women's historians had also begun to question the traditional periodization and to seek other ways to organize history, while family historians had begun to include questions about women in their work. Both Cott and Pleck in their introduction, and Degler in his preface, spoke of the distance between women's and family history and the need for them to recognize their connections. *A Heritage of Her Own* gathered together a collection of articles published throughout the 1970s by both women's and family historians that demonstrated the value of the quantitative and social-science-based methodologies used in family history for tackling questions about ordinary women; the articles showed how quantitative and qualitative evidence could validate each other. *At Odds* intermingled information and ideas from both women's and family history to attempt a synthetic overview examining the historical questions rising from women's individuality versus the surrender of individuality demanded by the family.[2]

By the 1980s there had occurred an increased sensitivity to gender in family history and an increased sensitivity to women's family context in women's history. The basic difference now remains one of perspective. Family historians see gender as one category among others, while women's historians see gender as the focal category around which institutions such as the family are structured. As a result of this difference in perspective, questions of women and the family continue to be addressed in greater depth by historians of women than by historians of the family. This chapter will trace some of the ways women's historians have added to the growth of knowledge about family history, specifically in areas concerning work, sexuality, and life roles.

WOMEN AND THE PREMODERN FAMILY

One of the earliest set of questions addressed concerned women, the family, and work. The questions arose out of contemporary white middle-class women's concerns for career equality with men in the public arena. How to juggle family and work outside the home became a major concern, and women's historians looked to the past for answers. On a deeper level they looked for the roots of the family/work dichotomy that had framed the dilemma.

The rediscovery of the work of Mary Sumner Benson, Elisabeth Anthony Dexter, and Julia Cherry Spruill set the context of the debate in colonial and revolutionary American women's history in the early 1970s.[3] All emphasized the variety of public work open to seventeenth- and eighteenth-century white American married women, including participation in historically "masculine" occupations like tanning and silversmithing. They detailed the lives of women who started and operated successful businesses or performed management tasks such as running a plantation, shop, or inn. They suggested to contemporary historians that during the colonial period, due to the flexibility of frontier conditions and women's value to the household as producers of goods, wives had more equality in the family and freedom to work outside the home than they would in the nineteenth century when these conditions changed. Because men's and women's work roles in the household blurred during the colonial and revolutionary periods, women were not subject to restrictions on working outside the home that would later become common, and women's work outside the home was socially acceptable in a way it would not be by the nineteenth century. Gerda Lerner first laid out this theoretical overview of colonial women's position, and it remained the dominant interpretation for several years.[4] Mary Beth Norton challenged this view in 1976. Her study of Loyalist women's claims for compensation after the American Revolution showed that these women at least were more domestic, very few worked outside the home or had masculine occupations if they did. In *Liberty's Daughters* (1980) she made the case that in eighteenth-century America married women were not relatively equal partners with men, and that they did not often take part in businesses outside the home.[5]

That same year Degler in *At Odds* also saw a clear gender division of tasks within the colonial household and made the point that it was widows more often than married women with husbands who participated in public work. Lyle Koehler, in her book on seventeenth-century New England women, also saw few women engaged in business. She found most married women's public work was an extension of women's gendered family work, as women filled jobs as wet nurses, dame school teachers, and healers. It remained for Laurel Thatcher Ulrich in *Good Wives* (1982) to reconcile the seemingly conflicting information into a new interpretation of the interaction of wives, family, and outside work roles. In the hierarchical family accepted by colonial Americans, a woman could work at anything, "as long as it furthered the good of her family and was acceptable to her husband." On those terms married women worked at every variety of occupation during the seventeenth and eighteenth-centuries, work socially sanctioned because it was done either as deputy husband or to conserve or enhance family comfort or survival. On the other hand, most colonial women did live domestic lives, "suggesting that even in America ideology was more permissive than reality."[6]

The needs of the household a woman lived in and the support or lack of support she received from it defined the boundaries of women's work options. This perspective has proved adaptable not only to New England, but to other regions, races, and classes. For African and native American slave women, however, this caveat held a twist. These women could do any work that furthered the good of their white household, or was accepted by the head of that household. Thus Phyllis Wheatley could become a poet, supported by the members of her white household, while other African American women and their daughters found themselves daily at hard labor in the fields—work not usually expected of their white counterparts. The same sanctions applied to enslaved native American women. So little is known about free African American women in the colonial period that no generalizations have been made, and even the basic work remains to be done in examining the roles of both white and black households and families on their public work lives. The work of African and native American slave women for their own families, kin, or local slave communities as they developed on plantations and in towns of the North and South has remained almost as invisible. Evidence exists that women grew gardens to supplement family food and raised chickens for sale to whites. As part of their work for the white household, slave women by the eighteenth century were spinning cloth and making clothing, most of which was to be used by slaves, which may have given them a sense of working for their own people.[7]

The history of free native American women during the colonial period is sparse but suggests that these women, while coming from diverse cultures, all participated in work that was divided according to gender, but the divisions were not the same as those expected of white colonial women. Reversing European expectations, farming generally was not seen as a man's occupation in native American societies. Although there is evidence men helped with certain jobs, such as the breaking up of the ground, native American women were usually the principal farmers, working in the fields and bringing in the crops. Europeans, as they came into contact with native Americans, tried to encourage them to adopt the gender relations expected in European societies. Thus men were induced to farm and women to spin and make cloth in the home, not work in the fields.[8]

In the realm of sexuality, colonial society expected women to be sexual beings. On the positive side, this meant sexual pleasure was an expectation for both men and women, ideally confined for whites within marriage where it was theoretically controlled against excess by the couple's orientation toward God. On the negative side, there was an underlying fear that women's sexuality could get out of hand, the most extreme example being through intercourse with the devil in witchcraft. Society attempted to control sexuality outside of marriage by external means, through laws and the courts. Nonmarital sex and bastardy, or the bearing of an illegitimate child, were crimes punishable by fines, whipping, or in the case of an indentured servant, by a lengthening of the time of service. Adultery was a capital crime, punishable by hanging, although in practice the charge was often reduced to a lesser one. Punishments varied by gender and colony. Sex between a married man and a single woman not promised to someone was not considered adultery, although sex between a married woman and any man was. In fornication cases in seventeenth-century Massachusetts, men generally received heavier sentences, both in fines and whippings, than women. Women generally received severer physical punishment in bastardy cases throughout the colonies. There was an economic component in the severity of the sentences for bastardy, which were meant to act as deterrents against other women having illegitimate children. Such children of both free and indentured women might have to be supported by public taxes, while pregnancy cheated a master of an indentured servant's work time. For African American slave women, however, it was not considered a crime to have an illegitimate child, because a slave child was a potential source of income, which was worth the loss of work time that pregnancy entailed.[9]

Although virginity before first marriage was the ideal, premarital pregnancy was a common phenomenon among white women in colonial America, ranging from 10 percent to 33 percent in some areas and time periods. There were no social sanctions if marriage followed such pregnancies. Historians now see premarital pregnancy as one way daughters and sons used to break with parental control of marriage toward the end of the eighteenth century, as society moved from premodern to modern family structure.[10]

Birth control was not a social issue. Fertility in marriage was the ideal. But as a private issue, there is some evidence that married (and single) women practiced birth control through *coitus interruptus*, and that women tried to control the spacing of children in marriage through breast-feeding, a nonreliable personal method, but a seemingly effective social method. On average a married woman would breast-feed a child from twelve to eighteen months and could expect to have a child every two years or so.[11]

Abortion was also not a social issue. The fetus was not considered to have a soul until "quickening," movement within the womb, which in general did not occur until the fourth month. It was considered a crime to attempt abortion after quickening, but not before. As a private issue, there is no way to tell how often abortion was used by married women, although there is some evidence that single women tried various plants and poisons to induce miscarriage and in some cases practiced infanticide in an attempt to avoid bastardy charges.[12]

In terms of women's roles in the life course, for white women marriage was intended to be for life. In the South, due to the dominance of the Anglican religion, no absolute divorce was possible. A man and woman could legally separate with some difficulty, but no legal remarriage was allowed. In New England, especially Connecticut, divorce was a civil not a church matter, and marriage was considered as a contract that could be dissolved, which made remarriage without legal penalty possible, although divorce remained rare. Desertion by both men and women served as an informal method of divorce. One of the things colonists remarked on about native Americans during the colonial period was the ease of divorce among them. Among the Iroquois, for example, usually by mutual agreement the man would leave and the woman kept the children, if there were any, and the couple would be free to start over. Like white women, African and native American women were perceived as sexual beings. Colonial society believed in control of sexuality through relationships, and slave women, from the little we know, were encouraged to marry, although such marriage was not seen by white society as legally binding and therefore not necessarily for life.[13]

Among white women marriage was also primarily an economic arrangement and usually settled by the fathers; love was not expected before marriage, although ideally regard would grow within marriage. This gradually gave way in the late eighteenth century to an emphasis among daughters and sons on love before marriage, and the choice of partners gradually came to be decided by the children themselves, rather than controlled by the parents. Again, this was a sign of the new modern family structure replacing the premodern family. Nancy Cott, in studying eighteenth-century divorce records in New England, found evidence of expectations of romantic love toward the end of the century, which added corroboration to the switch to a new idea of marriage and the family at that time.[14]

Study of African societies suggests patterns expected by slave women brought from Africa in the seventeenth and eighteenth centuries. Africans often lived in extended families built around same-sex adult siblings, whether male or female, living with spouses and children in compounds. Sexuality was viewed as normal and healthy. Marriage, as in European societies, was an economic transaction between two families, not between individuals, and most societies accepted premarital sex. Children were important, but parenting was a role exercised by all adults in a compound, although the actual parents had the chief responsibility. What could be adapted from African patterns in America depended on where a woman found herself, whether she was one of a few black people in an area or part of a larger black community. Evidence shows that marriage remained important to African American women. Patterns that developed included long-distance marriage, where one spouse lived on a different farm or plantation from the other and visited when possible. Free choice in marriage seems to have been the rule, although a master could interfere and make choices for the slaves. Nothing is known about slave patterns of divorce during this period, except that in this, too, the master could interfere.[15]

The terms of pregnancy and childbirth marked the bounds of women's lives more surely than the seasons marked the days of colonial farmers. Laurel Thatcher Ulrich writes of women's seasons of reproduction, for white women the constant two-year cycle of pregnancy, childbirth, and lactation. More than any other role, "reproduction was the axis of female life." Reproduction was also surrounded for women by their own rituals, shared with other women, kin, and neighbors: a gathering together of women, special groaning cakes and beer, a "sitting up" week of visiting after the birth in towns and cities, the use of special garments passed on from mother to daughter, possibly a "weaning journey," a trip by the mother to visit relatives without the child to facilitate the end of breast-feeding.[16]

Joan Rezner Gunderson suggests that slave women had a different season for pregnancy, that they tended to have babies from May to October in King William Parish, Virginia, while white women usually gave birth from October to November. Gunderson speculates that opportunities to be with men were greater during the summer season for African American women and in the winter season for white women. She also suggests that black women breast-fed longer, as much as three years, according to customs brought from Africa. Childbirth was shared with at least one other woman, the midwife.[17]

Ulrich shows how white colonial motherhood differed from later nineteenth-century motherhood. She describes mothering as "extensive rather than intensive.... Mothering meant generalized responsibility for an assembly of youngsters rather than concentrated devotion to a few." The need to mother children from other families present in the household through the placing-out system of apprenticeship, and the use of older children as caretakers of younger children, suggest this. Child-rearing was not the chief occupation of the household and neither was it the chief occupation of its mistress; it was one responsibility among many. The most successful mother was the one who had numerous descendents, the "fruitful vine." Fertility, more than sentiment, made a woman's motherly reputation. Moreover, the mother was not perceived as the primary parent. The father, as the children's moral teacher and guardian of their souls, held that position. In case of divorce or separation, the father by law assumed guardianship of the children.[18]

In becoming a wife, a white woman became involved in a mesh of mutual duties and responsibilities within the family. She was subordinate to her husband, and often acted as his second-in-command, but everyone else in the family, servants and children, was subordinate to her in the "great chain of being." She entered into some of the decision making in the family, in some places being required along with her husband to sign or mark children's apprenticeship papers, or assent to the selling of property.[19]

Widowhood was a precarious role for most white women during the colonial period. Many women were left with little, and especially in the South quick remarriage was the pattern. Widows were guaranteed a third of their husband's estate as their portion, which provided some security to wealthier women. Widows also threw off their *femes covert* status and could own property, keep their own wages and profits, make contracts, borrow and loan money, all the things that they could not do normally within marriage, although it has been difficult to tell whether women perceived this as any kind of advantage. Wealthy widows who remarried could set up prenuptial agreements by which they could keep control of their property, but this occurred rarely and largely as protection so that the children of the former marriage would not lose their inheritance.[20]

One last role expected of white women during the colonial period was that of daughter. Daughters were expected to leave home and to become part of another family. Therefore, since families conserved wealth, daughters were usually not left large amounts of property in wills and most land went to sons. They did generally inherit their mother's personal items and property and were supplied with a dowry when they married. Daughters usually left home between the ages of ten and twelve as part of the "putting out" system in New England, to learn the arts of keeping house from another woman. Up to that time they were probably baby tenders in their mother's seasons of reproduction, or workers in the household economy beginning around the age of five. Spinning became a job for daughters in the eighteenth century. A girl's first menstruation does not seem to have been a notable event.

Little is known about slave women in the roles of mothers, wives, or daughters during the colonial period. Norton suggests that in the eighteenth century slave mothers tended to transmit skills they learned, such as dairying or midwifery, to daughters.[21]

Native Americans had diverse courtship and marriage customs. Marriage was not necessarily for life as divorce was common and by relatively simple mutual agreement. In many tribes, the mother's family was the primary family and the mother kept the children. Native American women also attempted to regulate the spacing of children by lactation and nursed for a longer time period than white women, some for as much as three or four years. Some tribes practiced polygamy, and a woman might be one of several wives, part of a system that spread out the work of the household. Childbirth usually took place in a special hut away from the family living area. Puberty was a time of initiation into adulthood among many peoples through special ceremonies, isolation, or training by older women. Mothers in general taught daughters, while men taught sons.[22]

WOMEN AND THE MODERN FAMILY

Beginning in the revolutionary period and extending most visibly through the first half of the nineteenth century, women's work and family obligations changed as a new type of family and new social organizations occurred. What resulted for women was the development of the ideology of domesticity, which placed men and women in separate spheres and which made public work no longer socially acceptable for married, middle-class women, excluding them from paid middle-class occupations and careers. Barbara Welter early identified this domesticity, which made woman "the hostage in the home." At first historians focused on the oppressiveness of domesticity and saw the first half of the nineteenth century as a nadir for women. The theory was that as women lost productive power in the home with the development of industrialization, they lost importance in society and gave up actual family power for idealized "influence." Ann Douglas called the loss of spinning and cloth production to factories "feminine disestablishment" and "the end of mother-power."[23]

This interpretation began to be challenged on closer examination of the period. In 1973, Kathryn Kish Sklar suggested that women helped both to create and promote domesticity in the nineteenth century because of the positive advantages the idea held for them. Norton later made the case that domestic pursuits had not had much value in the eighteenth century, whereas in the nineteenth century they were revalued and given social respect. Other historians also found that the new ideology helped to raise women's status in family and society. As America struggled to adapt ideas and institutions to democratic rather than hierarchical ideals, a separate sphere for women seemed to promote democracy within the family. In theory separate spheres gave women their own autonomous realm of authority, whereas in the eighteenth-century household the husband as family head claimed all authority. For example, when county fairs were first held, prizes for cooking and women's productivity were awarded to the husband, not the wife, because they were seen as household products under control of the male head of the household. The ideology of domesticity also helped develop the idea of women's moral superiority to men, whereas in the eighteenth century women were seen as the daughters of Eve and potentially morally weak.[24]

Over the years there has been some reevaluation of the extent to which the "assignment of spheres" influenced middle-class women economically. Many of these women got around this prohibition by doing things that were "not really work," such as writing for magazines. Some women ran schools with their husbands. As Joan Jensen has demonstrated, in the mid-Atlantic states middle-class rural women retained roles as producers of products in rural households in the nineteenth century, replacing the making of cloth and textiles with the making of butter which they sold to earn extra money. Suzanne Lebsock has noted in her study of antebellum Petersburg, Virginia, that town life was still a "half-farming life" in the first half of the nineteenth century, with people keeping various animals and growing gardens and orchards from which they intended to make money. She also suggests that married women in antebellum Petersburg continued to work if they made enough money to make it worthwhile, for example, at millinery.[25] Nevertheless the evidence shows that middle-class women were gradually squeezed out of activities and occupations in which they had formerly participated, for example as doctors, midwives, attorneys of record, and businesswomen.[26] As wages became the standard for public work, it became socially unacceptable for married middle-class women to have paying occupations.

Many white married women worked outside the home in an unpaid capacity in organizations that helped the poor, widows, and orphans, in missionary societies to bring religion to the frontier, in moral reform societies, in abolition, and in women's rights. This organization of married women to work outside the home is one of the phenomena of the nineteenth century. In the antebellum period, most of the women involved lived in New England and the mid-Atlantic states. After the Civil War, this work spread to other parts of the country, involving increasingly large numbers of women.

At first historians studied women's reform work as a response to the Second Great Awakening and a reaction to the doctrine of the spheres. Then Mary Ryan studied the connections of women's unpaid public work with family development in the nineteenth century. She discovered that the type of associations women participated in or founded depended on the type of family they belonged to and the status and economic needs of that family. She argued that in revival and reform work women helped create the middle-class family and stabilize their own families within the new class.[27] Nancy Hewett later showed the different family backgrounds of the middle-class women who belonged to three distinct networks of reform in Rochester, New York, between 1822 and 1872. She adds: "Varied patterns of private domesticity thus helped to shape varied patterns of public activism."[28]

The artificial separation of women's public work into paid (recognized) work and unpaid (unrecognized) work may have also hidden changes in family dynamics. There is a need to study how women's reform work influenced or was influenced by relationships between husband and wife, mother and children, as growing numbers of women became involved throughout the 1800s. Free African American women received more support to participate in radical reform than white women, since that reform involved their communities. In the North women were encouraged within growing antebellum African American communities to belong to abolition organizations and to participate in charitable and reform work; and in marked difference from white gender conventions, women's speaking in public was accepted by the African American male community at a time when white women struggled against the resistance of white men. The case of Maria Stewart provides an exception to this, apparently because she spoke critically of the efforts of African American men who then turned against her.[29]

Suzanne Lebsock, in the most complete study of free African American women of the early nineteenth century, showed that a significantly higher percentage, for example, 16.1 percent of 124 laundresses and seamstresses versus 1.1 percent of their 92 white counterparts were married. Of factory workers, 20.5 percent of 293 African American women were married, while among whites only 7.8 percent of 269 women were married.[30] Other historians have documented this as a trend continuing into the twentieth century. A consistently higher proportion of African American wives has participated in the work force than white wives of either the working or middle classes. Lebsock found that economic necessity was not the only consideration, because African American women who did not need to work continued to do so, although for many women this was the major motivation. Elizabeth Pleck, in a study of African American and Italian American women in Buffalo, New York, during the last part of the nineteenth century also suggested that African American women might be responding to some different expectations about women in their culture and were aided by a different pattern of child-rearing to pursue such a course. She found that even when husbands' income was the same, African American women worked more often than Italian women. In Italian families close supervision of children was the cultural norm, while African American families raised children to be self-reliant.[31]

The strictures of domesticity against wives working also did not apply to the white women of the developing industrial working class. Factories often hired families rather than individuals, and husbands, wives, and children each had their part in the factory work. In the late eighteenth and early nineteenth century these families were not paid as individuals but as households, and the wages were given to the head of the household, whether male or female.[32] Christine Stansell has demonstrated the importance of married working-class women and daughters in New York City in the antebellum period to the "family wage economy," in which parents and children pooled their wages for family survival. Stansell suggests that the urban worker's household remained very much like the colonial household in its lack of privacy, its hierarchy, and its dependence on a family-oriented economy to which everyone contributed.[33] The continuation of a household economy not only among the developing urban working class, but also in rural areas, among southern antebellum families and Irish and German immigrant families that became working class, reinforces the point that those directly affected by the development of the new modern family in the antebellum period were actually a very small part of the population.

The family wage economy led to different combinations of wage work, domestic work, and unpaid work (such as children scavenging on the streets or helping mothers with piece work) than the colonial household had provided, and Stansell suggests that this eventually undermined both parental and male authority in the household. Both Stansell and writers on later immigrant experience see tensions developing within the family as daughters and sons faced conflicts between giving their wages to the family or spending them as they wished. It seems that by the period after 1810 workers were being paid as individuals rather than as families.[34]

The ideology of domesticity did not apply to the work of slave women because the household continued to be the model for rural and plantation life, and African American women, while there was some gender differentiation in their work, ultimately worked at anything the head of the white household deemed necessary. Work for the white household was made to take precedence over work for their own families, and often the latter work was taken out of a woman's hands. Care of children was given to "grannies" helped by young girls in group day-care situations. In smaller places, the white wife might assume day-care duties while the black woman worked in the fields. Housework was communal in varying degrees, as groups of women spun cloth and made clothes for the whole slave community, or two or three times a year gangs went through the slave quarters of larger places cleaning and whitewashing. Housework was sometimes communal in the slave quarters as women washed clothes together on Saturdays. Through this type of work slave women gained a sense of responsibility in working for the slave community as a whole. But Jacqueline Jones suggests that "slave women deprived of the ability to cook for their own kinfolk or discipline their own children felt a keen sense of loss."[35] Part of the meaning of freedom after the Civil War for African American women would be to be able to put their families and their community first, instead of the white master's wishes.

Domesticity did affect some native American women. Adoption of farming for men and housewifery for women in the European pattern changed the Iroquois "quasi-matriarchal system," as the important relationship structure shifted from mother-daughter to husband-wife. This meant a loss of status for women in the tribe. The same type of thing seems to have happened to women among the Cherokee. During the antebellum period Indian agents and missionaries encouraged women to become domestic in the European sense to further assimilation of these people into "acceptable" ways of living.[36]

The second half of the nineteenth century saw the gradual disintegration of the spheres as middle-class women entered formerly closed professions and achieved rigorous higher education, but these were usually daughters and not married women, and they did not join the paid public work force as a group until the twentieth century. Daughters who married were often constrained to give up paid public work, and a significant number of middle-class women made choices between family or career. The number of sex-segregated occupations grew developing along the pattern of middle-class family relationships of men and women. As Dee Garrison shows for librarians, these patterns were hierarchical, paternal, and placed women in the position of public wives. Thus family structure was provided for the single daughters and widows who made up the female library profession. The family roles of these women also influenced the shape the jobs took, as women became library hostesses and caretakers of children in the public realm.[37]

For African American women freedom first affected work patterns, because right after the Civil War women refused to work for whites and African American men wanted their wives to stay at home. Jones has shown that this was probably as much to get away from physical and sexual abuse at the hands of white employers as to adhere to the domestic ideal of white society. As sharecropping became the dominant pattern for African American family work in the South, it allowed women to work with and for their own African American families and to assume gender-differentiated tasks important to their nuclear families rather than to a white household. As families migrated to southern towns and cities and then to the cities of the North, the pattern of married women working was gradually reasserted, both out of economic necessity and for other reasons tied to the family, such as the desire to educate children. But most women worked with other members of their families as field hands in the South. In cities in the South most married African American women worked at home as washerwomen or took in boarders, while young unmarried women held most of the domestic service jobs.[38] Just as for white women, although a few years later in the last half of the nineteenth century and on a more limited scale, professional jobs for African American women began to open up, particularly teaching and writing. A small number of women became doctors and, in the early twentieth century, lawyers.

In the new waves of European immigration that began during the late nineteenth century and continued into the twentieth, most women contributed to a family wage economy, even though a common pattern among many immigrant groups was that the wife did not work outside the home. Often the wife took in piecework put out by factories or took in boarders, the traditional ways married women helped family economics.

Significant change occurred in expectations of white women's sexuality in the nineteenth century. Middle-class white women gradually began to be perceived as sexless beings. Purity was reinforced as the ideal for daughters and "passionlessness," as Nancy Cott named it, became the ideal for married women. At first women's historians concentrated on this as a negative phenomenon for women. From emphasis on sex as a pleasurable and healthy passion in advice books of the seventeenth and eighteenth centuries, such books by the mid-nineteenth century were emphasizing the need for self-control in sex and warning of the dangers of sexual excesses of all types. The middle-class ideal shifted from balanced sexual love in marriage to concentration on spiritual love as the most worthy, a love that minimized or totally cut out the importance of sexual activity. Marital continence began to be valued. Although looking back we might consider this to be dangerously repressive in light of Freudian ideas, historians have found this shift to have had value for middle-class women. It de-emphasized them as sex objects, turning sex, which had been an area of criticism about women in the eighteenth century, into an area of strength. This stress on women's spiritual capacities over sexual desires also helped create the idea of women's moral superiority to men and gave women higher status in society. A change that accompanied this shift was a reduction of middle-class women's fertility rates throughout the nineteenth century, from an average of almost eight children per family to between three and four per family by the end of the century.[39]

Birth control became a social issue in the nineteenth century as married white women began to limit their fertility and men were encouraged to have smaller families in order to do better in the business world. Daniel Scott Smith, using fertility studies, was able to chart the decreasing fertility of nineteenth-century middle-class women and link it to evidence that women wanted and intended to control the amount of conception. His information was reinforced by Laurence Glasco's study of Irish, German, and native-born whites living in Buffalo, New York, in 1855. In looking at the fertility rates of the three groups, he discerned that those of the native-born women were so reduced as to suggest controlled conception, while the fertility rates of the two ethnic groups suggested uncontrolled conception. African American women's fertility decreased by one-third between 1880 and 1910, and urban fertility rates were half those of rural African American women. Jones suggests this was due to poor conditions rather than conscious desire, but the pattern seems similar to what was happening to other women as America industrialized and urbanized.[40]

Birth control during most of the nineteenth century meant the use of abstinence, *coitus interruptus*, and douching; again, like breast-feeding these were not reliable methods for individuals, but it has been suggested they work to help bring average fertility rates down for a society. The use of artificial devices was frowned upon as they became available during the last half of the century. They were seen as methods that would promote "free love"—socially uncontrolled sexuality outside the marriage bonds—whereas the goal of the small group of radicals who called for "voluntary motherhood" in the last part of the century was restraint of sexuality within the marriage bond.[41]

African American, native American, Mexican American, and white working-class women became counterfoils to white middle-class women in the sexual realm. As these white women were perceived as increasingly asexual, the "Jezebel" image of black women's uncontrolled sexuality justified white exploitation of black women. Free African American women in the North were urged by antebellum black newspapers to adopt domestic qualities and particularly to be asexual in public. African American women were assumed by whites to be more sexual and more open to the advances of men. This differentiated them from white women and put them outside the accepted boundaries of womanhood so that they did not have to be treated as white women were treated, and the sexual victimization of African American slave women by white men was justified. This same type of rationalization concerning African American women remained after the Civil War and the end of slavery to justify continued exclusion of African American women from the role of the "lady," who was entitled to the sexual protection of white men and not their exploitation. Native American and Mexican American women faced the same type of stereotyping as they became exotic sensual women in the white public's awareness. The white working class retained eighteenth-century ideas of women that emphasized their sexuality and sexual weakness, and as classes began to be differentiated, such women became sexual targets for upper- and middle-class "gentlemen." Stansell argues that through the first half of the nineteenth century, with the development of a working-class culture, there gradually grew up a sense of class protectiveness for women, but that the working-class family in general was more flexible about daughters' sexuality, as long as it did not interfere with the family wage economy.[42]

Pregnancy outside marriage ceased to be a formal crime in the nineteenth century and instead became a matter of social sanction. A middle-class woman who became pregnant out of wedlock could expect to lose her family's support and her class affiliation and be downgraded to the working class or lower. Working-class families were more flexible in this respect. A woman who bore an illegitimate child might still make a respectable working-class marriage later in life. African American women were not included in middle-class sanctions. Like working-class women, slave women were not barred from respectability due to premarital pregnancy, partly due to the permissibility of such activity in several African cultures that slaves came from, and also because of the realities of slave life, which demanded that women become "breeders" early. The community tolerated sexual experimentation and pregnancy by teen women, but this experimentation was apparently controlled by verbal criticism within the community that defined the boundaries of the acceptable and unacceptable. Generally sexual activity was expected to lead to stable, long-term relationships in the women's early twenties. This was one way to insure stability of relationships when they were not assured by formal means structured by society. Birth control was not a visible issue for African American women, who were encouraged by white masters to have children, although for many it remained a personal issue as they faced the dilemma of having children who themselves would become slaves.[43]

By the second half of the nineteenth century abortion had become a social issue as doctors perceived married white women to be using abortion for family limitation. Abortion in this context became a threat to the family, and the first movement to make abortion illegal began during this period, bolstered by the insistence that conception marked the beginning of life for the impregnated egg and not "quickening," as had been the former standard. The years from 1860 to the 1880s saw a series of laws enacted in many states prohibiting abortion. In 1881, for example, New York passed a law in which abortion became a felony offense. Carroll Smith-Rosenberg and James Mohr have suggested that this occurred partly out of a struggle for status and power among allopaths or "regular" doctors, who were prohibited by the Hippocratic oath from performing abortions, and the "irregulars," eclectics, homeopaths, and others who were not prohibited from performing abortions, and partly as an attack on married women's seemingly increasing autonomy within the home.[44]

Middle-class women also found the debate over work and higher education tied more and more to their sexuality. Some doctors argued that brain work diverted blood or other essential supplies from the ovaries and womb, ultimately resulting in sterility or "female troubles" for such women. Doctors argued that menstruation made women erratic every month, so how could they be trusted with a profession or the reins of government? For the protection of their health women were urged to stay in their own sphere, and women's illnesses were used to explain women's natural inferiority to men and unfitness for higher education and men's sphere.[45]

Prostitution also became a social issue in the nineteenth century, as social purity increasingly became a goal pursued by middle-class women. In moral reform societies of the early nineteenth century women sought to end the sexual double standard which allowed married men to philander. In the social purity movement of the latter half of the century, by fighting prostitution women and men were setting boundaries against types of sexuality that should not be allowed within the family and promoting "middle-class sex"—"sober, proper, modest, conformist." Prostitution itself visibly became big business in the latter half of the century as "red light districts" became notorious in many cities and many types of houses of prostitution grew up, reflecting the new class organization of society.[46]

Middle-class white women's life-role expectations changed significantly as a result of the shift from the premodern to the modern family structure. Marriage, while still for life, became a personal rather than a family choice throughout the century, a choice based no longer primarily on property considerations but on the presence of affection between the parties. This meant a slow but steady increase in divorce over the century as marriages did not meet the emotional expectations of the people involved and as alternate economic opportunities for single women opened up. Still, divorce continued to be a difficult option for women throughout the century.

Herbert Gutman has shown the importance of marriage for slave women and men. Although denied legal marriage, slaves used various formal and informal ceremonies, from the use of an African American or white minister in a traditional ceremony to jumping over a broomstick, to mark their commitment to each other. Gutman also detailed how after the Civil War freedmen and women made great efforts to have their marriages legalized.[47]

Childbirth was increasingly attended by male doctors among urban middle-class women, although midwives continued to deliver the children of the poor, working-class, immigrant and rural families into the twentieth century. This led to the end of childbirth as a women's ritual and to the increasing privatization of childbirth, a sign of the developing private modern family.[48] Middle-class white motherhood became a sacred role in the nineteenth century. It began with the establishment of what Linda Kerber calls "Republican Motherhood" after the Revolution, the renewed importance of the mother as the creator of good citizens for the Republic, which opened education first as a practice and then as a profession for republican daughters. Women gradually became the primary parents, responsible for the moral and spiritual guidance of children now perceived as potential little angels rather than sinful beings. The ideal became to concentrate intense care on fewer children, and childrearing became the primary function of the modern home around which everything else revolved.[49]

Motherhood for African American women was not perceived by whites to be important unless it was directed toward whites, as in the stereotype of the Mammy, the black surrogate mother of white children, who alone of slave women fulfilled the conditions of "true womanhood" to be pure, pious, domestic, and submissively loyal and faithful to her white family. Catherine Clinton called the Mammy "the positive emblem of familial relations between black and white." As Deborah Gray White, Clinton, and Elizabeth Fox-Genovese have detailed, the Mammy was "pure," usually an older woman past her sexual years; "pious," steeped in trust in God and hope in life after death; "domestic," running the white household and nurturing white children; and "submissive," that is, loyal and faithful to the white family. The Mammy, as White states, represented both the "idealized slave" and the "idealized woman." Catherine Clinton found that there were actually not many African American women who played the Mammy role during the antebellum period, when the legend grew. But historians have discovered that among African American women themselves motherhood was a primary source of a woman's identity. For many women married to men who lived on other plantations or farms, wifehood was a part-time role only, but children were always present. Slave women suffered from their inability to give all the care they desired to children. Freedom for African American women would include the ability to mother children and, when they worked outside the home, often it was to benefit their children.[50]

In wifehood, white middle-class women supposedly moved toward autonomy with men and their spheres. But although the hierarchy of the great chain of being was destroyed as a motivation for men's and women's roles in the nineteenth century, science stepped in and fixed the races and the sexes in a new hierarchical order of ascendency. Scientists discovered, for example, women's brains to be smaller and weigh less than men's, which led to the interpretation that they were inferior to men's, although this difference is negated when body size and weight are taken into consideration. White men's brains were also said to have a more complex structure, more concavities and whorls than women's or those of African Americans. This new hierarchical structure worked against the development of democracy in the home and in the spheres.[51]

The Married Women's Property Acts, which began to be passed in 1839, gradually improved married women's position and the worst features of the *femes covert* system. But originally, as Lebsock has shown, these laws were passed for reasons of men's self-interest. During the depressed era of the 1840s, giving women control over property meant preserving it from seizure in case the husband went into debt and bankruptcy. Only gradually, as the laws were amended later in the century, were women's interests, such as control of children or control of their own wages, introduced into these laws.[52]

Deborah Gray White has argued that wifehood for African American slave women meant a more egalitarian and independent relationship than white women could expect to attain. African American slave women could not depend on husbands for the protections and economic provision that white women expected, nor was there much property to be controlled in the marriage. Thus the underlying supports for male dominance did not exist in slave society and slavery itself fostered self-reliance and discouraged overdependence on any one person who might be sold away or be seen once every few weeks or months. White argues that slave husbands and wives were equal partners in the relationship, but that this equality was "founded on complementary roles, roles that were different yet so critical to slave survival that they were of equal necessity." Since marriage was not legally recognized, divorce was informal in the slave community and apparently not condemned by the community. Jones agrees with White that African American women were not as dependent as white women and had more equal relationships as wives, but adds that after freedom, "black men headed the vast majority of southern rural families, and they self-consciously ruled their wives and children."[53]

Little is known about free African American women and families during the early nineteenth century. Lebsock found a disproportionately higher number of households headed by free black women in Petersburg, Virginia during this antebellum era, for many possible reasons. Consistently, more women were manumitted than men, which led to an imbalance; also some women were married to slaves or involved with white men and therefore not officially in households with men in charge; also, if a woman wanted to free kinfolk, she might think twice about marriage, which would make her a *femes covert* and mean her property and wages would be transferred to her husband. Although Gutman has proven conclusively the predominance of two-parent households among African American people, he noted the presence of some female-headed households even on antebellum plantations. This pattern of African American women heading households more than white women has been a consistent one into the twentieth century, particularly in urban areas. From 1880 to 1915 about 25 to 30 percent of urban black families in the South were headed by women, according to Jones. Hope of greater economic opportunities and the difficulties of sharecropping without a husband could account for the migration of women with children to cities. To counter the assertion that the female-headed household is socially pathological, Jones has seen it as a result of economic problems, while Lebsock and Farnham have suggested that in some cases this may be an African American cultural alternative family form.[54]

Those women who remained in working-class and immigrant versions of the premodern family household did not even have the illusion of democracy provided by the spheres for most of the nineteenth century. These households remained openly paternal with women in their deputy-husband positions, but this gave women some status as the custom developed that the husband's and children's paychecks would go to the wife, who managed the household accounts and bought household necessities, ideally in consultation with her husband. Working-class daughters in cities gradually began to leave home and live away from the family before marriage, usually with other young women in boarding houses or apartments. Earning money apparently gave Polish women bargaining power in their families according to their financial contributions, but to other immigrants such as Italian women, earning power did not result in increased influence in the family, probably because male authority in Italy had not depended on being a constant breadwinner.[55]

Responses to widowhood during the nineteenth century began to show a mixed pattern. Lebsock discovered that women who could afford to in Petersburg did not remarry, suggesting a desire to preserve their autonomy and avoid renewed male dominance. From impressionistic evidence on older women in the nineteenth century, it appears that many lived with children or relatives if they did not remarry.[56]

WOMEN AND THE CONTEMPORARY FAMILY

In the ninteenth century the ideal of the middle-class family was democracy, but for most the reality remained a hierarchy. The history of the contemporary family, which becomes visible around 1920, is the history of changing family dynamics, focused on the rooting out of hierarchy and the attempt to make democracy a reality. The changes that have occurred, whether in the realm of work, sexuality, or life roles, have emphasized the growing autonomy and individuality of family members. At the same time, these changes have provoked attempts to preserve the authoritarian and hierarchical family as an unchanging ideal. The debate over women's roles in the family reflects these underlying issues.

In the twentieth century the most important trends concerning women, the family, and work have been the entrance of married middle- and working-class women into public work, and since World War II the increasing number of middle-class mothers moving into jobs. In 1900 5.6 percent of married women in the United States worked. By 1987 56 percent of married women were working. As late as 1940, only 8.6 percent of mothers with children under eighteen years old were working. By 1987, 60.2 percent of all mothers with children under eighteen were working and 53.1 percent of all mothers with preschool-age children were working. Various reasons contributed to this change: periodic economic hardship during the century, which led women to work through necessity; the rise of mass consumer culture and the need for two paychecks to buy consumer goods to maintain or enhance quality of life; the stress in Freudian psychology and the women's movement on the importance of women's self-fulfillment over self-sacrifice; and the egalitarian ideals of the contemporary family. Among working-class women, the ending of both the availability of home piecework from industry and of widespread child labor gradually forced working-class wives and mothers to look for public work to help the family economy. When World War II made women's public work a patriotic duty, married middle- and working-class women with children as well as childless wives were drawn into the work force and remained, in spite of campaigns after the war to send them back into the home. One result of this has been the new legitimacy of day care as a social issue. Day care for poor mothers had received some support during the New Deal period. With the influx of middle-class women into the work force in World War II, day care received government attention in the Lanham Act in a limited yet precedent-setting attempt to take care of the children of working mothers. By the 1980s day care had gained new political impetus through the growing involvement of middle-class mothers in professional and service jobs.[57]

The twentieth century has also seen a struggle to readjust the ideology of domesticity to keep pace with changing times. Women's work outside the home was fought as detrimental to family life and denigrated as an attempt by women to earn "pin money" for their own individual pleasure. Gradually as more women were employed, the rationale of women working outside the home changed to stress the women's work as family work, done from necessity or to provide extra money for family needs, rather than being an issue of women's freedom to choose such work. The "true woman" has been replaced by the "superwoman," who in the ideal manages both household duties and a high-paying career. When housework seemed minimized during the turn of the century by the development of commercial bakeries and food producers, the growth of ready-made clothing, and an emphasis on the use of machines to make home work easier, proponents of domesticity attempted to make housework a profession, in line with the widespread professionalization of public work in the late nineteenth and early twentieth centuries. Under the leadership of Ellen Richards, home economics developed as a field, and in the Progressive era Christine Fredericks attempted to organize housework on the model of office organization and to make housewives home managers. But the widespread adoption of home economics programs in the first thirty years of the century had various motives. Colleges saw it as a way to provide higher education that did not leave women unfit for family life. High schools set up programs partially as a means of social control over the new waves of immigrants coming into America from the 1890s through the 1930s. Home economics was seen as a way to teach immigrant girls American values and thereby assimilate them and their actual and potential families more quickly into American society.[58]

Within the middle-class home itself a trend in the twentieth century has been the gradual end of the use of servants in favor of home technology, beginning in the Northeast in the first half of the century and spreading to the south and west by the 1960s. This occurred for many reasons: the opening of better-paying, higher-status jobs to minority women in business and factories; the end of large-scale immigration; the development of apartment living; the rising cost of domestic service and the difficulty of obtaining it; the availability of such things as washing machines and vacuum cleaners and the emphasis on consumer buying. One unexpected result was that household technology raised the standard of cleanliness expected in a twentieth-century American house and did not give women the leisure from housework that had been anticipated. Another unanticipated result of the loss of servants and the rise in women working, combined with the new contemporary expectations of marriage and fatherhood, was that husbands began helping more around the house. According to William Chafe, patterns of sex-segregated work at home were gradually influenced by "patterns of sharing" as husbands washed dishes, did laundry, or chauffeured children. Although women still have most of the responsibility for housework and child care, middle-class men have steadily increased the amount of work they do in the household. The equal sharing of household duties has become a new ideal for some middle-class families with two working spouses.[59]

In the twentieth century, the nineteenth-century ideal of romantic, spiritual love has slowly been replaced with that of romantic, sexual love, epitomized by the 1970s catchphrase, "the joy of sex." All women are expected to be sexual beings, and sex is once again viewed as healthy and pleasurable, especially when confined within marriage. Birth control went from being a radical issue at the beginning of the twentieth century to respectability by the 1920s. It became linked to the use of devices such as the condom or the diaphragm, then in the 1960s to birth control pills and the IUD. This type of birth control, seen as a threat to the family in the nineteenth century, now became respectable in the twentieth with the return of sexual pleasure as a marriage goal, and with the ideal of "every child a wanted child" espoused by Margaret Sanger. The birthrate has continued to go down for almost every group of Americans except recent immigrants throughout the twentieth century, until now it is under two children per family.[60]

Abortion has again become a social issue in the last twenty years, corresponding to the revival of feminism and ideas of women's equality on the one hand and fears for the traditional family on the other. In the 1960s states began to broaden the grounds for legal abortion and in 1973 the Supreme Court in *Roe* v. *Wade* ruled that a woman in her first trimester of pregnancy had a right to abortion and that state interference in this was unconstitutional. In the fall of 1989, the Supreme Court in *Webster* v. *Reproductive Services* began to place restrictions on women's right to abortion, and at this writing abortion is again a volatile issue.[61]

Other social issues that have surfaced in the past twenty years are related to sexual violence toward women and children. Rape, first outside marriage and then within, and wife beating have been the two issues that have primarily concerned women. These became public matters as a result of the women's movement and as part of the increasing concern over the rights of individuals within families. Both have been linked to actual or perceived threats to the traditional male-dominated, authoritarian power structure in the family. It is probably fair to say that all family violence, whether it concerns child abuse, husband bashing, wife beating, or parent abuse, occurs because of expectations of or a desire for dominance and power or control by one family member over others, for whatever reasons.[62]

As the idea of marriage changed to emphasize partnership in the early twentieth century, divorce became a major social issue. In 1900, one in twelve marriages ended in divorce; in 1980, one in two marriages ended in divorce. Before the end of the nineteenth century divorce was an individual problem, but not a social problem. People got divorced but had to cope with it as individuals. Society's position was that divorce was abnormal and potentially sinful. Divorce became a social problem when it became a widespread middle-class problem and when ideas about the family and marriage began to change. The family had been perceived as something fixed forever, but in the twentieth century the family began to be perceived as a social organism, evolving just as humans were evolving. The growth in importance of individualism as a value in American society translated in marriage into a relationship in which self-fulfillment replaced self-sacrifice as the goal. Women's improving economic condition and social advances made it easier for women to turn to divorce as an alternative to continuing an unsatisfactory marriage.[63]

Ideas about divorce have changed through the centuries. In the nineteenth century divorce meant there was something wrong with a person's character. At the turn of the twentieth century divorce was blamed on social and economic causes over moral ones—chiefly industry, the growth of cities, and the women's movement. From the 1920s to the 1950s marriage problems leading to divorce were seen as psychopathological. Maladjusted adults got divorced, and divorce was the sign of an immature, unstable person, who was often sexually inept as well. As a result the divorced home was perceived as the "broken home," and broken homes led to broken lives. The public debate over divorce was actually a debate over the state of the family in American life, whether the family was being destroyed as a social institution or merely evolving into a different form as society changed. There has been a periodical resurgence of this debate throughout the twentieth century. William O'Neill has argued that divorce is not a flaw but an essential feature of the contemporary family, and that family dissolution rates have actually been lower in the twentieth century than the nineteenth, due to the lowering of disruptions from death of a spouse.[64]

Childbirth in the twentieth century became the realm of the doctor as midwives were squeezed out of rural practice and out of working with immigrant and working-class women. One of the results of this has been that pregnancy was gradually treated as a disease or illness, which often necessitated surgery to bring about a favorable outcome. A response to this in the last twenty years has been a reemphasis of the naturalness of childbirth among middle-class women. Breast-feeding, which went out in favor of the bottle among the middle class from about 1920 to 1950, has since reasserted itself as an ideal.[65]

The beginning of the twentieth century saw an attempt to professionalize motherhood as well as housework. Scientific motherhood became the goal, and motherhood became detached from maternal instinct and became perceived as something a woman could learn. In the late 1940s and 1950s, white mothers were accused of "Momism"—overprotection of their children, especially boys. African American, urban, working-class women faced their own charges of Momism in the Moynihan Report of 1965, where they were accused of inadequate or dominating parenting of their children, again especially boys. The report recommended enlistment in the armed forces for young African American men, "an utterly masculine world . . . a world away from women." At the same time, both African American and white men were being encouraged to assume more responsibilities as fathers in the family. The nineteenth-century conception of motherhood as sacred has lingered on into the twentieth century, but the goal now is quality time, not quantity time spent with children. The ideal has expanded to include fathers having equal responsibility as children's care givers. Surrogate motherhood, which became an issue in the 1980s, went against prevailing ideals of motherhood as a personal growth experience for women and a bonding experience between mother and child.[66]

Within the contemporary family ideal, wifehood has moved toward equality. Sheila Rothman calls the new ideal of the contemporary family circa the 1920s that of the "wife-companion," an equal partner not a subordinate deputy husband. The thought was that as the wife fulfilled her own personal needs instead of sacrificing them, her husband and family benefited. But the idea that the husband should rule the household has remained as an influential counterfoil to the new ideal. In the 1960s, the African American woman's role as wife as well as mother was challenged by the Moynihan Report. Urban, African American, working-class and lower-class wives were described as perpetuating a matriarchy in which they dominated their husbands, reversing expected roles of husband and wife. The solution to the problem, the report's writers averred, was the reaffirmation of the male's role as head of the household through programs that would help promote and maintain this status, while the wife should take her place as deputy husband. The premises of this report have been strongly attacked and discredited in the 1970s and 1980s, but the struggle continues over whether women should play an egalitarian or a secondary role in the African American family.[67]

Widowhood has become a stage during which women live alone as long as possible, and then usually end up in nursing homes rather than living with their children. This is partly a result of the new emphasis on individualism in the family and the transition from traditional family dynamics, in which children had the duty and obligation to care for parents as long as they lived, to a dependence on help outside family sources such as pensions and Medicare.[68]

NEW DIRECTIONS FOR FAMILY HISTORY

Family history, like women's history, unthinkingly accepted the nineteenth-century dichotomy between public and private life, and the family's role in American history has been perceived primarily as part of the private realm. But the work of women's historians has shown this to be a false dichotomy for women and for the family unit as well. Stansell, in studying the development of industry in antebellum New York City, shows the extent to which the early industrial pattern borrowed the household pattern and how closely the early industrial model replicates the family model. Mary Ryan linked the growth of the middle class with certain family strategies in the early nineteenth century. These works show that the private is indeed the political and that the family and society do not belong to separate spheres, but are twined together in as yet largely unexamined ways. More attention needs to be paid to the replication of family structures, roles, and patterns in the public world and what this has meant in the overall development of American society.

Within the family, women's history has led family historians to examine power relationships among family members and how these have changed over time. Along with this, women's historians have suggested the existence of women's family culture; that is, separate beliefs and values, rituals and practices that women share with other women and that are incorporated into family structures at different times and places. Micaela Di Leonardo has identified what she calls "kinwork," the time and effort needed to keep up with relatives (and friends), which commonly falls to women within families. Smith-Rosenberg first identified women's homosocial networks and sometimes erotic love of other women, which took place within a family framework in the nineteenth century. Ulrich's study of women's trading networks in colonial America suggests important differences in the way women and men operate, as well as arguing that these networks were as important to family survival as those of men.[69] More exploration is needed in gender-related areas to illuminate this distinctively feminine subculture within the family.

NOTES

1. This information on the differences between family and women's history comes from: Joan Wallach Scott, *Gender and the Politics of History* (New York: Columbia University Press, 1988); Louise A. Tilly, "Women's History and Family History: Fruitful Collaboration or Missed Connection?," *Journal of Family History* 12 (1987): 303–15; Elizabeth H. Pleck, "Women's History: Gender as a Category of Historical Analysis," in *Ordinary People and Everyday Life Perspectives in the New Social History*, ed. James B. Gardner and George Rollie Adams, (Nashville, Tenn.: The American Association for State and Local History, 1983), 51–65; Maris A. Vinovskis, "American Families in the Past," in *Ordinary People and Everyday Life*, 115–37; Carl Degler, *At Odds: Women and the Family in America from the Revolution to the Present* (New York: Oxford University Press, 1980); Nancy F. Cott and Elizabeth H. Pleck, eds., *A Heritage of Her Own: Toward a New Social History of American Women* (New York: Simon and Schuster, 1979); Gerda Lerner, "Placing Women in History: Definitions and Challenges," *Feminist Studies* 3 (1975): 5–14. There are numerous other articles that address the issues of women's and family history separately.

2. Cott and Pleck, *A Heritage of Her Own*, 9–24; Degler, *At Odds*, v–x.

3. Elisabeth Anthony Dexter, *Women in Colonial Affairs* (Boston: Houghton Mifflin, 1924); Mary Sumner Benson, *Women in Eighteenth-Century America: A Study of Opinion and Social Usage* (New York: Columbia University Press, 1935); Julia Cherry Spruill, *Women's Life and Work in the Southern Colonies* (New York: W. W. Norton & Company, 1938).

4. Gerda Lerner, "The Lady and the Mill Girl: Changes in the Status of Women in the Age of Jackson, 1800–1840," *Midcontinent American Studies Journal* 10 (1969): 5–14; reprinted in *A Heritage of Her Own*.

5. Mary Beth Norton, "Eighteenth-Century American Women in Peace and War: The Case of the Loyalists," *William and Mary Quarterly* 3d Ser. 33 (1976): 386–409; idem., *Liberty's Daughters: The Revolutionary Experience of American Women, 1750–1800* (Boston: Little, Brown and Company, 1980).

6. Degler, *At Odds*, 363, 365; Lyle Koehler, *A Search for Power: The 'Weaker Sex' in Seventeenth-Century New England* (Urbana: University of Illinois Press, 1980), 114–22; Laurel Thatcher Ulrich, *Good Wives: Image and Reality in the Lives of Women in Northern New England, 1650–1750* (New York: Alfred A. Knopf, 1982), 38.

7. Norton, *Liberty's Daughters*, 32; Joan Rezner Gundersen, "The Double Bonds of Race and Sex: Black and White Women in a Colonial Virginia Parish," *Journal of Southern History* 52 (1986): 366–67.

8. Anthony Wallace, with the assistance of Sheila C. Steen, *The Death and Rebirth of the Seneca* (New York: Random House, 1969; Vintage Books, 1972), 24; Charles Hudson, *The Southeastern Indians* (Knoxville: University of Tennessee Press, 1976); Norton, *Liberty's Daughters*, 18–20.

9. John Demos, *A Little Commonwealth: Family Life in Plymouth Colony* (New York: Oxford University Press, 1970), 96–97; Ulrich, *Good Wives*, 94; Koehler, *A Search for Power*, 316–17; Spruill, *Women's Life*, 320; Christie Farnham, "The Position of Women in the Slave Family," in *Major Problems in American Women's History*, ed. Mary Beth Norton (Lexington, Mass.: D. C. Heath and Company, 1989), 159–70.

10. Lois Green Carr and Lorena S. Walsh, "The Planter's Wife: The Experience of White Women in Seventeenth-Century Maryland," *William and Mary Quarterly*, 3rd series, 34 (1977): 542–71. Reprinted in *A Heritage of Her Own*, 29, 42–43; Daniel Blake Smith, *Inside the Great House: Planter Family Life in Eighteenth-Century Chesapeake Society* (Ithaca, N.Y.: Cornell University Press), 139–40; Joan M. Jensen, *Loosening the Bonds: Mid-Atlantic Farm Women, 1750–1850* (New Haven, Conn.: Yale University Press, 1986), 13.

11. Ulrich, *Good Wives*, 135, 139; Daniel Blake Smith, *Inside the Great House*, 138–39; Jensen, *Loosening the Bonds*, 29.

12. Carroll Smith-Rosenberg, "The Abortion Movement and the AMA, 1850–1880," in *Disorderly Conduct: Visions of Gender in Victorian America* (New York: Oxford University Press, 1985), 219; Spruill, *Women's Life*, 325–26; Koehler, *A Search for Power*, 205; see also James Mohr, *Abortion in America: The Origins and Evolution of National Policy* (New York: Oxford University Press, 1978).

13. Wallace, *Death and Rebirth*, 26; Carolyn Niethammer, *Daughters of the Earth: The Lives and Legends of American Indian Women* (New York: Macmillan Co., 1977), 96; see also John Upton Terrell and Donna M. Terrell, *Indian Women of the Western Morning: Their Life in Early America* (New York: The Dial Press, 1974).

14. Daniel Blake Smith, *Inside the Great House*, 140–50; Nancy F. Cott, "Eighteenth-Century Family and Social Life Revealed in Massachusetts Divorce Records," *William and Mary Quarterly*, 3rd series, 33 (1976): 586–614. Reprinted in *A Heritage of Her Own*, 122–24.

15. Farnham, "The Position of Women," 159–70.

16. Ulrich, *Good Wives*, 126, also ch. 7, "Travail."

17. Gunderson, "The Double Bonds," 361, 363–64.

18. Ulrich, *Good Wives*, 157–59.

19. Demos, *A Little Commonwealth*, 88–89.

20. Carr and Walsh, "The Planter's Wife," 35–36, 39, 40; Ulrich, *Good Wives*, 7, 38, 249 n.6; Daniel Blake Smith, *Inside the Great House*, 238–42; Alexander Keyssar, "Widowhood in Eighteenth-Century Massachusetts: A Problem in the History of the Family," *Perspectives in American History* 8 (1974): 83–119. Reprinted in *Women's Experience in America: An Historical Anthology*, ed. Esther Katz and Anita Rapone (New Brunswick, N.J.: Transaction Books, 1980), 47–48.

21. Norton, *Liberty's Daughters*, 30–31.

22. Niethammer, *Daughters of the Earth*, 7–8, 23–24, 38–39, 91–93, 96.

23. Barbara Welter, "The Cult of True Womanhood: 1800–1860," *American Quarterly* 18 (1966): 151–75. Reprinted in *Dimity Convictions*; Ann Douglas, *The Feminization of American Culture* (New York: Avon Books, 1977), 50, 55. See also

Gerda Lerner, "The Lady and the Mill Girl: Changes in the Status of Women in the Age of Jackson, 1800–1840." *Midcontinent American Studies Journal* 10 (1969): 5–14; reprinted in *A Heritage of Her Own*, 182–84.

24. Kathryn Kish Sklar, *Catharine Beecher: A Study in American Domesticity* (New Haven, Conn.: Yale University Press, 1973); Norton, *Liberty's Daughters*, 36–39.

25. Jensen, *Loosening the Bonds*, 79–91; Suzanne Lebsock, *The Free Women of Petersburg: Status and Culture in a Southern Town, 1784–1860* (New York: W. W. Norton & Company, 1984), 149–50.

26. Lerner, "The Lady and the Mill Girl," 115–17.

27. Mary Ryan, *Cradle of the Middle Class: The Family in Oneida County, New York, 1790–1865* (Cambridge: Cambridge University Press, 1981), 60, 84–92, 99.

28. Nancy Hewitt, *Women's Activism and Social Change: Rochester, New York, 1822–1872* (Ithaca, N.Y.: Cornell University Press, 1984), 67.

29. James Oliver Horton, "Freedom's Yoke: Gender Conventions among Antebellum Free Blacks," *Feminist Studies* 12 (1986): 62–63.

30. Lebsock, *Free Women*, 188.

31. Lebsock, *Free Women*, 188; Elizabeth Pleck, "A Mother's Wages: Income Earning among Married Italian and Black Women, 1896–1911," in *A Heritage of Her Own*, 367–92; Claudia Goldin, "Female Labor Force Participation: The Origin of Black and White Differences, 1870 and 1880," *Journal of Economic History* 37 (1977): 87–108; Jacqueline Jones, *Labor of Love, Labor of Sorrow: Black Women, Work, and the Family from Slavery to the Present* (New York: Random House, 1985), 113, 162.

32. Women's history at first concentrated on women's experiences as individuals becoming industrial workers in the nineteenth century, and thus primarily on the experience of single women at Lowell, without much family context. A book that pointed women's historians toward women's family experiences in factory work was Anthony Wallace's *Rockdale* (1972), which suggested the importance of families working together as units in early mills that were not such showplaces as Lowell. See also Mary Blewett, "The Divisions among the Shoebinders," in *Major Problems in American Women's History*, 188–99.

33. Christine Stansell, *City of Women: Sex and Class in New York, 1789–1860* (Urbana: University of Illinois Press, 1987), 52.

34. Stansell, *City of Women*, 53; Lois Rita Helmbold, "Beyond the Family Economy: Black and White Working-Class Women during the Great Depression" *Feminist Studies* 13 (1987): 629–55.

35. Jones, *Labor of Love*, 29; Dorothy Sterling, ed., *We Are Your Sisters: Black Women in the Nineteenth Century* (New York: W. W. Norton & Company, 1984), 5–7.

36. Wallace, *Death and Rebirth*, 28, 310–13; Mary E. Young, "Women, Civilization, and the Indian Question," in *Clio Was a Woman: Studies in the History of American Women*, ed. Mabel E. Deutrich and Virginia C. Purdy (Washington, D.C.: Howard University Press, 1980), 98–110.

37. Dee Garrison, "The Tender Technicians: The Feminization of Public Librarianship, 1876–1905," in *Clio's Consciousness Raised: New Perspectives on the History of Women*, ed. Mary S. Hartman and Lois Banner (New York: Harper Colophon Books, Harper and Row, 1974), 158–78.

38. Herbert Gutman, *The Black Family in Slavery and Freedom, 1750–1925* (New

York: Random House, 1976), 443; Jones, *Labor of Love*, 149–50.

39. Nancy Cott, "Passionlessness: An Interpretation of Victorian Sexual Ideology, 1790–1850," in *A Heritage of Her Own*, 162–81.

40. Daniel Scott Smith, "Family Limitation, Sexual Control, and Domestic Feminism in Victorian America," in *A Heritage of Her Own*, 222–45; Laurence A. Glasco, "The Life Cycles and Household Structure of American Ethnic Groups: Irish, Germans, and Native-born Whites in Buffalo, New York, 1855," in *A Heritage of Her Own*, 268–89; Jones, *Labor of Love*, 123.

41. Linda Gordon, *Woman's Body, Woman's Right* (New York: Penguin Books, 1976), 95–115.

42. Stansell, *City of Women*, 95–96, 179–80.

43. Deborah Gray White, *Ar'n't I a Woman? Female Slaves in the Plantation South* (New York: W. W. Norton & Company, 1985), 97–98; Gutman, *Black Family*, 60–73, 114; on birth control methods used by slaves see Gutman, 80–82, long footnote.

44. Smith-Rosenberg, *Disorderly Conduct*, 217–44; see also James Mohr, *Abortion in America: The Origins and Evolution of National Policy* (New York: Oxford University Press, 1978), chs. 3–6.

45. John S. Haller Jr. and Robin M. Haller, *The Physician and Sexuality in Victorian America* (Urbana: University of Illinois Press, 1974), 47–87.

46. Ibid., 237–70.

47. Gutman, *Black Family*, 270–77, 412–17.

48. Catherine M. Scholten, " 'On the Importance of the Obstetrik Art': Changing Customs of Childbirth in America, 1760–1825," *William and Mary Quarterly* 3rd series, 34 (1974): 426–45. Reprinted in *Women's America: Refocusing the Past*, ed. Linda K. Kerber and Jane De Hart Mathews (New York: Oxford University Press, 1982), 51–65.

49. Linda Kerber, *Women of the Republic: Intellect & Ideology in Revolutionary America* (Chapel Hill: University of North Carolina Press, 1980).

50. White, *Ar'n't I a Woman*, 58–61; Catherine Clinton, *The Plantation Mistress: Women's World in the Old South* (New York: Pantheon Books, 1982), 202; Gutman, *Black Family*, 443; Elizabeth Fox-Genovese, *Within the Plantation Household: Black and White Women of the Old South* (Chapel Hill: The University of North Carolina Press, 1988), especially pages 162, 291–92.

51. Haller and Haller, *Physician and Sexuality*, 48–61.

52. Lebsock, *Free Women*, 54–86.

53. White, *Ar'n't I a Woman*, 158, 159, 157; Jones, *Labor of Love*, 104.

54. Lebsock, *Free Women*, 87–111; Gutman, *Black Family*, 117, 119; Farnham, "The Position of Women," 163–69; Jones, *Labor of Love*, 112, 186.

55. Susan Estabrook Kennedy, *If All We Did Was to Weep at Home: A History of White Working-Class Women in America* (Bloomington: Indiana University Press, 1979), 56–57.

56. Lebsock, *Free Women*, 26–27; Jones, *Labor of Love*, 114.

57. Sheila M. Rothman, *Woman's Proper Place: A History of Changing Ideals and Practices, 1870 to the Present* (New York: Basic Books, 1978), 222–23, 289; Mark S. Hoffman, ed., *The World Almanac and Book of Facts, 1989* (New York: World Almanac, 1988), 157.

58. Barbara Ehrenreich and Deirdre English, *For Her Own Good: 150 Years of*

the Experts' Advice to Women (New York: Doubleday, Anchor Books, 1978); Glenna Matthews, *"Just a Housewife": The Rise and Fall of Domesticity in America* (New York: Oxford University Press, 1987); Maxine Seller, "The Education of the Immigrant Woman, 1900–35," in *Women's America: Refocusing the Past*, 242–56.

59. Ruth Schwartz Cowan, "The 'Industrial Revolution' in the Home: Household Technology and Social Change in the Twentieth Century," *Technology and Culture* 17 (January, 1976): 1–23. Reprinted in *Women's America: Refocusing the Past*, 324–38; William H. Chafe, *The American Woman: Her Changing Social, Economic, and Political Roles, 1920–1970* (New York: Oxford University Press, 1972), 222.

60. Rothman, *Women's Proper Place*, 194; Gordon, *Women's Body*, 186–245; Steven Mintz and Susan Kellogg, *Domestic Revolutions: A Social History of American Family Life* (New York: The Free Press, 1988), 203.

61. Chafe, *American Woman*, 241; Rothman, *Women's Proper Place*, 285–88.

62. Susan Brownmiller, *Against Our Will: Men, Women, and Rape* (New York: Simon and Schuster, 1975); Elizabeth Pleck, *Domestic Tyranny: The Making of Social Policy against Family Violence from Colonial Times to the Present* (New York: Oxford University Press, 1987); Mildred Daley Pagelow, *Family Violence* (New York: Praeger, 1984).

63. William O'Neill, *Divorce in the Progressive Era* (New Haven, Conn.: Yale University Press, 1967), 20–21, 31.

64. O'Neill, *Divorce*, 31.

65. Jenny Carter and Terese Duriez, *With Child: Birth through the Ages* (Edinburgh, Scotland: Mainstream Publishing, 1986), 146–48, 170–87; Janice M. Morse, Margaret J. Harrison, Karen M. Williams, "What Determines the Duration of Breastfeeding?," in *Childbirth in America: Anthropological Perspectives*, Karen L. Michaelson, et al., eds. (South Hadley, Mass.: Bergin & Garvey, Publishers, 1988), 262.

66. Betty Friedan, *The Feminine Mystique* (New York: Dell Publishing Co., 1963); Gutman, *Black Family*, 464–65, 468; Daniel Patrick Moynihan, "The Negro Family: The Case for National Action," reprinted in Lee Rainwater and William L. Yancey, *The Moynihan Report and the Politics of Controversy* (Cambridge, Mass.: MIT Press, 1967), 39–124, quote on p. 42; Jones, *Labor of Love*, 312–13.

67. Rothman, *Women's Proper Place*, 6; Rainwater and Yancey, *Moynihan Report*, 76–77; for arguments against the Moynihan Report see Rainwater and Yancey, also Paula Giddings, *When and Where I Enter: The Impact of Black Women on Race and Sex in America* (New York: Bantam Books, 1984), ch. 18, and Patricia Hill Collins, "A Comparison of Two Works on Black Family Life," *Signs* 14 (1989): 875–84.

68. Lois Rita Helmbold discusses the breakdown of the traditional system, especially under stress, in "Beyond the Family Economy: Black and White Working-Class Women during the Great Depression," *Feminist Studies* 13 (1987): 629–55.

69. Micaela Di Leonardo, "The Female Work of Cards and Holidays: Women, Families, and the Work of Kinship," *Signs* 12 (1987): 440–53; Carroll Smith-Rosenberg, "The Female World of Love and Ritual: Relations between Women in Nineteenth Century America," in *Disorderly Conduct*, 53–76; Laura Thatcher Ulrich, "Housewife and Gadder: Themes of Self-Sufficiency and Community in

Eighteenth-Century New England," in *"To Toil the Livelong Day": America's Women at Work, 1780–1980*, ed. Carol Groneman and Mary Beth Norton (Ithaca, N.Y.: Cornell University Press, 1987), 21–34.

REFERENCES

Benson, Mary Sumner. *Women in Eighteenth-Century America: A Study of Opinion and Social Usage.* New York: Columbia University Press, 1935.

Brownmiller, Susan. *Against Our Will: Men, Women, and Rape.* New York: Simon and Schuster, 1975.

Carter, Jenny, and Terese Duriez. *With Child: Birth through the Ages.* Edinburgh, Scotland: Mainstream Publishing, 1986.

Chafe, William H. *The American Woman: Her Changing Social, Economic, and Political Roles, 1920–1970.* New York: Oxford University Press, 1972.

Clinton, Catherine. *The Plantation Mistress: Women's World in the Old South.* New York: Pantheon Books, 1982.

Collins, Patricia Hill. "A Comparison of Two Works on Black Family Life." *Signs: A Journal of Women in Culture and Society* 14 (1989): 875–84.

Cott, Nancy F., and Elizabeth H. Pleck, eds. *A Heritage of Her Own: Toward a New Social History of American Women.* New York: Simon and Schuster, 1979.

Degler, Carl N. *At Odds: Women and the Family in America from the Revolution to the Present.* New York: Oxford University Press, 1980.

Demos, John. *A Little Commonwealth: Family Life in Plymouth Colony.* New York: Oxford University Press, 1970.

Deutrich, Mabel E., and Virginia C. Purdy, eds. *Clio Was a Woman: Studies in the History of American Women.* Washington, D.C.: Howard University Press, 1980.

Dexter, Elisabeth Anthony. *Women in Colonial Affairs.* Boston: Houghton Mifflin Co., 1924.

Di Leonardo, Micaela. "The Female Work of Cards and Holidays: Women, Families, and the Work of Kinship." *Signs: Journal of Women in Culture and Society* 12 (1987): 440–53.

Douglas, Ann. *The Feminization of American Culture.* New York: Alfred A. Knopf, 1977.

Ehrenreich, Barbara, and Deirdre English. *For Her Own Good: 150 Years of the Experts' Advice to Women.* New York: Doubleday, Anchor Books, 1978.

Friedan, Betty. *The Feminine Mystique.* New York: Dell Publishing Co., 1963.

Gardner, James B., and George Rollie Adams, eds. *Ordinary People and Everyday Life: Perspectives in the New Social History.* Nashville, Tenn.: The American Association for State and Local History, 1983.

Giddings, Paula. *When and Where I Enter: The Impact of Black Women on Race and Sex in America.* New York: Bantam Books, 1984.

Goldin, Claudia. "Female Labor Force Participation: The Origin of Black and White Differences, 1870 and 1880." *Journal of Economic History* 37 (1977): 87–108.

Gordon, Linda. *Woman's Body, Woman's Right: A Social History of Birth Control in America.* New York: Penguin Books, 1976.

Groneman, Carol, and Mary Beth Norton, eds. *"To Toil the Livelong Day": America's Women at Work, 1780–1980*. Ithaca, N.Y.: Cornell University Press, 1987.

Gundersen, Joan Rezner. "The Double Bonds of Race and Sex: Black and White Women in a Colonial Virginia Parish." *Journal of Southern History* 52 (1986): 351–72.

Gutman, Herbert G. *The Black Family in Slavery and Freedom, 1750–1925*. New York: Random House, 1976.

Haller, John S., Jr. and Robin M. Haller. *The Physician and Sexuality in Victorian America*. Urbana: University of Illinois Press, 1974.

Hartman, Mary S., and Lois Banner, eds. *Clio's Consciousness Raised: New Perspectives on the History of Women*. New York: Harper and Row, Harper Colophon Books, 1974.

Helmbold, Lois Rita. "Beyond the Family Economy: Black and White Working-Class Women during the Great Depression." *Feminist Studies* 13 (1987): 629–55.

Hewitt, Nancy. *Women's Activism and Social Change: Rochester, New York, 1822–1872*. Ithaca, N.Y.: Cornell University Press, 1984.

Hoffman, Mark S., ed. *The World Almanac and Book of Facts, 1989*. New York: World Almanac, 1988.

Horton, James Oliver. "Freedom's Yoke: Gender Conventions among Antebellum Free Blacks." *Feminist Studies* 12 (1986): 51–76.

Hudson, Charles. *The Southeastern Indians*. Knoxville: University of Tennessee Press, 1976.

Jensen, Joan M. *Loosening the Bonds: Mid-Atlantic Farm Women, 1750–1850*. New Haven, Conn.: Yale University Press, 1986.

Jones, Jacqueline. *Labor of Love, Labor of Sorrow: Black Women, Work, and the Family from Slavery to the Present*. New York: Random House, 1985.

Katz, Esther, and Anita Rapone, eds. *Women's Experience in America: An Historical Anthology*. New Brunswick, N.J.: Transaction Books, 1980.

Kennedy, Susan Estabrook. *If All We Did Was to Weep at Home: A History of White Working-Class Women in America*. Bloomington: Indiana University Press, 1979.

Kerber, Linda. *Women of the Republic: Intellect and Ideology in Revolutionary America*. Chapel Hill: University of North Carolina Press, 1980.

Kerber, Linda K., and Jane De Hart Mathews, eds. *Women's America: Refocusing the Past*. New York: Oxford University Press, 1982.

Koehler, Lyle. *A Search for Power: The "Weaker Sex" in Seventeenth-Century New England*. Urbana: University of Illinois Press, 1980.

Lebsock, Suzanne. *The Free Women of Petersburg: Status and Culture in a Southern Town, 1784–1860*. New York: W. W. Norton & Company, 1984.

Lerner, Gerda. "The Lady and the Mill Girl: Changes in the Status of Women in the Age of Jackson, 1800–1840." *Midcontinent American Studies Journal* 10 (1969): 5–14.

———. "Placing Women in History: Definitions and Challenges." *Feminist Studies* 3 (1975): 5–14.

Matthews, Glenna. *"Just a Housewife": The Rise and Fall of Domesticity in America*. New York: Oxford University Press, 1987.

Michaelson, Karen L., et al. *Childbirth in America: Anthropological Perspectives.* South Hadley, Mass.: Bergin & Garvey, Publishers, 1988.

Mintz, Steven, and Susan Kellogg. *Domestic Revolutions: A Social History of American Family Life.* New York: The Free Press, 1988.

Mohr, James. *Abortion in America: The Origins and Evolution of National Policy, 1800–1900.* New York: Oxford University Press, 1978.

Niethammer, Carolyn. *Daughters of the Earth: The Lives and Legends of American Indian Women.* New York: Macmillan Co., 1977.

Norton, Mary Beth. "Eighteenth-Century American Women in Peace and War: The Case of the Loyalists." *William and Mary Quarterly* 3d Ser. 33 (1976): 386–409.

———. *Liberty's Daughters: The Revolutionary Experience of American Women, 1750–1800.* Boston: Little, Brown and Company, 1980.

———. *Major Problems in American Women's History.* Lexington, Mass.: D. C. Heath and Company, 1989.

O'Neill, William. *Divorce in the Progressive Era.* New Haven, Conn.: Yale University Press, 1967.

Pagelow, Midred Daley. *Family Violence.* New York: Praeger, 1984.

Pleck, Elizabeth H. *Domestic Tyranny: The Making of American Social Policy against Family Violence from Colonial Times to the Present.* New York: Oxford University Press, 1987.

Rainwater, Lee, and William L. Yancey. *The Moynihan Report and the Politics of Controversy.* Cambridge, Mass.: MIT Press, 1967.

Rothman, Sheila M. *Woman's Proper Place: A History of Changing Ideals and Practices, 1870 to the Present.* New York: Basic Books, 1978.

Ryan, Mary P. *Cradle of the Middle Class: The Family in Oneida County, New York, 1790–1865.* Cambridge: Cambridge University Press, 1981.

Scott, Joan Wallach. *Gender and the Politics of History.* New York: Columbia University Press, 1988.

Sklar, Kathryn Kish. *Catharine Beecher: A Study in American Domesticity.* New Haven, Conn.: Yale University Press, 1973.

Smith, Daniel Blake. *Inside the Great House: Planter Family Life in Eighteenth-Century Chesapeake Society.* Ithaca, N.Y.: Cornell University Press, 1980.

Smith-Rosenberg, Carroll, ed. *Disorderly Conduct: Visions of Gender in Victorian America.* New York: Oxford University Press, 1985.

Spruill, Julia Cherry. *Women's Life and Work in the Southern Colonies.* New York: W. W. Norton & Company, 1938.

Stansell, Christine. *City of Women: Sex and Class in New York, 1789–1860.* Urbana: University of Illinois Press, 1987.

Sterling, Dorothy, ed. *We Are Your Sisters: Black Women in the Nineteenth Century.* New York: W. W. Norton & Company, 1984.

Terrell, John Upton, and Donna M. Terrell. *Indian Women of the Western Morning: Their Life in Early America.* New York: The Dial Press, 1974.

Tilly, Louise A. "Women's History and Family History: Fruitful Collaboration or Missed Connection?" *Journal of Family History* 12 (1987): 303–15.

Ulrich, Laurel Thatcher. *Good Wives: Image and Reality in the Lives of Women in Northern New England, 1650–1750.* New York: Alfred A. Knopf, 1982.

Wallace, Anthony. *Rockdale: The Growth of an American Village in the Early Industrial*

Revolution. New York: Alfred A. Knopf, 1978.

Wallace, Anthony, with the assistance of Sheila C. Steen. *The Death and Rebirth of the Seneca*. New York: Random House, 1969.

Welter, Barbara. "The Cult of True Womanhood: 1800–1860." *American Quarterly* 18 (1966): 151–75.

White, Deborah Gray. *Ar'n't I a Woman? Female Slaves in the Plantation South*. New York: W. W. Norton & Company, 1985.

9

African American Families

Karen Anderson

No system of family relations has received as much scholarly and public attention in the past generation as that of the African American family. Much of that attention has derived from efforts to derogate black culture by labeling it "matriarchal" and thereby to discount black political claims. Many scholars have focused on issues of illegitimacy, family structure, and authority patterns, often using white family patterns as an implicit norm. Those who offer different perspectives on black families have been thrown on the defensive by the power of sexism to set the terms under which American political culture interprets class and race relations.[1]

More recently, some scholars of African American families have viewed their differences from white patterns as strengths. Some have found the origins of black family structures and roles in African customs. Many have concluded that these patterns developed or persisted because they enabled blacks to survive despite the racism and economic oppression they experienced in the United States.[2]

The "strengths"-of-black-families school has drawn some criticism, although it remains central to scholarly work in the field, especially among historians. In 1976, Nathan Hare objected to this approach, stating that it failed "to distinguish between a family form that merely represents adaptation to oppression and a family form or culture of resistance, between a culture of choice and a culture of necessity." Recently, some feminist scholars have questioned whether a family system predicated on gender oppression can be construed as emancipatory.[3]

As the various debates over African American families reveal, it is important to analyze the effects of a sentimentalized family ideal drawn from the perspective of white middle-class males on academic understandings of families. It is also essential to make explicit one's assumptions regarding the interconnections among families, social relations, and institutional structures at the societal level. This chapter begins, therefore, with a discussion of the theoretical frameworks underlying its historical analysis.[4]

FAMILIES, POWER, AND SOCIAL HIERARCHY

Understanding family dynamics and their connections to other institutions and to the construction of social relations is no simple matter. As Coppelia Kahn has observed, "the family is both the first scene of individual development and the primary agent of socialization, it functions as a link between psychic and social structures, and as the crucible in which gender [and other] identity is formed." Family members experience their kin relations as personal, unique, and individual, while enacting them within a system of norms and institutional arrangements created and enforced from outside. Thus, the hegemony of men and parents within families is simultaneously personal and political.[5]

Families embody and engender contradictions. Family members simultaneously bring to their relations common and competing interests. They experience family life as a locus of pressures toward cooperation and conflict, autonomy and connection, selfishness and sacrifice for the common good. Because families organize and express relations of intimacy, sexuality, power, and authority, their dynamics come freighted with powerful emotions.[6]

Moreover, those relations are organized hierarchically. By virtue of their gender, age, marital status, and other attributes, individuals within families perform different roles with different cultural and political meanings. In addition, they occupy different relationships to other social institutions. Thus, attempts to devise a unitary characterization of families are inadequate—they fail to capture the complexities of the internal and external relations of family life.

In modern societies, hierarchies and conflicts within families are exacerbated by the family's relationship to other institutions and the systems of social relations their custodians attempt to construct. In the United States, family relations have been highly politicized. From the colonial period, policymakers have legislated and classified family relations in the interests of various institutions and social groups. Those who hold power in various interconnected institutions—church, state, economy—have intervened to support the family norms and power relations they believe to be required by their institutions. Family relations, however, are not a simple reflection or creation of other institutional arrangements in society; nor can they be understood in isolation from their institutional setting. Because families serve as a repository of cultures under attack and as a site for interrelated political struggles, they reveal the processes whereby social relations are constructed with particular clarity.[7]

This is especially the case with racial ethnic families. In any historical period, they are created by women and men acting within a set of constraints and possibilities they did not choose. The dynamism of family systems derives from the interactions between human beings struggling to secure power, dignity, and well-being and political, economic, and cultural arrangements at the societal level. As Maxine Baca Zinn has noted, "rather than treating them as survivals from a former time, ethnic families may actually be seen as new forms of social life that are generated, revived and transformed by distinct forces in modern society."[8]

Moreover, although many ethnic groups have experienced similar pressures—discrimination, impoverishment, and cultural stigma—they have also varied in their political, economic, and cultural relations to dominant social groups and in their constructions of relations of gender and generation within families. For all the pressures to conformity, then, family structures and dynamics have been highly variable in the United States.

AFRICAN AMERICAN FAMILIES IN
HISTORICAL PERSPECTIVE

The historical experience of African Americans that sets them apart from other groups in American society is the fact that they were enslaved by whites for centuries. For generations, scholars have assumed the saliency of that experience in the development of black family relations and have attempted to interpret its meanings for contemporary African American family patterns. In most cases, scholars who conclude that slavery had a long-term impact on black families also assume that its effects were detrimental, specifically because it precluded the full development of the patterns of monogamous marriage and patriarchal authority that were normative in white, middle-class culture.[9]

Some scholars of slavery have sought to retain that normative view while undermining the stigmatizing effects of the "pathologies" school by emphasizing the similarities between enslaved families and white family systems. Herbert Gutman, for example, revised previous understandings of slave families by documenting the prevalence of long-term monogamous unions on large plantations, the patterns of naming for fathers that reflected and constituted a formal paternal role under slavery, and the efforts of emancipated blacks to reconstruct families that had been divided by sale and war.[10]

Eugene Genovese attempted to "redeem" African American women from charges of undue familial power by noting the ways in which "
"did everything possible to strengthen their men's self-esteem a'

defer to their leadership." Under his construction of slave gender relations, women's "voluntary" subordination to men was the precondition for an "approximation to a healthy sexual equality." By defining racism as a form of masculine dispossession, he could also conclude that black women's identification with the patriarchal power of black men constituted an essential dimension in their own resistance to racial degradation. Genovese lauded black women for their willingness to maintain black men's interrelated claims to power over women and self-esteem without noticing the implicit lack of egalitarian reciprocity in the relations he described.[11]

Similarly, Elizabeth Fox-Genovese concludes that the slave community "naturally viewed the reestablishment of gender relations as the necessary foundation for long-term collective resistance." According to Fox-Genovese, slavery had created a dissonance between the roles of women and men and their gender relations, and had robbed African American men of "all the normal attributes of male power: legal and social fatherhood, the control of property, the ability to dominate households." She further argues that the oppression of slavery rendered gender irrelevant in slave women's lives and had an atomizing effect on the slave community. Even in discussing the rape of enslaved women by white men, Fox-Genovese concludes that "as a slave woman and her master confronted each other, the trappings of gender slipped away. The woman faced him alone. She looked on naked power."[12]

In *Labor of Love, Labor of Sorrow*, Jacqueline Jones concurs with Genovese that women and men supported men's roles as providers and protectors. She further claims that black men and women chose a traditional division of labor within the slave family and community. According to Jones, this choice defined a strategy of resistance to white slaveholders who otherwise undermined gender distinctions in work by assigning women to field labor. The strength of the view that conventional gender roles constituted a culture of resistance created by African Americans ignores the role of African custom and of white work allocations and gender conventions in shaping slave family relations.[13]

Deborah Gray White, by contrast, has concluded that slave marriages were characterized by a complementary equality grounded in women's autonomy from their husbands, the lack of structural supports for male dominance, and women's contributions to their family's subsistence and well-being. At the same time, she provides evidence of violence against women and marital conflict over domestic power relations in slave families. Under this construction, sexism is reduced to individual acts by apparently aberrant men rather than examined for its roots in the condition of enslaved blacks.[14]

Taken together, these works constitute a dangerous line of "defense" against the "pathologies" school. Most legitimize white norms and the patriarchal family relations they mandate, and all discount gender as a source of oppression in African American women's lives. Moreover, they tend to efface unique elements in the African American construction and experience of gender and sexuality under slavery and afterward. As Susan Mann has observed, these and other scholars have been quite reluctant to label African American families patriarchal or to investigate the institutional bases for patriarchal power among enslaved or emancipated blacks.[15]

The meanings of slavery for black family relations were complex. In some ways, slave family and gender systems resembled those found in other social groups in significant ways. The gender division of labor and authority within black families prescribed domestic work, child nurture, and the maintenance of kin relations for women, and an attempt by men to serve as protectors and providers. As John Campbell's work demonstrates, men used the leverage they had in the economy to provide some resources to their families and enhance their power in the family.[16]

Enslaved black men, however, lacked the institutional basis to carry out their role expectations fully or to secure the degree of male dominance prevalent among free whites. Under slavery, husbands and wives frequently lived on different plantations, had some decisions about family made for them, and sometimes experienced white intervention in marital relations. Men could not fully enact the provider and protector roles in families, and parental powers to socialize, train, and discipline children remained subject to the requirements of the system of white planter power. Within these limits, black norms sanctioned some level of deference to male authority, especially in interactions with outsiders, and required that black women provide ego support and domestic services to black men.[17]

Black men could not control black women's labor or sexuality in the ways free white men believed appropriate for themselves. Under slavery, arduous daily work characterized black women's lives, providing uncongenial soil for the development of mores stressing feminine weakness or incompetence. The politics of race and sex—expressed in the systematic sexual abuse of black women by white men—also precluded the enforcement by black men of norms of premarital chastity for black women.[18]

The institution of slavery also affected gender and family relations among free blacks in the South. Suzanne Lebsock found considerable discord between free black women and men in her study of antebellum Petersburg. According to Lebsock, this derived from women's willingness to assert their prerogatives in a context in which deference to their men brought little benefit. Observing that family harmony and integrity are sometimes predicated on women's subordination, she concluded that "insofar as conflict grew out of leverage and assertiveness on the part of women, it was a sign of health."[19]

EMANCIPATION, POWER, AND FAMILY RELATIONS

After the abolition of slavery, blacks found that the context within which they were to create and sustain family life had changed substantially. Women and men assumed greater power in the allocation of labor and distribution of resources within families. The affective and economic dimensions of family life were connected in new and sometimes disconcerting ways. These interconnections simultaneously strengthened and undermined postwar families.

When emancipation changed the conditions of male-female relations among blacks, a complex pattern of cooperation and conflict ensued. Men's claims to patriarchal power received some support from institutional arrangements and postwar conditions. Indeed, white planters relied on patriarchal family relations to discipline their labor force. As Susan Mann has documented, women's economic dependence on men was pronounced, given men's greater access to land in the rural economy.[20]

Women's ability to secure rural work was hampered by white preferences for male labor, the danger of sexual exploitation in jobs that entailed working under direct white supervision, and women's responsibility for the care of others. Women had difficulty negotiating tenancy arrangements—the main form of rural labor—unless they had husbands or older sons to assist in farm work. The Freedmen's Bureau often allocated less land to female-headed households than to those headed by men. If they were to remain in the rural sector, many had to rely on wage labor, the bottom of the economic ladder in the rural economy. The plantation economy thus made manifest men's economic contributions to family support and provided some incentives for the maintenance of family integrity.[21]

The gender and generational division of labor in black families derived from white power, the demographic composition of families, and from conflicts and negotiations between black women, men, and children. Whites' ability to control economic conditions virtually ensured the availability of women and children for paid labor in the southern economy. Economic clout was sometimes backed by physical coercion. E. Franklin Frazier reported the case of a single mother with a sick infant who had been beaten by her landlord in order to force her to leave her baby unattended and work in the fields.[22]

In many tenant households, the amount of time a woman could spend with her young children depended on the presence of older children to

replace her in field work. This may have been the case in urban economies as well. A Women's Bureau study of women workers in 1920
revealed that employed black women in Jacksonville, Florida were less
likely to have employed children over the age of eighteen in the household than white women workers.[23]

Susan Mann, however, overstates the degree to which the postwar
plantation economy imposed male dominance within African American
families. The economic oppression of black men encouraged women's
employment and contributed to the formation of family structures that
gave women alternatives to marriage. As a result, the sources and degree
of male authority in black households were both unclear and contested
in the postwar period.[24]

Neither the structure of the economy nor the organization of gender
relations enabled black women to rely solely on the nuclear family for
support. The inadequate and insecure wages of women and men, the
migration of child earners, the death of husbands, and failed marriages
prompted black women to turn to other kin for assistance. In a complex
system of reciprocity, they often brought dependents into their families
and shared resources with others outside their households. As black
women negotiated the interconnections between affective and economic
relationships within the family, they sought power commensurate with
their needs, and their material and other contributions to family welfare.
In so doing, they altered and extended the mutable family system they
had helped to devise under slavery.

Women's work responsibilities were reinforced by the economic position of black men and its effects on their family roles. When confronted
with the closed system under which they were expected to earn a livelihood, some black men grew discouraged and abandoned the breadwinning responsibility to women. Others left when their inability to
secure work created family strains. From the point of view of many black
women, it constituted an evasion of an onerous responsibility that was
then shifted solely to them.[25]

The family economy thus assumed various forms, as family members
negotiated their material and emotional relationships within a context
of extreme economic oppression. The lack of a normative consensus
between women and men regarding appropriate authority patterns in
the household and the contradictory implications of southern economic
structures for family power dynamics created a pattern of conflict and
relative instability in black family lives. This was exacerbated by high
rates of widowhood and by the decisions of older children to leave in
order to search for better work opportunities, to establish their own
families, or to gain some autonomy from the nuclear family.

The sparse data on household structures offer only a suggestive
glimpse of the flexibility and variability of black family structures or of

the extent of women's responsibility for the support of others. Knowing how many households are male-headed or how many are extended does not enable us to describe very specifically the dynamics of household composition. They do not reveal the compatibilities and tensions between the affective and economic relationships within families or the connections among women's kin work, their productive work, and their family status.[26]

Family structures derived from the choices made by blacks in a context in which virtually no other institutions provided assistance in the care of dependents, and family property and incomes were exceedingly low. Extraordinary poverty and family instability among blacks made a system of extended kinship ties and responsibilities an imperative. Black women often adopted orphaned children and those whose parents could not offer adequate support or care. Although black families tried to support aging parents whenever possible and were more likely to take in such dependents than to take in workers who produced income, they could not always balance their income and their responsibilities to others.[27]

As a result, many black women found themselves responsible for the support of their children and other dependents. After emancipation, many were unable or unwilling to continue or reestablish their slave marriages. Some women could not locate their husbands or found that they had remarried. For others freedom meant the right to renounce husbands whom they found incompatible. Those who had borne children by their masters could expect little assistance from them in providing for their offspring. A few attempted to get the Freedmen's Bureau to enforce child support payments from the white fathers, but they usually did not succeed. Others found it impossible to marry because so many black men had died during the Civil War.[28]

Not surprisingly, then, black women were more likely to head families and to do so at a younger age than was true of white women. Herbert Gutman's data from representative southern communities in the 1880 census revealed that women headed 13 to 18 percent of rural black families and 26 to 31 percent of urban black families. Black women in their twenties were two to four times more likely to be family heads than white women of the same age. As Gutman points out, most black families included adult men, but many black women assumed the full breadwinner burden for extended periods in their lives.[29]

A relatively high incidence of female-headed families persisted well into the twentieth century. The continuing pattern of marriage to older men and the mortality rates caused by poverty contributed to high rates of widowhood for black women. A 1938 study revealed that 48 percent of the wives of black Georgia men aged sixty-five were under the age of fifty-five. Such arrangements worked to the economic disadvantage of middle-aged women, who were often burdened with aging husbands unable to work or widowed at a young age with little means to secure a livelihood in the rural economy unless they had older children present in the household.[30]

Not only did black women experience high rates of widowhood, but also they experienced desertion more often than white women and, whatever the cause, they lost their husbands at a substantially earlier age than whites. In their study of families in Philadelphia between 1850 and 1880, Furstenberg, Hershberg, and Modell found that at least one quarter of married black women with children reported themselves as widowed by the time they reached their forties. It is probable that many of these women had been deserted, as Elizabeth Pleck's more detailed work has revealed for Boston in this period. Data from the 1940 census confirms the persistence of these patterns over time. In 1940, 15.8 percent of black women were classified as widowed, compared to 11.1 percent of white women. Among those aged fifty to fifty-four, 31.5 percent of black and 14.5 percent of white women reported themselves as widowed. Of those who reported themselves as married in 1940, 4 percent of white and 14 percent of black women had husbands absent. In the urban areas, 5 percent of white and 19 percent of black married women did not live with their husbands.[31]

At the same time, marriage rates were higher among blacks than whites, especially at young ages. In 1940, 60.4 percent of nonwhite women aged twenty to twenty-four had not married, while 73.5 percent of white women in the same age group remained single. The combination of high marriage rates and high rates of female-headed families reflects a pattern of serial monogamy and the effects of a normative system that did not require marriage to legitimize pregnancies.[32]

Although single black women were more likely to have children than whites, many of these women later married. As one mother said of her daughter who had borne a child outside of marriage: "She started to get married, but didn't; liable to marry after while." As the frequency of remarriage indicates, black women sought marriage rather than the long-term maintenance of female-headed households. Marriages frequently failed as a consequence of external pressures and black women's willingness to struggle for greater compatibility and egalitarianism in their unions.[33]

The community condemned those who remained in an unhappy union more than those who separated. These mores reflected and reinforced women's marital power by sanctioning women's refusal to remain in oppressive marriages. The reasons most commonly given by women for ending their marriages were marital violence and the failure of their husbands to contribute to their support. Several women told Johnson that they left their husbands because they were "jest too mean." One separated from her mate because "he fight so I jest couldn't live with him. He treat me so bad."[34]

Much of the violence in these households stemmed from disputes over the degree of authority men could claim, especially in establishing norms for sexual conduct. Many couples reported disputes over the wife's infidelity—real and perceived. In some cases, the threat of violence from husbands supported the sexual double standard within marriage. In others it contributed to marital instability and to women's preference for informal liaisons. Some women found that men's expectations of dominance increased after marriage: "Soon as you marry a man he starts mistreating you, and I'm not going to be mistreated no more." Couples who had established stable unions reported that they had successfully placed jealousy behind them. One man, married for forty years, concluded that "when you jealous you don't live long."[35]

The persistence of the problem of wife abuse over such a long period of time bespeaks the inability of men to establish the kind of dominance they expected. Poverty and racism strained family relations and reduced men's ability to establish an uncontested authority. They lacked the status and income advantage over women that characterized white marriages and sustained stable but unequal unions. The frequency with which black women chose to fight back and/or to leave abusive husbands indicates that black men's domestic power was neither ideologically nor economically secured.[36]

Men's inability to dictate the terms of gender relations in black families did not mean that these families were either matriarchal or egalitarian. Instead, a complex pattern of deference and assertion characterized black women's unions. As Delia Harris observed: "You promised to 'bey the man, but before you finish it's cussing, honey." Despite their efforts to secure greater marital power, black women faced marital inequality because they did not have sufficient power outside of marriage to create relationships on their terms. They were able to shape the normative structure of gender relations in the black community enough to secure support from others when they decided to forgo marriage, but not enough to enforce egalitarian relationships on would-be patriarchs.[37]

Black women's willingness to leave oppressive marriages derived from and necessitated a flexible family system that would provide a safety net for female-headed households. The contested nature of gender relations among blacks thus contributed to the development of a family system in which women chose to rely on their own labor and on their kin work to secure multiple sources of support for their dependents. Because black women often could not earn enough to support themselves and others, even at the most minimal level, the organization of family earning and consumption patterns fundamentally affected their well-being.[38]

As Elizabeth Pleck has noted, "it was personally trying to belong to a family system that made so many demands." Although they provided security in the face of poverty, complex networks of kin also created competing demands for resources and emotional support. Obligations to extended kin strained some marriages. The incorporation of new people into the household sometimes added to family conflict, especially when that new person was a stepfather. One woman remembered that "my stepfather was so mean to us, Mamma's children, that we had to go stay with my grandmother. He wouldn't let Mamma keep us."[39]

By the 1910s, industrial development in the North and crises in southern agriculture foretold the processes that would change the conditions for African American family life in the coming decades. Growing numbers of black families began migrating to northern cities, pushed by poverty and racism in the rural South and lured by the promise of better jobs in the factories of the North. There they confronted new problems and possibilities in the urban environment. In the 1930s, the Great Depression culminated decades of declining economic conditions with a massive displacement of blacks from the rural sector and caused dire destitution. Many African Americans headed north in search of work or welfare.

In the northern cities, overcrowding and discrimination in housing promoted a lively street culture as blacks sought space to escape domestic pressures and to express their individuality. That street culture, however, occupied the intersection of various systems of power where possibilities for oppression and liberation coexisted. Because it fragmented families by gender and generation and because it offered commercial and sexual temptations, ghetto life challenged black women's moral authority as mothers and as managers of a family economy.[40]

Those temptations posed various threats to family integrity and well-being, including those of infidelity, squandering of family resources, and desertion. They also eroded parental authority in a context in which adult women's need for assistance from older children was growing. For daughters coming of age in urban ghettos, the new commercialized sexuality could mean new possibilities for their sexual exploitation in a masculinist urban culture.[41]

Neither family, nor church, nor community, however, provided an antidote to dangerous urban attractions. The anonymity of urban life, the availability of social and recreational activities outside the supervision of church and family, and individual access to money in a wage economy reduced the importance of kin relations and increased the significance of peer groups in social life.[42] As in other working-class households in this period, the rise of a consumer culture altered family relations.[43]

Integration into an urban wage economy increased pressures on black marriages. Greater instability in black men's employment patterns, coupled with the diminished social controls of urban life, promoted marital instability. As in the countryside, marriages often foundered as women and men disagreed about issues of economic obligation, fidelity, and physical abuse. Blues singer Ida Cox expressed women's vulnerability as follows: "Southern men will stick by you when the Northern men can't be found."[44]

These tensions were greatly exacerbated by the Depression. As Jacqueline Jones notes, it is impossible to disentangle the economic roots of family conflict and disintegration in this period, although male unemployment and women's access to welfare and other sources of support outside of marriage both contributed to family instability. Despite changes in work roles imposed by the urban economy, men and women continued to create a livelihood and seek emotional support in an interdependent, but fragile, family system.[45]

THE END OF THE PLANTATION AND THE CRISIS OF THE MODERN AFRICAN AMERICAN FAMILY

Nothing, however, was more important for the transformation of black status and family relations in the twentieth century than the dismantling of the plantation economy in the South. Although that system had been eroding for decades, economic changes initiated during World War II provided the impetus for its destruction, ending its stranglehold on black workers and black lives. In addition, the conditions blacks encountered in the wartime economy foretold the difficulties they would face in the postwar era.[46]

Racial discrimination in housing, day care, transportation, and commercial establishments affected family decisions. Facing uncertain employment circumstances and lacking adequate housing and day care, many women workers chose to leave their children with relatives when they migrated to new communities. Although this practice had deep historical roots, its persistence during the war years derived from the lack of institutional support for black family integrity. Long after the war ended, public policy decisions would affect African American families in profoundly important ways.[47]

In the postwar years, the decline of home-based employment, most notably in agriculture and as laundresses, necessitated a movement of married women workers into jobs outside the home. As a result of these structural shifts, the historic tension between their responsibilities as breadwinners and as homemakers was intensified. Consequently, the employment rates of black married women grew more slowly than those of white wives in the postwar period. In order to balance their support and caretaking duties, some black women went on welfare; many relied even more heavily on the family networks that had sustained them under the plantation system.

Black women and men found that they needed whatever assistance they could get in their struggle to secure a livelihood in the postwar economy. Millions moved to the cities in this period, with little cushion against the vicissitudes of an urban wage economy. They had virtually no savings and were entirely dependent on wage work for support. Moreover, racism and their late entry into competition for urban jobs impeded their mobility. As a result, black women and men have faced chronic unemployment and all the problems associated with urban poverty.[48]

Reduced demand for workers in the rural sector and discrimination in urban jobs created a new class of black dependents—many of them women and children—whose claims to support strained traditional welfare and employment practices in the North as well as the South. The increasing reliance of African-American women on public assistance as a source of support in a discriminatory economy fueled a backlash and provided a convenient scapegoat for those attempting to stem the tide of change. The "welfare mother" has joined the "black rapist" as a central mythic figure in America's racial politics, revealing their changed character.[49]

In the last few decades, public officials have subjected blacks to heightened scrutiny and regulation of their private lives, especially in the areas of gender relations, sexuality, and reproduction. Teenage motherhood and the rise of female-headed families have become convenient explanations for the persistence of black poverty, despite the fact that the pregnancy rates of black teens have decreased consistently since the 1950s. Politicians who have directed their attention to the problem of welfare—rather than those of education, jobs, and wages for women and men—have often obscured and exacerbated problems in the black family, while professing to solve them. Not coincidentally, they have also capitalized politically by heaping abuse on women whose public dependence has come to be defined as a private failure with dangerous social consequences.[50]

The family and economic problems confronting blacks in the postwar era did not originate in welfare policies, however. Their causes were multiple, deriving from historic and continuing patterns of racism and discrimination, the legacy of earlier black family traditions, and the intensified pressures confronting blacks in an urban environment. For African-American women, especially, the ghetto has been hostile terrain. Marked culturally as masculine space, the streets of the ghetto have signified the denial of their maternal authority and of their personal autonomy and safety.[51]

Most important, they have symbolized conflicts between women and men as they try to establish the norms whereby they are to provide economic security, emotional support, and dignity to one another in a society unwilling to provide regular jobs and adequate incomes for blacks. The debate over black "matriarchy" and male "absence" from families has obscured the profound economic and emotional interdependence between African American women and men and the heightened tensions over the terms of their mutual needs in recent decades. Poor black men's increasing loyalty to a peer group and a masculine identity defined in street culture has conflicted with women's attempts to enforce a stronger domestic orientation by men. These conflicts have worsened as life in inner-city America has become more precarious and dangerous.[52]

The result of heightened gender conflict has been an increase in marital dissolution among blacks accompanied by a growing reluctance on the part of black women to marry at all. By the 1980s, two-thirds of adult black women were living without husbands, and the majority of black children were living apart from their fathers. This rise in female-headed families has meant an increase in black women's breadwinning responsibilities that has far outstripped their gains in income in the postwar era.[53]

At the same time, black family structures—and women's roles and position within them—have become more varied as some blacks have experienced occupational mobility in the postwar period. African American family dynamics vary with the migration status, place of residence, region, education, and income of family members. Across the social spectrum, however, black families have been affected by public policy decisions often taken without regard for their effects on black well-being.

Indeed, many African American families experienced heightened stresses. The movement of blacks to the cities, their placement in the secondary sector of the urban labor force, and the systematic frustration of their attempts to enter the American mainstream took an enormous toll on black family life. Increased dependence on wage work for a livelihood in a context of pervasive discrimination intensified economic pressures in the lives of women and men.

At the same time, urbanization and the increasing importance of the mass media in their lives dramatically increased black interaction with a national culture. This exposure to middle-class possibilities heightened black expectations but did not offer a means for the elimination of barriers to their achievement. According to Kenneth Clark, the contrast between ghetto realities and media-sponsored aspirations had a profoundly demoralizing effect on many blacks, who interpreted "their predicament as a consequence of personal disability or as an inherent and imposed powerlessness which all Negroes share." Family life became a major theater within which black despair was enacted and reproduced, prompting Paula Giddings to conclude that "giving Blacks half a loaf in exchange for acculturation into American society had a more dire impact on the Black family than slavery, war, or racial violence."[54]

Whereas the rural economy had encouraged marriage by linking women's access to agricultural work to a family system of labor and making men's breadwinning efforts visible, the postwar urban environment intensified marital conflict and instability. As a hedge against masculine failure, many poor black men attempted to limit their affective and economic commitments to families. Many black women experienced that distancing as a betrayal and concluded that men were unreliable as partners and providers. Inevitably, men who chose to limit their family commitments found that their strategies had backfired as their marital performance fell short of their wives' expectations, contributing to high rates of separation and divorce. The result for many poor men and women was that they had become, in the words of Jean Carey Bond and Pat Peery, "hateful partners in a harrowing dance."[55]

As a result of their own experiences, many African American mothers convey deeply contradictory messages to their daughters. Virtually all socialize their daughters to a primary emotional and sexual orientation to men—a message reinforced in black popular culture. At the same time, many also encourage them to view men with great suspicion and to develop some independence in case their heterosexual relationships do not work out. They label men's abuse as wrong to a greater degree than is true in many other social groups, while conveying the message that it is unrealistic to expect real respect or mutuality from men.[56]

From their first adolescent courtships through their adult encounters, poor black women and men warily negotiate the meanings of sexuality and parenthood for their emotional and economic ties to one another. Among adolescents, young men pressure women for sexual relationships in order to affirm their masculinity and adult status. At all ages, many women seek commitment in their sexual relationships for the sake of their emotional and economic security. Men, however, are often reluctant to assume the risks associated with the breadwinner role and approach marriage and fatherhood ambivalently.[57]

Those men who marry find that the vagaries of the secondary labor market exert enormous pressures on them. The low wages and high unemployment rates in secondary sector jobs constantly threaten their ability to support their families adequately. Many men experience the loss of a job as a serious blow to their self-esteem. By virtue of their economic and emotional ties to men, women become the inevitable witnesses to masculine failure. Because women symbolize and press the families' claims to men's earnings, men usually turn to street culture for ego support when frustrated by their inability to meet their wives' expectations. There they can seek out other women or their masculine peer group for uncritical approval. As Elliot Liebow observed, the latter defines a lesser standard of masculine worth and offers a man relationships in which he can be "a person in his own right... noticed by the world he lives in." These friends, however, stand "unrevealed to one another," able to offer support only to the degree that they maintain distance.[58]

Some poor men have treated their income as an individual asset unavailable to the family except as a "gift," expecting their wives to support the children. Others have given their children little time or attention—a problem that occurs frequently among whites as well. It is hardly surprising that some black women have concluded that "men are no good" and have experienced men's tenuous ties to their families as a betrayal. One such woman discounted men's professions of concern for their children as follows: "They say they love them. Shit. If they love them, would they let them go hungry? In raggedy-ass clothes? They don't love them. Children are just a tie to a man." Gail Stokes articulated the anger of women forced to assume the main breadwinning responsibility:

My belly rose and swelled year after year from the implantations of your seed, while you cursed my pregnancies, forgetting that they were all mainly the product of your sexual pleasures. But you didn't mind letting the consequences rain heavily upon my nappy head.... Yes, I know your pay isn't much and your opportunities are limited, but when you squander away what little you do make and the same little that I count on so desperately, how else can I react?[59]

The anger of these women suggests the toll taken by chronic poverty and gender conflicts over economic responsibilities. Their despair exacerbated by racism, many African Americans find the maintenance of relationships difficult. That this is not true in all cases is important, however. Examining stable and competent black families in this period reveals the meanings of mobility for black families and the structural supports essential to family cohesion.

Dorothy Bolden, for example, attributed the success of her second marriage to the fact that she and her husband were jointly responsible for breadwinning and child care. Her husband was fortunate in that his employment was steady, although poorly paid. She worked in domestic service and his schedule at work enabled him to supervise their children in the afternoons. She explained: "I was lucky. My husband always got off at one or two o'clock during the daytime, and I have a wonderful husband. I was lucky to have a husband to share the responsibility."[60]

Their relationship exemplified several elements critical for family integrity and economic well-being among African Americans—regular work for men, women's employment, and relatively egalitarian gender practices. Those black families in which men have jobs that offer more security and higher incomes experience greater marital stability. Families with incomes above the poverty line experienced less stress and deprivation, with the result that marital harmony and stability were enhanced.[61]

A significant component of that stability was the sense that crises were temporary and that family members could cope. One working-class black mother of four described her response to her husband's hospitalization after he sustained a serious injury at work:

I worked three days [a week] then, but the Welfare Department, the State, they helped us, and we kept our bills paid up. When I look back on it, I don't really think it was a bad time. You know, we still had our needs, and we had everything paid, our rent, and we kept everything going, but we didn't get anything else. ... 'Cause you know, time be worse at that time, but it's gone and then you look back at it, and then you say, "Well, I was really blessed in a way because...he was not paralyzed."

That family's ability to manage was predicated on its previous strength, the probability that the husband could return to his job as a construction foreman, and the availability of welfare to see them through the crisis.[62]

At the same time, economic mobility has not eased the dual burden of employment and family work for most working-class and middle-class black women. Indeed, black mobility rests firmly on the two-earner family. Women's employment outside the home, even when their children are young, has been essential to black mobility as well as to the maintenance of middle-class status. Maternal employment, especially when it was adequately compensated, has increased the economic well-being and stability of black families.[63]

Social mobility for blacks, however, does not automatically create nuclear families supported by men. Jesse Bernard's study of marital status differences by race and class found that black men's rates of marital stability increased with economic mobility, but that they were significantly less likely to be living in stable first marriages than whites with comparable occupational or income status. This is partly because many upwardly mobile blacks bring with them distrust and conflicts rooted in their previous poverty and have to manage the tensions generated between nuclear families and other kin when some relatives remain impoverished.[64]

Economics alone, however, cannot explain the origins of female-headed families. Labor force discrimination against minority men can contribute to the emergence of female-headed families, but does not fully account for it. Women's active assertion of their prerogatives in heterosexual unions, a dynamic that has either been overlooked or condemned by most scholars, has also promoted the rise of families headed by women.[65]

As in the past, black women have defined norms of reciprocity in their relationships that they expect men to honor. Indeed, Robert Blood and Donald Wolfe found in their 1960 study that black women of all social classes expressed greater dissatisfaction with the emotional, companionate, and financial dimensions of their marriages than did white women in the same income groups. Although Blood and Wolfe implied that black women were not sufficiently grateful to their husbands, one might conclude instead that they held to a higher standard of mutual responsibility in marriage than prevailed among whites of the same social classes. As Audre Lorde has noted, "Female-headed households in the Black community are not always situations by default."[66]

Black women's willingness to leave unions in which that standard has been breached derives in part from their faith in their ability to support themselves. As May Anna Madison explained, "A black man can't do any more to me than I will let him do because I can and have taken care of myself." Blanche Scott, who had worked for pay all her life, left her husband in 1946 because "he was wild. He's run around with women and drink. He had done me so bad, I just left him." Maya Angelou left her white husband in the 1950s, despite the fact that she would have to seek employment, having concluded that "women who accepted their husbands' inattention and sacrificed all their sovereignty for a humiliating marriage [were] more unsavory than the prostitutes who were drinking themselves awake in the noisy bar."[67]

Many African American women have viewed employment as a means to set some limits on the power of men in their lives. Janie Cameron Riley stated that she could not understand why white women put up with their husbands' liaisons with black women, given that white women had more opportunities than black women. For Riley, it was inconceivable that a woman would put up with such conduct when she could support herself. Others also concluded that white women were more willing than black to accept oppressive conditions in their marriages. Nancy White observed: "When you come right down to it, white women just *think* they are free. Black women *know* they ain't free. Now, that is the most important difference between the two.... The white women would be all right if they would just stop paying any attention to them sorry menfolks of theirs."[68]

In all social classes, married black women are more likely than white women to work for pay, whether their husbands are opposed, neutral, or in favor of their employment. Their decisions to work for pay do not necessarily indicate power over their husbands' actions or an equal voice in other marital decisions regarding the gender division of labor, money, sexuality, or companionship. Indeed, their decisions to work may derive in part from their lack of power over other domains of their marriages and in part from their willingness to assert themselves in those areas of the marriage where they can act autonomously. Their low marriage rates testify to their inability to impose their standards of marital reciprocity in a society hostile to their implementation.[69]

Unable to compel the full emotional allegiance or economic assistance of the men they loved, some found themselves settling for "love on men's terms." Those terms sometimes included the requirement that women tolerate infidelity. In a social group where the number of men is lower than the number of women, some women have decided, however reluctantly, to "share" their men with others. Others stayed in oppressive unions while they tried to tame their husbands' "wildness."[70]

Poor men's terms usually included a willingness to contribute to the support and nurture of families, but to do so on a voluntary and often limited basis. In fact, Liebow found that poor men were often most willing to do so in contexts where the formal claims on their support were weakest—as stepfathers or "boyfriends" in the household—rather than within marriage. When the expectations of them were low, their participation garnered them more credit. Nonmarital unions, thus, have offered men a way to realize the rewards of family life—and contribute to family well-being—with less pressure and stress.[71]

Given these dynamics, it is not surprising that the number of black women heading families has increased dramatically, especially since the 1960s. The proportion of black women who are married and living with their husbands declined from 52 percent in 1947 to 34 percent in 1980. Compared to white women, black women were less likely to marry, more likely to be divorced or separated, and less likely to remarry after a divorce. As black women's marriage and remarriage rates have declined, marital pregnancy rates have fallen more rapidly than nonmarital pregnancy rates. By the 1980s, most black babies were born outside of wedlock and the majority of black children were not living with their fathers. To an even greater extent than in the past, black women had become breadwinners.[72]

Even moreso than for other women, heading a family means poverty for black women. Their limited work opportunities have kept most black female-headed families well below the official poverty line. Moreover, their ability to use the law to secure financial assistance from the fathers of their children has been hampered by their high rates of illegitimacy and the poverty of the children's fathers. In 1978, only 28.8 percent of unmarried black mothers had court orders mandating child support payments, compared to 43.8 percent of Hispanics and 70.7 percent of whites.[73]

As a result, poor black women often had to rely on "street corner strategies" to secure some support from the fathers of their children and other men in their lives. This has often entailed entering men's spaces—the streets, for example—in order to ask them for money. These strategies worked to some degree; 69 percent of the Aid to Families with Dependent Children (AFDC) fathers in Carol Stack's study contributed some financial and nurturing assistance to their children. In order to wrest money from men who were otherwise reluctant to volunteer their help, black women have had to sacrifice dignity and privacy.[74]

These changes in their economic roles and needs have not been accompanied by the wider employment opportunities they necessitate. Black women's economic dependence (on men and the state) therefore has increased. At the same time, the urban wage economy has provided only low wages and insecure employment for most black men. As a result, neither black women nor black men have the structural supports necessary to enact their role responsibilities in the family.

Moreover, economic oppression dramatically heightens gender conflict among blacks. Women's efforts to keep their marriages intact often founder in the face of their husbands' unemployment and the temptations of street culture for discouraged men. As in the past, they have been willing to struggle with their men in order to secure more egalitarian relationships. Black women's willingness to forgo unpromising marriages or to leave bad relationships has not created egalitarianism in gender roles. The disparity between their gender ideals and the terms of their relationships bespeak black women's limited power in the domestic realm. It also reveals the inadequacies of individualistic strategies unsupported by the values or practices of the larger society.[75]

The economic marginality of black women and men created a material interdependence, but not a mutually acceptable normative structure that defined their economic or emotional obligations to one another. Many men expected to be able to dictate the household division of labor and to enforce a double standard in marital norms regarding sexuality. For some, violence served as a tool of last resort, the weapon of those for whom material, political, and ideological dominance were not fully available. Women's resistance to masculine authority was occasioned by those same circumstances. Their economic position, however, did not offer them advantages over men or enable them to secure egalitarian relationships.[76]

Only when good jobs and public power are as available to African American women and men as to others can the pressures on their families be eased sufficiently so that they can define a gender system based on shared responsibility and mutual trust. Until then, the crisis in black family life will continue, orchestrated by those who believe that neglect can be benign and that subordination is the price women must pay for economic well-being and marital stability.

NOTES

1. The Moynihan Report, of course, represents the exemplary statement of this position. U.S. Department of Labor, *The Negro Family: The Case for National*

Action, by Daniel P. Moynihan (Washington, D.C.: Government Printing Office, 1965); Paula Giddings, *When and Where I Enter: The Impact of Black Women on Race and Sex in America* (New York: Bantam Books, 1984), 252–53; Lee Rainwater and William L. Yancey, eds., *The Moynihan Report and the Politics of Controversy* (Cambridge: MIT Press, 1967); Patricia Hill Collins, "A Comparison of Two Works on Black Family Life," *Signs: A Journal of Women in Culture and Society* 14 (Summer 1989): 875–84; Maulanga Karenga, "Social Ethics and the Black Family: An Alternative Analysis," *The Black Scholar* (September/October 1986): 41–54; Bettina Aptheker, *Woman's Legacy: Essays on Race, Sex, and Class in American History* (Amherst: University of Massachusetts Press, 1982), 129–51.

2. Eleanor Engram, *Science, Myth, Reality: The Black Family in One-Half Century of Research* (Westport, Conn.: Greenwood Press, 1982), 24–28; Joyce Ladner, *Tomorrow's Tomorrow: The Black Woman* (Garden City, N.Y.: Doubleday and Co., 1971); Carol B. Stack, *All Our Kin: Strategies for Survival in a Black Community* (New York: Harper and Row, 1974); Andrew Billingsley, *Black Families in White America* (Englewood Cliffs, N.J.: Prentice-Hall, 1968). They have, however, drawn contradictory conclusions regarding the power dynamics within black families before, during, and after slavery.

3. Nathan Hare, "What Black Intellectuals Misunderstand about the Black Family," *Black World* 25 (March 1976): 4–14; Audre Lorde, *Sister/Outsider: Essays and Speeches* (Trumansburg, N.Y.: The Crossing Press, 1984). See also the debates in *The Black Scholar* 10 (May-June 1979).

4. Engram, *Science, Myth, Reality*, pp. 24–28.

5. Coppelia Kahn, "Excavating 'Those Dim Minoan Regions': Maternal Subtexts in Patriarchal Literature," *Diacritics* 12 (Summer 1982): 33; Colin Bell and Howard Newby, "Husbands and Wives: The Dynamics of a Deferential Dialectic," in *Dependence and Exploitation in Marriage and Work*, ed. Diana Leonard Barker and Sheila Allen (New York: Longman, 1976), 152–68.

6. Nancy Chodorow, "Family Structure and Feminine Personality," in *Woman, Culture, and Society*, ed. Michelle Zimbalist Rosaldo and Louise Lamphere (Stanford, Calif.: Stanford University Press, 1974), 43–66.

7. Linda Gordon, "Child Abuse, Gender, and the Myth of Family Independence," *Child Welfare* 64 (May-June 1985): 213–24; Marylynn Salmon, *Women and the Law of Property in Early America* (Chapel Hill: University of North Carolina Press, 1986). As Karen Sacks has noted, neither Marxist nor Freudian theory adequately explains these dynamics. Karen Sacks, "What's a Life Story Got to Do with It?" in *Interpreting Women's Lives*, ed. Personal Narratives Group (Bloomington: Indiana University Press, 1989), 85–95; Collins, "A Comparison of Two Works on Black Family Life," 875–84.

8. Engram, *Science, Myth, Reality*; Jane Collier, Michelle Z. Rosaldo, and Sylvia Yanagisako, "Is There a Family? New Anthropological Views," in *Rethinking the Family: Some Feminist Questions*, ed. Barrie Thorne with Marilyn Yalom, (New York: Longman, 1982), 25–39; Rosalind Pollack Petchesky, "Antiabortion, Antifeminism, and the Rise of the New Right," *Feminist Studies* 7 (Summer 1981): 206–46; Maxine Baca Zinn, "Chicano Family Research: Conceptual Distortions and Alternative Directions," *Journal of Ethnic Studies* 7 (Fall 1979): 57–71.

9. Billingsley, *Black Families in White America*, 48–69; Deborah Gray White, *Ar'n't I a Woman?: Female Slaves in the Plantation South* (New York: W. W. Norton

& Company, 1985), 13–25; E. Franklin Frazier, *The Negro Family in the United States* (Chicago: University of Chicago Press, 1939).

10. Herbert G. Gutman, *The Black Family in Slavery and Freedom, 1750–1925* (New York: Random House, 1976). Deborah Gray White has cautioned, however, that long-term marriages do not necessarily indicate marital harmony or choice in women's lives. White, *Ar'n't I a Woman?*, 149–53.

11. Eugene Genovese, *Roll, Jordan, Roll: The World the Slaves Made* (New York: Pantheon Books, 1974), 482–501.

12. Elizabeth Fox-Genovese, *Within the Plantation Household: Black and White Women of the Old South* (Chapel Hill: University of North Carolina Press, 1988), 30, 49, 330–33, 373–74. This book is often muddled, contradictory, and surprisingly obtuse regarding the dynamics of gender and sexuality in the antebellum South.

13. Jacqueline Jones, *Labor of Love, Labor of Sorrow: Black Women, Work, and the Family from Slavery to the Present* (New York: Basic Books, 1985), 11–43.

14. White, *Ar'n't I a Woman?*, 142–60.

15. Susan A. Mann, "Slavery, Sharecropping, and Sexual Inequality," *Signs: A Journal of Women in Culture and Society* 14 (Summer 1989): 774–98.

16. Suzanne Lebsock, *The Free Women of Petersburg: Status and Culture in a Southern Town, 1784–1860* (New York: W. W. Norton & Company, 1984); Jones, *Labor of Love, Labor of Sorrow*, 38; Claudia Goldin, "Female Labor Force Participation: The Origin of Black and White Differences, 1870 and 1880," *Journal of Economic History* 37 (March 1977): 87–108; Genovese, *Roll, Jordan, Roll*, 482–501; John Douglass Campbell, "The Gender Division of Labor, Slave Reproduction, and the Slave Family Economy on Southern Cotton Plantations" (Ph.D. diss., University of Minnesota, 1988). Deborah Gray White, by contrast, notes that black women also helped to provision their families and concludes that men had no economic basis for authority. White, *Ar'n't I a Woman?*, 13–25.

17. John W. Blassingame, *The Slave Community: Plantation Life in the Ante-Bellum Slave South* (New York: Oxford University Press, 1972), 77–103; White, *Ar'n't I a Woman?*, 142–60.

18. Gutman, *The Black Family*, 60–67, 81; Lebsock, *The Free Women of Petersburg*, 87–111. According to Lebsock, free black women often chose to establish informal unions rather than marriage in order to preserve their autonomy.

19. Lebsock, *The Free Women of Petersburg*, 87–111.

20. Mann, "Slavery, Sharecropping, and Sexual Inequality," 774–98.

21. Elizabeth Hyde Botume, *First Days among the Contrabands* (New York: Arno Press and the *New York Times*, 1968), 151; Charles L. Flynn, Jr., *White Land, Black Labor: Caste and Class in Late Nineteenth-Century Georgia* (Baton Rouge: Louisiana State University Press, 1983), 66; Jones, *Labor of Love, Labor of Sorrow*, 62, 73; Thomas J. Edwards, "The Tenant System and Some Changes Since Emancipation," *Annals of the American Academy of Political and Social Science* 49 (September 1913): 38–46; Dolores Janiewski, *Sisterhood Denied: Race, Gender, and Class in a New South Community* (Philadelphia, Pa.: Temple University Press, 1985), 17–18, 38, 42–44.

22. Jacqueline Jones claims, by contrast, that the gender division of labor among African Americans in the rural South was simply chosen by them. Jones, *Labor of Love, Labor of Sorrow*, 3, 13–14, 36, 38, 41, 46, 57, 59, 62, 78; U.S.

Children's Bureau, "Maternity and Child Care in Selected Rural Areas in Mississippi," by Helen M. Dart, Publication no. 88 (Washington, D.C.: Government Printing Office, 1921), 35; U.S. Children's Bureau, "Rural Children in Selected Counties of North Carolina," by Francis Sage Bradley and Margaretta A. Williamson, Publication no. 33 (Washington, D.C.: Government Printing Office, 1918); Frazier, *The Negro Family in the United States*, 141; Elizabeth Rauh Bethel, *Promiseland: A Century of Life in a Negro Community* (Philadelphia, Pa.: Temple University Press, 1981), 47, 162.

   23. Bethel, *Promiseland*, 47, 162; U.S. Women's Bureau, "Family Status of Breadwinning Women in Four Selected Cities," Bulletin 23 (Washington, D.C.: Government Printing Office, 1925), 37–38.

   24. Mann, "Slavery, Sharecropping, and Sexual Inequality," 774–98.

   25. Jones, *Labor of Love, Labor of Sorrow*, 104–5.

   26. Gutman, *The Black Family*, 433; Crandall A. Shifflett, "The Household Composition of Rural Black Families: Louisa County, Virginia, 1880," *Journal of Interdisciplinary History* 6 (Autumn 1975): 235–60. Pleck has shown that longitudinal data reveal more family instability than the data used in most studies. Elizabeth Hafkin Pleck, *Black Migration and Poverty: Boston, 1865–1900* (New York: Academic Press, 1979).

   27. Shifflett, "The Household Composition of Rural Black Families," 235–60; Janice L. Reiff, Michel R. Dahlin, and Daniel Scott Smith, "Rural Push and Urban Pull: Work and Family Experiences of Older Black Women in Southern Cities, 1880–1900," *Journal of Social History* 16 (Summer 1983): 39–48.

   28. Peter Kolchin, *First Freedom: The Response of Alabama's Blacks to Emancipation and Reconstruction* (Westport, Conn.: Greenwood Press, 1972), 62–63; Leon F. Litwack, *Been in the Storm So Long: The Aftermath of Slavery* (New York: Alfred A. Knopf, 1979), 227–42.

   29. Gutman, *The Black Family*, 489–500.

   30. Johnson, *Shadow of the Plantation*, 57, 77–78; Memo, W. R. Williamson to Wilbur Cohen, 24 August 1938, Records of the Department of Health, Education, and Welfare, RG 47, Box 31, SSA, Office of the Commissioner, National Archives.

   31. Frank F. Furstenberg, Jr., Theodore Hershberg, and John Modell, "The Origin of the Female-Headed Black Family: The Impact of the Black Experience," *Journal of Interdisciplinary History* 6 (Autumn 1975): 211–33. Whether the pattern found by Furstenberg, et al. explains dynamics in the South remains to be seen. U.S. Bureau of the Census, Sixteenth Census of the United States: 1940, *Population*, Vol. 4: 17, 25. It is difficult to separate the widowed from the separated because some with absent husbands reported themselves as widows. Pleck, *Black Migration and Poverty*, 161–96.

   32. U.S. Bureau of the Census, Sixteenth Census of the United States: 1940, *Population*, Vol. 4: 17.

   33. Frazier, *The Negro Family*, 114.

   34. Johnson, *Shadow of the Plantation*, 75–80.

   35. Johnson, *Shadow of the Plantation*, 51–53, 83; Hortense Powdermaker, *After Freedom: A Cultural Study in the Deep South* (New York: The Viking Press, 1939), 157–74, 192–96.

   36. Lebsock, *The Free Women of Petersburg*, 87–111. Jacqueline Jones's reliance

on poverty alone as an explanation for domestic abuse obscures the fact that violence also occurs in economically secure households and ignores the interactive dimension of gender relations. Jones, *Labor of Love, Labor of Sorrow*, 102–4; Lenore E. Walker, *The Battered Woman* (New York: Harper Colophon Books, 1979), 127–44.

37. Charles L. Perdue, Jr., Thomas E. Barden, and Robert K. Phillips, eds., *Weevils in the Wheat: Interviews with Virginia Ex-Slaves* (Charlottesville: University of Virginia Press, 1976), 131; John Blassingame, ed., *Slave Testimony: Two Centuries of Letters, Speeches, Interviews, and Autobiographies* (Baton Rouge: Louisiana State University Press, 1977), 644.

38. Bethel, *Promiseland*, 52. Bethel's finding that sons in landowning families stayed in the community and sometimes worked their parents' land indicates the importance of land to the retention of the labor power of sons for the natal household.

39. Johnson, *Shadow of the Plantation*, 78; Pleck, *Black Migration and Poverty*, 196; "Bachelor Mothers," Federal Writers' Project, Folder 183, Southern Historical Collection, University of North Carolina; "I'd Like to Have a Coca Cola," Federal Writers' Project, Folder 216, Southern Historical Collection, University of North Carolina.

40. Abraham Epstein, *The Negro Migrant in Pittsburgh* (1918; reprint, New York: Arno Press and the *New York Times*, 1969), 50; Jones, *Labor of Love, Labor of Sorrow*, 181–95.

41. Powdermaker, *After Freedom*, 232, 236, 254, 272–73; Janiewski, *Sisterhood Denied*, 139–40.

42. St. Clair Drake and Horace R. Cayton, *Black Metropolis: A Study of Negro Life in a Northern City* (New York: Harper and Row, 1962), 2: 568; Linda Dahl, *Stormy Weather: The Music and Lives of a Century of Jazzwomen* (New York: Pantheon Books, 1984), 15. The nexus between money and sex was exemplified by the fact that women singers could earn larger tips when their lyrics were suggestive.

43. Pleck, *Black Migration and Poverty*, 161–96; Clyde Vernon Kiser, *Sea Island to City: A Study of St. Helena Islanders in Harlem and Other Urban Centers* (New York: AMS Press, 1967), 201–15; Jones, *Labor of Love, Labor of Sorrow*, 182–95.

44. Drake and Cayton, *Black Metropolis*, Vol. 2: 581–88; Jones, *Labor of Love, Labor of Sorrow*, 186, 198, 225; Daphne Duval Harrison, "Black Women in the Blues Tradition," in *The Afro-American Woman: Struggles and Images*, ed. Sharon Harley and Rosalyn Terborg-Penn (Port Washington, N.Y.: Kennikat Press, 1978), 61. Elizabeth Pleck has concluded that disease, sterility, urbanization, and poverty caused the black pattern of marital instability and female-headed households in cities. Pleck, *Black Migration and Poverty*, 161–96.

45. Jones, *Labor of Love, Labor of Sorrow*, 186, 198, 225.

46. Jay R. Mandle, *The Roots of Black Poverty: The Southern Plantation Economy after the Civil War* (Durham, N.C.: Duke University Press, 1978), 98–104, 117–22.

47. General Comments of Workers, Baltimore, Md., Women's Bureau, RG 86, Box 1541, National Archives.

48. Mandle, *The Roots of Black Poverty*, 98–104, 117–22.

49. Ibid. Aptheker, *Woman's Legacy*, 129–51.

50. Aptheker, *Woman's Legacy*, 129–51.

51. Ann Petry, *The Street* (Boston: Beacon Press, 1985); Lee Rainwater, *Behind Ghetto Walls: Black Families in a Federal Slum* (Chicago: Aldine Publishing Company, 1970); Robert Staples, ed., *The Black Family: Essays and Studies* (Belmont, Calif.: Wadsworth Publishing Company, 1971), 3; Michele Wallace, *Black Macho and the Myth of the Superwoman* (New York: Warner Books, 1980), 66–68, 149.

52. Robert Staples, "The Dyad," in Staples, ed., *The Black Family*, 74–83; Rainwater, *Behind Ghetto Walls*; Stack, *All Our Kin*, 109–13. Staples has concluded that conflict and hostility are so endemic that "it makes little sense to create a myth about the happiness or stability of Black marriages."

53. William Julius Wilson, *The Truly Disadvantaged: The Inner City, the Underclass, and Public Policy* (Chicago: University of Chicago Press, 1987), 77–92; Andrew J. Cherlin, *Marriage, Divorce, Remarriage* (Cambridge, Mass.: Harvard University Press, 1981), 93–112.

54. Hylan Lewis, *Blackways of Kent* (Chapel Hill: University of North Carolina Press, 1955), 30–39; Kenneth B. Clark, *Dark Ghetto: Dilemmas of Social Power* (New York: Harper Torchbooks, 1965), 12; Giddings, *When and Where I Enter*, 256.

55. Lee Rainwater, *Behind Ghetto Walls*, 150–63, 170–75; Gail A. Stokes, "Black Woman to Black Man," in Staples, ed., *The Black Family*, 159–61; Elliott Liebow, *Tally's Corner: A Study of Negro Streetcorner Men* (Boston: Little, Brown and Company, 1967), 70–78, 95, 115; Ladner, *Tomorrow's Tomorrow*, 66, 188; Stack, *All Our Kin*; Lee Rainwater, "Husband-Wife Relations," in Staples, ed., *The Black Family*, 163–66; Sarah Webster Fabio, "Blowing the Whistle on Some Jive," *The Black Scholar* 10 (May-June 1979): 57; Clark, *Dark Ghetto*, 70–74; Jean Carey Bond and Pat Peery, "Has the Black Man Been Castrated?" in Staples, ed., *The Black Family*, 140–44.

56. Gloria I. Joseph and Jill Lewis, *Common Differences: Conflicts in Black and White Feminist Perspectives* (Boston: South End Press, 1981), 127–48, 178–230; Patricia Hill Collins, "The Meaning of Motherhood in Black Culture and Black Mother-Daughter Relationships," *Sage* 4 (Fall 1987): 3–10.

57. Ladner, *Tomorrow's Tomorrow*, 201–12, 231; Liebow, *Tally's Corner*, 70, 76–78, 115; Clark, *Dark Ghetto*, 70–74.

58. Liebow, *Tally's Corner*, 60–63, 206–7, 213; Lillian Rubin, *Intimate Strangers: Men and Women Together* (New York: Harper and Row, 1983).

59. Lee Rainwater, "Husband-Wife Relations," in Staples, ed., *The Black Family*, 163–66; Ladner, *Tomorrow's Tomorrow*, 66, 188; Liebow, *Tally's Corner*, 95; Gail A. Stokes, "Black Woman to Black Man," in Staples, ed., *The Black Family*, 159–61; Mollie Crocker Dougherty, *Becoming a Woman in Rural Black Culture* (New York: Holt, Rinehart, and Winston, 1978), 24; Fabio, "Blowing the Whistle on Some Jive," 57. The problems African American women face in securing support for their children are quite similar to those white women experience after a divorce. The reluctance of men to support their children except under certain conditions raises serious questions about policies that assume a "trickle down" pattern from men to women and children. Terry Arendell, *Mothers and Divorce: Legal, Economic, and Social Dilemmas* (Berkeley: University of California Press, 1986).

60. Nancy Seifer, ed., *"Nobody Speaks for Me": Self-Portraits of American Working Class Women* (New York: Simon and Schuster, 1976), 149; Jerry M. Lewis and John G. Looney, *The Long Struggle: Well-Functioning Working-Class Black Families*

(New York: Brunner/Mazel, Publishers, 1983).

61. Jessie Bernard, "Marital Stability and Patterns of Status Variables," *Journal of Marriage and the Family* 28 (November 1966): 421–39; J. Richard Udry, "Marital Instability by Race, Sex, Education, and Occupation Using 1960 Census Data," *American Journal of Sociology* 72 (September 1966): 203–9; John H. Scanzoni, *The Black Family in Modern Society* (Boston: Allyn and Bacon, 1971); Lewis and Looney, *The Long Struggle*.

62. Lewis and Looney, *The Long Struggle*, 2.

63. Harriette Pipes McAdoo, "Factors Related to Stability in Upwardly Mobile Black Families," *Journal of Marriage and the Family* 40 (November 1978): 761–76; Giddings, *When and Where I Enter*, 247–48; Lewis and Looney, *The Long Struggle*, 94–95.

64. Bernard, "Marital Stability," 421–39; Udry, "Marital Instability," 203–9; Scanzoni, *The Black Family*.

65. Marietta Morrissey, "Female-Headed Families: Poor Women and Choice," in *Families and Work: Towards Reconceptualization*, ed. Naomi Gerstel and Harriet Engel Gross (Philadelphia, Pa.: Temple University Press, 1987), 302–14. Mexican American families, by contrast, have relatively low proportions of female-headed families despite high poverty rates.

66. Robert O. Blood, Jr., and Donald M. Wolfe, *Husbands and Wives: The Dynamics of Married Living* (New York: The Free Press, 1960), 108–9, 171, 182, 195, 197, 214–15, 223–24; Scanzoni, *The Black Family*, 201–3; Gwendolyn Brooks, "Why Negro Women Leave Home," *Negro Digest* 9 (March 1951): 26–28; Robert Staples, "The Myth of the Black Matriarchy," in Staples, ed., *The Black Family*, 157; Lorde, *Sister/Outsider*, 51.

67. Blanche Scott Oral History, 11 July 1979, Southern Oral History Project, RG 4007, Southern Historical Collection, University of North Carolina; Maya Angelou, *Singin' and Swingin' and Gettin' Merry Like Christmas* (Toronto: Bantam Books, 1977), 39; John L. Gwaltney, *Drylongso: A Self-Portrait of Black America* (New York: Random House, 1980), 171.

68. Janie Cameron Riley and Lottie Phillips Oral History, 6 June 1975, Southern Oral History Project, RG 4007, Southern Historical Collection, University of North Carolina; Gwaltney, *Drylongso*, 147; Judith Rollins, *Between Women: Domestics and Their Employers* (Philadelphia, Pa.: Temple University Press), 175.

69. Bart Landry and Margaret Platt Jendrek, "The Employment of Wives in Middle-Class Black Families," *Journal of Marriage and the Family* 40 (November 1978): 787–97; Ladner, *Tomorrow's Tomorrow*, 44–46, 184–88.

70. Liebow, *Tally's Corner*, 137–60; Audrey B. Chapman, "Male-Female Relations: How the Past Affects the Present," in *Black Families*, 2d ed., ed. Harriette Pipes McAdoo (Newbury Park, Calif.: Sage Publications, 1988), 195–96; Lewis and Long, *The Long Struggle*, 111.

71. Ladner, *Tomorrow's Tomorrow*, 33–38; Liebow, *Tally's Corner*, 83–91; Lee Rainwater, "Husband-Wife Relations," in Staples, ed., *The Black Family*, 163–66.

72. Given other changes in the patterns of black response to census takers in this period, it is possible that these statistics overstate the change. It is not clear whether black women report their common law relationships as marriages as readily as they did in the past. Cherlin, *Marriage, Divorce, Remarriage*, 93–112; Arthur J. Norton and Jeanne E. Moorman, "Current Trends in Marriage and

Divorce," *Journal of Marriage and the Family* 49 (February 1987): 3–14. Although female-headed families have also increased among whites, the proportion of black families with children that were headed by women was more than three times the rate for white families in 1983. Ruth Sidel, *Women and Children Last: The Plight of Poor Women in Affluent America* (New York: The Viking Press, 1986), 18. William Wilson has concluded that the rise in female-headed families occurred as a consequence of a lack of "marriageable" black men. Whether his definition of marriageable coincides with that of African American women is not clear. Wilson, *The Truly Disadvantaged*, 66–71, 77–92.

73. U.S. Bureau of the Census, "Child Support and Alimony: 1978," *Current Population Reports*, ser. P–23, no. 106, p. 3.

74. Liebow, *Tally's Corner*, 76; Stack, *All Our Kin*, 71.

75. But see Giddings, *When and Where I Enter*, 252–53, 256; Roi Ottley, "What's Wrong with Negro Women?" *Negro Digest* (December 1950): 71–75; St. Clair Drake, "Why Men Leave Home," *Negro Digest* 8 (April 1950): 25–27; Brooks, "Why Negro Women Leave Home," 26–28; Joseph and Lewis, *Common Differences*, 178–230.

76. Powdermaker, *After Freedom*, 165, 169–74. The experiences of black women in this period confirm Rodman's conclusions that women's marital power is enlarged when men do not have a substantial material advantage over them and when gender ideologies validate women's claims to power. Hyman Rodman, "Marital Power and the Theory of Resources in Cultural Context," *Journal of Comparative Family Studies* 3 (Spring 1972): 50–69.

REFERENCES

Angelou, Maya. *Singin' and Swingin' and Gettin' Merry Like Christmas*. Toronto: Bantam Books, 1977.

Aptheker, Bettina. *Woman's Legacy: Essays on Race, Sex, and Class in American History*. Amherst: University of Massachusetts Press, 1982.

Arendell, Terry. *Mothers and Divorce: Legal, Economic, and Social Dilemma*. Berkeley: University of California Press, 1986.

Baca Zinn, Maxine. "Chicano Family Research: Conceptual Distortions and Alternative Directions." *Journal of Ethnic Studies* 7 (Fall 1979): 57–71.

Bell, Colin, and Howard Newby. "Husbands and Wives: The Dynamics of a Deferential Dialectic." In *Dependence and Exploitation in Marriage and Work*, ed. Dianna Leonard Barker and Sheila Allen, 152–68. New York: Longman, 1976.

Bernard, Jessie. "Marital Stability and Patterns of Status Variables." *Journal of Marriage and the Family* 28 (November 1966): 421–39.

Bethel, Elizabeth Rauh. *Promiseland: A Century of Life in a Negro Community*. Philadelphia, Pa.: Temple University Press, 1981.

Billingsley, Andrew. *Black Families in White America*. Englewood Cliffs, N.J.: Prentice-Hall, 1968.

Blassingame, John W. *The Slave Community: Plantation Life in the Ante-Bellum Slave South*. New York: Oxford University Press, 1972.

Blassingame, John, ed. *Slave Testimony: Two Centuries of Letters, Speeches, Interviews, and Autobiographies*. Baton Rouge: Louisiana State University Press, 1977.

Blood, Robert O., Jr., and Donald M. Wolfe. *Husbands and Wives: The Dynamics of Married Living*. New York: The Free Press, 1960.

Bond, Jean Carey, and Pat Peery. "Has the Black Man Been Castrated?" In *The Black Family: Essays and Studies*, ed. Robert Staples, 140–44. Belmont, Calif.: Wadsworth Publishing Company, 1971.

Botume, Elizabeth Hyde. *First Days among the Contrabands*. New York: Arno Press and the *New York Times*, 1968.

Brooks, Gwendolyn. "Why Negro Women Leave Home." *Negro Digest* 9 (March 1951): 26–28.

Chapman, Audrey B. "Male-Female Relations: How the Past Affects the Present." In *Black Families*, ed. Harriette Pipes McAdoo. 2d ed., 195–96. Newbury Park, Calif.: Sage Publications, 1988.

Cherlin, Andrew J. *Marriage, Divorce, Remarriage*. Cambridge, Mass.: Harvard University Press, 1981.

Clark, Kenneth B. *Dark Ghetto: Dilemmas of Social Power*. New York: Harper Torchbooks, 1965.

Collier, Jane, Michelle Z. Rosaldo, and Sylvia Yanagisako. "Is There a Family? New Anthropological Views." In *Rethinking the Family: Some Feminist Questions*, ed. Barrie Thorne with Marilyn Yalom, 25–39. New York: Longman, 1982.

Collins, Patricia Hill. "A Comparison of Two Works on Black Family Life." *Signs: A Journal of Women in Culture and Society* 14 (Summer 1989): 875–84.

———. "The Meaning of Motherhood in Black Culture and Black Mother-Daughter Relationships." *Sage* 4 (Fall 1987): 3–10.

Dahl, Linda. *Stormy Weather: The Music and Lives of a Century of Jazz Women*. New York: Pantheon Books, 1984.

Di Leonardo, Micaela. *The Varieties of Ethnic Experience: Kinship, Class, and Gender among California Italian-Americans*. Ithaca, N.Y.: Cornell University Press, 1984.

Dougherty, Mollie Crocker. *Becoming a Woman in Rural Black Culture*. New York: Holt, Rinehart, and Winston, 1978.

Drake, St. Clair. "Why Men Leave Home." *Negro Digest* 8 (April 1950): 25–27.

Drake, St. Clair, and Horace R. Cayton. *Black Metropolis: A Study of Negro Life in a Northern City*. Vol. 2. New York: Harper and Row, 1962.

Edwards, Thomas J. "The Tenant System and Some Changes since Emancipation." *Annals of the American Academy of Political and Social Science* 49 (September 1913): 38–46.

Engram, Eleanor. *Science, Myth, Reality: The Black Family in One-Half Century of Research*. Westport, Conn.: Greenwood Press, 1982.

Epstein, Abraham. *The Negro Migrant in Pittsburgh*. 1918. Reprint. New York: Arno Press and the *New York Times*, 1969.

Fabio, Sarah Webster. "Blowing the Whistle on Some Jive." *The Black Scholar* 10 (May-June 1979): 56–58.

Flynn, Charles L., Jr. *White Land, Black Labor: Caste and Class in Late Nineteenth-Century Georgia*. Baton Rouge: Louisiana State University Press, 1983.

Fox-Genovese, Elizabeth. *Within the Plantation Household: Black and White Women of the Old South*. Chapel Hill: University of North Carolina Press, 1988.

Frazier, E. Franklin. *The Negro Family in the United States*. Chicago: University of Chicago Press, 1939.

Furstenberg, Frank F., Jr., Theodore Hershberg, and John Modell. "The Origin of the Female-Headed Black Family: The Impact of the Black Experience." *Journal of Interdisciplinary History* 6 (Autumn 1975): 211–33.

Genovese, Eugene. *Roll, Jordan, Roll: The World the Slaves Made*. New York: Pantheon Books, 1974.

Gerson, Judith M., and Kathy Peiss. "Boundaries, Negotiation, Consciousness: Reconceptualizing Gender Relations." *Social Problems* 32 (April 1985): 317–31.

Giddings, Paula. *When and Where I Enter: The Impact of Black Women on Race and Sex in America*. New York: Bantam Books, 1984.

Goldin, Claudia. "Female Labor Force Participation: The Origin of Black and White Differences, 1870 and 1880." *Journal of Economic History* 37 (March 1977): 87–108.

Gordon, Linda. "Child Abuse, Gender, and the Myth of Family Independence." *Child Welfare* 64 (May-June 1985): 213–24.

Gutman, Herbert G. *The Black Family in Slavery and Freedom, 1750–1925*. New York: Random House, 1976.

Gwaltney, John L. *Drylongso: A Self-Portrait of Black America*. New York: Random House, 1980.

Hare, Nathan. "What Black Intellectuals Misunderstand about the Black Family." *Black World* 25 (March 1976): 4–14.

Harrison, Daphne Duval. "Black Women in the Blues Tradition." In *The Afro-American Woman: Struggles and Images*, ed. Sharon Harley and Rosalyn Terborg-Penn, 58–73. Port Washington, N.Y.: Kennikat Press, 1978.

Janiewski, Dolores. *Sisterhood Denied: Race, Gender, and Class in a New South Community*. Philadelphia, Pa.: Temple University Press, 1985.

Johnson, Charles S. *Shadow of the Plantation*. Chicago: University of Chicago Press, 1934. Reprinted, 1969, 1976.

Jones, Jacqueline. *Labor of Love, Labor of Sorrow: Black Women, Work, and the Family from Slavery to the Present*. New York: Random House, 1985.

Joseph, Gloria I., and Jill Lewis. *Common Differences: Conflicts in Black and White Feminist Perspectives*. Boston: South End Press, 1981.

Kahn, Coppelia. "Excavating 'Those Dim Minoan Regions': Maternal Subtexts in Patriarchal Literature." *Diacritics* 12 (Summer 1982): 32–41.

Karenga, Maulanga. "Social Ethics and the Black Family: An Alternative Analysis." *The Black Scholar* 17 (September/October 1986): 41–54.

Kiser, Clyde Vernon. *Sea Island to City: A Study of St. Helena Islanders in Harlem and Other Urban Centers*. New York: AMS Press, 1967.

Kolchin, Peter. *First Freedom: The Response of Alabama's Blacks to Emancipation and Reconstruction*. Westport, Conn.: Greenwood Press, 1972.

Ladner, Joyce. *Tomorrow's Tomorrow: The Black Woman*. Garden City, N.Y.: Doubleday and Co., 1971.

Landry, Bart, and Margaret Platt Jendrek. "The Employment of Wives in Middle-Class Black Families." *Journal of Marriage and the Family* 40 (November 1978): 787–97.

Lebsock, Suzanne. *The Free Women of Petersburg: Status and Culture in a Southern Town, 1784–1860*. New York: W. W. Norton & Company, 1984.

Lewis, Hylan. *Blackways of Kent*. Chapel Hill: University of North Carolina Press, 1955.

Lewis, Jerry M. and John G. Looney. *The Long Struggle: Well-Functioning Working-Class Black Families*. New York: Brunner/Mazel, Publishers, 1983.

Liebow, Elliott. *Tally's Corner: A Study of Negro Streetcorner Men*. Boston: Little, Brown and Company, 1967.

Litwack, Leon F. *Been in the Storm So Long: The Aftermath of Slavery*. New York: Alfred A. Knopf, 1979.

Lorde, Audre. *Sister/Outsider: Essays and Speeches*. Trumansburg, N.Y.: The Crossing Press, 1984.

McAdoo, Harriette Pipes, ed. *Black Families*. 2d ed. Newbury Park, Calif.: Sage Publications, 1988.

———. "Factors Related to Stability in Upwardly Mobile Black Families." *Journal of Marriage and the Family* 40 (November 1978): 761–76.

Mandle, Jay R. *The Roots of Black Poverty: The Southern Plantation Economy after the Civil War*. Durham, N.C.: Duke University Press, 1978.

Mann, Susan A. "Slavery, Sharecropping, and Sexual Inequality." *Signs: A Journal of Women in Culture and Society* 14 (Summer 1989): 774–98.

Morrissey, Marietta. "Female-Headed Families: Poor Women and Choice." In *Families and Work: Towards Reconceptualization*, ed. Naomi Gerstel and Harriet Engel Gross, 302–14. Philadelphia, Pa.: Temple University Press, 1987.

Norton, Arthur J., and Jeanne E. Moorman. "Current Trends in Marriage and Divorce." *Journal of Marriage and the Family* 49 (February 1987): 3–14.

Ottley, Roi. "What's Wrong with Negro Women?" *Negro Digest* 9 (December 1950): 71–75.

Perdue, Charles L., Jr.; Thomas E. Barden; and Robert K. Phillips, eds. *Weevils in the Wheat: Interviews with Virginia Ex-Slaves*. Charlottesville: University of Virginia Press, 1976.

Petchesky, Rosalind Pollack. "Antiabortion, Antifeminism, and the Rise of the New Right." *Feminist Studies* 7 (Summer 1981): 206–46.

Petry, Ann. *The Street*. Boston: Beacon Press, 1985.

Pleck, Elizabeth H. *Black Migration and Poverty: Boston, 1865–1900*. New York: Academic Press, 1979.

Powdermaker, Hortense. *After Freedom: A Cultural Study in the Deep South*. New York: The Viking Press, 1939.

Rainwater, Lee. *Behind Ghetto Walls: Black Families in a Federal Slum*. Chicago: Aldine Publishing Company, 1970.

———. "Husband-Wife Relations." In *The Black Family: Essays and Studies*, ed. Robert Staples, 163–66. Belmont, Calif.: Wadsworth Publishing Company, 1971.

Rainwater, Lee, and William L. Yancey, eds. *The Moynihan Report and the Politics of Controversy*. Cambridge: MIT Press, 1967.

Reiff, Janice L., Michel R. Dahlin, and Daniel Scott Smith. "Rural Push and Urban Pull: Work and Family Experiences of Older Black Women in

Southern Cities, 1880–1900." *Journal of Social History* 16 (Summer 1983): 39–48.

Rodman, Hyman. "Marital Power and the Theory of Resources in Cultural Context." *Journal of Comparative Family Studies* 3 (Spring 1972): 50–69.

Rollins, Judith. *Between Women: Domestics and Their Employers.* Philadelphia, Pa.: Temple University Press, 1985.

Rubin, Lillian. *Intimate Strangers: Men and Women Together.* New York: Harper and Row, 1983.

Sacks, Karen. "What's a Life Story Got to Do with It?" In *Interpreting Women's Lives: Feminist Theory and Personal Narratives,* ed. Personal Narratives Group, 85–95. Bloomington: Indiana University Press, 1989.

Salmon, Marylynn. *Women and the Law of Property in Early America.* Chapel Hill: University of North Carolina Press, 1986.

Scanzoni, John H. *The Black Family in Modern Society.* Boston: Allyn and Bacon, 1971.

Seifer, Nancy, ed. *"Nobody Speaks for Me": Self-Portraits of American Working Class Women.* New York: Simon and Schuster, 1976.

Shifflett, Crandall A. "The Household Composition of Rural Black Families: Louisa County, Virginia, 1880." *Journal of Interdisciplinary History* 6 (Autumn 1975): 235–60.

Sidel, Ruth. *Women and Children Last: The Plight of Poor Women in Affluent America.* New York: The Viking Press, 1986.

Stack, Carol B. *All Our Kin: Strategies for Survival in a Black Community.* New York: Harper and Row, 1974.

Staples, Robert, ed. *The Black Family: Essays and Studies.* Belmont, Calif.: Wadsworth Publishing Company, 1971.

———. "The Dyad." In *The Black Family: Essays and Studies,* ed. Robert Staples, 74–83. Belmont, Calif.: Wadsworth Publishing Company, 1971.

———. "The Myth of the Black Matriarchy." In *The Black Family: Essays and Studies,* ed. Robert Staples, 157. Belmont, Calif.: Wadsworth Publishing Company, 1971.

Sterling, Dorothy, ed. *The Trouble They Seen: Black People Tell the Story of Reconstruction.* Garden City, N.Y.: Doubleday and Co., 1976.

Stokes, Gail A. "Black Woman to Black Man." In *The Black Family: Essays and Studies,* ed. Robert Staples, 159–61. Belmont, Calif.: Wadsworth Publishing Company, 1971.

Udry, J. Richard. "Marital Instability by Race, Sex, Education, and Occupation Using 1960 Census Data." *American Journal of Sociology* 72 (September 1966): 203–9.

U.S. Bureau of the Census. *Child Support and Alimony: 1978.* Special Studies. *Current Population Reports,* ser. P–23, no. 106.

———. *Sixteenth Census of the United States: 1940, Population* Vol. 4. Washington, D.C.: Government Printing Office, 1942.

U.S. Children's Bureau. *Maternity and Child Care in Selected Rural Areas in Mississippi,* By Helen M. Dart. Publication no. 88. Washington, D.C.: Government Printing Office, 1921.

———. *Rural Children in Selected Counties of North Carolina,* By Frances Sage

Bradley and Margaretta A. Williamson. Publication no. 33. Washington, D.C.: Government Printing Office, 1918.

U.S. Department of Labor. *The Negro Family: The Case for National Action*, by Daniel P. Moynihan. Washington, D.C.: Government Printing Office, 1965.

U.S. Women's Bureau. *Family Status of Breadwinning Women in Four Selected Cities.* Bulletin 23. Washington, D.C.: Government Printing Office, 1925.

Wade-Gayles, Gloria. *No Crystal Stair: Visions of Race and Sex in Black Women's Fiction.* New York: The Pilgrim Press, 1984.

Walker, Lenore E. *The Battered Woman.* New York: Harper Colophon Books, 1979.

Wallace, Michele. *Black Macho and the Myth of the Superwoman.* New York: Warner Books, 1980.

White, Deborah Gray. *Ar'n't I a Woman?: Female Slaves in the Plantation South.* New York: W. W. Norton & Co., 1985.

Wilson, William Julius. *The Truly Disadvantaged: The Inner City, the Underclass, and Public Policy.* Chicago: University of Chicago Press, 1987.

Zinn, Maxine Baca. "Chicano Family Research: Conceptual Distortions and Alternative Directions." *Journal of Ethnic Studies* 7 (Fall, 1979): 57–71.

10

Native American Families

Nancy Shoemaker

In their classic study of the Navajo Indians, Kluckhohn and Leighton noted that the "importance of his relatives to the Navaho can scarcely be exaggerated. The worst that one may say of another person is, 'He acts as if he didn't have any relatives.' "[1] In all Indian societies, not just among the Navajos, the family was an important institution. The household, the extended family, and the kin-based clans commonly found among many Indian groups gave each individual a vast network of primary allegiances and largely determined each individual's place in the social, political, and economic activities of the community. The Native American family influenced political leadership and alliances and was the crucial means for mediating conflicts and minimizing wrongdoing. The family was also an economic unit, with clearly designated roles for each member of the family based on gender and age.

To further generalize about the Native American family is a risky venture, since many diverse cultures fall under the label "American Indian." Although regional and community studies are common vehicles for history generally, American Indian historians seem particularly focused on the tribal and regional distinctions of the people they study.[2] The majority of books in Native American history are tribal histories, histories of federal Indian policy, or histories of a particular tribe in the throes of a particular federal Indian policy. Integrating the varied histories of the Lakotas, Kickapoos, Klamaths, Menominis, Osages, Cherokees, and several hundred other Indian groups into a general discussion based on a theme, such as family history, emerges as an impossible albeit worthy task.

Research on the Native American family very roughly falls into four areas: historical demography, kinship, gender, and the effects of colonization on the family.[3] Since this volume covers the American family,

I will generally confine my discussion to 'Indians within U.S. borders, with some necessary references to Canada. The chronological focus will be the nineteenth and twentieth centuries, since very little is known about the Indian family in earlier periods. Before discussing the specific areas of research mentioned above, I will outline some of the problems and prospects of Native American family history as a field.

NATIVE AMERICAN HISTORY AND THE FAMILY

Despite the widespread recognition that the Native American family constituted the most essential association in Indian society, there has been little research into its history. For well over a century, anthropologists have been intrigued by the Native American family, historians less so. The social history movement in particular, and its accompanying fascination with the family, somehow bypassed the majority of scholars working in Indian history. Even now, as many scholars are turning to questions about Indian families in the past, they face a different set of problems from other family historians.

Since the academic study of Native Americans was long the domain of anthropologists, Indian history has developed into an interdisciplinary field. Although historians owe much to the curiosity of Lewis Henry Morgan and the later generations of anthropologists who besieged Indian reservations in the early twentieth century, anthropology has not, until recently, been sensitive to the historian's primary concern—change over time. Since anthropological fieldwork eventually becomes a valuable historical document, historians must constantly grapple with literature that is either entirely ahistorical or has a two-tiered depiction of historical change: the precolonization past appears as a static and pure culture, into which European contact introduced rapid, usually devastating changes. In reality, the most profound changes in Native American societies occurred gradually and subtly, making it impossible to judge when these pristine cultures described in the ethnographic literature were supposed to have existed and exactly when the scourge of Euroamerican influence destroyed traditions.

One difficulty hindering development of Native American family history as a field is that research models used by other historians are not easily adapted to the distinctive documentary record available for Indian history. Like black slaves and colonial women, Native Americans have left few of their own written records. Personal accounts, letters, and diaries written by Indians for an Indian audience are practically non-existent. But while other groups in American society have their histories partly recorded in tax lists, church and court records, and censuses, for Indians these resources are sporadic, available for some groups at some times. Although the wealth of records in federal archives, particularly the records of the Bureau of Indian Affairs, compensates somewhat for the lack of records on the local and state level, most federal records specifically relate to the Native American's unique political status: removal lists of property and improvements, personal money accounts, government boarding school records, and annuity lists and genealogies related to tribal enrollment.[4]

In the mid- to late nineteenth century, the federal government began enforcing exhaustive record keeping to assist in managing reservations and encouraging assimilation; yet this immense resource for Native American family history has barely been touched. Several scholars have explored the possibilities of using such federal records as removal censuses to explore assimilation and land allotment records to reveal changes in social structure and residence patterns.[5] Other attempts to use some of these valuable Indian records include the Newberry Library's American Indian Family History Project, which has collected in machine-readable form a variety of census data (both from the regular U.S. census and Bureau of Indian Affairs censuses) for five tribes in the period from 1885 to 1930.[6] In the future, there will no doubt be more similarly innovative research based on federal Indian records.

HISTORICAL DEMOGRAPHY

Native American historical demography has for the most part followed a different course from other research in American demographic history. The arrival of Europeans in the Americas led to devastating population losses for the native people and a continuing population decline that lasted several centuries. Naturally, this event has attracted much scholarly research. Most of this research has little bearing on the family, focusing instead on estimating precontact population totals and detailing the horrendous impact of European diseases. Estimates for the population size of North and South America in 1492 range from 8.5 million to over 100 million. This enormous range in precontact estimates weakens the credibility of all estimates, and in recent years the politics of native population estimates have become not only more blatant but also more divisive (the higher the native population at the time of contact, the more egregious the effects of colonization). Although estimating population totals based on the skimpiest of data often appears futile, this research has raised many provocative questions for which more and better data probably do exist. For instance, why did some groups survive while others did not? How were Indian fertility patterns affected by demographic collapse? And how do intermarriage and changes in ethnic identity influence our calculations of population size and demographic rates?[7]

Since S. Ryan Johansson's essay, "The Demographic History of the

Native Peoples of North America: A Selective Bibliography," provides an excellent overview of Indian mortality and fertility patterns from precontact times through the twentieth century, my review will be brief.[8] Life expectancy for Native Americans before European contact, estimated from the analysis of skeletal remains, was probably lower than that for Western Europe in the fifteenth century. Not until around 1900, however, are there adequate vital statistics and census data for American Indians. From these resources, we know that mortality rates for Native Americans in the early twentieth century were about double the rates for other Americans. Indian mortality began improving in the 1930s, when the federal government overhauled its reservation health programs, and there were even more rapid improvements in the postwar period. Now Indian mortality rates are close to the United States average, although the causes of death still vary widely from the norm, with Indians prone to high accidental death rates.[9]

Although all Indian groups suffered from excessively high mortality until recently, there were marked differences depending on the environment, economy, and the nature of Euroamerican contact. Johansson and Preston compared Hopi and Navajo demography using 1900 U.S. census data and showed that these two tribes, although sharing the same land-base, had very different mortality rates. The Navajos living on the Hopi reservation in Arizona had an estimated life expectancy at birth in the mid thirties while Hopi life expectancy at birth was estimated to be in the low twenties.[10] Smallpox had just raged through several Hopi villages in 1898 and partly explains the Hopis' high mortality. But also, the Hopis lived close together in compact villages, where epidemics could thrive and sanitary conditions could not have been ideal. Navajo families, whose livelihood (after the Spanish conquest of Mexico) depended on their large herds of sheep, lived far apart from other families and moved frequently throughout the year to take maximum advantage of the land's grazing capability. The Navajos, who were perhaps the fastest growing Indian tribe in the nineteenth and twentieth centuries, and the Hopis cannot be considered typical, but life expectancy for most Indian tribes in 1900 probably fell within that range of low twenties to mid thirties.

As with mortality, little is known about Native American fertility before 1900 except that it was high (probably total fertility ranged from five to seven children). Nearly universal marriage and a young marriage age contributed to this high fertility. Although Indian fertility was high by modern standards, there is some evidence suggesting that Euroamerican contact led to a fertility increase. Indian women may have increased their fertility to compensate for the higher mortality rate, but also intermarriage with whites seems to have increased fertility. Research on the fur trade has shown that Indian women married to white men and Métis or "mixed-bloods" (the racially mixed ethnic group that emerged from Indian-white interaction in the fur trade) had very high fertility.[11] The published figures for Native Americans from the 1910 U.S. census also showed that full-blood Indians had considerably lower fertility than mixed bloods.[12] Mixed-blood families had the high fertility rates typically found in frontier America, but it is not clear why this should be the case. Would racially mixed families behave more like whites, like Indians, or like something else?

Intermarriage with whites probably did lead to some changes in native childbearing attitudes and behavior. Missionaries and fur traders frequently commented on Indian childbearing practices, and so we know that in most Native American communities there was some concept of family limitation. References to abortion, infanticide, and the use of contraceptive charms and medicines occur frequently in the documents, but unfortunately give few clues as to whether native women's attempts to control their fertility were common, effective practices.[13] Also, by many accounts, Indian mothers breast-fed infants for several years, often until they gave birth to another child.[14] Since breast-feeding can depress fecundity, it may have served to limit fertility, either as a deliberate fertility control method or simply as a byproduct of mothers trying to ensure the nutritional health of their infants.

Two recent articles on the fertility decline among native people in Canada and among Alaska natives link lactation to changes in native fertility rates.[15] Both researchers suggest that native women, undergoing modernization, began breast-feeding for shorter periods of time, leading to a brief rise in fertility in the 1950s, followed by the anticipated modern fertility decline in the 1960s. However, since non-Indians, who presumably were not adjusting breast-feeding practices but were experiencing the postwar baby boom, showed a simultaneous rise in fertility followed by a decline, this latest research may exaggerate the role of lactation in explaining Indian fertility change.

Native American fertility probably has declined significantly in the past forty years, but short-term fluctuations, such as the postwar baby boom, obscure the long-term trend. In their research on differential trends in fertility during the baby boom, Rindfuss and Sweet found that American Indian fertility was the second highest after Mexican Americans. Like other subgroups of the U.S. population, Indian fertility rose during the 1950s and declined in the 1960s, but their fertility remained high.[16] More analysis of recent fertility could perhaps distinguish the Indian fertility transition from the short-term fluctuations.

More research is also needed on the demographic consequences of the urban migration of Native Americans, which began during World War II and rapidly accelerated during the 1950s and 1960s. Sociological research on urban Indian fertility suggests that urbanization did not always have the predictable effect of depressing fertility. Surveys conducted among several urban and rural Indian communities in the 1970s showed that urban Omahas had higher fertility and a higher ideal family size than rural Omahas, but the reverse pattern existed among the Seminoles in Florida.[17]

Compositional changes in the Native American population have complicated demographic research on American Indians. Between 1950 and 1960, when the U.S. Census Bureau initiated self-identification for race, the Native American population grew beyond what was demographically possible. The 1970 and 1980 censuses also reveal big leaps in the Indian population because more people identified themselves as Indian. Between 1950 and 1980, the U.S. Indian population more than tripled, from 357,000 to 1,364,000.[18] Part of this growth could be related to intermarriage. There are no clearcut rules about what race the children of intermarried parents are, and intermarriage between whites and Indians has always been high. Today, more than one-half of married Indians are married to non-Indians.[19] Changes in ethnic identity obscure whether observed changes in behavior are merely changes in the composition of the population.

KINSHIP

With a few exceptions, most of the literature on kinship in native societies has focused on kinship systems, the linguistic and cultural frameworks for understanding relationships. Lewis Henry Morgan, often referred to as the father of kinship studies, was the first to "discover" that Native Americans classified relatives differently from Euroamericans. In his research on the Iroquois in the mid-nineteenth century, he became intrigued by the matrilineal system, in which children inherited from their mothers, a woman's brother was father to her children, and a child's biological father was no relative at all. Further research showed enormous variety between Indian groups, which Morgan tried to explain as the product of recent historical change.[20]

Kinship studies continued to thrive in anthropology, particularly with Fred Eggan's efforts in the 1930s. After studying native languages and oral accounts, Eggan and other anthropologists described and diagramed the diverse ways in which Native American societies organized human relationships into a complex network of reciprocal relations and obligations. There is a vast anthropological literature on lineage (how individuals inherited clan membership, religious or political leadership positions, property); clan, band, or village endogamy or exogamy depending on the tribe; and the social behavior, ranging from joking and sexual flirtation to avoidance, dictated by a particular relationship in a particular culture. Structural-functionalism and acculturation theory replaced Morgan's use of evolutionary theory to explain the variety of kinship systems in American Indian cultures.[21]

Although relying on historical change to explain cultural differences between tribes, anthropologists studying kinship portrayed static societies. Kinship studies reputedly based on fieldwork from the 1930s through the 1950s make references to the importance of the horse and include comments like "raiding is an important economic activity," but make no mention of the increasing presence of automobiles, wage labor, and anthropologists on Indian reservations.[22] Most kinship studies analyzed native languages to reveal structure, leaving unanswered other important and interesting questions. For instance, once Native Americans exchanged their native languages for English, or in earlier periods for French and Spanish, how did they describe relationships? Native kin terms are not directly translatable, as is evident in the tongue-twisting prose of kinship analysis (e.g., the Crow kinship system is "the classification of the father's sister's female descendants through females with the father's sister, and their sons with the father, thus giving a definite descent pattern").[23] Did Indians adopt Euroamerican kinship systems along with the language, and if not, how did they arrive at meaningful kinship terms in the new language?

In most kinship studies, Indian kinship seems timeless and abstract, existing only in people's minds with little relationship to behavior. The more recent anthropological research on kinship tries to resolve some of these problems. Gary Witherspoon's kinship study of the Navajos tries to bridge the gap between culture and society by analyzing both the Navajo system for understanding relationships and actual residence patterns.[24] And anthropologist John Moore, in a provocative social history of the Cheyennes, rejects his predecessors' portrayals of Cheyenne kinship as static, arguing that the environment and changing residence patterns have brought about contradictions and changes in Cheyenne kinship.[25]

Perhaps the biggest flaw in the older kinship studies is that the search for structure disguised the great flexibility in Indian kinship behavior. In Native American societies, kinship did not always express biological relationships but also had a social use. Fictive kin and adoption were frequent, and individuals often used kin terms to make new social connections. Treaty and trade negotiations between Indians and whites were heavily laden with kin terms and reveal the many ways in which Native Americans adopted kin terms to establish bonds of respect, trust, and obligation. Kinship had to be flexible because such accidents of daily living as migration, mortality, and personality (some people just do not get along well together) would interfere in the realization of ideal relationships. An individual living in a matrilocal society cannot reside with his or her mother and her family if they are dead and will not reside with them if tension and constant arguing make everyone unhappy.

With kinship studies, anthropologists outlined the cultural rules, while

Native Americans autobiographies show that people did not always behave by the rules or even agree on what the rules were. Although most
autobiographies had non-Indian mediators who shaped the final product, a personal Indian perspective still emerges. In a detailed, intimate
account of his life, Hopi Indian Don Talayesva described how kinship
rules almost influenced behavior during his first serious romance, occurring with a fellow boarding school student around 1906.

One day Louise told me, to my surprise, that she was the daughter of my clan
brother, and therefore my clan daughter. She said that her father was Talas-
veyma of the Gray Hawk Clan, which is linked with the Sun and Eagle clans.
This was bad news for me. Her real father had lived with her mother, Kelmaisie,
only a short time. Then her stepfather, Kalmanimptewa, had married her mother
and raised several children. I had not known that Louise was the daughter of
my linked-clan brother and therefore my daughter. I knew that our relatives
would not like for us to be in love, and wondered what we could do. After we
had talked the matter over for a long time, I said, "Well, we have our agreement;
and I don't care what our relatives say. Your father is not supporting you, and
I will look out for you as long as my money lasts." But we were both worried
about it all.[26]

Later, when Louise's family discovered their engagement, her relatives
persuaded her not to see him again, but by then Talayesva was already
falling in love with someone else.

   A similar conflict between rules and desires appears in another autobiography, in which a Navajo man remembered a dance.

All at once a girl grabbed me. I didn't notice anything until she was dragging
me by the fire. When we got out of the shade I asked for her clan. She was Red
Clay, and so I went ahead and danced with her. When she let me go I went
back to sleep again. But then another girl grabbed me. This time I noticed her
as soon as she took hold of me, and I asked about her clan and her father's clan.
She said, "My father's clan is Bitter Water, and my clan is Salt." While she was
holding me a fellow said, "She's your granddaughter, because her mother's father
belongs to your clan." So she let me go, and I went back inside the shade and
lay down again. I was about to go to sleep when the same girl grabbed me. I
said, "You're my granddaughter." But she kept pulling on me, and so I went
and danced with her. I tried to get away, but she held me as tight as she could
and started dragging and pulling me out of the dance to where her mother and
the others were sitting. Her mother shook hands with me, and I said, "What's
the matter with this girl? She's my granddaughter. I told her to let me loose,
but she doesn't want to." Her mother laughed and said, "Well, she must like
you, and if she does, go with her, because she's always wanted to marry a man
of my father's clan. So you can take her right now."[27]

   Clearly, straightening out kin relationships was an important aspect
of social interaction. In both these stories, the narrators first established

the nature of the relationship and second recognized that marriage was not allowable. But then the individuals involved—the boy, the girl, and members of the family—made decisions about whether or not the rules should be followed. Most of the anthropological research on kinship focuses on the first and second steps to kin interaction, figuring out who is related to whom and realizing the ideal behavior accompanying that relationship. More research on actual behavior would perhaps reveal under what circumstances cultural rules were followed and how they changed.

Other research on kinship focuses on the role of the family in particular cultures or regions. This research, ascribing a functional purpose to the family, has explored how the family worked as an organizing framework for economic and political activities. Despite their variety, all Indian kinship systems were similar in that they allowed for people to have more relatives than in Euroamerican societies: native kinship terms tend to bring distant relatives closer. Many cultures even endowed individuals with several mothers or several fathers. Why did people want so many relatives? On a basic level, having many relatives probably was a useful insurance against deprivation in hard times, but much of this research suggests that the family served more specific purposes.

Historian Gary Anderson's research on the Dakota Indians in Minnesota in the mid-nineteenth century emphasizes the role of kinship in politics and trade. White traders married into Dakota families and formed trading networks through their native kinship alliances, and Dakota leaders like Little Crow became prominent with the support of powerful relatives including his father-in-law. Anderson credited his understanding of Dakota kinship to Ella Deloria's book *Speaking of Indians*, but their concepts of kinship seem somewhat at odds. In Anderson's work, kinship appears as a mechanism for men, both white and Indian, to accumulate wealth and political influence. Deloria, however, described kinship as a way to keep peace, to reinforce good feelings between people, and to subdue violence and anger between members of the same community.[28]

Long-standing debates on family hunting territories among the northeastern Algonquin Indians center on the family's role in land tenure. Among the Algonquins on the eastern edge of North America at the time of European contact, and today among northern Algonquins in Canada, families controlled territories of land and could sell, bequeath, or give away their rights to hunt on this land to other families. The debate has centered on whether this ownership of usufruct rights to clearly defined tracts of land was a functional strategy for beaver conservation or a shift to participation in a barter economy brought about by the fur trade.[29]

And among Northwest Coast Indians, family wealth largely determined social status. Extended families in the Northwest Coast also controlled resources within a certain area, but exploited these resources to accumulate wealth. An individual's status depended first on the family's wealth and second on his or her relationship to the family head. The debate here has focused less on the family than on the class structure of Northwest Coast Indian societies, whether there were three classes— a slave-owning class, a lower class, and a class of slaves—or two classes, one free and one slaves. Whatever the class structure, the family was the primary economic unit for resource acquisition and distribution.[30]

GENDER

Gender was perhaps the primary division within Native American societies, and within families gender was of the utmost importance since it usually determined each individual's contribution to the family economy.[31] Among the Iroquois and Plains Indians, women used to be the farmers while men were hunters and warriors. Among the Hopi, men farmed corn while women ground the corn and made baskets. In the Northwest and Great Lakes area, women dug for roots while men were hunters and warriors. Even the less frequent tasks like erecting a tipi or constructing a birchbark canoe incorporated a division of labor based on gender. Participation in social organizations, warrior societies for instance, and ceremonial activity also often depended on gender, with men usually taking on a more public role than women.

Although Native American societies had clearly defined roles based on gender, like kinship gender was not a biological classification but a social one. Much of the recent literature on gender in Indian societies focuses on the gender choices individuals were allowed to make.[32] Given the name *berdache* by the French, in some societies men could dress like women, take husbands, and do women's work if they preferred the social and economic role of women. Maria Chona, in her life story *Papago Woman*, talked about how her husband's brother, a "man-woman" would sometimes grind corn for her, "something my husband could never do even though he was kind. It would look too bad for a man to grind corn. I found the man-woman very convenient."[33]

Similarly, women who preferred the social and economic role of men could go to war and hunt if they favored those activities over women's activities. Pretty Shield, a Crow woman, proudly told a story about two women who went to fight with General Crook against the Sioux.

Yes, a Crow woman fought with Three-stars [Crook] on the Rosebud, *two* of them did, for that matter; but one of them was neither a man nor a woman. She looked like a man, and yet she wore woman's clothing; and she had the heart of a woman. Besides, she did a woman's work. Her name was Finds-them-

and-kills-them. She was not a man, and yet not a woman. She was not as strong as a man, and yet she was wiser than a woman. The other woman was a *wild* one who had no man of her own. She was both bad and brave, this one. Her name was The-other-magpie; and she was pretty.[34]

Although alternative gender roles were socially acceptable, it is not clear to what degree they were socially respectable. The literature on *berdache* tends to admire the openness in Indian societies while de-emphasizing the ambiguous social position left to people falling outside the two dominant gender roles. Pretty Shield's story is respectful of Finds-them-and-kills-them and The-other-magpie, but Pretty Shield also alludes to men not accepting *berdaches* and women in male roles, particularly as warriors. For the battle, Finds-them-and-kills-them dressed in men's clothes so as not to be ashamed if the Sioux discovered him to be a woman. And Pretty Shield says that the men would never tell this story about women fighting in battle, but that she will "not be stealing anything from the men by telling the truth."[35] Even though individuals could in many Native American societies choose a different gender role, few did.

Despite the flexibility of gender, there were many culturally defined social restrictions on what men and women could and could not do. In *The Ojibwa Woman*, one of the first monographs to study Indian women, anthropologist Ruth Landes argued that Ojibwa men and women led very different lives. Ojibwa society trained men and subjected them to rigid social regulations while women were left "to spontaneous and confused behavior." Men were taught not just the economic roles of hunting and trapping but also to value initiative and endurance. Sexual pursuit of women was also admirable male behavior. Women's work, such as fine beadwork, was valued, but women were generally not allowed the same honors as men.

While the women work, they talk. They talk a great deal, but never with idle hands. Men on the contrary can talk only when they are idle, from the nature of their work. In the absence of men, the women form a closed world where each woman is distinctive, where women's work is valued explicitly, and where women's values are pursued. It is completely dissociated from the world of men where women's work is conventionally ignored and where no individual woman is distinctive.[36]

Also, women could take on the male activities of hunting and trapping, and frequently did so in the absence of men, but it was not expected of them.

One feminist scholar has termed *The Ojibwa Woman* "male-centered," and it is indeed an excessively grim portrait of Indian women's lives.[37] However, some of the Landes's observations resound in other docu-

mentary records, particularly in autobiographical accounts encompass-
ing other tribes and time periods. Personal experiences described in
autobiographies confirm many of Landes's impressions about sexuality
and marriage, for instance. Ojibwa men, Landes claimed, pursued
women as a kind of achievement. Women were more likely expected to
be chaste. Several of the available autobiographies of Indian men give
sometimes detailed accounts of youthful sexual exploits, and the men
seem to have made great efforts to portray themselves as popular with
women.[38] In *Crashing Thunder*, a Winnebago man devoted many of his
stories to courtship and flirtation, describing himself as a resolute ladies'
man until his conversion to the Native American Church.[39]

Women's autobiographies suggest women held different attitudes
about sexuality, marriage, and the family. Crashing Thunder's sister, in
her life story *Mountain Wolf Woman*, told how her brother chose her first
husband for her, how she eventually left him, later marrying someone
else.[40] Maria Chona's family also arranged her first marriage, and she
also left her first husband after he brought home a second wife. Her
family quickly arranged a second marriage because they were unable to
support her.[41] Their marriages happened apparently without courtship
and quickly, at their family's behest, and although their first marriages
ended unhappily, the second marriages developed into long-lasting economic partnerships.

By far the most research in Indian women's history focuses on the
changes wrought by European contact, particularly addressing how colonization affected women's position in Native American societies. Two
general lines of interpretation emerge. One argument suggests that native women were able to survive colonization better than men because
their roles as wives and mothers offered continuity, while men's roles as
hunters and warriors were increasingly thwarted.[42] More often espoused
is the view that Indian women became subordinate to Indian men largely
because the biases of Western culture denied women opportunities. Men
were able to take advantage of the new opportunities offered by contact
and trade with Europeans, and men took over many of the productive
tasks of women, such as agriculture.[43] There are also several articles
which agree in substance with this viewpoint but which show how women
in some communities briefly managed to maintain the status quo despite
pressure from missionaries and traders.[44]

The fur trade brought native women into especially close contact with
European culture, often resulting in intensive, intimate relationships
between Native Americans and Europeans. European men formed liaisons, sometimes brief and sometimes lifelong, with Indian women. The
dearth of European women migrating to North America in the early
days of the fur trade and the urge to establish good trading networks
encouraged traders to seek Indian wives. For a while, the French gov-

ernment also promoted intermarriage as a means to settle Canada without draining France's population, although government officials later retracted this directive because the intermarried Frenchmen seemed to become more like Indians and less like Frenchmen.[45] Sylvia Van Kirk and Jennifer S. H. Brown have shown how Native American women participated fully in the fur trade by preparing hides and skins, trading, interpreting, and negotiating exchanges between their Indian communities and the communities of their white spouses. A new class or race, usually called Métis in Canada and mixed bloods in the United States, emerged from these mixed marriages. Mixed-blood women soon replaced Indian women as more desirable wives, and eventually traders sought white wives, who were other traders' daughters or recently imported European women. Race and gender became increasingly the determinants of success in fur trade society.[46]

As in the larger field of women's history, much of the research on Native American women asks questions about status and power. Separate spheres dominated in most Indian societies and particularly ruled over economic activity, but whether these gender distinctions between public and domestic activities indicated differences in women's political influence remains a prime research question for historians and anthropologists. Men usually did dominate in the public sphere, and their roles as hunters and warriors offered them the means to attract public recognition. With European contact, partly because Euroamerican men expected to deal with men, Indian men continued to dominate in the public sphere. Women's domestic roles, although productive and important to the family economy, were less dramatic and visible, especially to European observers. Although control of the public sphere is seen as a means to political power for men in American society, this was not necessarily true in Native American societies. Whether the available documentary resources, which are particularly scant for Indian women's history, will help resolve this issue awaits to be seen.

EFFECTS OF COLONIZATION

Research into the effects of colonization on the family is more amorphous than the debates on gender. The changes occurring in the Indian family since European colonization have been only sporadically investigated. Promising areas of research include household structure and Indian responses to the assimilation attempts of missionaries and government.

Native American residence patterns at the time of contact varied. The large matrilocal, multifamily households of the Iroquois and Hopi Indians have perhaps received the most attention, but were not typical.[47] Some societies were organized patrilocally, and many groups lived in nuclear family households but settled closely together in bands with other, related families. Underlying the diverse literature on Native American household structure is the consensus that colonization interrupted traditional living arrangements and, either through voluntary adaptations or the changing economic conditions for Indians, the nuclear family unit replaced the extended family.

Perhaps the most influential statement of this process is Anthony Wallace's *The Death and Rebirth of the Seneca*, a history of the prophetic movement that spread among the Iroquois in the early nineteenth century. Wallace proposed that the Handsome Lake religion articulated greater changes in Seneca society, particularly changes in the family. After the social and economic chaos of the American Revolution and the Senecas' confinement to reservations, the Senecas accepted Handsome Lake's advocacy of a new family structure, patriarchal and nuclear, more suitable to Euroamerican-style farming and reservation living.[48] However, other research has shown that one hundred years after Handsome Lake introduced the nuclear family ideal to the Iroquois, the Senecas still had a large number of extended-family households and tended to live in much more complicated households than white Americans.[49]

Although the evidence for Wallace's transformation of the Seneca family is sketchy, his model of family change is widely accepted. The nuclearization of the Indian family over time is a particularly popular approach for understanding changes in the Indian family, partly because the idea of large preindustrial families being modernized and nuclearized has seduced many believers.[50] However, this model is not entirely suitable for explaining changes in Native American households since there always was a range of household types among different Indian groups (from nuclear to multifamily).

Also, the nuclear family may not be the living arrangement colonized people adapt under economically dependent conditions. Native Americans were not modernized, they were colonized. Other literature on Indian households describes colonization's harsh effects on the family. After the gold rush in California, for instance, the demand for native labor scattered individual Indians across white households and rancheros, breaking up family units and consequently assisting in the rapid depopulation of California's Indians.[51] Sociological literature on contemporary Indian household structure, largely the work of Joseph Jorgensen and his students, has argued that large households among contemporary Native Americans are a functional response to poverty. Economically marginalized nuclear family fragments have consolidated households to share resources in an unstable economy; the more stable incomes provided by wage labor seemed to nuclearize families.[52]

Sociologists Sandefur and Sakamoto have also analyzed contemporary Indian household structure, using data from the 1980 census. Although nearly as poor as blacks, Native Americans had fewer female-headed households and more households headed by couples with children than either blacks or whites. They use these results to make poverty policy recommendations, but these results also suggest intriguing possibilities for historical research.[53] Poverty and economic dependency are not sufficient explanations for the distinct patterns in Indian household structure.

Besides having some as yet undefined influence on household structure, colonization affected the Native American family in other, more directly intrusive ways. Certainly, Euroamericans made great efforts to change the Indian family. Although we know a lot about these assimilationist forces, we know very little about how Native Americans responded. The most direct efforts to change Indian families came first from missionaries and later from the U.S. government.

Missionaries tried to enforce a new morality on Native Americans, and particularly preached against what they viewed as lax marriage customs—easy marriage, easy divorce. Their preachings clearly conveyed to the Indians what whites considered wrong or obscene or vulgar, but it is not clear to what degree missionaries actually changed Indian behavior. If the behavior went underground, it is harder for us to find out about it in existing records. Many Native Americans, although attracted by some aspects of Christianity, did not want to make the sacrifices in family life that missionaries demanded, sacrifices such as sending their children away to school, giving up all but one of their wives, and not being allowed to divorce a spouse.[54]

With very similar attitudes toward the Native American family, the government took on moral reform beginning in the late nineteenth century as it planned to assimilate Indians into mainstream society.[55] Reservations were to be eliminated and each individual endowed with a plot of land supposedly suitable for farming. In the 1880s, the government also began establishing courts of Indian Offenses on most reservations and paid native policemen to round up wrongdoers. The courts acted mostly as agents for mainstream American morality and decided on cases involving adultery and polygamy.[56] Simultaneously, Indian children were forced to attend school, frequently off-reservation boarding schools since the government considered Indian parents a bad influence.[57] Government boarding schools, designed to separate children from their native cultures, did create social distance between children and parents, and between Euroamerican-educated children and their peers with no school experience. Whether attitudes toward marriage and divorce changed is harder to detect. Eventually, polygamy was abandoned, but Native American resistance to the Euroamerican insistence on marriage for life may have survived long enough for Indians to see other Americans adopt a concept of marriage more like their own.

Histories of individual families during this "assimilation period" reveal dramatic changes occurring within a generation and suggest that models used by immigration historians could easily be applied to study the rapid transformations occurring in Native American communities. Language differences and the increased knowledge of English among the young may have affected intergenerational relationships. And conflicts between the traditional and the new were probably worked out in each family as decisions had to be made about economics, religion, and social customs. Despite the changes, there was continuity. A history of the LaFlesche family, for instance, shows a continuity of leadership. LaFlesche, Chief Iron Eyes, was an important Omaha chief whose children became influential administrators, teachers, and speakers for Indian rights on and off the reservation.[58] And the history of a Hidatsa family during the reservation period, which was reproduced for a museum exhibit and exhibit catalog, reveals rapid changes in material culture, but a constant interaction between traditional and new attitudes.[59]

CONCLUSION

Although previously American Indian historians have not devoted much of their research to family history, publications in the field during the past few years have shown more interest in exploring changes in the Native American family. Not only is there an increasing number of publications on the subject, but also the research questions seem to recognize better the importance of the family in Native American communities. American Indian historical demography seems to be focusing more attention on the dynamics of population growth—mortality, fertility, and marriage rates—as well as analyzing the effects of intermarriage and the changing composition of Native Americans as an ethnic group. The study of kinship systems has similarly given way to more research on how the cultural concepts structuring relationships influence and were influenced by behavior. Gender and the changing family under colonization continue to be fruitful areas for research.

Like other Americans, Indians have in the past few hundred years seen enormous changes in technology, economics, and society. Underlying these societal changes, however, was another tension: the transition from relative independence to political and economic dependence, from a band or tribal identity to a larger identity as members of a minority group. One essential question for historians is whether there is such a thing as a Native American family or whether there are just Chippewa families, Lakota families, Seminole families? Does the Native American family still reflect the diverse cultural heritage of American Indians, or has the economic and political situation of Indians led to another kind of family, which the label American Indian would inarguably encompass?

To understand historical changes in the Native American family, historians must weigh the competing effects of cultural continuity, changing economic conditions, and assimilationist pressures.

NOTES

1. Clyde Kluckhohn and Dorothea Leighton, *The Navaho*, rev. ed. (Cambridge, Mass.: Harvard University Press, 1974), 100.

2. The major reference works in the field reflect this emphasis on tribe and region, since most handbooks and bibliographies are organized by tribal, regional, and cultural distinctions. The premier reference book for Indian history in the United States and Canada is the *Handbook of North American Indians* put out by the Smithsonian Institution (William C. Sturtevant, general editor). Although the set consists of twenty proposed volumes, fewer than ten volumes have as yet appeared. Most of the volumes cover a particular region, and within each volume essays on the various tribes outline their history, material culture, and social organization. The Newberry Library's Bibliographical Series in Indian history is also an essential resource. This series includes a set of about twenty short guides, which typically survey the literature for a particular tribe or a group of tribes in a particular region. The two most recent volumes in the series have abandoned the regional and tribal emphasis in favor of bibliographical essays that review the latest research in such areas as the fur trade, the use of quantitative data and methods, Indian women, and twentieth-century Indian history. See William R. Swagerty, ed., *Scholars and the Indian Experience: Critical Reviews of Recent Writing in the Social Sciences* (Bloomington: Indiana University Press, 1984), and Colin G. Calloway, ed., *New Directions in American Indian History* (Norman: University of Oklahoma Press, 1988).

3. I will not talk about children since Margaret Connell Szasz has done that in her essay, "Native American Children," in Joseph M. Hawes and N. Ray Hiner, *American Childhood: A Research Guide and Historical Handbook* (Westport, Conn.: Greenwood Press, 1985): 311–42.

4. For a detailed description of federal Indian records in the National Archives in Washington, see Edward E. Hill, *Guide to Records in the National Archives of the United States Relating to American Indians* (Washington, D.C.: General Services Administration, 1981). Microfilmed records are catalogued in the National Archives publication *American Indians: A Select Catalog of Microfilm Publications* (Washington, D.C.: General Services Administration, 1984). The regional outposts of the national archives also have sizable collections of Indian records, and federal records for Oklahoma Indians are mostly at the Oklahoma Historical Society; see "Notes and Documents: Catalogue of Microfilmed Publications of the Archives and Manuscripts Division, Oklahoma Historical Society," *Chronicles of Oklahoma* 60 (Spring 1982): 74–87; (Summer 1982): 218–31; (Fall 1982): 348–59; (Winter 1982): 473–80.

5. William G. McLoughlin and Walter H. Conser, Jr., "The Cherokees in Transition: A Statistical Analysis of the Federal Cherokee Census of 1835," *Journal of American History* 64 (December 1977): 678–703; John H. Moore, "Aboriginal Indian Residence Patterns Preserved in Censuses and Allotments," *Sci-*

ence 207 (11 January 1980): 201–2; John H. Moore and Gregory R. Campbell, "An Ethnohistorical Perspective on Cheyenne Demography," *Journal of Family History* 14 (1989): 17–42.

6. The Newberry Library American Indian Family History Project developed out of a conference on quantitative methods in Indian history. Refer to the Center for the History of the American Indian, "Towards a Quantitative Approach to American Indian History," Occasional Papers Series 8 (Chicago, Illinois: Newberry Library, February 1987). A project of similar scale using Canadian censuses, church records, and land records and surveys produced a genealogical database for the Red River Métis community. See D. N. Sprague and R. P. Frye, *The Genealogy of the First Métis Nation: The Development and Dispersal of the Red River Settlement, 1820–1900* (Winnipeg, Manitoba: Pemmican Publications, 1983).

7. Russell Thornton provides a thorough summary of this literature in *American Indian Holocaust and Survival: A Population History Since 1492* (Norman: University of Oklahoma Press, 1987). See also Henry F. Dobyns, *Their Number Become Thinned: Native American Population Dynamics in Eastern North America* (Knoxville: University of Tennessee Press, 1983), and William M. Denevan, ed., *The Native Population of the Americas in 1492* (Madison: University of Wisconsin Press, 1976).

8. S. Ryan Johansson, "The Demographic History of the Native Peoples of North America: A Selective Bibliography," *Yearbook of Physical Anthropology* 25 (1982): 133–52. See also Henry F. Dobyns, *Native American Historical Demography: A Critical Bibliography* (Bloomington: Indiana University Press, 1976).

9. Johansson, "Demographic History"; S. B. D. Aberle, "Child Mortality among Pueblo Indians," *American Journal of Physical Anthropology* 16 (January-March 1932): 339–49; S. B. D. Aberle, "Maternal Mortality among the Pueblos," *American Journal of Physical Anthropology* 18 (January-March 1934), 431–35; Stephen J. Kunitz, *Disease Change and the Role of Medicine: The Navajo Experience* (Berkeley: University of California Press, 1983).

10. S. Ryan Johansson and S. H. Preston, "Tribal Demography: The Hopi and Navaho Populations as Seen through Manuscripts from the 1900 U.S. Census," *Social Science History* 3 (Fall 1978): 1–33.

11. Jacqueline Peterson, "Many Roads to Red River: Métis Genesis in the Great Lakes Region, 1680–1815," in *The New Peoples: Being and Becoming Métis in North America*, ed. Jacqueline Peterson and Jennifer S. H. Brown (Lincoln: University of Nebraska Press, 1985), 37–71; Jennifer Brown, "A Demographic Transition in the Fur Trade Country: Family Sizes and Fertility of Company Officers and Country Wives, Ca. 1759–1850," *The Western Canadian Journal of Anthropology* 6, no. 1 (1976): 61–71.

12. U.S. Bureau of the Census, *Indian Population of the United States and Alaska* (Washington, D.C.: Government Printing Office, 1915), 157–60.

13. James Axtell, ed., *The Indian Peoples of Eastern America: A Documentary History of the Sexes* (New York: Oxford University Press, 1981), 3–30; June Helm, "Female Infanticide, European Diseases, and Population Levels among the Mackenzie Dene," *American Ethnologist* 7 (May 1980): 259–85; William Engelbrecht, "Factors Maintaining Low Population Density among the Prehistoric New York Iroquois," *American Antiquity* 52 (1987): 13–27; John C. Ewers, "Contra-

ceptive Charms among the Plains Indians," *Plains Anthropologist* 15 (August 1970): 216–18; Ales Hrdlicka, "Physiological and Medical Observations among the Indians of the Southwestern United States and Northern Mexico," *Bureau of American Ethnology Bulletin* 34 (Washington, D.C.: Smithsonian Institution, 1908).

14. Hrdlicka, "Physiological and Medical Observations"; Leo W. Simmons, *Sun Chief: The Autobiography of a Hopi Indian* (New Haven, Conn.: Yale University Press, 1942), 34.

15. A. Romaniuk, "Increase in Natural Fertility during the Early Stages of Modernization: Canadian Indians Case Study," *Demography* 18 (May 1981): 157–72; Larry Blackwood, "Alaska Native Fertility Trends, 1950–1978," *Demography* 18 (May 1981): 173–79.

16. Ronald R. Rindfuss and James A. Sweet, *Postwar Fertility Trends and Differentials in the United States* (New York: Academic Press, 1977), ch. 5.

17. Margot Liberty, David V. Hughey, and Richard Scaglion, "Rural and Urban Omaha Indian Fertility," *Human Biology* 48 (February 1976): 59–71; idem., "Rural and Urban Seminole Fertility," *Human Biology* 48 (December 1976): 741–55.

18. U.S. Bureau of the Census, "We, the First Americans," (Washington, D.C.: Government Printing Office, December 1988); Jeffrey S. Passel and Patricia A. Berman, "Quality of 1980 Census Data for American Indians," *Social Biology* 33 (Fall-Winter 1986): 163–82. For a discussion on the changes in definition and ethnic identification of American Indians, see Thornton, *American Indian Holocaust and Survival*, ch. 8.

19. Gary D. Sandefur and Trudy McKinnell, "American Indian Intermarriage," *Social Science Research* 15 (1986): 347–71.

20. Lewis Henry Morgan, *Systems of Consanguinity and Affinity of the Human Family* (Washington, D.C.: Smithsonian Institution, 1871); Thomas R. Trautmann, *Lewis Henry Morgan and the Invention of Kinship* (Berkeley: University of California Press, 1987).

21. See for example Fred Eggan, *Social Organization of the Western Pueblos* (Chicago: University of Chicago Press, 1950); idem., "The Cheyenne and Arapaho Kinship System," in *Social Anthropology of North American Tribes*, ed. Fred Eggan (Chicago: University of Chicago Press, 1937), 35–95; idem., "Historical Changes in the Choctaw Kinship System," *American Anthropologist* 39 (1937): 34–52; Robert N. Bellah, *Apache Kinship Systems* (Cambridge, Mass.: Harvard University Press, 1952).

22. Bellah, *Apache Kinship*, 14.

23. Eggan, "Historical Changes in the Choctaw Kinship System," 36.

24. Gary Witherspoon, *Navajo Kinship and Marriage* (Chicago: University of Chicago Press, 1975).

25. John H. Moore, *The Cheyenne Nation: A Social and Demographic History* (Lincoln: University of Nebraska Press, 1987).

26. Simmons, *Sun Chief*, 111.

27. Walter Dyk, *Son of Old Man Hat: A Navajo Autobiography* (Lincoln: University of Nebraska Press, 1938).

28. Gary Clayton Anderson, *Kinsmen of Another Kind: Dakota-White Relations in the Upper Mississippi Valley, 1650–1862* (Lincoln: University of Nebraska Press,

1984); idem., *Little Crow: Spokesman for the Sioux* (St. Paul: Minnesota Historical Society, 1986); Ella Deloria, *Speaking of Indians* (New York: Friendship Press, 1944).

29. Frank G. Speck, "The Family Hunting Band as the Basis of Algonkian Social Organization," *American Anthropologist* 17 (1915): 289–305; William Christie MacLeod, "The Family Hunting Territory and Lenape Political Organization," *American Anthropologist* 24 (1922): 448–63; Rolf Knight, "A Re-examination of Hunting, Trapping, and Territoriality among the Northeastern Algonkian Indians," in *Man, Culture, and Animals: The Role of Animals in Human Ecological Adjustments*, ed. Anthony Leeds and Andrew P. Vayda (Washington, D.C.: American Association for the Advancement of Science, 1965), 27–42; Adrian Tanner, *Bringing Home Animals: Religious Ideology and Mode of Production of the Mistassini Cree Hunters* (New York: St. Martin's Press, 1979), 182–202; Eleanor B. Leacock, "The Montagnais 'Hunting Territory' and the Fur Trade," Memoir 78, American Anthropological Association, 1954.

30. Wayne Suttles, "Affinal Ties, Subsistence, and Prestige among the Coast Salish," *American Anthropologist* 62 (April 1960): 296–305; Philip Drucker, "Rank, Wealth, and Kinship in Northwest Coast Society," *American Anthropologist* 41 (January-March 1939): 55–65.

31. There are several good bibliographic resources for Indian women's history. See Rayna Green, *Native American Women* (Bloomington: Indiana University Press, 1983), or her article, "Review Essay: Native American Women," *Signs: Journal of Women in Culture and Society* 6 (Winter 1980): 248–67. There is also a thorough bibliography of Indian women with an emphasis on Indian women's autobiographies in Gretchen M. Bataille and Kathleen Mullen Sands, *American Indian Women: Telling Their Lives* (Lincoln: University of Nebraska Press, 1984). For a good sense of issues in the field, see the collection of essays on Sioux women in Patricia Albers and Beatrice Medicine, *The Hidden Half: Studies of Plains Indian Women* (Lanham, Md.: University Press of America, 1983).

32. Evelyn Blackwood, "Sexuality and Gender in Certain Native American Tribes: The Case of Cross-Gender Females," *Signs: Journal of Women in Culture and Society* 10 (Autumn 1984): 27–42; Charles Callender and Lee M. Kochems, "The North American Berdache," *Current Anthropology* 24 (1983): 443–70; Walter L. Williams, *The Spirit and the Flesh: Sexual Diversity in American Indian Culture* (Boston: Beacon Press, 1986).

33. Ruth M. Underhill, *Papago Woman* (New York: Holt, Rinehart, and Winston, 1979; Part 2 orig. pub. in 1936, American Anthropological Association Memoir 46), 64.

34. Frank Linderman, *Pretty Shield: A Crow Medicine Woman* (New York: Holt, Rinehart, and Winston, 1932), 228.

35. Ibid., 228.

36. Ruth Landes, *The Ojibwa Woman* (New York: Columbia University Press, 1938), vii, 18.

37. Green, *Native American Women*, 4.

38. Simmons's *Sun Chief* and Dyk's *Son of Old Man Hat* are especially detailed and candid. Before publishing *Sun Chief*, anthropologist Simmons suggested to Talayesva "that a few delicate items might be deleted for personal reasons," but Talayesva refused to edit what he saw as "the complete record of my life"

(p. xviii). Since Indian autobiographies were usually the product of a social interaction between Indians and their interviewer, typically an anthropologist or a writer for the popular press, any detectable gender differences in the texts could say more about the interviewer than the interviewee. Although male anthropologists collected mostly men's autobiographies and female anthropologists women's autobiographies, there is no reason to believe the interaction was similar.

39. Paul Radin, *Crashing Thunder* (New York: D. Appleton & Co., 1926).

40. Nancy Oestreich Lurie, *Mountain Wolf Woman, Sister of Crashing Thunder, The Autobiography of a Winnebago Indian* (Ann Arbor: University of Michigan Press, 1961).

41. Underhill, *Papago Woman*.

42. Marla N. Powers, *Oglala Women: Myth, Ritual, and Reality* (Chicago: University of Chicago Press, 1986).

43. Several of the articles in *Women and Colonization*, ed. Mona Etienne and Eleanor Leacock (New York: Praeger, 1980), address the changing economic roles for Indian women under European colonization. See particularly the Introduction, 1–24, and Eleanor Leacock's "Montagnais Women and the Jesuit Program for Colonization," 25–42; also Judith Brown, "Economic Organization and the Position of Women among the Iroquois," *Ethnohistory* 17 (1970): 151–67.

44. Diane Rothenberg, "The Mothers of the Nation: Seneca Resistance to Quaker Intervention," in *Women and Colonization*, Etienne and Leacock, 63–87; Karen Anderson, "Commodity Exchange and Subordination: Montagnais-Naskapi and Huron Women, 1600–1650," *Signs: Journal of Women in Culture and Society* 11, (1985): 48–62.

45. Olive Peterson Dickason, "From 'One Nation' in the Northeast to 'New Nation' in the Northwest: A Look at the Emergence of the Métis," in *The New Peoples*, Peterson and Brown, 19–36. For more on intermarriage between Indians and whites, see William J. Swagerty, "Marriage and Settlement Patterns of Rocky Mountain Trappers and Traders," *Western Historical Quarterly* 11 (April 1980): 159–80.

46. Sylvia Van Kirk, *Many Tender Ties: Women in Fur-Trade Society, 1670–1870* (Norman: University of Oklahoma Press, 1983); Jennifer S. H. Brown, *Strangers in Blood: Fur Trade Company Families in Indian Country* (Vancouver: University of British Columbia Press, 1980).

47. See for example Lewis Henry Morgan's classic *Houses and House-Life of the American Aborigines* (Washington, D.C.: Government Printing Office, 1881), and Peter M. Whiteley's discussion of Hopi households in *Deliberate Acts: Changing Hopi Culture through the Oraibi Split* (Tucson: University of Arizona Press, 1988).

48. Anthony F. C. Wallace, *The Death and Rebirth of the Seneca* (New York: Random House, 1969).

49. Nancy Shoemaker, "From Longhouse to Loghouse: Seneca Household Structure in the Nineteenth Century," *American Indian Quarterly*, forthcoming.

50. See for example Jon A. Schlenker, "An Historical Analysis of the Family Life of the Choctaw Indians," *The Southern Quarterly* 13 (July 1975): 323–34.

51. Albert L. Hurtado, " 'Hardly a Farm House—A Kitchen without Them': Indian and White Households on the California Borderland Frontier in 1860," *Western Historical Quarterly* 13 (July 1982): 245–70; idem., *Indian Survival on the*

California Frontier (New Haven, Conn.: Yale University Press, 1988).

52. Joseph C. Jorgensen, "Indians and the Metropolis," in *The American Indian in Urban Society*, ed. Jack O. Waddell and O. Michael Watson (Boston: Little, Brown and Company, 1971), 67–113; idem., *The Sun Dance Religion: Power for the Powerless* (Chicago: University of Chicago Press, 1972), ch. 4; Martha C. Knack, *Life Is with People: Household Organization of the Contemporary Southern Paiute Indians* (Socorro, N.M.: Ballena Press, 1980).

53. Gary D. Sandefur and Arthur Sakamoto, "American Indian Household Structure and Income," *Demography* 25 (February 1988): 71–80.

54. See Axtell, *The Indian Peoples of Eastern America*, a documentary collection that includes many missionary observations on the Indian family; and Henry Warner Bowden, *American Indians and Christian Missions: Studies in Cultural Conflict* (Chicago: University of Chicago Press, 1981).

55. Frederick E. Hoxie, *A Final Promise: The Campaign to Assimilate the Indians, 1880–1920* (Lincoln: University of Nebraska Press, 1984).

56. William T. Hagan, *Indian Police and Judges: Experiments in Acculturation and Control* (New Haven, Conn.: Yale University Press, 1966).

57. Robert A. Trennert, Jr., *Phoenix Indian School: Forced Assimilation in Arizona, 1891–1935* (Norman: University of Oklahoma Press, 1988); idem., "Victorian Morality and the Supervision of Indian Women Working in Phoenix, 1906–1930," *Journal of Social History* 22 (Fall 1988): 113–28.

58. Norma Kidd Green, *Iron Eye's Family: The Children of Joseph LaFlesche* (Lincoln, Nebr.: Johnsen Publishing Company, 1969).

59. Carolyn Gilman and Mary Jane Schneider, *The Way to Independence: Memories of a Hidatsa Indian Family, 1840–1920* (St. Paul: Minnesota Historical Society Press, 1987).

REFERENCES

Aberle, S. B. D. "Child Mortality among Pueblo Indians." *American Journal of Physical Anthropology* 16 (January-March 1932): 339–49.

————. "Maternal Mortality among the Pueblos." *American Journal of Physical Anthropology* 18 (January-March 1934): 431–35.

Albers, Patricia and Beatrice Medicine. *The Hidden Half: Studies of Plains Indian Women.* Lanham, Md.: University Press of America, 1983.

Anderson, Gary Clayton. *Kinsmen of Another Kind: Dakota-White Relations in the Upper Mississippi Valley: 1650–1862.* Lincoln: University of Nebraska Press, 1984.

————. *Little Crow: Spokesman for the Sioux.* St. Paul: Minnesota Historical Society, 1986.

Anderson, Karen. "Commodity Exchange and Subordination: Montagnais-Naskapi and Huron Women, 1600–1650." *Signs: Journal of Women in Culture and Society.* 11, no. 1 (1985): 48–62.

Axtell, James, ed. *The Indian Peoples of Eastern America: A Documentary History of the Sexes.* New York: Oxford University Press, 1981.

Bataille, Gretchen M., and Kathleen Mullen Sands. *American Indian Women: Telling Their Lives.* Lincoln: University of Nebraska Press, 1984.

Bellah, Robert N. *Apache Kinship Systems.* Cambridge, Mass.: Harvard University

Press, 1952.

Blackwood, Evelyn. "Sexuality and Gender in Certain Native American Tribes: The Case of Cross-Gender Females." *Signs: Journal of Women in Culture and Society* 10 (Autumn 1984): 27–42.

Blackwood, Larry. "Alaska Native Fertility Trends, 1950–1978." *Demography* 18 (May 1981): 173–79.

Bowden, Harry Warner. *American Indians and Christian Missions: Studies in Cultural Conflict.* Chicago: University of Chicago Press, 1981.

Brown, Jennifer S. H. "A Demographic Transition in the Fur Trade Country: Family Sizes and Fertility of Company Officers and Country Wives, Ca. 1759–1850." *The Western Canadian Journal of Anthropology* 6, (1976): 61–71.

———. *Strangers in Blood: Fur Trade Company Families in Indian Country.* Vancouver: University of British Columbia Press, 1980.

Brown, Judith. "Economic Organization and the Position of Women among the Iroquois." *Ethnohistory* 17 (1970): 151–67.

Callender, Charles, and Lee M. Kochems. "The North American Berdache." *Current Anthropology* 24 (1983): 443–70.

Calloway, Colin G., ed. *New Directions in American Indian History.* Norman: University of Oklahoma Press, 1988.

Deloria, Ella. *Speaking of Indians.* New York: Friendship Press, 1944.

Denevan, William M., ed. *The Native Population of the Americas in 1492.* Madison: University of Wisconsin Press, 1976.

Dobyns, Henry F. *Native American Historical Demography: A Critical Bibliography.* Bloomington: Indiana University Press, 1976.

———. *Their Number Become Thinned: Native American Population Dynamics in Eastern North America.* Knoxville: University of Tennessee Press, 1983.

Drucker, Philip. "Rank, Wealth, and Kinship in Northwest Coast Society." *American Anthropologist* 41 (January-March 1939): 55–65.

Dyk, Walter. *Son of Old Man Hat: A Navajo Autobiography.* Lincoln: University of Nebraska Press, 1938.

Eggan, Fred. "The Cheyenne and Arapaho Kinship System." In *Social Anthropology of North American Tribes,* ed. Fred Eggan, 35–95. Chicago: University of Chicago Press, 1937.

———. "Historical Changes in the Choctaw Kinship System." *American Anthropologist* 39 (1937): 34–52.

———. *Social Organization of the Western Pueblos.* Chicago: University of Chicago Press, 1950.

Engelbrecht, William. "Factors Maintaining Low Population Density among the Prehistoric New York Iroquois." *American Antiquity* 52 (1987): 13–27.

Etienne, Mona, and Eleanor Leacock, eds. *Women and Colonization: Anthropological Perspectives.* New York: Praeger, 1980.

Ewers, John C. "Contraceptive Charms among the Plains Indians." *Plains Anthropologist* 15 (August 1970): 216–18.

Gilman, Carolyn, and Mary Jane Schneider. *The Way to Independence: Memories of a Hidatsa Indian Family, 1840–1920.* St. Paul: Minnesota Historical Society Press, 1987.

Green, Norma Kidd. *Iron Eye's Family: The Children of Joseph LaFlesche.* Lincoln,

Nebr.: Johnsen Publishing Company, 1969.

Green, Rayna. *Native American Women: A Contextual Bibliography.* Bloomington: Indiana University Press, 1983.

————. "Review Essay: Native American Women." *Signs: Journal of Women in Culture and Society* 6 (Winter 1980): 248–67.

Hagan, William T. *Indian Police and Judges: Experiments in Acculturation and Control.* New Haven, Conn.: Yale University Press, 1966.

Helm, June. "Female Infanticide, European Diseases, and Population Levels among the Mackenzie Dene." *American Ethnologist* 7 (May 1980): 259–85.

Hill, Edward E. *Guide to Records in the National Archives of the United States Relating to American Indians.* Washington, D.C.: General Services Administration, 1981.

Hoxie, Frederick E. *A Final Promise: The Campaign to Assimilate the Indians, 1880–1920.* Lincoln: University of Nebraska Press, 1984.

Hrdlicka, Ales. "Physiological and Medical Observations among the Indians of the Southwestern United States and Northern Mexico." *Bureau of American Ethnology Bulletin* no. 34. Washington, D.C.: Smithsonian Institution, 1908.

Hurtado, Albert L. " 'Hardly a Farm House—A Kitchen without Them': Indian and White Households on the California Borderland Frontier in 1860." *Western Historical Quarterly* 13 (July 1982): 245–70.

————. *Indian Survival on the California Frontier.* New Haven, Conn.: Yale University Press, 1988.

Johansson, S. Ryan. "The Demographic History of the Native Peoples of North America: A Selective Bibliography." *Yearbook of Physical Anthropology* 25 (1982): 133–52.

Johansson, S. Ryan, and S. H. Preston. "Tribal Demography: The Hopi and Navaho Populations as Seen through Manuscripts from the 1900 U.S. Census." *Social Science History* 3 (Fall 1978): 1–33.

Jorgensen, Joseph G. "Indians and the Metropolis." In *The American Indian in Urban Society,* ed. Jack O. Waddell and O. Michael Watson, 67–113. Boston: Little, Brown and Company, 1971.

————. *The Sun Dance Religion: Power for the Powerless.* Chicago: University of Chicago Press, 1972.

Kluckhohn, Clyde, and Dorothea Leighton. *The Navaho.* Rev. ed. Cambridge, Mass.: Harvard University Press, 1974.

Knack, Martha C. *Life Is with People: Household Organization of the Contemporary Southern Paiute Indians.* Socorro, N.Mex.: Ballena Press, 1980.

Knight, Rolf. "A Re-examination of Hunting, Trapping, and Territoriality among the Northeastern Algonkian Indians." In *Man, Culture, and Animals: The Role of Animals in Human Ecological Adjustments,* ed. Anthony Leeds and Andrew P. Vayda, 27–42. Washington, D.C.: American Association for the Advancement of Science, 1965.

Kunitz, Stephen J. *Disease Change and the Role of Medicine: The Navajo Experience.* Berkeley: University of California Press, 1983.

Landes, Ruth. *The Ojibwa Woman.* New York: Columbia University Press, 1938.

Leacock, Eleanor B. "The Montagnais 'Hunting Territory' and the Fur Trade." Memoir 78. American Anthropological Association, 1954.

Liberty, Margot, David V. Hughey, and Richard Scaglion. "Rural and Urban

Omaha Indian Fertility." *Human Biology* 48 (February 1976): 59–71.

Liberty, Margot, Richard Scaglion, and David V. Hughey. "Rural and Urban Seminole Fertility." *Human Biology* 48 (December 1976): 741–55.

Linderman, Frank. *Pretty Shield: A Crow Medicine Woman.* New York: Holt, Rinehart, and Winston, 1932.

Lurie, Nancy Oestreich. *Mountain Wolf Woman, Sister of Crashing Thunder, The Autobiography of a Winnebago Indian.* Ann Arbor: University of Michigan Press, 1961.

MacLeod, William Christie. "The Family Hunting Territory and Lenape Political Organization." *American Anthropologist* 24 (1922): 448–63.

McLoughlin, William G., and Walter H. Conser, Jr. "The Cherokees in Transition: A Statistical Analysis of the Federal Cherokee Census of 1835." *Journal of American History* 64 (December 1977): 679–703.

Moore, John H. "Aboriginal Indian Residence Patterns Preserved in Censuses and Allotments." *Science* 207 (11 January 1980): 201–2.

———. *The Cheyenne Nation: A Social and Demographic History.* Lincoln: University of Nebraska Press, 1987.

Moore, John H., and Gregory R. Campbell. "An Ethnohistorical Perspective on Cheyenne Demography." *Journal of Family History* 14, (1989): 17–42.

Morgan, Lewis Henry. *Houses and House-Life of the American Aborigines.* Washington, D.C.: Government Printing Office, 1881.

———. *Systems of Consanguinity and Affinity of the Human Family.* Washington, D.C.: Smithsonian Institution, 1871.

Newberry Library Center for the History of the American Indian. "Towards a Quantitative Approach to American Indian History." Occasional Papers Series no. 8. Chicago, Illinois: February 1987.

"Notes and Documents: Catalogue of Microfilmed Publications of the Archives and Manuscripts Division, Oklahoma Historical Society." *Chronicles of Oklahoma* 60 (Spring 1982): 74–87; (Summer 1982): 218–31; (Fall 1982): 348–59; (Winter 1982): 473–80.

Passel, Jeffrey S., and Patricia A. Berman. "Quality of 1980 Census Data for American Indians." *Social Biology* 33 (Fall-Winter 1986): 163–82.

Peterson, Jacqueline, and Jennifer S. H. Brown, eds. *The New Peoples: Being and Becoming Métis in North America.* Lincoln: University of Nebraska Press, 1985.

Powers, Marla N. *Oglala Women: Myth, Ritual, and Reality.* Chicago: University of Chicago Press, 1986.

Radin, Paul. *Crashing Thunder.* New York: D. Appleton & Co., 1926.

Rindfuss, Ronald R., and James A. Sweet. *Postwar Fertility Trends and Differentials in the United States.* New York: Academic Press, 1977.

Romaniuk, A. "Increase in Natural Fertility during the Early Stages of Modernization: Canadian Indians Case Study." *Demography* 18 (May 1981): 157–72.

Sandefur, Gary D., and Trudy McKinnell. "American Indian Intermarriage." *Social Science Research* 15 (1986): 347–71.

Sandefur, Gary D., and Arthur Sakamoto. "American Indian Household Structure and Income." *Demography* 25 (February 1988): 71–80.

Schlenker, Jon A. "An Historical Analysis of the Family Life of the Choctaw

Indians." *The Southern Quarterly* 13 (July 1975): 323–34.

Shoemaker, Nancy. "From Longhouse to Loghouse: Seneca Household Structure in the Nineteenth Century." *American Indian Quarterly*. In Press.

Simmons, Leo. *Sun Chief: The Autobiography of a Hopi Indian*. New Haven, Conn.: Yale University Press, 1942.

Speck, Frank G. "The Family Hunting Band as the Basis of Algonkian Social Organization." *American Anthropologist* 17 (1915): 289–305.

Sprague, D. N., and R. P. Frye. *The Genealogy of the First Métis Nation: The Development and Dispersal of the Red River Settlement, 1820–1900*. Winnipeg, Manitoba: Pemmican Publications, 1983.

Sturtevant, William C., ed. *Handbook of North American Indians*. Washington, D.C.: Smithsonian Institution, 1978–.

Suttles, Wayne. "Affinal Ties, Subsistence, and Prestige among the Coast Salish." *American Anthropologist* 62 (April 1960): 296–305.

Swagerty, William R. "Marriage and Settlement Patterns of Rocky Mountain Trappers and Traders." *Western Historical Quarterly* 11 (April 1980): 159–80.

———. ed. *Scholars and the Indian Experience: Critical Reviews of Recent Writing in the Social Sciences*. Bloomington: Indiana University Press, 1984.

Szasz, Margaret Connell. "Native American Children." In *American Childhood: A Research Guide and Historical Handbook*, ed. Joseph M. Hawes and N. Ray Hiner, 311–42. Westport, Conn.: Greenwood Press, 1985.

Tanner, Adrian. *Bringing Home Animals: Religious Ideology and Mode of Production of the Mistassini Cree Hunters*. New York: St. Martin's Press, 1979.

Thornton, Russell. *American Indian Holocaust and Survival: A Population History since 1492*. Norman: University of Oklahoma Press, 1987.

Trautmann, Thomas R. *Lewis Henry Morgan and the Invention of Kinship*. Berkeley: University of California Press, 1987.

Trennert, Robert A., Jr. *Phoenix Indian School: Forced Assimilation in Arizona, 1891–1935*. Norman: University of Oklahoma Press, 1988.

———. "Victorian Morality and the Supervision of Indian Women Working in Phoenix, 1906–1930." *Journal of Social History* 22 (Fall 1988): 113–28.

Underhill, Ruth M. *Papago Woman*. 1936, part 2, Anthropological Association Memoir 46. New York: Holt, Rinehart, and Winston, 1979.

U.S. Bureau of the Census. *Indian Population of the United States and Alaska*. Washington, D.C.: Government Printing Office, 1915.

———. *We, the First Americans*. Washington, D.C.: Government Printing Office, 1988.

U.S. National Archives. *American Indians: A Select Catalog of Microfilm Publications*. Washington, D.C.: General Services Administration, 1984.

Van Kirk, Sylvia. *Many Tender Ties: Women in Fur-Trade Society, 1670–1870*. Norman: University of Oklahoma Press, 1983.

Wallace, Anthony F. C. *The Death and Rebirth of the Seneca*. New York: Random House, 1969.

Whiteley, Peter M. *Deliberate Acts: Changing Hopi Culture through the Oraibi Split*. Tucson: University of Arizona Press, 1988.

Williams, Walter L. *The Spirit and the Flesh: Sexual Diversity in American Indian Culture*. Boston: Beacon Press, 1986.

Witherspoon, Gary. *Navajo Kinship and Marriage*. Chicago: University of Chicago Press, 1975.

11

Immigrant Working-Class Families

Selma Berrol

This chapter will examine the experience of the Chinese, Eastern European Jewish, French Canadian, German, Irish, Italian, Mexican, and Slavic families that came to the major cities of the United States between 1840 and 1940. These groups were chosen because their numbers were large, their places of origin varied (thus allowing for comparisons), and except for the Germans, they settled mostly in urban areas. They also have been studied a great deal, making it possible to use the resulting scholarship to discern the trends and issues in the field. There has been no shortage of issues. As with many other topics in American history during the past thirty years, older views of the immigrant family have been attacked and revised. As of 1989, the contestants appear to have reached at least a temporary armistice, and a middle-of-the-road position on most issues has emerged.

Most prominent has been the matter of dysfunctional versus stable immigrant families. In the fifties, as William Thomas, Florian Znaniecki, and others had done before, Oscar Handlin found the uprooted Boston Irish family in disarray, and Caroline Ware presented the Italians of New York City's Greenwich Village in a similar light, as did Leonard Covello in regard to the "uptown" Italians of East Harlem.[1] Beginning in the 1970s, however, notably with Carol Groneman's dissertation on the Irish of the "Bloody Ould Sixth Ward" of New York City, in which she demonstrated that even the poorest Irish families in New York City, circa 1855, maintained close family ties, Caroline Golab, Kathleen Conzen, Richard Gambino, and John Bodnar, among others, have found much evidence of the persistence of family stability in spite of the buffeting immigrant families took from poverty, prejudice, and the enormous changes emigration from a rural agricultural culture to an urban industrial world required. Even when a symptom of disorganization like desertion is discussed, as Abigail Moore does in her essay on Eastern European Jewish family breakup, the cause is found to lie in a marriage already "enfeebled" in the old country. Similarly, whatever chaos existed in the Irish American family, Kirby Miller says, was the result of the poverty caused by an inequitable land system in Ireland.[2]

As is usual in scholarly research, interpretations rest on the sources read and the temper of the times. Earlier works on the immigrant family depended heavily on the reports of reformers and journalists who, for various reasons of their own, stressed what they found to be unpleasant. (Tamara Hareven calls them neo-romantics), emphasizing drink, dirt, and desertion, and blaming the victims rather than the society for their misfortunes. More recent scholarship, on the other hand, in an attempt to write history from the "bottom up," has been based on quantitative data such as the census, on interviews with survivors, and on insights born out of the ethnic pride that emerged in the late sixties. These studies have emphasized the responsibility of an exploitative industrial society for the newcomer's plight, which would have been much worse, they say, without the supportive family networks that marked immigrant communities. "Far from destroying relationships among kin," say Steven Mintz and Susan Kellogg, "immigration across the Atlantic strengthened family and kinship ties because families were the basic resource in effecting the immigrant's transition to the new environment." Virginia Yans-McLaughlin agrees, saying that kinship eased adjustment.[3]

At this writing, the revisionists appear to have won the day on the issue of family disorganization, but partly as a result of their victory other questions have emerged. Did the existence of strong family networks, and thus the persistence of ethnic attitudes, retard Americanization? Or did the desire to enter the American mainstream override ethnic customs, leaving family alliances intact but eroding more deep-seated ethnic influences? Which was more important in the shaping of the ethnic family, their cultural baggage or their American experiences? With many caveats, it appears that commonsense consensus has been reached on most of these matters.

The attitudes and behavior of the immigrant working class, it is more or less agreed, were the products of their past and their present. Richard Gambino, for example, points out that Italian Americans adapted new ways "when they were compatible with the family system and its values" and offers the fact that Italian daughters and wives worked outside the home (a new departure for this group) when necessary, but only at strictly regulated places and preferably with other Italians. Virginia Yans-McLaughlin also found this to be true, citing the work of Italian women and children camping out in groups to work in the Buffalo canneries. Tamara Hareven is less certain about immigrant adaptation and cautions that the immigrant family could only provide security and stability as the new environment and their economic status permitted.[4]

A survey of the field makes it clear that family arrangements and ethnic attitudes are processes rather than static conditions, and therefore they change as different opportunities and settings requiring different responses arise.[5] Depending on the group, when they arrived, and where they settled, old world values, customs, and practices were modified to a greater or lesser degree, at different rates of speed, with more or less conflict, to produce a third generation that included people who had little or no relation to their ethnic past, men and women who maintained a facade of identification (often merely culinary), as well as others whose values and attitudes were not very different from those of their grandparents.

After a brief examination of the relative importance of the nuclear family, also known as the stem or conjugal family, consisting of mother, father, and unmarried children; and the extended family, composed of grandparents, siblings, godparents, in-laws, nephews and nieces, in both place of origin and in the United States, the chapter will discuss the formation, structure, and operation of the nuclear family—with somewhat less attention given to the extended one. The conjugal family will be examined from several vantage points: the roles of fathers and mothers, fertility patterns, childrearing practices, and the intergenerational conflict that often resulted. How the family lived, including the place of home work and boarders in the household, is another area to be considered. The discussion will focus on the similarities and differences between the designated groups, changes resulting from emigration, and developments that emerged over time.

FAMILIES, NUCLEAR AND EXTENDED

Joseph Lopreato has provided a definition of the southern Italian family that can also be used to describe the family background of most of the Europeans who came to the United States between 1840 and 1940. "The typical patriarchal family of the southern Italian peasantry is ... a small group of unmarried siblings and their parents, closely knit together and disciplined to the idea that the major decisions of an individual's life ought to be made in accordance with the aims and good of the group as a whole as defined by the oldest active member of the family."[6] Micaela Di Leonardo adds an economic note: the southern Italian peasant family was "a pre-industrial rural agricultural or urban artisanal household which was itself a productive unit, including men, women and children."[7]

The nuclear family, of course, was not the exclusive creation of European immigrants. A description of the traditional Mexican American family includes exactly the same characteristics described in the others: male dominance, respect for elders, priority status for the conjugal unit, and only a little less importance for the extended one. All sources agree that a strong nuclear family was necessary for the protection of persons and property in most of the places immigrants came from; indeed, in many instances such as economic disasters and persecution, it was essential for survival. For these reasons, ties to parents and siblings usually took precedence over all others. The decision to emigrate, whether as a family, as was often the case with the French Canadians, the Irish, Germans, and Eastern European Jews, or as an individual, which was more likely among Slavs, Italians, and the Chinese, was usually a family decision based on consideration of what was best for the group as a whole. There are innumerable examples of family efforts to finance the emigration of one member (in Ireland, sometimes a man would use his wife's dowry to pay the passage of a younger brother across the ocean), and as the numerous travel agencies and "bankers" in every immigrant neighborhood demonstrated, family members in the United States would save and buy a ship ticket to bring others to the new world.[8]

This was often a great hardship; marriage might have to be postponed and personal comforts denied, but family honor required that it be done. Letters to the editor of the "Bintel-Brief" (bundle of letters) column of the *Jewish Daily Forward* testify to the pressure resulting from duty versus self-interest, especially when the request to send money home was for a family member who did not plan to emigrate. One correspondent called upon to provide what seemed to him to be a very large sum of money for his sister's dowry questioned whether the "bull" she was to marry was worth the cost! Sometimes an immigrant son or daughter could not send the expected funds and broke off all contact with his family rather than admit his lack of success in America.[9]

Perhaps because they were not sure that traditional obligations would be honored, parents sometimes objected to the departure of their children, fearing loss of support in their old age. It would appear that in most cases, they need not have worried. Among the Chinese it was said that family members "were like arms and legs" and must be supported, and Carol Groneman says that "the single-minded devotion with which the Irish immigrant continued to send money to Ireland attested to the strength of the family ties which even 3,000 miles of ocean could not break."[10]

In many respects—including the fact that the nuclear family in the country of origin was also part of an extended family defined by Richard Gambino as "all of the blood relatives including distant cousins, aunts and uncles, creating an extended clan [that was] traced through paternity and further enlarged by carefully selected outsiders called godparents"— the immigrant family of the late nineteenth and early twentieth centuries resembled the preindustrial American family of the seventeenth and early eighteenth centuries. By the time the Italians that Gambino speaks of arrived, however, the extended American family was much less prominent.[11]

The characteristics that marked the extended immigrant family such as solidarity, leadership by a senior male, and a lack of concern with individual behavior unless it affected the family unit, were no longer part of American mores because they were not appropriate to the industrial society that had emerged by the late nineteenth century. A major purpose of the extended family at any time and in any place was protection from hostile outsiders (including other extended families) and kin assistance. By the turn of the century, however, increasingly urbanized native-born Americans no longer needed the clan membership that had existed on the frontier. Newly arrived immigrants, however, exposed to a different kind of frontier, felt an acute need for kin and godparents, and thus the extended family, at least for the first two generations, played an important role in their lives.[12]

Indeed, this aspect of family life may have grown in importance when mass emigration began. A departing father, for example, whose closest relatives were too poor to care for his wife and children during his absence, might entrust them to more distant relatives and godparents (basically friends who were now seen as kin) while he went to America to work and save until he could bring them over. And if he should die in a strange land and his wife should also be lost to her children, the godparents would be responsible for the orphans. In general, the migration experience led many of the newcomers, because "of social obligations, charity, sentiment and economic considerations," to remain close to their extended families long after they arrived in the new land. Those such as the Chinese, who were rarely able to bring over relatives more distant than wives, felt the lack of grandparents very keenly, especially in terms of child care. Diane Mei Ling and Ginger Chih found that the absence of grandmothers and aunts often meant that young children were left alone because both parents had to work.[13]

The underlying raison d'être for both the closely knit nuclear family and the influential extended family was survival. Everyone—parents, children, grandparents and other relatives—had a better chance as a family unit that pooled its resources and shared its burdens than they would have had on their own. Family members were expected to cooperate for the good of all, and family solidarity was the basic code, born out of interdependence, not necessarily affection. Richard Gambino sees historical reasons for the importance of la famiglia to southern Italians: "vulnerable over the centuries to frequent invasions and domination by strangers, they endured and built their culture by sealing out the influence of strangers." William MacCready restates this idea: "The family" [in southern Italy] was the only social unit capable of defending its members from enemies." Seen in this light, its importance for groups who were targets of persecution, such as the Jews and the Irish, goes without saying.[14]

Claudia Goldin found that immigrants in late nineteenth-century Philadelphia followed "a family strategy—a set of interrelated family decisions involving economic and demographic variables," and Tamara Hareven says that French Canadian mill workers in New Hampshire decided who among them should go to work, "which son or daughter should start first, at what point a wife should stop, when she should return to work, and who should try to get work outside the mill."[15]

The family strategy of certain groups, such as French Canadians, Slavs, and Italians, among others, placed immediate income above mobility via formal education, and for this reason they preferred that their children go to work at the earliest possible age. John Bodnar, when speaking of working-class Slavic families, including Poles, thinks this was the result of traditional beliefs in mutual assistance rather than individual achievement, as well as "an assessment of what was needed to survive in America." From the vantage point of today, Slavic immigrants seem to have made the correct decision; other sources indicate that by exploiting themselves and their children, many first-generation families were able to buy land and/or houses, a feat that could not have been accomplished without the earnings of several family members.[16]

Chinese families, however, tried to "have it all" and expected their children to attend (and do well) in public school and Chinese school, share in the work of earning a living, and in the case of a daughter, manage the household. Jade Snow Wong says "the only goal [of her hardworking San Francisco family] was for all in the family to work, to save and to become educated." To a lesser extent, this was also the goal of many, although not all, Eastern European Jewish families, where it was customary for boys to attend *heder* (religious school) after public school as well as assist the family as newsboys and messengers. A Jewish education was not provided for girls, who therefore could do more in the household as well as help with the home work that took so much of their mother's time. The strategy of some immigrant families was entrepreneurial, albeit on a small scale. In such cases, notably again the Chinese and Eastern European Jews, mothers and fathers were partners in their "Ma and Pa" stores, and the children were their active assistants, expected to assume larger and larger responsibilities as they grew older.[17]

Among Mexican families, "the family [nuclear and extended] was the most important facet of life . . . relatives were the main focus of obligations and also a source of emotional and economic support." This could certainly be said about most immigrant families. Paul Siu's memorable study of the *Chinese Laundryman* speaks of direct appeals from the family in China to the absent member such as, "Ling marries. Send eight hundred dollars," and says that in the rare case that the request was denied, the nongiver was considered "non-virtuous" or "inhuman." Women, perhaps more than men, relied on an extended family at crucial moments. A new baby would probably be delivered by an outsider (a doctor or more likely a midwife), but it was sisters and sisters-in-law who would care for the older children, assist with the new baby, and keep the household going until the mother was on her feet again. Of even greater importance, relatives were a widow's only insurance if her husband died before her children were old enough to work.[18]

Contrary to parental fears, responsibility for elderly mothers and fathers was a recognized obligation even when their children crossed the ocean and never saw their family again. If the entire family lived in the United States, sons were expected to contribute financially to their parents' support and daughters were expected to take care of them physically. While this was surely a burden to some, a close-knit family was also a source of pride to others, even perhaps pleasure, as indicated by the frequent socializing that was a feature of immigrant family life. Grandparents, even when not in need, were an integral part of the family and, when not present in America, were often sorely missed. Immigrant apartments were decorated with family pictures, and some families "created their parlors as shrines to family culture [in order] to keep in touch with their roots and remembered past."[19]

MARRIAGE

The extended family was formed, except for the designation of godparents, without deliberate design; but the nuclear family was the result of careful marriage arrangements, an old-country process that continued in the United States whenever possible. Even when it proved impossible for an Italian immigrant father to find a suitable husband for his daughter as he had been able to do in his native village, he continued to resist her efforts to find one on her own. Some daughters rebelled; eager to get out "from under the skirt of [their] mother," they married the first man to come along and smile at them. Often an appropriate suitor appeared under the auspices of a matchmaker, a person (usually a woman) of real importance in the immigrant community. On the Lower East Side of New York they were paid 5 percent of the bride's dowry as well as a flat fee. Since their reward came from the bride's family, matchmakers paid close attention to the wishes of her mother and father, which were to have a son-in-law who would increase or at least maintain the prestige and prosperity of the family.[20]

It was much harder for Chinese men, often anxious to marry, to find a mate. The Chinese laborers who came to the United States during most of the nineteenth century were free to return home and marry or bring in a "picture bride" selected by the family, but the passage of the Scott Act in 1888, by stating that Chinese laborers would be barred from reentry if they left the United States, made such visits unlikely. The bachelor society thus created prevented them from finding a wife by traditional means. They could not be introduced to a prospective partner by their parents, nor would their mothers and fathers be expected to pay the bride's family for raising a well-bred daughter. The latter change might have come as a welcome relief to his parents but not to the lonely sojourner son, who for reasons of racism and the scarcity of Chinese women in the United States could not find a wife on his own. Until 1924 it remained possible to import a bride selected by his family, but after the passage of the National Origins Act, importation became virtually impossible (an exception was made for merchants' wives) and the gender imbalance in Chinatowns all over the United States grew worse.[21]

Those immigrants, male or female, who came to the United States alone, found their own mates, but those born here of immigrant parents usually found their partners through the same time-worn patterns that had shaped their parents' marriages, including, as noted earlier, the use of matchmakers. Mothers took a leading role in mate selection, although fathers could veto the choice. Love was of the least importance, perhaps preventing disillusion later on, says Virginia Yans-McLaughlin; the prospective partner's character and the status of the family one's child would be entering were much more significant. Two Irish proverbs said it all: "Beauty don't boil the pot" and "It's as easy to love a rich man as a poor one." Brides continued to come with dowries and were expected to become part of their husbands' families. If all other factors were satisfactory, age disparities were not considered a drawback, but marriage to a member of another ethnic group was proscribed except among Scandinavians, and German and British families living in rural areas, where the chances of finding a partner from one's own group were slim.[22]

In general, endogamy was the rule, and the wedding was one of the high spots of immigrant life because marriage, with few exceptions, was desired by most men and women (indeed, Jewish and Irish women often left kith and kin for just that purpose) and was considered to be a sacred lifetime bond. Amongst Orthodox Jews, for example, men and women were considered incomplete without a spouse and children. When emigration denuded their small town communities of eligible men, Jewish girls followed them across the sea and hoped to find the right man at family celebrations such as other peoples' weddings. The qualifications of a "Mr. Right" did change in America. He was much less likely to be the gifted student of the Torah and more likely to be an enterprising wage earner or budding entrepreneur.[23]

Italian women, as a rule, did not emigrate on their own, but they were still eager to marry rather than continue to work in factories. Some women wanted the status and attention they had been denied in their male-dominated families, others were trying to replace parental support lost through emigration, and still others, if they could find a native-born husband, saw marriage as a path to becoming an American lady. There were also negative reasons to marry, particularly to avoid the lowly and lonely status of being an old maid.

Occasionally a daughter would remain single in order to care for younger siblings or elderly parents, but this was the exception not the rule. Male immigrants also wanted to marry: for a home (being a boarder had its disadvantages) and for warmth and security in a foreign land. "In an unfriendly city, one did not dare remain single," says Donald Cole when speaking of Lawrence, Massachusetts. For many men economic considerations, just as in the peasant economies of Europe, also played a part. The instability of the American economy meant that two people might not live as cheaply as one, but that together they could survive.[24]

For all these reasons, with some exceptions, most immigrants married at a relatively young age. French Canadian women, however, preferred to marry late because becoming a wife did not mean liberation from mill work, but rather it added household management to their lives. Irish men and women also married late, continuing a pattern "born of the economic necessities of rural Irish life." In Buffalo from 1855 to 1895 the average age at marriage for Irish males was thirty-one, and for females thirty-five, in contrast to twenty-three and twenty-six for native-born men and women. Overall, more of the Irish married earlier in the United States than they had in Ireland, where the practice of one child inheriting the family farm deprived his siblings of a livelihood, but on the whole they were less likely to marry than other immigrant groups.[25]

Many Irish women did not come to the United States to find a husband; nor did they marry non-Irishmen. Their reluctance to wed was based on practical reasons: customarily a married woman did not work, and so lost the independence that her own income assured her as well as the ability to send money to her family in Ireland. Furthermore, the burden of a growing family would make home work more difficult, and there were dangers in marriage. Wife beating and alcoholism were not unknown, and desertion and widowhood were quite possible while divorce was not. As Hasia Diner points out, "because they had immigrated to the United States in order to better their lot . . . Irish women exchanged their roles as wage earners . . . for that of wives and mothers with a degree of circumspection."[26]

In view of prevailing peasant attitudes about what constituted a good wife, this is not surprising. William MacCready gives us the Sicilian view:

"Like a good weapon, she should be cared for properly; like a hat she should be kept straight; like a mule she should be given plenty of work and occasional beatings. Above all she should be kept in her place as a subordinate for there is no peace in a house where a woman leads a man." A Yiddish proverb says something similar in the form of a riddle: Why is a wife like a horse? Because without a kick she won't go.[27]

Unhappy marriages were commonplace in any ethnic group, both in America and Europe and for both men and women. For some, their home was a prison where a domineering wife or husband was transformed into a hated warden. In the Jewish communities of Eastern Europe separation, whether tacit (the husband, under the guise of piety and love of learning, resided in his rabbi's home) or actual (wives returned to their parents' home), was uncommon partly because of community pressures, but it did occur. In the United States, parental or community havens were much scarcer, and outside mediation was harder to find. An immigrant wife, for example, could not leave an abusive or adulterous husband because she had neither a trade nor a family, and very possibly she could not speak English.

The problems within some marriages were not insignificant. Long separations were often the cause. One lonely wife, left alone in Europe, referred to her status as "living widowhood," to which her husband responded by saying that he would never abandon her. But even with reassurances, the absences bred suspicions. What was he doing for sex and companionship in America? What was she doing back home without a husband to protect her? In extreme cases a newly married man, expecting to emigrate without his bride, avoided consummation of the marriage in order to test his wife's fidelity upon his return.[28]

Even when a marriage survived separation, it might fall apart at the reunion. In many cases the wife that had been acceptable in the old country was unacceptable in the new one: a "greenhorn" who spoke, dressed, kept house, and behaved very differently from the American women with whom the husband was now familiar. She was an embarrassment. In the Jewish community divorce was possible, although for practical reasons an infrequently used option.

For all groups, the poor man's divorce—desertion—was more common. A widely read newspaper, the *Forward*, had a column entitled "The Gallery of Missing Husbands," accompanied by photographs of the absent men that helped the National Desertion Bureau, created by a consortium of Jewish organizations, to find them. It was a large enough problem for these same Jewish welfare organizations to press for laws that would make desertion a felony, and one such act was passed in New York State in 1905. If it had been enforced, Italian husbands were not likely to be targets. Unlike the 50 percent rate of desertions Abigail

Moore found in the 16,000 cases (all Jews) she studied, statistics for Italians indicated a very low desertion or divorce rate.[29]

FAMILY STRUCTURE

There is universal agreement that most immigrant nuclear families were, in varying degrees, paternalistic. John Bodnar, writing about Poles; Leonard Covello, Donna Gabbaccia, Richard Gambino, and Joseph Lopreato on Italians; Jade Snow Wong on the Chinese; and Joan Moore on the Mexicans, all stress the significant role of the father as the head of the household. There were, however, chinks in his armor: Cole describes the changes that took place when a son began to earn more than his father or, in times of depression, was able to get the job his father could not. Partly to maintain the husband's superior status and partly to protect her honor, Polish, Italian and Jewish wives were not encouraged to work outside the home, although economic requirements often took precedence over a husband's wishes.[30]

Whether she did outside work or not, however, an immigrant mother was a most significant part of the family. Gambino says "the father is the head of the family [but] the mother is the center." Lopreato says the patriarchal family in Italy is a myth perpetrated by wives who acknowledged their husbands as the head of the family but who also exercised a strong hand, particularly, Gabaccia says, when it came to choosing mates for their children. Although Paul Siu saw the Chinese wife as subservient (her husband's housekeeper, not his partner), Wong summarizes the mother-father issue for her Chinese American family thusly: "father was the unquestioned head" but "mother was the mistress in domestic affairs," and together they presented a "united front" to their children.[31]

One of the most surprising results of newer explorations into ethnic family history is the emergence of the "closet mama," that is, the discovery that in many immigrant families that appeared to be patriarchal, the mother exercised considerable power. Reminiscent of an old joke in which a husband says "I decide all the important issues—will there be war or peace in the world and who will be elected president, while my wife decides the minor ones—how to spend our money, whom our children should marry, where we should live, and so on,"—the earlier view of the all-powerful authoritarian father figure should be modified. This is not the result of work done by feminist historians; rather it emerges in the books written by Leonard Covello, Richard Gambino, and Irving Howe, as well.

One of the reasons for earlier assumptions about wifely subservience came from the married woman's desire to preserve traditional appearances. To protect their husbands' status, mothers often resorted to 'gimmicks' such as insisting that a child's earnings be handed to the father (who then turned it over to her for disposal) or warning a misbehaving child to "just wait until your father comes home." In reality, as one second-generation Italian woman described her marriage: "The most important thing is that a man wants to be the head of the family but in a roundabout way, I get my way. So he's the boss, but I get my way if I know how to work it." In one regard, the emergence of a significant mother should not come as a surprise. Immigrants, like other people in the late nineteenth and early twentieth centuries, consciously or not, subscribed to the doctrine of separate spheres for men and women, and the realm reserved for the latter was often quite satisfying to many of them. For all women, immigrants or native-born, there was often pride and status in being a wife and mother, and pleasure in serving a husband and children. In short, the picture of the miserable and subservient wife needs adjustment.[32]

Further reinforcement of the mother's importance comes from Richard Gambino, who points out that the early death of a mother was considered a much greater tragedy than the premature death of a father, partly because the father's place could be taken by an older son to whom the mother would give the same respect as she had to her husband, but no daughter could take the place of the giver of affection, the family mediator and role model. Furthermore, as Sydney Weinberg makes clear, some Jewish mothers continued a historic tradition by assuming the entire responsibility for the support of the family in addition to performing vital duties such as supplying the physical needs of her husband and children and controlling family expenditures. Corinne Krause reinforces this by saying that it was the mother's responsibility to see that "signs of well-being emanated from the household." Thus, she was expected to keep the house, manage the finances, and do whatever "best served the interests of the family" including, for the wife of an Italian barber, laundering the towels he used in his shop![33]

What emerges from this is the importance of the mother in the totality of the family; missing is information on a woman's life if she was the only parent. The absence of data is not difficult to explain. Until recent years, in spite of the fact that the early death of the major breadwinner was a frequent occurrence, female-headed households were not as abundant as they are today. Certainly they existed; immigration fiction is replete with the difficulties experienced by the entire family when the mother had to assume the role of provider, and the reports of various do-gooders make it clear that her road was often rocky. Contemporary scholarship, however, has not devoted a great deal of attention to this aspect of family history, although both Kathleen Conzen and Hasia Diner have found that the female-headed household was quite significant among Irish families.[34]

CHILDREARING

In spite of marrying later than the norm for most men and women, Irish Americans had a high fertility rate. In Italian families, and probably others, men and women sometimes differed on the number of children that was desirable, but since most immigrant families did not practice birth control and many feared abortion, their disagreements were moot. Much to the horror of the WASP restrictionists, immigrant families were large. One of the reasons was economic; as in Europe, a child's labor was a means of support for the family, and high children's mortality rates meant that it was necessary to have many. Interestingly, when an effective child labor law was passed in New Hampshire, the fertility rate of the French Canadian families dropped.[35]

Economics aside, immigrant mothers and fathers had other reasons for wanting children. Removal from their family of origin led to a desire to recreate one in the new world; children healed the wounds of separation and raised the status of both mother and father. The latter's image was enhanced by visible signs of his virility; contrariwise, a wife's barrenness made her an object of pity or worse. As time went on and more children survived, many immigrant families began to see that less could be more, that is, that the family as a whole might benefit if there were fewer demands on its purse. Until this happened, however, dolls were not needed in most immigrant families because there was always a new baby to play with. More realistically, older girls were kept from school when their mother's duties (the family washing, for example) left the babies uncared for, and in general, children were often cast into the role of surrogate parents to their younger siblings. The youngest child in the family was the most fortunate: there were no babies to take care of but there were older brothers and sisters to learn from, and the family might be less likely to need the income a child could earn.[36]

But most immigrant working-class families for a long time did need a child's wages. John Bodnar believes "that most [of them] were able to operate within a margin of comfort only to the degree that they could count on steady contributions from their laboring children of both sexes." As a result, he goes on to say, "Young Poles, Slovaks and Croatians were regularly sent to work and asked to relinquish all wages . . . for use by the entire household." Sometimes children under fourteen were expected to do only part-time work and thus could continue at school, but more often a younger boy would be trained to follow in his father's footsteps or apprenticed to someone else to learn a different occupation.[37]

In the latter instance he lived at his master's home, an arrangement that did not add to his family's income but did save them the money it would otherwise take to feed and clothe him. His sister might also not live at home because she would be in service as a domestic worker, living in her employer's home. Other young workers lived with their families and assisted with the obiquitous home work, making artificial flowers or removing basting stitches, while waiting to enter a factory. An account of an ordinary day in an Italian household in 1905 describes the work of two tiny girls on artificial flowers: "The three year old worked on the petals, her older sister (four years old) separated stems and dipped them in paste while their mother and grandmother placed the petals on the stems." All of this brought a mere ten cents per hour into the family coffers.[38]

Chinese children were assigned tasks as early as possible so that their parents could work. Jade Snow Wong says that at eleven years old she was expected to shop for the family's food before going to public school, from which she returned home to cook dinner before going to Chinese school, finally coming home to clean up. Girls, Chinese or not, often contributed more to the family than their brothers partly because they kept less for themselves. Hareven found that in the French Canadian families she studied, daughters gave 95 percent of their wages to the family while sons gave only 83 percent. Girls were also expected to deny themselves education, finery, and pleasures if their earnings could assist their brothers' occupational mobility.[39]

Although they seemed to understand that large families and grinding poverty made it difficult for parents to give their offspring much affection, memoirs and oral histories demonstrate that immigrant children missed the attention very much. Mothers were distracted and harassed but usually physically present. Fathers, on the other hand, who left for work before their children awoke and returned after they went to sleep, were not present. Some regretted this, as a portion of a poem by Morris Rosenfeld entitled "My Little Boy" indicates:

> Ere dawn my labor drives me forth
> I have a little boy at home
> That seldom do I see
> Ere dawn my labor drives me forth
> 'Tis night when I am free
> A stranger am I to my child
> And strange my child to me.[40]

Other men, however, shunned childrearing and took little responsibility for their children except to administer physical punishments. Mothers did this as well, and most immigrant families were quite authoritarian. Part of the reason for this was worry because poor neighborhoods offered temptations and dangers. Parents feared that their children would be victims or delinquents. Girls were a special concern and a double problem. Their virginity had to be protected and their dowry provided. Sending them to work would help achieve one goal but might endanger the other. No wonder Italians had a saying that graphically expressed their feelings: "I have six children, two sons and four burdens!"[41]

Mothers were demanding teachers and trainers who prepared their girls for marriage and motherhood; fathers tried to inculcate in their sons the ability to deal with the outside world by fair means or foul. Jewish parents pushed their children hard, sometimes to do well at school, sometimes to start businesses, often to aim for the professions rather than settle for manual labor. Chinese parents demanded silence, punctuality, attentiveness, good table manners, and in general molded their youngsters to be "trouble free, unobtrusive, quiescent and cooperative." They also told them they were smarter and came from a greater culture than Caucasian children and held them to standards of perfection. Although sons were the most valued and received the best treatment (in all ethnic groups sons seem to do nothing in the family kitchen except eat there), Chinese daughters were also considered worthy of education.[42]

This was not true for other groups, including Poles and Italians. One Italian mother justified keeping her daughter out of school by saying "Why should she learn to write? She'd only write to her boyfriends!" Even the Eastern European Jews, who did view formal education more favorably than other immigrant groups, did not see much point in educating daughters who, it was expected, would spend their adult lives as homemakers and mothers, not as career women. The one exception to this view was teaching. A teacher-daughter could never attain the status of her brother the doctor but was certainly admired over women who did factory work. Until the late thirties, however, in many urban school systems including New York's, a married woman (unless her husband was disabled) could not be a teacher, and thus the girl who chose that path and stayed on it was doomed to be a spinster, a condition many parents dreaded.[43]

It is widely accepted that Italian families did not see formal education as a route to upward mobility for their children of either sex. From several sources we learn that *ben educato*, that is, training a child to be attuned to the family's welfare, was the goal. There are several historical reasons for this. For one thing, nothing in the experience of the emigrants from southern Italy or Sicily had indicated that schooling had improved their children's chances for survival, and family considerations, always uppermost, indicated that it was better to keep them working on the land. Dire poverty in America plus the fact of opportunities for children to earn money led to a continuation of the attitudes of the homeland.

This, however, did not mean that Italian parents opposed any kind of training for their sons. They favored a *practical* education, which would teach a trade, and tried to apprentice a boy to a master craftsman for this purpose. Many Italian parents believed that the school personnel were their enemies because they tried to inculcate values hostile to traditional attitudes. Virginia Yans-McLoughlin sums up the matter: "Buffalo Italians apparently believed that family interests were better served by property ownership and financial security than by children's education." Some parents were angry enough with American ways to "pour a malediction on Columbus and his great discovery!"[44]

In an extremely interesting article on changing educational strategies among immigrant generations, Miriam Cohen points out that these negative attitudes were not cast in concrete. If the family could forgo their wages, a prospect that was more and more real as their time in America lengthened, more and more Italian families accepted the idea that schooling beyond the primary grades was beneficial, especially completing a vocational course of study. Furthermore, as infant mortality rates declined, Cohen says, so did fertility rates, and "with fewer children to support, it made more sense to invest greater resources in education, even for girls."

Girls were still expected to work and contribute to the household but the nature of their work changed. By the 1930s manufacturing jobs became less important for women and opportunities in clerical and sales work rose steadily. To gain white-collar work, a high school commercial course was essential and so more and more Italian daughters enrolled for such training. Much of this was also true for Jewish girls, and by the early forties, more second-generation daughters than sons were likely to be high school graduates. Cohen sums up the matter: age-old convictions about the propriety of education for males and females changed along with economic and social realities.[45]

There does not seem to have been as much change in Slavic attitudes to schooling, although as John Bodnar makes clear, when their desperate need for income decreased somewhat, a small number of Slavic parents were willing to sacrifice for a child's education. Interestingly, the children did not respond, and whether because of a "deep sense of obligation" or simply dislike of formal education, left school for work at the earliest opportunity. Eastern European Jewish children reacted differently. When economic circumstances permitted, perhaps having internalized a traditional value that said it was a child's duty to bring *nachus* (honor, satisfaction) to his or her family, Jewish sons and daughters completed secondary school in larger numbers than their peers.[46]

MARGINAL MEN AND WOMEN

In some respects, children who spurned schooling and stayed in similar occupations and the same social class as their parents suffered less than those who were encouraged to separate from their parents' traditions and join the American mainstream. The problems of the "marginal man and woman" were real enough for the educational philosopher John Dewey to express concern about the "denationalization" of immigrant children by the public schools. The pressure to Americanize was very strong (the district superintendent of the Lower East Side schools in New York, Julia Richman, spoke of "wresting" the immigrant child from his parents), and many children responded affirmatively. The young men in Jerre Mangione's novel, *Mount Allegro*, said they wanted to be like most people and "most people, they realized as they grew older, were not Sicilians." Harry Roskolenko, the son of Eastern European Jewish immigrants, remembers that outside of home he and his siblings saw themselves as Americans, but to their parents they were only Jews. What was a child to believe?[47]

Anzia Yezierska wrote a famous book on this theme. *The Children of Loneliness* of the title were the millions of "immigrant youth wandering between worlds that are at once too old and too new to live in." Maxine Hong Kingston's memoir bears this out. In her home a child's silence was greatly valued but in school teachers demanded that she speak out. Unable to accommodate herself to these conflicting demands, she remained silent and "flunked" kindergarten. Other sources confirm the fact that Chinese culture rewards silence and inconspicuousness while punishing outspoken behavior.[48]

Anecdotal evidence indicates both the feelings of the marginal immigrant child and the difficulties of adjusting to them. Rosemary Prosen, daughter of Slovenian immigrants, recalls that as a young child she was ashamed of things she saw as Slovenian: that her mother never sat down to eat with the family, that her father drank heavily, and that the furniture and linens in her home were made from scrap wood and feed bags. Her goal was to remove herself from her parents' environment as soon as possible.[49]

The result of school and, to a certain extent, peer pressure was to create a marginal child, attached by bonds of affection and respect to the traditional practices of his or her parents but also eager to be free of some of them. What made the problem worse was the confusing message they got from their parents, many of whom wanted them to succeed in the outside world while still following traditional patterns. Children made a variety of adjustments to this dilemma. Speaking of the Italians, Joseph Lopreato says: "Some stayed as Italian as possible, some rebelled as much as possible and the majority remained apathetic and gradually became assimilated." Much of this could also be said for other second- and third-generation immigrants although the rate of speed varied a great deal and Slavic, especially Polish, children were less likely than others to succumb to mainstream pressures.[50]

The most "rending confrontations" between rebellious children and their parents were connected to marriage, languages, and in the case of orthodox Eastern European Jews, piety. There were monumental struggles between young women who wanted to marry for love and their parents who wanted them to marry for security and continuation of the family's traditions. In many homes, children refused to use the family tongue, and despairing mothers grew furious when they could not communicate with their offspring nor they with her. Sometimes the break was irreparable, as was the case when fifteen-year-old Harry Roskolenko battled his father physically, while defying his insistence that he follow orthodox Jewish religious practices, and finally ran away to sea.[51]

THE IMMIGRANT HOUSEHOLD

These battles, bitter as they were, were conducted in full view and hearing of all the occupants of an immigrant household because few working-class homes offered opportunities for seclusion. According to Ruth Schwartz Cowan and her husband Neil, authors of *Our Parents' Lives*, personal privacy was not high on the Eastern European Jews' list of priorities in the old country or the new, and even when improved finances made better housing possible, children did not have separate beds, let alone bedrooms. A contemporary observer described living conditions in a 1905 Russian Jewish apartment in this way:

A family consisting of a husband, wife and six to eight children whose ages range from less than one to twenty-five years live under the following conditions. The parents occupy the small bedroom together with two, three or even four of the younger children. In the kitchen, on cots and on the floor, are the older children, in the front room two or more lodgers sleep on the floor or on cots and in the fourth room sleep two lodgers who desire to have separate rooms.

The Cowans received a similar description from one of their sources: "There were two bedrooms. Three of my brothers were in one room: they all slept together in one bed, a double bed. I slept in the other room with my mother because I was the only daughter. My father slept on a folding cot in the dining room with my youngest brother." Under such circumstances, one wonders at the high fertility rates of immigrant families, but the probable answer is that nature finds a way.[52]

Many sources cite the importance of the kitchen in the immigrant household, although reasons for its centrality differ. Donald Cole found the room and particularly the stove (a large, imposing item in an early twentieth-century kitchen), symbolic of the peasant hearth and the warmth that it provided. Irving Howe agrees that the kitchen was the warmest and brightest room in the apartment because both the heat and electricity were turned off in all the other rooms in order to save on utility bills. One could also argue that the kitchen was the most important room because food in many immigrant families was "the center of existence."[53]

The same, entirely logical, concern with money resulted in another characteristic of the immigrant household, the boarder. Deplored by progressive reformers as the "lodger evil," the boarder, whether a relative or a stranger, was of the utmost value to struggling families. John Bodnar estimates that boarders could add twelve to sixteen dollars a week to family income. The practice was also beneficial to the boarder. It was cheaper than renting a single room and allowed the newly arrived immigrant to save money that might enable him to bring relatives over sooner.

In some immigrant communities, Pittsburgh for one, the shortage of women in the early years of settlement made communal-type bachelor apartments essential, but living with a family, especially if the mother was a good cook, was preferable. In German households in Milwaukee the boarder was likely to be an apprentice, and Italians also tended to take in nonrelatives as boarders. Eastern European Jews, on the other hand, were much more likely to make space available for relatives. Irving Howe says that Lower East Side children were reluctant to go to school because they feared that their beds would have been given to a newly arrived relative while they were gone, and many of the elderly men and women interviewed by the Cowans complained of sharing their beds with unfamiliar relatives some of whom, as one woman complained, had smelly feet.[54]

Donald Cole found that in 1912, 50 percent of the working-class families in Lawrence, almost all immigrants, took in boarders, and a study of living conditions in New York City in 1910 reported that 80 percent of the Eastern European Jewish families and 24 percent of Italians but only 6 percent of the Irish had boarders. Nonquantitative descriptions bear this out. Observers noted that Jews preferred to lease larger and better apartments and take in boarders to pay the rent, while Italians were more likely to take smaller places and fewer boarders, and the Irish rarely took any at all.[55]

In spite of the reservations previously noted, the Cowans' respondents did not express serious objections to this enforced intimacy with relatives. Most of them said "that was the way things were," from which the authors concluded that "hospitality was more important to the immigrants than single room occupancy." Housing reformers, however, believed that the physical environment determined a child's life chances, and they were horrified. "It [the lodger evil] frequently leads to the breaking up of homes and families, to the downfall and subsequent degraded career of young women, to grave immoralities—in a word to the profanation of the home." Not because of the reformers' protests but rather because of changing economic conditions, boarders became less important in the immigrant household economy, but the change could not have brought joy to progressive hearts. For a while (although when work in the garment industry slackened, boarders reappeared), home work, mostly subcontracting on clothing, took the place of lodgers, bringing its own problems and not making tenement apartments any more livable.[56]

For Jews the household as workshop continued patterns established in their villages of origin, which was also true for the custom of living behind the store. In many poor neighborhoods, a small number of rooms could be rented along with a shop, and whole families grew up in such quarters. There were many advantages: mothers could manage household chores and be close to their children (arguments that were also made for home work), spell their husbands—and children, as they grew older, could do the same. Certainly money was saved on rent and more money could be earned because the store could be opened earlier and closed later if the proprietor was on the premises twenty-four hours a day. Sometimes whole factories grew up in this fashion. Jade Snow Wong tells about the denim factory her parents operated in San Francisco where a flood of orders could relegate the family to the basement of the shop, leaving their former living quarters to the workers and their sewing machines. Another version of this was living above the store. Even when he could well afford to house his family elsewhere, many an immigrant entrepreneur preferred to live as close as possible to his place of business.[57]

It requires only a little imagination to recognize the difficulties inherent in keeping crowded quarters in old tenements clean and orderly. Again, housing reformers deplored the prevailing disorder and dirt. Immigrant women hated the situation, but not for the same reasons. They found housework in America much harder than in their places of origin, both because there were fewer grandmothers or spinster relatives with whom to share it and also because it was more complicated. In addition to the need to do unfamiliar tasks such as cleaning the woodwork and washing the windows, the immigrant housekeeper had to cope with frequent moves. In search of better quarters when affordable, or lower rents when times were hard, or to live closer to the father's workplace, or to be nearer to job opportunities for wives and children, immigrant families moved very often. Indeed, residential mobility often took the place of more elusive social and economic mobility.[58]

Overall, it appears that immigrant families resembled each other more than might be expected given the differences in places of origin, religion, time of arrival in the United States, reasons for emigrating, and varying degrees of adjustment in the new world. This, however, should not come as a great surprise. Family structures and strategies were similar because they were dictated by the same forces—the need for survival and a desire for improvement. Pragmatists all, Jews, Italians, Slavs, the Irish, French Canadians, the Chinese, and other groups not discussed in this chapter took what they valued from their past and adjusted it (at varying rates of speed and to varying degrees) to what they found in America. By so doing, albeit at considerable cost, a large number created moderately successful lives.

NOTES

1. William Thomas and Florian Znaniecki, *The Polish Peasant in Europe and America* (New York: Dover Press, 1958); Oscar Handlin, *Boston's Immigrants, 1790–1865* (Cambridge, Mass.: Harvard University Press, 1941); Caroline Ware, *Greenwich Village* (New York: Harper and Row, 1935); Leonard Covello, *The Social Background of the Italo-American School Child* (Leiden, Netherlands: E. J. Brill, 1967).

2. Carol Groneman, "The Bloody Ould Sixth Ward," (Ph.D. diss., University of Rochester, 1973); Caroline Golab, "The Impact of the Industrial Experience on the Immigrant Family," in *Immigrants in Industrial America*, ed. Richard Erlich, 1–32 (Chapel Hill: University of North Carolina Press, 1977); Kathleen Conzen, *Immigrant Milwaukee, 1836–1860* (Cambridge Mass.: Harvard University Press, 1976); Richard Gambino, *Blood of My Blood: The Dilemma of Indian Americans* (Garden City, N.Y.: Doubleday and Co., 1974); John Bodnar, Roger Simon, and Michael Weber, *Lives of Their Own: Blacks, Italians and Poles in Pittsburgh, 1900–1960* (Urbana: University of Illinois Press, 1982); Abigail Moore, "Marital Discord among New York Jews," paper delivered at the Organization of American Historians meeting, 10 April 1980; Kirby Miller, *Emigrants and Exiles: The Irish Exodus to America* (New York: Oxford University Press, 1985).

3. Steven Mintz and Susan Kellogg, *Domestic Revolution: A Social History of American Family Life* (New York: The Free Press, 1988), 87; Virginia Yans-McLaughlin, *Family and Community: Italian Immigrants in Buffalo, 1880–1930* (Ithaca, N.Y.: Cornell University Press, 1977), 56–57; Tamara Hareven, "Family and Work Patterns of Immigrant Laborers in a Planned Industrial Town, 1900–1930," in *Immigrants in Industrial America*, ed. Richard Erlich, p. 63.

4. Gambino, *Blood*, 13; Yans-McLaughlin, *Family and Community*, 187; Hareven, "Family and Work Patterns," 49.

5. "Family Patterns," in *Harvard Encyclopedia of American Ethnic Groups*, ed. Stephen Thernstrom (Cambridge, Mass.: Harvard University Press, 1980), 345.

6. Joseph Lopreato, *Italian Americans* (New York: Random House, 1970), 59.

7. Micaela Di Leonardo, *The Varieties of Ethnic Experience: Kinship, Class, and Gender among California Italian-Americans.* (Ithaca, N.Y.: Cornell University Press, 1984), 65.

8. David Alvirez, Frank Bean, and Dorie Williams, "The Mexican American Family," in *Ethnic Families in America*, ed. Charles Mindel and Robert Habenstein (New York: Elsevier, 1981), 274; Miller, *Emigrants*, 483; Harry Roskolenko. "America the Thief," in *The Immigrant Experience*, ed. Thomas Wheeler (New York: Dial Press, 1971), 156.

9. Abraham Karp, *Golden Door to America* (New York: The Viking Press,

1976), 143; Hyman Cantor, "Autobiography," typescript, 62; Miller, *Emigrants*, 485–86.

10. Paul Siu, *The Chinese Laundryman in America*, ed. John Kuo Wei (New York: New York University Press, 1987), 157; Groneman, "The Bloody Ould Sixth Ward," 55.

11. Gambino, *Blood*, 3.

12. "Family Patterns," *Harvard Encyclopedia*, 346.

13. Yans-McLaughlin, *Family and Community*, 61, 75, 77; Joan Moore, *Mexican Americans* (Englewood Cliffs, N.J.: Prentice-Hall, 1970), 105; Diane Mei Ling and Ginger Chih, *A Place Called Chinese America* (San Francisco: Organization of Chinese Americans, 1982), 72.

14. Gambino, *Blood*, 32; William C. MacCready, "The Persistence of Ethnic Variation in American Families," in *Ethnicity in the United States*, ed. Andrew Greeley (New York: John Wiley and Sons, 1974), 161.

15. Claudia Goldin, "Family Strategies and the Family Economy in the Late Nineteenth Century," in *Work, Space, Family and Group Experience in the Nineteenth Century*, ed. Theodore Hershberg (New York: Oxford University Press, 1981), 278; Hareven, "Family and Work Patterns," 61.

16. John Bodnar, "Schooling and the Slavic American Family, 1900–1940," in *American Education and the European Immigrant: 1840–1940*, ed. Bernard Weiss (Urbana: University of Illinois Press, 1982), 91.

17. Jade Snow Wong, "Puritans from the Orient," in *Immigrant Experience*, ed. Wheeler, 109; Sydney Stahl Weinberg, "Jewish Mothers and Immigrant Daughters," *Journal of American Ethnic History* 6 (Spring 1987): 40; idem., *The World of Our Mothers: The Lives of Jewish Immigrant Women* (Chapel Hill: University of North Carolina Press: 1988), 137; Roskolenko, "America the Thief," 166; Mei Ling and Chih, *Chinese America*, 61.

18. Moore, *Mexican American*, 104; Siu, *Chinese Laundryman*, 156, 162; Elizabeth Ewen, *Immigrant Women in the Land of Dollars* (New York: Monthly Review Press, 1985), 132; Gambino, *Blood*, 26.

19. Mei Ling and Chih, *Chinese America*, 72; Ewen, *Immigrant Women*, 158.

20. Lopreato, *Italian Americans*, 68; Gary Mormino and George Pozzetta, *The Immigrant World of Ybor City: Italians and Their Latin Neighbors in Tampa, 1885–1985* (Urbana: University of Illinois Press, 1987), 255; Irving Howe, *World of Our Fathers* (New York: Harcourt Brace Jovanovich, 1976), 219.

21. Mei Ling and Chih, *Chinese America*, 61; Wong, "Puritans," 121.

22. Yans-McLaughlin, *Family and Community*, 95; Weinberg, *World of Our Mothers*, 205; Gambino, *Blood*, 7; Bodnar, *Lives*, 100–101; Richard Bernard, *The Melting Pot and the Altar* (Minneapolis: University of Minnesota Press, 1980), 124–25; Miller, *Emigrants*, 405.

23. Weinberg, *World of Our Mothers*, 23; Ewen, *Immigrant Women*, 226, 228, 233, 235; Yans-McLaughlin, *Family and Community*, 82.

24. Weinberg, *World of Our Mothers*, 208, 210; Ewen, *Immigrant Women*, 229; Donald Cole, *Immigrant City* (Chapel Hill: University of North Carolina Press, 1963), 102; Miller, *Emigrants*, 407; Mintz and Kellogg, *Domestic Revolutions*, 88.

25. Hareven, "Family and Work," 62; Hasia Diner, *Erin's Daughters in America: Irish Immigrant Women in the Nineteenth Century* (Baltimore, Md.: Johns Hopkins University Press, 1983), 46; Ellen Horgan Biddle, "The American Catholic Irish

Family," in *Ethnic Families in America*," ed. Mindle and Habenstein, 95.

26. Diner, *Erin's Daughters*, 50, 51, 69.

27. MacCready, "Ethnic Variations," 160.

28. Karp, *Golden Door*, 143–44; Moore, "Marital Discord," 2; Weinberg, *World of Our Mothers*, 129; Maxine Seller, *Immigrant Women* (Philadelphia, Pa.: Temple University Press, 1981), 118.

29. Seller, *Immigrant Women*, 119; Karp, *Golden Door*, 121; Moore, "Marital Discord," 9; Robert Orsi, *Madonna of 116th Street* (New Haven, Conn.: Yale University Press, 1985), 25; Howe, *Fathers*, 177; Yans-McLaughlin, *Family and Community*, 86; Ewen, *Immigrant Women*, 230.

30. Bodnar, *Lives*, 93; Cole, *Immigrant City*, 101; Covello, *Italo-American School Child*, 237; Moore, *Mexican Americans*, 104.

31. Gambino, *Blood*, 6; Lopreato, *Italian Americans*, 58; Donna Gabaccia, *From Sicily to Elizabeth Street* (Albany: State University of New York Press, 1984), 4; Wong, "Puritans," 107; Sui, *Chinese Laundryman*, 164.

32. Gambino, *Blood*, 7; Howe, *Fathers*, 172; Weinberg, "Mothers and Daughters," 45–46, 47; Covello, *Italo-American School Child*, 237; Weinberg, *World of Our Mothers*, 140; Jill Quadagno, "The Italian American Family," in *Ethnic Families in America*, ed. Mindel and Habenstein, 77.

33. Gambino, *Blood*, 24; Weinberg, "Mothers and Daughters," 44; Corinne Krause, "Urbanization without Breakdown," *Journal of Urban History* 4 (May 1978): 297.

34. Pietro Di Donato, *Christ in Concrete* (Indianapolis, Ind.: Bobbs-Merrill, 1939); Conzen, *Immigrant Milwaukee*, 51; Diner, *Erin's Daughters*, 45.

35. Tamara Hareven, "Family and Work," 63.

36. Ewen, *Immigrant Women*, 135; Cole, *Immigrant City*, 105; Lawrence Glasco, "The Life Cycles and Household Structures of American Ethnic Groups," in *A Heritage of Her Own: Toward a New Social History of American Women*, ed. Elizabeth Pleck and Nancy Cott (New York: Simon and Schuster, 1979), 283; Hareven, "Family and Work," 63; Krause, "Urbanization," 296; Howe, *Fathers*, 268.

37. Bodnar, *Lives*, 92, 95; Bodnar, "Schooling," 82.

38. Thomas Kessner and Betty Caroli, "New Immigrant Women at Work: Italians and Jews in New York City, 1880–1905," *Journal of Ethnic Studies* 5 (Winter 1978): 22.

39. Glasco, "Life Cycles," 277, 283, 285; Hareven, "Family and Work," 62, 64; Wong, "Puritans," 118–19; Mei Ling and Chih, *Chinese America*, 70.

40. Karp, *Golden Door*, 133–34; originally published in *"Songs of Labor" and Other Poems* (1914) by R. J. Badge, trans. Rose Pastor Stokes and Helena Frank.

41. Weinberg, *World of Our Mothers*, 29, 32; Karp, *Golden Door*, 132, Yans-McLaughlin, *Family and Community*, 159.

42. Howe, *Fathers*, 261; Gambino, *Blood*, 20; Wong, "Puritans," 115; Mei Ling and Chih, *Chinese America*, 74.

43. Kessner and Caroli, "New Immigrant Women," 24; Howe, *Fathers*, 266; Helena Lopata, "Polish American Families," in *Ethnic Families in America*, ed. Mindel and Habenstein, 26.

44. Lopreato, *Italian Americans*, 83; Gambino, *Blood*, 226, 227; Yans-McLaughlin, *Family and Community*, 77; Ewen, *Immigrant Women*, 157; Bodnar, *Lives*, 95; Quadagno, "Italian American Family," in *Ethnic Families in America*, ed. Mindel and Habenstein, 64.

45. Miriam Cohen, "Changing Education Strategies among Immigrant Generations," *Journal of Social History* 15 (Spring 1982): 448, 451, 457.

46. Bodnar, "Schooling," 84; Bernard Farber, Charles Mindel, and Bernard Lazerwitz, "Jewish American Families," in *Ethnic Families in America*, ed. Mindel and Habenstein, 375.

47. Jerre Mangione, *Mount Allegro: A Memoir of Italian American Life* (New York: Columbia University Press, 1981); Martin Dann, "Little Citizens: Working Class and Immigrant Childhood in New York City, 1890–1915" Ph.D. diss., City University of New York 1978), 387; Julia Richman, National Education Association, *Proceedings*, National Education Association 1905: 115; Quote, Lopreato, *Italian Americans*, 66–67; Roskolenko, "America the Thief," 258.

48. Anzia Yezierska, *The Children of Loneliness* (New York: Funk & Wagnalls, 1923), 101; Lucy Jen Huang, "The Chinese American Family," in *Ethnic Families in America*, ed. Mindel and Habenstein, 125; Maxine Hong Kingston, "A Song For a Barbarian Reed Pipe," in *Immigrant Women*, ed. Seller, 291.

49. Rosemary Prosen, "Looking Back," in *Growing Up Slavic in America*, ed. Michael Novak, (EMPAC!): 1976, 3, 4–5.

50. Howe, *Fathers*, 180; Gambino, *Blood*, 33–34; Lopreato, *Italian Americans*, 69.

51. Seller, *Immigrant Women*, 124; Roskolenko, "America the Thief," 176.

52. Neil Cowan and Ruth Schwartz Cowan, *Our Parents' Lives* (New York: Basic Books, 1989), 44–48; Karp, *Golden Door*, 128.

53. Cole, *Immigrant City*, 107; Howe, *Fathers*, 171.

54. Cowan and Cowan, *Parents'*, 45, 50; Bodnar, *Lives*, 103, 105; Krause, "Urbanization," 296; Howe, *Fathers*, 171.

55. Cole, *Immigrant City*, 108; Cowan and Cowan, *Parents'*, 48, 49; Mintz and Kellogg, *Domestic Revolutions*, 93; Glasco, "Life Cycles," 278; Karp, *Golden Door*, 143; Conzen, *Immigrant Milwaukee*, 55–56.

56. Cowan and Cowan, *Parents'*, 48–49.

57. Cowan and Cowan, *Parents'*, 54–55; Wong, "Puritans," 109.

58. Ewen, *Immigrant Women*, 148, 151; Golab, "Impact of Industrialization," 2.

REFERENCES

Alvirez, David, Frank Bean, and Dorie Williams. "The Mexican American Family." In *Ethnic Families in America*, ed. Charles Mindel and Robert Habenstein, 269–92. New York: Elsevier, 1981.

Bernard, Richard. *The Melting Pot and the Altar*. Minneapolis: University of Minnesota Press, 1980.

Biddle, Ellen. "The American Catholic Irish Family." In *Ethnic Families in America*, ed. Charles Mindel and Robert Habenstein, 86–114. New York: Elsevier, 1981.

Bodnar, John. "Schooling and the Slavic American Family, 1900–1940." In *American Education and the European Immigrant: 1840–1940*, ed. Bernard Weiss, 78–95. Urbana: University of Illinois Press, 1982.

Bodnar, John, Robert Simon, and Michael Weber. *Lives of Their Own: Blacks,*

Italians and Poles in Pittsburgh, 1900–1960. Urbana: University of Illinois Press, 1982.

Brown, Charlotte, Paula Hyman, and Sonya Michel. *The Jewish Woman in America.* New York: Dial Press, 1976.

Cantor, Hyman. "Autobiography," typescript at YIVO, New York City.

Cohen, Miriam. "Changing Educational Strategies among Immigrant Generations." *Journal of Social History* 15 (Spring 1982): 443–60.

Cole, Donald. *Immigrant City.* Chapel Hill: University of North Carolina Press, 1963.

Conzen, Kathleen. *Immigrant Milwaukee 1836–1860.* Cambridge, Mass.: Harvard University Press, 1976.

Covello, Leonard. *The Social Background of the Italo-American School Child.* Leiden, Netherlands: E. J. Brill, 1967.

Cowan, Neil, and Ruth Schwartz Cowan. *Our Parents' Lives.* New York: Basic Books, 1989.

Dann, Martin. "Little Citizens: Working Class and Immigrant Childhood in New York City, 1890–1915." Ph.D. diss., City University of New York, 1978.

Di Donato, Pietro, *Christ in Concrete.* Indianapolis, Ind.: Bobbs-Merrill, 1939.

Di Leonardo, Micaela. *The Varieties of Ethic Experience: Kinship, Class, and Gender among California Italian-Americans.* Ithaca, N.Y.: Cornell University Press, 1984.

Diner, Hasia. *Erin's Daughters in America: Irish Immigrant Women in the Nineteenth Century.* Baltimore, Md.: Johns Hopkins University Press, 1983.

Ewen, Elizabeth. *Immigrant Women in the Land of Dollars.* New York: Monthly Review Press, 1985.

"Family Patterns." In *Harvard Encyclopedia of American Ethnic Groups,* ed. Stephen Thernstrom, 345–54. Cambridge, Mass.: Harvard University Press, 1980.

Farber, Bernard, Charles Mindel, and Bernard Lazerwitz. "Jewish American Families." In *Ethnic Families in America,* ed. Charles Mindel and Robert Habenstein, 350–85. New York: Elsevier, 1981.

Fernandez-Marina, Eduardo Ramon, Maldonado-Sierra, and Richard Trent. "Three Basic Themes in Mexican and Puerto Rican Family Values." *Journal of Social Psychology* 48 (1958): 167–81.

Gabaccia, Donna. *From Sicily to Elizabeth Street.* Albany: State University of New York Press, 1984.

Gambino, Richard. *Blood of My Blood: The Dilemma of Italian Americans.* Garden City, N.Y.: Doubleday and Co., 1974.

Glasco, Lawrence. "The Life Cycles and Household Structures of American Ethnic Groups." In *A Heritage of Her Own: Toward a New Social History of American Women,* ed. Elizabeth Pleck and Nancy Cott, 268–89. New York: Simon and Schuster, 1979.

Golab, Caroline. "The Impact of the Industrial Experience on the Immigrant Family." In *Immigrants in Industrial America,* ed. Richard Erlich, 1–32. Chapel Hill: University of North Carolina Press, 1977.

Goldin, Claudia. "Family Strategies and the Family Economy in the Late Nineteenth Century." In *Work, Space, Family and Group Experience in the Nineteenth Century,* ed. Theodore Hershberg, 277–310. New York: Oxford University Press, 1981.

Groneman, Carol. "The Bloody Ould Sixth Ward." Ph.D. diss. University of Rochester, 1973.

Haines, Michael. "Poverty, Economic Stress and the Family in a Late Nineteenth Century American City: Whites in Philadelphia." In *Work, Space Family and Group Experience in the Nineteenth Century*, ed. Theodore Hershberg, 240–76. New York: Oxford University Press, 1981.

Handlin, Oscar. *Boston's Immigrants, 1790–1865*. Cambridge, Mass.: Harvard University Press, 1941.

Hareven, Tamara. "Family and Work Patterns of Immigrant Laborers in a Planned Industrial Town, 1900–1930." In *Immigrants in Industrial America*, ed. Richard Erlich, 47–66. Chapel Hill: University of North Carolina Press, 1977.

Howe, Irving. *World of Our Fathers*. New York: Harcourt Brace Jovanovich, 1976.

Huang, Lucy Jen. "The Chinese American Family." In *Ethnic Families in America*, ed. Charles Mindel and Robert Habenstein, 115–42. New York: Elsevier, 1981.

Karp, Abraham. *Golden Door to America*. New York: The Viking Press, 1976.

Kessner, Thomas and Betty Caroli. "New Immigrant Woman at Work: Italians and Jews in New York City, 1880–1905." *Journal of Ethnic History* 5 (Winter 1978): 19–32.

Kingston, Maxine Hong. "A Song for a Barbarian Reed Pipe." In *Immigrant Women*, ed. Maxine Seller, 290–97. Philadelphia, Pa.: Temple University Press, 1981.

Krause, Corinne. "Urbanization without Breakdown: Italian, Jewish and Slavic Women in Pittsburgh, 1908–1945." *Journal of Urban History* 4 (May 1978): 291–306.

Lopata, Helena. "Polish American Families." In *Ethnic Families in America*, ed. Charles Mindel and Robert Habenstein, 17–42. New York: Elsevier, 1981.

Lopreato, Joseph. *Italian Americans*. New York: Random House, 1970.

MacCready, William C. "The Persistence of Ethnic Variation in American Families." In *Ethnicity in the United States*, ed. Andrew Greeley, 157–67. New York: John Wiley and Sons, 1974.

Mangione, Jerre. *Mount Allegro: A Memoir of Italian American Life*, New York: Columbia University Press, 1981.

Mangione, Jerre. "Talking American." In *Children of the Uprooted*, ed. Oscar Handlin, 355–69. New York: Grosset & Dunlap, 1968.

Mei Ling, Diane, and Ginger Chih. *A Place Called Chinese America*. San Francisco: Organization of Chinese Americans, 1982.

Miller, Kirby. *Emigrants and Exiles: The Irish Exodus to America*. New York: Oxford University Press, 1985.

Mintz, Steven, and Susan Kellogg. *Domestic Revolutions: A Social History of American Family Life*. New York: The Free Press, 1988.

Moore, Abigail. "Marital Desertion among New York Jews." Paper presented at the Organization of American Historians meeting, April 1980.

Moore, Joan. *Mexican Americans*. Englewood Cliffs, N.J.: Prentice-Hall, 1970.

Mormino, Gary, and George Pozzetta. *The Immigrant World of Ybor City: Italians and Their Latin Neighbors in Tampa, 1885–1985*. Urbana: University of Illinois Press, 1987.

National Education Association. *Proceedings*, National Education Association, 1905.

Orsi, Robert. *Madonna of 116th Street*, New Haven, Conn.: Yale University Press, 1985.

Prosen, Rosemary. "Looking Back." In *Growing Up Slavic in America*, ed. Michael Novak, 1976, 1–8, an EMPAC! publication.

Quadagno, Jill. "The Italian American Family." In *Ethnic Families in America*, ed. Charles Mindel and Robert Habenstein, 61–85. New York: Elsevier, 1981.

Roskolenko, Harry. "America the Thief." In *The Immigrant Experience: The Anguish of Becoming American* ed. Thomas Wheeler, 151–78. New York: Dial Press, 1971.

Seller, Maxine, ed. *Immigrant Women*. Philadelphia, Pa.: Temple University Press, 1981.

Siu, Paul. *The Chinese Laundryman in America*. Ed. John Kuo Wei Tchen. New York: New York University Press, 1987.

Thomas, William, and Florian Znaniecki. *The Polish Peasant in Europe and America*. New York: Dover Press, 1958.

Ware, Caroline. *Greenwich Village*. New York: Harper and Row, 1935.

Weinberg, Sydney Stahl. "Jewish Mothers and Immigrant Daughters." *Journal of American Ethnic History* 6 (Spring 1987): 39–55.

———. *The World of Our Mothers: The Lives of Jewish Immigrant Women*. Chapel Hill: University of North Carolina Press, 1988.

Wong, Jade Snow. "Puritans from the Orient." In *The Immigrant Experience: The Anguish of Becoming American*, ed. Thomas Wheeler, 107–31. New York: Dial Press, 1971.

Yans-McLaughlin, Virginia. *Family and Community: Italian Immigrants in Buffalo, 1880–1930*. Ithaca, N.Y.: Cornell University Press, 1977.

Yezierska, Anzia. *The Children of Loneliness*. New York: Funk & Wagnalls, 1923.

Selected Bibliography

Aaron, Daniel, and Robert Bendiner, eds. *The Strenuous Decade: A Social and Intellectual Record of the Nineteen-Thirties*. New York: Anchor Books, 1970.

Aberle, S. B. D. "Child Mortality among Pueblo Indians." *American Journal of Physical Anthropology* 16 (January–March 1932): 339–49.

———. "Maternal Mortality among the Pueblos." *American Journal of Physical Anthropology* 18 (January–March 1934): 431–35.

"ACLI. Analysis Shows Effect of Maturing Members of Baby Boom." *The National Underwriter: Life and Health Insurance Edition* 85 (1981): 5.

Adamic, Louis. *My America, 1928–1938*. New York: Harper and Brothers, 1938.

Agee, James, and Walker Evans. *Let Us Now Praise Famous Men*. Boston: Houghton Mifflin Co., 1941; New York: Ballantine Books, 1966.

Albers, Patricia, and Beatrice Medicine. *The Hidden Half: Studies of Plains Indian Women*. Lanham, Md.: University Press of America, 1983.

Albrecht, M. C. "The Relationship of Literature and Society." *American Journal of Sociology* 59 (March 1954): 425–36.

Allen, David Grayson. *In English Ways: The Movement of Societies and the Transferal of English Local Law and Custom to Massachusetts Bay in the Seventeenth Century*. Chapel Hill: University of North Carolina Press, 1981.

Allen, Margaret. "The Domestic Ideal and the Mobilization of Woman Power in World War II." *Women's Studies International Forum* 6 (1983): 401–12.

Anderson, Gary Clayton. *Kinsmen of Another Kind: Dakota-White Relations in the Upper Mississippi Valley: 1650–1862*. Lincoln: University of Nebraska Press, 1984.

———. *Little Crow: Spokesman for the Sioux*. St. Paul: Minnesota Historical Society, 1986.

Anderson, Joseph M. *Population Change and the American Labor Market: 1950–2000*. U.S. Congress. House. Select Committee on Population, Hearings on the Consequences of Changing U.S. Population: Baby Boom and Bust. 95th Cong. 2d sess., 2 June 1978, 781–804.

Anderson, Karen. "Commodity Exchange and Subordination: Montagnais-Naskapi and Huron Women, 1600–1650." *Signs: Journal of Women in Culture and Society* 11, no. 1 (1985): 48–62.

———. *Wartime Women: Sex Roles, Family Relations, and the Status of Women during World War II.* Westport, Conn.: Greenwood Press, 1981.

Anderson, Terry L., and Robert Paul Thomas. "The Growth of Population and Labor Force in the 17th-Century Chesapeake." *Explorations in Economic History* 15 (1978): 290–312.

Anderson, Virginia DeJohn. "Migrants and Motives: Religion and the Settlement of New England, 1630–1640." *New England Quarterly* 58 (1985): 339–83.

Angell, Robert C. *The Family Encounters the Depression.* New York: Charles Scribner's Sons, 1936.

Angelou, Maya. *I Know Why the Caged Bird Sings.* New York: Random House, 1969.

———. *Singin' and Swingin' and Gettin' Merry Like Christmas.* Toronto: Bantam Books, 1977.

Aptheker, Bettina. *Woman's Legacy: Essays on Race, Sex, and Class in American History.* Amherst: University of Massachusetts Press, 1982.

Arendell, Terry. *Mothers and Divorce: Legal, Economic, and Social Dilemmas.* Berkeley: University of California Press, 1986.

Argersinger, Jo Ann E. *Toward a New Deal in Baltimore: People and Government in the Great Depression.* Chapel Hill: University of North Carolina Press, 1988.

Aries, Philippe. *Western Attitudes toward Death from the Middle Ages to the Present.* Trans. Patricia M. Ranum. Baltimore, Md.: Johns Hopkins University Press, 1974.

Auwers, Linda. "Fathers, Sons, and Wealth in Colonial Windsor, Connecticut." *Journal of Family History* 3 (1978): 136–49.

Axtell, James, ed. *The Indian Peoples of Eastern America: A Documentary History of the Sexes.* New York: Oxford University Press, 1981.

———. *The School upon a Hill: Education and Society in Colonial New England.* New Haven, Conn.: Yale University Press, 1974.

"Babies Bottom Out: A 'Maybe Boom.'" *Science News* 112 (1977): 101.

"Baby Boom Families." *American Demographics* 4 (1982): 46–47.

Baca Zinn, Maxine. "Chicano Family Research: Conceptual Distortions and Alternative Directions." *Journal of Ethnic Studies* 7 (Fall 1979): 57–71.

Bailyn, Bernard. *Education in the Forming of American Society: Needs and Opportunities for Study.* Chapel Hill: University of North Carolina Press, 1960.

———. *Voyagers to the West: A Passage in the Peopling of America on the Eve of the Revolution.* New York: Alfred A. Knopf, 1986.

Baker, Paula. "Domestication of American Politics." *American Historical Review* 89 (1984): 620–49.

Baker, Russell. *Growing Up.* New York: Congdon & Weed, 1982.

Bakke, E. Wight. *Citizens without Work: A Study of the Effects of Unemployment upon the Workers' Social Relations and Practices.* New Haven, Conn.: Yale University Press, 1940.

Baltes, Paul B., David L. Featherman, and Richard M. Lerner, eds. *Life-Span Development and Behavior.* Vol. 8. Hillsdale, N. J.: Lawrence Erlbaum Associates, 1988.

Bane, Mary Jo. *Here to Stay: American Families in the Twentieth Century.* New York: Basic Books, 1976.

Barabba, Vincent P. *Effects of Population Change on Voting Behavior and Other Aspects of Lifestyle.* U.S. Congress. House. Select Committee on Population, Hearings on the Consequences of Changing U.S. Population: Baby Boom and Bust. 95th Cong. 2d sess., 23 May 1978, 369–83.

Barker, Dianna L., and Sheila Allen, eds. *Dependence and Exploitation in Marriage and Work.* New York: Longman, 1976.

Basch, Norma. *In the Eyes of the Law: Women, Marriage and Property in Nineteenth-Century New York.* Ithaca, N.Y.: Cornell University Press, 1982.

Bataille, Gretchen M., and Kathleen Mullen Sands. *American Indian Women: Telling Their Lives.* Lincoln: University of Nebraska Press, 1984.

Baym, Nina. *Women's Fiction: A Guide to Novels by and about Women in America, 1820–1870.* Ithaca, N.Y.: Cornell University Press, 1978.

Beales, Ross W., Jr. "In Search of the Historical Child: Miniature Adulthood and Youth in Colonial New England." *American Quarterly* 27 (1975): 379–98.

Bean, Frank D. "The Baby Boom and Its Explanations." *Sociological Quarterly* 24 (1983): 353–65.

Bean, Frank D., and Linda Aiken. "Intermarriage and Unwanted Fertility in United States." *Journal of Marriage and the Family* 38 (1976): 61–72.

Behrman, S. J., Leslie Corsa, Jr., and Ronald Frudman, eds. *Fertility and Family Planning.* Ann Arbor: University of Michigan Press, 1969.

Bellah, Robert N. *Apache Kinship Systems.* Cambridge, Mass.: Harvard University Press, 1952.

Bellah, Robert, et al. *Habits of the Heart: Individualism and Commitment in American Life.* Berkeley: University of California Press, 1985.

Benes, Peter, ed. *Early American Probate Inventories.* The Dublin Seminar for New England Folklife, Annual Proceedings, 1987. Boston: Boston University Scholarly Publications, 1989.

———, ed. *Families and Children.* The Dublin Seminar for New England Folklife, Annual Proceedings, 1985. Boston: Boston University Scholarly Publications, 1987.

Bennett, Shelia K., and Glen Elder, Jr. "Women's Work in the Family Economy: A Study of Depression Hardship in Women's Lives." *Journal of Family History* 4 (Summer 1979): 153–76.

Benson, Mary Sumner. *Women in Eighteenth-Century America: A Study of Opinion and Social Usage.* New York: Columbia University Press, 1935.

Berelson, B., and Patricia J. Salter. "Majority and Minority Americans: An Analysis of Magazine Fiction." *Public Opinion Quarterly* 10 (Summer 1946): 168–90.

Berger, Bennett M. *Looking for America: Essays on Youth, Suburbia, and Other American Obsessions.* Englewood Cliffs, N.J.: Prentice-Hall, 1971.

———. *Working Class Suburb.* Berkeley: University of California Press, 1971.

Berger, Brigitte, and Peter Berger. *The War Over the Family: Capturing the Middle Ground.* Garden City, N.Y.: Doubleday and Co., 1983.

Berger, Brigitte, and Sidney Callahan, eds. *Child Care and Mediating Structures.* Washington, D.C.: American Enterprise Institute for Public Policy Research, 1979.

Berkin, Carol, and Clara Lovett, eds. *Women, War, and Revolution.* New York: Holmes and Meier, 1980.

Berkner, Lutz. "The Stem Family and the Developmental Cycle of the Peasant Household: An Eighteenth-Century Austrian Example." *American Historical Review* 77 (April 1972): 398–418.

Bernard, Jessie. *The Future of Marriage.* New York: Bantam Books, 1972.

———. *The Future of Motherhood.* New York: The Dial Press, 1974.

———. "Marital Stability and Patterns of Status Variables." *Journal of Marriage and the Family* 28 (November 1966): 421–39.

Bernard, Richard. *The Melting Pot and the Altar.* Minneapolis: University of Minnesota Press, 1980.

Bernstein, Irving. *A Caring Society: The New Deal, the Worker, and the Great Depression.* Boston: Houghton Mifflin Co., 1985.

———. *The Lean Years: A History of the American Worker, 1920–1933.* Boston: Houghton Mifflin Co., 1966.

Bethel, Elizabeth Rauh. *Promiseland: A Century of Life in a Negro Community.* Philadelphia, Pa.: Temple University Press, 1981.

Billingsley, Andrew. *Black Families in White America.* Englewood Cliffs, N.J.: Prentice-Hall, 1968.

Bird, Caroline. *The Invisible Scar.* New York: David McKay, 1966.

Blackwelder, Julia Kirk. "Letters from the Great Depression." *Southern Exposure* 6 (Fall 1978): 73–77.

———. "Quiet Suffering: Atlanta Women in the 1930s." *Georgia Historical Quarterly* 61 (Summer 1977): 112–24.

———. *Women of the Depression: Caste and Culture in San Antonio, 1929–1939.* College Station: Texas A & M University Press, 1984.

Blackwood, Evelyn. "Sexuality and Gender in Certain Native American Tribes: The Case of Cross-Gender Females." *Signs: Journal of Women in Culture and Society* 10 (Autumn 1984): 27–42.

Blackwood, Larry. "Alaska Native Fertility Trends, 1950–1978." *Demography* 18 (May 1981): 173–79.

Blake, Judith, and Prithwis das Gupta."Reply to: Reproductive Motivation versus Contraceptive Technology: Is Recent American Experience an Exception?" *Population and Development Review* 4 (1978): 326–29.

Blake, Judith, and Prithwis das Gupta. "Reproduction Motivation versus Contraceptive Technology: Is Recent American Experience an Exception?" *Population and Development Review* 1 (1975): 229–49.

Blalock, Herbert M., Jr., ed. *Sociological Theory and Research: A Critical Appraisal.* New York: Free Press, 1980.

Blassingame, John W. *The Slave Community: Plantation Life in the Ante-Bellum Slave South.* New York: Oxford University Press, 1972.

———, ed. *Slave Testimony: Two Centuries of Letters, Speeches, Interviews, and Autobiographies.* Baton Rouge: Louisiana State University Press, 1977.

Bloch, Ruth H. "American Feminine Ideals in Transition: The Rise of the Moral Mother, 1785–1815." *Feminist Studies* 4 (1978): 101–26.

Blood, Robert O., Jr., and Donald M. Wolfe. *Husbands and Wives: The Dynamics of Married Living.* New York: The Free Press, 1960.

Blum, John. *V Was For Victory: Politics and American Culture During World War II.* New York: Harcourt Brace, Jovanovich, 1976.

Blumstein, Philip, and Pepper Schwartz. *American Couples: Money, Work, Sex.* New York: William Morrow, 1983.

Bodle, Wayne. "The 'Myth of the Middle Colonies' Reconsidered: The Process of Regionalization in Early America." *Pennsylvania Magazine of History and Biography* 113 (1989): 527–48.

Bodnar, John, Roger Simon, and Michael Weber. *Lives of Their Own: Blacks, Italians and Poles in Pittsburgh, 1900–1960.* Urbana: University of Illinois Press, 1982.

Bolin, Winifred D. Wandersee. "The Economics of Middle-Income Family Life: Working Women during the Great Depression." *Journal of American History,* 65 (June 1978): 60–74.

Botume, Elizabeth Hyde. *First Days among the Contrabands.* New York: Arno Press and the *New York Times,* 1968.

Bowden, Harry Warner. *American Indians and Christian Missions: Studies in Cultural Conflict.* Chicago: University of Chicago Press, 1981.

Bowen, Murray. *Family Therapy in Clinical Practice.* New York: Jason Aronson, 1978.

Boyer, Paul, and Stephen Nissenbaum. *Salem Possessed: The Social Origins of Witchcraft.* Cambridge, Mass.: Harvard University Press, 1974.

Boyett, Gene W. "Aging in Seventeenth-Century New England." *New England Historical and Genealogical Register* 134 (1980): 181–93.

Brandt, Lillian. *An Impressionistic View of the Winter of 1930–1931 in New York City.* New York: Welfare Council of New York City, 1932.

Breen, T. H., and Stephen Foster. "Moving to the New World: The Character of Early Massachusetts Immigration." *William and Mary Quarterly* 3d ser., 30 (1973): 189–222.

Breines, Wini. "Domineering Mothers in the 1950s: Image and Reality." *Women Studies International Forum* 8 (1985): 601–8.

Bremer, William W. "Along the 'American Way': The New Deal's Work Relief Programs for the Unemployed." *Journal of American History* 62 (December 1975): 636–52.

———. *Depression Winters: New York Social Workers and the New Deal.* Philadelphia, Pa.: Temple University Press, 1984.

Bremner, Robert H., et al., eds. *Children and Youth in America: A Documentary History.* Vol. 1, *1600–1865.* Cambridge, Mass.: Harvard University Press, 1970.

Bremner, Robert H., and Gary W. Reichard, eds. *Reshaping America: Society and Institutions, 1945–1960.* Columbus: Ohio University Press, 1982.

Brobeck, Stephen. "Images of the Family: Portrait Paintings as Indices of American Family Culture, Structure, and Behavior, 1730–1860." *Journal of Psychohistory* 5 (1977): 81–106.

Brooks, Gwendolyn. "Why Negro Women Leave Home." *Negro Digest* 9 (March 1951): 26–28.

Brown, Charlotte, Paula Hyman, and Sonya Michel. *The Jewish Woman in America.* New York: The Dial Press, 1976.

Brown, Dorothy M. *Setting a Course: American Women in the 1920s.* Boston: Twayne

Publisher 1987.

Brown, Jennifer, S. H. "A Demographic Transition in the Fur Trade Country: Family Sizes and Fertility of Company Officers and Country Wives, Ca. 1759–1850." *The Western Canadian Journal of Anthropology* 6, no. 1 (1976): 61–71.

———. *Strangers in Blood: Fur Trade Company Families in Indian Country.* Vancouver: University of British Columbia Press, 1980.

Brown, Judith. "Economic Organization and the Position of Women among the Iroquois." *Ethnohistory* 17 (1970): 151–67.

Brownmiller, Susan. *Against Our Will: Men, Women, and Rape.* New York: Simon and Schuster, 1975.

Brumberg, Joan Jacobs. *Fasting Girls: The Emergence of Anorexia Nervosa as a Modern Disease.* Cambridge, Mass.: Harvard University Press, 1988.

Buel, Joy Day, and Richard Buel, Jr. *The Way of Duty: A Woman and Her Family in Revolutionary America.* New York: W. W. Norton & Company, 1984.

Buerkel-Rothfuss, N., and S. Mayes. "Soap Opera Viewing: The Cultivation Effect." *Journal of Communication* 31 (Summer 1981): 108–15.

Bumpass, Larry L., and James A. Sweet. "Differentials in Marital Instability: 1970." *American Sociological Review* 37 (1972): 754–66.

Burnham, John. *Paths into American Culture: Psychology, Medicine, and Morals.* Philadelphia, Pa.: Temple University Press, 1988.

Bushman, Richard. "Family Security in the Transition from Farm to City, 1750–1850." *Journal of Family History* 6 (Fall 1981): 238–56.

Butz, William P., and Michael P. Ward. "Baby Boom and Baby Bust: A New View." *American Demographics* 1 (1979): 11–17.

———. "The Emergence of Countercyclical U.S. Fertility." *American Economic Review* 69 (1979): 318–28.

Byers, Edward. "Fertility Transition in a New England Commercial Center: Nantucket, Massachusetts, 1680–1840." *Journal of Interdisciplinary History* 13 (1982): 17–40.

Byrne, Harriet A. *The Effects of the Depression on Wage Earners' Families.* Women's Bureau, Bulletin no. 108. Washington, D.C.: Government Printing Office, 1933.

Cable, Mary. *The Little Darlings: A History of Child Rearing in America.* New York: Charles Scribner's Sons, 1975.

Cain, Glen. *Married Women in the Labor Force: An Economic Analysis.* Chicago: University of Chicago Press, 1966.

Calhoun, Arthur W. *A Social History of the American Family from Colonial Times to the Present.* 3 vols. Cleveland, Ohio: The Arthur H. Clark Company, 1917–1919. Reprint. New York: Barnes & Noble, 1945.

Calloway, Colin G., ed. *New Directions in American Indian History.* Norman: University of Oklahoma Press, 1988.

Calvert, Karin. "Children in American Family Portraiture, 1670 to 1810." *William and Mary Quarterly* 3d ser., 39 (1982): 87–113.

Calverton, Victor F., and Samuel D. Schmalhausen, eds. *The New Generation: The Intimate Problems of Modern Parents and Children.* New York: Macaulay, 1930.

Campbell, Arthur A. "Baby Boom to Birth Dearth and Beyond." *Annals of the American Academy of Political and Social Science* 435 (January 1978): 40–59.

Campbell, D'Ann. *Women at War with America: Private Lives in a Patriotic Era.* Cambridge, Mass.: Harvard University Press, 1984.

Cannell, M. O., A. C. Orr, and M. Leuck. "Children of Working Mothers." *American Demographics* 5 (1982): 6–12.

Cantor, Hyman. "Autobiography." Typescript at YIVO, New York City.

Cantor, Muriel G., and Suzanne Pingree. *The Soap Opera.* Beverly Hills, Calif.: Sage Publications, 1983.

Caplow, Theodore, et al. *Middletown Families: Fifty Years of Continuity and Change.* Minneapolis: University of Minnesota Press, 1982.

Carr, Lois Green, and Lorena S. Walsh. "The Planter's Wife: The Experience of White Women in Seventeenth-Century Maryland." *William and Mary Quarterly* 3d ser., 34 (1977): 542–71.

Carr, Lois Green, Philip D. Morgan, and Jean B. Russo, eds. *Colonial Chesapeake Society.* Chapel Hill: University of North Carolina Press, 1988.

Carroll, Peter N. *It Seemed Like Nothing Happened: The Tragedy and Promise of America in the 1970's.* New York: Holt, Rinehart, and Winston, 1982.

Carter, Hugh, and Paul Glick. *Marriage and Divorce: A Social and Economic Study.* Cambridge, Mass.: Harvard University Press, 1976.

Carter, Jenny, and Terese Duriez. *With Child: Birth through the Ages.* Edinburgh, Scotland: Mainstream Publishing, 1986.

Castleman, Harry. *Watching TV—Four Decades of American Television.* New York: McGraw-Hill, 1982.

Cates, Gerald L. " 'The Seasoning': Disease and Death among the First Colonists of Georgia." *Georgia Historical Quarterly* 64 (1980): 146–58.

Cavan, Ruth S., and Katherine H. Ranck. *The Family and the Depression: A Study of One Hundred Chicago Families.* Chicago: University of Chicago Press, 1938.

Censer, Jane Turner. *North Carolina Planters and Their Children, 1800–1860.* Baton Rouge: Louisiana State University Press, 1984.

Chafe, William H. *The American Woman: Her Changing Social, Economic, and Political Roles, 1920–1970.* New York: Oxford University Press, 1972.

———. *The Unfinished Journey: America since World War II.* New York: Oxford University Press, 1986.

———. *Women and Equality: Changing Patterns in American Culture.* New York: Oxford University Press, 1977.

Chambers-Schiller, Lee Virginia. *Liberty, A Better Husband: Single Women in America, The Generations of 1780–1840.* New Haven, Conn.: Yale University Press, 1984.

Charles, Searle F. *Minister of Relief: Harry Hopkins and the Depression.* Syracuse, N.Y.: Syracuse University Press, 1963.

Cherlin, Andrew J. "Changing Family and Household: Contemporary Lessons from Historical Research." *Annual Review of Sociology* 9 (1983): 51–66.

———. "The 50's Family and Today's," *New York Times,* 18 November 1981, 1:31.

———. *Marriage, Divorce, Remarriage.* Cambridge, Mass.: Harvard University Press, 1981.

―――. "Remarriage as an Incomplete Institution." *American Journal of Sociology* 84 (1978): 634–50.

Chilman, Catherine. *Adolescent Sexuality in a Changing American Society.* New York: John Wiley and Sons, 1983.

Chodorow, Nancy. *Reproduction of Mothering: Psychoanalysis and the Sociology of Gender.* Berkeley: University of California Press, 1978.

Clague, Ewan, and Powell Webster. *Ten Thousand Out of Work.* Philadelphia: University of Pennsylvania Press, 1931.

Clark, Charles E., et al., eds. *Maine in the Early Republic: From Revolution to Statehood.* Hanover, N.H.: University Press of New England, 1988.

Clark, Clifford Edward. *The American Family Home, 1800–1960.* Chapel Hill: University of North Carolina Press, 1986.

―――. "Domestic Architecture as an Index to Social History: The Romantic Revival and the Cult of Domesticity in America, 1840–1870." *Journal of Interdisciplinary History* 7 (1976): 33–56.

Clark, Kenneth B. *Dark Ghetto: Dilemmas of Social Power.* New York: Harper Torchbooks, 1965.

Clayton, Richard R., and Harwin L. Vocc. "Shacking Up: Cohabitation in the 1970s." *Journal of Marriage and the Family* 39 (1977): 273–83.

Clinton, Catherine. *The Plantation Mistress: Women's World in the Old South.* New York: Pantheon Books, 1982.

Clive, Alan. "Women Workers in World War II: Michigan as a Test Case." *Labor History* 20 (1979): 44–72.

Coale, Ansley. *The Growth and Structure of Human Populations.* Princeton, N.J.: Princeton University Press, 1972.

Coale, Ansley J., and Melvin Zelnik. *New Estimates of Fertility and Population in the U.S.: A Study of Annual White Births from 1855 to 1960 and of Completeness of Enumeration in the Censuses from 1880 to 1960.* Princeton, N.J.: Princeton University Press, 1963.

Cogan, Frances. *All-American Girl: The Ideal of Real Womanhood in Mid-Nineteenth-Century America.* Athens: University of Georgia Press, 1989.

Cohen, Henry S. "Connecticut's Divorce Mechanism: 1636–1969." *American Journal of Legal History* 14 (1970): 34–54.

Cohen, Miriam. "Changing Educational Strategies among Immigrant Generations." *Journal of Social History* 15 (Spring 1982): 443–60.

Cohen, Sheldon S. "The Broken Bond: Divorce in Providence County, 1749–1809." *Rhode Island History* 44 (1985): 66–79.

―――. " 'To Parts of the World Unknown': The Circumstances of Divorce in Connecticut, 1750–1797." *Canadian Review of American Studies* 11 (1980): 275–93.

―――. "What Man Hath Put Asunder: Divorce in New Hampshire, 1681–1784." *Historical New Hampshire* 41 (1986): 118–41.

Cohen, Wilbur J., and Charles F. Westoff. *Demographic Dynamics in America.* New York: The Free Press, 1977.

Cohn, Henry S. "Connecticut's Divorce Mechanism: 1636–1969." *American Journal of Legal History* 14 (1970): 34–54.

Cole, Donald. *Immigrant City.* Chapel Hill: University of North Carolina Press, 1963.

Cole, Thomas R. "Family, Settlement, and Migration in Southeastern Massa-
    chusetts, 1650–1805: The Case for Regional Analysis." *New England His-
    torical and Genealogical Register* 132 (1978): 171–85.
Collins, Patricia Hill. "A Comparison of Two Works on Black Family Life." *Signs:
    A Journal of Women in Culture and Society* 14 (Summer 1989): 875–84.
———. "The Meaning of Motherhood in Black Culture and Black Mother-
    Daughter Relationships." *Sage* 4 (Fall 1987): 3–10.
Conrad, Laetitia M. "Some Effects of the Depression on Family Life." *Social
    Forces* 15 (1936–1937): 76–81.
Conzen, Kathleen. *Immigrant Milwaukee 1836–1860.* Cambridge, Mass.: Harvard
    University Press, 1976.
Coontz, Stephanie. *The Social Origins of Private Life: A History of American Families,
    1600–1900.* London: Verso, 1988.
Cott, Nancy F. *The Bonds of Womanhood: "Woman's Sphere" in New England, 1780–
    1835.* New Haven, Conn.: Yale University Press, 1977.
———. "Divorce and the Changing Status of Women in Eighteenth-Century
    Massachusetts." *William and Mary Quarterly* 3d ser., 33 (1976): 586–614.
———. "Eighteenth-Century Family and Social Life Revealed in Massachusetts
    Divorce Records." *Journal of Social History* 10 (1976): 20–43.
———. "Notes toward an Interpretation of Antebellum Childrearing." *The Psy-
    chohistorical Review* 6 (Spring 1978): 4–20.
———. "Young Women in the Second Great Awakening in New England."
    Feminist Studies 3 (Fall 1975): 15–29.
Cott, Nancy F., and Elizabeth H. Pleck, eds. *A Heritage of Her Own: Toward a
    New Social History of American Women.* New York: Simon and Schuster,
    1979.
Cottle, Thomas J. *Time's Children: Impressions of Youth.* Boston: Little, Brown and
    Company, 1971.
Covello, Leonard. *The Social Background of the Italo-American School Child.* Leiden,
    Netherlands: E. J. Brill, 1967.
Cowan, Neil, and Ruth Schwartz Cowan. *Our Parents' Lives.* New York: Basic
    Books, 1989.
Cowan, Ruth Schwartz. "The 'Industrial Revolution' in the Home: Household
    Technology and Social Change in the 20th Century." *Technology and Cul-
    ture* 17 (1976): 1–23.
———. *More Work for Mother: The Ironies of Household Technology from the Open
    Hearth to the Microwave.* New York: Basic Books, 1983.
Crandall, John C. "Patriotism and Humanitarian Reform in Children's Litera-
    ture, 1825–1860." *American Quarterly* 21 (1969): 3–22.
Cressy, David. *Coming Over: Migration and Communication between England and
    New England in the Seventeenth Century.* New York: Cambridge University
    Press, 1987.
———. "The Seasonality of Marriage in Old and New England." *Journal of
    Interdisciplinary History* 16 (1985): 1–22.
Crouse, Joan M. *The Homeless Transient in the Great Depression: New York State,
    1929–1941.* Albany: State University of New York Press, 1986.
Crouse, Nellis M. "The Causes of the Great Migration, 1630–1640." *New England
    Quarterly* 5 (1932): 3–36.

Dahl, Linda. *Stormy Weather: The Music and Lives of a Century of Jazzwomen.* New York: Pantheon Books, 1984.

Danziger, Sheldon H., and Daniel H. Weinberg, eds. *Fighting Poverty: What Works and What Doesn't.* Cambridge, Mass.: Harvard University Press, 1986.

Davidoff, Leonore, and Catherine Hall. *Family Fortunes: Men and Women of the English Middle Class, 1780–1850.* London: Hutchinson, 1987.

Davidson, James West, and Mark Hamilton Lytle, eds. *After the Fact: The Art of Historical Detection.* 2d ed. New York: Alfred A. Knopf, 1986.

Davis, Kingsley. *The American Family in Relation to Demographic Change.* Commission on Population Growth and the American Future, Research Reports, 1, Demographic and Social Aspects of Population Growth. Washington, D.C.: Government Printing Office, 1972.

Deetz, James. *In Small Things Forgotten: The Archeology of Early American Life.* Garden City, N.Y.: Doubleday and Co., 1977.

Degler, Carl N. *At Odds: Women and the Family in America from the Revolution to the Present.* New York: Oxford University Press, 1980.

Deloria, Ella. *Speaking of Indians.* New York: Friendship Press, 1944.

deMause, Lloyd, ed. *The History of Childhood.* New York: Psychohistory Press, 1974.

D'Emilio, John, and Estelle B. Freedman. *Intimate Matters: A History of Sexuality in America.* New York: Harper and Row, 1988.

Demos, John. "The American Family in Past Time." *American Scholar* 43 (1974): 422–46.

———. "Developmental Perspectives on the History of Childhood." *Journal of Interdisciplinary History* 2 (1971): 315–27.

———. *Entertaining Satan: Witchcraft and the Culture of Early New England.* New York: Oxford University Press, 1982.

———. "Families in Colonial Bristol, Rhode Island: An Exercise in Historical Demography." *William and Mary Quarterly* 3d ser., 25 (1968): 40–57.

———. *A Little Commonwealth: Family Life in Plymouth Colony.* New York: Oxford University Press, 1970.

———. "Notes on Life in Plymouth Colony." *William and Mary Quarterly* 3d ser., 22 (1965): 264–86.

———. *Past, Present, and Personal: The Family and the Life Course in American History.* New York: Oxford University Press, 1986.

———. "Underlying Themes in the Witchcraft of Seventeenth-Century New England." American Historical Review 75 (1970): 1311–26.

Demos, John, and Sarane Spence Boocock, eds. *Turning Points: Historical and Sociological Essays on the Family.* Chicago: University of Chicago Press, 1978.

Demos, John, and Virginia Demos. "Adolescence in Historical Perspective." *Journal of Marriage and the Family* 31 (1969): 632–38.

Denevan, William M., ed. *The Native Population of the Americas in 1492.* Madison: University of Wisconsin Press, 1976.

Deutrich, Mabel E., and Virginia C. Purdy, eds. *Clio Was a Woman: Studies in the History of American Women.* Washington, D.C.: Howard University Press, 1980.

Dexter, Elisabeth Anthony. *Women in Colonial Affairs.* Boston: Houghton Mifflin Co., 1924.

Di Leonardo, Micaela. "The Female Work of Cards and Holidays: Women, Families, and the Work of Kinship." *Signs: Journal of Women in Culture and Society*. 12 (1987): 440–53.

———. *The Varieties of Ethnic Experience: Kinship, Class, and Gender among California Italian-Americans*. Ithaca, N.Y.: Cornell University Press, 1984.

Diner, Hasia. *Erin's Daughters in America: Irish Immigrant Women in the Nineteenth Century*. Baltimore, Md.: Johns Hopkins University Press, 1983.

Dobyns, Henry F. *Native American Historical Demography: A Critical Bibliography*. Bloomington: Indiana University Press, 1976.

———. *Their Number Become Thinned: Native American Population Dynamics in Eastern North America*. Knoxville: University of Tennessee Press, 1983.

Donegan, Jane. *Women and Men Midwives: Medicine, Morality and Misogyny in Early America*. Westport, Conn.: Greenwood Press, 1978.

Dorn, Harold F. "Pitfalls in Population Forecasts and Projections." *Journal of the American Statistical Association* 45 (1950): 311–34.

Dougherty, Mollie Crocker. *Becoming a Woman in Rural Black Culture*. New York: Holt, Rinehart, and Winston, 1978.

Douglas, Ann. *The Feminization of American Culture*. New York: Alfred A. Knopf, 1977.

Drake, St. Clair. "Why Men Leave Home." *Negro Digest* 8 (April 1950): 25–27.

Drake, St. Clair, and Horace R. Cayton. *Black Metropolis: A Study of Negro Life in a Northern City*. Vol. 2. New York: Harper and Row, 1962.

Drucker, Philip. "Rank, Wealth, and Kinship in Northwest Coast Society." *American Anthropologist* 41 (January–March 1939): 55–65.

DuBois, Ellen. *Feminism and Suffrage: The Emergence of an Independent Women's Movement in America*. Ithaca, N.Y.: Cornell University, 1978.

DuBois, Ellen, et al. "Politics and Culture in Women's History: A Symposium." *Feminist Studies* 6 (1980): 26–64.

Dumas, David W. "The Naming of Children in New England, 1780–1850." *New England Historical and Genealogical Register* 132 (1978): 196–210.

Dunn, Richard S. "The Barbados Census of 1680: Profile of the Richest Colony in English America." *William and Mary Quarterly* 3d ser., 26 (1969): 3–30.

———. "The Social History of Early New England." *American Quarterly* 24 (1972): 661–79.

Dunn, Richard S., and Mary Maples Dunn, eds. *The World of William Penn*. Philadelphia: University of Pennsylvania Press, 1986.

Duvall, Evelyn M. *Family Development*. Philadelphia, Pa.: J. B. Lippincott, 1967.

Dye, Nancy Schrom, and Daniel Blake Smith. "Mother Love and Infant Death, 1750–1920." *Journal of American History* 73 (1986): 329–53.

Dyk, Walter. *Son of Old Man Hat: A Navajo Autobiography*. Lincoln: University of Nebraska Press, 1938.

Dyke, Bennett, and Warren T. Morrill, eds. *Genealogical Demography*. New York: Academic Press, 1980.

Earle, Alice Morse. *Child Life in Colonial Days*. New York: Macmillan Co., 1899.

———. *Home Life in Colonial Days*. New York: Macmillan Co., 1898.

Easterlin, Richard A. *The American Baby Boom in Historical Perspective*. New York: National Bureau of Economic Research, 1962.

———. "The American Baby Boom in Historical Perspective." Occasional Paper no. 79. Washington, D.C.: National Bureau of Economic Research, 1962.

———. Birth and the Fortune: The Impact of Numbers on Personal Welfare. New York: Basic Books, 1980.

———. "The Conflict between Aspirations and Resources." Population and Development Review 2 (September/December 1972): 417–26.

———. "Demographic Influences on Economic Stability: The United States Experience." Population and Development Review 4 (1978): 1–22.

———. "Here Comes Another Baby Boom." The Wharton Magazine (Summer 1979): 29–33.

———. Population, Labor Force, and Long Swings in Economic Growth. New York: National Bureau of Economic Research, 1968.

———. "What Will 1984 Be Like? Socioeconomic Implications of Recent Twists in the Age Structure." Demography 15 (1978): 397–432.

Edwards, Thomas J. "The Tenant System and Some Changes since Emancipation." Annals of the American Academy of Political and Social Science 49 (September 1913): 38–46.

Eekelaar, John M., and Sanford N. Katz, eds. Marriage and Cohabitation in Contemporary Societies: Areas of Legal, Social, and Ethical Change. Toronto: Buttersworths, 1979.

Eggan, Fred. "Historical Changes in the Choctaw Kinship System." American Anthropologist 39 (1937): 34–52.

———, ed. Social Anthropology of North American Tribes. Chicago: University of Chicago Press, 1937.

———. Social Organization of the Western Pueblos. Chicago: University of Chicago Press, 1950.

Ehrenreich, Barbara. Hearts of Men: American Dreams and the Flight from Commitment. Garden City, N.Y.: Doubleday and Co., 1983.

Ehrenreich, Barbara, and Deirdre English. For Her Own Good: 150 Years of the Experts' Advice to Women. New York: Doubleday, Anchor Books, 1978.

Elbert, Sarah. A Hunger for Home: Lousia May Alcott's Place in American Literature. New Brunswick, N.J.: Rutgers University Press, 1987.

Elder, Glen H., Jr. Children of the Great Depression: Social Change in Life Experience. Chicago: University of Chicago Press, 1974.

———. "History and the Family: The Discovery of Complexity." Journal of Marriage and the Family 43 (August 1981): 439–519.

———, ed. Life Course Dynamics: Trajectories and Transitions, 1968–1980. Ithaca, N.Y.: Cornell University Press, 1985.

———. "Military Times and Turning Points in Men's Lives." Developmental Psychology 22 (March 1986): 233–45.

———, ed. Transitions: The Family and the Life Course in Historical Perspective. New York: Academic Press, 1978.

———. "Families and Lives: Some Developments in Life-Course Studies." Journal of Family History 12 (1987): 179–199.

Elkind, David. The Hurried Child: Growing Up Too Soon. Reading, Mass.: Addison-Wesley, 1981.

Engram, Eleanor. Science, Myth, Reality: The Black Family in One-Half Century of Research. Westport, Conn.: Greenwood Press, 1982.

Epstein, Abraham. *The Negro Migrant in Pittsburgh.* 1918. Reprint. New York: Arno Press and the *New York Times,* 1969.

Epstein, Barbara. *The Politics of Domesticity: Women, Evangelism, and Temperance in Nineteenth-Century America.* Middletown, Conn.: Wesleyan University Press, 1981.

Erlich, Richard, ed. *Immigrants in Industrial America.* Chapel Hill: University of North Carolina Press, 1977.

Espenshade, Thomas, and William Serow, eds. *The Economic Consequences of Slowing Population Growth.* New York: Academic Press, 1978.

The Ethics Committee of the American Fertility Society. "Ethical Considerations of the New Reproductive Technologies." *Fertility and Sterility* 46, supplement 1 (1986): 1–94.

Etienne, Mona, and Eleanor Leacock, eds. *Women and Colonization: Anthropological Perspectives.* New York: Praeger, 1980.

Ewen, Elizabeth. *Immigrant Women in the Land of Dollars.* New York: Monthly Review Press, 1985.

Ewers, John C. "Contraceptive Charms among the Plains Indians." *Plains Anthropologist* 15 (August 1970): 216–18.

Fabio, Sarah Webster. "Blowing the Whistle on Some Jive." *The Black Scholar* 10 (May–June 1979): 56–58.

Faderman, Lillian. *Surpassing the Love of Men: Romantic Friendships and Love between Women from the Renaissance to the Present.* New York: William Morrow & Co., 1981.

Faragher, John. "Old Women and Old Men in Seventeenth-Century Wethersfield, Connecticut." *Women's Studies* 4 (1976): 110–31.

Farber, Bernard. *Guardians of Virtue: Salem Families in 1800.* New York: Basic Books, 1972.

Farley, Reynolds, and Albert I. Hermalin. "Family Stability: A Comparison of Trends between Blacks and Whites." *American Sociological Review* 36 (1971): 1–17.

Fass, Paula. *The Damned and the Beautiful: American Youth in the 1920's.* New York: Oxford University Press, 1977.

Federal Writers Project. *These Are Our Lives.* 2d ed. Chapel Hill: University of North Carolina Press, 1969.

Fellman, Anita Clair, and Michael Fellman. *Making Sense of Self: Medical Advice Literature in Late Nineteenth-Century America.* Philadelphia: University of Pennsylvania Press, 1981.

Fernandez-Marina, Ramon, Eduardo Maldonado-Sierra, and Richard Trent. "Three Basic Themes in Mexican and Puerto Rican Family Values." *Journal of Social Psychology* 48 (1958): 167–81.

Filene, Peter Gabriel. *Him/Her/Self: Sex Roles in Modern America.* 2d ed. Baltimore, Md.: Johns Hopkins University Press, 1986.

Finkelstein, Barbara, ed. *Regulated Children/Liberated Children: Education in Psychohistorical Perspective.* New York: Psychohistory Press, 1979.

Fischer, David Hackett. *Albion's Seed: Four British Folkways in America.* New York: Oxford University Press, 1989.

———. "Forenames and the Family in New England: An Exercise in Historical Onomastics." *Chronos* 1 (1981): 76–111.

Flaherty, David H. *Privacy in Colonial New England.* Charlottesville: University Press of Virginia, 1972.

Fleming, Sandford. *Children and Puritanism: The Place of Children in the Life and Thought of the New England Churches, 1620–1847.* New Haven, Conn.: Yale University Press, 1933.

Flynn, Charles L., Jr. *White Land, Black Labor: Caste and Class in Late Nineteenth-Century Georgia.* Baton Rouge: Louisiana State University Press, 1983.

Fowler, William M., Jr., and Wallace Cole, eds. *The American Revolution: Changing Perspectives.* Boston: Northeastern University Press, 1979.

Fox, Vivian C. "Is Adolescence a Phenomenon of Modern Times?" *Journal of Psychohistory* 5 (1977): 271–90.

Fox, Vivian C., and Martin H. Quitt, eds. *Loving, Parenting and Dying: The Family Cycle in England and America, Past and Present.* New York: Psychohistory Press, 1980.

Fox-Genovese, Elizabeth. *Within the Plantation Household: Black and White Women of the Old South.* Chapel Hill: University of North Carolina Press, 1988.

Frazier, E. Franklin. *The Negro Family in the United States.* Chicago: University of Chicago Press, 1939.

Freedman, Deborah. "Fertility, Aspirations, and Resources: A Symposium on the Easterlin Hypothesis." *Population and Development Review* 2 (1976): 411–15.

Freedman, Estelle. "The New Woman: Changing Views of Women in the 1920's." *Journal of American History* 61 (1974): 372–93.

———. "Sexuality in Nineteenth-Century America: Behavior, Ideology and Politics." *Reviews in American History* 10 (1982): 196–215.

Freedman, Ronald, Deborah Freedman, and Arland Thornton. "Changes in Fertility Expectations and Preferences between 1962 and 1977: Their Relation to Final Parity." *Demography* 17 (1980): 365–78.

Freeman, Jo. *The Politics of Women's Liberation.* New York: David McKay, 1975.

Friedan, Betty. *The Feminine Mystique.* New York: Dell Publishing Company, 1963.

Frost, Jerry W. "As the Twig Is Bent: Quaker Ideas of Childhood." *Quaker History* 60 (1971): 67–87.

———. *The Quaker Family in Colonial America: A Portrait of the Society of Friends.* New York: St. Martin's Press, 1973.

Fuchs, Victor R. *How We Live.* Cambridge, Mass.: Harvard University Press, 1983.

Furstenberg, Frank, et al. *Adolescent Mothers in Later Life.* New York: Cambridge University Press, 1987.

Furstenberg, Frank F., Jr., Theodore Hershberg, and John Modell. "The Origin of the Female-Headed Black Family: The Impact of the Black Experience." *Journal of Interdisciplinary History* 6 (Autumn 1975): 211–33.

Gabaccia, Donna. *From Sicily to Elizabeth Street.* Albany: State University of New York Press, 1984.

Gabin, Nancy. "Women Workers and the UAW in the Post–World War II Period: 1945–1954." *Labor History* 21 (1979–80): 5–30.

Galenson, David W. " 'Middling People' or 'Common Sort'?: The Social Origins of Some Early Americans Reexamined." *William and Mary Quarterly* 3d ser., 35 (1978): 499–524; with a rebuttal by Mildred Campbell, 525–40.

Gallman, James M. "Determinants of Age at Marriage in Colonial Perquimans County, North Carolina." *William and Mary Quarterly* 3d ser., 39 (1982): 176–91.

———. "Mortality among White Males: Colonial North Carolina." *Social Science History* 4 (1980): 295–316.

Gambino, Richard. *Blood of My Blood: The Dilemma of Italian Americans.* Garden City, N.Y.: Doubleday and Co., 1974.

Gans, Herbert J. *The Levittowners.* New York: Columbia University Press, 1967.

———. *Popular Culture and High Culture.* New York: Basic Books, 1974.

Gardner, James B., and George Rollie Adams, eds. *Ordinary People and Everyday Life: Perspectives in the New Social History.* Nashville, Tenn.: American Association for State and Local History, 1983.

Garrett, W. Walton. "Filial Responsibility Laws." *Journal of Family Law* 18 (1979–80): 804–8.

Gaylin, Willard, et al. eds. *Doing Good: The Limits of Benevolence.* New York: Random House, 1978.

Geddes, Gordon E. *Welcome Joy: Death in Puritan New England.* Ann Arbor, Mich.: UMI Research Press, 1981.

Gemery, Henry A. "Disarray in the Historical Record: Estimates of Immigration to the United States, 1700–1860." *Proceedings of the American Philosophical Society* 133 (1989): 123–27.

———. "Emigration from the British Isles to the New World, 1630–1700: Inferences from Colonial Populations." In *Research in Economic History: A Research Annual* 5, ed. Paul Uselding, 179–231. Greenwich, Conn.: JAI Press, 1980.

Genovese, Eugene. *Roll, Jordan, Roll: The World the Slaves Made.* New York: Pantheon Books, 1974.

Gerson, Judith M., and Kathy Peiss. "Boundaries, Negotiation, Consciousness: Reconceptualizing Gender Relations." *Social Problems* 32 (April 1985): 317–31.

Gerstel, Naomi, and Harriet Engle Gross, eds. *Families and Work: Towards Reconceptualization.* Philadelphia, Pa.: Temple University Press, 1987.

Giddings, Paula. *When and Where I Enter: The Impact of Black Women on Race and Sex in America.* New York: Bantam Books, 1984.

Gilman, Carolyn, and Mary Jane Schneider. *The Way to Independence: Memories of a Hidatsa Indian Family, 1840–1920.* St. Paul: Minnesota Historical Society Press, 1987.

Glass, D. V., and D. E. C. Eversley, eds. *Population in History: Essays in Historical Demography.* Chicago: Aldine Publishing Co., 1965.

Glendon, Mary Ann. *Abortion and Divorce in Western Law.* Cambridge, Mass.: Harvard University Press, 1987.

———. *The New Family and the New Property.* Toronto: Butterworths, 1981.

Goldin, Claudia. "Female Labor Force Participation: The Origin of Black and White Differences, 1870 and 1880." *Journal of Economic History* 37 (March 1977): 87–108.

Goldman, Eric F. "The Emerging Upper American." *American Demographics* 3 (1981): 20–23.

Goldman, Nancy, ed. *Female Soldiers: Combatants or Non-Combatants? Historical and Contemporary Perspectives.* Westport, Conn.: Greenwood Press, 1982.

Gordon, Linda. "Child Abuse, Gender, and the Myth of Family Independence." *Child Welfare* 64 (May–June 1985): 213–24.

———. *Heroes of Their Own Lives: The Politics and History of Family Violence, Boston, 1880–1960.* New York: The Viking Press, 1988.

———. *Woman's Body, Woman's Right: A Social History of Birth Control in America.* New York: Penguin Books, 1976.

Gordon, Michael, ed. *The American Family in Social-Historical Perspective.* 3d ed. New York: St. Martin's Press, 1983.

Gordon, Michael, and M. Charles Bernstein. "Mate Choice and Domestic Life in the Nineteenth-Century Marriage Manual." *Journal of Marriage and the Family* 32 (1970): 665–74.

"Go West Small Fry." *American Demographics* 4 (November 1982): 12.

Graebner, William. *A History of Retirement: The Meaning and Function of an American Institution, 1885–1978.* New Haven, Conn.: Yale University Press, 1980.

Greeley, Andrew, ed. *Ethnicity in the United States.* New York: John Wiley and Sons, 1974.

Green, Norma Kidd. *Iron Eye's Family: The Children of Joseph LaFlesche.* Lincoln, Nebr.: Johnsen Publishing Company, 1969.

Green, Rayna. *Native American Women: A Contextual Bibliography.* Bloomington: Indiana University Press, 1983.

———. "Review Essay: Native American Women." *Signs: Journal of Women in Culture and Society* 6 (Winter 1980): 248–67.

Greenberger, Ellen, and Laurence Steinberg. *When Teenagers Work: The Psychological and Social Costs of Adolescent Employment.* New York: Basic Books, 1986.

Greene, Jack P. "Autonomy and Stability: New England and the British Colonial Experience in Early Modern America." *Journal of Social History* 7 (1974): 171–94.

———. *Pursuits of Happiness: The Social Development of Early Modern British Colonies and the Formation of American Culture.* Chapel Hill: University of North Carolina Press, 1988.

Greene, Jack P., and J. R. Pole, eds. *Colonial British America: Essays in the New History of the Early Modern Era.* Baltimore, Md.: Johns Hopkins University Press, 1984.

Greenstein, Robert. "Prisoners of the Economy." *New York Times Book Review,* 25 October 1987, 46.

Greider, William. "The Unlucky Cohort." *American Demographics* 1 (1979): 2–3.

Greven, Philip J., Jr. "Family Structure in Seventeenth-Century Andover, Massachusetts." *William and Mary Quarterly* 3d ser., 23 (1966): 234–56.

———. *Four Generations: Population, Land, and Family in Colonial Andover, Massachusetts.* Ithaca, N.Y.: Cornell University Press, 1970.

———. "Historical Demography and Colonial America: A Review Article." *William and Mary Quarterly* 3d ser., 24 (1967): 438–54.

———. *The Protestant Temperament: Patterns of Child-Rearing, Religious Experience, and the Self in Early America.* New York: Alfred A. Knopf, 1977.

———. "Youth, Maturity, and Religious Conversion: A Note on the Ages of Converts in Andover, Massachusetts, 1711–1749." *Essex Institute Historical Collections* 108 (1972): 119–34.

Grier, George. *The Baby Bust.* Washington, D.C.: Center for Metropolitan Studies, 1971.

Grigg, Susan. "Women and Family Property: A Review of U.S. Inheritance Studies." *Historical Methods* 22 (1989): 116–22.

Griswold, Robert. *Family and Divorce in California, 1850–1890: Victorian Illusions and Everyday Realities.* Albany: State University of New York Press, 1982.

Grobstein, C., M. Flower, and J. Mendeloff. "Frozen Embryos: Policy Issues." *New England Journal of Medicine* 312 (1985): 1584–88.

Groneman, Carol. "The Bloody Ould Sixth Ward." Ph.D. diss., University of Rochester, 1973.

Groneman, Carol, and Mary Beth Norton, eds. *"To Toil the Livelong Day": America's Women at Work, 1780–1980.* Ithaca, N.Y.: Cornell University Press, 1987.

Gross, Robert A. *The Minutemen and Their World.* New York: Hill & Wang, 1976.

Grossberg, Michael. *Governing the Hearth: Law and Family in Nineteenth-Century America.* Chapel Hill: University of North Carolina Press, 1985.

Grubb, Farley. "Servant Auction Records and Immigration into the Delaware Valley, 1745–1831: The Proportion of Females among Immigrant Servants." *Proceedings of the American Philosophical Society* 133 (1989): 154–69.

Gundersen, Joan Rezner. "The Double Bonds of Race and Sex: Black and White Women in a Colonial Virginia Parish." *Journal of Southern History* 52 (1986): 351–72.

Gutman, Herbert G. *The Black Family in Slavery and Freedom, 1750–1925.* New York: Random House, 1976.

Gwaltney, John L. *Drylongso: A Self-Portrait of Black America.* New York: Random House, 1980.

Haber, Carole. *Beyond Sixty-Five: The Dilemma of Old Age in America's Past.* Cambridge and New York: Cambridge University Press, 1983.

Hagan, William T. *Indian Police and Judges: Experiments in Acculturation and Control.* New Haven, Conn.: Yale University Press, 1966.

Hagood, Margaret Jarman. *Mothers of the South: Portraiture of the White Tenant Farm Woman.* Chapel Hill: University of North Carolina Press, 1939. Reprint. New York: W. W. Norton & Company, 1977.

Hale, Nathan. *Freud and the Americans: The Beginnings of Psychoanalysis in the United States, 1876–1917.* New York: Oxford University Press, 1971.

Halem, Lynne Carol. *Divorce Reform: Changing Legal and Social Perspectives.* New York: The Free Press, 1980.

Hall, Jacquelyn Dowd. "Partial Truths." *Signs: Journal of Women in Culture and Society* 14 (1989): 902–11.

Haller, John S., Jr., and Robin M. Haller. *The Physician and Sexuality in Victorian America.* Urbana: University of Illinois Press, 1974.

Handler, Jerome S., and Robert S. Corruccini. "Weaning among West Indian

Slaves: Historical and Bioanthropological Evidence from Barbados." *William and Mary Quarterly* 3d ser., 43 (1986): 111–17.

Handlin, Oscar. *Boston's Immigrants, 1790–1865.* Cambridge, Mass.: Harvard University Press, 1941.

———, ed. *Children of the Uprooted.* New York: Grosset & Dunlap, 1968.

Handlin, Oscar, and Mary F. Handlin. *Facing Life: Youth in the Family in American History.* Boston: Little, Brown and Company, 1971.

Hardin, Garrett, ed. *Population, Evolution and Birth Control.* San Francisco: W. H. Freeman Co., 1969.

Hare, Nathan. "What Black Intellectuals Misunderstand about the Black Family." *Black World* 25 (March 1976): 4–14.

Hareven, Tamara K. *Anonymous Americans: Explorations in Nineteenth-Century Social History.* Englewood Cliffs, N.J.: Prentice-Hall, 1971.

———, ed. *Family and Kin in Urban Communities, 1700–1930.* New York: New Viewpoints, 1977.

———. "The Family Process: The Historical Study of the Family Cycle." *Journal of Social History* 7 (Spring 1974): 322–29.

———. *Family Time and Industrial Time: The Relationship between the Family and Work in a New England Industrial Community.* Cambridge: Cambridge University Press, 1982.

———. "Origins of the 'Modern Family' in the United States." *Journal of Social History* 17 (1983): 338–44.

———, ed. *Transitions: The Family and the Life Course in Historical Perspective.* New York: Academic Press, 1978.

Hareven, Tamara K., and K. J. Adams, eds. *Aging and Life Course Transitions: An Interdisciplinary Perspective.* New York: Guilford Press, 1982.

Harley, Sharon, and Rosalyn Terborg-Penn, eds. *The Afro-American Woman: Struggles and Images.* Port Washington, N.Y.: Kennikat Press, 1978.

Harrington, Michael. *The Other America: Poverty in the United States.* New York: Macmillan Co., 1963.

Harris, P.M.G. "The Demographic Development of Colonial Philadelphia in Some Comparative Perspective." *Proceedings of the American Philosophical Society* 133 (1989): 262–304.

Hart, Jeffrey. *When the Going Was Good! American Life in the Fifties.* New York: Crown, 1982.

Hartman, Mary S., and Lois Banner, eds. *Clio's Consciousness Raised: New Perspectives on the History of Women.* New York: Harper and Row, Harper Colophon Books, 1974.

Hartmann, Susan. *The Home Front and Beyond: American Women in the 1940's.* Boston: Twayne, 1982.

Hasting, Robert J. *A Nickel's Worth of Skim Milk, A Boy's View of the Great Depression.* Carbondale: Southern Illinois University Press, 1972.

Hauser, Philip. "A New Tidal Wave of Births." *New York Times*, 25 February 1971.

Hawes, Joseph. *Children in Urban Society: Juvenile Delinquency in Nineteenth-Century America.* New York: Oxford University Press, 1971.

Hawes, Joseph M., and N. Ray Hiner, eds. *American Childhood: A Research Guide and Historical Handbook.* Westport, Conn.: Greenwood Press, 1985.

Hayden, Dolores. *The Grand Domestic Revolution: A History of Feminist Designs for American Homes, Neighborhoods, and Cities.* Cambridge, Mass.: MIT Press, 1981.

Hecht, Irene W. D. "The Virginia Muster of 1624/5 as a Source for Demographic History." *William and Mary Quarterly* 3d ser., 30 (1973): 65–92.

Heiss, J. "On the Transmission of Marital Instability in Black Families." *American Sociological Review* 37 (1972): 82–92.

Helm, June. "Female Infanticide, European Diseases, and Population Levels among the Mackenzie Dene." *American Ethnologist* 7 (May 1980): 259–85.

Helmbold, Lois Rita. "Beyond the Family Economy: Black and White Working-Class Women during the Great Depression." *Feminist Studies* 13 (1987): 629–55.

Henderson, Rodger C. "Demographic Patterns and Family Structure in Eighteenth-Century Lancaster County, Pennsylvania." *Pennsylvania Magazine of History and Biography* 114 (1990): 349–83.

———. "Matters of Life and Death: A Demographic Analysis of 18th-Century Lancaster Reformed Church Records." *Journal of the Lancaster County Historical Society* 91 (1987/88): 43–77.

Henretta, James A. "Families and Farms: *Mentalité* in Pre-Industrial America." *William and Mary Quarterly* 3d ser., 35 (1978): 3–32.

———. "The Morphology of New England Society in the Colonial Period." *Journal of Interdisciplinary History* 2 (1971): 379–98.

Henslin, James, ed. *Studies in the Sociology of Sex.* New York: Appleton-Century Crofts, 1971.

Hersh, Blanche Glassman. *The Slavery of Sex: Feminist-Abolitionists in America.* Urbana: University of Illinois Press, 1978.

Hershberg, Theodore, ed. *Philadelphia: Work, Space, Family, and Group Experience in the Nineteenth Century: Essays toward an Interdisciplinary History.* New York: Oxford University Press, 1981.

Hetherington, Mavis. "Effects of Father Absence on Personality Development in Adolescent Daughters." *Developmental Psychology* 7 (1972): 313–26.

Hewitt, Nancy. *Women's Activism and Social Change: Rochester, New York, 1822–1872.* Ithaca, N.Y.: Cornell University Press, 1984.

Higgs, Robert, and H. Louis Stettler III. "Colonial New England Demography: A Sampling Approach." *William and Mary Quarterly* 3d ser., 27 (1970): 282–94.

Hill, Edward E. *Guide to Records in the National Archives of the United States Relating to American Indians.* Washington, D.C.: General Services Administration, 1981.

Hill, Reuben. "Methodological Issues in Family Development Research." *Family Process* 3 (March 1964): 186–206.

Hill, Robert B. *Strengths of Black Families.* New York: Emerson Hall, 1971.

Hiner, N. Ray. "Adolescence in Eighteenth-Century America." *History of Childhood Quarterly* 3 (1975): 253–80.

———. "The Child in American Historiography: Accomplishments and Prospect." *Psychohistory Review* 7 (1978): 13–23.

———. "Cotton Mather and His Female Children: Notes on the Relationship between Private Experience and Public Thought." *Journal of Psychohistory* 13 (1985): 33–49.

——. "The Cry of Sodom Enquired into: Educational Analysis in Seventeenth-Century New England." *History of Education Quarterly* 13 (1973): 3–22.

——. "Wars and Rumors of Wars: The Historiography of Colonial Education as a Case Study in Academic Imperialism." *Societas* 8 (1978): 89–114.

Hiner, N. Ray, and Joseph M. Hawes, eds. *Growing Up in America: Children in Historical Perspective.* Urbana: University of Illinois Press, 1985.

Hodgson, Godfrey. *America in Our Time.* Garden City, N.Y.: Doubleday and Co., 1976.

Hoffer, Peter C., and N.E.H. Hull. *Murdering Mothers: Infanticide in England and New England, 1558–1803.* New York: New York University Press, 1981.

Hoffert, Sylvia. *Private Matters: American Attitudes toward Childbearing and Infant Nurture in the Urban North, 1800–1860.* Urbana: University of Illinois Press, 1989.

Hoffman, Marks S., ed. *The World Almanac and Book of Facts, 1989.* New York: World Almanac, 1988.

Hoffman, Ronald, and Peter J. Albert, eds. *Women in the Age of the American Revolution.* Charlottesville: University Press of Virginia, 1989.

Hogg, Margaret H. *The Incidence of Work Shortage: Report of a Survey by Sample of Families Made in New Haven, Connecticut, in May–June, 1931.* New York: Russell Sage Foundation, 1932.

Homan, Walter Joseph. *Children & Quakerism: A Study of the Place of Children in the Theory and Practice of the Society of Friends, Commonly Called Quakers.* Berkeley, Calif.: Gillick Press, 1939. Reprint. New York: Arno Press, 1972.

Horton, James Oliver. "Freedom's Yoke: Gender Conventions among Antebellum Free Blacks." *Feminist Studies* 12 (1986): 51–76.

Howard, George Elliott. *A History of Matrimonial Institutions Chiefly in England and the United States with an Introductory Analysis of the Literature and the Theories of Primitive Marriage and the Family.* 3 vols. Chicago: University of Chicago Press, 1904. Reprint. New York: Humanities Press, 1964.

Howe, Irving. *World of Our Fathers.* New York: Harcourt Brace Jovanovich, 1976.

Hoxie, Frederick E. *A Final Promise: The Campaign to Assimilate the Indians, 1880–1920.* Lincoln: University of Nebraska Press. 1984.

Hrdlicka, Ales. "Physiological and Medical Observations among the Indians of the Southwestern United States and Northern Mexico." *Bureau of American Ethnology Bulletin* no. 34. Washington, D.C.: Smithsonian Institution, 1908.

Hudson, Charles. *The Southeastern Indians.* Knoxville: University of Tennessee Press, 1976.

Humphries, Jane. "Women, Scapegoats and Safety Valves in the Great Depression." *Review of Radical Economics* 8 (Spring 1976): 98–121.

Hunt, Morton M. *Sexual Behavior in the 1970s.* Chicago: Playboy Press, 1974.

Hurtado, Albert L. " 'Hardly a Farm House—A Kitchen without Them': Indian and White Households on the California Borderland Frontier in 1860." *Western Historical Quarterly* 13 (July 1982): 245–70.

——. *Indian Survival on the California Frontier.* New Haven, Conn.: Yale University Press, 1988.

Innes, Stephen. *Labor in a New Land: Economy and Society in Seventeenth-Century Springfield*. Princeton, N.J.: Princeton University Press, 1983.

———, ed. *Work and Labor in Early America*. Chapel Hill: University of North Carolina Press, 1988.

Isaac, Rhys. "Order and Growth, Authority and Meaning in Colonial New England." *American Historical Review* 76 (1971): 728–37.

Jackson, Kenneth. *Crabgrass Frontier: The Suburbanization of the United States*. New York: Oxford University Press, 1984.

Jacobs, Rita P. "Making Sense of the Recent Past." *American Quarterly* 36 (1984): 581–86.

Jacoby, Russell. *Social Amnesia: A Critique of Conformist Psychology from Adler to Laing*. Boston: Beacon Press, 1975.

Janiewski, Dolores. *Sisterhood Denied: Race, Gender, and Class in a New South Community*. Philadelphia, Pa.: Temple University Press, 1985.

Jedrey, Christopher M. *The World of John Cleaveland: Family and Community in Eighteenth-Century New England*. New York: W. W. Norton & Company, 1979.

Jeffrey, Kirk. "The Family as Utopian Retreat from the City." *Soundings* 55 (1972): 21–41.

———. "Marriage, Career, and Feminine Ideology in Nineteenth-Century America: Reconstructing the Marital Experience of Lydia Maria Child, 1828–1874." *Feminist Studies* 7 (1981): 113–30.

Jensen, Joan M. *Loosening the Bonds: Mid-Atlantic Farm Women, 1750–1850*. New Haven, Conn.: Yale University Press, 1986.

Johansson, S. Ryan. "The Demographic History of the Native Peoples of North America: A Selective Bibliography." *Yearbook of Physical Anthropology* 25 (1982): 133–52.

Johansson, S. Ryan, and S. H. Preston. "Tribal Demography: The Hopi and Navaho Populations as Seen through Manuscripts from the 1900 U.S. Census." *Social Science History* 3 (Fall 1978): 1–33.

Johnson, Charles S. *Shadow of the Plantation*. Chicago: University of Chicago Press, 1934. Reprinted, 1969, 1976.

Johnson, Paul E. "The Modernization of Mayo Greenleaf Patch: Land, Family, and Marginality in New England, 1766–1818." *New England Quarterly* 55 (1982): 488–516.

Johnston, Denis Foster. "The Aging of the Baby Boom Cohorts." *Statistical Reporter* 76 (1976): 161–65.

———. "Population and Labor Force Projections." *Monthly Labor Review* 96 (1973): 8–17.

Jones, Jacqueline. *Labor of Love, Labor of Sorrow: Black Women, Work, and the Family from Slavery to the Present*. New York: Random House, 1985.

Jones, Kathleen W. "Sentiment and Science: The Late Nineteenth Century Pediatrician as Mother's Advisor." *Journal of Social History* 17 (1983): 79–96.

Jones, Landon Y. "The Emerging Superclass." *American Demographics* 3 (1981): 30–35.

———. *Great Expectations: America and the Baby Boom Generation*. New York: Ballantine Books, 1980.

———. "My Son, The Doctor of Cab Driving." *American Demographics* 2 (1980): 20.

Jorgensen, Joseph G. "Indians and the Metropolis." In *The American Indian in Urban Society*, ed. Jack O. Waddell and O. Michael Watson, 67–113. Boston: Little, Brown and Company, 1971.

———. *The Sun Dance Religion: Power for the Powerless*. Chicago: University of Chicago Press, 1972.

Joseph, Gloria I., and Jill Lewis. *Common Differences: Conflicts in Black and White Feminist Perspectives*. Boston: South End Press, 1981.

Kahn, Coppelia. "Excavating 'Those Dim Minoan Regions': Maternal Subtexts in Patriarchal Literature." *Diacritics* 12 (Summer 1982): 32–41.

Kaledin, Eugenia. *Mothers and More: American Women in the 1950's*. Boston: Twayne, 1984.

Kalter, Joanmarie. "Television as Value Setter: Family," *TV Guide*, 23–29 July 1988, 5–15.

Kammen, Michael. "Changing Perceptions of the Life Cycle in American Thought and Culture." *Proceedings of the Massachusetts Historical Society* 91 (1979): 35–66.

Kantrow, Louise. "Life Expectancy of the Gentry in Eighteenth and Nineteenth-Century Philadelphia." *Proceedings of the American Philosophical Society* 133 (1989): 312–27.

Karenga, Maulanga. "Social Ethics and the Black Family: An Alternative Analysis." *The Black Scholar* 17 (September/October 1986): 41–54.

Karlsen, Carol F. *The Devil in the Shape of a Woman: Witchcraft in Colonial New England*. New York: W. W. Norton & Company, 1987.

Karp, Abraham. *Golden Door to America*. New York: The Viking Press, 1976.

Katz, Esther, and Anita Rapone, eds. *Women's Experience in America: An Historical Anthology*. New Brunswick, N.J.: Transaction Books, 1980.

Katz, Michael B. *In the Shadow of the Poorhouse: A Social History of Welfare in America*. New York: Basic Books, 1986.

Katz, Michael B., Michael J. Doucet, and Mark J. Stern. *The Social Organization of Early Industrial Capitalism*. Cambridge, Mass.: Harvard University Press, 1982.

Katz, Stanley N., ed. *Colonial America: Essays in Politics and Social Development*. Boston: Little, Brown and Company, 1971.

Kealey, Linda, ed. *A Not Unreasonable Claim: Women and Reform in Canada, 1880–1920*. Toronto: The Woman's Press, 1979.

Kelley, Mary. *Private Women, Public Stage: Literary Domesticity in Nineteenth-Century America*. New York: Oxford University Press, 1984.

———, ed. *Women's Being, Women's Place: Female Identity and Vocation in American History*. Boston: G. K. Hall & Co., 1979.

Kelly, R. Gordon. *Mother Was a Lady: Self and Society in Selected American Children's Periodicals, 1865–1890*. Westport, Conn.: Greenwood Press, 1974.

Kelly, William R., and Phillips Cutright. "Economic and Other Determinants of Annual Change in U.S. Fertility: 1917–1976." *Social Science Research* 13 (1984): 250–67.

Keniston, Kenneth. *The Uncommitted: Alienated Youth in American Society*. New York: Harcourt, Brace & World, 1965.

Keniston, Kenneth, and the Carnegie Council on Children. *All Our Children: The American Family under Pressure.* New York: Harcourt Brace Jovanovich, 1977.

Kennedy, Susan Estabrook. *If All We Did Was to Weep at Home: A History of White Working-Class Women in America.* Bloomington: Indiana University Press, 1979.

Kerber, Linda. "The Republican Mother: Women and the Enlightenment, An American Perspective." *American Quarterly* 28 (1976): 187–205.

———. "Separate Spheres, Female Worlds, Woman's Place." *Journal of American History* 75 (1988): 9–39.

———. *Women of the Republic: Intellect and Ideology in Revolutionary America.* Chapel Hill: University of North Carolina Press, 1980.

Kerber, Linda K., et al. "Beyond Roles, Beyond Spheres: Thinking About Gender in the Early Republic." *William and Mary Quarterly* 3d ser., 46 (1989): 565–85.

Kerber, Linda K., and Jane De Hart Mathews, eds. *Women's America: Refocusing the Past.* New York: Oxford University Press, 1982.

Kern, Louis. *An Ordered Love: Sex Roles and Sexuality in Victorian America.* Chapel Hill: University of North Carolina Press, 1977.

Kessler-Harris, Alice. *Out to Work: A History of Wage-Earning Women in the United States.* New York: Oxford University Press, 1982.

Kessner, Thomas, and Betty Caroli. "New Immigrant Woman at Work: Italians and Jews in New York City, 1880–1905." *Journal of Ethnic History* 5 (Winter 1978): 19–32.

Kett, Joseph F. *Rites of Passage: Adolescence in America, 1790 to the Present.* New York: Basic Books, 1977.

Keyfitz, Nathan. "The Baby Boom Meets the Computer Revolution." *American Demographics* 6 (1984): 22.

Keyssar, Alexander. "Widowhood in Eighteenth-Century Massachusetts: A Problem in the History of the Family." *Perspectives in American History* 8 (1974): 83–119.

Kiefer, Monica. *American Children through Their Books, 1700–1835.* Philadelphia: University of Pennsylvania Press, 1948.

Kierner, Cynthia A. "Family Values, Family Business: Work and Kinship in Colonial New York." *Mid-America* 71 (1989): 55–64.

Kiser, Clyde Vernon. *Sea Island to City: A Study of St. Helena Islanders in Harlem and Other Urban Centers.* New York: AMS Press, 1967.

Kiser, Clyde, et al. *Trends and Variations in Fertility in the United States.* Cambridge, Mass.: Harvard University Press, 1968.

Klarman, Herbert E., ed. *Empirical Studies in Health Economics: Proceedings of the Second Conference on the Economics of Health.* Baltimore, Md.: Johns Hopkins University Press, 1970.

Klein, Randolph Shipley. *Portrait of an Early American Family: The Shippens of Pennsylvania Across Five Generations.* Philadelphia: University of Pennsylvania Press, 1975.

Klepp, Susan E. "Demography in Early Philadelphia, 1690–1860." *Proceedings of the American Philosophical Society* 133 (1989): 85–111.

———. "Fragmented Knowledge: Questions in Regional Demographic History."

Proceedings of the American Philosophical Society 133 (1989): 223–33.

Kluckhohn, Clyde, and Dorothea Leighton. *The Navaho.* Rev. ed. Cambridge, Mass.: Harvard University Press, 1974.

Knack, Martha C. *Life Is with People: Household Organization of the Contemporary Southern Paiute Indians.* Socorro, N. Mex.: Ballena Press, 1980.

Koehler, Lyle. *A Search for Power: The "Weaker Sex" in Seventeenth-Century New England.* Urbana: University of Illinois Press, 1980.

Kolchin, Peter. *First Freedom: The Response of Alabama's Blacks to Emancipation and Reconstruction.* Westport, Conn.: Greenwood Press, 1972.

Komarovsky, Mirra. *The Unemployed Man and His Family: The Effects of Unemployment upon the Status of the Man in Fifty-Nine Families.* New York: Dryden Press, 1940.

Kramer, Rita. *In Defense of the Family: Raising Children in America Today.* New York: Basic Books, 1983.

Krause, Corinne. "Urbanization without Breakdown: Italian, Jewish and Slavic Women in Pittsburgh, 1908–1945." *Journal of Urban History* 4 (May 1978): 291–306.

Kreps, Juanita, ed. *Women and the American Economy.* Englewood Cliffs, N.J.: Prentice-Hall, 1976.

Kuhn, Anne. *The Mother's Role in Childhood Education: New England Concepts, 1830–1860.* New Haven, Conn.: Yale University Press, 1947.

Kulikoff, Allan. *Tobacco and Slaves: The Development of Southern Cultures in the Chesapeake, 1680–1800.* Chapel Hill: University of North Carolina Press, 1986.

Kunitz, Stephen J. *Disease Change and the Role of Medicine: The Navajo Experience.* Berkeley: University of California Press, 1983.

Lacey, Barbara E. "The World of Hannah Heaton: The Autobiography of an Eighteenth-Century Connecticut Farm Woman." *William and Mary Quarterly* 3d ser., 45 (1988): 280–304.

Ladd-Taylor, Molly. *Raising a Baby the Government Way: Mothers' Letters to the Children's Bureau, 1915–1932.* New Brunswick, N.J.: Rutgers University Press, 1986.

Ladner, Joyce. *Tomorrow's Tomorrow: The Black Woman.* Garden City, N.Y.: Doubleday and Co., 1971.

Land, Aubrey C., Lois Green Carr, and Edward C. Papenfuse, eds. *Law, Society, and Politics in Early Maryland: Proceedings of the First Conference on Maryland History, June 14–15, 1974.* Baltimore, Md.: Johns Hopkins University Press, 1977.

Landes, Ruth. *The Ojibwa Woman.* New York: Columbia University Press, 1938.

Landry, Bart, and Margaret Platt Jendrek. "The Employment of Wives in Middle-Class Black Families." *Journal of Marriage and the Family* 40 (November 1978): 787–97.

Landsman, Ned C. "Ethnicity and National Origin among British Settlers in the Philadelphia Region: Pennsylvania Immigration in the Wake of *Voyagers to the West.*" *Proceedings of the American Philosophical Society* 133 (1989): 170–74.

Lantz, Herman R., et al. "Pre-Industrial Patterns in the Colonial Family in America: A Content Analysis of Colonial Magazines." *American Sociological Re-*

view 33 (1968): 413–26.

Lasch, Christopher. *Haven in a Heartless World: The Family Besieged.* New York: Basic Books, 1977.

———. *The Minimal Self: Psychic Survival in Troubled Times.* New York: W. W. Norton & Company, 1984.

Laslett, Peter. *The World We Have Lost: England Before the Industrial Age.* New York: Charles Scribner & Sons, 1965.

Laslett, Peter and Richard Wall, ed. *Household and Family in Past Time.* Cambridge: Cambridge University Press, 1972.

Leacock, Eleanor B. "The Montagnais 'Hunting Territory' and the Fur Trade." *Memoir* 78. American Anthropological Association, 1954.

Leasure, J. William. "United States Demographic and Family History." *Historical Methods* 16 (1983): 163–68.

Leavitt, Judith Walzer. *Brought to Bed: Childbearing in America, 1750–1950.* New York: Oxford University Press, 1986.

———. " 'Science' Enters the Birthing Room: Obstetrics in America since the Eighteenth Century." *Journal of American History* 70 (1983): 281–304.

Lebsock, Suzanne. *The Free Women of Petersburg: Status and Culture in a Southern Town, 1784–1860.* New York: W. W. Norton & Company, 1984.

Lee, R. D. "Aiming at a Moving Target: Period Fertility and Changing Reproductive Goals." *Population Studies* 34 (1980): 205–26.

Leeds, Anthony, and Andrew P. Vayda, eds. *Man. Culture, and Animals: The Role of Animals in Human Ecological Adjustments.* Washington, D.C.: American Association for the Advancement of Science, 1965.

LeMasters, E. E. *Blue-Collar Aristocrats: Life-Styles at a Working-Class Tavern.* Madison: University of Wisconsin Press, 1975.

Lemay, J. A. Leo, ed. *Robert Bolling Woos Anne Miller: Love and Courtship in Colonial Virginia, 1760.* Charlottesville: University Press of Virginia, 1990.

Lerner, Gerda. "The Lady and the Mill Girl: Changes in the Status of Women in the Age of Jackson, 1800–1840. *Midcontinent American Studies Journal* 10 (1969): 5–14.

———. 'Placing Women in History: Definitions and Challenges." *Feminist Studies* 3 (1975): 5–14.

LeShan, Eda. *The Conspiracy against Childhood.* New York: Atheneum, 1967.

Levinger, George, et al., eds. *Divorce and Separation: Conditions, Causes, and Consequences.* New York: Basic Books, 1979.

Levitan, Sar A., and Richard S. Belous. *What's Happening to the American Family?* Baltimore, Md.: Johns Hopkins University Press, 1981.

Levitan, Sar A., and Clifford M. Johnson. *Beyond the Safety Net: Reviving the Promise of Opportunity in America.* Cambridge, Mass.: Ballinger, 1984.

Levitan, Sar A., William B. Johnston, and Robert Taggart. *Minorities in the United States: Problems, Progress, and Prospects.* Washington, D.C.: Public Affairs Press, 1975.

Levy, Barry. *Quakers and the American Family: British Settlement in the Delaware Valley.* New York: Oxford University Press, 1988.

———. " 'Tender Plants': Quaker Farmers and Children in the Delaware Valley, 1681–1735." *Journal of Family History* 3 (1978): 116–35.

Lewis, Hylan. *Blackways of Kent.* Chapel Hill: University of North Carolina Press,

1955.

Lewis, Jan. "Domestic Tranquillity and the Management of Emotions among the Gentry of Pre-Revolutionary Virginia." *William and Mary Quarterly* 3d ser., 39 (1982): 135–49.

———. *The Pursuit of Happiness: Family and Values in Jefferson's Virginia.* Cambridge: Cambridge University Press, 1983.

———. "The Republican Wife: Virtue and Seduction in the Early Republic." *William and Mary Quarterly* 3d ser., 44 (1987): 689–721.

Lewis, Jan, and Kenneth A. Lockridge. " 'Sally Has Been Sick': Pregnancy and Family Limitation among Virginia Gentry Women, 1780–1830." *Journal of Social History* 22 (1988): 5–19.

Lewis, Jerry M., and John G. Looney. *The Long Struggle: Well-Functioning Working-Class Black Families.* New York: Brunner/Mazel, Publishers, 1983.

Liberty, Margot, David V. Hughey, and Richard Scaglion. "Rural and Urban Omaha Indian Fertility." *Human Biology* 48 (February 1976): 59–71.

Liberty, Margot, Richard Scaglion, and David V. Hughey. "Rural and Urban Seminole Fertility." *Human Biology* 48 (December 1976): 741–55.

Liebow, Elliott. *Tally's Corner: A Study of Negro Streetcorner Men.* Boston: Little, Brown and Company, 1967.

Linderman, Frank. *Pretty Shield: A Crow Medicine Woman.* New York: Holt, Rinehart, and Winston, 1932.

Lingeman, Richard R. *Don't You Know There's a War On? The American Home Front, 1941–1945.* New York: G. P. Putnam's Sons, 1970.

Litwack, Leon F. *Been in the Storm So Long: The Aftermath of Slavery.* New York: Alfred A. Knopf, 1979.

Lockridge, Kenneth A. *The Diary and Life of William Byrd II of Virginia, 1674–1744.* Chapel Hill: University of North Carolina Press, 1987.

———. *A New England Town: The First Hundred Years, Dedham, Massachusetts, 1636–1736.* New York: W. W. Norton & Company, 1970.

———. "The Population of Dedham, Massachusetts, 1636–1736." *Economic History Review* 2d ser., 19 (1966): 318–44.

Logue, Barbara J. "The Whaling Industry and Fertility Decline: Nantucket, Massachusetts, 1660–1850." *Social Science History* 7 (1983): 427–56.

Lopreato, Joseph. *Italian Americans.* New York: Random House, 1970.

Lorde, Audre. *Sister/Outsider: Essays and Speeches.* Trumansburg, N.Y.: The Crossing Press, 1984.

Lowitt, Richard, and Maurine Beasley, eds. *One Third of a Nation: Lorena Hickok Reports on the Great Depression.* Chicago: University of Illinois Press, 1983.

Luker, Kristin. *Abortion and the Politics of Motherhood.* Berkeley: University of California Press, 1984.

Lunberg, Ferdinand, and Marynia Farnham. *Modern Woman: The Lost Sex.* New York: Harper and Brothers, 1947.

Lurie, Nancy Oestreich. *Mountain Wolf Woman, Sister of Crashing Thunder, The Autobiography of a Winnebago Indian.* Ann Arbor: University of Michigan Press, 1961.

Lynd, Robert S. "Family Members as Consumers." *Annals of the American Academy of Political and Social Sciences* (1932): 86–93.

Lynd, Robert S., and Helen Merrell Lynd. *Middletown: A Study in Modern American*

Culture. New York: Harcourt, Brace & World, 1929.

———. *Middletown in Transition: A Study in Cultural Conflicts*. New York: Harcourt, Brace & World, 1937.

Lystra, Karen. *Searching the Heart: Women, Men, and Romantic Love in Nineteenth-Century America*. New York: Oxford University Press, 1989.

McAdoo, Harriette Pipes, ed. *Black Families*. Beverly Hills, Calif.: Sage Publications, 1981.

———, ed. *Black Families*. 2d ed. Newbury Park, Calif.: Sage Publications, 1988.

———. "Factors Related to Stability in Upwardly Mobile Black Families." *Journal of Marriage and the Family* 40 (November 1978): 761–76.

McCarthy, James. "A Comparison of the Probability of the Dissolution of First and Second Marriages." *Demography* 15 (1978): 345–59.

Maccoby, Eleanor, Theodore Newcomer, and Eugene Hartley, eds. *Readings in Social Psychology*. New York: Holt, Rinehart, and Winston, 1958.

McCracken, Grant. "The Exchange of Children in Tudor England: An Anthropological Phenomenon in History Context." *Journal of Family History* 8 (1983): 303–13.

McCue, Julia. "Baby Boom's New Echo." *Editorial Research Reports* 26 (1981): 471–88.

McDannell, Colleen. *The Christian Home in Victorian America, 1840–1900*. Bloomington: Indiana University Press, 1986.

MacDonald, Maurice, and Ronald Rindfuss. "Earnings, Relative Income, and Family Formation." *Demography* 18 (1981): 123–36.

McElvaine, Robert S. *Down and Out in the Great Depression: Letters from the 'Forgotten Man'*. Chapel Hill: University of North Carolina Press, 1983.

Macfarlane, Alan. *The Family Life of Ralph Josselin, a Seventeenth-Century Clergyman: An Essay in Historical Anthropology*. Cambridge: Cambridge University Press, 1970.

McGovern, James R. "The American Woman's Pre-World-War Manners and Morals." *Journal of American History* 55 (1968): 315–33.

———. "David Graham Phillips and the Virility Impulse of Progressives." *New England Quarterly* 34 (1966): 333–48.

Mack, Raymond W. *Transforming America: Patterns of Social Change*. New York: Random House 1967.

Macklin, Eleanor D. "Nonmarital Heterosexual Cohabitation." *Marriage and Family Review* 1 (1978): 1–12.

MacLeod, Anne. *A Moral Tale: Children's Fiction and American Culture, 1820–1860*. Hartford, Conn.: Anchor Books, 1975.

MacLeod, William Christie. "The Family Hunting Territory and Lenape Political Organization." *American Anthropologist* 24 (1922): 448–63.

Mahler, Margaret S., Fred Pine, and Anni Bergman. The *Psychological Birth of the Human Infant: Symbiosis and Individuation*. New York: Basic Books, 1975.

McLoughlin, William G., and Walter H. Conser, Jr. "The Cherokees in Transition: A Statistical Analysis of the Federal Cherokee Census of 1835." *Journal of American History* 64 (December 1977): 679–703.

McNall, Sally Allen. *Who Is in the House: A Psychological Study of Two Centuries of Women's Fiction in America, 1795 to the Present*. New York: Elsevier, 1981.

Manchester, William. *Glory and the Dream: A Narrative History of America, 1932–*

1972. Boston: Little, Brown and Company, 1974.

Mandle, Jay R. *The Roots of Black Poverty: The Southern Plantation Economy after the Civil War*. Durham, N.C.: Duke University Press, 1978.

Mangione, Jerre. *Mount Allegro: A Memoir of Italian American Life*. New York: Columbia University Press, 1981.

Mann, Susan A. "Slavery, Sharecropping, and Sexual Inequality." *Signs: A Journal of Women in Culture and Society* 14 (Summer 1989): 774–98.

Marcy, Peter T. "Factors Affecting the Fecundity and Fertility of Historical Populations." *Journal of Family History* 6 (1981): 309–26.

Marsh, Margaret. *Suburban Lives*. New Brunswick, N.J.: Rutgers University Press, 1990.

Marshall, Victor W., ed. *Later Life: The Social Psychology of Aging*. Beverly Hills, Calif.: Sage Publications, 1986.

Masnick, George S., and Joseph A. McMalls, Jr. "Those Perplexing U.S. Fertility Swings: A New Perspective on a 20th Century Puzzle." *PRB Report* (1978): 1–10.

Mason, Karen Oppenheimer, John L. Czajka, and Sara Arber. "Change in U.S. Women's Sex-Role Attitudes, 1964–1974." *American Sociological Review* 41 (1976): 573–96.

Masters, Ardyce. "Stumbling into the History of Childhood." *Journal of Psychohistory* 16 (1988): 173–75.

Matthews, Glenna. *"Just a Housewife":The Rise and Fall of Domesticity in America*. New York: Oxford University Press, 1987.

May, Elaine Tyler. *Great Expectations: Marriage and Divorce in Post-Victorian America*. Chicago: University of Chicago Press, 1980.

————. *Homeward Bound: American Families in the Cold War*. New York: Basic Books, 1988.

Mechling, Jay. "Advice to Historians on Advice to Mothers." *Journal of Social History* 9 (1975): 44–63.

Mei Ling, Diane, and Ginger Chih. *A Place Called Chinese America*. San Francisco: Organization of Chinese Americans, 1982.

Mellor, George R. "Emigration from the British Isles to the New World, 1765–1775." *History: The Journal of the Historical Association* 40 (1955): 68–83.

Menard, Russell R. "From Servant to Freeholder: Status Mobility and Property Accumulation in Seventeenth-Century Maryland." *William and Mary Quarterly* 3d ser., 30 (1973): 37–64.

————. "The Growth of Population in the Chesapeake Colonies: A Comment." *Explorations in Economic History* 18 (1981): 399–410. Reply by Terry L. Anderson. "From the Parts to the Whole: Modeling Chesapeake Population": 411–14.

————. "Was There a 'Middle Colonies Demographic Regime'?" *Proceedings of the American Philosophical Society* 133 (1989): 215–18.

Menken, Jane, James Trussell, and Susan Watkins. "The Nutrition Fertility Link: An Evaluation of the Evidence." *Journal of Interdisciplinary History* 11 (1981): 425–41.

Michaels, Joanne. *Living Contradictions: The Women of the Baby Boom Come of Age*. New York: Simon and Schuster, 1982.

Michaelson, Karen L., et al. *Childbirth in America: Anthropological Perspectives*.

South Hadley, Mass.: Bergin & Garvey, Publishers, 1988.

Milden, James Wallace, comp. *The Family in Past Time: A Guide to the Literature.* New York: Garland Publishing, 1977.

Milkman, Ruth. "Organizing the Sexual Division of Labor: Historical Perspectives on 'Women's Work' and the American Labor Movement." *Socialist Review* 49 (1980): 95–150.

———. "Women's Work and the Economic Crisis: Some Lessons from the Great Depression." *Review of Radical Political Economics* 8 (1976): 73–97.

Miller, Douglas T., and Marion Nowak. *The Fifties: The Way We Really Were.* Garden City, N.Y.: Doubleday and Co., 1977.

Miller, Kirby. *Emigrants and Exiles: The Irish Exodus to America.* New York: Oxford University Press, 1985.

Miller, Marc. "Working Women and World War II." *New England Quarterly* 53 (1980): 52–61.

Milne, Ann. "Family Structure and the Achievement of Children." Paper presented at the Conference on Education and the Family, Office of Educational Research and Improvement, U.S. Office of Education, Washington, D.C., 17–18 June 1988.

Mindel, Charles, and Robert Habenstein, eds. *Ethnic Families.* New York: Elsevier, 1981.

Mintz, Steven. *A Prison of Expectations: The Family in Victorian Culture.* New York: New York University Press, 1983.

Mintz, Steven, and Susan Kellogg. *Domestic Revolutions: A Social History of American Family Life.* New York: The Free Press, 1988.

———. "Recent Trends in American Family History: Dimensions of Demographic and Cultural Change." *Houston Law Review* 21 (1984): 792–93.

Modell, John. *Into One's Own: From Youth to Adulthood in the United States, 1920–1975.* Berkeley: University of California Press, 1989.

———. "Normative Aspects of American Marriage Timing since World War II." *Journal of Family History* 5 (1980): 210–34.

Mohr, James. *Abortion in America: The Origins and Evolution of National Policy, 1800–1900.* New York: Oxford University Press, 1978.

Molen, Patricia A. "Population and Social Patterns in Barbados in the Early Eighteenth Century." *William and Mary Quarterly* 3d ser., 28 (1971): 287–300.

Moller, Herbert. "Sex Composition and Correlated Culture Patterns of Colonial America." *William and Mary Quarterly* 3d ser., 2 (1945): 113–53.

Monroe, Day. *Chicago Families: A Study of Unpublished Data.* Chicago: University of Chicago Press, 1932.

Moore, Charles Guy. *Baby Boom Equals Career Bust.* U.S. Department of Health, Education and Welfare. Office of Education. Washington, D.C.: 1977. 18 pp; *ERIC Document Reproduction Service,* ED 145411, 1971.

Moore, Joan. *Mexican Americans.* Englewood Cliffs, N.J.: Prentice-Hall, 1970.

Moore, John H. "Aboriginal Indian Residence Patterns Preserved in Censuses and Allotments." *Science* 207 (11 January 1980): 201–2.

———. *The Cheyenne Nation: A Social and Demographic History.* Lincoln: University of Nebraska Press, 1987.

Moore, John H., and Gregory R. Campbell. "An Ethnohistorical Perspective on

Cheyenne Demography." *Journal of Family History* 14, (1989): 17–42.

Moran, Gerald F. "Religious Renewal, Puritan Tribalism, and the Family in Seventeenth-Century Milford, Connecticut." *William and Mary Quarterly* 3d ser., 36 (1979): 236–54.

Moran, Gerald F., and Maris A. Vinovskis. "The Puritan Family and Religion: A Critical Reappraisal." *William and Mary Quarterly* 3d ser., 39 (1982): 29–63.

Morantz-Sanchez, Regina Markell. *Sympathy and Science: Women Physicians in American Medicine.* New York: Oxford University Press, 1985.

Morgan, Edmund S. *American Slavery, American Freedom: The Ordeal of Colonial Virginia.* New York: W. W. Norton & Company, 1975.

———. *The Puritan Family: Religion and Domestic Relations in Seventeenth-Century New England.* 1944. Revised edition. New York: Harper & Row, 1966.

———. "The Puritans and Sex." *New England Quarterly* 15 (1942): 591–607.

———. "The Puritan's Marriage with God." *South Atlantic Quarterly* 48 (1949): 107–12.

Morgan, Lewis Henry. *Houses and House-Life of the American Aborigines.* Washington, D.C.: Government Printing Office, 1881.

———. *Systems of Consanguinity and Affinity of the Human Family.* Washington, D.C.: Smithsonian Institution, 1871.

Morgan, Winona L. *The Family Meets the Depression.* Minneapolis: University of Minnesota Press, 1939.

Mormino, Gary, and George Pozzetta. *The Immigrant World of Ybor City: Italians and Their Neighbors in Tampa, 1885–1985.* Urbana: University of Illinois Press, 1987.

Morrison, Peter A. "Demographic Trends That Will Shape Future Housing Demand." *The Rand Paper Series P–5596* (1978).

———. "The Future Demographic Context of the Health Care Delivery System." *Rand Publication Series: N–1347–NICHD* (1979).

Motz, Marilyn Ferris. *The True Sisterhood: Michigan Women and Their Kin, 1820–1920.* Albany: State University of New York Press, 1983.

Motz, Marilyn Ferris, and Pat Brown, eds. *Making the American Home: Middle Class Women and Domestic Material Culture, 1840–1940.* Bowling Green, Ohio: Bowling Green University Press, 1988.

Mowrer, Ernest. *Family Disorganization: An Introduction to a Sociological Analysis.* Chicago: University of Chicago Press, 1932.

Murray, Charles. *Losing Ground: American Social Policy, 1950–1980.* New York: Basic Books, 1984.

———. "No. Welfare Isn't Really the Problem." *Public Interest* 84 (Summer, 1986): 3–11.

Murray, John P. *Television and Youth: 25 Years of Research and Controversy.* Stanford, Wash.: Boys Town Center, 1980.

Murrin, John M. "Review Essay." *History and Theory* 11 (1972): 226–75.

Neugarten, Bernice L., John W. Moore, and John C. Lowe. "Age Norms, Age Constraints, and Adult Socialization." *American Journal of Sociology* 70 (May 1965): 710–17.

Newberry Library Center for the History of the American Indian. "Towards a Quantitative Approach to American Indian History." Occasional Papers

Series no. 8. Chicago, Illinois: February 1987.

Niethammer, Carolyn. *Daughters of the Earth: The Lives and Legends of American Indian Women.* New York: Macmillan Co., 1977.

Nooter, Eric, and Patricia U. Bonomi, eds. *Colonial Dutch Studies: An Interdisciplinary Approach.* New York: New York University Press, 1988.

Norton, A. J. "Keeping Up with Households." *American Demographics* 5 (February 1983): 17–21.

Norton, Arthur J., and Jeanne E. Moorman. "Current Trends in Marriage and Divorce." *Journal of Marriage and the Family* 49 (February 1987): 3–14.

Norton, Mary Beth. "Eighteenth-Century American Women in Peace and War: The Case of the Loyalists." *William and Mary Quarterly* 3d ser. 33 (1976): 387–409.

———. "The Evolution of White Women's Experience in Early America." *American Historical Review* 89 (1984): 593–619.

———. "Gender and Defamation in Seventeenth-Century Maryland." *William and Mary Quarterly* 3d ser. 44 (1987): 3–39.

———. *Liberty's Daughters: The Revolutionary Experience of American Women, 1750–1800.* Boston: Little, Brown and Company, 1980.

———, ed. *Major Problems in American Women's History.* Lexington, Mass.: D. C. Heath and Company, 1989.

Norton, Susan L. "Marital Migration in Essex County, Massachusetts, in the Colonial and Early Federal Periods." *Journal of Marriage and the Family* 35 (1973): 406–18.

———. "Population Growth in Colonial America: A Study of Ipswich, Massachusetts." *Population Studies* 25 (1971): 406–18.

"Notes and Documents: Catalogue of Microfilmed Publications of the Archives and Manuscripts Division, Oklahoma Historical Society." *Chronicles of Oklahoma* 60 (Spring 1982): 74–87; (Summer 1982): 218–31; (Fall 1982): 348–59; (Winter 1982): 473–80.

O'Brien, Margaret Steinfels. *Who's Minding the Children? The History and Politics of Day Care in America.* New York: Simon and Schuster, 1973.

Office of Educational Research and Improvement, U.S. Department of Education. *Youth Indicators 1988.* Washington, D.C.: Government Printing Office, 1988.

Ogburn, William F. "The Changing Family." *The Family* 19 (July 1938): 139–43.

———. "Recent Changes in Marriage." *American Journal of Sociology* 41 (November 1935): 285–98.

O'Keefe, Doris. "Marriage and Migration in New England: A Study in Historical Population Geography." Department of Geography, Syracuse University, *Discussion Papers Series*, no. 16, June 1976.

O'Neill, William. *Divorce in the Progressive Era.* New Haven, Conn.: Yale University Press, 1967.

———, ed. *Insights and Parallels: The Problems and Issues of American Social History.* Minneapolis, Minn.: Burgess Publication Co., 1973.

"Openers: Job Jumping." *American Demographics* 2 (June 1980): 10.

Oppenheimer, Valerie Kincade. "The Easterlin Hypothesis: Another Aspect of the Echo to Consider." *Population and Development Review* 2 (1976): 433–57.

————. *The Female Labor Force in the United States.* Berkeley: University of California Press, 1970. Reprint. Westport, Conn.: Greenwood Press, 1976.

————. "The Sociology of Women's Economic Role in the Family." *American Sociological Review* 42 (1977): 387–406.

Orsi, Robert. *Madonna of 116th Street.* New Haven, Conn.: Yale University Press, 1985.

Osterud, Nancy, and John Fulton. "Family Limitation and Age at Marriage: Fertility Decline in Sturbridge, Massachusetts, 1730–1850." *Population Studies* 30 (1976): 481–94.

Ottley, Roi. "What's Wrong with Negro Women?" *Negro Digest* 9 (December 1950): 71–75.

Packard, Vance. *Our Endangered Children: Growing Up in a Changing World.* Boston: Little, Brown and Company, 1983.

Pagelow, Mildred Daley. *Family Violence.* New York: Praeger, 1984.

Papashvily, Helen. *All the Happy Endings.* New York: Harper and Row, 1956.

Patterson, James T. *America's Struggle against Poverty, 1900–1980.* Cambridge, Mass.: Harvard University Press, 1981.

Peck, Ellen, and Judith Senderowitz, eds. *Pronatalism: The Myth of Moms and Apple Pie.* New York: Crowell, 1974.

Peiss, Kathy, and Christina Simmons, eds. *Passion and Power: Sexuality in History.* Philadelphia, Pa.: Temple University Press, 1989.

Perdue, Charles L., Jr., Thomas E. Barden, and Robert K. Phillips, eds. *Weevils in the Wheat: Interviews with Virginia Ex-Slaves.* Charlottesville: University of Virginia Press, 1976.

Personal Narratives Group, eds. *Interpreting Women's Lives: Feminist Theory and Personal Narratives.* Bloomington: Indiana University Press, 1989.

Petchesky, Rosalind Pollack. "Antiabortion, Antifeminism, and the Rise of the New Right." *Feminist Studies* 7 (Summer 1981): 206–46.

Peterson, Jacqueline, and Jennifer S. H. Brown, eds. *The New Peoples: Being and Becoming Métis in North America.* Lincoln: University of Nebraska Press, 1985.

Petry, Ann. *The Street.* Boston: Beacon Press, 1985.

Phillips, Roderick. *Putting Asunder: A History of Divorce in Western Society.* New York: Cambridge University Press, 1988.

Pivar, David. *Purity Crusade: Sexual Morality and Social Control, 1868–1900.* Westport, Conn.: Greenwood Press, 1973.

Plane, David A. "A Systemic Demographic Efficiency Analysis of United States Interstate Population Exchange, 1935–1980." *Economic Geography* 60 (1984): 294–312.

Platt, Anthony. *The Child Savers: The Invention of Delinquency.* Chicago: University of Chicago Press, 1969.

Pleck, Elizabeth H. *Black Migration and Poverty: Boston: 1865–1900.* New York: Academic Press, 1979.

————. *Domestic Tyranny: The Making of American Social Policy against Family Violence from Colonial Times to the Present.* New York: Oxford University Press, 1987.

————. "Two Worlds in One: Work and Family." *Journal of Social History* 9 (Winter 1976): 178–95.

Pleck, Elizabeth H., and Nancy F. Cott, eds. *A Heritage of Her Own: Toward a New Social History of American Women*. New York: Simon and Schuster, 1979.

Pleck, Elizabeth H., and Joseph H. Pleck, eds. *The American Man*. Englewood Cliffs, N.J.: Prentice-Hall, 1980.

Powdermaker, Hortense. *After Freedom: A Cultural Study in the Deep South*. New York: The Viking Press, 1939.

Powell, Chilton L. "Marriage in Early New England." *New England Quarterly* 1 (1928): 323–34.

Powers, Marla N. *Oglala Women: Myth, Ritual, and Reality*. Chicago: University of Chicago Press, 1986.

Pruette, Lorine. *Women Workers through the Depression*. New York: Macmillan Co., 1934.

Pugh, David. *Sons of Liberty: The Masculine Mind in Nineteenth-Century America*. Westport, Conn.: Greenwood Press, 1983.

Quinn, David B., ed. *Early Maryland in a Wider World*. Detroit, Mich.: Wayne State University Press, 1982.

Radin, Paul. *Crashing Thunder*. New York: D. Appleton & Co., 1926.

Radway, Janice A. *Reading the Romance: Women, Patriarchy, and Popular Literature*. Chapel Hill: University of North Carolina Press, 1984.

Rainwater, Lee. *Behind Ghetto Walls: Black Families in a Federal Slum*. Chicago: Aldine Publishing Company, 1970.

Rainwater, Lee, and William L. Yancey, eds. *The Moynihan Report and the Politics of Controversy*. Cambridge, Mass.: MIT Press, 1967.

Reed, James. *Private Vice to Public Virtue: The Birth Control Movement and American Society since 1830*. New York: Basic Books, 1978.

Reiff, Janice L., Michel R. Dahlin, and Daniel Scott Smith. "Rural Push and Urban Pull: Work and Family Experiences of Older Black Women in Southern Cities, 1880–1900." *Journal of Social History* 16 (Summer 1983): 39–48.

Reisman, David. *Abundance for What? and Other Essays*. New York: Doubleday, 1964.

Rindfuss, Ronald R., and James A. Sweet. *Postwar Fertility Trends and Differentials in the United States*. New York: Academic Press, 1977.

Robey, Bryant. "Baby Boom Economics." *American Demographics* 5 (1983): 38–41.

Robey, Bryant, and Cheryl Russell. "Trends: A Portrait of the American Worker." *American Demographics* 6 (1984): 17–21.

Robinson, Paul H. *The Modernization of Sex*. New York: Harper and Row, 1976.

Rodgers, Roy H. *Improvement in the Construction and Analysis of Family Life Cycle Categories*. Kalamazoo: Western Michigan University Press, 1962.

Rodman, Hyman. "Marital Power and the Theory of Resources in Cultural Context." *Journal of Comparative Family Studies* 3 (Spring 1972): 50–69.

Rollins, Judith. *Between Women: Domestics and Their Employers*. Philadelphia, Pa.: Temple University Press, 1985.

Romaniuk, A. "Increase in Natural Fertility during the Early Stages of Modernization: Canadian Indians Case Study." *Demography* 18 (May 1981): 157–72.

Rosaldo, Michelle Zimbalist, and Louise Lamphere, eds. *Women, Culture and Society*. Stanford, Calif.: Stanford University Press, 1974.

Rosenberg, Charles E. "Sexuality, Class, and Role in Nineteenth-Century America." *American Quarterly* 25 (May 1973): 131–53.

Ross, Heather, and Isabel B. Sawhill. *Time of Transition: The Growth of Families Headed by Women*. Washington, D.C.: The Urban Institute, 1975.

Ross, John A., ed. *International Encyclopedia of Population*. New York: McMillan, 1982.

Rothman, David. *Conscience and Convenience: The Asylum and Its Alternatives in Progressive America*. Boston: Little, Brown and Company, 1980.

Rothman, Ellen K. *Hands and Hearts: A History of Courtship in America*. New York: Basic Books, 1984.

———. "Sex and Self-Control: Middle-Class Courtship in America, 1770–1870." *Journal of Social History* 15 (1982): 409–25.

Rothman, Sheila M. *Woman's Proper Place: A History of Changing Ideals and Practices, 1870 to the Present*. New York: Basic Books, 1978.

Rotundo, E. Anthony. "American Fatherhood: A Historical Perspective." *American Behavioral Scientist* 29 (1985): 7–25.

Rubin, Eva R. *The Supreme Court and the American Family: Ideology and Issues*. Westport, Conn.: Greenwood Press, 1986.

Rubin, Lillian. *Intimate Strangers: Men and Women Together*. New York: Harper and Row, 1983.

Rupp, Leila. *Mobilizing Women for War: German and American Propaganda, 1939–1945*. Princeton, N.J.: Princeton University Press, 1978.

Russell, Louise B. *The Baby Boom Generation and the Economy*. Washington, D.C.: Brookings Institute, 1982.

———. "The Baby Boom Generation and the Labor Market in the Next Decade." *World Future Society Bulletin* 17 (1983): 20–22.

Russett, Cynthia. *Sexual Science: The Victorian Construct of Womanhood*. Cambridge: Cambridge University Press, 1989.

Rutman, Darrett B., and Anita H. Rutman. "Of Agues and Fevers: Malaria in the Early Chesapeake." *William and Mary Quarterly* 3d ser., 33 (1976): 31–60.

———. *A Place in Time: Middlesex County, Virginia, 1650–1750*. New York: W. W. Norton & Company, 1984.

Rutman, Darrett B., Charles Wetherell, and Anita H. Rutman. "Rhythms of Life: Black and White Seasonality in the Early Chesapeake." *Journal of Interdisciplinary History* 11 (1980): 29–53.

Ryan, Mary P. *Cradle of the Middle Class: The Family in Oneida County, New York, 1790–1865*. Cambridge: Cambridge University Press, 1981.

———. *The Empire of the Mother: American Writing about Domesticity, 1830–1860*. New York: Haworth Press, 1982.

———. *Womanhood in America*. New York: New Viewpoints, 1979.

———. *Women in Public: Between Banners and Ballots*. Baltimore, Md.: Johns Hopkins University Press, 1990.

Ryder, Norman B. "The Cohort as a Concept in the Study of Social Change." *American Sociological Review* 30 (December 1965): 834–61.

———. "The Future of American Fertility." *Social Problems* 26 (1979): 359–69.

Ryder, Norman B., and Charles F. Westoff. *Reproduction in the United States.* Princeton, N.J.: Princeton University Press, 1971.

Ryerson, Alice Judson. "Medical Advice on Child Rearing, 1550–1900." *Harvard Educational Review* 31 (1961): 302–23.

Sagarin, Edward, ed. "Sex and the Contemporary American Scene." *Annals of the American Academy of Political and Social Science* 376 (March 1968).

Salerno, Anthony. "The Social Background of Seventeenth-Century Emigration to America." *Journal of British Studies* 19 (1979): 31–52.

Salmon, Marylynn. *Women and the Law of Property in Early America.* Chapel Hill: University of North Carolina Press, 1986.

Samuelson, Robert J. "Baby Boom Talk." *National Journal* (1979): 191.

———. "Look Closely, and the Recovery Starts to Make Some Sense." *American Banker* 149 (1984): 8–10.

Sandefur, Gary D., and Trudy McKinnell. "American Indian Intermarriage." *Social Science Research* 15 (1986): 347–71.

Sandefur, Gary D., and Arthur Sakamoto. "American Indian Household Structure and Income." *Demography* 25 (February 1988): 71–80.

Saveth, Edward N. "The Problem of American Family History." *American Quarterly* 21 (1969): 311–29.

Scanzoni, John H. *The Black Family in Modern Society.* Boston: Allyn and Bacon, 1971.

Scharf, Lois. *To Work and to Wed: Female Employment, Feminism, and the Great Depression.* Westport, Conn.: Greenwood Press, 1980.

Scharf, Lois, and Joan M. Jensen, eds. *Decades of Discontent: The Women's Movement, 1920–1940.* Westport, Conn.: Greenwood Press, 1983.

Schlenker, Jon A. "An Historical Analysis of the Family Life of the Choctaw Indians." *The Southern Quarterly* 13 (July 1975): 323–34.

Schlesinger, Elizabeth Bancroft. "Cotton Mather and His Children." *William and Mary Quarterly* 3d ser., 10 (1953): 181–89.

Schlossman, Steven L. *Love and the American Delinquent: The Theory and Practice of "Progressive" Juvenile Justice, 1825–1920.* Chicago: University of Chicago Press, 1977.

Schneider, Carl E. "Moral Discourse and the Transformation of American Family Law." *Michigan Law Review* (1985): 1803–79.

Schnucker, R. V. "The English Puritans and Pregnancy, Delivery and Breast Feeding." *History of Childhood Quarterly* 1 (1974): 637–58.

Schofield, Roger. "Historical Demography in the 1980s." *Historical Methods* 18 (1985): 71–75.

Scholten, Catherine M. *Childbearing in American Society, 1650–1850.* New York: New York University Press, 1985.

———. " 'On the Importance of the Obstetrik Art': Changing Customs of Childbirth in America, 1760 to 1825." *William and Mary Quarterly* 3d ser., 34 (1977): 426–45.

Scott, Donald M., and Bernard Wishy, eds. *America's Families: A Documentary History.* New York: Harper and Row, 1982.

Scott, Joan Wallach. *Gender and the Politics of History.* New York: Columbia University Press, 1988.

Scott, Loren C. "Demographic Shifts and the Economy of the 1980's." *Louisiana Business Review* 44 (1980): 2–5.

Seifer, Nancy, ed. *"Nobody Speaks for Me": Self-Portraits of American Working Class Women.* New York: Simon and Schuster, 1976.

Selig, Robert A. "Emigration, Fraud, Humanitarianism, and the Founding of Londonderry, South Carolina, 1763–1765." *Eighteenth-Century Studies* 23 (1989): 1–23.

Seller, Maxine, ed. *Immigrant Women.* Philadelphia, Pa.: Temple University Press, 1981.

Seward, Ruby Ray. *The American Family: A Demographic History.* Beverly Hills, Calif.: Sage Publications, 1978.

———. "The Colonial Family in America: Toward a Socio-Historical Restoration of Its Structure." *Journal of Marriage and the Family* 35 (1973): 58–70.

Shammas, Carole. "The Domestic Environment in Early Modern England and America." *Journal of Social History* 14 (1980): 3–24.

Shammas, Carole, Marylynn Salmon, and Michael Dahlin. *Inheritance in America: From Colonial Times to the Present.* New Brunswick, N.J.: Rutgers University Press, 1987.

Shifflett, Crandall A. "The Household Composition of Rural Black Families: Louisa County, Virginia, 1880." *Journal of Interdisciplinary History* 6 (Autumn 1975): 235–60.

Shimkin, Demitri B., Edith M. Shimkin, and Dennis A. Frate, eds. *The Extended Family in Black Societies.* Chicago: University of Chicago Press, 1978.

Shoemaker, Nancy. "From Longhouse to Loghouse: Seneca Household Structure in the Nineteenth Century." *American Indian Quarterly.* In Press.

Shumsky, Neil Larry. "Parents, Children, and the Selection of Mates in Colonial Virginia." *Eighteenth-Century Life* 2 (1976): 83–88.

Sidel, Ruth. *Women and Children Last: The Plight of Poor Women in Affluent America.* New York: The Viking Press, 1986.

Simler, Lucy, and Paul G. E. Clemens. "The 'Best Poor Man's Country' in 1783: The Population Structure of Rural Society in Late-Eighteenth-Century Southeastern Pennsylvania." *Proceedings of the American Philosophical Society* 133 (1989): 234–61.

Simmons, Christina. "Companionate Marriage and the Lesbian Threat." *Frontiers* 4 (1979): 54–59.

Simmons, Leo. *Sun Chief: The Autobiography of a Hopi Indian.* New Haven, Conn.: Yale University Press, 1942.

Singell, Larry D. "Some Private and Social Aspects of Labor Mobility of Young Workers." *Quarterly Review of Economics and Business* 6 (1966): 19–28.

Siu, Paul. *The Chinese Laundryman in America.* Ed. John Kuo Wei Tchen. New York: New York University Press, 1987.

Sklar, Kathryn Kish. *Catharine Beecher: A Study in American Domesticity.* New Haven, Conn.: Yale University Press, 1973.

———. "Hull House in the 1890s: A Community of Women Reformers." *Signs: Journal of Women in Culture and Society* 10 (1985): 658–77.

Slater, Peter Gregg. *Children in the New England Mind: In Death and in Life.* Hamden, Conn.: Archon Books, 1977.

———. " 'From the *Cradle* to the *Coffin*': Parental Bereavement and the Shadow of Infant Damnation in Puritan Society." *Psyhohistory Review* 6 (1977–78): 4–24.

Smith, Billy G. "The Family Lives of Laboring Philadelphians during the Late Eighteenth Century." *Proceedings of the American Philosophical Society* 133 (1989): 328–32.

Smith, Daniel Blake. "Autonomy and Affection: Parents and Children in Eighteenth-Century Chesapeake Families." *Psychohistory Review* 6 (1977–78): 32–51.

———. *Inside the Great House: Planter Family Life in Eighteenth-Century Chesapeake Society.* Ithaca, N.Y.: Cornell University Press, 1980.

———. "Mortality and Family in the Colonial Chesapeake." *Journal of Interdisciplinary History* 8 (1978): 403–27.

———. "The Study of the Family in Early America: Trends, Problems, and Prospects." *William and Mary Quarterly* 3d ser., 39 (1982): 3–28.

Smith, Daniel Scott. " 'All in Some Degree Related to Each Other': A Demographic and Comparative Resolution of the Anomaly of New England Kinship." *American Historical Review* 94 (1989): 44–49.

———. "Child-Naming Practices, Kinship Ties, and Change in Family Attitudes in Hingham, Massachusetts, 1641 to 1880." *Journal of Social History* 18 (1985): 541–66.

———. "The Demographic History of Colonial New England." *Journal of Economic History* 32 (1972): 165–83.

———. "The Estimates of Early American Historical Demographers: Two Steps Forward, One Step Backward, What Steps in the Future?" *Historical Methods* 12 (1979): 24–38.

———. "Family Limitation, Sexual Control, and Domestic Feminism in Victorian America." *Feminist Studies* 1 (1973): 40–58.

———. "Parental Power and Marriage Patterns: An Analysis of Historical Trends in Hingham, Massachusetts." *Journal of Marriage and the Family* 35 (1973): 419–28.

———. "A Perspective on Demographic Methods and Effects in Social History." *William and Mary Quarterly* 3d ser., 39 (1982): 442–68.

Smith, Daniel Scott, and Michael S. Hindus. "Premarital Pregnancy in America, 1640–1971: An Overview and Interpretation." *Journal of Interdisciplinary History* 5 (1975): 537–70.

Smith, James Morton, ed. *Seventeenth-Century America: Essays in Colonial History.* Chapel Hill: University of North Carolina Press, 1959.

Smith, James P., and Finis Welch. "No Time to Be Young: The Economic Prospects for Large Cohorts in the United States." *Population and Development Review* 7 (1981): 71–83.

Smith-Rosenberg, Carroll, ed. *Disorderly Conduct: Visions of Gender in Victorian America.* New York: Oxford University Press, 1985.

Smith-Rosenberg, Carroll, and Charles Rosenberg. "The Female Animal: Medical Views of Woman and Her Role in Nineteenth-Century America." *Journal of American History* 60 (1973): 332–56.

Snowden, R., G. D. Mitchell, and E. M. Snowden. *Artificial Reproduction: A Social Investigation.* London: George Allen and Unwin, 1983.

Soloman, Barbara. *In the Company of Educated Women: A History of Women and*

Higher Education in America. New Haven, Conn.: Yale University Press, 1985.

Somerville, James K. "Family Demography and the Published Records: An Analysis of the Vital Statistics of Salem, Massachusetts." *Essex Institute Historical Collections* 106 (1970): 243–51.

Sommerville, C. John. "English Puritans and Children: A Social-Cultural Explanation." *Journal of Psychohistory* 6 (1978): 113–37.

Sorensen, Aage B., Franz E. Weinert, and Lonnie R. Sherrod, eds. *Human Development and the Life Course.* Hillsdale, N.J.: Lawrence Erlbaum Associates, 1986.

Souden, David. " 'Rogues, Whores and Vagabonds': Indentured Servant Emigrants to North America, and the Case of Mid-Seventeenth-Century Bristol." *Social History* 3 (1978): 23–41.

Spain, Daphne, and Suzanne M. Bianchi. "How Women Have Changed." *American Demographics* 5 (1983): 18–25.

Speck, Frank G. "The Family Hunting Band as the Basis of Algonkian Social Organization." *American Anthropologist* 17 (1915): 289–305.

Speth, Linda E., and Alison Duncan Hirsch. *Women, Family, and Community in Colonial America: Two Perspectives.* New York: Haworth Press, 1983.

Spicker, Stuart F., Kathleen M. Woodward, and David D. Van Tassel, eds. *Aging and the Elderly: Humanistic Perspectives in Gerontology.* Atlantic Highlands, N.J.: Humanities Press, 1978.

Sprague, D. N., and R. P. Frye. *The Genealogy of the First Métis Nation: The Development and Dispersal of the Red River Settlement, 1820–1900.* Winnipeg, Manitoba: Pemmican Publications, 1983.

Spruill, Julia Cherry. *Women's Life and Work in the Southern Colonies.* New York: W. W. Norton & Company, 1938.

Spurlock, John. *Free Love: Marriage and Middle-Class Radicalism in America, 1825–1860.* New York: New York University Press, 1988.

Stack, Carol B. *All Our Kin: Strategies for Survival in a Black Community.* New York: Harper and Row, 1974.

Stanley, Thomas J., and George P. Moschis. "American Affluence." *American Demographics* 6 (1984): 28–33.

Stannard, David E. "Death and the Puritan Child." *American Quarterly* 26 (1974): 456–76.

————. *The Puritan Way of Death: A Study in Religion, Culture, and Social Change.* New York: Oxford University Press, 1977.

Stansell, Christine. *City of Women: Sex and Class in New York, 1789–1860.* Urbana: University of Illinois Press, 1987.

Staples, Robert. "Toward a Sociology of the Black Family: A Theoretical and Methodological Assessment." *Journal of Marriage and the Family* 33 (1971): 119–38.

————, ed. *The Black Family: Essays and Studies.* Belmont, Calif.: Wadsworth Publishing Company, 1971.

Starkey, Marion L. *The Devil in Massachusetts: A Modern Enquiry into the Salem Witch Trials.* New York: Alfred A. Knopf, 1949.

————. "The Easiest Room in Hell." *Essex Institute Historical Collections* 92 (1956): 33–42.

Stearns, Carol Z., and Peter Stearns. "Victorian Sexuality: Can Historians Do It Better?" *Journal of Social History* 18 (1985): 625–34.

Stearns, Peter N. *Be a Man! Males in Modern Society.* New York: Holmes & Meier Publishers, 1979.

Steffen, Charles G. "The Sewall Children in Colonial New England." *New England Historical and Genealogical Register* 131 (1977): 163–72.

Steinberg, Ira S. *The New Lost Generation: The Population Boom and Public Policy.* New York: St. Martin's Press, 1982.

Steiner, Gilbert Y. *The Futility of Family Policy.* Washington, D.C.: Brookings Institution, 1981.

Sterling, Dorothy, ed. *The Trouble They Seen: Black People Tell the Story of Reconstruction.* Garden City, N.Y.: Doubleday and Co., 1976.

———, ed. *We Are Your Sisters: Black Women in the Nineteenth Century.* New York: W. W. Norton & Company, 1984.

Sternlieb, George, and James W. Hughes. "Running Faster to Stay in Place—Family Income and the Baby Boom." *American Demographics* 4 (1982): 16–19.

Stockwell, Edward G. *Population and People.* Chicago: Quadrangle Books, 1968.

Stone, Lawrence. *The Family, Sex and Marriage in England, 1500–1800.* New York: Harper and Row, 1977.

Stott, William. *Documentary Expression and Thirties America.* New York: Oxford University Press, 1973.

Stouffer, Samuel A., and Paul E. Lazarsfeld. *Research Memorandum on the Family in the Depression.* Bulletin no. 29. New York: Social Science Research Council, 1937.

Stowe, Steven. *Intimacy and Power in the Old South: Ritual in the Lives of the Planters.* Baltimore, Md.: Johns Hopkins University Press, 1987.

Straub, Eleanor. "United States Government Policy toward Civilian Women during World War II." *Prologue* 5 (1973): 240–54.

Strickland, Charles. "A Transcendental Father: The Childrearing Practices of Bronson Alcott." *Perspectives in American History* 3 (1969): 5–73.

———. *Victorian Domesticity: Families in the Life and Art of Louisa May Alcott.* University: University of Alabama Press, 1985.

Strong, Bryan. "Toward a History of the Experiential Family: Sex and Incest in the Nineteenth Century Family." *Journal of Marriage and the Family* 35 (1973): 457–66.

Sturtevant, William C., ed. *Handbook of North American Indians.* Washington, D.C.: Smithsonian Institution, 1978–.

Susman, Warren I. *Culture as History: The Transformation of American Society in the Twentieth Century.* New York: Pantheon Books, 1984.

Suttles, Wayne. "Affinal Ties, Subsistence, and Prestige among the Coast Salish." *American Anthropologist* 62 (April 1960): 296–305.

Sutton, John R. *Stubborn Children: Controlling Delinquency in the United States, 1640–1981.* Berkeley: University of California Press, 1989.

———. "Stubborn Children: Law and the Socialization of Deviance in the Puritan Colonies." *Family Law Quarterly* 15 (1981): 31–64.

Swagerty, William R. "Marriage and Settlement Patterns of Rocky Mountain

Trappers and Traders." *Western Historical Quarterly* 11 (April 1980): 159–80.

———, ed. *Scholars and the Indian Experience: Critical Reviews of Recent Writing in the Social Sciences*. Bloomington: Indiana University Press, 1984.

Sweezy, A. "The Economic Explanation of Fertility Changes in the United States." *Population Studies* 25 (1971): 255–67.

Tanner, Adrian. *Bringing Home Animals: Religious Ideology and Mode of Production of the Mistassini Cree Hunters*. New York: St. Martin's Press, 1979.

Tarter, Jeffrey. "The Baby Boom: Where Have All the Children Gone." *Inc.* 2 (1980): 78–80.

Tate, Thad W., and David L. Ammerman, eds. *The Chesapeake in the Seventeenth Century: Essays on Anglo-American Society*. Chapel Hill: University of North Carolina Press, 1979.

Tavris, Carol, and Carole Offir. *The Longest War: Sex Differences in Perspective*. New York: Harcourt Brace Jovanovich, 1977.

Taylor, Karen. "Disciplining the History of Childhood." *Journal of Psychohistory* 16 (1988): 189–90.

Taylor, Robert M., Jr., and Ralph J. Crandall, eds. *Generations and Change: Genealogical Perspectives in Social History*. Macon, Ga.: Mercer University Press, 1986.

Teitelbaum, Lee E. "Moral Discourse and Family Law." *Michigan Law Review* (1985): 430–34.

Temkin-Greener, H., and A. C. Swedlund. "Fertility Transition in the Connecticut Valley: 1740–1850." *Population Studies* 32 (1978): 27–41.

Terkel, Studs. *Hard Times: An Oral History of the Depression*. New York: Avon Books, 1970.

Terrell, John Upton, and Donna M. Terrell. *Indian Women of the Western Morning: Their Life in Early America*. New York: The Dial Press, 1974.

Terrill, Tom E., and Jerrold Hirsch. *Such as Us: Southern Voices of the Thirties*. New York: W. W. Norton & Company, 1978.

Theriot, Nancy. *The Biosocial Construction of Femininity: Mothers and Daughters in Nineteenth-Century America*. Westport, Conn.: Greenwood Press, 1988.

Thernstrom, Stephen, ed. *Harvard Encyclopedia of American Ethnic Groups*. Cambridge, Mass.: Harvard University Press, 1980.

Thomas, William, and Florian Znaniecki. *The Polish Peasant in Europe and America*. New York: Dover Press, 1958.

Thompson, R. "Seventeenth-Century English and Colonial Sex Ratios: A Postscript." *Population Studies* 28 (1974): 153–65.

Thompson, Roger. "Adolescent Culture in Colonial Massachusetts." *Journal of Family History* 9 (1984): 127–44.

———. "Attitudes towards Homosexuality in the Seventeenth-Century New England Colonies." *Journal of American Studies* 23 (1989): 27–40.

———. "Popular Attitudes towards Children in Middlesex County, Massachusetts, 1649–1699." *Journal of Psychohistory* 13 (1985): 145–58.

———. *Sex in Middlesex: Popular Mores in a Massachusetts County, 1649–1699*. Amherst: University of Massachusetts Press, 1986.

Thompson, Thomas C. "The Life Course and Labor of a Colonial Farmer." *Historical New Hampshire* 40 (1985): 135–55.

Thorne, Barrie, with Marilyn Yalom, ed. *Rethinking the Family: Some Feminist Questions.* New York: Longman, 1982.

Thornton, Russell. *American Indian Holocaust and Survival: A Population History since 1492.* Norman: University of Oklahoma Press, 1987.

Thurston, Flora M. *A Bibliography of Family Relationships.* New York: National Council of Parent Education, 1932.

Tiffin, Susan. *In Whose Best Interests? Child Welfare Reform in the Progressive Era.* Westport, Conn.: Greenwood Press, 1982.

Tilly, Louise A. "Women's History and Family History: Fruitful Collaboration or Missed Connection?" *Journal of Family History* 12 (1987): 303–15.

Tompkins, Jane. *Sensational Designs: The Cultural Work of American Fiction, 1790–1860.* New York: Oxford University Press, 1985.

Tracy, Patricia J. "Re-Considering Migration within Colonial New England." *Journal of Social History* 23 (1989): 93–113.

Trautmann, Thomas R. *Lewis Henry Morgan and the Invention of Kinship.* Berkeley: University of California Press, 1987.

Treckel, Paula A. "Breastfeeding and Maternal Sexuality in Colonial America." *Journal of Interdisciplinary History* 20 (1989): 25–51.

Trennert, Robert A., Jr. *Phoenix Indian School: Forced Assimilation in Arizona, 1891–1935.* Norman: University of Oklahoma Press, 1988.

———. "Victorian Morality and the Supervision of Indian Women Working in Phoenix, 1906–1930." *Journal of Social History* 22 (Fall 1988): 113–28.

Trout, Charles H. *Boston, the Great Depression and the New Deal.* New York: Oxford University Press, 1977.

Tufte, Virginia, and Barbara Myerhoff, eds. *Changing Images of the Family.* New Haven, Conn.: Yale University Press, 1979.

Udry, J. Richard. "Marital Instability by Race, Sex, Education, and Occupation Using 1960 Census Data." *American Journal of Sociology* 72 (September 1966): 203–9.

Uhlenberg, Peter. "Cohort Variations in Life Cycle Experiences of U.S. Females." *Journal of Marriage and the Family* 36 (May 1974): 284–92.

———. "A Study of Cohort Life Cycles: Cohorts of Native Born Massachusetts Women, 1830–1920." *Population Studies* 23 (1969): 407–20.

Uhlenberg, Peter, and David Eggebeen. "The Declining Well-Being of American Adolescents." *Public Interest* 85 (Winter 1986): 25–38.

Ulrich, Laurel Thatcher. *Good Wives: Image and Reality in the Lives of Women in Northern New England, 1650–1750.* New York: Alfred A. Knopf, 1982.

———. *A Midwife's Tale: The Life of Martha Ballard, Based on Her Diary, 1785–1812.* New York: Alfred A. Knopf, 1990.

Underhill, Ruth M. *Papago Woman.* 1936, part 2, Anthropological Association Memoir 46. New York: Holt, Rinehart, and Winston, 1979.

U.S. Bureau of the Census. Special Studies, *Child Support and Alimony: 1978. Current Population Reports,* ser. P–23, no. 106.

———. *Indian Population of the United States and Alaska.* Washington, D.C.: Government Printing Office, 1915.

———. *Sixteenth Census of the United States: 1940, Population.* Vol. 4. Washington, D.C.: Government Printing Office, 1942.

————. *We, the First Americans.* Washington, D.C.: Government Printing Office, 1988.

————. *Who's Minding the Kids?* Washington, D.C.: Government Printing Office, 1987.

U.S. Children's Bureau. *Maternity and Child Care in Selected Rural Areas in Mississippi,* by Helen M. Dart. Publication no. 88. Washington, D.C.: Government Printing Office, 1921.

————. *Rural Children in Selected Counties of North Carolina,* by Frances Sage Bradley and Margaretta A. Williamson. Publication no. 33. Washington, D.C.: Government Printing Office, 1918.

U.S. Congress. Joint Economic Committee. *Studies in Public Welfare.* Washington, D.C.: Government Printing Office, 1974.

U.S. Department of Labor. *The Negro Family: The Case for National Action,* by Daniel P. Moynihan. Washington, D.C.: Government Printing Office, 1965.

U.S. Department of Labor. Bureau of Labor Statistics. *Employment in Perspective: Working Women.* Washington, D.C.: Government Printing Office, 1982.

Uselding, Paul, ed. *Research in Economic History: A Research Annual 5.* Greenwich, Conn.: JAI Press, 1980.

U.S. National Archives. *American Indians: A Select Catalog of Microfilm Publications.* Washington, D.C.: General Services Administration, 1984.

U.S. Women's Bureau. *Family Status of Breadwinning Women in Four Selected Cities.* Bulletin 23. Washington, D.C.: Government Printing Office, 1925.

Vaile, Roland S. *Research Memorandum on Social Aspects of Consumption in the Depression.* New York: Social Science Research Council, 1937.

Van Kirk, Sylvia. *Many Tender Ties: Women in Fur-Trade Society, 1670–1870.* Norman: University of Oklahoma Press, 1983.

Van Tassel, David, ed. *Aging, Death and the Completion of Being.* Philadelphia: University of Pennsylvania Press, 1979.

Vaughan, Jerry L. "The Major Impacts of the Baby Boom upon American Life, 1945–2050." Arlington, Va.: *ERIC Document Reproduction Service,* ED 230478, 1983.

Verduin, Kathleen. " 'Our Cursed Natures': Sexuality and the Puritan Conscience." *New England Quarterly* 56 (1983): 220–37.

Veroff, Joseph, Elizabeth Douan and Richard A. Kulka. *The Inner America: A Self Portrait from 1957 to 1976.* New York: Basic Books, 1981.

Vinovskis, Maris A. "Angels' Heads and Weeping Willows: Death in Early America." *Proceedings of the American Antiquarian Society* 86 (1976): 273–302.

————. *An "Epidemic" of Adolescent Pregnancy?: Some Historical and Policy Considerations.* New York: Oxford University Press, 1988.

————. "Family and Schooling in Colonial and Nineteenth-Century America." *Journal of Family History* 12 (1987): 19–37.

————. *Fertility in Massachusetts from the Revolution to the Civil War.* New York: Academic Press, 1981.

————. "From Household Size to the Life Course: Some Observations on Recent Trends in Family History." *American Behavioral Scientist* 21 (November/December 1977): 263–87.

————. "Recent Trends in American Historical Demography: Some Methodological and Conceptual Considerations." *Annual Review of Sociology* 4 (1978): 603–27.

Volpe, E. Peter. *Test-Tube Conception: A Blend of Love and Science*. Macon, Ga.: Mercer University Press, 1987.

Waciega, Lisa Wilson. "A 'Man of Business': The Widow of Means in South-eastern Pennsylvania." *William and Mary Quarterly* 3d ser., 44 (1987): 40–64.

Waddell, Jack O., and O. Michael Watson, eds. *The American Indian in Urban Society*. Boston: Little, Brown and Company, 1971.

Wade-Gayles, Gloria. *No Crystal Stair: Visions of Race and Sex in Black Women's Fiction*. New York: The Pilgrim Press, 1984.

Wagner, Peter. "A Note on Puritans and Children in Early Colonial New England." *Amerikastudien* 25 (1980): 47–62.

Walker, Lenore E. *The Battered Woman*. New York: Harper Colophon Books, 1979.

Wall, Richard, Jean Robin, and Peter Laslett, eds. *Family Forms in Historic Europe*. Cambridge: Cambridge University Press, 1983.

Wallace, Anthony. *Rockdale: The Growth of an American Village in the Early Industrial Revolution*. New York: Alfred A. Knopf, 1978.

Wallace, Anthony. *The Death and Rebirth of the Seneca*. New York: Random House, 1969.

Wallace, Michele. *Black Macho and the Myth of the Superwoman*. New York: Warner Books, 1980.

Wallerstein Judith S., and Joan B. Kelley. "Children and Divorce: A Review." *Social Work* 24 (1979): 472.

———. *Surviving the Breakup: How Children and Parents Cope with Divorce*. New York: Basic Books, 1980.

Walsh, Lorena S. "The Historian as Census Taker: Individual Reconstitution and the Reconstruction of Censuses for a Colonial Chesapeake County." *William and Mary Quarterly* 3d ser., 38 (1981): 242–60.

———. "Staying Put or Getting Out: Findings for Charles County, Maryland, 1650–1720." *William and Mary Quarterly* 3d ser., 44 (1987): 89–103.

Walsh, Lorena S., and Russell R. Menard. "Death in the Chesapeake: Two Life Tables for Men in Early Colonial Maryland." *Maryland Historical Magazine* 69 (1974): 211–27.

Walters, Leroy. "Human in Vitro Fertilization: A Review of the Ethical Literature." *The Hastings Center Report* 9 (1979): 23–43.

Walters, Ronald. "The Family and Antebellum Reform." *Societas* 3 (1973): 221–32.

Wandersee, Winifred D. *Women's Work and Family Values, 1920–1940*. Cambridge, Mass.: Harvard University Press, 1981.

Ware, Caroline. *Greenwich Village*. New York: Harper and Row, 1935.

Ware, Susan. *Holding Their Own: American Women in the 1930s*. Boston: G. K. Hall & Co., 1982.

Waters, John J. "Family, Inheritance, and Migration in Colonial New England: The Evidence from Guilford, Connecticut." *William and Mary Quarterly* 3d ser., 39 (1982): 64–86.

———. "Naming and Kinship in New England: Guilford Patterns and Usage,

1693–1759." *New England Historical and Genealogical Register* 138 (1984): 161–81.

———. "Patrimony, Succession, and Social Stability: Guilford, Connecticut, in the Eighteenth Century." *Perspectives in American History* 10 (1976): 129–60.

———. "The Traditional World of the New England Peasants: A View from Seventeenth-Century Barnstable." *New England Historical and Genealogical Register* 130 (1976): 3–21.

Watson, Alan D. "Household Size and Composition in Pre-Revolutionary North Carolina." *Mississippi Quarterly* 31 (1978): 551–69.

Wattenberg, Esther. "The Fate of Baby Boomers and Their Children." *Social Work* 31 (1986): 20–28.

Watters, David H. " 'I Spake as a Child': Authority, Metaphor and *The New England Primer*." *Early American Literature* 20 (1985/86): 193–213.

Weinberg, Sydney Stahl. "Jewish Mothers and Immigrant Daughters." *Journal of American Ethnic History* 6 (Spring 1987): 39–55.

———. *The World of Our Mothers: The Lives of Jewish Immigrant Women*. Chapel Hill: University of North Carolina Press, 1988.

Weiner, Nella Fermi. "Baby Bust and Baby Boom: A Study of Family Size in a Group of University of Chicago Faculty Wives Born 1900–1934." *Journal of Family History* 8 (1983): 279–91.

Weisberg, D. Kelly. " 'Under Greet Temptations Heer': Women and Divorce in Puritan Massachusetts." *Feminist Studies* 2 (1975): 183–94.

Weiss, Bernard, ed. *American Education and the European Immigrant: 1840–1940*. Urbana: University of Illinois Press, 1982.

———. *Going It Alone: The Family Life and Social Situation of the Single Parent*. New York: Basic Books, 1979.

Weitzman, Lenore J. *The Divorce Revolution: The Unexpected Social and Economic Consequences for Women and Children*. New York: The Free Press, 1985.

Welch, Finis. "Effects of Cohort Size on Earnings: The Baby Boom Babies Financial Bust." *Journal of Political Economy* 87 (1979): 565–97.

Wells, Robert V. "The Demography of a Region: Historical Reality or Historian's Creation." *Proceedings of the American Philosophical Society* 133 (1989): 219–22.

———. "Family History and Demographic Transition." *Journal of Social History* 9 (1975): 1–19.

———. "Family Size and Fertility Control in Eighteenth-Century America: A Study of Quaker Families." *Population Studies* 25 (1971): 73–82.

———. "Marriage Seasonals in Early America: Comparisons and Comments." *Journal of Interdisciplinary History* 18 (1987): 299–307.

———. *The Population of the British Colonies in America before 1776: A Survey of Census Data*. Princeton, N.J.: Princeton University Press, 1975.

———. "Quaker Marriage Patterns in a Colonial Perspective." *William and Mary Quarterly* 3d ser., 29 (1972): 415–42.

———. *Revolutions in Americans' Lives: A Demographic Perspective on the History of Americans, Their Families, and Their Society*. Westport, Conn.: Greenwood Press, 1982.

———. *Uncle Sam's Family: Issues in and Perspectives on American Demographic His-*

tory. Albany: State University of New York Press, 1985.

Welter, Barbara. "The Cult of True Womanhood: 1800–1860." *American Quarterly* 18 (1966): 151–75.

———. *Dimity Conventions: The American Woman in the Nineteenth Century*. Athens. Ohio University Press, 1976.

Wertz, Richard W., and Dorothy C. Wertz. *Lying-In: A History of Childbirth in America*. New York: The Free Press, 1977.

Westin, Jeane. *Making Do: How Women Survived the '30s*. Chicago: Follett Publishing Company, 1976.

Westoff, Charles. "Baby Boom Critic: Theory a Bust." *The Wharton Magazine* (1979): 66–67.

———. "The Decline of Fertility." *American Demographics* 1 (1979): 16–19.

———. "The Decline of Unplanned Births in the United States." *Science* 191 (1976): 38–41.

———. "The End of 'Catholic' Fertility." *Demography* 16 (1979): 209ff.

———. "Some Speculations on the Future of Marriage and Fertility." *Family Planning Perspectives* 10 (1978): 79–83.

Westoff, Charles F., et al. *Toward the End of Growth: Population in America*. Englewood Cliffs, N.J.: Prentice-Hall, 1973.

Westoff, Charles, and Larry Bumpass. *The Later Years of Childbearing*. Princeton, N.J.: Princeton University Press, 1970.

Westoff, Charles, and R. Parke, eds. *Demographic and Social Aspects of Population Growth*. Vol. 1. Commission on Population Growth and the American Future. Washington D.C.: Government Printing Office, 1972.

Westoff, Charles F., Robert Potter, and Philip Sagi. *The Third Child*. Princeton, N.J.: Princeton University Press, 1963.

Weyrauch, Walter O., and Sanford N. Katz. *American Family Law in Transition*. Washington, D.C.: Bureau of National Affairs 1972.

Whaley, Charles E. "The Major Impacts of the Baby Boom Cohort upon American Life, Past, Present and Future." Arlington, Va.: *ERIC Document Reproduction Service*, ED 231–709, 1983. 35 pp.

Wheeler, Thomas, ed. *The Immigrant Experience: The Anguish of Becoming American*. New York: Dial Press, 1971.

White, Deborah Gray. *Ar'n't I am Woman? Female Slaves in the Plantation South*. New York: W. W. Norton & Company, 1985.

White, R. Clyde, and Mary K. White. *Research Memorandum on Social Aspects of Relief Policies in the Depression*. New York: Social Science Research Council, 1937.

Whiteley, Peter M. *Deliberate Acts: Changing Hopi Culture through the Oraibi Split*. Tucson: University of Arizona Press, 1988.

Whitney, Herbert A. "Estimating Precensus Populations: A Method Suggested and Applied to the Towns of Rhode Island and Plymouth Colonies in 1689." *Annals of the Association of American Geographers* 55 (1965): 179–89.

Wickens, James F. *Colorado in the Great Depression*. New York: Garland, 1979.

Williams, J. M. *Human Aspects of Unemployment and Relief*. Chapel Hill: University of North Carolina Press, 1933.

Williams, Walter L. *The Spirit and the Flesh: Sexual Diversity in American Indian Culture*. Boston: Beacon Press, 1986.

Wilson, William Julius. *The Truly Disadvantaged: The Inner City, the Underclass, and Public Policy.* Chicago: University of Chicago Press, 1987.

Winn, Marie. *Children without Childhood.* New York: Pantheon Books, 1983.

———. *The Plug-In Drug.* New York: The Viking Press, 1977.

Wishy, Bernard. *The Child and the Republic: The Dawn of Modern Child Nurture.* Philadelphia: University of Pennsylvania Press, 1968.

Witherspoon, Gary. *Navajo Kinship and Marriage.* Chicago: University of Chicago Press, 1975.

Withey, Lynne E. "Household Structure in Urban and Rural Areas: The Case of Rhode Island, 1774–1800." *Journal of Family History* 3 (1978): 37–50.

Wokeck, Marianne S. "German and Irish Immigration to Colonial Philadelphia." *Proceedings of the American Philosophical Society* 133 (1989): 128–43.

Wolf, Stephanie Grauman. *Urban Village: Population, Community, and Family Structure in Germantown, Pennsylvania, 1683–1800.* Princeton, N.J.: Princeton University Press, 1977.

Wolfstein, Martha. "Fun Morality: An Analysis of Recent American Child Training Literature." *Journal of Social Issues* 7 (1951): 15–21.

Woloch, Nancy. *Women and the American Experience.* New York: Alfred A. Knopf, 1984.

Wood, Ann Douglas. "The 'Scribbling Women' and Fanny Fern: Why Women Wrote." *American Quarterly* 28 (1971): 3–24.

Wright, Gwendolyn. *Building the Dream: A Social History of Housing in America.* 2d ed. Cambridge, Mass.: MIT Press, 1983.

———. *Moralism and the Model Home: Domestic Architecture and Cultural Conflict in Chicago, 1873–1913.* Chicago: University of Chicago Press, 1980.

Wyatt-Brown, Bertram. *Southern Honor: Ethics and Behavior in the Old South.* New York: Oxford University Press, 1982.

———. "Three Generations of Yankee Parenthood: The Tappen Family, a Case Study of Antebellum Nurture." *Illinois Quarterly* 38 (Fall 1975): 12–28.

———. *Yankee Saints and Southern Sinners.* Baton Rouge: Louisiana State University Press, 1985.

Yankelovich, Daniel. *New Rules: Searching for Self-Fulfillment in a World Turned Upside Down.* New York: Random House, 1981.

Yans-McLaughlin, Virginia. *Family and Community: Italian Immigrants in Buffalo, 1880–1930.* Ithaca, N.Y.: Cornell University Press, 1977.

Yezierska, Anzia. *The Children of Loneliness.* New York: Funk & Wagnalls, 1923.

Young, Pauline V. "Human Cost of Unemployment." *Sociology and Social Research* 17 (March–April 1933): 361–69.

———. "The New Poor." *Sociology and Social Research* 17 (January–February 1933): 234–42.

Zaretsky, Eli. *Capitalism, The Family, and Personal Life.* New York: Harper and Row, 1973.

Zawadzki, Bohan, and Paul Lazarsfeld. "The Psychological Consequences of Unemployment." *Journal of Social Psychology* 6 (May 1935): 224–51.

Zinn, Maxine Baca. "Chicano Family Research: Conceptual Distortions and Alternative Directions." *Journal of Ethnic Studies* 7 (Fall 1979): 57–71.

Zuckerman, Michael, ed. *Friends and Neighbors: Group Life in America's First Plural Society*. Philadelphia, Pa.: Temple University Press, 1982.
———. "William Byrd's Family." *Perspectives in American History* 12 (1979): 255–311.

Index

ilies, 48; role of, in television families, 184; and sex, 195; sexual abuse of, increase in, 202; school age, and working mothers, 243; and single parent household, 198; and social anxiety, 195; socialization of, in colonial families, 48; of tenant farmers, as a social problem, 145; and street scavenging in the nineteenth century, 235; and "tender years" doctrine for custody, 191; and two parent household, 198; wanted, and rise of birth control movement, 245; welfare of, and no-fault divorce system, 194; welfare of, following divorce, 192; and women's roles during World War II, 162; work of, in the nineteenth century, 234; young, as typical of families during 1940s and 1950s, 166

child savers, rise of professionalism among, 128

child saving, 128, 149 n.11; as organized professional academic activity, 128; and progressivism, 149 n.11; as a reform movement in early twentieth century, 128

child studies, expertise in 1930s, 128

child support, 192, 193, 266, 277, 283 n.59; difficulties for African American women, 283 n.59; and divorced white women's difficulties, 283 n.59; and Freedmen's Bureau, 266; payments for, laws regarding, 192; payments for, role of government, 193; racial differences in, 277

Chinese Laundryman, 324–325

Chodorow, Nancy, 100

Chona, Maria, author of *Papago Woman*, 300, 302

Christianity, as a critique of Native American patterns of life, 305

cities, northern, and family life among African Americans, 269

Civilian Conservation Corps (CCC), 141

Civil Works Administration (CWA), 142

Clark, Clifford, 89–90

Clark, Kenneth, and demoralization among African Americans, 272

class, 11, 234; influence of, on work by married women in the nineteenth century, 234; as a variable in the study of family history, 11

classes, social among Northwest Coast Indians, 300

Cleaveland, John, 41

Cleaveland family, 50

Clinton, Catherine, and "Mammy" stereotype, 241

Coca-Cola, 25

Cogan, Frances, 93

cohabitation, 185, 191, 193; and courts, 193; entitled to protection from hostile regulation, 191; by unmarried couples, increase of, 185

Cohen, Miriam, and changing attitudes regarding education among immigrants, 334

Cohen, Sheldon, 51

coitus interruptus, 228, 237; as a birth control technique in the nineteenth century, 237; as a means of birth control during the colonial period, 228

Cole, Donald, 327, 336, 337; and importance of kitchens in immigrant households, 336–337; and study of immigrant marriage patterns, 327

college, 104, 187, 244; women's enrollment in the late nineteenth century, 104; and women's graduation rates, increase of, during the 1950s, 187; and women's preparation for family life, 244

colonization, European and Native American family, 303–306

Colorado, and cotton production, 136

companionship, and marriage during the 1930s, 131–134

Comstock, Anthony, 106

and impact on family life during the 1930s, 131

United States, and attacks on Native American families, 305

University of North Carolina Press, 144

urbanization, and impact on Native American fertility, 295

U.S. Bureau of Indian Affairs, and records as sources for family history, 293

U.S. Bureau of the Census: and recording of Native American population, 296; and rising living standards after World War II, 164

U.S. Children's Bureau, 107, 203; and study of child abuse, 203; creation of, 107

Utah, and children's rights, 192

values, 135, 187, 188; family, shift in, since 1950s, 187–188; family-centered, during the 1930s, 135

Van Kirk, Sylvia, and Jennifer S. H. Brown, and study of Indian women, 303

venereal disease, and nineteenth-century women's fears, 96

violence, 192, 193, 196, 202, 203, 246, 262, 267, 268, 278, 327; domestic, among African Americans, 278; domestic, and courts, 193; domestic, and social class, 202; domestic, changes in laws regarding since 1960, 192; domestic, study of since World War II, 202–203; family, as a reason for Irish women not marrying, 327; marital, among African Americans, 267–268; sexual, against women and children, increase of, in twentieth century, 246; and slave women, 262; and television, studies of impact on children, 196

Virginia, 37, 230; and Bacon's Rebellion, 37; and pregnancy cycles of slave women during the colonial period, 230

virginity, 189; of women, at marriage, decline in numbers, 185; decline of, for women at marriage in 1960s, 189

wages, 136, 137, 205; family, paid to head of hispanic families, 136–137; federal minimum, effect of, 205

Wallace, Anthony, 251 n.32, 304; and study of family work in factories, 251 n.32; and study of religion among the Seneca, 304

"The Waltons" (television program), 183

Ward, M. P., and baby boom, 167

Ware, Caroline, and study of immigrant families, 319

Waters, John J., 47, 51

Watson, John, 108, 163; and behaviorist childrearing, 163

Wayland, Francis, Rev., 99–100

weaning, 43, 230; ceremony at end of, during the colonial period, 230; process of in colonial period, 43

Webster v. Reproductive Services, and restrictions on abortion rights, 246

Weinberg, Sydney, 132, 133, 330; and Jewish mothers, 330

welfare, 50, 198, 201, 204, 206, 269–271; and African American women after World War II, 270–271; and children who had participated in head start, 198; laws, and overhaul by U.S. government in 1988, 206; as a lure to African Americans to northern cities, 269; policies, and impact on black families, 204: rolls, in colonial Virginia, 50; and teenage pregancies, 201

Wells, Robert, 3, 7, 41–42

Welter, Barbara, 92, 102, 232; and domesticity, 232

West Indies, 36

wet-nursing, practice of, in colonial period, 43

About the Contributors

KAREN ANDERSON is an associate professor of history and director of the Women's Studies Program and the Southwest Institute for Research on Women at the University of Arizona. Her publications include *Wartime Women: Sex Roles, Family Relations, and the Status of Women during World War II*; *Changing Our Minds: Feminist Transformations of Knowledge*; and numerous articles on women's history and women and work. She is currently writing a historical study of Mexican American, native American, and African American women entitled *Changing Woman: Racial Ethnic Women in Modern America*.

ROSS W. BEALES, JR., is a member of the Department of History, College of the Holy Cross, in Worcester, Massachusetts. A historian of colonial America, his special interests include the history of the family and communities, and he is currently completing a study of "The Worlds of Ebenezer Parkman: Family, Religion, and Community in Eighteenth-Century Westborough, Massachusetts."

SELMA BERROL is Professor of History at Baruch College, City University of New York. She is a specialist in American immigration history with special emphasis on immigration and ethnicity in New York City. She is the author of *Immigrants at School: New York City, 1898–1914*; *Getting Down to Business: A History of Baruch College in the City of New York*; and numerous articles on the public schools and immigrant children, and German Jewish/Russian Jewish tensions.

MARILYN DELL BRADY teaches American family history, women's history, and African American history at Virginia Wesleyan College. She recently completed her Ph.D. at the University of Kansas, writing her dissertation on motherhood in selected women's autobiographies. Her other research interests include the black clubwomen's movement and Quaker women in Philadelphia in the 1790s.

MARGARET M. CAFFREY is Assistant Professor of History at Memphis State University, where she teaches U.S. and women's history. She is the author of *Ruth Benedict: Stranger in This Land* and is currently researching the women's emancipation movement in the Progressive era.

JOSEPH M. HAWES is Professor of History at Memphis State University, where he teaches courses on the history of American children and the American family. He is the author of *Children and Urban Society* and the coeditor (with N. Ray Hiner) of *Growing Up in America*; *American Childhood*; and *Children in Historical and Comparative Perspective* (forthcoming). He is currently at work on a history of the children's rights movement.

LAURA McCALL received her Ph.D. from the University of Michigan, where she examined gender expectations in early American literature. She teaches American socio-intellectual and European history at Western State College of Colorado. Her content analysis of *Godey's Lady's Book* was recently published in the *Journal of the Early Republic*. She is presently investigating masculine and feminine perceptions of the land in the decades preceding the Civil War.

STEVEN MINTZ is Associate Professor of History at the University of Houston and has been Visiting Scholar at Harvard University's Minda de Gunzberg Center for European Studies. His publications include *A Prison of Expectations: The Family in Victorian Culture* and *Domestic Revolutions: A Social History of the American Family* (coauthored with Susan Kellogg). He serves as a consultant in American family history at the Smithsonian Institution's National Museum of American History and as the editor of the *American Social Experience* (New York University Press).

ELIZABETH I. NYBAKKEN is Associate Professor of History at Mississippi State University, where she teaches courses in colonial America, social history, and women's history. She is the author of *The Centinel: Warnings of a Revolution* and articles on eighteenth-century culture and religion. She is currently working on a biography of the Reverend Dr. Francis Alison, an eighteenth-century Presbyterian educator and cleric.

JUDITH SEALANDER is Professor of History at Wright State University, Dayton, Ohio, where she teaches U.S. and women's history. Her publications include *As Minority Becomes Majority: Federal Reaction to the*

Phenomenon of Women in the Work Force, 1920–1963 and *"Grand Plans": Business Progressivism and Social Change in the Ohio Miami Valley, 1890– 1929.* She is currently at work on a study of the rise of multinational corporations in the late nineteenth century.

NANCY SHOEMAKER is a doctoral student in history at the University of Minnesota, where she is working on a study of native American fertility in the twentieth century. She has worked on the American Indian Family Project at the Newberry Library's D'Arcy McNickle Center for the History of the American Indian and has published articles in the *Western Historical Quarterly* and *American Indian Quarterly.*

MARIS A. VINOVSKIS is Professor of History at the University of Michigan, where he teaches U.S. family history and social history. Among his publications are *Demographic History and the World Population Crisis; Education and Social Change in Nineteenth-Century Massachusetts* (with Carl Kaestle); *Fertility in Massachusetts from the Revolution to the Civil War; The Origins of Public High Schools: A Re-Examination of the Beverly High School Controversy,* and *An "Epidemic" of Adolescent Pregnancy? Some Historical and Policy Perspectives.*

WINIFRED D. WANDERSEE is Dewar Professor of History at Hartwick College, Oneonta, New York, where she teaches modern American political and social history, women's history, and the history of American public policy. Her publications include *Women's Work and Family Values, 1920–1940* and *On the Move: American Women in the 1970s.* She is currently working on a biography of Frances Perkins, Secretary of Labor for Franklin D. Roosevelt.